TEACHING and LEARNING
the Language Arts

TEACHING and LEARNING the Language Arts

SECOND EDITION

Edna P. DeHaven

University of Oregon

LITTLE, BROWN AND COMPANY

Boston   Toronto

Library of Congress Cataloging in Publication Data

DeHaven, Edna P.
    Teaching and learning the language arts.

    Bibliography: p.
    Includes index.
    1. Language arts (Elementary) I. Title.
LB1576.D33   1983   372.6′044   82-18006
ISBN 0-316-17935-3

Library of Congress Catalog Card No. 82–18006

ISBN 0-316-17935-3

9 8 7 6 5 4 3 2 1

MV

Published simultaneously in Canada
by Little, Brown & Company (Canada) Limited

Printed in the United States of America

CHAPTER OPENING PHOTOGRAPH CREDITS
Chapters 1, 2, 3, 4, 6, 8, 10, and 11 by Peter Vandermark. Chapters 5 and
13 used courtesy of Madelyn Olson at Lane County Education Service
District. Chapter 7 © 1980 by Laimute E. Druskis/Jeroboam, Inc. Chapters
9 and 12 used courtesy of the Eugene, Oregon School District 4J.

CREDITS AND ACKNOWLEDGMENTS
Michael Halliday, from *Learning How To Mean.* London: Edward Arnold.
New York: Elsevier—North Holland, 1975, pp. 19–21. Reprinted by
permission of the author.

Reprinted from *English for a New Generation* by H. P. Guth. Copyright 1973,
with permission of Webster/McGraw-Hill.

Lefevre, from *Linguistics and the Teaching of Reading.* New York: McGraw-
Hill, 1982, pp. 90–91. Copyright © 1980 by McGraw-Hill. Reprinted by
permission.

Fry, from *Elementary Reading Instruction.* New York: McGraw-Hill, 1982, p.
217. Reprinted by permission.

Geneva Smitherman, from *Talkin' and Testifyin'.* Copyright © 1977 by
Geneva Smitherman. Reprinted by permission of Houghton Mifflin
Company.

continued on page 528

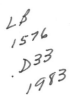

Preface

As in the first edition, this edition of *Teaching and Learning the Language Arts* continues to serve a two-fold purpose: to help teachers develop a knowledge base of current language arts information and to offer practical guidelines and suggestions for planning effective programs. The content of the book has been shaped by the questions and concerns expressed by pre-service and in-service teachers; it reflects their quest for a rational, stimulating, and balanced approach to teaching the language arts.

In preparing this edition, newer research findings and educational trends have been thoughtfully considered and appropriately incorporated throughout the text. New material on oral language development, writing, schema theory, teacher effectiveness, electronic technology, and special children placed in regular classrooms is included.

The first edition of *Teaching and Learning the Language Arts* was written primarily as a textbook for teachers-in-training. However, because of such features as the breadth and depth of content, the research base, the attention to current curriculum issues, and the many teaching suggestions, experienced teachers and other graduate students have also found the book to be a welcome and useful resource.

Today's language arts teachers face an interesting challenge. The uses of language are many and cut across all areas of the curriculum. They encompass a broad range of knowledge, skills, abilities, and appreciations. At the same time, the users of language — the children in the classrooms — present a range of backgrounds, interests, and attitudes. Such an array of factors clearly speak to the need to "tailor make" the language arts curriculum appropriate to each classroom of children. Somehow the teacher must decide what to teach and how to teach it.

Teaching and Learning the Language Arts is designed to help teachers meet the challenge. It offers a comprehensive and objective look at language and language learning and assists teachers in developing a conceptual framework for making rational decisions about language arts instruction. The book recognizes children's need to master skills, not because skills are an end in themselves, but because skills are essential components of the communication code. Many practical and creative language activities provide opportunities for children to practice language and to assimilate newly formed concepts and skills into their oral and written language. Attention is given to the importance of both cognitive and affective learning and to individual differences among children. Throughout the book the interrelationships among the language arts are emphasized, and there are many suggestions for enhancing learning through integration.

The book follows a developmental sequence. The first section focuses on teaching and learning about language as a communication process. Chapters include specific information about the English language system, the history of English (including the origin of family and place names), varieties of English, and various approaches to the study of grammar. Then, building on this foundation of linguistic knowledge, the second section examines separately each of the major areas of the language arts curriculum. These areas include oral language, listening, creative drama and puppetry, expository and narrative writing, spelling, handwriting, reading, and children's literature and poetry. The third and final section concentrates on planning and managing the total language arts program. Here we first look at handicapped, multicultural, and gifted and talented children in the regular classroom, and then turn our attention to the formulation of goals and objectives, grouping and instruction, and the uses of human and material resources in language arts programs. Of particular interest is the section on computers and other electronic devices in educational settings.

The format of the chapters in the first two sections is designed to facilitate the processing of information and to set program development resource material apart for ready reference. The format of the chapters generally includes:

a brief preview

questions to focus attention and stimulate thinking

a presentation and discussion of pertinent literature and research discussion of important concepts and special concerns

practical teaching suggestions and examples of lessons

a summary of the chapter

followed by

cognitive and affective learning objectives

suggested learning activities

selected references for further reading

The final section follows a similar format with changes appropriate to the content.

Many people have contributed to the writing of this book. Children, teachers, and graduate and undergraduate college students have all provided insights about the teaching and learning of language. I am particularly grateful to my colleagues Helen Tyler, Dorothy Latham, and Glenn Ellen Brun for their interest and helpful suggestions. Mylan Jaixen of Little, Brown deserves special credit for his guidance and encouragement in the planning and preparation of this book.

I would also like to thank the following people, who helped in the initial planning and development for this edition and in making this edition better than the first: Joanne Golden, University of Delaware; Eugene Irving, Illinois State University; Noel Jones, University of North Carolina — Wilmington; Linda Lamme, University of Florida; Marvin Marion, Missouri Western State College; Judy Meagher, University of Connecticut; Raymond Rodriguez, University of Colorado — Colorado Springs; Marilou Sorenson, University of Utah; Shane Templeton, Emory University; and Laverne Warner, Sam Houston State University.

E. P. D.
Eugene, Oregon

Brief Contents

Contents

TEACHING and LEARNING
the Language Arts

1

The Nature of Language and Language Teaching

*Language . . . is the key to all human activities. It is the vehicle
through which the world can be understood and appreciated; without
language, people are isolated and helpless.*

Gertrude Boyd (1976)

CHAPTER PREVIEW

So far as we know only humans have developed an oral language
system. This chapter is about that language, what it is and how we
use it. It begins with a broad look at language as communication
and then focuses on specific components and features of language
as a highly developed and functional system. From this frame of
reference, we will explore the nature of language teaching and
learning and suggest implications for a language arts program.

QUESTIONS TO THINK ABOUT AS YOU READ

How might our lives as humans be different if we had never
developed a language system?

In what ways does language reflect and serve our cultural society?

What is the overall design of our language system?

How are the language arts interrelated?

How has the more recent work of linguists influenced language arts
programs?

As a language arts teacher, what kinds of knowledge do I need and
what should I be able to do?

What kinds of decisions will I need to make?

How do learning objectives facilitate instruction?

The Importance of Language

Imagine that all human beings possessed small computerized screens
remotely controlled by language impulses to the brain. Whenever we
used language — whether consciously or unconsciously, in public or
in private — the words would automatically appear on our screen.

How interesting that might be! In addition to the words that you are now reading, for example, your screen would also record your daydreams, your anxieties, and your momentary reactions to people and things in your environment.

Now further suppose that you don't want to have anything so personal as your thoughts recorded for others to see. You decide to keep your screen absolutely blank. What could you do without transmitting language impulses? What wouldn't involve language in some way?

It is very difficult, of course, to think of anything that does not involve either internal or external use of language. Even nonlanguage activities, such as walking the dog or washing the car, tend to elicit thought. While you are engaged in physical movements so well learned that conscious thought is not required, your mind is actively remembering, associating, and organizing. Language is consciously or unconsciously associated with nearly everything we do. It is a personal matrix for receiving, processing, and sharing ideas and information.

The need for language is a basic premise underlying language teaching and learning. This concept should be clearly understood by teachers and children alike. Language makes functional and creative exploration of the world possible. It allows us to interpret experience, to form concepts and see relationships. Facility in language is essential to the personal and corporate qualities of life.

Language and Communication

Communication is a broad term that includes but is not limited to language. It may be thought of as the transmission of a message between two or more beings. At the very least, it requires a sender and a receiver, a message, and some medium or channel to carry the signal. Communication may be transmitted and received through any of the sensory perception channels: visual, auditory, olfactory, gustatory, or tactile.

Sometimes communication takes place through more than one channel concurrently. For example, among humans an auditory "I am angry," may be accompanied by visual communication of "I am angry," on the person's face, and tactile communication of "I am angry," through the person's fist.

The way in which messages are transmitted and received is called a *communication system*. Communication systems range from simple to complex. That is, communication may occur through a single channel of sensory perception or many channels. It may be limited to a single message, or it may carry an infinite number of messages through intricate variations.

One way to gain an understanding and appreciation of our language is to compare it to other communication systems. Children find this approach very interesting, and, in studying how other systems work, they make many discoveries about their own language. Communication among animals has fascinated people for centuries, and the topic provides an engaging way to approach the study of the nature of language with children. The material that follows is intended to supply some background information about animal communication systems and to suggest a frame of reference for thinking about the human language system. As you read, think about the possibilities for using this and related information (see the references at the end of the book) to teach children about the language they use. The Suggested Learning Activities section at the end of the chapter suggests some ways of teaching this information.

Animal Communication

Communication is not limited to humans. Scientists tell us that all living creatures have some type of communication. In a single-cell animal it may be the simple tactile awareness of another. More complex forms of animal life perform more obvious acts of communication, such as producing signals.

Most communication among animals is closely related to their survival and basic needs. For example, common communication signals include ways to mark territory, to indicate sex, to recognize rank and group, to assemble or disperse, to give alarm, and to announce location. Communication, particularly in the lower animals, is limited and appears to be more reflexive or intuitive than conscious. It occurs as a response to a biological or emotional urge. It may seem absurd to say that protozoa communicate; yet, in some way, the cells influence one another to form an organism.

The way animals communicate is, of course, limited by the physical as well as the mental capabilities of a species. Sebeok (1972) reports that the great majority of animals are deaf, dumb, and blind. He explains, "true hearing and functional sound occur only in two phyla: the Arthropods and the Chordates, and even in every class of Arthropods a majority of the species is deaf and dumb." (p. 95) Sebeok goes on to suggest that chemical signaling, involving scent production and the sense of smell, may be found among all animals.

There is considerable evidence to support such a theory. Many animals, including dogs, mark their territory with urine. Another example is the stag, which communicates with two different scents, each emanating from a separate gland. It exudes one scent to mark the trail and keep the herd together. It uses the other to signal territory and ward off rival males.

Visual communication plays an important role among sighted animals. The bear, for example, marks its territory by making deep scratches in trees with its claws and teeth. It stands on its hind legs and makes its marks as high as possible. Thus it not only marks its territory but indicates its size to any potential opponent. Numerous other examples of visual communication are found in the animal world, such as the preening of birds, the facial expressions of monkeys, and the aristocratic walk of a buck that has just won a battle.

Research on animals' ability to communicate through sound has generated considerable interest. Dolphins, for example, have been found to use a sonar or echo system to locate objects under water just as bats do in the air. They are able to reproduce a rather wide repertoire of sounds including human laughter and human and electronic whistles.

A fascinating study documenting the use of multisensory communication among honeybees was conducted by Karl von Frisch (1954). Professor von Frisch found that honeybees use a variety of senses in communicating the source of food through patterned movements he called *dances*. He identified two kinds of dances, the round dance and the wagging dance.

The *round dance* was used when the food source was near the hive. In it, the foraging bee returned to the hive fresh with the smell of honey and began whirling around in circles, first to the right and then to the left (Figure 1-1). Other bees followed, trying to keep their feelers in contact with the tip of the forager's abdomen, in what Frisch described as "a perpetual comet's tail of bees." The dance abruptly ended and the foraging bee hurried out of the hive to get more honey. The other bees didn't follow then, however, but appeared later at the food source. Von Frisch pointed out that the dance normally took place in the darkness of a closed hive, and thus the communication was not visual, but was achieved through touch and smell.

When the source of food was farther away, at least 50 to 100 meters, Frisch found that the honeybees used a *wagging dance*. In the wagging dance, the forager bee made a semicircle, then returned to the starting point in a straight line. It then repeated the movement in the opposite direction, completing a full circle. The straight run of the dance involved a "wagging" of the bee's abdomen (Figure 1-2).

Through the wagging dance, the bee communicated the distance and the direction of the food source. The number of waggles indi-

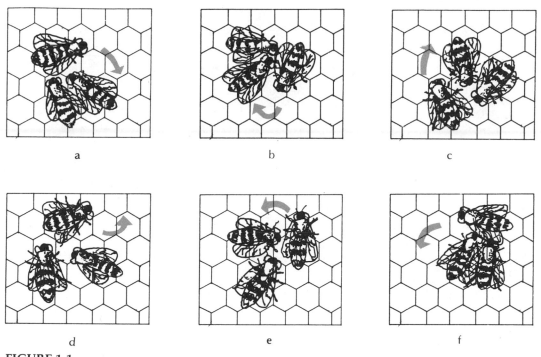

FIGURE 1-1
The Round Dance.

From Karl von Frisch, *The Dancing Bees*, copyright 1954. Used by permission of the author and Springer-Verlag, Heidelberg.

cated the distance, and the angle of the straight line indicated the direction of food in relation to the position of the sun.

Human Language

The theory is frequently espoused that language is uniquely human and that language ability is what sets humans apart in the animal kingdom. Jacques Monod goes even further to hypothesize that language led to the evolution of man. He says, "Language was not only the product but one of the initial conditions of this evolution" (1971, p. 129).

Monod explains that different organisms respond to environment in different ways, that selective pressures within an organism itself, as well as within the environment, determine evolutionary change. He believes that the development of *Homo sapiens* as a separate species goes back to a crucial, initial "choice" of rudimentary symbolic communication that set the species on a different evolutionary path.

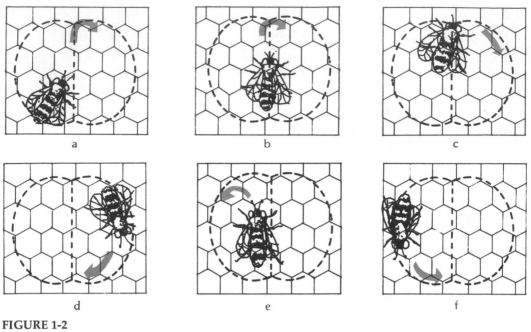

FIGURE 1-2
The Wagging Dance.

From Karl von Frisch, *The Dancing Bees,* copyright 1954. Used by permission of the author and Springer-Verlag, Heidelberg.

Each choice in the evolutionary process created new selective pressures that were binding on the future of the species. *Homo sapiens* continued to make selections that favored the development of linguistic ability. And this ability, in turn, led to greater development of the brain, and, hence, to human intelligence.

Be that as it may, it is readily apparent that language has played, and continues to play, a significant role in human accomplishments. Why this is true may best be understood by considering the potential of human language in comparison to the communication systems of animals.

Humans rely on senses for communicating, just as animals do. Facial expressions and gestures, perfumes and hair dressings, a touch or a hug, laughter or screams all have their counterpart in the animal kingdom. But in addition to the nonverbal communication systems shared with animals, humans have developed another option for communicating through sensory channels — a highly involved language system that allows much richer representation and sharing of meaning than any known system of animal noises.

Language is the chief means of communication among humans

and provides certain advantages over animal communication systems. Animal communication, as far as we know, consists of learned or intuitive responses triggered by immediate stimuli. Their responses are perfunctory rather than cognitive. Humans, on the other hand, can communicate about intangible things removed from the present. Therefore, we are not limited to "now" and "here" but are able to talk about things in the past and in the future without sensory referents.

Language permits the exchange of an unlimited number of perceptions and ideas. Everything animals can communicate, humans can say through language — plus much more. Once the language system is acquired, anything that is thought about can be communicated. By selecting and combining words according to the rules of the language system, we can generate an infinite set of messages that can be understood by others within the language community.

That a relationship exists between language and the cognitive achievements of humans seems obvious. Perhaps most significant in this relationship is the fact that the symbolic nature of language permits both delayed recall and speculation about the intangible and nonexistent. By encoding past experiences into verbal symbols, humans can collect those experiences and formulate generalizations about them. In this way, we can sort information and organize it in our computerlike brain. As new situations are encountered, appropriate information can be retrieved to enhance understanding or aid in problem-solving. Moreover, it is language that allows us to apply knowledge gained through ideas and experiences — others' as well as our own. Through creative uses of language we can mentally explore the unknown and structure abstract knowledge.

Language Defined

Linguists define language as *a system of arbitrary vocal symbols through which members of a group communicate.* This definition contains several concepts that help us to understand what language is and how it works. We will examine them individually.

Language is systematic Language is consistent and predictable. It follows patterns or rules that allow an infinite number of communications. We do not learn to speak and understand a discrete number of messages. Rather, we develop an intuitive knowledge of the language system, which allows us to generate and receive messages that are totally new to us.

Language is arbitrary Elements of a language system are arbitrarily determined. A four-legged, furry animal with a wagging tail could be called "womp" or "flatchet" just as well as "dog." But somewhere in the history of the English language, *dog* became the verbal symbol for that animal. Such decisions reflect the need for members of a group to share common language elements. Individuals cannot utter any string of sounds in any order and expect others to understand them. Communication is dependent on an established system, and decisions about the elements within that system are necessarily arbitrary.

Language is primarily vocal Language is based on a set of speech sounds produced by the vocal organs of the body. Words are made by combining those sounds. Speech was the primary form of language. Writing developed thousands of years later.

Language is symbolic Words create images of objects and things and allow us to talk about them when they are not present. A word is not the thing, it is an abstract symbol. For example, when we hear the sound symbols /d/ /o/ /g/, we translate the symbols into a mental image of a dog.[1] The symbolic nature of our language allows us to think and talk about abstract ideas such as democracy and love, as well as about concrete objects and things.

The purpose of language is group communication The need for communication among members of a group gives rise to language. The language that develops belongs to the group and binds its members together. They in turn are responsible for knowing the language; it is a prerequisite for functional membership in the group.

Language Functions

The uses of language derive from the needs and customs of a given society. In addition to using language to think, to communicate information, and to direct behavior, we use language in social and very personal ways. Language is an important aspect of human relationships. Consider its use in greetings, conversations, organizational meetings, ceremonies, and informal written communications. It is also used as an expression of emotion, as a release from tension, as a reaction to an emergency, and as a means of sharing unique personal perceptions.

DeStefano (1978, p. 116) gives seven universal functions of language originally identified by Halliday (1975):

> *Instrumental language.* "I want" or "I need." Language used to satisfy needs or desires. Often takes the form of a request.
>
> *Regulatory language.* "Do this," or "Get out of here!" or "Stop it!" For controlling others.

[1] Symbols written between slash marks represent sounds, not letters.

Interactional language. "Will you play with me?" or "Let's go for a walk together." For establishing relationships, defining them, and maintaining them. Also for participating in social behavior.

Personal language. "I'm going to be a doctor." or "I think . . ." For expressing individuality, to give personal opinions and feelings.

Imaginative language. "Let's pretend" or "Once upon a time," etc. Used to create a world of one's own.

Heuristic language. "Why?" "What's that for?" or "Why is the sky blue?" or "Why do people talk differently?" For exploring the world, for finding things out.

Informative language. "I've got something to tell you." For conveying information.

To be competent users of language, children need to be aware of its functions and to develop skill in using it for different purposes. A balanced language program gives attention to the full range of language functions. Through many different activities children discover the relationships of language choice and language function and become flexible and competent in using language appropriately.

Our Language System

In the normal course of growing up, each of us has acquired language with little thought about the regularities of the system or how its units combine to form meaningful utterances. Linguists, however, have spent a great deal of time analyzing our language system, and they have identified both its components and its design.

Sounds and Words

A *phoneme* is the smallest significant unit of sound in our language. For example, the word "cat" has three phonemes: /c/ /a/ /t/. Each is a distinctly different sound, and each is essential to the word. Changing any one of the sounds would result in a different word. Linguists have identified about forty-four different phonemes in our language. Some linguists use a slightly higher figure, and others identify fewer phonemes, but the difference is small.

Phonemes are represented in writing by *graphemes*. There is not a consistent one-to-one phoneme-grapheme correspondence, however; some phonemes are represented by different graphemes in different words (e.g., *full*, *phone*, and lau*gh*), and different phonemes may be represented by a common grapheme (e.g., *chance*, *chef*, and *chorus*).

Morphemes are made up of phonemes. Linguists define a morpheme as the smallest unit of meaning. The word *cat* has just one morpheme but *cats* contains two. When we add the letter *s* to a word we add another morpheme because *s* signals plurality; it has meaning. The word *gentlemanly* contains three morphemes: *gentle*, *man*, and *ly*. Each part of the word means something and is therefore classified as a morpheme.

Morphemes are further classified as *bound* or *free*. A bound morpheme can never stand alone as a word; it must be attached to one or more other morphemes to form a word. The *s* in *cats* and the *ly* in *gentlemanly* are bound morphemes. *Cat*, *gentle*, and *man*, on the other hand, may be used as separate words and are classified as free morphemes.

Intonation

Every language has particular sound characteristics. Even when we can't understand what a speaker is saying we can often identify what language he or she is speaking by its overall sound. It is the *intonation* system of our language that gives it its unique rhythm and sound. Some linguists call this system the *suprasegmental phonemes* of language. Three elements — pitch, stress, and juncture — are used in combination to produce the distinctive sound patterns of English.

Pitch refers to how high or low a sound is made. Linguists distinguish four levels to describe pitch in speech: low, medium, high, and very high. Varying the pitch makes language melodic. A rise or fall in pitch at the end of a sentence also tells us whether it is a question or a statement.

Stress refers to the amount of emphasis given to each word in a sentence. For example, try reading a sentence in different ways. Stress the italicized word in each sentence that follows and notice the difference it makes in the meaning of the sentence.

Jack doesn't like salami sandwiches.

Jack doesn't *like* salami sandwiches.

Jack doesn't like *salami* sandwiches.

Jack doesn't like salami *sandwiches*.

Juncture refers to the slight break or pause between words or sentences. The words *night rate* and *nitrate* are spelled differently, yet they are composed of identical phonemes. The difference in pronunciation is one of juncture.

Syntax

Syntax refers to the arrangement of words in sentences. To be meaningful a sentence must follow a grammatical pattern. The string of words *Be must out garbage taken the,* is not a grammatical sentence. When the same words are arranged in a different order, however, they convey meaning: *The garbage must be taken out.* The way words are arranged in sentences is important to meaning.

Some words, particularly adverbials, may be used in more than one place in a sentence. *Yesterday I went to the library,* or *I went to the library yesterday,* have the same meaning and are equally grammatical. However, notice the difference in these two sentences.

The flea bit the dog.

The dog bit the flea.

Identical vocabulary arranged in grammatical but different ways may convey very different meaning.

Language Arts in Today's Schools

Up to this point we have been thinking about the nature of language and how it functions as a communication system. This is important background, because language is what language arts teaching and learning are all about. Language is both the foundation on which a program is built and the source of supply for continuing growth.

The term *language arts* describes a wide range of school activities designed to help children become knowledgeable about language and use language effectively. It implies that learning to use language involves art as well as functional language skills. Language arts as a school subject inherently suggests a developing awareness of the forms and variations of language and an appreciation of the intricacies of learning to use language effectively.

Interrelationships Among the Language Arts

The language arts are commonly classified according to the tasks involved: *listening, speaking, reading,* and *writing.* These tasks may in turn be classified as receptive (listening and reading) and expressive (speaking and writing). Another way of classifying them would be as oral activities (listening and speaking) and written activities (reading and writing). Such a variety of possible classification schemes attests to the commonality of skills among the various language arts.

In the early childhood years, listening and speaking are closely intertwined. Listening is a major avenue of learning. Through listening, children acquire knowledge of their world translated into language. They learn vocabulary through repeated associations of objects and their vocal symbols; they assimilate syntactic patterns by hearing those patterns spoken over and over. Although very young children do not speak in the whole sentence patterns that they hear, research indicates that they are, nevertheless, thinking in sentence equivalents. As their language performance develops, they gradually expand their beginning minimum utterances to include all the surface elements of adult language. Listening provides the models for oral language development.

The similarity of skills among the four language arts makes learning in one area complementary to that in another area. Although each task may involve different cognitive processes, many skills involving language and thought are used in all language arts activities. In both reading and writing, for example, children use their knowledge of such things as vocabulary, inflected forms of words, sentence structure, and punctuation.

The relatedness of the language arts is graphically represented in Figure 1-3. The four categories — listening, speaking, reading, and writing — are shown as having overlapping sets of skills and abilities that operate within a universe of language. Cognition, at the center of the universe, is reflected in both the content and the process of using language. It is the mind that controls our capacity for knowing and thinking and allows us to organize and share knowledge through the language system.

The Role of Research

Language arts programs are continually being influenced by research studies. Findings of investigations point out possible implications of instructional practices and suggest specific ways of altering and improving the language arts curriculum. One such area of research, *linguistics*, has had a considerable effect on language arts instruction. It has led both to broader content in language arts programs and to changes in approaches to the study of language. Linguistics, defined as the *scientific study of language*, includes many areas of specialization such as phonology (language sounds), orthography (spelling), syntactic structures (grammar), dialectology (language

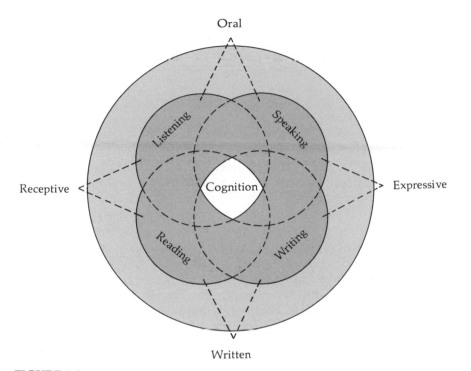

FIGURE 1-3
The Universe of Language.

variation), graphemics (the writing system), and sociolinguistics (variation in language structure and usage according to social situations).

Linguists collect and analyze language data and formulate rational generalizations about language and its use. Their findings have greatly increased the body of knowledge available for study. Furthermore, the scientific method for studying language developed by modern linguistics has filtered down to language arts instruction in the classroom. The method provides a process model for studying language that enables students to recognize and understand patterns and regularities of language rather than simply to memorize definitions and rules. The scientific approach has been particularly noticeable in the study of grammar, as we will see in Chapter 3.

A closely related research field, *psycholinguistics*, combines cognitive psychology and linguistic research. Psycholinguists are interested not only in language itself, but also in how the human brain acquires and processes language. Psycholinguistic research is concerned with the developmental aspects of language and with the factors that tend to limit or facilitate language growth. Although psycholinguistics is most often associated with reading, it clearly has significance for other areas, particularly curriculum planning for language arts in the elementary school. Psycholinguistic studies yield an important body of information about the learning of language and suggest developmental mental processes that ought to be consciously fostered in schools.

Yet another field of recent research, *teacher effectiveness*, has helped to identify instructional practices associated with maximum learning. Researchers in this field consistently report the importance of planned instruction and learner attentiveness. Learning has been found to be most effective when teachers have clearly identified instructional objectives, structure their lessons to achieve the desired learning, guide children through the learning experience, provide adequate demonstrations or examples to develop understanding, and give children opportunities to use what they have learned in meaningful follow-up activities.

The way in which time is spent in the classroom is also important. Effective teaching and learning requires focused attention; thus teaching strategies should include ways to actively involve the learner and elicit responses. Appropriate pacing of lessons is also crucial. There must be time to think and assimilate, yet the lesson must not drag and allow the learner's attention to wander.

The Language Arts Curriculum

From the foregoing discussion, it has probably become apparent that today's language arts curriculum is broadly based. If the scope of the curriculum seems overwhelming, it may be helpful to think of teaching and learning activities under two general headings: those which focus on developing knowledge and understanding of language and those which focus on developing language skills. These are essentially complementary curricular concerns, and a good language arts program must include both. Emphasis on skill development to the exclusion of understanding and appreciation of the use of those skills is both inefficient and ineffective. At the same time, knowledge about language without the ability to apply that knowledge to real-life situations also is inadequate.

What and *how much* to teach in a language arts curriculum is a continuing controversy. The current trend seems to be toward a greater emphasis on teaching specific competencies, or skills. In some school districts the emphasis on skill development may discourage using additional time for studying language as a discipline. However, the study of language is a worthy use of school time. From a humanistic point of view, language is seen as a reflection of that which makes us human, as embracing the whole of our heritage. It is a composite of our knowledge, our *modus operandi,* our emotions, and our creative potential. It reflects the total life and culture of a people. Additionally, the study of language provides a broader perspective for understanding and acquiring specific skills. It helps children see skills not as ends in themselves, but as necessary conventions of a highly developed communication system.

An adequate curriculum ought to include both knowledge about language and skill development in functional and artistic uses of language. It should reflect children's developmental levels and their need to make sense out of what they learn, to integrate new knowledge with existing language structures. In addition, a sound curriculum is one in which conscious attention to the development of positive attitudes and appreciations overlies the whole instructional program.

The Language Arts Teacher

Because teachers of language arts face a many-faceted task, they need to be well prepared academically. They need to be competent users of language, so they will be good models. They also need to accept and value the language children bring with them to school, and use that language as a base for additional learning. A good knowledge of language and how it is used leads to a sense of confidence and facilitates creative teaching. The ability to conceptualize the structure and function of language enables teachers to identify the knowledge and skills children need and to break complex concepts and abilities into lesson-sized experiences.

Teachers need to know how to diagnose, plan, and instruct in consistent and meaningful ways. But that is not enough. The way teachers interact with children is also important. They need to be able to stimulate children's interest in language and to motivate them to learn the skills they need. Successful teachers show a genuine interest in children and notice how children respond in specific learning situations. They realize that teaching involves listening as well as talking. By getting to know the children in their classroom well, they can fine tune their teaching strategies for maximum effectiveness.

There is another aspect of teaching that is sometimes overlooked. It has to do with the teacher's attitude toward all or part of the language arts curriculum, the *content* of language arts. What the teacher thinks and feels is clearly communicated even when it is not spoken. Teachers need to realize this and to deal with it consciously. For example, unless teachers value handwriting, children are apt to feel that it is unimportant and make little progress. To bring language teaching alive teachers need to show an interest in the fascinating world of language and to indicate by their attitude that the study and use of language are both challenging and satisfying.

Meeting the Needs of the Learner

Children grow and mature, both physically and mentally, in their own unique ways. Modern educators realize this fact and seek to modify instruction to meet the children's individual needs. They continuously evaluate each child's competencies and learning needs. They listen critically to children's oral responses and assess their writing. They analyze habits children have consciously or unconsciously developed and watch for evidence of attitudes and interest in learning.

Strategies for individualizing instruction fall into two major categories: *expansion* and *remediation*. Although each category has a somewhat different focus, they are by no means mutually exclusive. Teaching strategies to expand children's language abilities build on what children already know and the patterns they already use. Carefully planned activities challenge children to use language in new situations, to discover effective ways to express a felt communication need. Children are thus encouraged to develop an increasingly greater breadth and depth of language power.

Remediation has the same ultimate goal but aims at correcting an existing language problem. In remediation one focuses on analyzing and treating deviations that retard or block language achievement. Remedial instruction therefore requires a clear definition of what are "normal," or appropriate uses of language. Its techniques are designed to overcome learning barriers and to help children acquire a level of language competence commensurate with their general level of development. In using this approach, however, one must be careful not to denigrate the child's home language since that will accomplish little. Rather, one should help the child to become aware of and to choose appropriate options in particular social contexts.

Evaluation is a prerequisite for determining and planning the kind and amount of instruction in each category for each child. Mastery of basic skills is essential, but we must also realize that excessive drill on skills that children already possess is a boring waste of time. Instruction should be more than remediation. The best language arts instruction builds on children's existing competencies and keeps children at the growing edge of their knowledge and skills. At the same time, it emphasizes mastery of skills that underlie more complex abilities and that, if not learned, limit children's progress.

A Self-Assessment for Language Arts Teachers

As stated earlier, language arts teachers need to have both a background of knowledge about language and a well-developed set of skills for helping children expand and refine their language competence. The statements in the self-assessment that follows are representative of the knowledge and skills you should have to teach language arts in the elementary school. Read each statement thoughtfully, and mark where you stand on the continuum between weak and strong as you begin this study.

When you have completed the self-assessment, you will have a profile of some important facets of your language arts teaching competency. Look at your profile carefully, and identify the areas in which you need to improve. Then, as you read on through this book, pay particular attention to the sections that deal with your weaker areas. It will also be helpful to read additional materials from the list of selected references and to observe children using and learning language as much as you can.

	Weak				Strong
	1	2	3	4	5
1. I can define and explain the process of communication.	___	___	___	___	___
2. I can discuss the similarities and differences between animal and human communication systems.	___	___	___	___	___
3. I can explain the subsystems of language.	___	___	___	___	___
4. I know the history of our language and can discuss major influences in its development.	___	___	___	___	___
5. I can define *grammar* and *usage*.	___	___	___	___	___
6. I can model standard English usage.	___	___	___	___	___
7. I can discuss language varieties from a linguistic point of view.	___	___	___	___	___
8. I can explain developmental stages in children's acquisition and development of language.	___	___	___	___	___
9. I can discuss the interrelationships of language and thinking.	___	___	___	___	___
10. I can discuss the role of language in our society.	___	___	___	___	___

11. I can identify and discuss problems of bilingual learners.   ___ ___ ___ ___ ___

12. I can define the organs of speech and describe how different sounds are made.   ___ ___ ___ ___ ___

13. I can identify formal and informal oral language skills and plan effective oral language instruction.   ___ ___ ___ ___ ___

14. I can explain the importance of listening.   ___ ___ ___ ___ ___

15. I can identify different kinds of listening.   ___ ___ ___ ___ ___

16. I can model effective listening behavior.   ___ ___ ___ ___ ___

17. I can identify and teach listening skills.   ___ ___ ___ ___ ___

18. I can explain the rationale for including creative drama in the language arts.   ___ ___ ___ ___ ___

19. I can discuss the relative importance of *process* and *product* in creative drama.   ___ ___ ___ ___ ___

20. I can identify and teach creative drama skills.   ___ ___ ___ ___ ___

21. I can use creative drama to develop skills and understandings in other areas of the curriculum.   ___ ___ ___ ___ ___

22. I can explain the process of writing and how it differs from speaking from a linguistic point of view.   ___ ___ ___ ___ ___

23. I can identify prerequisite skills for written composition and can plan appropriate instruction to develop readiness.   ___ ___ ___ ___ ___

24. I know what skills and techniques are involved in effective written composition and can help children become more effective writers.   ___ ___ ___ ___ ___

25. I can identify different types of writing situations and provide a balanced writing program.   ___ ___ ___ ___ ___

26. I can explain why the words in our language are spelled as they are.   ___ ___ ___ ___ ___

27. I can explain phoneme-grapheme relationships and identify generalizations that should be taught.   ___ ___ ___ ___ ___

28. I can discuss the validity and use of word lists   _____ _____ _____ _____ _____
    in a spelling program.

29. I know how different learning modalities affect   _____ _____ _____ _____ _____
    children's progress in learning to spell and can
    help children find an effective method of study.

30. I can explain the importance of involving   _____ _____ _____ _____ _____
    children in evaluation of their own spelling
    performance.

31. I can discuss the history of writing and the   _____ _____ _____ _____ _____
    importance of writing to modern-day society.

32. I can serve as a good model for manuscript and   _____ _____ _____ _____ _____
    cursive writing.

33. I can plan an efficient and effective teaching   _____ _____ _____ _____ _____
    strategy for teaching beginning manuscript
    writing and for the transition to cursive
    writing.

34. I can identify common writing errors and   _____ _____ _____ _____ _____
    provide effective remediation.

35. I can explain the integral and reciprocal nature   _____ _____ _____ _____ _____
    of reading and the other language arts.

36. I can discuss reading as a communication   _____ _____ _____ _____ _____
    process.

37. I can provide reading instruction as an integral   _____ _____ _____ _____ _____
    part of the language arts.

38. I can explain the meaning of the term *good*   _____ _____ _____ _____ _____
    children's literature.

39. I can identify children's interests and suggest   _____ _____ _____ _____ _____
    appropriate materials.

40. I can identify common forms of children's   _____ _____ _____ _____ _____
    literature.

41. I can identify concepts and understandings   _____ _____ _____ _____ _____
    which the study of literature should help
    children develop.

42. I can identify goals for an effective language   _____ _____ _____ _____ _____
    arts program.

43. I can define cognitive and affective instructional objectives and explain their function in developing a language arts curriculum. ____ ____ ____ ____ ____

44. I can plan ways to integrate language arts in other areas of the curriculum. ____ ____ ____ ____ ____

45. I can discuss the ways school and community expectations affect a language arts program. ____ ____ ____ ____ ____

46. I can identify individual differences among children and plan appropriate instruction to meet children's needs. ____ ____ ____ ____ ____

47. I can train and use volunteers to assist children in improving their language arts ability. ____ ____ ____ ____ ____

48. I can evaluate and select language arts textbooks and other materials. ____ ____ ____ ____ ____

Using Learning Objectives

Good teaching has direction. It follows a plan of instruction based on the school's instructional goals, the individual needs of children, and the philosophy of the teacher. Although the way something is taught may vary from one situation to another, teaching must be purposeful to be effective. We must know what our objectives are before we can formulate plans for instruction.

Learning objectives are derived from the mass of information related to a given topic or area of study. Once you have attained a background of knowledge about some aspect of the language arts, the next step is to identify what to teach to children. When you determine what you want them to know and to be able to do, you are formulating objectives.

Learning objectives are of two types: cognitive and affective. *Cognitive* objectives deal with intellectual development, whereas *affective* objectives are concerned with feelings and attitudes. Both types are important in the elementary school, for it is here that the skills, attitudes, and values are developed that influence children's later habits and accomplishment. For a detailed explanation of the hierarchical levels of cognitive and affective behavior, see *Taxonomy of Educational Objectives: Cognitive Domain* by Bloom et al. (1956) and *Taxonomy of Educational Objectives Handbook II: Affective Domain* by Krathwohl, Bloom, and Masia (1968).

Learning objectives for each area of the language arts are listed near the end of each chapter in this book. They are designed to help you identify significant concepts, abilities, and attitudes that will enhance children's understanding and mastery of language. The objectives provide a framework for designing and developing language arts instruction.

Cognitive objectives are stated as generalizations and may be translated into behavioral objectives by rewriting them to include demonstrable specifics (stating what the child will be able to do under what conditions). If you need help in writing objectives in behavioral terms, see *Preparing Instructional Objectives* by Mager (1962). You will notice that affective objective statements tend to be long range and less precisely measurable than cognitive objectives. The formation of attitudes, appreciations, and values is most often the result of different experiences that occur over a period of time. Although a single experience may spark obvious interest, it is frequently difficult to determine just when lasting achievement of affective objectives has been attained.

In Summary

Language is defined as a system of arbitrary vocal symbols through which members of a group communicate. As far as we know, language as such is a form of communication unique to human beings. It has certain advantages over other communication systems. Among them are the potential for an infinite number of messages, and the provision for communicating abstract ideas and for communicating about the past and future as well as the present.

Our language system consists of units of sound (phonemes), which are combined to form units of meaning (morphemes). A word is made up of one or more morphemes. Words are arranged in sentences according to certain meaningful and grammatical patterns. The intonation system (pitch, stress, and juncture) also conveys meaning and gives English its unique rhythm and sound.

The language arts curriculum includes both the study of language (linguistics) and the development of language skills and abilities. It is designed to help children learn about their language — its history and development, the varieties of English, and the sound and grammatical systems. It is intended to develop children's competence in using receptive language (listening and reading) and expressive language (speaking and writing). Language arts teachers need to be knowledgeable about language and be able to guide children's continual growth in the various components of the language arts.

Learning Objectives

COGNITIVE OBJECTIVES

Primary Grades

Children will

know that animal communication is limited to members of the animal's group.

know that the way animals communicate is different from the way humans communicate.

understand words as sets of sounds that stand for things.

understand that a word can mean whatever a group of people decide it should mean.

understand that members of a group must all know the language if they are to communicate.

be able to group words together to form grammatical sentences.

realize that changing the order of words in a sentence may change the meaning of a sentence.

Middle Grades

Children will

maintain all primary-grade objectives.

be able to describe different communication systems.

be able to explain why most communication systems are limited in kind and number of possible messages.

be able to discuss language as a communication system.

understand the need to know about and be able to use the language system.

understand that human language allows people to communicate anything they can think about.

AFFECTIVE OBJECTIVES

Children will

be interested in finding out about other communication systems.

want to know more about the human language system.

appreciate the advantages of using language to communicate.

value becoming proficient in using their language.

Suggested Learning Activities

Many activities can be used to meet more than one language arts objective. In addition, language activities are often related to other areas of the curriculum and may meet objectives in those areas also. Before you begin any activity, be certain that it is appropriate for your specific objective(s) and the age of the children you teach. Always follow up each activity with a brief discussion or summarization of what has been learned.

Talking Animals. Show the children pictures of animals (e.g., a dog wagging its tail, a horse bucking, a lion snarling, etc.) and ask them what feelings or thoughts they think each animal is communicating. Then have them sug-

gest what the animal might be saying if it could talk (e.g., "I'm glad to see you." "Get off my back." "You'd better watch out."). Write the sentences neatly on strips of paper and display them as captions under the pictures on a bulletin board. Or, make the pictures and captions into a book and place it on the reading table. (This idea may be developed within a language experience approach to reading.)

Animal Antics. Discuss ways that animals communicate. Let each child pick an animal he or she wants to be. Then have the children space themselves so that they do not touch each other. (The activity may be performed in the gym, but that large a space is not necessary.) Say sentences and have children try to communicate the ideas of the sentences as their animals might. For example, you might say:

I am happy today.

I'm looking for something good to eat.

The sun is hot.

I smell an enemy.

I guess I'll take a nap.

Mood music may be played to heighten the children's imagination.

Secret Codes. Have each child choose a partner and then devise a code and exchange secret messages. Examples could include new alphabet symbols such as 1 = a, 2 = b, 3 = c, etc., or new phoneme-grapheme symbols such as ✶ = /ă/, + = /ā/, ◯ = /ä/, ⌇ = b, ♡ = c, etc.

Signal Systems. Report on signalling systems for sending messages (e.g., wigwag, Morse code, Indian smoke signals, trail signs, railroad signals, and referee signals, etc.).

Animal Watching. Through reading books, watching films, or observing live animals, collect data about the ways animals communicate. Make a bar graph to show how many different messages each animal is known to communicate.

Nonverbal Communication. Working in pairs, the children make a chart of messages they can communicate through gestures and facial expressions. Before they can list a message on the chart, it must be demonstrated by one partner and correctly identified by the other without any exchange of language.

Naming Game. Pass out a different but common object to each child (pen, eraser, chalk, toothbrush, paper clip, etc.). Have the children decide what they would call their object if they were seeing it for the first time. Then have them plan a brief speech to introduce the "new" object to the class. For example, a pen might be renamed a "blit" and presented as follows: "This is a blit. It is blue but blits come in all colors. They are useful in writing neat papers. The ink in this blit dries very fast and there is never a smudge or smear on your paper. The blit is designed to fit into your pocket."

Tell Me a Story. Select a familiar nursery rhyme or story and retell it using different names or words for key characters and objects. For example, *The Three Bears* could be *The Three Marts* who went for a walk in the tooze while Blonwon visited their hosh, etc.

Communicating Without Words. Divide the children into groups of three to five. Give each group a slip of paper on which a single message is written. After a brief planning time, let the children take turns acting out or in some way trying to convey their message without speaking words or forming words with their lips. Include messages of varying difficulty such as: "It is a hot day." "We had chicken for dinner yesterday." "I am hungry." "I want to go fishing

FACIAL EXPRESSION	WHAT IT TELLS	GESTURE	WHAT IT TELLS

next summer." "The hotel is a tall building." When all groups have had a turn, discuss which messages or parts of messages were most difficult and why. Then discuss and list the advantages of our language system.

Scrambled Sentences. Pass out envelopes that contain a sentence cut up into separate words. Have the children arrange the words to form a sentence and decide whether there is more than one possible arrangement.

Signs and Symbols. Make a collection of signs and symbols that humans use to communicate (e.g., highway signs, skull and crossbones, signs on restroom doors, directional arrows, etc.).

Heraldry. Look at examples of coats-of-arms, crests, and shields from the days of knighthood. Discuss what the elements in the designs stand for. Have each child design his or her family coat-of-arms and explain its meaning.

Suggestions for Further Reading

Boyd, Gertrude. *Linguistics in the Elementary School.* Itasca, Ill.: F. E. Peacock, 1976.

Denham, Carolyn, and Ann Lieberman, eds. *Time to Learn.* Washington, D.C.: National Institute of Education, 1980.

DeStefano, Johanna S. *Language, the Learner and the School.* New York: John Wiley and Sons, 1978.

*Gallant, Roy A. *Man Must Speak: The Story of Language and How We Use It.* New York: Random House, 1969.

*Gilbert, Bil. *How Animals Communicate.* New York: Pantheon Books, 1966.

*Pei, Mario. *All About Language.* Philadelphia: Lippincott, 1954.

  * Easy books.

2
Our English Language

Since very ancient times men have been interested in their languages. As one of the most remarkable, complex, and familiar attainments, language has excited their curiosity. It is so much a part of their human existence that to understand themselves they have seen that they must first understand language.

H. A. Gleason, Jr. (1965, p. 28)

CHAPTER PREVIEW

Have you ever wondered why you are served *pork* chops but never *pig* chops? Hidden away in the history of language are the answers to many such puzzling "why" and "how" questions about the words we use. This chapter will give you some important background about the history of language. Although the chapter is primarily informational, knowledge of the origins of language should cause you to generate many ideas for classroom activities. The first part of the chapter contains a brief overview of the periods of English language history, including some of the major events and influences that helped to shape our language. Then there is an explanation of how words are added to our ever-changing and expanding language and some information about the fascinating topic of name origins. Finally, there is a discussion of how the history of language fits into the language arts program and there are some specific examples of lessons.

QUESTIONS TO THINK ABOUT AS YOU READ

How did the history of England affect the English language?

Which events are particularly significant? Why?

How is our language today different from that of early England?

Why did English change when it was brought to America?

What are some ways that new words are added to our language?

Where did our family and place names come from?

What should children know about the history of language?

The History of Language

No one really knows how language began. Linguistic history can be traced back only to known languages and known events that shaped the development of language, leaving the evolution of first utterances to speculation. One of the better known theories of the origin of language is termed the "bow-wow" theory. In this theory it is supposed that words evolved from the noises associated with certain things, such as the bark of a dog, the babble of a brook, and the rushing of the wind. In another theory, called the "ding-dong" theory, language results from noises made by man in reaction to outside forces, just as a bell rings when someone pushes or pulls it. The "pooh-pooh" theory explains language as man's spontaneous reaction to things in the same way that we say "Ouch!" or "Oh!" Yet another theory suggests that language may have evolved from the emotional, songlike outpourings of primitive man.

Perhaps we will never know just how our language began, but we do know that language has grown and changed as a reflection of movements of people and events in history. Any living language constantly changes, and English is no exception. The change, of course, is slow and almost imperceptible until we make comparisons over a considerable period of time.

Linguists divide the languages of the world into *families.* English belongs to the Indo-European or Aryan family. The branches of this family include Indian, Iranian, Armenian, Hellenic, Albanian, Italic, Celtic, Balto-Slavonic, and Teutonic (Bryant, 1962, pp. 10–12). English comes from the Teutonic, or Germanic, branch. This origin has been determined on the basis of such common features as sound, structure, and vocabulary. Because of the similarities, linguists believe that all the languages in the group are variants of the same original language.

The history of the English language is arbitrarily divided into three periods: Old English, Middle English, and Modern English. Within these blocks of time it is possible to identify certain events that significantly shaped the language we know today, but in doing this it is important to keep in mind that these events seldom produced immediate change. The development of our language is really one continuous story of interaction and gradual change. Language is always in a state of becoming. It is continually shaped by the slow, casual death of features that have ceased to serve a purpose and the assimilation of new creations that have survived the rigors of day-by-day field-testing.

The Old English Period (450–1100)

The first language identified in what is now Great Britain was Celtic. The people who lived there were called Celts, not because of their race but because they spoke the Celtic language. Only two groups of the original Celts, however, maintained their separate identity, the Picts in the north and the Scots in the west.

The Celts were ruled by Rome from about the middle of the first century to the fifth century. There is no literary language from this period and there is little evidence to suggest that the Celts had much influence on the English language. Some Celtic place names such as Kent, Avon, and Dover remain, however.

The beginning of English The story of English as a distinct language really begins with the collapse of the Roman Empire. When the Roman legions left Britain in the fifth century, the Celtic people, who had not had to defend themselves for several hundred years, were attacked by marauding Picts and Scots. The Celts appealed to Germanic tribes from Northern Europe for help, offering them land in return for protection.

The appeal brought assistance, but it also brought increasing numbers of Angles, Saxons, Jutes, and probably some Frisians, who came to help and stayed. Fierce seesaw battles raged for some 200 years as the Celts resisted the invasion. Eventually the Northern European tribes were successful in taking over the country, and the Celts were forced to flee for their lives to the mountains and outer areas of the country. Tales of the period survive in the legends of King Arthur.

The victorious tribes settled in various areas of Britain, the Angles in the north and central part of the country, the Saxons in the south, and the Jutes in the southeastern corner and the Isle of Wight (see Figure 2-1). The language they spoke belonged to the Teutonic or Germanic branch of the Indo-European family of languages. It was called Anglo-Saxon after the two dominant tribes, but it is more commonly known today as Old English. The name England also came from the Angles. At first the country was called "Angleland" after them, then "Engleland," and finally "England."

The Latin influence In 597 another historical event occurred that had linguistic implications. Roman missionaries under the leadership of St. Augustine introduced Christianity into England and brought Latin into the country as their working language. One result of their coming was the infusion of a number of Latin religious terms into English. These were "borrowed" or added to the existing language, a practice that has continued to the present time.

More than 450 words of Latin origin can be found in Old English. Some of these were doubtlessly already a part of the language before

FIGURE 2-1
Settlement of Early Britain.

the coming of the missionaries as a result of the Roman occupation and other contacts with Roman merchants. It is difficult to determine when specific Latin words came into use, because of the lack of written language. At any rate, by the end of the Old English period, a number of words of Latin origin were firmly established in the language. Among these were: *stræt* (street), *mil* (mile), *weall* (wall), *win* (wine), *cese* (cheese), *disc* (dish), *cytel* (kettle), *nunne* (nun), *candel* (candle), *organa* (organ), *preost* (priest), *psealm* (psalm), *scol* (school), *tempel* (temple), and *magister* (master).

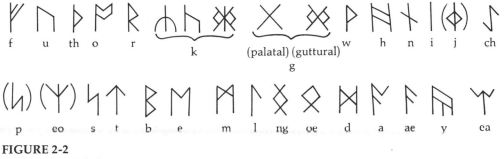

FIGURE 2-2
The Runic Alphabet.

From *The World Book Encyclopedia.* © 1982 World Book-Childcraft International, Inc. Used by permission.

The runic alphabet Before the coming of the missionaries, writing was apparently limited to the runic alphabet (see Figure 2-2). It was not used for literary purposes, however, and its origin and use remain shrouded in mystery. It is believed that the alphabet was derived from early Greek and Roman symbols, but clues to its origin are quite limited. Runic inscriptions on monuments, coins, and jewelry have been found that date back to around A.D. 200. Only a few people knew the runic alphabet, and it is thought that the symbols were used primarily for rituals and magic. The story is told of a lovely maiden who lay seriously ill. The wisest doctors could neither explain her illness nor effect a cure. Finally, runic symbols were discovered carved into the frame of her wooden bed. The runes were removed, and the maiden, freed from the awful curse, immediately became well.

The Danish influence About 790 the Danes became a serious threat to England. Battles between the English and the Danes raged for nearly ninety years. At last the Danes gained the upper hand, and in the peace of Wedmore they were granted official control of more than half of England. The exciting and gory tales of this period have come down to us in the story of *Beowulf.*

The language of the Danes was similar to that already in use in England. Many words were in fact identical in the two languages because of the common Germanic origin. Some remnants of specific Danish influence can be found, however, in place names such as those ending in *-by, -thorp, -beck,- dale,* and *-thwaite.* Words with the *sk* sound are another reminder of the Danes (*sky, skill, skin, scrub, scrape,* etc.). Prior to the Danish invasion this sound was not found in Old English. Old English did have an *sc* spelling but it was pronounced /sh/ and the spelling was later changed to *sh* (*scyrte–shirt, scip–ship, sceal–shall, fisc–fish,* etc.).

A look at Old English Old English looks very much like a foreign language to us now. Our language has undergone so much change since that time that we have to study Old English just as we would a foreign language in order to read and understand it. A sample is included here to show you what it was like (Figure 2-3). The selection is from a sermon by Aelfric, a man Pyles calls "the greatest prose writer of the Old English period" (1964, p. 133). In this selection Aelfric tells about the martyrdom of Christian soldiers in Asia Minor.

When you read this selection you probably noticed that some of the symbols were different from those used in our writing today and that the language was rather cryptic, even when translated. If you could hear the selection read you would also notice a difference in specific sounds of the language. That is because some of the symbols were not pronounced as we pronounce them today. In addition Old English had some sounds that we no longer use, and it had not yet acquired some of our modern sounds.

The vocabulary of Old English was also quite different. More than half of the words we currently use have been derived from French and Latin, and these had not yet been incorporated into the language. Old English words were almost entirely of Teutonic origin, and many of them have been lost through the years. Baugh reports, for instance, that 85 percent of the words in an Old English dictionary are no longer in use. In spite of this high figure, however, the words from Old English that have survived carry a heavy communication load in modern English. They are the common words that we use over and over (for example, *animal, home, house, man, woman, wife, eye, ear, son, brother, daughter, young, good, ride, love, help, sit, drink, eat, write, sing, learn, climb, was, were, drive, bite, floor, find, would,* and *should*).

The grammar of Old English was also quite different from that of Modern English. You may have noticed in the selection from Aelfric that the arrangement of words in the sentences did not follow the pattern you expected. That is because Old English was a highly *inflected* language and word order was not as important for meaning as it is today. An inflected language has many different forms of words, created most frequently by adding suffixes to indicate both grammatical and semantic information. Just for nouns alone there were inflections to indicate whether the word was masculine, feminine, or neuter; singular or plural; and whether the noun was the subject or

FIGURE 2-3 (*facing page*)

From *The Origins and Development of the English Language* byThomas Pyles, © 1964 by Harcourt Brace Jovanovich, Inc. Reprinted by permission of the publisher.

WĒ   WYLLAÐ   ĒOW   GERECCAN   ÞÆRA   fēowertigra
We   want   [to] you   to tell   of the   forty

cempena   ðrōwunge   þæt   ēower   gelēafa   þē   trumre
soldiers   [the] suffering,   that   your   belief   the   firmer

      sȳ.   þonne   gě   gehȳrað   hū   þegenlice   hī   þrōwodon
may be,   when   ye   hear   how   thanelike   they   suffered

for   crīste·   On   þæs   cāseres   dagum   þe   wæs   gehāten
for   Christ.   In   that   Caesar's   days   who   was   called

licinius   wearð   āstyred   mycel   ēhtnys   ofer   þā
Licinius   was   stirred up   much   persecution   over   the

crīstenan·   swā   þæt   ælc   crīsten   mann   sceolde   be
Christians,   so   that   each   Christian   man   should   by

his   āgenum   fēore   þām   hǣlende   wiðsacan   and   tō
his   own   life   the   Saviour   deny   and   to

hǣðenscype   gebūgan·   and   þām   dēofolgyldum   drihtnes
heathenship   bow,   and   to the   idols   [the] Lord's

wurþmynt   gebēodan·   Þā   wæs   geset   sum   wælhrēowa
honor   submit.   Then   was   set   some   bloodthirsty

dēma   agricolaus   gecīged·   on   ānre   byrig   sebastia   gehāten·
judge   Agricolaus   called   in   a   city   Sebastia   called,

on   þām   lande   armenia·   Se   foresǣde   dēma   wæs   swīðe
in   the   land   Armenia.   The   aforesaid   judge   was   very

ārlēas·   crīstenra   manna   ēhtere   and   arod   tō
merciless,   [of] Christian   men   [a] persecutor   and   ready   to

dēofles   willan·   Þā   hēt   se   cwellere   þæs
[the] devil's   will.   Then   ordered   the   murderer   the

cāseres   cempan   ealle   geoffrian·   heora   lāc   þām
Caesar's   soldiers   all   to offer   their   sacrifices   to the

godum·
gods.

an object, whether it showed possession, and, in some instances, whether it expressed a means or agency. Because the form of individual words in Old English clearly indicated their use and function in a sentence, word order was less important.

In comparison, Modern English has very few inflections. Only three inflected forms, for example, are common to nouns today: those to signal number, possession, and gender. Nouns usually form a plural by adding *-s* or *-es* (*dog–dogs*, *fox–foxes*). They usually show possession by adding *'s* or just *'* (singular possessive: *dog's*; plural possessive: *dogs'*). In addition some nouns indicate gender by adding *-or* or *-ess* (*actor–actress*). The specific use of a noun, such as whether it is the subject or the object of the sentence, is indicated by word order rather than by inflected form. In the sentences *The dog ran after the boy*, and *The boy ran after the dog*, there is no need to change the spelling of *boy* or *dog* to signal who is doing what. The position of each word in the sentence establishes its use.

Our practice of combining words to form compounds had its genesis in Old English. *Barn*, for instance, is from a compound of two words *bere* (barley) and *ærn* (building). It meant a place for storing barley. *Daisy* comes from *dæg* (day) and *ēage* (eye); *window* comes from *vindr* (wind) and *ēage* (eye).

The use of synonyms also date back to the Old English period. Jesperson points out seventeen expressions for the sea in the epic poem *Beowulf (brim, flod, garsecg, hæf, heaðu, holm, holmwylm, hronrad, lagu, mere, merestræt, sæ, seglrad, stream, wæd, wæg, yþ)*, and thirteen more in other poems of that period *(flodweg, flodwielm, flot, flotweg, holmweg, hronmere, mereflod, merestream, sæflod, sæholm, sæstream, sæweg, yþmere)* (1955, p. 53).

The Middle English Period (1100–1500)

A period of comparative calm followed the Scandinavian invasion of Britain. Although the English had paid a big price to the invaders, the two groups had a common ancestry and were alike in other ways. The conquered and the conquerors settled into a reasonably peaceful period.

Then in 1065 Edward the Confessor, king of England, died without an heir. The nobles of England named Harold, son of the powerful Earl Godwin, as the new king. Over in France, however, William, Duke of Normandy, claimed that Edward had promised the crown to him. He gathered his army and invaded England. At the Battle of Hastings, in 1066, Harold was killed by an arrow in his eye, and the leaderless English were summarily defeated by William. The victorious William then proclaimed himself William the Conqueror, king of England, and proceeded to conquer the rest of England.

The Norman French rule Thus the British people came under the feudal rule of the French aristocracy. King William brought in his Norman friends to be the lords and ladies of England. He gave them land and set them up as the ruling class. Important positions and great estates were all held by the French aristocracy. French became the language of the government and schools (except in those which used Latin), but English continued to be the main language of the common people. Latin was used for religious purposes and for legal documents.

Both the French and the English people varied in their mastery of the other language. Some became bilingual, but most of them learned only a few phrases. The French did not consider themselves English and generally resisted learning the English language. They learned only as much as they had to to rule the common people, to travel, and to carry on their business affairs. All the while the masses of people continued to speak English, and so the two languages existed side by side. This coexistence of the two languages is reflected today in our language; we still have two words for some things or ideas (*child/infant, freedom/liberty, lamb/mutton, happiness/felicity*).

Coexistent languages At the beginning of the Middle English period English and French were still coexistent but polarized languages in England, with French the prestigious language. However, before the close of the period English had been revived as the accepted language. Baugh (1957) notes that by the end of the thirteenth century there were indications that the French language was losing its hold on England and that the tendency to speak English was becoming constantly stronger. He cites as evidence the number of monas teries and schools that had adopted rules *requiring* students to use French "lest the French language be completely disused."

Renewed interest in English The renewed interest in English came about as a result of several factors. The importance of a language is largely determined by the importance of the people who speak it, and by this time the English speaking people were gaining more recognition. Because the feudal system was giving way to free tenancy of land, the general condition of the masses improved. An epidemic known as "the Black Death" killed many of the working class and created a shortage of labor, which in turn increased the economic importance of the working class. The rise of craftsmen and the rise of the merchant class also came about during this same period. The French oppression of the English people tended to create a strong national feeling and a determination to preserve their identity and their language. The fact that the French spoken in England was considered inferior by Frenchmen on the continent also contributed to the weakened position of the French language.

The English that emerged at the end of the period was quite different from that used at the beginning of the Middle English period. The sounds of the language, the vocabulary, and the grammar had all changed. For a comparison of English from around the beginning of the eleventh century and the end of the fourteenth century look at the two versions of the Lord's Prayer in Figure 2-4.

The Old English practice of regularly stressing first syllables and carefully enunciating inflected endings created a harsh and strident sound. French words, on the other hand, were usually stressed on the last syllable. Thus, when French words were combined with English words in a sentence, the overall sound of the language was quite different from that of Old English. The variation in stress cre-

Fæder ure þu þe eart on heofonum, si þin nama gehalgod;	Oure fadir þat art in heuenes, halwid be þi name;
tobecume þin rice;	þi reume or kyngdom come to þe;
gewurþe þin willa on eor-ðan swa swa on heofonum.	be þi wille don in herþe as it is don in heuene.
Urne gedæghwamli-can hlaf syle us to dæg;	Yeue to vs to day oure eche dayes bred;
and forgyf us ure gyltas, swa swa we forgyfað urum gyltendum.	and foryeue to vs oure det-tis, þat is, oure synnys, as we foryeuen to oure det-touris, þat is, to men þat han synned in vs.
And ne gelæd þu us on costnunge, ac alys us of yfele.	And lede vs not in to temptacion, but delyuere vs from euyl.
Soþlice.	Amen, so be it.

FIGURE 2-4

From Thomas Pyles, *The English Language: A Brief History*, copyright © 1968, p. 39. Reprinted by permission of Holt, Rinehart and Winston, publishers.

ated an ebb and flow of speech sounds and a more interesting rhythmic pattern.

The change in stress also had an effect on English grammar. The endings of words began to be enunciated less clearly, and gradually many of the inflections from the Old English period were lost. The reduction of the number of inflected forms in Middle English was necessarily accompanied by the establishment of word order to signal meaning. For example, we say

> The *paint* is thick.
>
> I am going to *paint* the house.
>
> Hand me the *paint* brush.
>
> The clerk mixed the *paint*.
>
> The machine squirted some color into the *paint*.

All of these sentences use the same spelling of the word *paint*. We understand the word's meaning and its relationship to other words in the sentences because of its position. The word order makes it clear whether paint is the subject, verb, adjective, direct object, or indirect object.

The vocabulary of Middle English had also changed. To communicate with the working class, the ruling class had to learn some common English words; the working class likewise had to become familiar with some French words. Because French was the language of the schools and the new universities, any commoner who wished to become educated and to improve himself had to learn French. Marriages sometimes occurred between the French and the English, particularly in outlying regions. Although French did not become the common language of England, it was inevitable that it should exert a considerable influence on the English language. Many words of French origin were incorporated into the English language (*army, navy, choir, faith, sermon, duke, prince, servant, gown, jewel, fruit, liquor, art, harmony, literature, painting, science, chapter, letter,* and *volume,* to name a few).

The Modern English Period (1500–)

Before we consider the influences that continued to shape our language during the Modern English period, we should note that the Norman Conquest was the last time England was invaded and conquered by a foreign power with another language. Subsequent years and events continued to bring about change in the language, but

English never again had to compete with another language for national supremacy. By the beginning of the Modern English period, English was well established as the oral and literary language of a recognized nation.

The first two centuries in the Modern English period set the trend for continued development of the English language. It was a time of renewed interest in the arts and in learning in general; of unprecedented travel and intellectual opportunities. Language, quite naturally, grew and changed.

Factors that influenced the language The invention of the printing press in the middle of the fifteenth century had far-reaching effects on all languages. It was introduced into England by William Caxton in 1476. Many important works were translated into English and printed. By 1640 there were over 20,000 titles in English. Whereas books had once been an expensive luxury that only a few could afford, they were now available to everyone. In addition, the many books in print provided models of the language and promoted a trend toward standards and uniformity in language.

Aided by the advent of the printing press, education made rapid progress. Working conditions for the masses also improved, and people found themselves with leisure time. Therefore, more and more people of all classes learned to read and write, creating a demand for language and literature greater than ever before. Recognition of the great store of knowledge and experience preserved in the classics brought renewed interest in the work of Greek and Latin writers. People discovered that these early writers dealt with their concerns and desires. They also found that reading literature stimulated their thinking and helped them understand their own lives.

By the early Modern English period a greater social consciousness was developing. Lines between classes were less distinct, and it was possible for someone from a lower class to move to a higher one. To do so, of course, meant acquiring the language and social graces characteristic of the higher class. Thus, those who desired to improve their social position became more aware of language differences and sought to acquire the recognized standards of grammar and pronunciation.

Mobility also greatly influenced language in the Modern English period. Trade and travel flourished. The people of England as well as those on the Continent extended their contacts around the globe. Improvements in transportation and a greater interest in products and ideas from abroad brought about a rapid expansion of vocabulary and an increased interest in language in general.

The borrowing of words Under the influence of the Renaissance, writers freely borrowed from the classical languages of Latin and

Greek. Many of the words they introduced in writing, however, were never incorporated into the language. *Allect, adminiculation, improperations, incurvate,* and *subdichotomies* are among the examples given by Alexander of "words . . . that did not take root in the language." Alexander concludes that "In the long run the language seems to assimilate those words which have a useful function to fulfill and to reject most of the others" (1969, p. 100).

There were strict differences of opinion concerning the widespread borrowing of words during the early part of the Modern English period. Some people believed that the English language should remain "pure" — that it should not be adulterated with words from other languages. These purists labelled borrowed foreign words as *inkhorn* terms. Many of the controversial terms they were concerned about did come into common use. Words such as *industry, maturity,* and *temperance* are examples of inkhorn terms that we find quite useful today.

Perhaps word borrowing is an inevitable linguistic process. At any rate, Baugh (1957) reports that English has adopted words from more than fifty languages. From the classics, for example, we have *disrespect, excursion, education, emancipate, exist, sordid, urge,* and *meditate* directly from Latin, and *catastrophe, lexicon,* and *anonymous* directly from Greek. Another group of words such as *emphasis, climax, chaos,* and *system* came from Greek through Latin. Other foreign words that have been incorporated into the speech and writing of Modern English are the French words *alloy, bizarre, detail, entrance, equip, mustache, progress, shock, ticket, vogue,* and *volunteer;* the Italian words *balcony, cameo, design, influenza, granite, stanza, trill, umbrella, violin,* and *volcano;* and the Spanish words *alligator, apricot, banana, barricade, cannibal, embargo,* and *potato.*

Changes in the Sounds of English

It is easy to see that the English language changed considerably between the fifth century and the time it was brought to America by the early colonists. Any living language changes over a period of time, and English was no exception. The original Celtic tongue was infused and augmented through contributions (many of them forced) from the early Romans; Christian missionaries; the Angles, Saxons, and Jutes; the Danes; the French; and finally, the world of trade and of classical literature. Little by little the language grew. New words came into use and old words died out. Pronunciations changed, sometimes drastically. Two of the major pronunciation changes are

of particular importance: those which resulted from the loss of inflections and those in pronunciation of long vowels.

The loss of inflections As noted earlier in this chapter, many of
the inflections of Old English gradually weakened and finally
dropped from the language. Alexander says, "Because so many final
vowels, which had already been weakened in M. E., vanished completely by the modern period, the three stages of the language, O.
E., M. E. and Mod. E, are often called respectively the period of 'full
endings,' the period of 'reduced endings,' and the period of 'lost
endings' " (1969, p. 112). He cites the following examples as illustrations:

O.E.	M.E.	Mod. E
cēp*an*	kep*ee(n)*	keep
heort*e*	hert*e*	heart
nam*a*	nam*e* (*e* still pronounced)	name (*e* silent)
luf*u* (noun)	love (*e* still pronounced)	love (*e* silent)
luf*ian* (verb)	love(*n*) (*e* still pronounced)	love (*e* silent)
waēr*on*	were(*n*) (*e* still pronounced)	were (*e* silent)
stān*as*	stoon*es* (*e* still pronounced)	stones (*e* silent)

Notice that in the transition from inflected to uninflected word
forms, an unaccented *e* sound was common at the end of words. By
Modern English times the *e* was no longer pronounced, but it nevertheless remained in the spelling of the words.

The great vowel shift The second major group of sound changes
concerned the pronunciation of long vowel sounds. It is known as
"the great vowel shift." These changes are thought to have occurred
around the end of the Middle English period and the beginning of
the Modern English period. Malmstrom describes the changes that
took place as follows: "The low and mid vowels moved upward; the
highest vowels moved downward and acquired front or back off-
glides, becoming diphthongs" (1977, p. 60). Alexander describes the
shift as "a series of changes which affected the long vowels of M.E.
and gradually transformed them into quite different sounds in Mod.
E. It is the most revolutionary and far-reaching sound change during

the history of the language and naturally took a long time to complete" (1969, p. 114).

Pyles provides the following example to illustrate the differences between our modern long vowel sounds and their counterparts in Old English:

ā was as in Modern English *calm* (*hām* "home"),

ē approximately as in *late* (*mētan* "to meet"),

ī as in *need* (*rīdan* "to ride"),

ō approximately as in *hope* (*fōda* "food"), and

ū as in *school* (*hūs* "house"). (1968, p. 12)

The differences between the pronunciations of the vowel sounds in these examples and our pronunciation of long vowels today is significant (e.g., *calm*/*came*). It is also interesting to note that while this great change was taking place in the pronunciation of long vowels, the pronunciation of short vowels underwent comparatively little change.

Other pronunciation changes The silent letters in modern word spelling illustrate other pronunciation changes. For example, the initial consonant is no longer sounded in such words as *know*, *knot*, and *knee*; *gnaw*, *gnat*, and *gnarl*; *wrap*, *wreath*, and *wreck*; and *pneumonia*. Other silent letters that were once pronounced include the *gh* in such words as *night*, *sight*, and *naught*; and the *b* in *lamb* and *comb*, and the *t* in *castle* and *whistle*. Each of these changes, of course, affected a limited number of words. However, they illustrate pronunciation changes that have contributed to imperfect letter-sound spelling in modern day English.

American English

The language in the early colonies was essentially that of seventeenth-century British English. There was much that was different in America, however, and the speakers of English soon found their vocabularies inadequate. To fulfill their need for verbal labels, they acquired many Indian words. Among them were *raccoon*, *squaw*, *pecan*, *chipmunk*, *wigwam*, *moose*, *skunk*, *oppossum*, *canoe*, *toboggan*, *moccasin*, *mackinaw*, *tapioca*, *hominy*, *succotash*, and *pone*.

Our American language heritage also includes numerous examples of the colonists' ingenuity in combining or creating words and expressions to fill their linguistic needs. They added words such as *bluff, foothill, gap, divide,* and *underbrush* to the language to describe physical features for which they knew no words. Their knack for picturesque words and phrases is illustrated in such expressions as *bullfrog, garter snake, groundhog, warpath, crazy quilt, sidewalk, an ax to grind, face the music, fly off the handle,* and *bury the hatchet.*

Not all of the colonists were English, of course, and words from other countries soon became a part of the American language. For example, from the Dutch we acquired *waffle, cruller, coleslaw, cookie, Yankee, stoop, snoop, boss, Santa Claus,* and *dope.* From the French came *chowder, shanty, prairie, butte, cent, dime, portage, cache, levee, bayou, caribou, pumpkin,* and *bureau.* From the German came *frankfurter, hamburger, noodle, sauerkraut, kindergarten, pretzel, wiener,* and *lager.* The later influence of Spanish colonists contributed such words as *hammock, chocolate, mosquito, coyote, chili, patio, rodeo, corral, lariat, cinch, sombrero, lasso, incommunicado, vigilantes,* and *canyon.* The African brought *banjo, chigger, goober* (peanut), *gumbo, hoodoo, jazz, juke,* and *zombi.*

In trying to provide labels for things in their new environment, the colonists sometimes assigned a new meaning to an already established word. For example, they used the English name *robin* to identify an American bird quite different from the English robin. They also used the word *corn* for a new grain the Indians taught them to grow. In England the word *corn* meant any kind of grain.

The Birth of New Words

The vocabulary of our language continues to be expanded. Occasionally a new discovery or a new situation necessitates the deliberate creation of a new word. More often, though, words just seem to evolve, and we are quite unaware of when or how a particular new word came into the language. As we look back at this evolution, however, we can determine the way in which many of our present-day words were acquired. The following are some of the more common sources.

Borrowing Words from other languages are incorporated into our existing vocabulary. Examples: *halt* (German), *zany* (Italian), *parka* (Eskimo), *tycoon* (Japanese), *polka* (Czechoslovakian), and *poker* (French).

Change in word meaning The meaning of a word shifts so that a word already in the vocabulary acquires a different meaning. Examples: *quick* (formerly meant alive), *gripe* (formerly, to grip or hold), *nice* (formerly, foolish), *governor* (formerly, pilot), and *rheumatism* (formerly, a cold in the head). The meanings of some words have been expanded (e.g., *cavalcade* once meant on horseback), and the meanings of others have narrowed (e.g., *undertaker* once meant simply someone who undertook to do a job).

Functional change Words come to be used in different ways. For example, a noun may be used as a verb — *eye* (to eye something), *book* (to book a person), and *elbow* (to elbow one's way through a crowd); verbs may be used as nouns — *show* (to put on a show), *find* (a real find), *shave* (a close shave), and *hit* (scored a direct hit). (A functional change heard recently in a classroom: "We had a *fun* time.")

Compounding Two or more words are combined to form one word. Examples: *breakfast, skyscraper, overgrown, Christmas, backyard, paperback, overshadow, ovenproof, outstanding,* and the more recently formed *upcoming*.

Morphemic combinations Words are formed by combining roots or by combining roots and affixes. Many scientific words have been formed in this way. Examples: *telescope, astronaut, retrorocket, winterize, expertise, booklet, subway, overdose, New Yorker, communism,* and *coeducation*.

Acronyms Initial letters or parts of words are combined to form a new word. Examples: *laser* (light amplification by stimulated emission of radiation), *scuba* (self-contained underwater breathing apparatus), *radar* (radio detecting and ranging), *motel* (motor + hotel), *smog* (smoke + fog), *twirl* (twist + whirl), *grumble* (growl + rumble), and *flurry* (fly + hurry).

Shortening Parts of words are deleted to form a shorter word. Examples: *bike* (bicycle), *pup* (puppy), *props* (properties), *photo* (photograph), *bus* (omnibus), *cab* (cabriolet), and *wig* (periwig). The shortened word may form a new part of speech. Examples: *enthuse* (enthusiasm), *orate* (orator), and *edit* (editor).

Names of people and places Words may come from the name of a person or place associated with the things they describe. Examples: *pasteurize* (from Louis Pasteur who discovered the process), *cardigan* (from the Earl of Cardigan who insisted on having his sweaters open down the front), *silhouette* (from Etienne de Silhouette, the French controller-general who tried to simplify French finances), *braille* (from Louis Braille who developed the braille alphabet), *valentine* (from St. Valentine who is said to have sent the first valentine), *cantaloupe* (from Cantalupe, a country home of the Pope where cantaloupes were grown), *tuxedo* (from a club named for Tuxedo Park, New York), and *uranium* (from the planet Uranus).

Myths and legends The names of characters and places in myths and legends have been the sources of a number of words. Examples:

narcissism, stoical, herculean, titan, nymph, echo, siren, hero, demigod, and *oracle.*

Slang Slang terms tend to be short-lived. However, some slang words have achieved common usage over a period of time. Examples: *boom, slump, row* (disagreement), *crank* (grouch), *fad, joke, grit, pluck,* and *joint.* The term *slang* is thought to be a shortened form of *thieves' language,* which was a jargon spoken by thieves and criminals during the Middle Ages in England.

Coining Some words are simply created. They may result from the need to name a new product or they may be made up words that seem to fit a particular situation. Examples: *nylon, kodak, freon, teflon, zip, wheeze, bang, meow, breathalyzer,* and *umpteen.*

The Origin of Names

Family Names

Personal names appear to have been among the earliest forms of language. Family names, however, have a more recent origin. When people lived together in small family groups one name was adequate. But with greater mobility and larger social structures some means of finer identification became necessary. Just as we use a phrase to identify someone ("the one who sang the solo" or "the one who whistles like a bird"), people in earlier periods of time began to add descriptive phrases to point out which "Mary" or "John" they were referring to. If the description was apt it continued to be used. In time it was shortened to one word and became a second name for the person.

Surnames were not hereditary at first. A descriptive name given to an individual might continue to be used even when the description was no longer appropriate, but it was not passed on to the next generation. In most countries family names were first inherited among the nobles and landowners. Their names were derived from their estates, and it was only natural that the sons inherit the name along with the landholdings. By the end of the fourteenth century, family names were generally hereditary for everyone in England. Some countries on the continent had established the practice earlier, and in some countries it did not evolve until later.

Most surnames can be classified as one of four kinds of descriptions: location, occupation, parental name, or personal characteristic.

Names from locations Telling where someone lives or where he or she came from is a natural way of pointing out which person we mean. It was a common means of identification when people had only one name. In this way John from Hebden could be distinguished from another John who came from Hazon. Or, if the person was an established member of the community, the identification might point out some geographical feature near where the person currently lived, such as a hill or stream. Gradually these descriptive phrases took on the form of a second name. For example, John who lived on a hill would be known as John *Hill* and John who lived near a ford in the river would be known as John *Ford*. Sometimes two or more words were combined to form a name. The John who lived below the forest would be called John *Underwood* and John who lived near a church on the hill would be called John *Churchill*.

Surnames that were derived from places include *Forest, Field, Brook(s), Banks, Green* (village green), *Ridgeway, Baum* (tree), *Moore, Well(s), Lane, Meadows, Poole, Steinway* (stone road), *Thorpe* (village), *Scroggins* (thicket), and *Vanderpool* (pond).

Another interesting group of names from places had to do with the practice of identifying a public house or inn by a picture signboard. In some countries public houses were required by law to display an identifying sign. Because so many people couldn't read, the sign was a simple picture such as a key, spear, swan, bell, cock, ball, or horse. These too were used as descriptions of people who worked or lived there. John from an inn bearing the sign of a ball, for instance, would be known as John *Ball*.

An original name was quite often corrupted or changed in form over a period of time. For example the English *-ham* meaning "meadow on a stream" is part of many English names. Often, however, the original *-ham* has taken a different form: *-am, -um, -om, -man, -nam, -num, -son*, and *-hem* (Smith, 1973). Such corruptions occurred with many names and added greatly to the total number of family names.

Names from occupations Occupations were another natural way of identifying or pointing out someone. In earlier times people usually learned a trade when they were young and followed it all their lives. Thus people's occupations were readily associated with their names. Family names that have come from occupations include *Smith, Arrowsmith, Goldsmith, Miller, Weaver, Cook, Baker, Carpenter, Mason, Taylor, Shepherd, Fletcher* (maker of arrows), *Butler, Harper, Hunter, Potter, Fisher, Bowman, Sawyer, Bailey* (bailiff), *Ambler* (horseman), *Foster* (forester), *Turner* (woodworker), and *Honeyman*.

Names from parents Some names were derived from parental given names, usually the father's. This practice led to the many name endings that mean "son of" or "descendant of" in the various languages. *Patronymic* names, those derived from the father, are common among people from all countries. In English and Swedish the "son of" designation is simply *-son* attached to the father's name. For example, *Johnson* means "son of John" or "John's son." Other endings, according to Smith (1973), include -*sen* in Danish and Norwegian names, -*ian* in Armenian, -*nen* in Finnish, -*poulos* in Greek, and -*wicz* in Polish. Prefixes denoting "son" are the Scottish and Irish *Mac* or *Mc*, the Norman *Fitz*, and the Welsh *Ap*. The prefix *O'* in Irish names is used to denote "grandson of." *Di* and *de* may show familial relationship as in *Di Bernardo* ("son of Bernardo"), but the *de* prefix is also used in the sense of "from" as in *De Ville* ("one who came from Ville — town, city") or "the" as in *De Smet* ("the metal worker").

Patronymic names have also been corrupted and changed. Sometimes a current name may reflect a shortened form of an original affix. Spellings may also be changed in other ways. *Dickens* and *Dixon*, for example, are variant forms of *Dickson*. *Price* is a shortened form of *Aprice* and *Davis* was derived from *Davidson*.

Names from personal characteristics Perhaps the most interesting names are those which originated as nicknames. Just as we today tend to identify someone as "the cautious one," "the crabby one," "the blond," unusual qualities of character, attitudes, or physical appearance resulted in epithets that evolved into names. In some names the original meaning is still clearly evident, whereas in others the form requires translation. Names that came about as the result of physical characteristics include *Long, Lang, Longman, Tallman,* and *Longfellow* to describe someone who was noticeably tall; and *Reid, Reed, Read, Ruff, Russ, Russel, Ruddy, Rousseau, Rouse, Larouse, Roth,* and *Flynn* to indicate a red-haired person. Other examples of names given because of hair or skin coloring include *Boyd* (yellow-haired), *Fairfax* (fair haired), *Weiss* (fair in coloring), and *Schwartz* (dark in coloring). Names reflecting other physical characteristics include *Cruickshanks* (crooked leg), *Small, Strong, Armstrong, Gross* (big), *Cameron* (twisted nose), and *Campbell* (twisted mouth).

American Place Names

The history of our country is written in our place names. Each period of exploration, colonization, or expansion added new names to the land. A close look at the names on a map of the United States shows striking patterns of settlement. For example, English names abound in the northeastern states, French names around the Great Lakes and the Mississippi, Dutch names around New York, and Spanish names in the Southwest.

Names from former homes Many place names reflect ties to a former home. Some colonial place names were direct transplants of names from the colonists' former country: *New Hampshire* from Hampshire in England, *New Jersey* from the Island of Jersey in the

English Channel, *Plymouth* from Plymouth, England, and *New Netherlands* from the Dutch colonists' homeland. Explorers and colonists also named places for members of royalty in their home country. *New Orleans*, for example, was named by a French explorer in honor of the Duke of Orleans, and *Virginia* was named for Queen Elizabeth I, "the Virgin Queen." In later periods of settlement people continued to name their new homes for other places they had lived.

Indian names Indian place names stretch across the country. No less than twenty-six states derive their names from Indian words. The list includes *Massachusetts, Connecticut, Minnesota, Missouri, Oklahoma*, and *Kansas*. Many large cities, lakes, and rivers also bear Indian names. *Peoria*, for example, came from Indian words meaning "place of fat beasts," and *Chicago* meant "place of skunk smells."

Spanish names The Spanish influence is strongly reflected in the names of the Southwest. Names such as *San Jose, Los Angeles, Los Alamos, San Pedro, Las Cruces, Rio Grande, La Mesa, La Habra*, and *Palos Verdes* verify the importance of the Spanish in the early settlement of this part of the United States.

Names for explorers Even before the colonists began to give names to the land, there were places on the map bearing the names of early explorers. Information from each exploration was carefully recorded, and any new discoveries were customarily given the name of the explorer who first discovered them. Thus, such places as the *Hudson River, Gray's Harbor*, the *Straits of Juan de Fuca, Lake Champlain, McKenzie River, Pike's Peak, Vancouver Island*, and *Mt. McKinley* stand in tribute to the adventuresome men whose names they bear.

Names for geographic features People in all times seem to have assigned names that describe geographic features, such as *Cumberland Gap, Woodland, Cascade*, and *Oakland*. Many such names were added during the period of westward expansion. As the pioneers moved westward they sent scouts ahead of the wagon train to look the land over and report back. The scouts' descriptions of "the spring where oak trees grow," or "high, rocky mountains," or "swift river," were well remembered because the future well-being of those in the wagon train depended on such information. Many of these colorful descriptions evolved into place names along the way.

Names for leaders and heroes National leaders and heroes also account for a large number of place names. *Washington* is reported to be the most popular of American place names, but other names such as *Lincoln, Jackson, Franklin*, and *Jefferson* are also found in several states.

Every locality seems to have its fascinating names, names that may not appear on a map unless it shows a very small area in considerable detail. Unfortunately, the interesting origins of some names have long since been forgotten, but quite often the stories behind local names live in the memory of older residents or are preserved in the publications of state or county historical societies. In a rural area of Oregon, for example, the *Row River* stands as a reminder of a continual feud between two families who lived on opposite sides of the stream. Other local place names such as *Chickahominy Creek, Gate Creek, Jumpoff Joe Creek, Loon Lake, Elkhead, Wolf Creek, Deadwood, Buck Ford, Salmon River, Hoodoo Butte, Tombstone Summit, Wildcat Mountain, Lookingglass,* and *Cape Foulweather* suggest pieces of the area's history and lore.

Teaching and Learning About Language History

At this point you may be saying to yourself, "This is all very interesting, but how does it relate to teaching the language arts?" There are several possible answers to that question. First of all, knowing about the language we use and how it is related to our own history helps us identify with it. Language is a part of our heritage right along with our grandparents and aunts and uncles. It is a part of us.

Studying the history of language is an aid to vocabulary development and spelling. The history of a word brings it to life and gives it a special personality. Knowing it helps children remember it. Children also gain new dimensions of meaning and understand why words are spelled as they are. For example, words such as *mother, father, house,* and *daughter* are no longer mere verbal symbols; they are a reminder of life in the days of the Anglo-Saxons and the sounds of the language in that period.

The history of language seems to fascinate young and old alike. Children's natural curiosity about language can be a great asset in teaching and learning to use language effectively. When children are interested in language they develop an ear for it and become more aware of significant features. Thus they develop a keener appreciation of language and become more proficient in using it.

There are several ways to help children tune in to their language. You may use an informal approach and include brief but interesting side trips into the history of language whenever the opportunity arises or you may prefer to develop a more formal, teacher-directed unit plan. Most important, get in the habit of being curious about language yourself and you will begin to see all sorts of possibilities for exploring it with children. Begin by collecting resource material and reading about the history of language. A number of books, some written at the level children can read by themselves, are available. (See the references at the end of the book for suggestions.)

If you prefer the incidental approach, arm yourself with knowledge (file cards are useful) and then periodically share interesting things with your class. You might tell them interesting histories of one or two words or point out some historical fact related to the language they are using. Or, you might occasionally call children's attention to a particular word in their reading and ask them to hypothesize about its origin. Children should then be encouraged to check out their hypotheses using the sources available. New words or uncommon ways of using established words are frequently heard on television and radio or read in current newspapers and magazines (e.g., *econocar*, *gasohol*, and *weatherwise*). Sharing these words informally is another way of raising children's level of language consciousness.

With older children you may want to develop a unit on the history of language. Books, pictures, films, and recordings offer many possibilities for *learning about language* and *learning to use language* at the same time. Reading, viewing, listening, dramatizing, discussing, and writing are all helpful for discovering the history of language. A language time line showing the various influences on the English language is one way of organizing the unit and recording information. Colorful illustrations (e.g., a feudal castle, King Arthur, an American Indian) and examples of words added during each period stimulate interest. Learning activity packages and learning centers offer other organizational structures (see Chapter 13).

In Summary

The history of the English language is arbitrarily divided into three periods: Old English, Middle English, and Modern English. What is known as the Old English language was brought to the British Isles by invading Germanic tribes of Angles, Saxons, and Jutes. Few traces of the earlier Celtic language remain. During this period Christianity was introduced into England and Latin became the language of the church. Old English was very different from our modern English: words were both spelled and pronounced differently, and it was a highly inflected language (special endings of words indicated grammatical use).

The Middle English period began with the invasion of the Norman French. As a result, French became the language of the ruling class; and it existed side by side with the English of the working class. The two groups learned varying amounts of the other's language, but neither language completely dominated. Nevertheless, the English language changed considerably during the period. Many French words were incorporated into English. In addition, many of the inflected endings of words were weakened or dropped. As this period merged into the next the pronunciation of long vowels underwent marked change.

At the beginning of the Modern English period, the printing press was invented, making books more accessible. Working conditions improved, and people had more time for leisure activities. Improved transportation brought increased travel and trade. There was also a renewed interest in the classics. All of these factors influenced the growth and change in the English language.

The English language was further affected when it came to America with the colonists. Colonists from other countries and the native Indians added words. When there was no word for a particular situation, the colonists created one. Hence, American English came to differ from British English.

The derivation of place and family names is another aspect of language history. Family names evolved as a means of identification. Most frequently they derive from the place of residence, occupation, parental name, or a personal characteristic. Many place names reflect the language of the area's first settlers. Other names may record vivid descriptions of places as seen by early settlers.

Learning Objectives

COGNITIVE OBJECTIVES

Primary Grades

Children will

know that our language began in England hundreds of years ago.

know that many different languages are spoken in the United States.

know that English has always been the main language in the United States.

know that we have borrowed many words from other languages.

know that our names have meaning.

Middle Grades

Children will

maintain all primary-grade objectives.

be able to discuss events in history that brought about changes in our language.

be able to discuss our language as a multi-cultural heritage.

be able to discuss ways new words are added to our language.

be able to discuss the origin of surnames.

be able to give examples of descriptive surnames originally used for identification.

be able to discuss the origin of place names.

be able to give examples of place names that came from descriptions, from other places, from Spanish and Indian words, and from names of famous people.

AFFECTIVE OBJECTIVES

Children will

show an interest in our language heritage.

enjoy listening to stories of historical events that shaped our language.

be curious about our language.

seek origins of familiar words and phrases.

be alert to interesting personal and place names and try to analyze them.

Suggested Learning Activities

Days of the Week. Have children look up the origin of the names of the days of the week and report back to class. (Names of the months may be used also.)

Role-playing. Divide the class into groups of three and role-play a scene between a French landowner and two English serfs. The landowner is demanding more work, but the serfs are unable to understand what he wants. Plan the characterization carefully. The children may use gibberish instead of regular language.

Literature and Language. Read selections from children's versions of *Beowulf* and *Robin Hood.* Relate the events in those stories to linguistic history.

Learning to Read Etymologies. General reference dictionaries give brief etymologies of many words, but some are difficult to read because symbols and abbreviations are used. However, learning how to decipher a historical path leading up to current use can be an interesting challenge to older children. Here are examples from two dictionaries for the word fraction:

frac tion [ME fraccioun, fr. LL *fraction-, fractio* act of breaking, tr. L *fractus,* pp. of *frangere* to break — more at BREAK][1]

frac tion [Middle English *fraccioun,* from Late Latin *fractus,* past participle of *frangere,* to break. See bhreg- in Appendix.][2]

Students using the Merriam Webster dictionary will need to refer to the list of abbreviations (p. 31a in the 1974 edition) to interpret the meaning of the etymology as given. Guide children through the process with several different words, having them look up the abbreviations

and then restate the information in their own words.

Word Shopping. Make a set of cards by printing a common word from Old English or from a foreign country on each card. Write the origin on the back. Display the word cards around the room. The children should take turns selecting a word and guessing where it came from. If they are correct they may keep the card. If not, they put it back and the turn goes on to the next child.

Word Histories. Give the children a list of words from names such as *davenport, sandwich, maverick, graham, bowie, silhouette,* and *pasteurize* and have them find the origin of each word.

What's That Word. Give the children the forms of words in Old English and Middle English and have them try to guess the modern word.

Old English	Middle English	Modern English
belle	belle	(bell)
singan	singen	(sing)
fæder	fader	(father)
cū	cou	(cow)
fōda	fode	(food)
hliehhan	laughen	(laugh)
scöl	scole	(school)
sprecan	speken	(speak)
fæstan	fasten	(fast)
heall	halle	(hall)

Wonder Words. Pose questions that challenge children to discover interesting stories behind words or phrases. For example:

Is a water witch wet or dry?

Why isn't a teddy bear called a freddy bear?

How could someone meet his or her Waterloo without going to Belgium?

---

[1] Webster's New Collegiate Dictionary. Springfield, Massachusetts: G. & C. Merriam Company, 1974.

[2] The American Heritage Dictionary of the English Language. Boston: Houghton Mifflin Company, 1979.

If rhubarb isn't a fruit, what is it?

How many gadflies could sit on the back of a horse?

Children may write other, similar questions and post them on a specially designated bulletin board.

Word Search. Have children skim through a page or column of the newspaper or a book they are reading and list all the compound words they find. Have them identify the words that make up each compound word and tell the meanings of the parts separately and in combination.

Heads and Tails. Over a period of time the children should watch for and collect common prefixes and suffixes and learn their meaning. They need not have a long list; a few of the more common words will be more useful. Make various shaped heads, bodies, and tails of animals (large enough to write on). Print the prefixes on heads, suffixes on tails, and appropriate root words on the bodies. Mix all the pieces up and then have the children try to put them together to form words (and animals).

Roots and Trees. Give the children a list of five to ten common roots. Have them find the origin and meaning of each root and all the words they can that are derived from the root. Possible roots include: *aqua, audio, auto, bio, geo, graph, meter, micro, phone,* and *tele.* A bulletin board of simple cutouts of bare trees may be used to display the children's findings. Print the root across the roots of the tree and print words from the roots on the branches.

Common Names. Give the children a copy of the fifty most common names in Table 2-1. Let them find the meaning of as many names as they can. Then have them try to explain why each name became so widely used. For example, there were many kinds of Smiths (blacksmiths, locksmiths, etc.).

Naming Game. After the children have learned the four major ways that people got names (location, occupation, parental name, or personal characteristic) pass out lists of questions such as those which follow and have the children think of appropriate names.

What name would you give the first person to live on the moon?

What name would you give someone who eats lots of pizza?

What would you name a good athlete?

What would you name someone who lives behind the gym?

Popular Names. Find out the most popular last names in your town or city. Let each child take a section of the telephone book (if it isn't too large) and find which names appear the most times. Then, from these lists, compile a list of the ten most popular names. (If you teach in a large city, you may want to have the children find the most popular names beginning with "S" or "T", for example, rather than the whole telephone book.)

Variation: Examine a list of names of school children and determine the most popular first or last names (or both).

United States History. Let the children select an area on a map of the United States. Have them write a list of place names and find the origin of each name they can. See what the names tell about the early settlement of the area. The Great Lakes region, the lower Mississippi, and the Southwest are particularly good for this exercise.

Local History. Help the children list place names in your locality. Then plan to interview older residents to find out the origin of names. Discuss how to initiate an interview and what questions the children might ask during the interview.

TABLE 2-1. Common Surnames in the United States

RANK	NAME	ESTIMATED NUMBER	RANK	NAME	ESTIMATED NUMBER
1.	Smith	1,258,010	26.	Baker	213,490
2.	Johnson	938,880	27.	King	210,400
3.	Brown	701,940	28.	Roberts	199,370
4.	Miller	663,850	29.	Phillips	182,760
5.	Jones	663,420	30.	Evans	180,620
6.	Williams	660,160	31.	Turner	170,340
7.	Davis	532,960	32.	Rogers	156,820
8.	Anderson	448,470	33.	Edwards	155,280
9.	Wilson	399,590	34.	Bell	141,500
10.	Taylor	357,220	35.	Bailey	131,910
11.	Thomas	354,910	36.	Fisher	129,950
12.	Moore	352,760	37.	Bennett	128,400
13.	Martin	337,960	38.	Brooks	122,650
14.	White	337,010	39.	Foster	117,380
15.	Thompson	328,110	40.	Butler	116,590
16.	Jackson	308,680	41.	James	102,470
17.	Harris	289,080	42.	Cohen	102,200
18.	Lewis	256,980	43.	Jenkins	100,750
19.	Allen	243,450	44.	Ellis	91,940
20.	Nelson	243,370	45.	Jordan	90,740
21.	Walker	243,020	46.	Burke	89,360
22.	Hall	242,170	47.	Elliott	86,030
23.	Robinson	231,980	48.	Johnston	84,570
24.	Green	220,430	49.	Black	80,720
25.	Adams	216,400	50.	Owens	78,670
				Total	14,095,720

Suggestions for Further Reading

Alexander, Henry. *The Story of Our Language.* Garden City, N.Y.: Doubleday, 1969.

Baugh, Albert C. *A History of the English Language.* 2nd ed. Appleton-Century-Crofts, 1957.

Boyd, Gertrude. *Linguistics in the Elementary School.* Itasca, Ill.: F. E. Peacock, 1976.

Jespersen, Otto. *Growth and Structure of the English Language,* 9th ed. Garden City, N.Y.: Doubleday, 1955.

Malmstrom, Jean. *Understanding Language, A Primer for the Language Arts Teacher.* New York: St. Martin's Press, 1977.

Pyles, Thomas. *The English Language: A Brief History.* New York: Holt, Rinehart and Winston, 1968.

Smith, Elsdon C. *The Story of Our Names.* New York: Harper and Row, 1950.

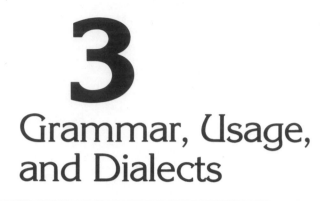

3

Grammar, Usage, and Dialects

Language . . . is a two-level system. In the case of spoken language, the two levels of the system are related to sound and meaning, and the task of the language learner is to construct a set of rules that will enable him to translate from one to the other. Many linguists refer to the two levels of language as surface and deep structure, with syntax, or grammar, as the set of rules that permits the language user to operate between the two.

Frank Smith (1973, p. 139)

CHAPTER PREVIEW

Think about these two sentences: "Pipe down!" "Kindly reduce the magnitude of your utterances." Are both sentences grammatical? Is one *better* than the other? A linguistic approach to the study of language analyzes; it *describes* rather than *prescribes*. Grammar, usage, and dialects are considered as different, but related, aspects of the language system. In this chapter we present background information concerning each area of study and suggest how the areas may be dealt with in the elementary language arts curriculum.

QUESTIONS TO THINK ABOUT AS YOU READ

What is the "grammar debate"?

How does "new" grammar differ from "old" grammar?

What are some linguistic terms associated with the study of grammar?

What and how might I teach children about grammar?

What does *usage* really mean?

Why should children learn standard English usage?

Who speaks a dialect?

What factors are known to influence the development and retention of dialects?

English Grammar

Grammar has long been the "bad medicine" of children's school years. Many parents and teachers alike have taken the position that grammar is good for children even though they don't like it. I recently sat among a group of junior high school parents and heard them plead for more grammar teaching. One parent expressed the widespread belief that only the teaching of grammar (specifically the diagramming of sentences) would reverse the universal downward trend in children's writing ability. That, of course, is not supported by research.

What grammar is and why it is taught is confusing to many people. Reasons for teaching grammar tend to be vague but on the order of "It's good for them." Most people who advocate the teaching of grammar believe that it will ultimately improve students' abilities to speak and write the "correct" forms of English. The teaching of grammar is commonly associated with the teaching of correct usage (particularly of verbs), drill on parts of speech, and the diagramming of sentences. When that approach is used, it is little wonder that grammar has been such a distasteful and neglected subject.

Grammar has been succinctly defined as a study of the morphology and syntax of a language. This means that grammar has to do with the form and function of words and the way they are combined to form sentences. In essence, grammar is a study of how language works. Additional information about the specific content of grammar will follow in the discussion of different teaching approaches.

Research does not give strong support to the belief that knowledge of grammar improves speaking or writing ability. Some research reports suggest that the transformational-generative approach may be helpful, but the evidence, taken as a whole, is far from conclusive. Another point to keep in mind is that an in-depth study of grammar requires a high level of abstract thinking, and is thus unsuited to the cognitive level of elementary schoolchildren.

Since these things are true, you are probably wondering if you should even teach grammar at all. And that is a legitimate question. Some people argue that a basic understanding of grammar and grammatical terms is necessary for discussing speech and writing and that grammar should be learned in order to be able to talk about the effective ways to use language. Others suggest that the study of grammar is a model of analytic thinking and that children benefit from such a systematic study. Another common response is that grammar is an essential component of any language system, and because our language is very personal and important in our lives, children ought to know how it works. Knowledge of any process, be it computing or deep sea diving, leads to a sense of confidence and control. Learning about language not only can help children to gain an understanding of a system they already use, but it can alert them to the intricacies and potential uses of the system. Personal experiences in teaching grammar have shown that children have a natural interest in their language and that they enjoy exploring it *when an inductive laboratory approach is used*. Teaching grammar through rote memorization belies the fact that although our language is systematic, it is a dynamic and changing language with infinite possibilities for communicating information and ideas.

Perhaps the grammar debate should focus not on whether to teach grammar, but on what the content of grammar should be, what teaching techniques should be used, and how much time should be spent studying grammar.

Approaches to Teaching Grammar

Grammar teaching has changed considerably in recent decades. Traditional grammar, the only approach to teaching grammar for many years, was prescriptive. That is, it said in effect, this is the way grammar ought to be used and any other way is incorrect. Traditional grammarians assumed that language was static; thus grammar could be taught as an absolute. Later, under the impetus of Sputnik and growing pressure to advance scientific knowledge, linguists began to apply scientific approaches to the study of language in schools. The result was the introduction of the *new English.*

The new English was a rather comprehensive linguistic study designed to help children understand and appreciate what language is, where it came from, and how it works. Perhaps the most important aspect of the new English was the entirely new way of looking at grammar. In the linguistic approach the study of grammar became an analytical study of the structure of contemporary English. Furthermore, usage was studied as a separate area from grammar, because it is a matter of word choice rather than function.

Brief summaries of approaches to grammar are presented here in historical sequence. The purpose of this discussion is to present an overview of the content of grammar and to help you gain a basic understanding of implications for instruction. The references at the end of the book will help you to pursue the study of grammar further.

The Traditional Approach

Traditional grammar was based on the grammar of Latin. Latin was thought to be the natural and perfect language, and the scholars who first set down English grammar had been schooled in Latin. Therefore, traditional grammarians sought to refine and purify English and make it a "cultured language" by using a grammatical structure similar to that of Latin. To do this they established rules based on Latin.

Today's linguists, however, argue the inappropriateness of trying to fit English into a Latin mold. The contrasts between Latin and English are significant. Latin is a highly inflected language and Modern English is not. An example given by Guth illustrates the differences between the Latin and English forms of nouns.

> The Latin framework provided a poor fit for the modern languages to which it was applied. The *farther* a modern language had moved away from the original Indo-European grammatical system, the harder it became to fit modern facts into an ancient frame. Discussing the noun, the traditional grammarian was thinking of the Latin system of cases — with the noun changing its *form* depending on whether it was used as subject, object, possessive, and the like:

nominative	(subject form)	*vir*	the *man*
genitive	(possessive)	*viri*	the *man's*
dative	(indirect object)	*viro*	(for) the *man*
accusative	(object form)	*virum*	the *man*
ablative	(instrumental)	*viro*	(by) the *man*

> The basic difficulty here is that the English noun no longer has any "cases": Where a Latin noun had four or five different forms for different slots in a sentence, the plain form of the English noun serves as an *all-purpose* form. Only a possessive form survives as a kind of linguistic fossil; and its use is optional (the *cat's* whiskers, or the whiskers *of the cat*). (1973, pp. 42, 43)

Traditional grammar relies heavily on the use of definitions. It defines a sentence as "a group of words that express a complete thought." The eight parts of speech are defined as follows:

A *noun* is the name of a person, place, or thing.

A *verb* expresses action or a state of being.

A *pronoun* is used in place of a noun.

An *adjective* modifies a noun or a pronoun.

An *adverb* modifies a verb, an adjective, or another adverb.

A *preposition* shows relationship.

A *conjunction* is a connecting word.

An *interjection* expresses strong feeling.

Typically, children are expected to memorize these definitions and then apply them in naming the parts of speech in a given sentence. One shortcoming of traditional grammar is that the definitions do not adequately describe or explain the patterns of our language. All of the italicized words in the following sentences would be classified as "adverbs," yet they serve very different functions.

John likes to hang *around* after school.

The fire was *very* hot.

Sue dances *divinely.*

The doctor is *not* in his office.

Another question about the adequacy of traditional grammar arises when a word fits one definition yet is used for another way in a sentence. For example, try to determine the part of speech for each word in the following sentence (using the preceding definitions):

Our team mascot faces numerous outside pressures.

This sentence illustrates the ambiguity of traditional definitions for determining parts of speech. (Did you label *team, mascot, faces, outside,* and *pressures* all as nouns?) As Guth (1973) points out, the "all-purpose form" of English words requires a different system of classifying parts of speech.

Diagramming, often a part of traditional grammar study, may be used to show the relationship of words in a sentence. Essentially it identifies the meaning-bearing words of the sentence — the noun, verb, and direct object or complement, if there is one — and then places modifiers under the words they modify. The sentence *The boy ate apples yesterday* appears in Figure 3-1.

Traditionally, correctness is an integral part of grammar instruction, and children are often drilled on what is deemed correct grammar. The varieties of English, the natural growth and change of a

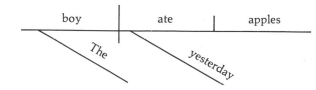

FIGURE 3-1

living language, and the relationships between grammar and reading and writing are seldom considered in traditional grammar programs.

The contributions of traditional grammar and its potential for the study of language should not be underestimated, however. Traditional grammar does provide a system for analyzing language, and we are currently seeing renewed interest in its use. Many of its shortcomings can be minimized by stressing a conceptualization of a language scheme rather than the memorization of definitions and rules.

The Structural Approach

Structural linguists, responding to the inadequacies of traditional grammar, developed a new system for analyzing language objectively. One very significant feature of structural grammar is that it *describes* grammar rather than *prescribes* it. The linguistic approach espouses a study of language based on the concept that oral language is the primary form of language. Writing is but a record of spoken language. Structural grammarians consider the whole of language including its phonemic system (the sounds of language), its morphological system (the form of words), and its syntactic system (the structure and function of words in sentences). Some of these aspects of language have already been discussed in Chapter 1.

Working from a corpus of sentences, structural grammarians identify basic sentence patterns and describe the form and function of words in each pattern. Lefevre lists four basic patterns with their variations (1964, pp. 90, 91):

Pattern One.   A. Noun–Verb
Example: Bob plays.

B. Noun–Verb–Adverb
Example: Bob plays well.

C. Noun–Verb–Adjective
Example: Bob arrives hungry.

Pattern Two.   Noun–Verb–Noun
Bob plays ball.

Pattern Three.   A. Noun–Verb–Noun–Noun
Example: Bob calls his dog Spot.

B. Noun–Verb–Noun–Noun
Example: Bob gives Spot milk.

Pattern Four.   A. Noun–Linking Verb–Noun
Example: Bob is a boy.

B. Noun–Linking verb–Adjective
Example: Bob is strong.

C. Noun–Linking verb–Adverb
Example: Bob is here.

Those sentence patterns illustrate the underlying structure of all sentences. They can be varied by expanding, rearranging, and combining.

In structural grammar the traditional eight parts of speech are reduced to four form classes and several structure words. The *form classes* are Class 1: *nouns;* Class 2: *verbs;* Class 3: *adjectives;* and Class 4: *adverbs.* Form class words carry the main load of communication in sentences; they are sometimes called "full" words because they have referents or can be represented in some way. Class designation is determined by analyzing the forms of a word (e.g., *talk, talked, talking*) and its function in a sentence. *Structure words,* or "empty" words have little or no lexical meaning. Their function is to specify or point out form class words (*the* apple, *my* pen) and to grammatically "glue" the sentence together. Structure words include noun markers (*a, an, the, this, each*) verb markers (*was, have, is, will*), question markers (*who, why, how, when*), phrase markers (*above, through, upon, into*), clause markers (*since, although, before, because, whether*), conjunctions (*and, but, for, so*), and intensifiers (*very, really, pretty, little, most*).

Rote memorization of definitions of form class words is not encouraged. Rather, the form class of a word is determined by analyzing the word's form and its function in the sentence. For example, to determine whether a word is a noun, children see if it could pattern with a noun marker ("some ———" or "a/an ———") or if it would fit in a noun frame ("———is here").

One way to diagram sentences in structural grammar involves a series of enclosures or "boxes," to show the relationship and function of the words in sentences. First the major parts of a sentence, the subject and predicate, are identified, and then other boxes are drawn within those boxes to show progressively more specific analysis.

| The | little | | dog | | scratched | | its | head. |

The Transformational-Generative Approach

In 1957 Noam Chomsky published a book, *Syntactic Structures,* that was to have great influence on the teaching of grammar. The approach he introduced has been called variously *transformational gram-*

mar, generative grammar, or *transformational-generative grammar.* Whereas the structural approach described the structure of language as it is used, the transformational-generative (TG) grammarians recognized an additional need to describe the process underlying the structure of sentences. The TG approach is concerned with identifying and analyzing the rules of language that native speakers of English acquire and use intuitively in producing grammatical sentences.

Chomsky explains that sentences have both a surface structure and a deep structure. The *surface structure* has to do with the form of a sentence, what is actually said or written; and the *deep structure* has to do with the meaning of the sentence, the underlying structure on which the surface form is based. For example, *Sandy hit the ball,* and *The ball was hit by Sandy,* are essentially the same in their deep structure; yet the sentences appear different at the surface level. The second sentence is a transformation of the first. On the other hand, some sentences with similar surface structures may be traced to different deep structures. The sentences *John is easy to see* and *John is eager to see* (C. Chomsky, 1969), are similar in appearance but different in meaning. In the first sentence John is the one who is seen and in the second sentence, he is the one who sees.

A study of TG grammar, then, is an analysis and explanation of the language system we acquire and use intuitively. It identifies two related types of rules for achieving linguistic competence: those for generating basic language units — *phrase structure rules* — and those for rearranging or combining the basic units into other forms or surface structures — *transformational rules. Kernel sentences* are the basic language units from which all other sentences are formed. They are simple, active, positive, declarative sentences without added phrases or details. The patterns identified in structural grammar are kernel sentences. In generating, or constructing, a sentence, a native speaker of English unconsciously follows certain rules that result in grammatical utterances. Phrase structure rules describe that process.

A basic set of phrase structure rules follows. It is essentially a series of linguistic equations by which a sentence is gradually broken down into smaller and smaller components. The first rule identifies the two parts of a sentence, the noun phrase (NP) and the verb phrase (VP). Then, step by step, elements on the right are further expanded or explained.

Rule 1.　　S $\longrightarrow$ NP + VP

Rule 2.　　NP $\longrightarrow \begin{Bmatrix} DP + N \\ Pro \end{Bmatrix}$

Rule 3.　　VP $\longrightarrow$ Aux + MVP

Rule 4.   Aux⟶Tns = (M) + (have + en) + (be + ing)

Rule 5.   Tns⟶$\begin{Bmatrix} \text{past} \\ \text{present} \end{Bmatrix}$

Rule 6.   MVP⟶V + (NP) + (Place) + (Time) + (Man)

Key:

S	= sentence
NP	= noun phrase
VP	= verb phrase
DP	= determiner phrase
N	= noun
Pro	= pronoun
Aux	= auxiliary
MVP	= main verb phrase
Tns	= tense
M	= modal

Linguistic equations are similar to mathematical equations. The elements to the left of the arrow are equal to those on the right. In reading the rules, the arrow is read "consists of" or "may be rewritten as." When elements are enclosed in brackets it means that one of those elements will always be present. Parentheses indicate optional elements. Other phrase structure rules may be added to identify noun features such as common/proper, abstract/concrete, mass/count, singular/plural, and animate/inanimate.

TG grammar uses a "tree" diagram to graphically portray the structure of sentences. Each phrase structure rule is systematically followed and the choices plotted at each step. This produces a branching diagram. For example, *The horse was munching its hay,* would look like Figure 3-2.

Phrase structure rules describe kernel sentences, the deep structure of language. Additional rules, called *transformational rules,* explain how kernel sentences are rearranged or combined to create various surface structures. Transformations may become quite complex, but some are fairly simple. For example, look at this transformation of a kernel sentence to a question:

Mary is going to town. ⟹ Is Mary going to town?

(Notice the use of the double-barred arrow to signal a transformation.) This yes-or-no question transformation involves only a change in word order and punctuation. This is another example of a transformation:

Herman threw the ball. ⟹ The ball was thrown by Herman.

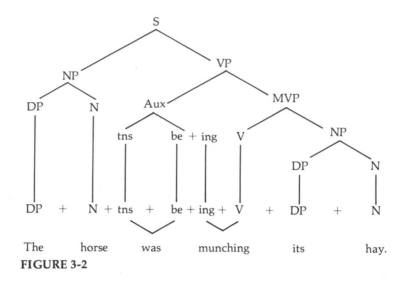

FIGURE 3-2

The process for changing a kernel sentence to passive voice includes the following steps: the second noun phrase (*the ball*) is moved to the initial position in the sentence, an auxiliary verb (*was*) is added, the verb is changed to its past participle, and the word *by* is added.

In a TG grammar approach, transformations are analyzed and described. Possible transformations include embeddings (combined sentences), passive transformation, negative transformations, various kinds of question transformation (who, what, where, when, why), and combinations of these (negative question: George can make candy. ⟹ George can not make candy. ⟹ Can't George make candy?)

Modern linguists vary in their acceptance of TG grammar, and variations and alternatives continue to be proposed. Nevertheless, TG grammar promises to have a lasting effect on language arts curricula in the schools. It represents one of the most important ideas in the history of language study. TG grammar is particularly well suited to research, and it has contributed a wealth of new insights to our understanding of language.

Grammar in the Elementary Classroom

An examination of language arts guides published by school districts and newer editions of published language arts textbooks indicates considerable emphasis on teaching grammar in the elementary school. At the same time research to support such a position cannot be found. Rather, most scholars agree that a formal study of grammar before the seventh grade is neither desirable nor effective.

Children learn language and learn about language by using it. The teaching of grammar at the elementary level ought to be an exploratory, inquisitive look at how our language works. Children need many opportunities to experiment with language, to form hypotheses, and to discover forms and systems. To provide these opportunities, teachers must have a good understanding of grammar and be able to think creatively about ways to help children become more aware of language and to discover the processes they already use. In one sense what is taught at this level might be considered "pre-grammar" or "readiness" for more formal grammar study. In a strict sense, however, when children discover the forms and functions of words in sentences and how words are strung together to make sentences, they are learning grammar itself.

Grammar in the elementary school must be addressed within the context of language children know and use. Children's own language is a rich source of "raw material" for inductively studying aspects of grammar. For example, sentence sense may be developed in the context of a writing workshop. As children are discussing their writing in a small group, pick out a string of words a child has written and ask the group whether or not the string is a sentence. Have children explain why they think it is or isn't. Using this technique with children prods them to think about sentence structure and to test their hypotheses about language.

Another time you might lift a well-written sentence from a child's paper and write it on the board or overhead projector. After reading the entire sentence together, children can think of other words that might be substituted for one of the words in the sentence. List their suggestions under the word as in the following examples.

> The beggar saw the food.
>   dog
>   monster
>   etc.

> John took out the garbage.
>   ashes
>   clothes
>   etc.

You may or may not use the term *noun* at this point. Although terminology is not particularly important in itself, it is convenient for communicating. Children seem to have little difficulty picking up grammatical terms that are used incidentally during an activity.

Another grammar activity might involve embedding (inserting) descriptive words and phrases from one kernel sentence into another. Point out two or more kernel sentences a child has written and ask the group if anyone can think of a way to make the sentences into one good sentence. For example:

Mary had a dog.
The dog was black.   〉   Mary had a black dog.

The same procedure may be followed at more advanced levels to teach coordination and subordination of kernel sentences.

Jack ordered a milkshake.   Jack ordered a milkshake but Jim
Jim ordered a Coke.   〉   ordered a Coke.

The children became frightened.   The children became frightened
They were alone.   〉   when they were alone.

Children in the elementary school can learn about grammar through any number of interesting language activities. For example, they may experiment with word order (*The dog chased the skunk.* / *The skunk chased the dog.*) They may pick out name words (*pig, car, ax, doctor*). They may have a word hunt to find words that are used in place of nouns (*he, it, they*). They may find words in sentences that tell how (*quickly, well, cautiously*). They may analyze and compare different kinds of kernel sentences (N–V–N, N–Lv–N) and then find other sentences that follow the same pattern. Or, they may analyze how sentences are changed to form questions (*This is an apple pie./Is this an apple pie? Jacob wrote a poem./What did Jacob write?*).[1]

Activities for teaching grammar concepts are available in many published language arts textbooks and materials. These often combine aspects of traditional, structural, and transformational grammars and lend themselves to a variety of programs. Be aware, however, that they may present aspects of grammar rather than be a comprehensive language program. Any such activities must, of course, be selected to fit your program and the developmental level of individual students within your classroom.

Usage

Boyd describes usage as "the attitudes that speakers of a language have toward different aspects of their language — that is, certain pronunciations, words, and grammatical forms" (1976, p. 8). Usage

---

[1] Bill Martin's *Sounds of Language Series*, published by Holt, Rinehart and Winston, suggests many interesting ways to explore the grammar of our language.

is not the same as grammar. It has to do with social acceptability —
with group consensus of propriety — and it should not be confused
with the grammatical construction of a sentence.

Patterns of usage are acquired in the normal course of learning a
language; they are "picked up" from the language environment.
Thus the language used in the home is the dominant influence on
children's speech habits. In a broader social setting their home-rooted
language may appear noticeably different from that of the larger
influential group. The study of usage in the schools is intended to
help children deal with that divergence. It should help children become flexible in using language so that they can function and be
respected in groups outside their immediate environment.

Usage is highly situation-dependent for most people. The choices
a person makes when engaged in an informal conversation with
friends are usually different from the choices made in public uses of
language. Speakers and writers characteristically move back and
forth between levels of usage in accordance with what they perceive
as appropriate. Even young children have been observed to vary
their language from one situation to another.

Perhaps no other aspect of language teaching generates more
intense discussion than usage. The controversy stems from a lack
of agreement in (1) defining an acceptable level of usage and (2)
setting instructional goals. Some people stress the function of language to communicate and disregard the importance of usage.
Others place high value on traditional standards of usage as a mark
of culture.

Teachers' divergent attitudes toward usage are illustrated in a
study by Pooley (1972). In the study, 1,000 junior and senior high
school English teachers evaluated the acceptability of selected usage
items. Their responses indicated a range from "acceptable anywhere" to "not acceptable" on a four-point scale. In response to *If
everybody would proofread carefully they would make fewer mistakes,* for
example, 64 teachers indicated that they would accept the usage in
all levels of communication, 289 indicated they would accept it in
informal speaking and writing, 373 indicated mere tolerance, and 250
indicated that the usage was not acceptable.

Perhaps the most significant finding from this study is that English
teachers are becoming more tolerant of usage that would have been
universally condemned in the past. And this trend is not limited to
teachers. Distinctions between certain word choices (e.g., *dived/dove,
hanged/hung the killer, reared/raised, It is I/It is me*) have nearly disappeared in all but formal speech and writing.

In planning usage instruction it seems important to realize that
there are differences among the users of any language and that these
differences are normal. Children's utterances reflect their language

experiences. The language they bring to school has been shaped by the language patterns they have heard in their homes and community since birth. Their ears are tuned to the home-rooted language of their environment, and it is their functional (and often vivid) mode of expression. If children are to change the way they speak they must have experiences with the alternatives to the extent that the alternatives become a familiar and viable choice.

Because language reflects the experiences of each individual, language is always very personal. It is important for teachers to realize how tightly each child's self-concept is wrapped up in his or her language. Children's language represents the people and experiences that are closest to them. Criticizing children's language is criticizing their world. It may be devastating to children and may result in a marked decrease in language output.

At the same time ability to use the universal or standard code of English has pragmatic value for individuals. There is little question that knowing only the language of a subgroup limits opportunities outside that group. This applies to either end of the educational continuum — to members of a highly learned philosophical society who use extremely formal language as well as to members of a ghetto neighborhood who have developed their unique language patterns. From a practical standpoint, inability to use standard English often limits freedom of choice in economic and social matters. We need not agree whether such forms as *ain't* or *he done it* should be acceptable to realize that people who persist in such usage do have more limited economic and social choices. Movement within the mainstream of our society necessitates ability to use language according to certain standards. Furthermore, it is argued that teachers have the moral responsibility to teach children facility in standard English and that not to do so deprives children of their educational rights.

Teaching standard English does not mean forcing children to exchange one form of language for another. It does not impugn the informal language of a group but focuses on language as it is used by most well-educated speakers in the country. Children learning standard English are somewhat like those learning English as a second language. Standard English does not replace a child's home-grown language; it merely expands the child's linguistic ability. Just as a foreign language allows the speaker a choice of language in certain situations, so knowledge of standard English allows children to make language choices dependent on the situation.

Teachers should not expect or insist that children adopt more formal language immediately. This is extremely difficult for children to do. They generate the forms they use through internalized rules, and these rules are very resistant to change. Repeatedly correcting children seldom effects lasting change; it is more apt to signal rejection of their language and bring resentment and frustration.

Usage choices are strongly related to affective development, and even people who can speak in standard forms will not choose to do so unless use of those forms satisfies their social and psychological needs, or at least is not perceived to be in conflict with those needs. Affective changes usually occur over a period of time. This can be discouraging to teachers. However, given time, social need, a rich array of language input, and a variety of interactive communication experiences, most children will develop the ability to speak appropriately in formal as well as informal situations.

One way to approach usage is to look at the many varieties of English objectively. Through a study of regional and social dialects that neither condemns nor condones, children can see their own differences in perspective. A study of dialects leads naturally to the generalization that people from different groups need a universal code or way of speaking to communicate efficiently and effectively outside their group. An awareness of language difference provides a base for examining which forms of communication are standard, or most common, throughout the United States.

Young children's deviations from standard forms may merely indicate that they are still acquiring the language system. This is particularly true of irregular verb forms (e.g., *maded, hided*). Such variations reflect maturational differences that will disappear with acquisition of intuitive grammar rules.

Teachers and others outside a particular speech community provide important models. As school personnel work with children day after day — interacting, talking, and paraphrasing — the sometimes strange sounds of language spoken outside the local community become familiar. Less directly, television, radio, films, and tapes offer a range of other language opportunities. Children gradually develop a listening repertoire and become aware of other language options.

It is important to give children opportunities to experience using standard English in nonthreatening situations. Participating in choral reading, oral reading of plays, stories, and poems, or oral language games paves the way for children to work out their own structures. Oral games and activities in which children repeat or generate practice sentences are generally more effective than "fill-in-the-blanks" exercises. New patterns must first be developed in the ear. Written lessons also yield fewer responses in a given amount of time and provide less efficient learning.

Familiar games can often be adapted to give children purposeful practice in using particular forms. For example, "Button, Button" can provide practice in using *don't have* in lieu of *ain't got*. In the game, one child goes through the motions of giving a button to each child and carefully slips the button to someone without anyone else knowing. Then the child who is "It" must guess who has the button. The dialog follows:

It: Button, Button,
          Who has the button?
          Mark, do you have the button?
Mark: No, I don't have the button.
It: (goes on to another child and repeats . . .)

A slightly more sophisticated question-and-answer situation might be devised for various kinds of usage practice. The following example could be used to practice *have gone*.

Teacher: George, have you ever gone to Disneyland?
George: No, I haven't gone to Disneyland but I have
            gone to San Francisco.
Teacher: Janet, have you ever gone to San Francisco?
Janet: Yes, I have gone to San Francisco and I have
            gone skiing on Mt. Hood.
Teacher: Josh, have you ever gone skiing on Mt. Hood?
etc.

Instruction in usage ought to include helping children learn to make choices about the appropriateness of words in specific situations. Such an activity might be to read a story to the class and then talk about the writer's choice of words and other possible choices. Continue the discussion by identifying the author's probable audience and evaluating the appropriateness of his or her choices for that group. Let children suggest how the story might have differed if the author were telling it to a neighbor or to a group of university presidents. In similar activities, children might consider how various people — television personalities, ministers, neighbors, teenagers, athletes, doctors, and salespeople — would talk in different situations. As much as possible children should have opportunity to engage in conversation with various other adults. Such activities will give children a broader perspective of language as it is used by a larger population and help them make appropriate choices in using language.

In teaching usage at the elementary level, the teacher should first evaluate the children's forms that are most noticeably different from common usage. (The summary of common usage problems that follows and the list of verb forms in Table 3-1 may be used as checklists.) Select only a few forms to develop at a time. Then plan activities to help children become aware of possible choices and to tune their ears to the preferred forms. Follow up with many opportunities to prac-

TABLE 3-1. VERB FORMS

PRESENT TENSE	PAST TENSE	PAST PARTICIPLE (HAVE + -EN)	PRESENT TENSE	PAST TENSE	PAST PARTICIPLE (HAVE + -EN)
am, is	was	been	lie (to recline)	lay	lain
are	were	been			
beat	beat	beaten	raise (to elevate)	raised	raised
become	became	become			
begin	began	begun	ride	rode	ridden
blow	blew	blown	ring	rang	rung
break	broke	broken	rise	rose	risen
bring	brought	brought	run	ran	run
burst	burst	burst	say	said	said
buy	bought	bought	see	saw	seen
catch	caught	caught	send	sent	sent
choose	chose	chosen	set (to place)	set	set
come	came	come			
do	did	done			
draw	drew	drawn	shake	shook	shaken
drink	drank	drunk	shine (the sun)	shone	shone
drive	drove	driven			
eat	ate	eaten	shine (to polish)	shined	shined
fall	fell	fallen			
fly	flew	flown	shrink	shrank	shrunk
freeze	froze	frozen	sing	sang	sung
get	got	got, gotten	sink	sank	sunk
give	gave	given	sit	sat	sat
go	went	gone	speak	spoke	spoken
grow	grew	grown	spring	sprang	sprung
hang (to punish)	hanged	hanged	steal	stole	stolen
			sting	stung	stung
hang (an object)	hung	hung	strike	struck	struck
			swear	swore	swore
hear	heard	heard	swim	swam	swum
hit	hit	hit	swing	swung	swung
hurt	hurt	hurt	take	took	taken
know	knew	known	tear	tore	torn
lay (to place)	laid	laid	throw	threw	thrown
			wear	wore	worn
lead	lead	led	write	wrote	written

tice their new skill and make the options of usage truly theirs. The sample lesson (Figure 3-3) illustrates a practice exercise that might be used as a follow-up to an oral lesson on *There is* and *There are*. It would be used to extend oral usage practice to written language once

Using Is or Are after There

> There **is** one snake in the big box.
> There **is** one mouse in the little box.

> There **are** two snakes in the big box.
> There **are** two mice in the little box.

The sentences in both boxes begin with **there**.
Read the sentences in the red box.

• Is each sentence about one thing or more than one thing?

• Which form of **be**—**is** or **are**—is the verb in each sentence?

Read the sentences in the blue box.

• Is each sentence about one thing or more than one thing?

• Which form of **be**—**is** or **are**—is the verb in each sentence?

For Practice

■ Choose **is** or **are** to complete each sentence. Write the sentence.

1. There ||||||||||||| seven people in the room.
2. There ||||||||||||| some pencils in the cupboard.
3. There ||||||||||||| a plant on the windowsill.
4. There ||||||||||||| many fish in that river.
5. There ||||||||||||| only one cookie left.
6. There ||||||||||||| a good show on TV now.
7. There ||||||||||||| three robins on the lawn.
8. There ||||||||||||| two sails on that boat.
9. There ||||||||||||| a cabin near the lake.
10. There ||||||||||||| a bug on your arm.
11. There ||||||||||||| two cakes in the oven.
12. There ||||||||||||| some new books on the shelf.

Remember

Some sentences begin with There is **or** There are.

Sentences about one person or thing begin with There is.

Sentences about more than one person or thing begin with There are.

◆ If you need more help, turn to page 48 of your Practice Handbook.

children have tuned their ears to the pattern. Children might also create their own sentences using *There is* and *There are*.

Summary of Common Usage Problems

Nouns

plural forms (*child–childs, mouse–mouses*)

slang terms (*kids, cops*)

Pronouns

as object of preposition (*Give it to Mark and I. It was between you and she.*)

in subject (*Us girls worked hard. Randy and me ran.*)

in series (*I and Maggie*)

redundancy (*Harry he, The boys they*)

colloquialism (*hisn, yourn, theirself, hisself*)

Verbs

subject and verb agreement (*he don't, they wasn't, I says*)

form (*I seen, they done*)

colloquialism (*busted, clumb*)

Adjective

colloquialism (*gooder, bestest*)

Adverb

adjective for adverb (*She did good.*)

Determiners

a and an (*a elephant, a octopus*)
this and these (*these kind*)
these and them (*them apples*)

Double negatives

I didn't do nothing.

Semantic confusion

between/among, may/can, teach/learn, leave/let.
bigger/biggest, stronger/strongest

FIGURE 3-3 *(facing page)*

From Kitzhaber, Kitzhaber, DeHaven, Salisbury, and Jones, *Spectrum of English*, Level 6, copyright 1978, p. 93. Reprinted by permission of Glencoe Press, publisher.

Verbs that do not follow the regular pattern for forming the past tense (*-ed* or *-d*) and the past participle (*have* + *-en*) are often confusing to children (and adults). Table 3-1 includes some of the verb forms that may be troublesome.

English Dialects

Variations in the English language have existed since the early days of its development in Britain. Whenever people are closely associated for social or economic purposes they bring together certain language habits to form a speech community. Such groups have formed and reformed throughout the history of our language. Through this process the language of each existing group develops unique sets of features. These varieties of English are called *dialects*.

Dialects reveal settlement history. Although increased mobility and instant communication with any place in the United States have tended to modify and lessen dialects somewhat, differences continue to exist. A study of the speech of a given area reveals much about the social and geographic history of the area's people.

Dialects originated in this country with the early colonists. Variations existed even among groups of English colonists. They emigrated from different dialectal areas of Britain and, once they were here, they did little traveling or intermingling to wear away the sharp differences in their language. Through remnants of language spoken in the various colonies, dialect geographers have been able to plot the linguistic areas of the early colonies. According to Shuy (1967) the major dialect areas have been identified and classified as Northern, Midland, and Southern.

As the colonists moved about and gradually pushed farther west, they took their language with them. Expansion of the country shows a general movement from the East to the West. However, the rise of manufacturing brought about considerable northern movement to the larger cities and industrial areas. The map in Figure 3–4 traces the movements of dialects across the United States as the population moved westward.

With the rise of cities, the larger urban areas tended to set the cultural pattern for surrounding areas. The dialect of the urban area

FIGURE 3-4   *(facing page)*
The Main Dialect Areas of the United States.

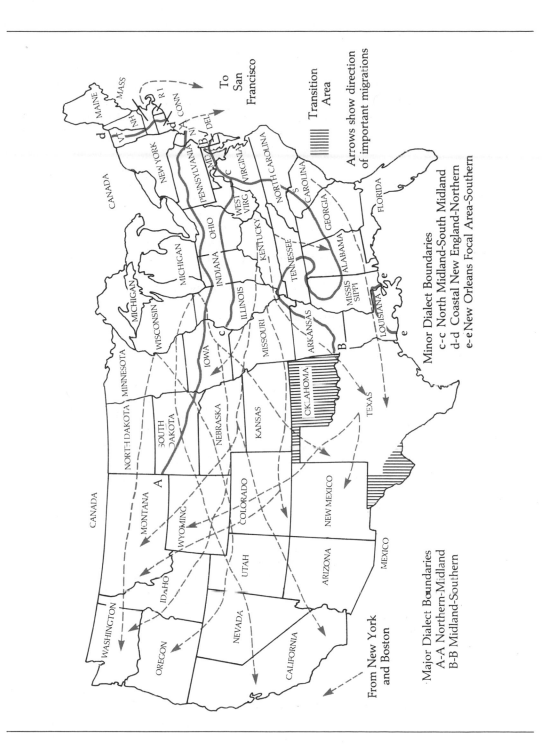

To San Francisco

Transition Area

Arrows show direction of important migrations

Minor Dialect Boundaries
c-c North Midland-South Midland
d-d Coastal New England-Northern
e-e New Orleans Focal Area-Southern

Major Dialect Boundaries
A-A Northern-Midland
B-B Midland-Southern

From New York and Boston

had prestige within the larger area. However, no one dialect ever exerted enough influence to create one national prestige dialect as had been the case in England. (There the dialect of London came to be known as "the King's English.") One reason for this lack is the size of our country. Another is the conscious or unconscious adherence to unique language features as a reflection of pride and loyalty to a particular group or area and a desire to maintain that identity. Bailey and Robinson comment

> American English dialects have been the object of strong feeling from the earliest days of settlement along the Atlantic seaboard. Although it might seem that the frontier spirit and democratic vistas would encourage tolerance and diversity of ways of speaking, the best evidence we have suggests that language — then as now — was a means of asserting unity within parts of the community; rustic backwoodsmen scorned the fancy talk of town and villages, society folk agreed with English visitors in looking with amused contempt on the speech of the unlettered. From the sometimes uneasy interaction of the settled and the unsettled in colonial days emerged some of the differences that came to distinguish American from British English. (1973, p. 151)

Black dialect was one of the earliest variations of English and certainly one of the most interesting. Smitherman traces its beginning "at least as far back as 1619 when a Dutch vessel landed in Jamestown with a cargo of twenty Africans" (1977, p. 5). She explains that as additional blacks were brought into the country from various African tribes, an English-African language gradually developed. It was the language used to communicate between slaves and masters and between fellow slaves.

Smitherman describes the dialect

> In a nutshell: Black Dialect is an Africanized form of English reflecting Black America's linguistic-cultural African heritage and the conditions of servitude, oppression and life in America. Black Language is Euro-American speech with an Afro-American meaning, nuance, tone, and gesture. The Black Idiom is used by 80 to 90 percent of American blacks, at least some of the time. It has allowed blacks to create a culture of survival in an alien land, and as a by-product has served to enrich the language of all Americans. (pp. 2, 3)

Geography is an important factor in the development and preservation of dialects. In the early days of our country, natural geographic barriers such as rivers and mountains often influenced patterns of settlements, and hence the language of a particular part of the country. Once people were settled in an area, the difficulty of transportation caused them to limit their association to other settlers near them. This resulted in "pockets" of dialects with distinctive language features. Many of these early language pockets continue to exist. Shuy (1967) mentions, for instance, that the Connecticut River still separates *pahk the cah* from *park the car*.

Language in the western United States tends to be a linguistic blend reflecting the influence of settlers from nearly every other area of the country. Many of the patterns of speech provide evidence of intermingling and partial adoption of a variety of dialects. Larger urban centers have had comparatively little influence on stabilizing the speech in their areas. This is probably due, at least in part, to the high mobility rate and the continual shuffling and intermingling of language patterns.

Dialect geographers have been mapping the regional speech patterns of the United States for many years. To do so they collect data from hundreds of people of various ages, occupations, and levels of education. Findings are then plotted on a map so that dominant patterns in areas become visible (see Figure 3-5). From these studies dialect geographers have found three clearly defined differences among dialects. They involve pronunciation, vocabulary, and verb forms. Different language habits were not found to be "mistakes" but variations according to a definite pattern or system.

Even dialects that are sometimes labeled nonstandard adhere to well-developed rules. Black dialect, for example, has a clearly definable grammar. The rules differ from those of standard English only in the surface structure. To illustrate this point, Labov explains that the absence of the verbs *is, have,* and *will* in black sentence structures results from "a low-level rule which carries contractions one step farther to delete single consonants" (1974, pp. 143–44). Referring to the sentence *They mine,* Labov states,

> the deletion of the *is* or *are* in nonstandard Negro English is not the result of erratic or illogical behavior: it follows the same regular rules as standard English contraction. Wherever standard English can contract, Negro children use either the contracted form or (more commonly) the deleted zero form. Thus *They mine* corresponds to standard *They're mine,* not to the full form *They are mine.* (p. 144)

Smitherman suggests that the grammar of black dialect reflects the influence of West African languages. She lists "a few of the West African rules that were grafted onto early Black English, and which still operate in Black English today" (1977, pp. 6–7):

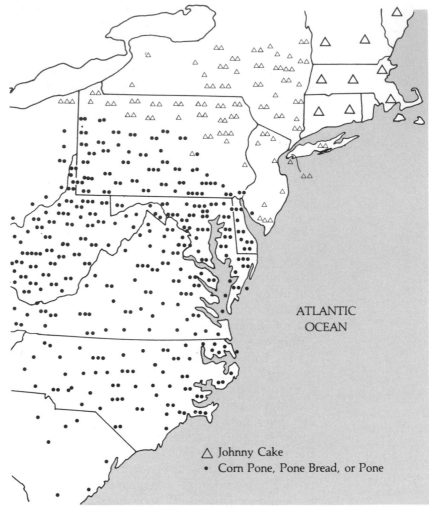

FIGURE 3-5
Mapping Dialect Information.

From Roger W. Shuy, *Discovering American Dialects*, p. 43. Copyright © 1967 by the National Council of Teachers of English. Reprinted by permission of the publisher and the author.

Grammar and Structure Rule in West African Languages	Black English
repetition of noun subject with pronoun	*My father, he work there.*
questions patterns without *do*	*What it come to?*

same form of noun for singular and plural	*one boy; five boy*
no tense indicated in verb; emphasis on manner or character of action	*I know it good when he ask me.*
same verb form for all subjects	*I know; you know; he know; we know; they know*

The vocabulary and grammar used in various American dialects has been found to be related to such factors as age, education, geographic region, ethnic and experiential background, and position in the community. In addition, a person's language tends to vary from one situation to another. It depends on such factors as the purpose of the communication, the formality of the occasion, the audience (public or private), and the form of communication (speaking or writing).

Everyone speaks a dialect of some sort. Even among members of a speech community, no two people speak in exactly the same way, although the differences may be very small. Children growing up in the same family often have unique words for things or special ways of expressing themselves. These individual language idiosyncrasies make up a person's *idiolect,* or personal language.

Dialects in the Classroom

The reality of dialects suggests two teaching goals: (1) helping children learn about dialects, and (2) teaching children whose dialect includes variant linguistic patterns. They are closely related. Humane and effective teaching of oral and written English depends on an objective attitude toward language variation, a recognition of the historical and situational significance of dialects.

A study of dialects and idiolects helps children develop a greater language consciousness. Listening for differences in pronunciation or names for things develops skill in listening and helps children become aware of nuances of language, the options available to speakers of English, and the effect of certain choices. It also allows children to examine their own language habits and to compare them with others'.

For example, the dialect features identified by Shuy (1967, pp. 17–24) might be used to generate discussion about dialect differences (e.g., family word for father — *dad, daddy, father, pa, papa, pappy, paw, pop;* a carbonated drink — *pop, soda, soda pop, tonic, soft drink;* a time of day — *quarter before eleven, quarter of eleven, quarter till eleven, quarter to eleven, 10:45*). Or, following a study of dialect differences, children might prepare a checklist or questionnaire and conduct a mini-field study of dialect differences in their school or immediate neighborhood.

Lessons for exploring dialects are found in several elementary language arts textbooks. One example is shown in Figure 3-6. The lesson develops the concept of regional differences in vocabulary. The activity in which children are asked to explain the meaning of words common to certain regional dialects illustrates one way to create an awareness and interest in dialectal differences. The lesson could be extended through children's reading. Books such as *The Empty Schoolhouse* by Carlson, *The Jack Tales* by Chase, *Strawberry Girl* by Lenski, and *The Little House on the Prairie* and others by Wilder will provide many words and expressions from given periods of history or geographic areas.

In Summary

Designing a grammar of the English language is a difficult and continuous task. Early grammarians, using a Latin model, devised a scheme that prescribed grammatically correct sentences. Their approach has come to be known as traditional grammar. Later linguistic approaches include structural and transformational-generative grammars. They describe language as it is currently used. Structural grammarians have identified the components of language and the patterns for combining those patterns into sentences. Transformational-generative grammarians continue to be concerned with the processes underlying utterances. They have attempted to describe those processes through phrase structure and transformation rules.

Throughout history languages have united groups of people. In the United States immigration, geographical barriers, and socioeconomic differences have created varieties of English. Variety is natural and to be expected. Standard English is the master language of the country, however, because it is the language spoken by most of the people. Ability to use standard English makes it possible to communicate with people in various subgroups.

Study of grammar and usage patterns of standard English is a part of the elementary school language arts curriculum. The study is usu-

FIGURE 3-6   *(pages 83–85)*

Reprinted from *American Language Today, Orange Rain* by C. Nachbar, R. W. L. Smith, E. H. Schuster, C. P. Anderson, B. Friedberg, D. A. Sohn, copyright 1974 with permission of Webster/McGraw-Hill.

● **What is a regional vocabulary?** People with different jobs sometimes use the same word. But the word can mean
A something different to each one. What kind of *shot* does a doctor give you? What kind of *shot* does a photographer take?

The two kinds of shots are quite different because the doctor and photographer are talking about different things.

B There is another kind of special vocabulary that works in another way. It uses different words to talk about the same thing. This kind of vocabulary is called a *regional vocabulary*. It is used in a certain region or part of the country.

A regional vocabulary belongs to the kind of English we use for *local purposes*. We all learn a local way of talking. We might call our local talk *LP* English.

A regional vocabulary does not belong to the kind of English we use for *general purposes*. We can use general purpose English to talk to almost anyone, anywhere. We might call this general purpose talk *GP* English.

Look at the picture below. Can you understand what the people are talking about?

D Remind the children to think back to the discussion of various jobs for ideas about what job they might pretend to have. Give them time to prepare a list of words before they play "Who am I?"

● In this lesson, the children explore regional vocabularies, or dialects.

A The doctor gives a shot of medicine with a needle. The photographer takes a shot, or picture, with his camera.

B In this text, regional dialects are called *Local Purpose English,* or *LP* English. The standard dialect is called *GP,* or *General Purpose,* English.

You might note that a dialect includes distinctive features of vocabulary, pronunciation, grammar, and usage. Also, it will be helpful to remember that GP English and LP English are not the only varieties of our language. Between these are many forms of standard English with a regional flavor.

Skills development,
pp. 238–239
Listening: good discussion
behavior.
Oral language: contributing
ideas; usage.
Visual literacy: getting
information from pictures.
Thinking skills: interpretation.

A *Snail* means the shelled
animal to most people, but it
has an added regional meaning
in San Francisco.

B The sweet breakfast roll
might have gotten that name
from its rolled-up shape.

The children should now be
able to explain the picture in
terms of the misunderstanding
of a regional word.

C Examples might help with
this concept. You might use
some American words taken
from British English that are
no longer in British usage,
such as: *fall* (autumn), *gully*
(channel made by running
water) *rare* (slightly cooked).

What do you think the boy means when he says, "I
had two snails for breakfast this morning?" Do you think
he actually ate two snails?

Does it help if you know that the boy is in San Francisco and the girl is in Chicago? Do you think that *snail*
means the same thing—everywhere? Or does it have a
special regional meaning? If so, does it have a special
meaning in San Francisco or in Chicago?

A   What is the GP English meaning of *snail?*

In the regional LP English of San Francisco, *snail*
also has another meaning. It means a sweet breakfast
B roll. Can you think of any reason for calling a sweet roll
a snail? Now can you explain the picture? Why did the
girl from Chicago say "ugh"?

Have you ever moved from one place to another?
After you moved did you ever use a word that other people did not understand? Do you know someone from
another part of the country? Does his vocabulary have
some different words from yours?

C   The English language is changing all the time, but
it doesn't change everywhere in exactly the same way.
Sometimes a new word stays in just one region. And
sometimes an older word is dropped in every place except
one. It remains in the regional vocabulary of that one
area.

Sometimes a word adds a meaning—but not everywhere. *Snail* picked up an extra meaning in San Francisco.
Does *snail* have an extra meaning for you?

238

Look very carefully at the pictures on the next page. Decide what you would call the thing shown in each one.
The pictures will help you answer the questions.

Each question contains a word from a regional vocabulary. Decide what the word means. Then think of an answer to the question. Your answer should show that you know what the word means.

A

1 Massachusetts: What is your favorite kind of *tonic?*
2 Rhode Island: You aren't afraid of a *dandle,* are you?
3 Ohio: Do you like *Dutch cheese* in your salad?
4 Georgia: Did you ever see a chicken in a *spider?*
5 Connecticut: How loud is the bark of an *angle dog?*
6 Texas: How many wings has a *mosquito hawk?*

Discuss your answers with your classmates. Try to agree on what each special word means.

A Synonyms for the regional words include the following (you might suggest some the children have not heard):

1 *tonic:* soda pop, soda water, soda, pop, soft drink.
2 *dandle:* seesaw, teeter-totter, teeterboard, tinter, tilt, tippity bounce, ridy-horse, kicky-horse.
3 *Dutch cheese:* cottage cheese, pot cheese, smearcase, curd cheese, clabber cheese, homemade cheese, cream cheese, sour-milk cheese.
4 *spider:* frying pan, skillet, creeper.
5 *angle dog:* earthworm, angleworm, eaceworm, red worm, rainworm, ground worm, fishworm, night crawler.
6 *mosquito hawk:* dragonfly, darning needle, snake doctor, spindle, snake feeder.

ally approached as an exploration of language and how language is used — both by subgroups and by the country as a whole. Children are taught to use standard English as the language of the majority. Flexibility in using language appropriately is stressed, and speech patterns of subgroups are respected.

Learning Objectives

COGNITIVE OBJECTIVES

Primary Grades

Children will

know that there are different kinds of words.

know that a sentence is composed of different kinds of words.

know that word order in sentences is important.

be able to recognize sentences and nonsentences.

be able to speak and write grammatical English sentences.

be able to identify noun phrases and verb phrases (subjects and predicates) in sentences.

be able to phrase questions.

know that people do not all talk the same way.

know that variation in speech is to be expected.

be able to recognize differences in speech.

Middle Grades

Children will

maintain all primary-grade objectives.

be able to explain the function of nouns, verbs, adjectives, and adverbs in sentences.

know that nouns express number and that they may show possession.

know that verbs express past and present time.

know that when a form of *be* is used as an auxiliary, an *-ing* form is added to the main verb.

know that when a form of *have* is used as an auxiliary, an *-en* form is added to the main verb.

be able to recognize determiner phrases.

be able to make several different sentences (transformations) from one kernel sentence.

be able to listen to their own speech and recognize patterns that differ significantly from standard English usage.

acquire alternate usage forms and use them in appropriate situations.

be able to discuss variations in English that reflect regional, social, and age differences.

be able to give examples of dialect differences in pronunciation, vocabulary, and grammar.

be able to formulate generalizations about language from data.

AFFECTIVE OBJECTIVES

Children will

be curious about the way English "works."

enjoy exploring our language system.

want to learn to improve their ability to communicate effectively.

respect the language of others.

appreciate the rich variety and beauty of expression in our language as the contributions of groups within our pluralistic society.

Suggested Learning Activities

Building Sentences. Make sets of words with a separate set for each part of speech (use different colors): nouns, verbs, adjectives, and adverbs. Pass out a set to each of four children and let them try to make a sentence from the words in their set. Discuss why this won't work and what they need to put with their kind of word to make sentences. The children should then select words from other sets to make sentences. A sample follows:

Set 1: Nouns	Set 2: Verbs	Set 3: Adjectives	Set 4: Adverbs
turtles	walk	happy	slowly
dogs	drink	old	loudly
porcupines	cry	little	carefully
babies	attack	dirty	wildly

Quite young children can do this activity, but they may need to have the words read to them and work under close supervision. The exercise may be varied for older children by giving them lists of words and having them see how many different (but grammatical) sentences they can make from just those sixteen words. They will find many unique combinations.

This exercise may also be used to develop vocabulary. Include interesting words that children are not likely to know (*sentimental, portly, judicious, contemptuous*). After they have looked the meaning up, the exercise will give them practice in using the words.

Sentence Roll. Get some small plastic foam blocks. Write noun words on all faces of one, verbs on another, adjectives on one, and adverbs on another. Let the children roll the blocks and try to make a sentence from the words that are facing up. They must decide if the words can be arranged to form a grammatical sentence. If they cannot, have the children tell what would need to be changed or added for the sentence to be grammatical.

Sentence Tags. For this activity you will need a supply of key tags and a board with nails or hooks to hang them on. Write noun phrases (subjects) and verb phrases (predicates) on the separate key tags. The children should find two parts that go together and hang them together on the board.

Substitution. Read a line of the poem "Jabberwocky" and have the children think of real words that might be substituted. They may also make up their own sentences with nonsense words for their classmates to "figure out."

Chop-chop. Write kernel sentences on separate pieces of paper. Give the children scissors and some blank pieces of paper. The children should cut the sentences apart and insert parts into other sentences to combine ideas. They may write any necessary additional words (*that, because, after*) on the blank paper and insert them into the sentences.

Expanding Kernel Sentences. Give the children a kernel sentence such as "Mother bought candy at the store yesterday." Have them make as many different sentences as possible from the one kernel sentence. Examples include:

Candy was bought at the store yesterday by Mother.

Who bought candy at the store yesterday?

Did Mother buy candy at the store yesterday?

What did Mother buy at the story yesterday?

Common Nouns and Proper Nouns. Prepare worksheets with two columns, one for common nouns and one for proper nouns. Write a word in one or the other column and have the children supply the missing word. For example:

Common Nouns	Proper Nouns
1. television program	_____
2. _____	Pontiac
3. _____	*The Wind in the Willows*
4. girl	_____
5. city	_____

Talking Mirrors. This is an activity to help children become familiar with standard English usage. It can be used in teaching any new speech pattern. First, construct one or more sentences that use the identified pattern (e.g., "I'm *not* going to tell you.") on the board. Have children repeat the sentences to become familiar with them. Children face each other in pairs. One is designated to be the mirror. The first child says a sentence and the mirror must repeat it exactly, including the intonation pattern and facial expressions. Children try to think of different ways to say the same sentence and challenge their "mirror's" ability to mimic them. If a child fails to match his/her partner, this cracks the mirror and the pair must begin again. (Devise a plan for alternating turns at being mirrors.)

Word Forms. Make a chart with columns for nouns, adjectives, verbs, and adverbs. Supply one form of a word on each line. Have children think up a sentence in which the word is used in that form. Then have them think of sentences in which other forms of the word are used. Determine the part of speech and write the word in the proper square. For example:

NOUN	ADJECTIVE	VERB	ADVERB
beauty	beautiful	beautify	beautifully
curiosity			
	winning		
		frighten	
			laughingly

Clothespin Match. Print base words on a cardboard circle (as spokes of a wheel) and print word endings on snap clothespins. The children should match words and possible endings by clipping the clothespins onto the end of words (see Figure 3-7). Note: Be careful of words such as *running* (doubled consonant) and *making* (dropped *e*). A supply of blank squares will allow the children to write a needed letter or to blot out an extra letter. The squares can then be clipped in place with the clothespin. Variation: Write contractions on clothespins (e.g., *don't*) and base words (e.g., *do not*) on the circles.

Word Mobiles. The children should select a word and find as many forms of it as possible (e.g., *joke, jokes, joked, joking, jokingly, joker, jokers*). Then they should write each word on a strip of cardboard and string the words up in mobile fashion. Wire from old coat hangers and nylon fish line are good for this, but any kind of stick and thread will do.

Note: this activity is especially good for unusual forms of words such as *be: am, is, are, was, were, been, being.*

Jargon. Most trades and professions use some words related to their work that are not generally well known. Have the children compile word lists of specilized vocabularies by occupations. Parents, friends, and how-to-do-it books are helpful sources.

Slang Dictionaries. Have the children begin this activity by examining their own vocabularies for slang. Then, as a class, set up the format for making a slang dictionary. Examine dictionaries used in the classroom to discover what information is given for each entry. Then have the children prepare a full entry for each of

FIGURE 3-7
Clothespin Match.

their slang terms. The activity may be continued over a period of time with children adding new terms as they discover them.

Names for Things. Make a bulletin board of pictures of things that are called by different names in different parts of the United States, e.g., frying pan, bag, ear of corn, skunk, bucket, etc. (See Shuy, 1967 for additional ideas.) Have the children find as many names for each item as possible and add the names under each picture in caption fashion.

Dialects in Literature. Read selections from literature that contain examples of dialects and discuss the variations. For example:

"Jack and Jill went up the hill / To *fetch* a *pail* of water."

"The queen of hearts / *She* made some tarts."

"Tom, Tom, the piper's son / Stole a pig and away he *run*."

With rings on her fingers, / And bells on her toes, / She *shall* have music wherever she goes."

The children may find examples to share in their reading. Folktales are rich sources of dialect but there are many stories such as *Little Britches* and *Tom Sawyer* that are good too.

Merry/Mary/Marry. After discussing dialects, help the children plan and carry out a pronunciation study. To keep it simple, the children might check with neighbors and friends the pronunciation of a few pairs or groups of words that are frequently pronounced differently. Variations should be noted and data kept on where each respondent grew up. Plot the class findings on charts or graphs to discover patterns. Words that might be used include *greasy/grassy* (the /s/ /z/ sound); *witch/which* (the /w/ /wh/ sound); *cot/caught* (the medial vowel sound); and *merry/Mary/marry* (the medial vowel sound).

Suggestions for Further Reading

Elgin, Suzette Haden. *A Primer of Transformational Grammar for Rank Beginners*. Urbana, Ill.: National Council of Teachers of English, 1975.

Fromkin, Victoria, and Robert Rodman. *An Introduction to Language*, 2nd ed. New York: Holt, Rinehart & Winston, 1978.

Reed, Carroll E. *Dialects of American English*, rev. ed. Amherst, Mass.: University of Massachusetts Press, 1977.

Shuy, Roger W. *Discovering American Dialects*. Champaign, Ill.: National Council of Teachers of English, 1967.

Weaver, Constance. *Grammar for Teachers, Perspectives and Definitions*. Urbana, Ill.: National Council of Teachers of English, 1979.

4
Oral Language

The specific communication skill which is most critical for the fully functioning individual in modern society and for success in any academic area is proficiency in the use of oral language.

Wilma Possien (1969, p. 8)

CHAPTER PREVIEW

Reading and writing account for only a small part of language usage. Historically, developmentally, and quantitatively, oral language takes precedence. It is not only the primary mode of communication, but the foundation for other modes. Therefore oral language ought to receive a great deal of attention in language arts programs. In this chapter we will look at developmental patterns of language and analyze the relationship of language and thinking. We will discuss important elements of speech and then suggest oral language activities for elementary schoolchildren.

QUESTIONS TO THINK ABOUT AS YOU READ

What is the sequence of language development?

How do linguists explain the process of learning language?

How is language related to thinking?

What is the sound system of English and how are the sounds made?

What is "good speech"?

What can be done about children's speech problems?

What kinds of speech activities are appropriate for elementary schoolchildren?

Learning Language

We tend to take the ability to speak for granted. It is largely an unconscious act and is so intimately interwoven in all that we think or do that we are hardly aware of the art and skill involved. Speaking and listening, reciprocal acts, are amazingly complex interactional processes requiring the orchestration of a wide range of mental, physical, and social skills.

Because the language of young children sounds much like that of adults, it is easy to ignore important developmental aspects of language learning. We may assume that children have a greater understanding than they actually do. By the time children reach school age they have usually become quite proficient in language. Research shows that most five-year-old children have acquired the sound system of English, are able to generate all the basic sentence patterns, and can use language to serve their immediate purposes. Even so, their language should not be considered equivalent to adults'. Young children are not only incapable of forming abstract concepts and generating and comprehending complex sentence structures, but their understanding of the social contexts of language is limited.

Stages of Development

In acquiring language, children progress through identifiable stages. The first stage we notice is *babbling*. Here the language sounds children make are largely unconscious and accidental, but from this experimental play with sounds the elements of speech ultimately emerge.

During the second six months of life children begin to make sounds more closely related to actual speech. From a range of nearly all the speech sounds they will eventually use (and possibly others that will be discarded because they are not part of the set of English sounds), a baby begins to focus on certain sounds and combinations of sounds. During this stage children typically utter combinations of consonants made in the front of the mouth and vowels made at the back of the mouth. This pattern gives rise to the sounds of ma-ma and pa-pa, which proud parents label as first words.

Gradually children progress to a stage of one-word utterances. These utterances, termed *holophrastic speech*, are somewhat like one-word sentences. When children say "Drink," for example, they are really formulating something meaning "Give me a drink," or "I want a drink." McNeill points out, however, that holophrastic speech is not the same as sentence construction. He says "Holophrastic speech means that while children are limited to uttering single words at the beginning of language acquisition, they are capable of conceiving of something like full sentences." (1970, p. 20) The one-word utterances are neither precise words nor sentences to children. They refer to things and are often closely linked with action, but they are essentially a representation of an experience.

In the next stage of development, children produce two-word utterances composed of meaning-bearing words (*Bobby sock, bye-bye car, allgone cookie*). Gradually they create longer strings of words (*Put it box, Markie. Molly go potty.*) You will notice that function words are omitted and that the children do not use inflected forms of words. Such speech has been called *telegraphic speech* because it sounds much like a telegram, with nonessentials omitted.

Analysis of children's utterances at this stage suggests children's early sense of function and system in language. Bloom (1973) found that children's two-word utterances are remarkably regular in word order when the words are classified according to their semantic roles in a particular context. For instance, when a child points to his or her mother's stocking and says "Mommy sock" the utterance expresses a possessor-possession relation. If we take careful note of such relationships as agent-action ("Daddy fix"), action-object ("Push car"), or object-location ("Doggie outside"), it is clear that children rarely violate the word order that adults use.

Lindfors (1980) aptly summarizes: "One cannot help but be impressed by the evidence of pattern in this early period in the child's language development. The child's language is clearly rule governed and creative. The child seems not to be imitating other's comments, but rather expressing her own meanings creatively, within the set of structural possibilities her system allows" (p. 132).

As children continue to grow and develop their linguistic abilities, they gradually increase their vocabulary and move toward fully formed and complex sentence structures. The grammar rules that they seem to know "in their heads" become apparent in the surface structures of their speech. One example of their knowledge of rules is reflected in their attempt to regularize all noun and verb forms (e.g., *foots, mouses, goed, and digged*). These errors indicate that children have somehow extracted the rules for forming the plural of nouns and the past tense of verbs from language. In doing so they have overgeneralized, believing that *all* nouns and *all* verbs take these forms.

Another example of children's developing but incomplete knowledge of language structures is found in such constructions as *Why Johnny isn't eating?* This example shows that the child is in the process of acquiring the rules for transforming a kernel sentence to a why question. The child has mastered the regular subject verb order of sentences but has not yet internalized the rule for changing word order as part of the question transformation.

Research indicates that it is futile to attempt to teach children grammatical structures that they have not yet internalized. Children process only what they understand and ignore the rest. McNeill illustrates the point well with this dialog, in which a mother is trying to get her child not to use a double negative:

Child: Nobody don't like me.
Mother: No, say "nobody likes me."
Child: Nobody don't like me.
     [eight repetitions of this dialogue]
Mother: No, now listen carefully: say "nobody likes me."
Child: Oh! Nobody don't likes me. (1970, p. 106)

Studies of language development show that children's mastery of language structures may extend well into the elementary years. Although these years of language development have not been as well researched as the early acquisition period, it is evident that some structures are not acquired until around nine or ten years of age or even later.

One of the more difficult structures involves the use of subordinators. In one study Chomsky assessed children's ability to understand these two constructions involving the use of the subordinator *although:*

> Mother scolded Gloria for answering the phone, and I would have done the same.

> Mother scolded Gloria for answering the phone, although I would have done the same.

Chomsky found that many nine- and ten-year-olds had difficulty explaining what the sentence indicated *I would have done.* (1974, p. 62)

Another study by Chomsky (1969) points out children's difficulty in understanding sentences that vary from the usual noun-verb order of kernel sentences. In one part of the study reported, Chomsky showed children Bozo and Donald Duck dolls. When they understood the identity of the dolls and the meaning of the word *promise,* the children were given an opportunity to demonstrate their knowledge of sentence structures such as

> Bozo tells Donald to hop up and down. Make him hop.

> Bozo promises Donald to do a summersault. Make him do it.

> Donald promises Bozo to hop up and down. Make him hop.

The study showed that children had acquired the grammatical rule that the subject of a compliment verb is the noun phrase most closely preceding it (e.g., "Bozo tells Donald to hop up and down"), but that some of them were unaware of exceptions ("Donald promises Bozo to do a summersault") until around the age of ten.

Developmental studies of children's language have yielded significant information. Perhaps the most important point is that children are *in the process* of becoming competent receivers and producers of language. The level of instruction and our expectations of children ought to match their actual developmental level and keep them on the growing edge of expanding and refining their language.

The Process of Learning Language

Just how children acquire language has not been clearly resolved. One theory suggests that language is learned through imitation and positive reinforcement. For example, when a baby produces a familiar sound or word, it is rewarded by the tone of pleasure in its mother's voice or by a smile. Repeated experiences with similar positive reinforcement leads to the establishment of culturally significant speech habits. However, this theory fails to account for the fact that speech is largely creative rather than imitative. Children are continually generating utterances that they have never heard (e.g., "All-gone outside"). Furthermore, some of the word forms they use reflect their own unique attempts to regularize grammatical forms (e.g., "We goed to the circus").

Another theory holds that language development is innate; children acquire language ability naturally, just as they acquire other human abilities. Lenneberg (1972) theorizes that the rate of development is determined by maturation, which is controlled by the development of the brain. He places the critical period for acquiring language between birth and about age twelve, or the onset of puberty. Lenneberg claimed that both hemispheres of a child's brain are involved with language processing during this period of development.

A third theory explains the development of language in relation to cognitive processes. Those who hold this theory believe that humans are born with a capacity for language, which Chomsky calls a *Language Acquisition Device* (LAD); it allows them to process language and intuitively formulate rules for its use. Children are thought to develop language through a series of hypotheses and tests that result in their discovering the rules governing the use of language. Language learning takes place subconsciously as children interact with other language users. The so-called errors children make (*higher the rope, I gots it*) represent their overgeneralization about how language works. Environment, of course, plays a significant role in the cogni-

tive theory; children must have input on which to base generalizations. Children's experiences provide the laboratory for learning
language. However, their cognitive capacity at any given time determines what they can extract from language data.

Recent research has tended to focus on social context — the matrix
of experiences and interaction that enables children to develop a
sense of language. The learning environment is important because as
Platt explains,

> From the very beginning, babies interact with people in relation to the
> world of things, places, and events which surround them. These
> understood situations enable them to develop both meaning and
> language. Language is thus learned in the same way as everything else:
> through cognitive powers of inference, and through awareness of other
> people (1979, p. 621).

This point of view suggests that children combine previous linguistic knowledge with situation-specific perceptions to form hypotheses
about language. Then, in interactions with others, they try out their
hypotheses and receive feedback. Hypotheses are modified and the
process is repeated. Gradually children come to approximate the
norm and thus acquire communicative competence in that social context.

The home is the first social context in which children develop communicative competence. They acquire not only the vocabulary and
grammatical structures used in the home but also an awareness of
intent and appropriateness. When they enter school they encounter
another social context, one in which they may find themselves unable
to communicate effectively. Teachers, other adults, and peers are
often relative strangers, and children have little or no basis for hypothesizing effective interactional language in the new situation.
They must discover such things as how to initiate a conversation
when participants do not have a common background of knowledge,
how to take turns yet hold their own as a member of a large group,
what uses of language are considered appropriate, and how to interpret a speaker's intended meaning when it is not directly stated ("It's
getting noisy in here").

Furthermore, the teacher's vocabulary and nonverbal cues are apt
to be significantly different from those of the child's mother or care-
taker. Concepts for words frequently used in school, such as *word,
sentence, recess,* and *the office,* are likely to be ill-formed or unknown.

Research pertaining to the social context of learning indicates that
children learn to respond differently in different situations. For example, they may speak to peers differently than they speak to teach-

ers. When they dictate a story they may use language (including tone of voice) that is different from that of casual conversation. These kinds of behaviors are contextually learned.

Research also indicates that for many children, perhaps most, there is a decided need to facilitate transitions between the contexts of home and school. During a recent project in England I observed this being done quite successfully in several schools. The heads of these schools planned a range of activities designed to provide interface between the school and the community. Parents performed various tasks about the school, older ladies helped small groups of children with cooking projects, and young children came with their mothers to pick up older brothers and sisters and to see their rooms. Family possessions were proudly displayed to illustrate a particular study or area of interest. Teachers and school patrons worked side by side on fund-raising projects and community socials. School programs included activities that not only interested the children but required participation and verbal interaction. For example, planting, tending, and harvesting a school garden or watching performances by local and outside musicians, actors, and puppeteers created a need to communicate and expand their use of language. Plants, pets, cozy little bays and nooks for group work, and lunch served at small tables by "dinner ladies" helped bridge the gap between home and school. Furthermore, direct experience accompanied by purposeful verbal interaction provided a rich laboratory in which to generate and test hypotheses about language.

We must be careful not to assume that developing communicative competence in a variety of social contexts will interest only primary-grade teachers. Whenever children are learning to deal with language in a different context, the teacher should plan learning activities that help them make important discoveries in a supportive, nonthreatening environment. Children for whom English is a second language, speakers of a divergent dialect, mainstreamed children, and children from different cultural backgrounds all must learn the fundamentals of communication in the new context of school. Ultimately they will need to be sensitive to a variety of social contexts and to be able to communicate effectively in each.

Patterns of Development

Studies in language acquisition and development reveal several patterns that have implications for teaching. One pattern is that of seeing language as a "whole." Data suggest that children sense the larger system of language from the beginning. Although children's early utterances consist of single words, those words represent whole ideas. Then, as children progress in linguistic ability, their multiple-word utterances capture more and more of the essence of whole sentence structures. Later, when children are involved in conscious study of word order and other aspects of grammar, such lessons must relate principles and generalizations to larger, meaningful structures that children already possess.

Another pattern is that children first formulate gross language generalizations and then refine them. Eve Clark (1973), for example, reported this pattern in her study of the language development of young children. Initially children in her study called all four-legged, furry animals "doggie." Gradually they acquired a larger frame of reference. Through comparison and contrast they became aware that other features such as size and shape were significant for an animal to fit in the "doggie" classification. On the basis of additional knowledge, the children narrowed their original generalization. The example given previously of children using *foots* or *digged* demonstrates their natural tendency to overgeneralize, to apply a rule too broadly. Recognition of this pattern suggests the importance of planning many purposeful language activities that allow children to gather data and check out the accuracy of their generalizations.

A related pattern shows the interrelationship of language and activity in language acquisition. Young children accompany activity with speech (or, perhaps speech with activity), even when their language seems not to be intended for an audience. Later, language becomes an extension of the activity itself. Young children have a need to "do" language to learn it. Language learning is an active, though largely unconscious, process, and it requires much opportunity to associate language with actual experience.

Finally, research points out an overall pattern or inborn language clock for acquiring and developing language. Researchers have replicated the sequence of language development many times to verify its consistent time line. Although children develop at their own rates, the pattern of development is highly consistent. Teachers can plan for and encourage maximum progress by providing language activities that help children expand and refine their language skills and understandings. In addition, the perceptive teacher observes children's level of language development and avoids putting the children in stressful and frustrating situations.

Language and Thought

The language of elementary schoolchildren appears to be inextricably interwoven with thought. Sometimes as we watch children involved in solving a problem we can almost "read their minds" and write out a script of what is going on inside their heads. But the exact degree of convergence between language and thought remains somewhat elusive, because thinking is entirely private and activities or verbalizations that reflect thought are always subject to interpretation. Research has shed considerable light on the thinking process, however, and suggests guidelines for the kinds of language activities that are best suited to children at each age level.

A Developmental Process

Piaget's research on language and thought has been particularly helpful. He has identified stages that all children go through and has described the implications for children's language at each stage of development. He believes that children's progress from one stage to another is a gradual and predictable process of continuous learning. Piaget's stages are briefly summarized in this section to provide a general understanding of his theoretical framework. Before you read on, however, a word of caution should be given concerning his age classifications. It is important to understand that the age ranges given for each stage are only approximate. They should be thought of as a general guide; children older or younger may demonstrate the characteristics of a particular stage.

Piaget believed that thought is internalized action, at first independent of language. In the *sensorimotor* period (birth to age two), children's cognitive functions begin to develop through their perceptions of things in the immediate environment. They discover and "know" through movements and sensory experiences. Activities such as kicking, reaching, touching, and tasting provide experiences in sensorimotor learning. The child bumps a toy and it falls over; he or she drops a fresh egg and it splats on the floor. Through repeated experiences the child learns how things behave when he or she does certain things to them. The child is not, however, capable of any further explanation.

Around the age of two years, children enter the period of *symbolic function*. At this stage words for things are associated with images. (Piaget uses the term *images* to include the recall of any experience, not just visual experience.) Children begin to develop a thought-symbolizing process that enables them to use verbal symbols apart from their direct experiences. Words become signifiers for things that are not present, and children are able to recall and reconstruct experiences. For example, when a little girl glanced at the door and said, "Mommie go shopping?" she was demonstrating the stage of symbolic function.

Piaget felt that language was not essential to thought in children's early development. He believed that language develops as an accompaniment to thought and that the direct action-thought process of children in the early years can occur without language. Ginsburg and Opper explain,

> Despite his new ability at language, the child often thinks nonverbally. He forms mental symbols which are based on imitations of things and not on their names. Language does, however, make a contribution. For example, when an adult uses a word which refers to a *class* of things, the child is given a glimpse of one facet of adult reasoning. An adult's language forces the child, to some degree, to consider the word from a new perspective. Nevertheless, it is probably fair to say that the child's thought depends less on his language than his language does on his thought. (1969, p. 85)

The *preoperational stage* (ages four to seven) is characterized by children's egocentricism. Their language and thinking represent a very personal and limited point of view. For example, a child's perception of a fall: *The sidewalk tripped me*, and of a traffic light: *That light is looking at me*. Along with this egocentric interpretation of things, children tend to focus on certain features of a thing and ignore other, equally important features. They center on the original state or position of something and are unable to comprehend its transformation or change from one state to another. Piaget demonstrated with plasticene. In the experiment children are given two identical balls of plasticene. First they are asked if there is the same amount in each ball. If they say no, they are asked to take some away from the larger ball and make it equal to the other. The children watch as one ball is molded into the shape of a sausage and then they are asked whether the second ball and the sausage contain the same amount. Children in the preoperational stage lack the concept of conservation of substance and are unable to answer correctly. They do not comprehend that changing the shape of something doesn't change the amount of it.

Children at the preoperational level of development are also unable to see the relationship of two or more features or events. They cannot think about more than one aspect of a situation at a time. Events and features are merely juxtaposed and not meaningfully connected. This characteristic may also be observed in children's drawings. For example, in drawing a bicycle children may draw the chain but not connect it to the wheel, or the wheels may be detached from the other structures.

Children's language at this stage is ego-centered. They do not consider the needs of their listener but seem to assume that the listener shares their image and already knows what they are talking about. Their explanations frequently include pronouns without referents (*You move it over there and push the thing that way*). Important features or parts of a story are sometimes left out, even though children may remember the parts. They also have a tendency to group unrelated things together into a confused whole. If something doesn't fit, they put it in anyway, possibly filling in imagined details to their personal satisfaction.

Much of children's speech during the preoperational stage may not be intended as communication. According to Piaget there are three types of noncommunicative utterances: repetition, monologue, and collective monologue. *Repetition* is merely repeating or mimicking another's speech. Ginsburg and Opper further comment, "Very often too the child is not aware that he is merely repeating what another person has said, but believes that his statement is an original one" (1969, p. 87). The term *monologue* describes the speech of children when they are alone and just talking to themselves. Quite often a length soliloquy accompanies children's independent play. A similar situation may occur when children are playing together. Piaget called this speech *collective monologue*. It occurs when children talk to themselves while they are in a group of children. The speech is not intended for the other children, and the other children don't appear to be listening to it.

During the preoperational period important mental and linguistic growth occurs. Children gradually shed egocentric patterns of thinking and move into a period of operational thinking. Richmond describes how children's environment influences their development:

> The child's increasing social involvement during these years gives impetus to the development of his intellectual processes. . . . the sharing of materials, the sharing of experience in play, and the engagement in similar tasks, force upon the child a communal form of thought. The principal currency of his social interchange is language, and he is immersed in a sea of words which define and relate his social behaviours and his physical activities. Whether he likes it or not, the child begins to see his relationship to others as reciprocal and not unidirectional. (1970, p. 31)

The *concrete operations* stage (ages seven to eleven) is characterized by children's ability to focus on several features or dimensions of a situation simultaneously and to comprehend how they are related. Children are able to understand that something may be changed from one shape to another without changing its volume or weight (the principle of conservation). They are able to understand that once something has been acted on (e.g., molding the plasticene ball into a sausage) the process can be reversed to return the thing to its original condition (the principle of reversibility). Children's thinking no longer focuses on states; they are aware of processes, the actions performed on things. These new mental abilities allow children much greater flexibility in thinking. Now that they can perform mental actions involving more than one concept, they can relate, rearrange, separate, and recombine images in endless ways.

Children's mental operations at this stage, however, are limited to concrete images. They can perform mental activities only on the images that they have already stored away in their minds or that they can directly manipulate and observe in their present environment. They are unable to solve problems involving things and ideas outside this range of reality.

The egocentricity that characterized the preoperational stage is lost in the period of concrete operations. Children's speech becomes more socially oriented. They speak to communicate and they are aware of the listener as a vital part of communication. Because they can hold several images in their mind and attend to them at once, they are able to perform operations with verbal symbols. They can now systematically relate things to other conceptual structures or to sets of internalized rules. For example, they can classify (chickens, ducks, and geese are fowl), relate one concept to another (the heart pumps blood through the veins and arteries), formulate classifications (long and thick, short and thick, long and thin), and recognize cause and effect (when water is heated it turns to steam).

Given a challenging environment with many opportunities to form and act on mental images, children's language develops rapidly in the concrete operations period. Just as in the earlier stages, their direct experiences are the foundation of learning. Now, however, children are able to do more with those experiences. They are able to combine their experiential images and rearrange them to create more complex concepts and to expand previous ones.

As children emerge from the period of concrete operations they are quite different mentally and linguistically from the way they were at the beginning of the period. With a good foundation of experiences, children around the age of eleven are ready to move into a period of formal operations. Their thinking is no longer bound to realia; they can conceptualize through the symbol system of language alone. They can use words conceptually to organize classifications and subclassifications, to construct sets with common members, and to formulate hypotheses. Language has become more directly related to thought.

Encouraging Growth

Piaget's research makes it clear that the development of language and thought is something that occurs within the child and that it cannot be imposed from the outside. We can, however, set the stage for learning and help children develop to the limits of their cognitive power.

Experience coupled with purposeful use of language is a major key to development. As we pointed out earlier, children make inferences from the language they hear, and later, from the language they read. We can facilitate this process by providing them a rich and stimulating environment in which language is used naturally for various purposes. In such a setting children can associate language with things and experiences. Smith states,

> there is only one essential precondition for children to learn about language, and that is that it should make sense to them, both in its content and its motivation. Children come to understand how language works by understanding the purposes and intentions of the people who produce it, and they learn to produce language themselves to the extent that it fulfills their own purposes or intentions" (1979, p. 119).

Research has shown that the kinds of questions teachers ask point children toward various kinds of thinking. Through a carefully planned sequence of questions teachers can help children to develop thinking strategies and to communicate their thoughts effectively. One paperback book that you will surely find valuable in learning to do this is Sanders's (1966) *Classroom Questions, What Kind?* In this book he simplifies and explains Bloom's well-known *Taxonomy of Educational Objectives* (1956). Here are Sanders's *preliminary* definitions of Bloom's categories of thinking:

1. *Memory:* The student recalls or recognizes information.

2. *Translation:* The student changes information into a different symbolic form or language.

3. *Interpretation:* The student discovers relationships among facts, generalizations, definitions, values, and skills.

4. *Application:* The student solves a lifelike problem that requires the identification of the issue and the selection and use of appropriate generalizations and skills.

5. *Analysis:* The student solves a problem in the light of conscious knowledge of the parts and forms of thinking.

6. *Synthesis:* The student solves a problem that requires original, creative thinking.

7. *Evaluation:* The student makes a judgment of good or bad, right or wrong, according to standards he designates. (p. 3)

Each successive level in the hierarchy is dependent on lower levels. For example, the ability to *apply* knowledge (level 4) depends on ability to interpret relationships (level 3). That ability in turn depends on a level of comprehension that permits explaining or restating information in another way (level 2), and that is only possible if there is information to begin with (level 1).

Using carefully structured questions, the teacher can guide the children through thinking processes that they would not execute on their own. In planning a discussion with younger children or introducing an unfamiliar topic to older children, you will probably need to establish a firm knowledge base before moving to higher levels. When children are familiar with a topic, however, they may not need to begin at the first level and systematically pose questions at each level. Questions at more advanced levels require children to understand a concept at a lower level of the hierarchy. By analyzing children's answers to a higher-level question you can discover when a child has omitted an important thinking skill. By phrasing another question at the needed lower level you can help the child include that step in his or her response.

Helping children learn to think by posing appropriate questions takes skill and practice but is highly rewarding when you see your students expanding their thinking and dealing with problems in purposeful ways. These examples of questions will help you get started:

Memory level

Who is . . . ?
What is . . . ?
Where was . . . ?
What did . . . ?
How many . . . ?
When did . . . ?

Translation level

In your own words, tell . . .
How else might you say . . . ?
Which picture shows . . . ?
Describe . . .
Tell how . . .

Interpretation level

Compare . . .
Tell what you think . . .
Is . . . greater than . . . ?
Why is it called . . . ?
Explain why . . .
What caused . . . ?
What conclusion have you reached about . . . ?

Application level

When might you . . . ?
Where could you . . . ?
Which would you use if . . . ?
How will this affect . . . ?
Suggest [2] possible ways to . . .

Analysis level

Why is . . . ?
What evidence is there that . . . ?
In what way might . . . ?
Give some instances in which . . .
Which of these would . . . ?

Synthesis level

How many ways can you think of to . . . ?
What would happen if . . . ?
Devise a plan to . . .
How can you explain . . . ?

Evaluation level

Should . . . be permitted to . . . ? Why?
Is . . . accurate? Why do you think this?
Was it wrong (right) for . . . ? Why do you think so?
How well did . . . ?
What is the most important . . . ? Why?
What are the chances that . . . ?
Which of the following . . . ?

Speech Sounds

The production of speech sounds involves a cooperative interplay of several organs not intended primarily for speech. Speech begins with a flow of air from the lungs, passes through the vocal cords in the larynx, up the pharynx, where it either goes on through the mouth or the flow is diverted through the nasal passages. Once in the mouth, the passage of the air stream is further controlled by the soft palate, the tongue, and the lips (see Figure 4-1).

Linguists classify consonant sounds in two major ways: according to *where* the sounds are made and *how* they are made. Knowing the *where* and *how* of speech production is helpful in working with children who have difficulty making certain sounds. These are the classifications that describe *where* a sound is articulated:

Labial (lips): p, b, m, w

Labio-dental (lips and teeth): f, v

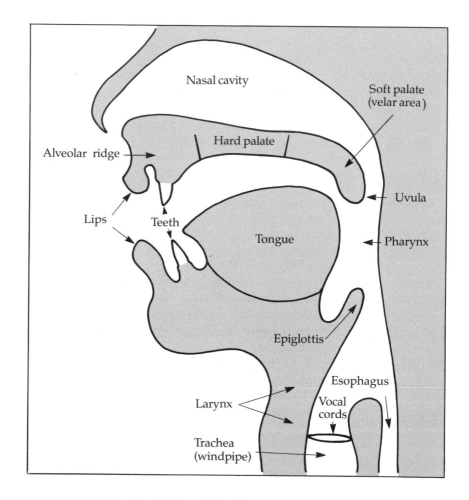

FIGURE 4-1

From Suzette Haden Elgin, *What Is Linguistics?* © 1973, p. 6. Reprinted by permission of Prentice-Hall, Inc., Englewood Cliffs, New Jersey.

Dental (teeth): voiced and voiceless th (ðθ)

Alveolar (behind upper teeth): t, d, s, z, l, r, n

Palatal (roof of mouth): ch, j, sh, zh

Velar (upper back of mouth): k, g, ng

Glottal (back of throat): h

You might try making each sound to get a feel for the position. As you do so, notice the shape of the tongue in producing different sounds.

The second way of classifying sounds has to do with *how* the breath stream is allowed to flow through the mouth. If the air stream is shut off and then suddenly released as in /b/ or /t/, the sound is called a *stop* or *plosive*. *Fricatives* are hissing sounds made by partially blocking the flow of air as in /f/ or /sh/. *Affricatives* are sounds that begin like a stop but end like a fricative as in /ch/ or /j/. *Nasal* sounds are made by partially blocking off the mouth cavity and sending air through the nasal passages as in /m/ or /n/. In producing *liquids* the air flow is obstructed but allowed to escape by lowering the sides of the tongue as in /l/ or /r/.

Consonant sounds may also be classified as *voiced* or *voiceless*. The vocal cords do not vibrate in the production of all sounds. For example, put your fingers on your throat and feel as well as listen while you make the sounds /t/ and /d/. The first is voiceless and the second is voiced. Other pairs of voiced and voiceless consonants are given in Table 4-1.

In making vowel sounds the breath stream is not restricted as it is when consonant sounds are made. Vowel sounds are made in different places in the mouth and are determined by the shape of the

TABLE 4-1. Classification of English Consonant Sounds by Place and Manner of Articulation

	STOPS	*FRICATIVES*	*AFFRICATIVES*	*NASALS*	*LIQUIDS*
Labial	p* b			m	
Labio-Dental		f* v			
Dental		θ* ð			
Alveolar	t* d	s* z			l r
Palatal		sh* zh	ch* j	n	
Velar	k* g			ng	
Glottal		h*			

From Suzette Haden Elgin, *What Is Linguistics?* © 1973. Adapted by permission of Prentice-Hall, Inc., Englewood Cliffs, New Jersey.
*Indicates voiceless

tongue. Read these sounds and notice how your tongue changes shape: /ē/, /ĭ/, /ĕ/, /ă/, /ə/. Now, by contrast, feel the difference in /ā/ and /aw/.

By the time children enter school most of them are able to produce most sounds. Templin's (1957) study reports the following ages as the times when 75 percent of the children in her study were able to produce certain sounds:

m, n, ng, p, f, h, w	3 years
y	3.5 years
k, b, d, g, r	4 years
s, sh, ch	4.5 years
t, th (voiceless) v, l	6 years
th (voiced), z, zh, j	7 years

Most speech production problems are minor and may be classified as substitutions (*wabbit* for *rabbit*), omissions (*member* for *remember*), insertions (*sherbert* for *sherbet*), and distortions (*leckercrick* for *electric*). Articulation problems tend to disappear as children get older, develop a better ear for language, and gain greater control over their individual speech instrument. Having children listen carefully while you say a word distinctly will help them become aware of differences. After modeling the word correctly ask them to repeat it. Continue this procedure on an informal and spontaneous basis from time to time.

Fingerplays, rhymes, and choral speech also provide interesting practice for specific sounds. Some examples of these activities are included in the activity section.

Listen carefully to children's speech and make a list of their variant patterns. This will give you data for analyzing the help they need. Errors that are merely immature speech may then be remediated in the classroom through speech activities that practice desirable patterns. You can make a simple speech assessment by drawing or glueing pictures of things whose names contain specific sounds onto cards and asking children to name the item. Use names that have a given sound at the beginning, middle, and end (e.g., *shoe*, *dishes*, and *fish*). Sometimes children have no difficulty pronouncing a sound at the beginning of a word but are unable to pronounce it in the middle or at the end of a word.

Another simple assessment tool is a series of questions that require children to use a particular sound. For example,

Which would you choose:

a rabbit or a rat?

a shark or a sheep?

a thin book or a thick book?

a new jacket or some jewelry?

etc.

Not all speech problems are simple, of course. Whenever children have a persistent speech handicap or one that appears to be more than a matter of habit or maturation or when they exhibit anxiety about their speech, they should be referred to a speech therapist. It is especially important to maintain a positive and supportive classroom atmosphere for these children, but they must not be made to feel "special." Calling attention to their handicap is emotionally threatening and tends to compound the problem.

Stuttering is one speech problem that calls for a specialist's help. However, certain guidelines may be useful until that help arrives. In general, stutterers need to feel accepted as normal and enjoyable individuals who just happen to have a stuttering problem. They should not be told to slow down or take a deep breath before they speak. Neither should they be "helped" by having you say words for them or praised for stuttering a fewer number of times during the day. These actions tell stutterers that you like them better when they don't stutter and only increase their anxiety. They need to accept themselves as they are and they need understanding (not pity or sympathy) from teachers and classmates.

Elements of Speech

Competence in using oral language essentially involves being able to express ideas clearly, interestingly, and appropriately. The purpose of speech and the nature of the situation suggest some special considerations, and we will look at some of the more common uses of speech in a moment. First we will consider some important elements of effective speech.

The Voice

Good speech is clear and distinct. It is melodic with appropriate variation in pitch and rhythm. Words are correctly pronounced, and the voice is modulated to produce a pleasing sound. The tempo varies somewhat with the situation in which the speech is made, but it is never too hurried or tiresomely slow.

Many children (and adults) are not at all conscious of their own voices. Thus improvement is not likely until they "tune in" to their own speaking habits. It is often helpful for children to listen to a variety of speech models and evaluate the qualities that make a voice pleasing and interesting to listen to. Television and radio provide a wide range, from character actors to eloquent speakers. Children's programs and recorded stories offer appropriate models for younger children. Samples from various sources may be tape recorded and then played back in the classroom for discussion.

As children discuss a favorite speaker, probe their thinking for *why* they enjoy that person. Write their descriptive words and phrases on the board. Then guide them in synthesizing the list into a model or set of guidelines for speaking. Copy the model onto a chart and display it in a prominent place. Children may then make tape recordings of their own speech and compare their talk with the model.

Audience Awareness

The egocentric nature of young children orients their use of oral language toward self-expression rather than the transmission of information. They tend to have little awareness or concern for their listener. Developing audience awareness in these children means helping them think about what they need to tell listeners and helping them speak distinctly and loudly enough to be heard. When children are telling something but failing to communicate, help them realize what additional information is needed. Capitalize on audience reactions to develop an awareness of the listener. For example, you might say, "I don't believe the children understand what you did. Where did you go? Who went with you?"

Older children also need to be aware of the informative purpose of speech and how they can best convey their ideas. They need to become flexible in using speech, adjusting their volume and tone to fit the situation. In considering their audience, children need to decide whether the size of the group requires them to project their voice or soften it so as not to disturb others outside the speech situation. They need to consider the background of the listener and how detailed they ought to be in presenting information or discussing ideas. In addition, they need to consider the speech situation and whether an informal or more serious approach is called for. Conversations, for example, seem stilted when a speaker talks in a loud, expository manner. A conversation suggests a more relaxed and intimate verbal exchange.

Nonverbal Communication

The often quoted "What you do speaks so loudly that I cannot hear what you say" is an apt admonition for all speakers. It is certainly true that nonverbal communication plays a tremendous role in communication. Children ought to be aware of this and learn to use nonverbal communication advantageously as they speak.

Tone has already been mentioned, but perhaps it should be included in this context as well. Children need to become aware of tones that may creep into their voices and create communication interference. Tones of contempt or condescension set up negative attitudes in listeners and cause them to distrust or tune out the speaker. A direct and unflinching manner conveys a sense of confidence. Tentativeness suggests an openness and invites discussion.

Body posture is closely related to tone. Whether a child is engaged in a conversation or presenting a report to the whole class, attentive body posture beckons responsive listening. Posture should be related to the situation. When children give a report to the class they should be encouraged to stand erect with their weight on both feet. In planning sessions, they may gather around a table or even sit on the floor. In any situation, they need to be aware that *how* they stand or sit conveys an important message. An alert body posture says in effect, "I'm saying something interesting and worth listening to."

Facial expressions are an important aspect of nonverbal communication. They reveal how speakers feel about what they are saying and about the people they are talking to. Eye contact lets listeners know that they are an essential part of the communication process, that the speaker is talking to them personally. An animated expression stimulates interest and develops an air of anticipation.

Children frequently use gestures when they talk and seldom need special emphasis in this area of nonverbal communication. It is more important to help them develop content for meaningful speech and gain confidence in talking to their peers than to spend time developing eloquent gestures. If, however, the children have annoying habits that distract from what they are saying, they will need to become aware of those habits and have help in changing them.

The Content of Speech

Content is the heart of communication. Because speaking skills involve having something to say, children ought to recognize their responsibility for meaningful content. Whether they are telling a joke or describing a sunset, their attentive listeners deserve to hear something worthwhile. This is not meant to suggest an overly critical approach, of course. Some children need a great deal of encouragement to say anything. It is important, however, for children to recognize speech as communication and to strive for purposeful and responsible use of language.

Organization of content is also important. Children may need help in keeping to the subject or in telling about one aspect of a topic or event at a time. Taping a conversation or report and then playing it back is one way to help children become aware of organization. Sketching a simple diagram on the board calls attention to the sequence in which the content of speech was presented and helps children recognize regressions and fault organization (Figure 4-2).

Vocabulary

An extensive vocabulary is important to good speech because it permits exact and colorful communication. A good vocabulary is directly related to the kinds of language activities children engage in and their attitude toward language. Words are only symbolic labels for things and concepts. Thus a large vocabulary will grow out of opportunities to establish connections between concepts and verbal symbols. Sensory experiences — seeing, feeling, touching, tasting, and smelling — stimulate concept formation. Children need to have such experiences in the company of knowledgeable others who can help them associate words with their experiences. They also need help in analyzing aspects of their perceptions and in attaching verbal labels to them. For example, on seeing a starfish children might talk about its size, shape, texture, how it moves, how it eats, what it eats, and where it lives. Such a discussion would make the experience more meaningful than merely looking at the starfish by themselves.

Literature is a rich source for vocabulary expansion. Reading to children, in addition to setting a time for them to read independently, is an important way for them to discover the use of words in meaningful contexts. Through stories children become acquainted with different denotations or meanings for words (*duck* as a bird, *duck* to get out of sight, *duck* cloth), dimensions of meaning (physical description, biological classification, habits, contrasting features, and function or use), and connotations (associated meanings such as the smell of a roasting duck). Each time children hear or read a word, it becomes a little more familiar. Gradually a concept is formed for the word and children are able to incorporate it in their speaking vocabulary.

A specific study of words may also yield new vocabulary. Noting morphemic elements of words, particularly common roots (*bio, geo, tele, scope, phone, gram*) and affixes (*un-, re-, sub-, -ment, -ly, -tion*) will

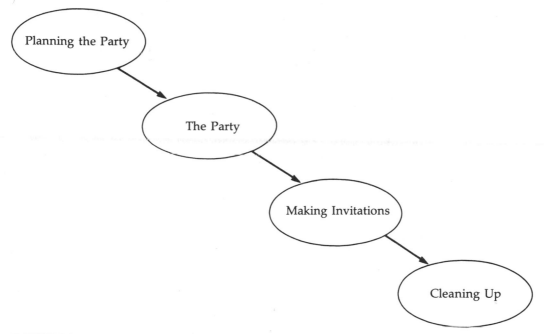

FIGURE 4-2

help children recognize familiar parts of words. Playing with words in puns, riddles, and jokes, or discovering word histories also stimulates interest in words and helps children expand their vocabulary.

Developing Speaking Abilities

Conversations

It is said that the art of conversation is dying out as a result of the time people spend passively viewing television. This may be true to some extent, but conversation still leads all other types of oral language activities. Learning to be a good conversationalist is an important lifetime skill. It provides satisfying experiences now and also prepares children to move into larger social settings as they mature. Conversation activities in the primary grades ought to encourage children to participate, to listen, to make worthwhile contributions, to take turns, and to be polite and considerate of others. In the middle grades, children's responsibilities for group participation ought to be further expanded to include more attention to content and to differing points of view.

Some children hesitate to participate in conversations either because they can't think of anything to say or because they are self-conscious about talking. Other children take an inordinate amount of time to say very little. Discussion of possible and appropriate topics is one way to attack these problems. Have children brainstorm on subjects for conversation — events in school, in their homes or neighborhoods, or things they have read about which interest them. Make a list of the topics they suggest. Then go through the list again to determine which ones would be easiest to talk about and with whom such a conversation might be most appropriate (grandmother, friend, new adult acquaintance, etc.). Point out that children can have a conversation about many things, but that the topics should interest all the people in the group. You may encourage shy children by helping them explore things they could add to a given conversation.

Another concept to develop is the reciprocal nature of speaking and listening. Children ought to realize that a good conversation occurs not when one person does all the talking but when members of a group listen and interact with the ideas of others. Conversation usually takes the form of a chain of topics, rather than focusing on one topic as in a discussion. Children must learn to listen to others, to keep up with the conversation, and to show consideration for others by waiting until another person has finished speaking before introducing a new topic.

Although children may have many opportunities to talk with others during the day, some time should be provided to analyze and practice the art of conversation. Divide the class into duos or trios and let the children converse about anything they wish. When the allotted time is up lead a brief discussion with such questions as: How did the conversation begin? (Who talked first? What did he/she say?) How many different things did your group talk about? How many people participated in the conversation? How was courtesy shown in your group? Calling attention to these points helps children become aware of conversation techniques and social responsibilities.

Discussions

Learning to participate effectively in group discussions seems particularly important in a day when so many real-life decisions are made in discussion sessions. Discussions are similar to conversations but are more structured: there is a definite goal and usually some preliminary planning and preparation. A discussion may take the form of pooling and synthesizing information about a given topic or it may involve group problem-solving. The discussion may also be a report in which members of a small group present information to a larger group.

The first step is to identify the purpose of the discussion. Every member of the group should clearly understand the problem or topic and be able to state the discussion task succinctly (e.g., "We are going to discuss what . . . ," or "We are going to discuss how . . . ," or "We are going to discuss why . . ."). Preparation for a discussion often requires additional background information, observable data, interviews of knowledgeable people, or reading. Having children help list subtopics or questions related to the major discussion purpose also gives direction and substance to a discussion.

A good discussion is a shared responsibility. Each member participates actively, with consideration for the contributions and opinions of others. Children should realize that participation is more than just giving important information. It also includes asking good questions, keeping the discussion on the topic, and helping resolve any differences.

Initially, children have to learn to take turns. One technique to encourage more equal participation is the *talking stick*. This idea is attributed to Indians in western Canada. It is said that they had an elaborately carved stick that carried the authority to speak. Each Indian in turn held the stick, spoke, and then passed it on to the next person in the circle. In this way everyone had a chance to speak without interruption. You can modify the talking stick idea with any handy but novel item. I found a Mexican chocolate beater to be an effective talking stick, but a special rock or button will do very well. Children should be encouraged to listen to what others say and plan what they will say without repeating what has already been said (unless it is an opinion poll). They may also need to be cautioned against taking too long a turn.

Another technique to encourage participation is to use an *inner circle* arrangement. Half of the class forms an inner circle and the rest of the class is seated around them in an outer circle. Only the children in the inner circle may talk. At the end of a given period of time (usually three to five minutes) the two groups exchange places and the discussion proceeds from where it left off. This exchange is repeated throughout the discussion.

A variation of the inner circle technique is to have the inner circle remain constant but with one empty chair. Anyone from the outer circle may take the chair temporarily to ask a question or make a contribution to the discussion and then return to his or her place in the outer circle.

The children ought to have both large-and small-group discussion experiences. Large-group discussions permit the teacher to model discussion behaviors for children to imitate. However, for learning and practicing discussion skills, it is advisable to break the class into smaller groups so that each child has a greater opportunity to participate and receive feedback. Small-group discussions can be used throughout the day to deal with topics, issues, and problems in various subject areas. Working in small groups greatly increases participation time for individual children and also helps some children overcome their egocentric behavior. Groups of five or six are about the right size. This number provides a range of personalities and ideas to deal with yet allows everyone in the group to participate frequently.

Designate one child in each group to be the discussion leader and rotate this role each time the groups meets. The discussion leader serves as the chairperson of the group with primary responsibility for keeping the group on task in a productive manner. Be certain, though, that the children do not rely too much on the leader and negate their cooperative responsibilities. It takes some time to develop cohesiveness and trust within a group. For this reason, the same children should stay in one group for a period of time. Rotating one member from each group every so often will provide fresh input to the group without major disruption. Figure 4-3 shows possible seating arrangements.

Evaluation following discussion sessions is an important learning tool. Children need to become aware of productive and unproductive behaviors to understand how their actions affect the ultimate outcome of a discussion. Evaluation identifies effective techniques and builds models that enable children to set meaningful discussion skill goals. Following a discussion, help the children identify examples of behavior that contributed positively to the discussion. Build on the children's strengths whenever possible. Focus on techniques and procedures rather than on individuals. These are some possible evaluation questions:

What were some good ideas you discussed?

Did you stick to the topic? If not, how did you get off the topic?

Did everyone participate in the discussion? If not, how might you have helped other children get into the discussion?

Did each of you talk as much as you wanted to? Why or why not?

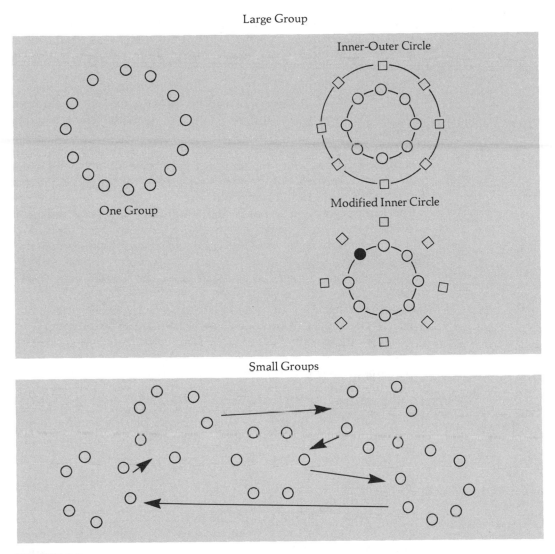

FIGURE 4-3
Possible Seating Arrangements for Group Discussions.

What things will you try to remember next time so you can have a good discussion?

Some important kinds of behavior follow. They suggest specific helping roles children can assume to facilitate discussions.

Giving information Knowledge is essential to any rational discussion. Participants must present pertinent information as a data base. They should include pieces of information from different points of view.

Clarifying Information must be understood to be used wisely. Clarifying behavior may be either *giving* explanatory information or *asking* for it. Clarification includes defining, describing, explaining, and qualifying.

Summarizing Organization is important to clear thinking and purposeful discussions. Summarizing at appropriate points helps children identify missing information and assess the direction of the discussion in terms of the stated purpose.

Checking perception What is said is not always what is heard or what is meant. Misperception can lead to serious communication problems. Paraphrasing what one thinks has been said helps ensure understanding and often avoids arguments. Anyone who takes issue with a point should make certain that he or she has correctly interpreted that point.

Hypothesizing As a discussion progresses, hypothesizing about solutions or results can provide a novel test situation for trying out ideas, or it can provide a mental leap for creative problem-solving or action.

Encouraging participation When members of a group are passive or shy they can be brought into productive roles when they are specifically asked for information or opinions.

Evaluating Evaluation is an ongoing part of discussions. It includes careful attention to relevancy, fact or opinion, practicality, and logic.

To help children become aware of facilitating behaviors, try tape recording a discussion session, then, together, listen and analyze what occurred. Children can (1) listen for examples of each of the helping behaviors, (2) identify instances when a particular behavior would have been helpful, and (3) identify a segment of the discussion that didn't go particularly well and discuss strategies that would have been better. Or, on occasion you may secretly assign a few children to play particular roles in a discussion. For example, one child might deliberately try to get the discussion off the subject, one might interrupt and try to talk all the time, and another might contribute nothing. Following the discussion children should discuss the behaviors and suggest ways to deal with them. Although negative behaviors are usually easier to identify, it is also important to recognize positive behaviors. A similar activity can be arranged in which certain children model desirable behaviors.

Interviews

The primary purpose of interviews, unlike that of conversations and discussions, is information. Whether the interviewer's style is formal or casual, his or her primary role is to inquire. Therefore interviews are more structured and require preplanning. Additionally, the interviewer may or may not be acquainted with the person being interviewed.

Opinion polls are one kind of interview. They are very impersonal and require interviewers to ask the same set of questions of every person they interview. Other types of interviews include talking to famous and interesting people about their lives or asking people about their views and ideas on some topic or issue.

In planning an interview children must first decide whom they wish to interview and what they want to find out. Then they are ready to develop a set of written interview questions to elicit the desired information. The questions they ask will depend on their purpose, their own interest, and how much information the interviewee is willing to give. The following questions (or adaptations to fit a particular situation) might be included.

1. What kinds of things do you do?

2. What do you find interesting about your job (position)?

3. What problems have you had and how have you overcome them?

4. What is the most important thing you have ever done? Please tell me about it.

5. How do you feel about [current concern]?

6. Is there something you would like to tell people (children)?

Once children have determined whom they wish to interview and what they want to find out, they should telephone or write to arrange an interview. They should tell who they are, state their purpose, and, if the person agrees to the interview, set a time and place. The day of the interview children should

arrive at the scheduled place at the scheduled time.

introduce themselves and state why they have come.

give a brief statement of what they know about the person being interviewed (e.g., "I understand you have lived in Podunk most of your life and that you have always been active in politics").

ask planned interview questions.

follow up with additional questions as necessary to clarify any points.

watch for relevant information not considered in planning the interview and pose appropriate additional questions.

summarize main points and give the person interviewed an opportunity to make clarifications or additions.

thank the person for his or her time, information, and interesting ideas.

An interview should be conducted in an efficient yet friendly manner. Children should realize that people's time is valuable and that granting them an interview is a courtesy. A follow-up note of appreciation would be appropriate if the person interviewed gives considerable time or effort to the interview.

Announcements and Directions

Making announcements and giving directions require extremely clear and concise use of language. Each detail is important and cannot be left out. Discuss the importance of giving complete information in announcements and make a list of the things that should be included. The list can then be made into a chart to serve as a checklist for children. Here is a sample chart:

> **Making Announcements**
> Tell what is happening.
> Tell where it will take place.
> Tell when it will take place.
> Tell what the purpose is.
> Tell who is responsible.

Children can also consider other possible kinds of announcements. For example, an announcement might concern something that is lost or found, public safety, or a car in a parking lot with its lights left on. The children will need to decide what information should be included in each situation.

Simulation exercises provide realistic practice in making announcements. Let children make up an announcement and present it to the class. If a microphone is available, it will add realism to the simulation. Even better, check with your principal to see if children might make morning announcements over the school's public address system.

Because children and adults are frequently asked for directions, skill in giving directions is particularly valuable. Listening to children's queries in the classroom will suggest many "real-life" opportunities for direction-giving activities. These might include how to use a piece of equipment (tape recorder, computer), how to make something (a book, a pinwheel), how to play a game (a board game, soccer), how to get to a particular place (a store, a theater), how to solve a problem (open a stuck bottle lid), or how to care for a pet.

Giving directions is similar to making announcements. Directions usually require more explanation and attention to sequence. Since one wrong step can make an entire set of directions useless, it is important to try out giving the directions while a partner performs the activity. If this isn't possible a simulation or a mental "walk-through" will help children develop the necessary skills.

Storytelling

Storytelling may involve an old or new creation. Children may retell a story they have previously heard or read, they may tell a cooperative story, or they may create a story of their own independently. In any case, a prerequisite for storytelling is a background of story experiences. Preparing to retell a favorite story is an excellent way to develop an awareness of plot and characterization. When children understand a story well and understand the characters' motives, they can concentrate on using their voices expressively and enunciating clearly.

Cooperative stories may be done in a round-robin manner in which children take turns telling a part of the story, or it may involve supplying parts of a story told by the teacher. The latter permits the teacher to give guidance in developing a story and in developing a story sense. It can be fascinating for all ages. The following example illustrates the latter type of cooperative story. A different child is called on to fill in each missing part of the story. Adjustments in the story may be made if the children's additions send the story in a somewhat different direction.

> Trudy lived in the heart of a very big forest. The trees were so tall and thick that she could not see their tops. The only place where bright sunshine reached the ground was by the big pool where the deer came to drink.
> Every day Trudy got up early, made her bed, ate her breakfast, and

went out into the woods to play. One day as she was playing she heard
_____. It was coming from a very large tree near the bent and
twisted one that creaked and groaned at night. She listened again and
she heard _____.

   Trudy was frightened, but she was also curious so she _____.
Closer and closer she crept toward the sound. Softly she stole through
the shadows until she was as close as from here to that chair. Then she
saw _____. It (they) was (were) _____ until she
happened to step on a twig that snapped. It (they) looked up and down
and all around. Then, presto! It (they) saw her and _____ and
_____.

   Trudy straightened herself up and ran as hard as she could back to
her house. Quickly she slammed and locked the door. Her heart beat
wildly and her face was burning hot. She held her breath for a long
moment and listened closely. All she heard was _____ and
_____.

When children create stories of their own they need to think carefully about how they will begin the story, who the characters will be,
where the story will take place, what sequence the action will follow
(plot), and how the story will end. They must also think about the
main events in the story and not get bogged down in unnecessary
details. Then they will need to practice telling the story several times
to perfect it before presenting it to a full audience. After they have
thought it through, they may tell it to a partner and get his or her
reaction. Or, they may tape record the story and play it back so they
can listen to it themselves. If possible, listen to the story with them
and use the experience to explore possibilities for further plot development, making the voice more expressive, telling events in sequence, choosing more appropriate words, etc.

Reports

Reporting begins in the first year of school and continues throughout a child's schooling. Many primary teachers set aside a period in
the day in which children show and tell about new and interesting
things and experiences. This is a simple form of reporting. The *Show
and Tell* period can be a valuable oral language activity if it is maintained as a time in which children practice good speaking and listening habits. However, the activity requires specific planning to make
it an interesting reporting situation with audience involvement. Otherwise Show and Tell may become dull routine with little or no educational value.

   Some teachers have found it useful to schedule groups of children
to share on specific days or to have children sign up for turns the day

before they share. Such plans give the children equal opportunity and make it easier for the teacher to see who needs to be encouraged to talk in front of the group and who needs help in planning an interesting presentation. Another technique teachers sometimes use when children are unduly repetitious or appear to have little of value to say is to specify a particular topic or type of sharing for each day. It should be pointed out that the teacher's role in Show and Tell is very important too. By paying close attention to the speaker a teacher provides a model of good audience behavior.

More formal reports may present information from the social studies or other content areas to the class. Good reports require thorough preparation, collecting and organizing information. The first step is to identify various aspects, or subtopics, of the main topic. These constitute a simple outline for students just beginning to develop outlining skills or become the skeleton of an outline for more advanced students. As the children read, the subtopics become reference points for relating information. Older children may write each subtopic on a separate card or sheet of paper and then jot down notes under each heading as they read.

It is well to keep in mind that children's cognitive structures are not fully developed until after the elementary school years and that finer points of outlining are almost certain to be beyond their conceptual level. Outlining is a complex skill involving summarizing, classifying, ranking, relating information, etc. A simple listing of subtopics, however, will help children relate what they read to the main topic and will help them keep on the topic while giving their report.

Because children think, talk, and read in sentences, notetaking is a skill that must be learned. Children need much help and practice in picking out and writing only the main words that carry the idea of a sentence. This is an important skill. It not only saves writing time but makes it easier for children to use their own words in making a report.

Oral reports may be presented in any number of interesting ways and should not be limited to talking from a set of notes. For example, children may use pictures, diagrams, charts, graphs, or maps to illustrate what they say. Or, they may prepare a diorama, a bulletin board, or a tabletop display. Different art media such as pencil, ink, crayon, paint, or charcoal may be used effectively on two- or three-dimensional visuals. Using attractive visuals makes a report more interesting and easier to understand.

When several children work together on the same topic, they may make a group presentation. A round-table discussion is one possibility. Each speaker in turn usually presents one aspect of the topic.

Then members of the group question each other to clarify points and to bring out additional information as they would in a regular discussion. Finally, the discussion is opened up for audience questions.

Another type of group presentation is an original play or puppet show. The content of the report is given in the lines of the characters. Suggestions for this kind of presentation may be found in Chapter 6.

Evaluation is a learning tool. After a report has been given, you might provide pertinent questions to help children identify strengths and weaknesses. The questions may be answered by the individual, by a small peer group, or in a teacher-pupil conference. Figure 4-4 follows a general format that may be adapted for specific situations. Such questions provide a framework for discussing a wide range of speech skills. It is important to discover the basis or explanation for each answer. For example, if the answer to question 1 is no, then children should try to discover *why* the audience lost interest. Was it an uninteresting topic? Was the speech too long? Was the speaker's voice monotonous?

Debates

Formal debate is usually reserved for secondary school, but mature elementary students enjoy the form also. It is a particularly good

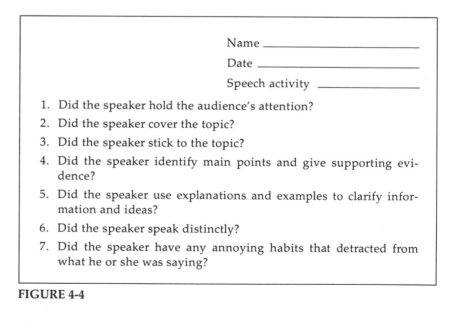

Name _____

Date _____

Speech activity _____

1. Did the speaker hold the audience's attention?
2. Did the speaker cover the topic?
3. Did the speaker stick to the topic?
4. Did the speaker identify main points and give supporting evidence?
5. Did the speaker use explanations and examples to clarify information and ideas?
6. Did the speaker speak distinctly?
7. Did the speaker have any annoying habits that detracted from what he or she was saying?

FIGURE 4-4

activity for educationally able children. For a simple debate, children select some controversial topic, such as year-round schools, and present the arguments for and against the idea. Two children present the argument for and two present the argument against. Then, each side has a chance for a brief rebuttal (final argument) to the opponents' views.

Debate is more formal than a round-table discussion: participants have only two opportunities to make their points: the presentation and the rebuttal. One needs a good knowledge of the topic and logical thinking in order to present a convincing argument. Critical listening skills are also needed, to present a good rebuttal in response to the opponents' argument. Debates develop listening skills for nonparticipants too. The audience usually becomes very involved in what the speakers are saying and thus listen attentively.

Time limits for each speaker may be set, but they usually are not necessary. Children seldom take more than a few minutes to present their arguments. Setting limits may even cause children to drag out what they have to say to fill up the time. A general consensus about which side presented the most convincing argument is usually evident. If not, you may want to select a panel of judges or ask the whole class to vote on the winning team.

Meetings

Children can learn the rudiments of parliamentary procedure as they deal with problems and situations within an ordinary classroom. A democratic classroom organization that meets regularly gives children an opportunity to participate in democratic procedures and to learn simple parliamentary rules. Interest in having their own class officers and holding class meetings is usually high. Some children may have additional learning experiences in various clubs outside of school.

Elected officers generally consist of a president and secretary and may include others if the class feels more are needed. Duties of each officer should be clearly established, and also who is next in line to serve in each office when an officer is absent. In the early primary grades the president may be responsible for such tasks as checking attendance and taking the lunch count each morning and the secretary may take care of recording the information and delivering it to the office. Younger children must, of course, be under close supervision whenever their skills are limited and accuracy is important. Also, in the lower grades children often have a short term of office, so that many children will have an opportunity to hold office.

Older children can assume many responsibilities through their class organization. For example, they may plan for parties, open houses, and other special events, or they may use their meeting to deal with school problems or concerns. Such activities provide many opportunities for learning about democratic processes through active participation.

The following parliamentary procedures are suggested for use in the elementary school:

The Order of the Meeting

1. The president calls the meeting to order.

2. The secretary reads the minutes of the last meeting.

3. The president asks for corrections or additions. If there are any, the secretary is instructed to incorporate them into the minutes and the minutes are accepted.

4. The president calls for business to come before the group. Each item of business is dealt with as it is presented before going on to another item.

5. The president adjourns the meeting.

Presenting an Item of Business

1. A child stands and addresses the chair: "Mister/Madam President."

2. The president recognizes the child by name: e.g., "George."

3. The child states his/her business: "I have a report about . . . ," or "I move that . . ."

4. When a motion is made another student must say, "I second it" (from his/her seat), or the motion is dropped.

5. If the motion is seconded, it is open for discussion. Each child who has something to say stands, addresses the chair, and waits to be recognized before going on.

6. The president calls for a voice vote: "All in favor of . . . say 'Aye.' " "All opposed say 'no.' " If there is a clear majority for the motion the president declares it passed: "The motion passed." If not, the president asks for a standing vote.

In Summary

Learning oral language is a developmental process. It begins with a baby's first sound and continues on beyond the elementary school years. By the time children come to school they have usually acquired a sizable vocabulary and the basic phonic and grammatical systems of their language. They have not acquired full control of the language, however. Their vocabulary and intuitive knowledge of language continues to grow and expand.

Research indicates a close relationship between language and thinking. It appears that children's ability to acquire and use language is influenced by their ability to think. Approximate ages at which children reach certain stages of development have been identified. This knowledge is important to teachers in understanding children's language ability and planning appropriate instruction.

Learning in the elementary school years is highly dependent on concrete experiences. Because children are generally unable to think abstractly until they near the end of the elementary school period, they need many opportunities to learn through activities and sensory stimuli. As you help children verbalize their experiences, you provide a meaning base for language and facilitate growth. A range of functional and creative language experiences may be used to stimulate the development of language competence in children.

Learning Objectives

COGNITIVE OBJECTIVES

Primary Grades

Children will

know that the lips, tongue, and teeth help make language sounds.

know that sounds must be clearly enunciated so others can understand what is said.

be able to change the volume and speed of their voice in different speech situations.

be able to share their thoughts effectively in speech.

be able to use expressive speech to add meaning and interest to what they say.

recognize conversation as a shared speech situation.

be able to tell things in sequential order.

be able to stick to a topic when they speak.

Middle Grades

Children will

meet all primary objectives.

be able to explain the interrelationship of speaking and listening.

be able to explain and use speech as a social as well as an intellectual tool.

demonstrate voice control and flexibility by effectively using the voice in many situations.

develop and expand their vocabularies.

be able to ask appropriate questions for gathering desired information.

be able to identify and explain possible purposes for giving a speech: to inform, to entertain, to convince, or to express feelings and emotions.

be able to identify behaviors that help or hinder in speech situations.

be able to organize a speech logically around important points or ideas.

be able to use speech effectively in various informal and formal situations.

be able to follow simple parliamentary procedure in business meetings.

AFFECTIVE OBJECTIVES

The student will

accept differences in language among peers.

maintain a cooperative and purposive attitude in carrying out speech activities.

share informal observations about public speech on radio, television, in movies, etc.

engage in self-evaluation of speech habits and skills, and set personal goals for improvement.

demonstrate a desire to help others improve their speech in tactful and supportive ways.

Suggested Learning Activities

Peeping Pete. Arrange objects that begin with a troublesome speech sound (e.g., letter, lemon, lettuce, light bulb, etc.) on a tray or table. Cover the tray with a cloth. Let the children take turns being Peeping Pete and looking under the cloth. Then ask, "What did you see, Peeping Pete?" and the child replies, "I saw . . ."

Mirror Talk. The children sit facing partners. One child silently forms a sentence with his or her mouth. The second child observes carefully and makes the same movement, adding the voice sounds. If he or she is incorrect, the action is repeated until the second child utters the sentence correctly. Then the children exchange roles.

If You Were a Flat Tire. Using objects that make familiar sounds, have the children pretend they are those objects. Let them tell what sound they would make and how they would make it. For example:

Teacher: If you were a flat tire, what sound would you make?
Child: Sssssssss.
Teacher: How would you make it?
Child: With my tongue and my teeth. [Demonstrates again.]

Favorite Places. Children are given time to think about a favorite place — either one they have seen or one they have read about. They may want to close their eyes and imagine the scene to bring it clearly into mind. Then, in small groups, they take turns describing the place. The other children try to visualize the place. Evaluation focuses on words or phrases that create visual imagery.

Character Comparisons. Ask children to think about two characters in a book or story (e.g., Mother Bear and Baby Bear in *The Three Bears* or Charles and Meg Murry in *A Wrinkle in Time*), then compare them. How are they alike? How are they different? What are some examples?

Marvelous Monsters. Children imagine a monster and describe it. Suggest that they think about what it looks like, what sounds it makes, how it lives, and what it does.

Instrument Landing. The object of this activity is to give clear enough directions to guide a pilot into an airport without mishap. Clear a "runway" on the floor. Blindfold one child, the pilot. Place harmless objects here and there on the runway (pillow, book, chair, etc.). One child is selected to be "in the tower" and verbally direct the pilot around each obstacle to the far end of the runway.

News Report. Children select news stories and advertisements from the local paper and put on the "Six O'clock News" complete with commercials. This can be done in small groups, with a different group responsible for the "broadcast" on different days.

Tongue Twisters #1. The children practice saying tongue twisters, enunciating each sound clearly. (*Betty Botter bought some butter . . . , How much wood would a woodchuck chuck . . . , She sells seashells by the seashore,* etc.)

Tongue Twisters #2. Let the children create sentences in which as many words as possible begin with the same sound or sound combination. For example,

Big black bugs buckle and bulge beneath the blue bundle.

Rich red roosters read riddles rapidly.

Expressive Alphabet. The children think of a story and then tell it expressively using only single letters of the alphabet in place of words. This means they must rely completely on voice control (intonation, speed, and volume) to convey the story and create suspense, humor, and excitement.

Pilot to Ground. Ask the children to imagine that they are an airplane pilot flying over the local city, town, or countryside. They radio back to the ground what they are seeing. At first they give a calm, rather routine report but then something exciting happens. Give them a few minutes to plan their monolog and then let them share their pilot-to-ground report with a group. Evaluate the changes in voice when the scene becomes exciting.

Time Warp Encounter. Groups of children select a famous historic person and plan an interview with the person (e.g., George Washington, Daniel Boone, Galileo, Betsy Ross, Sacajawea). The children will need to consider the period of time in which the person lived, where he or she lived, what the person did, what she or he hoped the lasting results would be, etc. To wrap up the interview, children ex-plain to the person what has since happened and why we still remember him or her.

Hear This. To help children learn to project their voices without shouting let them read or talk to each other with barriers or distance between them. Let them speak to each other from a distance on the playground, or, one child at a time can go into a closet or coatroom. Stress talking distinctly yet maintaining a well modulated, pleasant voice.

Poor Company. In groups of three, have the children plan and role-play a discussion in which one person exhibits undesirable speech habits (e.g., interrupts, talks too much, changes the topic, argues rudely, etc.). After a group has shared its scene with the class, the other children identify the player who is "poor company."

Twenty Questions. Pick a place that is familiar to everyone in the group, but do not reveal the place you have chosen. The children will try to find out where it is by asking questions that you must answer either yes or no. If they do not discover where it is after twenty questions you must tell them. Discuss which kinds of questions were most helpful in narrowing down the possibilities and identifying the place.

Fifty Words or Less. The children tell about a favorite movie or television program using no more than fifty words. To do so, they must limit what they say to main points in sequential order.

Finger Plays And Rhymes

Eensy, Weensy Spider

Eensy, weensy spider
  (Opposite thumbs and index fingers together, climb up each other.)
Climbed up the waterspout.
Down came the rain
  (Hands sweep down and out.)
And washed the spider out.
Out came the sun
  (Make circle with arms over head.)
And dried up all the rain.

So the eensy, weensy spider,
  (Same as before.)
Climbed up the spout again.

I'm a Little Teapot

I'm a little teapot, short and stout.
This is my handle,
  (Put one hand on hip.)
This is my spout.
  Extend other arm.)
When I get all steamed up, then I shout.
Just tip me over and pour me out.
  (Bend body toward "spout.")

This Little Fellow

This little fellow is ready for bed,
  (Hold up index finger.)
Down on the pillow he lays his head;
  (Lay finger on palm of other hand.)
Pulls up the covers, snug and tight,
  (Close up fingers.)
And this is the way he sleeps all night.
  (Close eyes.)
Morning comes and he opens his eyes,
  (Open eyes.)
Quickly he pushes the covers aside;
  (Open fingers.)
Jumps out of bed, puts on his clothes,
  (Opposite hand dress "fellow.")
And this is the way to school he goes.
  (Walk two fingers up opposite arm.)

Johnny's Hammer

Johnny hammers with one hammer, one ham-
  mer, one hammer,
  (Hit one fist on knee.)
Johnny hammers with one hammer, this fine
  day.
Johnny hammers with two hammers, two ham-
  mers, two hammers,
  (Two fists, two knees.)
Johnny hammers with two hammers, this fine
  day.
Johnny hammers with three hammers, three
  hammers, three hammers,
  (Add right foot.)
Johnny hammers with three hammers, this fine
  day.
Johnny hammers with four hammers, four

hammers, four hammers,
  (Add left foot.)
Johnny hammers with four hammers, this fine
  day.
Johnny hammers with five hammers, five ham-
  mers, five hammers.
  (Add head, nodding.)
Johnny hammers with five hammers, this fine
  day.
Johnny now is so tired, so tired, so tired,
  (Drooped position.)
Johnny now is so tired, this fine day.
Johnny goes to sleep now, sleep now, sleep
  now.
  (Nod head and close eyes.)
Johnny goes to sleep now, this fine day.
Johnny's waking up now, up now, up now,
  (Wake up and stretch.)
Johnny's waking up now, this fine day.

Jack-in-the-Box

Jack-in-the-box, all shut up tight,
  (Close fist around thumb; other hand on top
    for a lid.)
Not a breath of air or a ray of light,
How tired he must be, all folded up.
Let's open the lid,
  (Raise hand a little.)
And up he'll jump.
  (Remove hand; pop up thumb.)

The Beehive

Here is the beehive.
  (Make a loose fist with thumb inside.)
Where are the bees?
Hidden away where nobody sees.
Soon they come creeping out of the hive —
One! Two! Three! Four! Five
  (Extend one finger at a time.)

The Caterpillar

Fuzzy little caterpillar,
Crawling, crawling on the ground!
  (Close hands, only partially open to creep
    forward.)
Fuzzy little caterpillar,
Nowhere, nowhere to be found,
Though we've looked and hunted
Everywhere around!
  (Walk fingers around, looking.)

When the little caterpillar
Found his furry coat too tight,
  (Tight fists.)
Then a snug cocoon he made him
Spun of silk so soft and light;
  (Rotate thumb.)
Rolled himself away within it —
Slept there day and night.
  (Curl fingers over thumb.)
See how this cocoon is stirring!
Now a little head we spy —
  (Slowly enlarge hand, move thumb part way
    out.)
What! Is this our caterpillar
Spreading gorgeous wings to dry?
  (Stretch hand out.)
Soon the free and happy creature
Flutters gayly by.
  (Put backs of hands together near thumb, ex-
    tend thumbs out for body; flutter hands to
    make butterfly fly.)

Mrs. Pussy's Dinner

Mrs. Pussy, sleek and fat
  (Hold up thumb.)
With her kittens four,
  (Hold up 4 fingers.)
Went to sleep upon the mat
By the kitchen door.
  (Close hand.)
Mrs. Pussy heard a noise —
Up she jumped in glee:
  (Hand jumps up.)

"Kittens, maybe that's a mouse!
Let us go and see."
  (Finger circles as glasses.)
Creeping, creeping, creeping on,
Silently they stole;
  (Fingers creep.)
But the little mouse had gone
Back within its hole.
  (Thumb inside fist.)
"Well," said Mrs. Pussy then,
"To the barn we'll go;
  (Hands make gable.)
We shall find the swallow there
Flying to and fro."
  (Hands flying.)
So the cat and kittens four
Tried their very best;
  (Darting motion.)
But the swallows flying fast
  (Birds flying.)
Safely reached the nest!
  (Make nest.)
Home went hungry Mrs. Puss
And her kittens four;
  (Fingers walk.)
Found their dinner on a plate
By the kitchen door
  (Thumbs and fingers in a circle.)
As they gathered round the plate,
They agreed 'twas nice
That it could not run away
Like the birds and mice!
  (Lapping motion.)

Suggestions for Further Reading

Dale, Philip S. *Language Development*, 2nd ed. New York: Holt, Rinehart and Winston, 1976.

Elgin, Suzette Haden. *What Is Linguistics?* Englewood Cliffs, N.J.: Prentice-Hall, 1973.

Klein, Marvin L. *Talk in the Language Arts Classroom.* Urbana, Ill.: ERIC Clearinghouse on Reading and Communication Skills and National Council of Teachers of English, 1977.

Lindfors, Judith. *Children's Language and Learning.* Englewood Cliffs, N.J.: Prentice-Hall, 1980.

Pinnell, Gay Su, ed. *Discovering Language with Children.* Urbana, Ill.: National Council of Teachers of English, 1980.

Richmond, P. G. *An Introduction to Piaget.* New York: Basic Books, 1970.

Sanders, Norris M. *Classroom Questions: What Kinds?* New York: Harper and Row, 1966.

See Appendix A for multimedia resources.

5
Listening

The Child's Lament

Everyone listens to someone, *Everyone listens sometimes,*
And nobody listens to none. *And nobody listens never.*
But I wonder why *But I can't see*
They think that I *Why it should be*
Must listen to everyone! *That I must listen forever!*

Robert W. L. Smith (1974)

CHAPTER PREVIEW

In today's multimedia world listening may be the most important of all the language arts. Yet children (and adults) often hear without listening. The art of listening, *really* listening, involves an active mental process. In this chapter we will look at what listening is and at its cognitive demands for different purposes. We will also discuss factors that influence listening and suggest ways to help children develop listening skills.

QUESTIONS TO THINK ABOUT AS YOU READ

Is it necessary to *teach* listening? Why?

What factors influence effective listening?

How do listening tasks differ?

How does a teacher influence children's listening habits?

How can I help children develop listening skills?

Where does listening instruction fit into the total curriculum?

A Look at Listening

Sounds surround us. Unless we are aurally handicapped we can scarcely avoid listening. Children entering school have learned a great deal through their ears in just a few years. They do listen. But their listening habits are egocentric and selective; they listen to things that interest them at that moment.

Ability to listen is of the utmost importance, for listening is the primary source of language. It is the base on which all other language skills develop. Language comes first through the ears. A baby listens, then speaks, and later, learns to read and write. As language learning is expanded and developed, listening continues to be the primary channel for acquiring linguistic knowledge and skill.

Listening is an integral part of all language activities. Whether the activity is speaking, reading, or writing, it is somehow related to listening. For example, learning to read is learning to associate the spoken sounds of language with written symbols on a page and responding in the same way that one would to spoken language. To young children reading is the process of reconstructing talk that someone has encoded in symbols. Writing is the reverse process; it is making symbols to represent the words that are heard by the ears or in the mind.

More time is spent in listening than in any other language activity. It has been said that we listen a book a day, talk a book a week, read a book a month, and write a book a year. Wilt's (1950) classic study found that elementary schoolchildren spent two and one-half hours of a five-hour school day in listening. In addition to the time spent listening in school, activities outside of school are almost totally oral. Lundsteen (1971), for example, reports that between the ages of three and eighteen the average child spends 22,000 hours watching television.

It seems logical to assume that by the time we reach adulthood so much practice in listening would have resulted in a high level of listening ability. But that is not true. After extensive research Nichols reports, "Most of us operate at precisely a 25 percent level of efficiency when we listen to a ten-minute talk. And we know from research that the longer the talk the less the comprehension of it" (n.d., p. 1).

There is ample evidence that listening skills must be taught if they are to be acquired. Children do not need merely to listen more; they need to listen better. Lundsteen (1979) points out that children's experience with mass media involves passive listening. Watching television does not permit children to talk back or react to what they hear. Such activity forms poor listening habits and cuts down on more productive learning experiences. Children desperately need help in learning to think about and react to what they hear. They need listening lessons that cause them to question, to sort, to organize, to evaluate, and to choose. Instead of passively absorbing any message that might waft into their ears, they need to learn skills that will enable them to become connoisseurs and rational consumers of auditory input.

Cognitive Levels of Listening

We listen because we want to hear something. Even when listening conditions are less than ideal, we put forth extra effort to screen out distractions and focus on the source of input if we have sufficient motivation. Listening (meaning the full range of listening behaviors) involves several mental processes. If we examine our own listening behavior we will notice that the amount of effort and mental involvement varies considerably from one listening situation to another. In most instances the variation is directly attributable to our purpose and motivation for listening. Listening behaviors may be categorized according to the listener's cognitive involvement. These categories are: passive listening, listening for information, listening for understanding, critical listening, and appreciative listening.

Passive Listening

In passive listening, people hear — they physically receive the sounds — but have little or no mental response. This type of behavior ranges from marginal listening, in which listeners are only vaguely aware of sounds in the background, to hearing clearly but not processing messages contained in the sounds. For example, if you have the radio on while you are studying, you may be aware that there is music playing. However, if someone asks you to name the song that is playing you would have to "tune in" before you could answer. At other times you may be fully aware of your sound environment but make no effort to react to the sounds or even to remember them.

Passive listening can be deceptive to an observer. We think children are listening because they sit quietly and appear attentive. Actually, they may not be listening at all. Or they may be listening at the passive level and gaining little. Experienced teachers learn to watch for signs of passivity in their students. They plan frequent interactions to stimulate thinking and to pull passive listeners back into active listening.

Listening for Information

At the knowledge level listeners attend to stated information and concentrate on remembering what is said. As much information as possible is held in memory while the listener continues to collect additional knowledge.

Listening for information involves these cognitive abilities:

recalling known word meanings

deducing the meaning of unknown words from context

understanding the relationship of words in a sentence

recalling specifically stated facts and details

forming sensory impressions

following directions

paraphrasing spoken messages

Listening for Understanding

Listening for understanding involves the linking of ideas. It requires listeners to make associations and to see the relationships among ideas and pieces of information. Listeners use their information to solve problems or gain a comprehensive picture of a subject.

In listening to understand one uses the cognitive abilities for informational listening plus these:

associating ideas and information

relating past knowledge to new information

recognizing relationships of sequence, time and space, and cause and effect

summarizing

comparing and contrasting

identifying main ideas

classifying and organizing supporting information

making inferences

predicting or hypothesizing outcomes

Critical Listening

At the critical level, listeners must analyze what they hear and make judgments about it. Critical listeners do not accept information at face value; they probe below the surface. They assume a questioning attitude, looking for faulty logic, insufficient evidence, emotional appeal, etc.

In addition to all the lower cognitive abilities critical listening involves:

> determining relevant and irrelevant information
>
> separating fact from inference, supposition, or opinion
>
> identifying the author's purpose (to inform, to explain, to convince, to entertain, to express feelings)
>
> seeing implications
>
> recognizing different points of view
>
> detecting bias, prejudice, or propaganda
>
> comparing what is said with previous knowledge
>
> judging validity of information and generalizations
>
> drawing conclusions
>
> making recommendations

The affective dimensions of listening are inherent in listeners' behavior at each of the cognitive levels. How listeners feel about a particular listening task — how much they enjoy and value it — determines the amount of energy they are willing to expend. Their attitudes have evolved through a series of responses to past experiences. As a result they have learned to tune out, to remain passive, or to anticipate listening experiences positively. In teaching children to listen one must give attention to building interest in listening and developing a favorable attitude toward skills and abilities.

Appreciative Listening

Appreciative listening, the highest level, cuts across all cognitive and affective levels of listening. It involves a personal response to what is heard. Thus appreciative listening will vary according to the listener and the situation. We may simply appreciate the richness and melodic intonation of someone's voice; or, we may appreciate an opera because we have the musical background to examine critically the composition, the staging, the lighting, the costuming, the acting, and the musical abilities of the actors and orchestra. Our appreciation of what we hear reflects our reasons for listening, our background experiences, and our skill in listening.

Taylor's Listening Model

Taylor describes listening as having three hierarchical stages: hearing, listening, and auding. *Hearing* is the physical process of receiving and modifying sound waves in the ear. It depends on an individual's ability to locate the source of sounds, and to focus on and continue to receive auditory input. *Listening* refers to awareness of speech sounds and the processing of those sounds into meaningful units. It involves ability to analyze, organize, and associate sounds in relation to the situation and one's background of experiences. *Auding* is a term used to indicate a higher level of mental involvement that results in understanding or feeling. In auding one transfers the flow of words into meaning, using one's full range of critical thinking skills. Each stage depends on certain physical and mental abilities or processes. Figure 5-1 shows the three stages.

The Teacher as a Listening Model

Many children have never experienced a truly listening audience. Their background in listening consists mainly of television and catch-as-catch-can listening while in pursuit of another objective. Some children live in crowded conditions where little attention is given to any one individual. Others grow up in affluent homes but with little interpersonal communication, particularly any involving children. In some homes children's opinions and ideas are simply not valued.

The quality of children's listening experiences in school is crucial. The habits they form in their early years will most likely remain with them throughout their lives. Although the need for listening training is becoming more widely recognized, specific programs are rarely found beyond the elementary school, if at all.

Teachers should realize that they are models of listening behavior. The teacher is the center of much attention in a classroom as leader, organizer, arbiter, and instructor. Thus he or she becomes the listening model that all children in a classroom hold in common, and it is his or her listening behavior that is most frequently encountered by that group of children. The skills and attitudes exhibited by the teacher therefore become the yardstick for measuring the importance of listening habits.

FIGURE 5-1   *(facing page)*

From *Listening: What Research Says to the Teacher* by Stanford Taylor, copyright 1973. Reprinted by permission of the National Education Association, Washington, D.C.

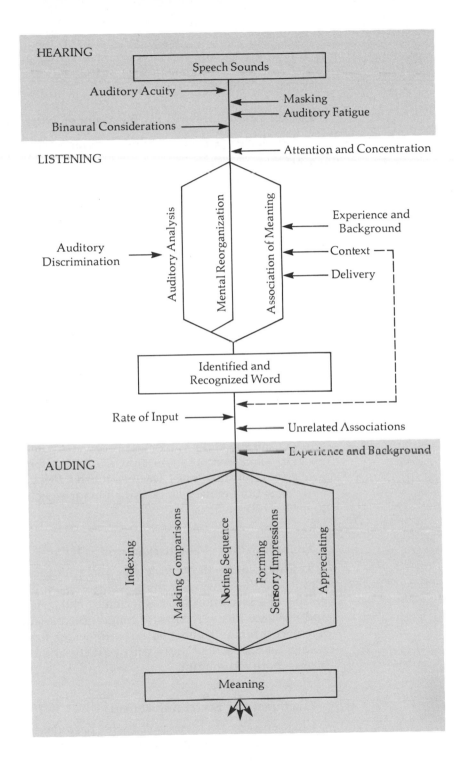

Analyzing your own listening behavior is the first step in planning a listening program. It is important for your actions to exemplify what you teach. To gain an idea of the kind of model you present, ask yourself these four questions:

1. Do I give the children my full attention when they speak?

2. Do I have eye contact with my students when they talk to me?

3. Do I indicate I am thinking about what the children say by making comments or asking clarifying questions?

4. Do I show enjoyment and appreciation when the children share humorous or especially appealing language?

Factors That Affect Listening

Auditory Acuity

When a child has a listening problem, physical loss of hearing may be a cause. Some symptoms of hearing loss are general inattention, moving closer to the speaker, cupping the hand to the ear or turning the head to the side, speaking too softly or too loudly, and asking you to turn up the volume during films or when using mechanical listening devices.

For a simple screening test, have the child face away from you and whisper questions for him or her to answer. Gradually move farther away to make hearing more difficult. An audiometer test is usually available in most districts. This is a reliable test given by a specialist, and you should request an examination for any child that you suspect to have a hearing loss.

Educational Level and Background

Research shows that intelligence and educational experience have high correlations with listening ability. Listening involves the processing of information and is affected by children's ability to organize and evaluate ideas. A broader range of experiences provides more reference points. Thus children with wider experiences can more readily associate new ideas with past experiences, and what they hear is more meaningful.

Emotional and Social Adjustment

Children who are preoccupied with personal feelings are less able to concentrate on outside stimuli. Well-adjusted and secure children operate from a positive base with fewer emotional distractions to impede mental processes.

Environment

Pleasant surroundings reasonably free from distractions make listening easier. A well-organized and friendly classroom atmosphere suggests a businesslike approach and lends importance to learning. Noise from outside or from within the room may mask or crowd out the sounds children are trying to attend to. Excessive movement or physical discomfort can also create distractions and make listening more difficult.

Attitude toward Listening

The child who really wants to do something usually does. Children need to feel that listening is important to them and that working to acquire skill is worthwhile. Using interesting topics for listening exercises helps keep their interest going. If you make frequent listening assessments so children can see their progress, you will encourage them to keep working toward additional goals.

Level of Difficulty of the Material

Listening to easy material holds little challenge for listeners. Unless listening yields new ideas or novel treatment of the familiar, the mind is not apt to stay at attention very long. On the other hand, material that demands intense concentration or is beyond comprehension also begs for diversion. To be effective, materials must be appropriate to children's experiential background and level of cognitive development. This means that listening activities should be based on materials at a comfortable yet stimulating level that encourages a reasonable cognitive "stretch."

Speaker's Voice and Delivery

An animated, well-modulated voice suggests the speaker has something interesting to say, and invites listening. Hesitation, repetition, distracting mannerisms, a monotonous voice, and an impersonal attitude are all hindrances to good listening. Teachers and children alike should be aware of the speaker's responsibility to listeners. The teacher's voice is usually dominant in a classroom. Teachers would do well to tape record their own voices and analyze their effects on listening behavior.

Planning a Listening Program

There is little question that children need to improve their listening skills. We have only to listen to the number of times teachers and parents implore children to listen, to realize that listening is not being performed at a satisfactory level. Yet according to Landry (1969), children in the primary grades are the best listeners. He states that the level of listening decreases with age.

Listening is a complex skill involving not only tuning in and receiving aural sounds, but mentally processing messages. Even motivated listeners need training to make use of their potential for effective and efficient listening. The assumption that children will learn to listen just as they learn to walk or talk is unfounded. Listening requires training just as reading or writing does. Children have to learn *how* to listen.

Various studies (Canfield, 1961; Fawcett, 1966; and Lundsteen, 1966) report that listening can be taught — that children's listening ability can be improved through instruction. Furthermore, direct instruction in a program designed to develop specific listening skills was found to be the most effective. Indirect instruction was found to produce some results, but improvement was not as great.

Getting Ready to Listen

Before children begin a specific listening task they need physical and mental preparation for listening. Preparation not only helps to ensure success in the activity but it also develops an attitude toward listening. It tells children that listening is important. Although it is true that listening conditions cannot always be modified and that good listeners need to be able to cope with distractions, preparing the physical environment as much as possible allows children to focus attention on the cognitive aspects of listening.

Physical preparation for listening might include attention to such conditions as:

1. *Proper room temperature and ventilation.* Listening requires concentration over an extended period of time. A stuffy or overheated room makes attention more difficult to maintain.

2. *Adequate body space.* Sociologists realize that each person is surrounded by a psychological bubble of private space. This space varies with the culture and with individuals within a culture. It isn't necessary for two people to touch physically to violate this territorial space. Any intrusion evokes a mental response rang-

ing from approval to defensiveness. But regardless of the response, violation is distracting and can have a negative influence on listening.

3. *Comfortable, alert posture.* Physical comfort helps children sustain listening attention. An attitude of appropriate physical alertness also encourages mental alertness.

4. *Elimination of unnecessary auditory distractions.* Excessive noise, particularly loud and piercing sounds, requires a great deal of effort to screen out. Poorer listeners may be completely distracted and unable to accommodate or process the content of the desired message.

Getting *mentally* ready to listen might include:

1. *Forming a mind set.* Motivation and anticipation are important prerequisites for effective listening. Children should want to listen and should expect to gain from the experience. Such an attitude helps them focus attention and leads to more productive listening.

2. *Getting oriented.* Children can listen more efficiently when they know something about the topic and the speaker. Brief introductory information or recall of previous knowledge helps establish a background and provides a frame of reference for collecting additional information.

3. *Setting a purpose for listening.* Having a reason for listening makes it a more purposeful activity and helps children plan a strategy of listening behavior. For example, instead of just asking children to listen to biographical information about a famous scientist, suggest what kinds of information to listen for. Knowing the purpose for listening directs attention and helps children organize what they hear.

The Content of the Listening Program

As you plan a listening program remember that the most effective instruction teaches specific listening skills. Thus, as you begin a program, decide what skills you want to teach and then plan lessons to develop them. You might use this skill list as the core of your program:

focus attention

hold information in memory

form sensory images

understand main ideas

pay attention to details

distinguish relevant from irrelevant

follow directions

organize information

infer

predict

sense emotional reaction

evaluate

draw conclusions

A Sample Lesson Plan

In planning a listening lesson, begin with an objective — what you want the children to be able to do. Then provide a listening experience that will help them develop the skill you have identified. Very often a listening lesson can be incorporated into some other curriculum area. For example, the following lesson might be part of a history study.

Objective:	To form sensory images from auditory descriptions.
Materials needed:	Paper and pencil for drawing.
Procedure:	Introduce lesson. Explain that the pioneers

didn't have tools like ours today. Most of their work was done by hand or with only a few simple tools. Often they made the tools themselves. Tell the children that you are going to read them a description of a tool the pioneers used for harvesting grain. They are to listen carefully and try to get a picture of the tool in their mind. Then read the following selection:

Pa and Uncle Henry were out in the field, cutting the oats with cradles. A cradle was a sharp steel blade fastened to a framework of wooden slats that caught and held the stalks of grain when the blade cut them. Pa and Uncle Henry carried the cradles by their long, curved handles,

and spun the blades into the standing oats. When they had cut enough to make a pile, they slid the cut stalks off the slats, into neat heaps on the ground.[1]

Without discussing the paragraph, pass out paper and pencils and have the children draw the cradle as they think it looked. When they have finished, read the selection again so they can see how well their drawings match the description.

The listening lesson in Figure 5-2 is an example of listening lessons included in language arts textbooks. It was designed to develop critical listening skills. The first page shows the page as it appears in the students' book. Teaching suggestions and the stories to be read are given only in the teacher's manual.

Listening Habits and Attitudes

Besides identifying specific skills, Nichols (n.d.) has identified some common habits that produce negative listening results. The teacher of listening should be aware of these and take positive action to try to keep children from forming them. Here are the ten bad listening habits Nichols identified from his research. Discussion and suggestions to prevent or remediate each habit are also given.

1. *Calling the subject dull.* Children may not be interested in a topic because they don't have enough background about it to understand and appreciate what the speaker is saying. Or, they may assume incorrectly that they know what a speaker will say.

   Positive approach: Children should be prepared for listening sessions. They should know enough about a topic to create an interest in it. Listening experiences should always be appropriate to the educational and interest level of the listeners, but children should also be encouraged to be open-minded and to search out new ideas.

2. *Criticizing the speaker.* The way a speaker looks, acts, and talks can divert attention from what is said. Poor listeners think about

[1] Wilder, Laura Ingalls. *Little House in the Big Woods.* Copyright: Laura Ingalls Wilder. (Scholastic Books Edition, 1979), p. 200.

FIGURE 5-2 (*pages 146–147*)

From *Language and How to Use It*, Book 3, by Andrew Schiller, et al. Copyright © 1973 by Scott, Foresman and Company. Reprinted by permission.

MATERIALS
Record 2, Side 2,
Listening Activities,
Bands 3, 4, 5, and 6

LISTENING FOR CLUES

Have you ever read an exciting mystery story and said to yourself, "Why I could solve a mystery like that"? Have you ever thought about being a detective someday? A good detective must have good eyes. He must be able to see everything—even small things like footprints and fingerprints. He must be able to figure out what the things that he sees might mean.

Does a good detective also have to be a good listener? Sometimes people tell him different stories about what happened. Is it important for the detective to listen carefully to each speaker? What do you think he is listening for?

If he is like most detectives, he probably is going to look and listen for clues. Do you know what a clue is? Sometimes just one little thing is the clue that will solve the whole mystery.

You are going to listen to some mysteries that were solved by boys and girls. If you listen carefully to what happened, you will hear the clue that will help *you* solve each mystery for yourself. After you hear each mystery, take turns telling the rest of the class what the clue was and how it helped you solve the mystery.

PAGE 89

EMPHASIS
Listening and logic go hand in hand in this lesson as pupils select the pertinent facts and discard the irrelevant in what they hear. Such evaluative listening helps pupils arrive at logical conclusions to solve capsule mysteries.

EXPLANATION
Use the silhouettes of hands and feet in the page decoration to suggest the idea of mystery to boys and girls. Lead discussion to the idea that a clue is anything that helps solve a mystery. Since children may believe clues to be only tangible bits of evidence—fingerprints, broken locks, etc.—bring out that detectives listen for clues as well as look for them.

When children have read page 89, tell them to consider every bit of information that is given to them in each story. The clue will be one bit of information that solves the mystery.

Discuss each mystery in turn as soon as pupils have heard it. The answers are given below for your convenience.
1. Since Willy cannot chew meat, he could not have chewed the slipper.
2. Jane was correct. Judy could not walk and therefore could not have left footprints. But her crawling would have flattened the grass.
3. The glasses must still be under the pillow. Larry could not have been reading in bed without his glasses.
4. The present was under the apple tree.

If any one of the mysteries is not solved, let children hear the story once more. Since they will then be familiar with the problem, most of them should discover the clue easily. However, you may wish to use these questions to focus attention on the exact nature of the needed information:
- What did Willy eat and why?
- How did Judy move around?
- When did Larry last wear his glasses?
- What was in the garden that changed with the seasons?

89

THE MYSTERY OF THE CHEWED SLIPPERS

Bob Jackson's big brother had a dog named Oscar, but Bob had always wanted a dog of his own. Finally his mother brought home a little puppy named Willy. Willy was too small to chew meat and so Bob fed him milk. Everyone liked Willy except Oscar. Oscar thought that one dog in a family was enough.

One day Bob and Mrs. Jackson walked into the kitchen and this is what they saw:

Willy was sleeping peacefully in his box. But beside him were all of the slippers in the house: Mr. Jackson's big brown leather ones, and Mrs. Jackson's little pink fluffy ones, and Bob's plaid wool ones, and his big brother's green ones. Big holes were chewed in all of them.

"Willy!" Mother cried. "Shame on you! I know that puppies like to chew slippers, but imagine chewing all of the slippers in the house!"

"Mother," said Bob, "Don't punish Willy. He didn't chew them. It must have been Oscar."

How did Bob know that?

A BARNYARD MYSTERY

Janet and Jane were twins who lived on a farm. They had a baby sister named Judy. Judy couldn't walk yet, but she loved to crawl around the farm and get into things. She liked to scare the chickens, pet the kittens, watch the cows, and pick the carrots that grew in a garden across the dirt road.

One day their mother had to drive into town for some groceries. "Take good care of Judy while I'm gone, girls," she told Janet and Jane. "Don't take your eyes off her for a minute and be sure that she doesn't crawl across the dirt road."

But after a while, Janet and Jane got interested in playing with their dolls and they forgot about Judy. When they finally remembered her, she was nowhere in sight.

Janet was very worried. "Where do you think she went, Jane?" she asked.

Jane said, "Let's look around for some clues."

They looked, but all they could see was the tall grass that grew in front of the cow pasture. Some of the grass had been flattened. Then they saw some footprints in the dust on the dirt road.

"Look at the footprints, Jane!" cried Janet. "Judy must have gone across the road again to pick carrots!"

"Don't be silly," replied Jane. "She went to look at the cows."

Who was right?

THE MYSTERY OF THE MISSING SPECTACLES

Larry O'Sullivan just got his first pair of glasses. He had to use them whenever he was reading or else he couldn't see the words. But then he lost them. He went to the Lost and Found window at school and said to the school secretary, "Miss King, do you have a pair of glasses with brown frames?"

Miss King frowned and looked in her drawer. "No, I'm sorry, Larry, I don't. When did you lose them?"

"I don't remember," Larry said.

"Can you remember when you last had them?" asked Miss King.

Larry replied, "I know I had them after school because I had to use them to play baseball. I took them off then and I think I put them in my jacket pocket. But I used them again after dinner to watch television. Then my mother made me wear them when I took my bath because she said that I never seem to see my dirt. And that was the last I saw of them."

Miss King said, "Did you do anything after your bath?"

"Well," said Larry, "I was reading a detective story in bed when I was supposed to be asleep. I used a flashlight so that my mother wouldn't see that the light in my room was on. But she came upstairs after I just got started on a really exciting chapter and I had to hide everything under the pillow."

Miss King smiled. "I think that if you have learned something about being a good detective, you will know where to look for your glasses."

Where were Larry's glasses?

THE MYSTERY OF THE HIDDEN PRESENT

Kathy loved her mother's garden. It had a wishing well, a goldfish pond, and an old apple tree with a swing. In the spring there were also daffodils, tulips, and lilacs growing in the garden. But in the winter, everything was covered with snow.

Kathy's mother liked to plan surprises. On Kathy's birthday she gave her this note. "To find your birthday present, you must solve this mystery. Your present is hidden under something in the garden. The something is pink in the spring and green in the summer and red in the autumn and bare in the winter."

Kathy thought for a minute and then she smiled and ran to get her present.

Where was Kathy's present hidden?

the speaker's qualities instead of the speech content. Good listeners try to understand and help the speaker.

Positive approach: Help the children recognize the reciprocal nature of speaking and listening and the responsibilities of both speakers and listeners. Show them that an audience can exert a positive or a negative influence on a speaker. An attitude of acceptance and an honest attempt to gain something from speakers will help put them at ease and let them focus their attention on the content of the speech. Also, children can learn to ask clarifying questions as a way of helping speakers organize their thoughts and share their knowledge more effectively.

3. *Getting overstimulated.* Strong emotional reactions overshadow important information and ideas. The mind gets stuck on one thought and fails to process additional content of the speech.

Positive approach: Children need to listen objectively. They need to learn to distinguish between fact and opinion and to refrain from evaluation until there is sufficient evidence for judgment. It is important to give children an opportunity to discuss various points of view. Being expected to accept something they disagree with leads to acquiescence or frustration.

4. *Listening only for facts.* Isolated facts are of little value. Good listeners concentrate on getting main ideas. Facts then fall into proper perspective within the framework of larger concepts.

Positive approach: Spend more time exploring associations and relationships. Concentrate on helping the children gain main ideas and give less reinforcement for verbatim repetition of information. Encourage the children to compare and contrast information as a means of forming generalizations.

5. *Trying to outline everything.* Outlining is often useful, but not all speeches lend themselves to such a structure. The good listener is flexible.

Positive approach: Help the children orient themselves to the style of the speaker and the content of the message. Discuss the need to tune in and sample the situation before planning a listening strategy. Provide a variety of listening experiences so that children have firsthand experience in listening for different purposes (e.g., for enjoyment, to detect propaganda, to judge the probable appeal of a new library book, etc.). Discuss the different types of listening required and help children plan appropriate listening strategies. Remember that writing is a laborious task for many elementary schoolchildren and that writing while they listen may be beyond their developmental ability level. If they take notes, emphasize the importance of brevity, of capturing the thought for later use rather than writing long and perfect sentences. Provide memory training to help the children remember what is said and negate the need to write everything down.

6. *Faking attention.* Assuming a listening pose does not ensure communication. Good listening is active. Nichols quotes a definition of attention as "a collection of tensions inside the listener" (n.d., p. 2).

   Positive approach: Listening instruction should include frequent stops to discuss, summarize, and react to what is heard. Active listening should be encouraged by monitoring expressions and calling on children to express evident thoughts: "Mark, what was your reaction to that point?" or "Mildred, you look troubled; what difficulty are you having with that idea?" Maintain an air of expectancy; assume that what the speaker says will stimulate children's thinking.

7. *Tolerating distraction.* Tuning in to annoying environmental factors or creating noise and squirms to distract others results in less efficient listening.

   Positive approach: Everyone has a critical level of tolerance. Some children may be able to tune out distractions that are overwhelming to others. Success begets success: successful listening experiences set the stage for more successful experiences. Encourage and accept honest complaints about distractions that they are unable to cope with. If possible, eliminate the problem. If it can't be eliminated, make arrangements to overcome the problem such as rearranging the seating or changing the source of input in some way. At the same time, help the children cope with and build their tolerance for distractions.

8. *Choosing only what's easy.* Poor listeners shun more serious presentations and select only the light and entertaining.

   Positive approach: Plan some listening experiences that require the children to expand and stretch their listening tastes and abilities. For example, if poetry is not their choice of listening fare, find a particularly interesting poem and help them learn to listen and enjoy it. Rewarding experiences show them that a little more effort is worthwhile and help them develop a new mind set toward more difficult listening.

9. *Letting emotion-laden words get in the way.* Words often have private connotations that incite emotional reaction. Poor listeners tune out and get side-tracked when they hear certain words.

   Positive approach: Recognize the difference between denotation and connotation of words. Help the children realize that their private meaning for words will be at least slightly different from other people's because they have had different experiences. Accept this as normal. You might make a list of words and phrases that have emotional appeal for children (medicine? cop? kill? good English? etc.). Then explore the denotation and connotation of the words and suggest possible synonyms. Being aware of their connotations for words may free children from some of the emotional interpretation. Or, if there is a less emotional synonym, children can mentally substitute the word when they listen instead of letting themselves get overly excited.

10. *Wasting the differential between speech and thought speed.* People are able to think at a faster rate than speakers speak. It is estimated that conversations take place at the rate of about 125 words per minute and speeches at 100 words per minute. Yet listeners are able to think at the rate of 400 to 500 words per minute. This time differential results in leftover thinking time, which allows the mind to stray off to unrelated thoughts. Then the content of the speech is temporarily or, in some instances, permanently lost.

    Positive approach: Talk about the differences in speech and thought speed. Older children can plan to use the differential to recall previous knowledge, to relate ideas, and to form generalizations and questions.

Integrating Listening Instruction

Every area of the curriculum provides opportunities for listening instruction. For example, in music children listen to learn the words or tune to a song; they listen for phrases; they listen to compare themes; they listen for the main idea or message of a song; or they listen to discover mood. In art children listen for directions; they listen to learn new vocabulary; they listen to discover the main events in an artist's life; they listen to compare the use of various media; and they listen to discover different ways to use a brush. In physical education children listen to learn how to play a game; they listen to evaluate their skills; and they listen to learn how to improve their skills.

Social studies offer many opportunities to teach and practice listening skills. For example, the children may listen to locate places, to summarize main points, to sequence events, to discover cause and effect, to evaluate the authenticity of material, to compare two or more accounts of an event, to classify, or to make generalizations. A similar list could be made for science. The important point is that listening is part of the entire school day. Almost everything children do involves listening.

Because listening is such a common activity, however, there is danger that it will not ever be *taught*, that there will be no planned program. Listening in the various curriculum areas must be taught if children are to make maximum gains in listening ability. Skills must be identified first, and then a program can be built to include practical application of those skills to listening situations throughout the school day.

Individualizing Listening Instruction

Children will vary in their listening ability just as they do in other areas. A good listening program should involve children in identifying their individual strengths and needs. It should also help them set appropriate objectives. Through class discussions, self-evaluations, and individual conferences, they can become aware of desirable listening behaviors and discover how to become better listeners.

A listening checklist provides a guide for developing good listening habits. The formulation of such a list can be a natural outgrowth of class discussions about listening skills and facilitating behaviors. In the early primary years children might come up with something like this:

Do I get ready to listen?

Do I look at the speaker?

Do I listen to what the speaker says?

Do I think about what the speaker says?

Can I tell someone else what I hear?

As children become more aware of listening skills and abilities their evaluation criteria will become more sophisticated. The following checklist (Kopp, 1967, p. 117) suggests points children in the higher levels might include.

Checking Up on My Listening

	Yes	No
1. Did I remember to get ready for listening?	___	___
a. Was I seated comfortably where I could see and hear?	___	___
b. Were my eyes focused on the speaker?	___	___
2. Was my mind ready to concentrate on what the speaker had to say?	___	___
a. Was I able to push other thoughts out of my mind for the time being?	___	___
b. Was I ready to think about the topic and call to mind the things I already knew about it?	___	___
c. Was I ready to learn more about the topic?	___	___
3. Was I ready for "take-off"?	___	___
a. Did I discover in the first few minutes where the speaker was taking me?	___	___
b. Did I discover his central idea so that I could follow it through the speech?	___	___
4. Was I able to pick out the ideas that supported the main idea?	___	___
a. Did I take advantage of the speaker's clues (such as first, next, etc.) to help organize the ideas in my mind?	___	___
b. Did I use extra "think" time to summarize and take notes — either mentally or on paper?	___	___
5. After the speaker finished and the facts were all in, did I evaluate what had been said?	___	___
a. Did this new knowledge seem to fit with the knowledge I already had?	___	___
b. Did I weigh each idea to see if I agreed with the speaker?	___	___

If you marked questions no, decide why you could not honestly answer them yes.

Many of the listening skills given earlier in this chapter may be appropriate for whole-class instruction. It is quite likely, for example, that most children will profit from experiences in following verbal directions or in judging the validity of information. However, the alert teacher needs to be aware of individual children's competencies in listening and to build on them. Although some practice is necessary to maintain skills, children need to be challenged to learn new skills and abilities. This may necessitate a special plan of instruction for more able listeners.

A listening center can provide appropriate individualized instruction for any age level. It should contain materials for children to practice skills. These might include tape recorded stories, puzzles, exercises, and recorded directions for making things. Once the skill list has been set up, activities can be indexed to skills so that children can work independently. Partners or small groups may work on a skill together. It is often helpful to have someone with whom to compare results or discuss ideas. Also, good readers can often help prepare tapes for use in the center, particularly for younger children. For more information on planning and organizing a listening center, see the section on learning centers in Chapter 12.

Television and radio offer several possibilities for valuable class or individual listening projects. Children's favorite programs may be used not only to develop specific listening skills, but to help children recognize the influence such listening and viewing experiences can have on their lives. Children need to learn to be wise consumers. Keeping a listening diary of the amount of time they spend listening to the radio or viewing television, the type of each program, and the listening skills required can help children become aware of limitations of their listening practice. Other possible learning experiences are retelling a story or episode, summarizing, stating main ideas, classifying programs, generalizing about characters ("What kind of a person is _____?") and giving details to support generalizations, identifying factual information and inference, comparing the content of a program with previously gained knowledge, and identifying the purpose of a program. Commercials, in particular, offer opportunities for developing critical listening skills. Recognizing the purpose of commercials and the techniques used to make a product attractive are especially important. Children might compile a list of products advertised, and the reasons given for purchasing them, including annotations for each reason as to whether it is based on fact, opinion, or inference. From these data children will be able to generalize about commercials. Experiences such as this develop important critical listening.

Listening Materials

Regular language arts textbooks have limited lessons on listening. Some series have none at all. Examine the textbooks you have available to see which listening skills are taught and how they are taught.

You may find that any attention to listening is incidental rather than a carefully planned program.

Several listening programs and materials are available commercially. Some of the better known programs include Education Development Corporation's *Countdown for Listening,* D. C. Heath and Company's *Listening-Reading Program,* and Science Research Associates' *Listening Skills Program. Listening Skills: An Introduction, Listen Well, Learn Well,* and *Your Communication Skills* by Coronet, and *Listening* by Churchill Films are some teaching films. Filmstrips on listening are also available from companies such as Coronet, Learning Corporation of America, and Filmstrip House. Various recordings of songs and stories offer a wealth of listening resources for the creative teacher.

Many books and materials already in the classroom may also be adapted for listening lessons. For example, reading materials such as the *Specific Skill Series* published by Barnell Loft, Ltd. or *Reading for Understanding* by Science Research Associates, may be used for oral comprehension as well as for reading comprehension.

A school library has a wealth of potential listening material. Children should be read to frequently to learn to enjoy the sounds and patterns of language. In addition to general listening experiences, however, selections may be used to develop specific listening skills. Don't forget the nonfiction section. Such topics as snakes, bees, fish, spiders, airplanes, boats, and bulldozers seem to hold universal appeal, and books on these topics provide excellent material for meaningful skill development.

Some books for young children are specifically written to call attention to listening. These include Paul Showers's *The Listening Walk,* Mary O'Neill's *What is that Sound!,* Don Safier's *The Listening Book,* and Margaret Wise Brown's noisy books — *The City Noisy Book, The Country Noisy Book, The Summer Noisy Book, The Winter Noisy Book, The Indoor Noisy Book, The Noisy Book, The Quiet Noisy Book,* and *The Seashore Noisy Book.*

Some of the best listening materials are those children design themselves. Planning listening experiences for others helps children become more conscious of their own listening habits and causes them to concentrate on ways to improve listening. For example, older children might closely tune their ears to sounds in the environment to tape record a series of sounds for a listener to identify. They might select and tape record a fiction or nonfiction selection with appropriate response questions. Or, they might listen critically to records, tapes, radio, or television to select appropriate examples of listening for different purposes. Projects to develop listening materials or "packages" can be a natural outgrowth of listening skill discussions or evaluations.

In Summary

Listening is an often neglected skill. Nevertheless it is very important inasmuch as children's speaking, reading, and writing are all affected by it. How well children listen depends on their background of experience; their physical, social, emotional, and cognitive development; and the content of the listening material.

Each listening situation requires a specific listening behavior. These behaviors range from passive listening to critical and appreciative listening. The purpose for listening in a given situation determines what kind of listening behavior is most appropriate.

Being a good listener entails the use of many skills. Instruction in listening helps children to become aware of these skills and to evaluate their own listening habits. It also provides opportunities to develop and practice skills in meaningful situations. Because listening is a part of the entire school day, it may be taught within the context of various subject areas.

Learning Objectives

COGNITIVE OBJECTIVES

Primary Grades

Children will

recall specific information.

identify the sequence of events.

follow directions.

explain how something functions.

relate (tell) stories or information accurately.

form mental images.

translate what is heard into written, graphic, musical, or dramatic form.

compare two stories or sources of information.

summarize information.

separate fact from fancy.

recognize cause and effect.

recognize implications.

listen for a specific purpose.

Middle Grades

Children will

maintain and expand all primary-grade listening objectives.

organize and classify information.

identify main ideas and supporting details.

apply a generalization to another situation.

identify relevant and irrelevant information.

identify bias, prejudice, or propaganda.

distinguish fact from opinion.

draw conclusions.

determine a speaker's purpose.

verify or discredit a statement.

suggest possible uses or further development of information.

plan and use an appropriate listening strategy.

AFFECTIVE OBJECTIVES

Children will

tune in to the sounds around them.

enjoy listening activities.

appreciate oral language as a means of communicating.

select a variety of active listening experiences.

appreciate the power of language to create enjoyment, emotion, and action.

be considerate of other listeners.

strive to improve their ability to listen.

develop new interests as a result of listening experiences.

Suggested Learning Activities

Messenger. Whenever possible give the children responsibility for carrying oral messages to the office or to other rooms. Stress the importance of listening and repeating accurate information.

Poetry Reading. Read poems that are likely to evoke children's feelings, moods, and emotions. Encourage the children to discuss how a poem makes them feel and try to identify why the poem affects them that way.

Song Stories. Have the children listen while you play a song. Let them tell the story from the song or suggest what might have led to the writing of the song.

Listen and Tell. Build a story one word at a time. The teacher says a beginning word such as "The" and the children in turn repeat what has been said and add one more word. For example, the first child might say, "The house," and the next child, "The house in," and so on around the group to complete a short story. Whenever a child misses a word a new story is begun.

Headliners. Read newspaper articles to the children and have them think of good headlines that contain the main idea of the article.

News Reporter. Read news or magazine articles to the children and have them listen for the five W's: *who, what, where, when,* and *why.*

The Informer. When children have been absent from class, give those who are present the assignment of summarizing and passing on orally the instructions and information about things the others have missed.

Listen and Act. Select a few paragraphs of narrative material from a book or story and

read it aloud. Divide the class into appropriately sized groups and let them act out what they heard. Share the productions with the total group and discuss any differences.

Behind the Lines. Read a conversation between two or more characters in a story or play. Have the children guess the story behind the conversation.

Unnamed Biographies. Read short biographies of well-known people, perhaps people the class is studying about. Have the students guess the identity of each person.

Peer Reports. Pair children off and have them interview each other about hobbies or special interests. Then have each child tell about the partner's hobbies or interests.

Meanings through Context. Select material that contains words the children do not know. Write the new words on the board without defining or explaining them. Read the selection and have the children try to figure out the meaning of each word from contextual clues.

Designing a Set. Read a story and have the children plan a stage setting adequate for acting it out.

Speech and Writing. Select a topic of current interest and lead a discussion. Make a tape recording of it. Have the children listen to the recording and compare speech to the way things are written in books. On the board make a list of the differences they notice. Discuss whether or not these differences are significant in developing listening skills.

Filmstrips. Read a selection from a social studies or science book and then have the children plan a filmstrip to illustrate the passage.

Sales Pitch. Record some radio advertisements. Let the children listen to them and analyze how the advertisers try to get people to buy their products.

One-sided Argument. Select a controversial topic and take the position that you know children favor (e.g., lunch menus, vacations). Write a paragraph presenting a strong argument for your position and deliberately leave out evidence that does not support it. Read the paragraph to the class and ask the children to criticize it objectively.

Relevant and Irrelevant. Have two children role-play an argument with deliberate inclusion of irrelevant statements. Then have the class critique the argument, citing the irrelevant statements.

Word Power. Ask the children to write the ten saddest words. Then ask them to write the ten happiest words. Compare the lists and discuss why the children associate words as being sad or happy. Discuss how these words make them feel when they hear them in speech.

Back It Up. Following the reading of a selection write a statement based on it that is true, partially true, or erroneous. Ask the children whether they agree that the statement is true and have them provide evidence from the selection to back up their position.

Title Critique. Tell the children the title of a short story and then read the story aloud to them. When you have finished, ask them to suggest other possible titles to the story. Write the original title and all their suggestions on the board. Then have them compare the merits of the various titles and decide which seems best and why.

Sneak Preview. Tell or read part of a story or historical event. Have the children think about what they have heard and then draw a picture of the next event. Let them share their pictures and explain why they think that event might happen.

Mind Pictures. Collect several pictures of the same subject, such as children playing, beach scenes, or picnics. Do not show the children the pictures. Describe one picture in the set and then show all of the pictures. Have the children identify the one you described.

What's Wrong with the Picture? Find a picture of a candy store, a bakery, or a fair. Without letting the children see the picture, describe what is in it but deliberately make some mistakes. You might say something is in one place when it is in another, or name the wrong shape or color; or you might say that something is there when it isn't. When you have finished describing the picture, show it to the children and let them tell what is wrong.

Important Character. Have the children listen to a story to determine which character is most important to the story. Ask each child to write down his or her choice on a slip of paper. Call on children to explain why they chose the character they did.

Comic Strip Stories. As you read a selection have the children listen to determine the sequence of main events. Then, working in small groups, let them share and compare their sequences and arrive at a consensus of the group. When they have done so they may draw a comic strip using a frame for each main event.

Categories. Assign categories of words to children (such as words that tell when, words that refer to people, or words that tell where). The children are to listen for words in their category while they listen to a selection. Several children may be assigned the same category so that they can compare their mental lists.

Who Said It? Read a play or a story with a considerable amount of dialog. When you are through, go back and read single speeches and ask children to identify the speaker.

Following Directions. Depending on the age of the children, give a series of directions for them to follow. For young children you might say, "Go to the door, turn around three times, and hop back to your seat." For older children you might say, "Trot to the cupboard; open the door; look in the box on the bottom shelf until you find a green clothespin; put it on the book on the third shelf and close the box; stretch your right arm and return to your seat." The other children must also listen closely to know whether actions are performed correctly.

Suggestions for Further Reading

Lundsteen, Sara W. *Listening: Its Impact on Reading and the Other Language Arts*. Urbana, Ill.: National Council of Teachers of English/ERIC, 1979.

Russell, David H., and Elizabeth F. Russell. *Listening Aids Through the Grades*. 2nd ed. New York: Teachers College Press, Columbia University, 1979.

Taylor, Stanford. *Listening: What Research Says to the Teacher*. Washington, D.C.: National Education Association, 1973.

Tiedt, Sidney W., and Iris M. Tiedt. *Language Arts Activities for the Classroom*. Boston: Allyn and Bacon, 1978.

Wagner, Guy. *Listening Games*. Darien, Conn.: Teachers Publishing Corporation, 1962.

See Appendix A for multimedia resources.

6
Creative Drama

*Dramatic Education is, therefore, not merely a way of looking at the
education process (a philosophy), or a way of helping the individual
develop (a psychology), or of assisting the individual to adjust to his
environment (a sociology); it is the basic way in which the human being
learns — and thus is the most effective method for all forms of
education.*

Richard Courtney (1968, p. 258)

CHAPTER PREVIEW

Do you remember as a child donning a grown-up's hat and
stepping into the world of make-believe? Creative drama is a natural
part of growing up and "trying on the world." It is at once an
exploration and an expression. As children play out a scene they are
experiencing life and acting out their conceptualization of it; therein
lies the foundation for speech and writing. This chapter is about
that process and how the rich resources of children's play and
creative drama relate to the language arts. First we will define
creative drama and discuss its place in elementary school programs.
From there we will proceed step-by-step to develop the knowledge
and skills involved in teaching creative drama (including the use of
puppets) as a language art.

QUESTIONS TO THINK ABOUT AS YOU READ

In what ways do creative drama and children's theater differ?

What is the value of creative drama in education?

How does creative drama fit into the language arts curriculum?

What skills enhance children's creative drama experience?

How can I teach creative drama effectively?

Where do puppets fit in? How are they related to creative drama
and the language arts?

What kinds of puppets are appropriate for children to make?

Children are scattered about the room — in aisles, in the space behind the teacher's desk, and in the open area by the classroom door.
They are crouching, their muscles taut as they slowly rise, bending
and struggling against an unseen something at their sides, then behind them, then above them. Then their strained countenances and

161

tense bodies slowly give way to radiant expressions and a firm, stalwart stance.

Assuming roles of young plants, these young children have just experienced a struggle for survival. They have grown untended through a tangle of fast growing weeds to reach the sunlight and establish their rightful place. Creative drama has taken these children through exploration of conflict stemming from their desire to live and grow in an already crowded environment. An analysis reveals several facts about the situation: the children were all acting simultaneously; there was no audience; the activity involved a thoughtful and totally consuming portrayal of each child's conceptualization of the struggle; and no one was wrong.

Creative drama is experience. It brings children to grips with reality in much the same way as firsthand experience. Playing out a scene causes children to analyze their knowledge and impressions and to translate what they know and feel into physical and emotional responses just as if they were responding to a real situation.

Creative drama produces a heightened sense of reality. Consciously performing an act often requires more thought than a spur-of-the-moment reaction. Thus when children plan what they are going to do, do it, and then evaluate the results, they develop a more thorough understanding. Common situations take on greater meaning; vague concepts become clearer. When children *are* someone or something they are no longer passive observers; they are participants. In *being* and *doing* they become both mentally and physically involved.

Creative drama helps children develop a greater awareness. Through guided explorations children gain insights about themselves as human beings. They discover their unstated personal objectives, how they usually approach situations, how they feel and react, and why they sometimes become frustrated. In creative drama children learn to look at experiences from another's point of view. They also learn how they are like others and how they are different. Working through guided situations, they increase their capacity to understand and empathize with others. In addition, creative drama encourages children to "tune in" to their environment, to become aware of factors that enhance experiences or that facilitate or inhibit.

Creative drama also helps children gain a sense of interrelationships. As they plan appropriate actions for themselves and others they expand their naturally egocentric point of view. They analzye how environment, time, space, and significant others influence what a person does. They begin to see how people and things depend on each other and to understand how they interact.

Creative drama helps develop both rational and creative thinking.

Dramatic experiences provide opportunities for children to practice consciously shaping experience. In playing out a scene children plan before they act. Then they evaluate and have another try. Such an approach helps them recognize and creatively cope with unalterable facts and elements (e.g., *it is raining*, or *you are late*, or *there are only two of you*). Because there is no one right way in creative dramatics, children are free to portray a scene as they interpret it, to create any alternative action that seems right to them. However, they must also deal with whatever situation they create. Thus they practice a range of cognitive skills such as identifying a specific objective or problem; identifying a related base of knowledge; exploring; selecting; organizing; and synthesizing the emotional, physical, and vocal content of the dramatic portrayal into a believable whole.

Creative Drama and Children's Theater

Creative drama should not be confused with children's theater. Although creative drama may lead to theatrical productions, the two are not the same, and it is important for teachers to understand the difference between them. Succinctly stated, creative drama is *process-oriented* and children's theater is *product-oriented*.

Moffett describes (creative) drama and theater in this way:

> Drama is the acting out of feeling and takes the point of view of the participant, for whom it exists; spectatorship is an irrelevance and, until a certain stage of development, a hindrance. Theater concerns performance before an audience, whose point of view is included and for whose benefit effects are calculated. (1973, p. 35)

Stewig summarizes some of the major distinctions between the two art forms in Table 6-1.

Creative drama emphasizes the development of each individual; product and audience are incidental. For example, children may replay a story over and over, changing it each time. They try out various ways of doing things, creatively expanding their knowledge and sensitivity. McCaslin states, "No matter how many times the story is played, it is done for the purpose of deepening understandings and strengthening the performers rather than perfecting a product" (1974, p. 7).

Creative drama helps children develop a better understanding of themselves and of others. As they explore and act out their impressions of people and events in their world, they develop a deeper sense of awareness and learn to analyze and to plan strategies for

TABLE 6-1

	SCRIPTED DRAMA	SPONTANEOUS DRAMA
Involvement	A few children can be involved, the rest must take backstage or other supportive jobs.	Involves all children in a variety of active roles.
Creativity encouraged	Close adherence to the script by the playwright is mandatory.	Children use story or other motivation as a springboard for their own creation.
Pressure to perform	High; children know audience is watching, done in surroundings with which child is often unfamiliar.	Low; if audience exists at all, it is small group of children's peers in the classroom situation with which they are familiar.
Need for props and equipment	Quite extensive; often these are not things children can create, but must be made for them by others.	Minimal or nonexistent; child uses creative imagination to evoke needed equipment, emphasis on refining movements (e.g., picking up a fork) to convey ideas.
Language learnings	Few; children are limited to understanding the uses the author has made of language.	Many; the situations presented challenge children to creative use of language, both verbal and nonverbal.

dealing with new situations. They also develop greater awareness and control of their bodies and minds and gain insights about group processes and individual human potential.

Children's theater, on the other hand, is product-oriented and more formal. The primary goal is a finalized production of a play for someone else's entertainment. Children's theater is audience-centered, and thus performance receives the major emphasis. This situation places constraints and pressures on the actors. It tends to lock them into a ready-made script, complete with staging and acting directions.

Whether children's theater, performed by children, should be a part of an elementary school curriculum is not a question of whether it is good or bad. Rather, it is a question of readiness, appropriateness, and whether the amount of time expended in such activities is educationally justifiable. Certainly children should *see* good theater, and some may benefit from participating in a formal play production. For many children, however, the large amount of time required for a theatrical production nets questionable results. Not only do many children lack the confidence and skills to create a satisfying performance for themselves or for their audience, but they might spend the time more profitably in another way.

Some drama leaders feel that any performance in front of an audience is harmful to children in that it interferes with their own free expression. Children are usually self-conscious in front of an audience, and their actions and words lack spontaneity and "rightness of the moment." Because they fear criticism they tend toward a safe and respectable performance rather than delving into and exposing their private thoughts and emotions.

Unless actors are quite skilled, their efforts are apt to be seen by an audience as merely humorous or clumsy. Such an audience reaction is devastating to the child and at cross-purposes to the goals of creative dramatics and education in general. Children who are laughed at or ridiculed soon learn to avoid getting into such situations, or they try to capitalize on the ludicrous to get more laughs.

Audience situations in creative drama are usually limited to sharing an interpretation or playing out a story for the rest of the group. Most of the time children are working simultaneously, either individually or in several small groups. Sharing is not done in the sense of giving a production for another group. The purpose of sharing is to demonstrate variations in interpretation and to facilitate learning through evaluation and discussion. Following the sharing of an activity children usually return to their groups to try out ways of improving what they are doing.

Way (1967) underscores the importance of concentrating on creative drama rather than children's theater in the early years. He suggests that both drama[1] and education may be defined simply as "to practice life." He emphasizes practice in the achievement of any human skill and urges teachers to provide dramatic opportunities for every child. He also points out the need to delimit the scope of dramatic activity if it is to serve education as practice for living. He says, "This becomes possible only if we discard the limitations of theatrical conventions and consider drama as a quite different activity, calling upon different standards of judgment and entirely different results. The aim is constant: to develop people, not drama" (p. 6).

Creative drama may sometimes lead to a production for an audience as an outgrowth of something the children are studying. However, the production phase of drama should not be forced or hurried. Children need a body of dramatic knowledge and skills before they

---

[1] Terms such as *drama, informal drama,* and *spontaneous drama* are used by some other writers to mean essentially the same thing as *creative drama* in this book.

can portray a character convincingly. In creative drama, as in any other area of the curriculum, activities should always be appropriate to the children's developmental level. It is important to help children develop necessary skills at their own individual levels and paces before they perform in front of an audience.

Children are often anxious to produce plays, and some children may be ready for such experience. The material must, however, be suitable and the production student-centered. Thus, children should have the opportunity for creative interpretation rather than following rigid and forced directions that they understand only vaguely. When these conditions are met, the overall results of an occasional play will probably be positive. One group of fifth-graders, for example, did an exemplary job of *The Wizard of Oz* entirely on their own. They practiced before and after school and during lunch and recess breaks. The final production for parents and peers was little short of amazing. Each child had a feel for his or her part, and the details of movement and staging had been thoroughly worked out. Effective costumes had been scrounged and improvised. When the wicked Witch died convincingly, some of the first-graders cried and not a single older student or adult snickered.

These young actors obviously were strongly motivated, to give so much of their free time. They had visualized, carefully planned, and practiced their parts until they felt confident in sharing their portrayal of the various characters. Cooperation and support among members of the group was evident. They had accomplished on their own what a creative drama teacher, had there been one, would have attempted to do. The audience situation was merely a natural outgrowth, a desire to share their work.

Children's Play as Dramatic Activity

Children dramatize bits of life in their play at an early age. They spontaneously greet an imaginary guest, put out a fire, drive a car, or call someone on the telephone with a striking sense of reality. Through dramatic play children reenact their own memorable experiences or enter into the experiences of others about them.

Children's dramatic play is whatever they want it to be at the moment. It needs no plot or particular structure. It may last only a few minutes or it may continue for some time. It may be an imaginary first-time encounter or a repetition of a familiar and enjoyable situation.

Dramatic play is an open-ended activity in which children explore, experiment, or reenact real life. It allows them to use limitless imagination or to reverse roles and put themselves in control of situations. Children often play the part of a parent or other significant adult, portraying that role as they perceive it. Observations of children engaged in dramatic play reveal much about them: their perceptions, their sense of relationships, their frustrations, their attempts to solve problems, and the things that delight them. Dramatic play mirrors both children's grasp of reality and their creativity.

A planned creative drama program in the school merely extends and builds on children's natural inclination to use drama as a way of learning. It provides opportunities to continue to use drama as a way of learning. It provides opportunities to continue playing out real-life situations and to be imaginative. It enhances their enjoyment through the development of sensory awareness, observation skills, and information-processing abilities.

Creative Drama as a Language Art

Although creative drama is recognized as a way of learning about and understanding oneself, others, and one's environment, it is ultimately communication. As such it belongs to the language arts. It is an expressive art, a way of communicating information and feelings to someone else. Furthermore, while exploring and developing the art of dramatic communication, one is helped with other aspects of receptive and expressive communication.

Creative drama provides the context for meaningful language growth. The language and thinking of children in the concrete operational stage of development depends on experience. Creative drama ties language to the real world of children. Through dramatic activities they reconstruct and rearrange their experiences; they act out their ideas by manipulating objects and events. Language is a natural and integral part of the process. It is both an extension and a symbol of the activity. To better understand this interrelationship, let us consider each of the language arts areas separately.

Oral Language

Creative drama stimulates conscious speech. It gives children a reason and a need to talk. It creates a language laboratory in which they must search out vocabulary and grammatical structures to communicate what they wish to express. Their discoveries about language are used immediately in meaningful situations, thus resulting in efficient and lasting learning.

The content of children's speech is also improved. In acting out scenes, children must visualize, associate, and infer. Situations become clearer. With this cognitive base, children are better able to think what to say and to organize their speech into more meaningful utterances.

Through creative drama children develop a greater consciousness of the sound of language. They increase their ability to discriminate language sounds and to reproduce them more accurately (Woolf and Myers, 1968). They also gain a better understanding of expressive speech and discover the ways pitch, stress, and juncture contribute to communication (Stewig, 1973). As they think about and plan characterizations, they become more aware of regional and social dialects and the use of different levels of language in different situations.

Initially, children may prefer to act out a scene without speech. In this way they can concentrate on the character and the situation without the added burden of formulating dialog. Gradually, however, dialog develops quite naturally as an accompaniment to action. But, whether children pantomime or use speech with their actions, they are developing language concepts. Language is inherent in the thought processes through which they mentally construct a situation and play out their ideas.

Listening

Listening is an important part of learning to work within a creative drama activity. Creative drama provides many opportunities for purposeful listening, and the need to listen is inherent in planning and playing out stories and ideas. The success with which children play out a scene or story is directly related to their ability to listen.

Opportunities for listening during a creative drama activity are numerous. For example, children listen to a story or idea to visualize and remember who the characters are, what they are like, what happens, where it happens, what causes it to happen, what the outcome is, and what sequence of events led to that outcome. Then they must listen as they plan, sharing and evaluating suggestions and determining what they will do. As they act they listen attentively as the story evolves, taking cues from others and creatively developing the story. They must also listen to themselves to use just the right words and expression to be the character they are portraying. When the story is finished they evaluate the effective parts and suggest how they might improve it. The activity continually involves tuning in and practicing listening skills.

The listening aspect of creative drama involves a wide range of skills. It includes discriminative and informational listening, inferential and applicative listening, and evaluative and creative listening.

These skills continue to improve through many well-planned and guided dramatic activities.

Reading

Creative drama enhances reading in several ways. Perhaps the most obvious effect is on comprehension. Because children's vocabulary and general language skills improve, they have a greater understanding of the printed page. They bring more to it, so they are able to take more away. Dramatic experiences give children a breadth and depth of understanding that enable them to comprehend nuances in written material often passed over by children who are less aware.

Sometimes a creative drama experience sparks children's interest in a particular topic and leads to additional reading. Children may simply become aware of something that intrigues them, or they may feel the need for a better understanding of something. Their extended interest may well focus on a particular character, especially if the person is well known and additional information is readily available.

Studies by Carlton and Moore (1968) indicated that creative drama significantly improved reading comprehension scores and that children also developed a greater interest in reading. This finding seems reasonable when we consider the effect of motivation on learning. To be motivated to read, children must have satisfying reading experiences. These experiences require more than merely decoding words. To comprehend and enjoy reading, children must be able to understand what words mean *in context.* The process of acting out, of doing, requires them to clarify the meaning of individual words and to comprehend the relationship of groups of words in sentences and paragraphs.[2] Such experiences enhance the meaning behind printed symbols and make reading materials come alive for children.

Creative drama develops personal knowledge of story design and plot development. This knowledge, in turn, heightens children's understanding and enjoyment of stories. Creative drama gives children firsthand experience in planning and acting the parts of a story: the beginning, the middle, and the end. They analyze motives for their action and become conscious of conflicting forces that complicate a plot and add interest. Such experiences help them think about and analyze the stories they read at more challenging and interesting levels of comprehension.

[2] See Ross and Roe (1977) for suggestions of dramatic activities designed to improve vocabulary and comprehension.

Writing

We might consider creative drama as readiness for creative writing. However, to do so would be greatly to limit it as an art and as a form of education. Certainly many of the objectives for creative drama are equally important for writing. Considering the two activities in a general sense, it is easy to see that a meaningful background of *being* experiences gives children a valuable perspective for writing. And, more specifically, *being* allows children to write vividly and with conviction. Creative drama and creative writing are in many ways similar modes of communicating. The main difference is that one is expressed visually and orally, and the other is expressed through written symbols.

Most creative drama is informal and spontaneous and does not need a script. However, for some children writing a script may be a natural outgrowth of an enjoyable dramatic activity. Perhaps a word of caution needs to be given, though, about *expecting* children to write down scenes and plays they have acted out. Writing is slow and laborious for most elementary schoolchildren, and attempting to script a play may be discouraging. How much script-writing children do should be determined by their motivation and abilities.

Slade points out, "A young child is quite incapable of the mastery of body and mind necessary in order to write down the flow of language and ideas found in its normal extempore work" (1955, p. 66). He suggests, however, that children may write descriptions of drama experiences. He feels that the emphasis for elementary-age children should be on developing "the love of language itself, which is stimulated both by the early actions to sounds and by the nurturing of Language Flow" (p. 66). He recommends a developmental sequence and states that "Play; Dramatic Play; improvisations; polished improvisations; some words written down; stories and dialogues copied from films, radio and life experiences; improved expression (coming from Language Flow) and improved writing ability mix with improvisation and begin to equal it" (p. 66).

Although creative drama need not lead to other oral or written language experiences, it may when appropriate. One natural way to integrate creative drama with writing is to use a brief dramatic warmup as a prewriting activity. Acting out an idea or some aspect of a planned writing task gets children mentally involved with what they are going to write about. Dramatizing intensifies children's feelings and facilitates a flow of language. For example, imagining and playing out the opening of a surprise package or a walk through a dark forest at night stimulates imagination and helps children think of something to write.

Creative drama can also complement practical writing. Creative drama experiences related to a particular problem or process generate thinking and necessitate the translation of thought into words and actions. In this way they help children comprehend difficult concepts in content areas and improve their ability to synthesize information. For example, when children are writing reports on the industries of a country, dramatizing work scenes in the industries is one way to develop a better understanding of the procedures and the processes involved. Dramatic explorations often lead to reports with greater clarity and vitality.

Creative drama also helps children understand and write from different points of view. Playing out a real or imagined situation (e.g., a conflict during the Revolutionary War period) helps children recognize other frames of reference and express varying points of view.

Reversing the order to write and then act what has been written can be a valuable experience also. Many original compositions of children lend themselves to dramatization and serve varied learning purposes. Using their own stories not only provides a source of ideas for dramatic activities but it provides feedback about children's writing as well. When children act out a story, they become aware of such problems as poor plot development, incongruencies, and lack of clarity in sequencing.

Creative Drama in the Elementary School Curriculum

There are two schools of thought about the place of drama in the curriculum. Some people believe that creative drama is a subject in its own right and that it should be taught separately. Slade (1955), for example, points out that there is a body of knowledge regarding drama just as there is for other arts such as music or painting. He favors teaching the elements of drama as a separate discipline.

Others point out that although there is a body of knowledge *about* drama, there is a lack of subject matter content for developing that knowledge. Therefore, any area of the curriculum may provide content for learning drama skills. Writers such as Way (1967) and Moffett (1973) suggest using drama throughout the school day to implement learning in various subject areas. In this way drama enhances subject matter learning, and the established curriculum provides the content for drama instruction.

Drama has a great deal to offer the learning process. As pointed out in the previous section, dramatic play is the way young children explore and get to know a wider range of experiences. Imagining they are someone or something provides practice in real-life experiences. In summarizing how drama and cognitive development are related Courtney states,

> There is a fundamental process to learning: perception, imitation and play, concept. We perceive an action or a process. We imitate the various elements within it, and then describe it (in dramatic play if we are a child or in words if we are an adult). This process culminates in the formation of the concept as a whole. (1968, p. 257)

Experiencing something results in greater and more lasting knowledge than merely hearing or reading about it. This is especially true for younger children with limited language and cognitive abilities. Everything that children need to learn cannot be experienced in the classroom, of course, but through the use of creative drama many experiences can be simulated to facilitate learning. On the basis of modern theories of cognition, Courtney offers this paradigm as the dramatic method of learning:

PERCEPTION - - - → ACTION - - → DESCRIPTION - - → THEORY
(dramatic
and/or
linguistic)

He says,

> The student should *watch* it, *do* it, *describe* it (in action and/or words), and then *theorize* about it. The "describe" part would be acted with the young child, a mixture of mimic actions and words if an adolescent, and purely in words if an adult (for the dramatic imagination has become internalized). (p. 258)

Components of the Dramatic Process

Awareness

The roots of meaningful experiences lie in the ability to receive and process perceptions. Such an awareness is the foundation of the dramatic process and of learning in general. Creative drama can help children become aware of themselves, of others, and of their environment. Awareness enhances the enjoyment of an experience and permits empathy with others. It allows children to intellectualize about situations and events and to exert rational control over them.

Becoming aware of self involves getting to know oneself as an individual — a distinct and unique human being. Creative drama helps children recognize feelings and emotions and understand how they are stimulated and expressed. It also helps them become aware that feelings and emotions influence what they do and how they do it.

Through creative drama children become aware of their physical and mental capabilities. They discover how the body moves in response to internal and external stimuli and how varying degrees and kinds of effort express attitudes and feelings. They come to recognize their voice as a physical instrument that they can control and use in different ways. Experiences in planning and shaping dramatic experiences help children become aware of themselves as rational and inventive beings, able to assimilate, judiciously organize, and create.

Awareness involves perceiving similarities and differences among people. It involves seeing them as individuals with feelings, emotions, and needs. Through creative drama children become aware of others as unique individuals. They become conscious of social interactions. They realize that what they do affects others, and in turn, that others affect them. Gradually children develop a greater sensitivity to others and a better understanding of themselves as social beings.

Becoming aware of one's environment involves tuning in to sensory experiences. Through creative drama children become more aware of visual, auditory, tactile, olfactory, and gustatory stimuli and the responses these stimuli evoke. They develop a sense of time and space and of mass and weight in relation to movement and plot development. They develop an awareness of how environmental factors influence individual and group activity.

Imagination

Imagination lets children reconstruct perceptions vividly in their minds. Because of imagination children can convincingly act out setting a table or walking in the rain. Activity becomes reality. Imagination lets children mentally become someone or something as they reenact an experience.

In addition, creative drama stimulates the imagination beyond the known. It encourages children to make mental leaps to create and explore what has not been experienced. Children may creatively mix known characters and settings with invented ones in play situations. They may bring inanimate objects to life or give existing creatures new powers. In doing these things, they must bring products of the imagination into clear focus so they can deal with them realistically.

Physical Control

Ability to control their movements is important for actors. Once children become aware of how they communicate actions and reflect feelings and attitudes through action, they need practice to gain control of their bodies. The first step is cognitive. Children must visualize what they wish to do and plan how they will do it. Then they must practice the action physically so that they can match what they do with what they visualize.

Concentration

Concentration involves sustained attention. Once children have planned what they will do they must try mentally to slip into the part and maintain it through to the end. Maintaining the characterization requires intense concentration. Children must learn to ignore all distractions and to think and respond in the manner of the character they are playing.

The level of concentration needed by actors requires considerable practice. Children should begin with short practice sessions requiring complete absorption in a task. (Not having an audience is essential at this point.) Concentration time can then be increased so that the children develop the ability to stay in character for longer periods of time.

Plot Development

Early dramatic encounters will most likely have little if any plot. There may be problems and conflicts, but in general the natural dramatic play of children will be "a slice of life," with everyday happenings that are not apt to build toward a climax. However, as children become older and their story background increases, they begin to play out familiar plots, often with new endings and other innovative changes throughout the story. They begin to have a sense of a developmental sequence — beginning, middle, and ending — in stories.

The *beginning* involves the *setting* (the time and place), the *characters* (who or what), and the *situation* (what the characters want to do). In it the basic elements of the story are established. It is an important part of the plot development because what the characters want to do provides the framework for the action of the story. The *middle* involves the problem(s) that the characters encounter in attempting to achieve their objective. Obstacles may arise from the setting (weather, terrain, darkness, etc.), from conflicts with other characters, or from conflicts within a character (illness, conscience, physical weakness, etc.). The plot develops as characters try to overcome an obstacle and reach their objectives. The *ending* evolves as the final outcome of the characters' struggle.

Characterization

To portray a character effectively one must synthesize an array of cognitive and physical skills. Awareness gives children the capacity to form a clear image of the characters they play. They must understand a character's feelings, attitudes, and patterns of speech and movement. They must develop a sense of relationships — cause and effect, time and space, human interactions, and environmental influences. As actors, children must not only maintain concentration and physical control, but synchronize mental and physical activities. An actor must have an understanding of objectives and motives and be able creatively to weave the elements of the plot together into a believable whole.

Language Development

Using language in creative drama involves a sense of "rightness," the ability to sense what to say and how to say it to enhance action. Children may not feel the need for language during early experiences in drama. Young children, for example, may be observed discussing what they are doing and making plans for an episode. Yet when they play it out they do not talk. The action may, however, be accompanied by or punctuated with appropriate sound effects. Gradually children feel the need for language to carry a story along and augment what they are able to convey through their acting.

Creative drama involves developing an ear for language. Children become aware of the melody of language and discover how intonation adds to the meaning of words. They become aware of the power of language to express feeling and emotion, and to elicit vivid imagery.

Teaching Creative Drama

Developing Specific Skills

Teaching creative drama is more than letting children act out stories. It includes helping them develop certain skills. Although children will encounter dramatic skills in playing out stories and ideas, they will grow most when they have opportunity to focus on specific skills. Improvement comes with awareness and practice of skills.

A skill exercise may be used as a short, separate activity or it may be used as a warmup activity at the beginning of a lesson. Quite often practice in a skill leads very naturally to a larger creative drama activity requiring or building on that skill.

The following examples of skill exercises are given by categories. The skills are, of course, overlapping. One activity might be used for more than one purpose. You will also find activities for skill practice in the activity section and in the references listed at the end of the book.

Sensory Awareness Exercises

(Children think without oral response during the activity.)

Close your eyes. Listen to sounds outside. . . . What are they? . . . Who or what is making each sound? . . . Listen to sounds in this room. . . . What do you hear? . . . Listen to sounds within yourself. . . . Can you hear yourself breathe? . . . Listen very closely to your heart. . . . Can you hear it beat? . . .

Close your eyes. Open your hand and lay it palm down on the surface in front of you [desk, floor, lap, etc.]. . . . Think how it feels. . . . Turn your hand over with the knuckle side down. . . . Is the sense of touch different in any way? . . . Make a fist and feel the same surface. . . . Now feel with just the tips of your fingers. . . .

Close your eyes and think of your favorite food. . . . Think how it smells . . . and looks. . . . Imagine you have a bite in your mouth and think how it feels as you chew it. . . . Now imagine taking a drink of milk. . . . How does the glass feel on your lips? . . . How does the milk taste and feel as it flows through your mouth and down your throat?

Look around the room and find as many straight lines as you can . . . in the floor . . . your desk [etc.]. . . . Look for circles. . . . Look for curved lines that are not circles. . . . Look for rectangles [or right angles, etc.]. . . . What patterns do the shapes make? . . .

Imagination Exercises

You are going to hear some sounds. Listen carefully and think what the sounds you hear might be. Close your eyes and listen. [Make a series of sounds such as tapping fingers on a hard surface, shuffling feet, crumpling paper, banging a door.] Keep your eyes closed and think about the sounds you heard. . . . Where might you be? What could be happening to make those sounds? . . . Listen again and try to visualize the situation. [Repeat exact sequence.] . . . Now open your eyes. Who would like to share their ideas? [The activity may be repeated with different sounds.]

Cup your hands together and imagine that you are holding a very small pet. . . . Look at it carefully so you can remember exactly how it looks. . . . What is it doing inside your hands? . . . How does it feel? . . . Touch your pet gently. . . . Make your pet feel comfortable. . . . Now put it away in your pocket or in your desk. . . . Be very careful not to hurt it. . . .

Concentration Exercises

Imagine that a mosquito is buzzing around you. . . . Keep your eyes on it. . . . Listen to its sound as it comes nearer . . . and moves farther away. . . . It is coming very close. . . . It lights on your arm. . . . Raise your other hand and try to sneak up on it and swat it. . . . You missed. . . . Watch it buzz around . . . and around. . . . Now it is on your knee. . . . Ready. . . . *You got it.*

You are going for a walk in the woods. You come to a stream, and the only way across the stream is to walk across on a log. Step up on the end of the log. . . . Feel it under your feet. . . . The log is not very large. . . . Slowly walk across it. . . . The stream under you is swift and cold. . . . You almost lost your balance. . . . Now you are moving all right again. Be careful. . . . Ah, you are across and you step down on good, firm earth again.

Movement Exercises

Make a tight fist. . . . Relax it and let it hang loose. . . . Make your hand as large as possible. . . . Make it as small as possible. . . . Make your hand show strength. . . . Make your hand appear weak. . . .

Move your hands slowly. . . . Fast. . . . See how many different shapes your hand can form. . . .

Stand right where you are and jog in place. . . . Pick up the pace a little. . . . Slower. . . . Now in slow motion. . . . Back to regular pace. . . . You are getting very tired. . . . You slow down. . . . There are heavy weights on your ankles. . . . You can hardly lift your feet. . . . Suddenly the weights are gone and you feel light as a feather. . . . You float over the ground. . . . Stop and sit down.

Imagine you are a leaf hanging on a limb. It is autumn and you are loosening from the branch. Think what kind of leaf you are. . . . What do you look like? Make the shape. . . . Gently fall to the ground. . . . A gentle wind rustles you. . . . It grows to a stronger breeze and moves you along. . . . The breeze becomes a whirlwind and you are caught up in it. . . . It dies down and you settle back on the ground.

Characterization Exercises

The scene is a street in your town. There are several people walking down the street. Be those people. Change characters as I tell you who the different people are. Walk and act as you think the person would.

You are a businessman or woman. Your boss has just bawled you out for something you didn't do right. You are very angry. . . . (How fast would you be walking? . . . How could your hands show how you feel? . . . What if someone accidentally bumped into you? . . .)

You are a young child with a new pair of shoes. Come out of the shoe store and walk down the street. (What emotion are you feeling? . . . How do you look at people you meet? . . . How do you walk in new shoes? . . .)

You are a grandmother or grandfather taking your grandchild for a walk. (How big is the child? . . . How do you feel about him or her? . . . What things might you point out along the street? . . . What would you do if you met someone you knew? . . .)

Your leg is in a cast and you are on crutches. (How do you feel about your situation? . . . Does it hurt? . . . Is it difficult to get through the crowd? . . . How do you respond if someone bumps into you? . . . Where are your eyes as you walk? . . .)

Imagine that you are a doctor. You have just received an emergency call and hurry out to your car. But . . . you cannot find your keys to unlock the door. Be the doctor.

Speech Exercises

Recite 'Hickory, dickory dock' as if it were a magic spell . . . in disgust . . . in pleading tones . . . as if it were terribly funny.

Get a partner. . . . One of you is Neighbor *A* and one of you is Parent *B*. Neighbor *A* has just rushed next door to inform Parent *B* that his or her child threw a ball through *A*'s window. Begin where *A* rings *B*'s doorbell.

Whisper 'How much wood would a woodchuck chuck' as loudly as you can. Do not hurry. Make each word distinct.

Plot Development Exercises

Give the children a problem and let them develop a plot around it:

It is after school and you are hungry. You start to look for something to eat. . . . (Where might you look? What trouble might you have before you got to eat?)

Give the children an object and let them develop a plot involving it:

Here is a ring [an empty gift box, a small spring and screw, or a letter, etc.]. Think of a story in which this thing is very important. . . . (Where did it come from? Who last had it? Where is it now and why is it there?)

Give the children an ending and let them develop the first part of the story:

Two children are hurrying home. One says, "What are we going to tell our folks?" The other child replies, "We might as well tell them the truth. They'd find out anyhow." (What has happened to the children? Did they cause it to happen? Was anyone else involved?)

Give the children a setting or mood and let them think of something that might happen there:

It was very cold. It was snowing hard and the wind blew the snow into big drifts against the buildings and fences. A snowplow had cleared the roads only a few minutes before, but the swirling snow made it difficult to see very far. (What might happen in such a situation? Who might be involved? Why would anyone want to be out in such a storm?)

The Teaching Cycle

Creative drama begins with *planning* — mentally "setting the scene." Children think and talk about what they might do in a given situation. If, for example, they are going to eat soup as a giant would, they need a few moments to think how large a giant is, how he would sit, hold a spoon, etc. The length of the planning time varies with the activity, depending on its complexity. It may be only a few moments for each child to think independently or it may involve a longer time in which the groups makes plans. The point is that children should be ready to act before they are placed in an acting situation. Ideas will flow more readily as children develop flexibility in thinking. The teacher's role during the planning state is to facilitate ideas and help children clarify them. The teacher acts as a stimulator and discussion leader, guiding children's thinking.

Acting out is the next step. It is a time for children to try out their ideas, to put their plans into action. As the situation indicates, children may act alone or in various sized groups. As they act, the teacher circulates about the room, posing questions or encouraging children. However, the teacher should not make either positive or negative comments, as they tend to curb creative thinking.

Evaluation follows action. Once children have planned and acted out an idea, they need time to reflect and to evaluate what they have done. This process may include a sharing of actions for others to observe, or children may simply discuss what did or didn't seem to go well. To begin such a discussion the teacher might mention some examples of effective acting he or she observed or might ask, "How did you feel about the way . . . ?" The discussion should be kept objective and positive. It should focus on effective techniques and possible ways to improve acting. Often the evaluation becomes a planning session for immediate replaying of an activity. Having an opportunity to do a scene again is a valuable learning situation.

Special Teaching Techniques

Getting Started Before beginning any activity be certain that *you* and *the class* are ready. To get yourself ready, think through what you need (if anything), what you will say and do, and what you expect from the class. Write out a lesson plan of the steps you will follow. Visualize the activity, taking into consideration the possible range of responses.

Getting your class ready involves making certain that they understand general procedures and that they know what they are going to do. Be definite about set procedures such as how they are to arrange themselves (in a line? in a circle? groups of three? scattered?), spacing (have children stretch their arms out in all directions to be certain they will not come into body contact with anyone else), what direction to move if they are moving en masse (clockwise in a circle? toward one end and then back?), and what signals you will use to begin and end an activity (e.g., "Wait until I say 'Curtain' to begin.").

Side-coaching   As children act, give encouragement in the form of side-coaching that does not interrupt their activity. Don't tell children what to do; pose a question or make a comment that will lead them to ideas and discoveries on their own and that will keep them mentally involved. For example, you might say, "How can your face show that you are in pain?" "Where did the sword strike?" "How else could you . . . ?" "Feel that hot sun beating down on you." "Smell that good, fresh air this morning." or "How would you open the door if you didn't know who was outside it?"

Pacing and Declimatizing   A percussion instrument such as a gong (one cymbal and a soft mallet will do), wood block, or tambourine makes an effective accompaniment for many activities. Recorded sounds or orchestral music may also be appropriate at times. Accompaniment helps control the speed, loudness, and intensity of an activity. Varying your own voice can also influence the pace and tenor for playing out a scene. Louder and faster sounds increase activity and suggest accelerated action and feeling, whereas softer and slower sounds have a calming affect.

When children are all playing at once, you will especially need to use a calming voice or accompaniment to end an activity and declimatize them. As they act, gradually drum or talk them down, getting slower and softer. Be certain that the children come to a full stop and settle into a comfortable position before beginning a discussion of the activity.

Participation and Discipline   When children discover that creative drama does not put them on the spot and they become involved in developing their own ideas, there is usually little problem either in getting them to participate or in discipline. Remember that children get most of their cues from you. Your careful planning and attitude should make it clear from the beginning that creative drama is a regular class and not a "fun and games" time. Try to maintain a warm, accepting, and thoughtful attitude. Give positive reinforcement to ideas and conscientious effort. Help children feel that what they are doing is worthwhile and enjoyable.

Older children who have not participated in dramatic activities before may be a bit shy initially. Plan activities that capture their interest and get them mentally involved. Keep them thinking and doing rather than watching. A peer audience can be threatening to children, especially when they are already self-conscious. If the children seem hesitant, try short experiences at first and gradually build toward more involved activities. Many concentration and imagination exercises can be performed while children are in their regular seating arrangement and this may help them feel secure. Larger movement exercises in space may begin from a crouched or seated position with all children moving from the particular position at the same time. Thought-provoking activities help children become involved and make creative drama a positive experience.

Costumes and Stage Props Creative drama does not require anything but the mind and the body. Elaborate costuming or staging may actually hinder children's inner visualization and portrayal of a character. In general, it is better to emphasize children's imaginative portrayals of characters in these early years, rather than to encourage them to become dependent on tangible properties.

Simple costumes and props, however, may facilitate development of imagination. A box of hats, for example, is almost certain to spark the imagination of young children and turn them into interesting characters. You may want to collect things for a dress-up box (such as hats, scarves, neckties, and aprons) to stimulate dramatic play in children's free time.

Large wooden cubes are versatile and provocative for designing sets. A few pieces placed side by side to cover an area can be used to suggest stepping up to another floor. In the hands of creative children, cubes can become seats, fences, fireplaces, or anything else the children want them to become.

Conflict Some kind of conflict is inherent in any story plot. If there is no problem, there can be no complication or climax. Children seem particularly intrigued by physical conflict, however, and this aspect of creative drama appears fairly soon in most classes. Physical conflict will have to be dealt with rationally; you cannot have children hitting each other in the name of creative drama.

Your natural impulse may be simply to say, "No fighting." But such an approach eliminates (or attempts to eliminate) a significant element of drama. It is better to help children analyze the situation to discover the most appropriate way for characters to handle conflict. For example, you might ask, "What is the problem between the two characters; why are they fighting? How else could they settle their dispute? Which of these ways do you think would be best? Why? Would working it out that way fit the nature of the characters?"

If your children feel that a fighting scene is indicated, then they need some help in doing it safely but realistically. You might begin by discussing the role of stunt men in movies and talk about how certain actions are faked, yet look real. Discuss dramatizing a fight and ask the children how it might be done to look real without actually touching or hurting each other. Lead them to discover the importance of an actor's reaction. If one actor swings at another and the second actor *acts* hurt, the audience will believe the blow scored its mark. Let the children practice reacting to an imaginary blow until they can do so convincingly. They may also need practice as the aggressor to convey a sense of power and force without actually hitting their victim.

Sources of Ideas

Ideas for creative drama lessons can come from anything children are learning about or have an interest in. They may stem from real experiences or be totally imaginary. It's a good idea to make a collection of ideas to help you find just the right situation to develop certain skills. The following categories suggest many possible lessons:

Pictures and photographs

of people (policeman, nurse, fairy godmother, grandparents)

of places (beach, mountains, museum, bus depot, courtroom)

of industries (toy factory, furniture factory, food-processing plant)

of products (new car, ballpoint pen, lock and key)

of entertainment (skiing, ball game, skating)

of fantasy (abstract designs, imaginary creatures)

of science (growth cycles, research laboratory, volcano)

of travel (trains, buses, airplanes, bicycles)

Music

instruments

records (2001: *A Space Odyssey, The Sorcerer's Apprentice, Grand Canyon Suite, Parade of the Wooden Soldiers*)

Objects

historical (coin, old book)

from nature (seashell, rock)

man-made (broken piece of glass, key)

Stories and books

adventure

biography

science fiction

historical

myths and legends

Newspapers

discoveries

events

comic strips

classified ads

Situations

no one was home

an early spring morning

the circus was in town

School subjects

story in reading class

scientific information

social studies concepts

math story problems

athletic events

First lines

"There in the fresh snow was the largest footprint the children had ever seen."

"As Mark walked home he kept thinking about what Old Gus had said. Maybe there really was something strange going on at night in the cemetery."

Last lines

"Finally the last car disappeared down the street."

"Marquita hugged her mother hard. It was so good to be home again."

Simple costume items

shoes

hats

badges

fancy jewelry

masks

capes

wigs

As you plan a lesson, identify a specific focus for the dramatization. A vague "Act out something in this picture" is almost certain to yield negative results. First, think what you want the children to gain from the experience. Do you want them to develop sensory awareness? to assume another's point of view? to develop a story? to create a mood? to understand cause and effect? to comprehend a process? Once you have identified the purpose of the activity, decide how you will guide children's thinking and prepare them for the experience. Planning with the children must include setting the parameters — *which* episode, *where, when,* and *who* or *what.* When you use a stimulus such as those we have suggested, you might begin by eliciting interpretations and ideas and then select one idea with good possibilities to act out; you might pose a problem suggested by the stimulus and have the group figure out a solution; or, you might prepare a questioning strategy that will lead the children into the activity. Whatever you choose, make certain that children are aware of their objective and that the nature of the activity has been adequately defined. Structure is important. It not only helps children feel "safe," but it gives the necessary focus to a task to allow productive and creative thinking.

Illustrative Lessons

Two examples of creative drama are given here. The first was planned solely as a creative drama lesson to develop specific drama skills. It illustrates a separate subject approach in which creative drama is taught for its own sake. The second example follows an integrated approach and illustrates how dramatic experience may evolve from ongoing classroom work. In the lesson a short dramatic activity was used as an interesting and effective way to help children develop an understanding of something they were studying. This is one way to include creative drama in the school day without adding another subject to the existing curriculum.

Lesson I: A Separate-Subject Approach

Background The lesson was used with second-graders. The objective was to help the children develop a concept of plot development: that a story has a beginning, middle, and end.

Warmup exercise To limber up the children's minds and bodies, the teacher began the lesson with a short movement exercise. First he asked the children to space themselves around the room so that they could reach in all directions without touching anyone else. Then he asked them to imagine that they were washing a big picture window with spray cleaner and a large cloth. They were given the signal to begin and they went to work. As they worked, the teacher side-coached: "See those fly specks. . . . You'll have to rub hard. . . . Reach up high to get the upper part of the window.   Higher Now the corners. . . . Now carefully go over the whole window with a clean part of your cloth. . . . Stand back and get a good look at it in the light. . . . Do you see any streaks? . . . You'd better take care of that one down there in the right hand corner. . . . That's good. . . . Stop." The children moved closer together and sat down on the floor.

Planning The teacher asked if anyone knew how the stores downtown got cleaned. Children suggested several ideas, but seemingly none of them had thought about it before. The teacher explained that businesses usually had people come in at night to clean while the stores were empty. He asked the children to close their eyes and imagine how a toy store would look at night after everyone had gone home. Then they opened their eyes and talked about the way they thought the store would look and the things that would need to be done to clean it up for morning: sweeping the floor, dusting, and cleaning the windows. The teacher asked how they might act out cleaning a toy store, and after some discussion the children decided that three people would do the cleaning and the rest of them would be toys.

Acting Three children from among the volunteers were chosen to be the cleaners, and the other children decided what toys they wanted to be and how they could make their bodies into that shape. When they were in character and ready, the teacher called "Begin" and the cleaners began to clean the store. After a few moments, he called, "Curtain," and the children sat down.

Discussing The teacher commended the children on their ability to hold still and to look like real toys that couldn't move. He asked if anyone had a problem. One of the cleaners suggested that they got in each other's way when they all tried to do the same thing and thought it would be better if they each did different jobs. The others agreed. One little girl said she was a ballerina doll but needed something to help hold her up. She decided to move where she could lean on the wall to keep her balance. One child didn't want to be a cleaner, but after someone else suggested that he could be the boss, the boy decided the plan was all right.

Then the teacher asked the children if they could think of anything interesting that might happen while the cleaners were in the toy store. Children suggested a robbery, someone getting hurt, and the lights going out so they couldn't see. The teacher wondered aloud if something might happen to the toys, too. Then someone suggested that the lights could go out and while they were out the toys would come to life. Another added that they could do the cleaning while the cleaners went to look for a way to turn the lights back on.

The teacher noted that the plan did sound like an interesting middle for their play and asked how they might end it. The children finally agreed that the lights would come on, the cleaners would come back to finish their jobs and find everything done. They would be surprised and leave.

Acting The children took their places again and the teacher reviewed what they were going to do: First the toys would be alone in the store. Then the cleaners would come in and start cleaning. The teacher would say "Click" when the lights went out and the cleaners would leave to find the fuse box. Then the toys would finish the cleaning just as the lights came back on and hurry back to their places. The cleaners would come in, be surprised, and leave. The children acted it out.

Discussing The teacher asked for volunteers to demonstrate their action for the rest of the class. Groups of four acted at a time and the class discussed which actions seemed most real. They talked about the parts of the play they liked best and about ways they could improve certain parts if they were to do it again. As a final summary the teacher asked the children to tell the three parts of their play: beginning, middle, and ending.

Although this lesson focused specifically on creative drama, you can see many interrelationships between the skills and understandings in the lesson and in other language arts lessons. Children were using language to help them conceptualize and organize and to communicate ideas. In addition, they were learning that character, setting, and situational problems contribute to plot development. This is an important understanding for writing and reading stories. Thus, the thinking and language skills children gained were not limited to creative drama. Many of them were related to the larger language arts curriculum, and children would encounter them again in other reading, writing, listening, and speaking contexts.

Lesson II: An Integrated Approach

Background A group of fourth-graders was studying pioneer life. Because they had never seen a real log cabin that had been built with hand tools, the teacher decided to use creative drama to develop an understanding of the process and the difficulties the pioneers encountered.

Planning The teacher showed the children outside and inside views of a log cabin. They talked about the kinds of material the pioneers used and where it came from. They had previously read a story in which there was a house-raising and had seen many modern homes being constructed. They talked about the kinds of tools the pioneers had to work with and made a list of the things that would have to be done to build a log cabin. Then groups were formed to act out each task and the children determined where in the room each activity should take place to simulate a community effort in building a log cabin.

Acting Children went to their places. The teacher said, "Begin," and they began working. As they worked, the teacher moved among the groups offering commendations and posing questions to shape thinking (e.g., "I can tell you have a heavy ax." "Why are you doing this and how do you feel about it?" "How big is that tree? How many chops will it take to cut it down?" "How might you hold your ax to take out the deepest bite?").

Discussing After a few minutes, the teacher called "Curtain" and asked the children to come back to their seats. She opened the discussion with "I could tell by the expressions on your faces that that was hard work. I could almost see the wood chips fly as your axes came down." Then she asked the children to describe at what point in the activity they had felt most like a pioneer. Children responded thoughtfully, describing high points. Then she asked them to compare building a log cabin with building a house today. A general discussion followed, with children pooling and clarifying their knowledge of building houses then and now. Then the teacher asked a final discussion question: "If you had the choice of having a log cabin built like the pioneers built them or of having a home built by a modern builder, which one would you choose, and why?" Again, many ideas having to do with size, work involved, facilities, and durability were explored. At the end of the activity there was little doubt that the children had a much better understanding of home construction and life in general during pioneer times.

In this situation, creative drama was used as a teaching tool. The primary objective of the lesson was to teach social studies concepts. However, the activity also gave children an opportunity to develop dramatic skills. In visualizing and acting out a real-life situation from earlier days, children were given practice in concentrating, in using their imagination, and in gaining physical control.

Puppets

Puppets provide another form of dramatic activity. Although they do not require children to respond with their own bodies, puppets stimulate oral language and involve most of the other elements of creative drama. Children who are hesitant to talk themselves are often quite comfortable talking through a puppet. Puppets are fun to make and offer many possibilities for creating a wide range of characters. There are suitable puppets for children at all levels of ability.

As a general rule children derive more satisfaction from simple puppets than they do from more difficult ones. They may lose interest if a puppet takes too long to make. Also, when operating a puppet demands too much attention, children are unable to get into character satisfactorily and have difficulty creating an adequate flow of language. In planning work with puppets, it is wise to consider the objectives of the lesson and then select the type of puppet that will best serve your purpose.

Stick Puppets

Head only A small sphere stuck on the end of a stick becomes a puppet in the imagination of children (Figure 6-1). For example, an eraser stuck on a pencil can be anything a child wants it to be. All you need is a supply of small dowels or other sticks and a variety of head shapes (styrofoam balls, rubber balls, ping pong balls, etc.).

Children draw or paint on features, then poke, tie, or glue the head to the stick, and the puppet is done.

Variations (Figure 6-2): Make the head on the back of a wooden spoon and there will be no need to attach another handle.

Stuff a piece of cloth or tissue for a head. Start with a square or circle of material. Wad up paper or other filling to make a ball, gather the material around it, and tie it to a stick. The sides of the cloth may hang down to make clothes for the puppet. Draw on features and decorate. (These puppets make especially good ghosts for Halloween.)

Whole body (Figure 6-3) Make children's drawings into puppets. Draw and cut figures from heavy paper and staple or glue them to sticks. A second identical shape may be attached to the other side of the stick for a back view. For three-dimensional figures shape them out of a modeling material that dries in the air. Be certain to make a hole for inserting the stick while the material is still pliable.

Variations of whole body puppets (Figure 6-4): Using heavy paper or tagboard, make the arms and legs as separate pieces and fasten them together at the joints with paper brads. Then attach the arms and legs to the rest of the body. Even though the children don't string these up as marionettes, the looseness of the figures provides some body movement.

Paper Bag Puppets

Use small paper bags to make talking puppets (lunch-size bags are good). Make a face on the bottom part of the bag by adding drawn or cut and glued paper features as shown in Figure 6-5. Add any other features appropriate to the character such as hair, glasses, mustache, ears, nose, etc. The entire bag may be colored (the body). To operate the puppets, children insert their hands up into the bags and open and close their hands to make the puppets open and close their mouths.

Paper Plate Puppets

The simplest paper plate puppet is the head-and-stick type in which the whole paper plate is used as a head puppet (Figure 6-6).

Variations of paper plate puppets: Cut a plate in two pieces and hinge the parts together on one side with a paper brad. This makes a big-mouthed puppet as shown in Figure 6-7. Fasten a stick to the back of each half so the operator can open and close the mouth.

Or, use two paper plates to make a puppet with pockets for the hands. Cut one plate in two and set it aside (Figure 6-8a). Fold the

FIGURE 6-1

FIGURE 6-2

FIGURE 6-3

FIGURE 6-4

FIGURE 6-5

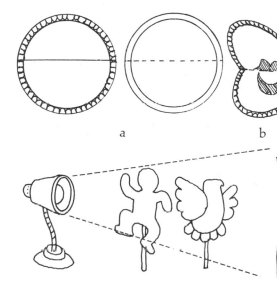

FIGURE 6-6

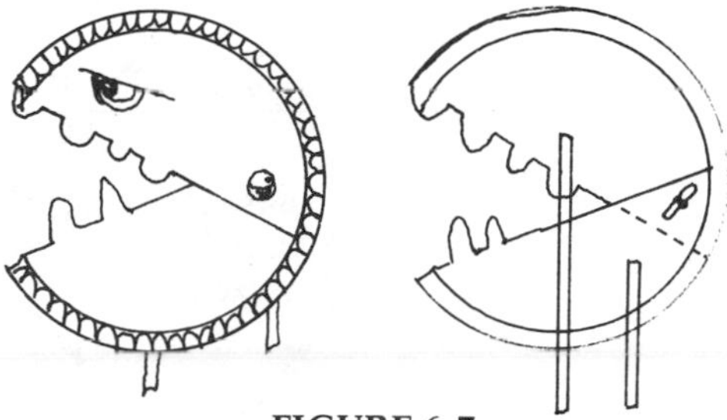

FIGURE 6-7

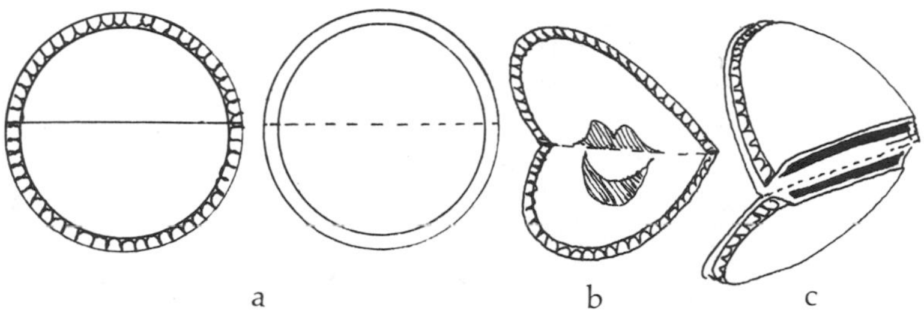

FIGURE 6-8　　　　a　　　　　　　　b　　　　　　c

FIGURE 6-9

FIGURE 6-10

FIGURE 6-11

FIGURE 6-12

FIGURE 6-13

FIGURE 6-14

FIGURE 6-15   a   b

other plate in half so the bottom sides are together. Open it back up and make a face on the plate, being careful to make the mouth right on the fold (Figure 6-8b). Glue the rims of the two paper plate halves to the first plate so that the concave surfaces are facing and the opening is opposite the fold (Figure 6-8c). (Let the glue dry thoroughly before children try to operate their puppets.) The children insert their fingers and thumbs into the slots to open and close the puppets.

Shadow Puppets

Shadow puppets are similar to stick puppets except that only the shape (the silhouette) is important. Cut figures out of cardboard or heavy paper (you may need to glue two thicknesses together) and attach them to thin sticks or stiff wire.

You will need an old sheet to serve as a screen, and a light (one with a reflector is best). The children move their puppets so they cast a shadow on the back of the screen as shown in Figure 6-9.

Finger Puppets

Finger puppets are made small enough to just fit on the tip of a finger. Children draw small heads or full body characters on heavy paper and cut them out. These are glued to bands that slip over the tips of the children's fingers (Figure 6-10).

Variations of finger puppets: Make full body puppets, but either leave off their legs or cut them after they are made. Cut finger-sized holes in the trunk of the body. Children insert their index and middle fingers through the holes to form legs as shown in Figure 6-11. (These are fun; the puppets can really walk!)

Glove and Sock Puppets

Use old mittens, gloves, or socks for ready-made hand puppets. On mittens and gloves the thumb forms the lower jaw for a side view of a character, or the palm or back can be the face.

Old socks can be used as is or cut across the toe and a mouth sewn in. Add button eyes, yarn hair, etc. to create the character (Figure 6-12).

Sewn Puppets

Sewn puppets are more difficult but versatile and fun to make. First, make a pattern like the one in Figure 6-13 that fits comfortably over a child's hand. Cut two pieces of felt or other cloth and sew them together to make a mitt. Younger children will need to make a simple running stitch and an outside seam. Older children might sew the right sides together and then turn the puppet to make the seams inside. (Perhaps a few parents would be willing to do this on a sewing machine.)

These basic patterns may then be decorated in any way to make different characters, either animal or human. (For some animals, such as a lion, the head should be made larger.) Glue or sew on clothing and features made from scraps (felt, yarn, lace, calico, buttons, braid, beads, etc.).

Mix and Match Puppets

By making separate heads and bodies, children may mix and match parts for greater variety of characters. The neck hole in the heads permits various bodies to be inserted for changes.

Children first make the heads by forming papier-mâché over a well-greased balloon (Vaseline is good) with an attached tube or roll of heavy paper for the neck. Let the head dry; deflate the balloon and remove. Paint features on the head and spray it with clear lacquer. Hair may be glued on.

The bodies are made much like those of sewn puppets but the head part is trimmed down to become the neck. Clothing may be made in any length and style (ball gowns, blue jeans, animal fur).

To use a puppet, place the body over the hand and add a head on top, as shown in Figure 6-14.

Marionettes

Marionettes can be quite complex, both to make and to operate. Younger children should make very simple ones by stringing such things as large beads, spools, clay balls, nuts, or cardboard circles (Figure 6-15a). Strings attached at the knee will make the puppet walk.

Older children may make doll like cloth bodies and separate clothing. These require a row of stitching at the joints so the puppet will bend. Strings are attached to the knees, wrists, head, and upper back. Threading the strings through a wooden frame as in Figure 6-15b helps keep the strings separated. Because these puppets are more difficult, children will need practice in learning to manipulate them.

Puppet Stages

Children often use puppets without any other props. However, if they prefer getting behind something so that only their puppets show, there are many ways to improvise a stage. The children may simply crouch down behind their desks and use the desk top as a stage, or they may devise a stage from classroom furniture. A small table turned on its side, a low portable counter or coat closet, a low screen, or a piece of paper or cloth stretched across a doorway also makes an effective stage.

A stage for stick puppets may be made from a cardboard box. Turn the box on its side and add scenery inside as in a diorama. Cut slots in the bottom of the box (the surface that was originally the side) so the puppets can be inserted and moved back and forth across the stage. (It is best to use popsicle sticks or tongue depressors in making puppets for this kind of stage.)

Box stages also work well for finger puppets. The slots, of course, will need to be cut wider to accommodate the children's fingers. Or, if puppets are not going to move around, cut round holes instead of slots.

Screen type stages are not difficult to make and are nice to have if you plan to do a lot with puppets. Use three large pieces of a building board material plus two strips for top and bottom braces. Assemble the sides and front with hinges so the screen can be folded up when not in use. Notch the strips to slide over the top and bottom edges of the screen and brace it firmly.

In Summary

Creative drama is a way of simulating real-life experiences in the classroom. It provides a laboratory for exploring and manipulating experiences and ideas. These activities are important for elementary schoolchildren because their learning is highly dependent on concrete experience; they learn by doing. For this reason creative drama ought to play an important role in the curriculum.

Creative drama is not the same as children's theater. It is concerned with process whereas the purpose of children's theater is production. Creative drama stimulates children's awareness and thinking by putting them right into the middle of a situation. It helps them get inside another person or thing and explore different points of view and ways of looking at situations. Through such creative drama experiences children learn to understand themselves, others, and their environment better. At the same time, they develop important language arts knowledge and skills.

Teaching creative drama is helping children learn to think logically and creatively and to control their actions. Exercises are designed to provide practice in concentration, in using imagination, in control of movement, in developing characterization, in using language effectively, and in dealing with problems through plot development. In short, creative drama lessons help children develop control of their minds and their bodies.

Puppets are another form of creative drama. In using puppets, children project their thoughts into the actions and words of puppet characters. Simple puppets are usually best, because they do not demand too much attention from children. Therefore, they allow children to think about what they are doing and saying.

Learning Objectives

COGNITIVE OBJECTIVES

Primary Grades

Children will

see themselves as unique individuals.

develop empathy.

be sensitive to their environment.

understand simple relationships.

increase the flow of ideas.

be able to plan and organize.

be able to think critically.

be able to communicate feelings and ideas.

expand their vocabulary and increase their fluency in oral language.

Middle Grades

Children will

improve and expand all primary-grade objectives.

be able to use language precisely to convey information, feelings, and moods.

understand time/space and cause/effect relationships.

be able to apply concepts of plot development in creating stories.

understand the interrelationships between people and their environment.

integrate the ideas of others into their own thinking.

develop an intellectual understanding of the art of drama.

AFFECTIVE OBJECTIVES

Children will

feel good about themselves.

develop independence in thought and action.

become sensitive to other people.

contribute and cooperate in group activities.

appreciate their environment.

enjoy communicating through creative drama.

appreciate drama as an art.

Suggested Learning Activities

DRAMATIC PLAY IDEAS

making cookies

cleaning up your room

a birthday party

bathing the dog

washing the car

going fishing

getting ready to go somewhere

putting out a fire

helping at an accident

building a road

moving day

finding buried treasure

EXPLORATION ACTIVITIES

Make your body as small as you can. . . . Now slowly change to make your body as large as you can. . . . Quickly get small again. . . . How do you feel? (Just think.) . . . Now get very small again. . . . How do you feel? What might you be?

Move only a part of your body at one time . . . right toes . . . right foot . . . right knee . . . right leg . . . left toes . . . left foot . . . left knee . . . left leg . . . your forehead . . . eyes . . . nose . . . mouth . . . tongue . . . head . . . your right thumb . . . right fingers . . . right hand . . . right elbow . . . right arm . . . left thumb . . . left fingers . . . left hand . . . left elbow . . . left arm . . . your shoulders . . . waist . . . hips . . . Now move all the parts of your body at once.

(This activity can also be done as cumulative action.)

There are three levels of movement: low, middle, and high. Move low in space. . . . Move low and slow. . . . What are you? (Think only.) . . . Move low and fast. . . . What are you? . . . Move slowly in middle space. . . . See how many different ways you can move slowly in middle space. . . . Move fast in middle space. . . . Move a different way. . . . Move high in space . . . higher . . . What moves this way? . . . Gradually move faster . . . faster . . . slower . . . slower . . . STOP.

Try saying "Hello" as many different ways as you can. What meaning is behind each way of saying it? (Discuss.)

(Follow the same procedure with "No" and "Come here.")

IMAGINATION ACTIVITIES

Walk in the wind.
   in deep snow.
   in the rain.
   in mud puddles.
   in soft sand.
   in tall grass.

Walk barefoot on gravel.
   on hot pavement.
   in mud.
   on a soft green lawn.
   in a cool mountain stream.

You are a big block of ice sitting in the hot sun. Slowly the heat of the sun causes you to melt. . . .

You are a balloon. Someone blows you up and ties a string around you. . . . They let go for just a moment and you rise up high in the air . . . and higher . . . and float along in the sky. . . . The wind blows you faster . . . and pulls you down toward the earth. . . . It stops and you float along again in the sky . . . under the warm sun. . . .

You are a piece of bread dough rolled up in a ball. Someone begins to knead you . . . this way . . . and that way. . . . They start to roll you out flat to make a cinnamon loaf. . . . You are very elastic and it is difficult to make you thin. . . . The rolling pin pushes hard on you, flattens you a little . . . but with each roll you creep back up a little. . . . Gradually you are stretched out flat. . . . They coat you with butter and cinnamon and sugar. . . . It tickles. . . . Gently they roll you up and put you in a pan to rise. . . .

Get into groups of three. Play catch with an imaginary ball. Feel its size and weight as you catch and throw it. (Vary the kind of ball: ping pong, baseball, football, basketball, etc.)

Get into groups of five and make a circle. Pass a lively, green frog around the circle . . . a thorny rose . . . sticky taffy . . . a shrunken head . . . an expensive vase . . . a heavy box . . . a kite with a long tail and a ball of string . . . a feather . . . a leaky bucket of dirty water. . . .

PANTOMIME

making a bed

brushing your teeth

mowing the lawn

opening a letter with a check to you

putting up an umbrella

getting into a car and starting it

looking up something in a dictionary

turning on the television and selecting a program

skating

walking into a room filled with stale smoke and leftover food

painting a picture

pushing a heavily laden wheelbarrow

getting something from a high shelf in the closet

playing with a kitten

eating spaghetti

watching a funny movie

EXPRESSING FEELINGS AND ATTITUDES

Show that you are frightened.
> you are happy.
> you are lazy.
> you are sad.
> you are suspicious.
> you are angry.
> you are strong.
> you are weak.
> you are tired.
> you are disgusted.
> you are sleepy.
> you are mean.

ADDING WORDS TO ACTION

You are a shopper in a busy store on a sale day. Crowds jostle you about but you are determined to get a bargain — and you do. Talk as if you were thinking out loud as you act out the scene.

You are a lost child in a supermarket. You can't find your mother anywhere. How do all those towering shelves look to you? the meat counter? the frozen food section? the bakery? Talk as if you are thinking out loud as you act out the experience.

You are a spectator at a ball game. Select any game you know well. What is happening? What should the players do? How should the referee call the plays? Talk as if you were thinking out loud as you act out the scene.

You are a child walking to school on the first day in a new school. What type of neighborhood are you in? Do you have to watch out for anything? Do you have to cross any streets? Does anyone join you? Talk as if you are thinking out loud as you walk along.

Imagine yourself as another person (a witch, a clown, a small child, a schoolteacher, a king or a queen, a lonely old lady, etc.) opening a birthday present. What do you think and do as you open the present? What is in the present? How do you feel about it? How will you respond to the giver (what will you do or say)? Talk as if you are thinking aloud as you open the present.

You are a well-dressed older man sitting on a park bench. Why are you here? What is the weather like? What can you see from where you sit? Does anyone or anything come near you? What are you thinking? Talk as if you were thinking out loud as you act out the scene.

PARTNER ACTIVITIES

Bus Driver and Rider. A rider discovers he or she doesn't have any money. What do the driver and the rider say and do? Act it out.

Employer and Employee. The employer is firing the employee. Decide what the job is and where the two are. What will each person say and do? Act it out.

Waitress and Unhappy Customer. Something is wrong with the food or service. What is the problem? What will the customer say and do?

How will the waitress handle the situation? Act it out.

Lost in a Cave. Two friends wander into an exciting-looking cave. Once inside, however, they can't find their way out. What is it like in there? How do they try to get out? What finally happens? Act it out.

Paper Boy/Girl and Customer. A customer telephones to find out why the paper hasn't been delivered. The paperboy or papergirl definitely remembers delivering it. What could have happened to it? Does the customer believe the child? What happens? Begin with the phone ringing. Act it out.

SMALL-GROUP ACTIVITIES

Time Machine. Imagine that a time machine has taken you back or ahead in time. Play out a family having breakfast. Talk about what you are eating and what each of you will do that day.

Baseball. Imagine that you are playing a game of baseball. Follow the ball with your eyes as it is pitched, caught, batted, etc. Plan the action and the dialog of the game. Then play it out.

Boston Tea Party. Imagine that you are the group of colonists disguised as Indians and act out throwing the tea overboard.

Vacation Planning. Imagine that you are a family trying to decide where you will go for your vacation this year. Discuss possible vacations and try to convince the others to want to go where you want to go.

Scenes from Poetry. Find poems that tell about interesting situations or activities ("Rodeo" by Lueders, "The Base Stealer" by Francis, "Child on Top of a Greenhouse" by Roethke, etc.) and act out the scene.

PLAYING A STORY

Choose an idea and develop it into a play. Plan a beginning, middle, and ending. Decide who the characters will be and the kind of person each will be.

It is dark and you are driving home from a long vacation. You take a shortcut through the mountains so you can get home sooner. It is a lonely road; you have not seen any other cars or houses since you left the main road. Your car begins to make a strange sound and then stops. . . .

It is after closing hours in a large department store when you discover that you have lingered too long. Everyone else is gone. You try each door, but they are all locked tight. . . .

Tomorrow is your mother's birthday and you are going to catch the bus to town to buy her a present. As you wait for the bus, a car comes by and stops. . . .

Your family has gone on a picnic. When you are ready to come home you can't find your dog. . . .

You have just moved into a new house and are surprised to find that a ghost lives there. It is not a haunting ghost, but a friendly ghost. It likes to go places with you and do things for you. Only you and your family can see it. No one else even knows that it exists. One day . . .

You are walking down a neighborhood street, and as you go by a house you happen to glance at the window and notice two people scuffling. One person is trying to escape. . . .

Two astronauts have just been shipwrecked on a strange planet. As they crawl out of their badly damaged spaceship they hear strange and beautiful music. . . .

Suggestions for Further Reading

Gardner, Richard. *101 Hand Puppets*. New York: David McKay Company, 1962.

Heinig, Ruth Beall, and Lydia Stillwell. *Creative Drama for the Classroom Teacher*. 2nd ed. Englewood Cliffs, N.J.: Prentice-Hall, 1981.

McIntyre, Barbara. *Creative Drama in the Elementary School*. Itasca, Ill.: F. E. Peacock, 1974.

Siks, Geraldine Brain. *Drama with Children*. New York: Harper and Row, 1977.

Stewig, John W. *Spontaneous Drama. A Language Art*. Columbus, Ohio: Charles E. Merrill, 1973.

Wagner, Betty Jane. *Dorothy Heathcote: Drama as a Learning Medium*. Washington, D.C.: National Education Association, 1976.

Way, Brian. *Development through Drama*. London: Longman, 1967.

7
Written Composition

History has taught us that writing is important to the individual during each stage of life. Learning to help children gain confidence and experience in writing is an important part of the classroom teacher's role. Even for the very young, writing is a means of thinking, learning, and being. Carefully stimulated and supported writing experiences enhance any child's development.

Haley-James (1981, p. ix)

___

CHAPTER PREVIEW

Think about the writing skills you use. How and when did you acquire them? Do you think you might have learned them in a better way? Just giving children writing assignments to do doesn't necessarily mean that they will develop skill in writing. It may only cause them to practice undesirable habits (and possibly even to hate writing). In this chapter we will examine the process of writing and what is involved in different kinds of writing. We will also identify skills that contribute to good writing and suggest ways to help children improve their writing ability.

QUESTIONS TO THINK ABOUT AS YOU READ

What does the writing process involve?

What kinds of writing should children experience in school?

How can I encourage children to write?

Why and how should children's writing be evaluated?

How can I help children develop needed writing skills?

What should I do if children don't want to write?

The ability to write is highly valued in our society. That fact is evident in the current concern over writing deficiencies among recent graduates. Young children sense the importance of writing and want to learn how to write. Long before most of them come to school they have experimented with lines of squiggles they call "writing." Although their attempts to write fail to communicate the messages in their heads to others at this stage, they are developing important concepts about writing and their efforts should be encouraged (Clay, 1982; King, 1980).

Careful nurturing is necessary if children are to become good writers. They not only need to develop facility in oral language, but they need to have appropriate experiences with written language. They need to be read to. They need opportunities to peruse and enjoy books on their own. They need to write and to observe others writing. They also need continued guidance in structuring their ideas and in learning the forms and conventions of writing.

The Writing Process

The process of writing — what writers actually do, the choices they make, and the factors inherent in their conscious and unconscious decisions — continues to intrigue and challenge teachers and researchers. The act of writing is both complex and abstract. As young children mature they discover that words do not unconsciously tumble out onto the page in response to thought or momentary impulse. Instead, one must hold thoughts in the mind while carefully translating words into their visual symbols. Writing is a demanding task, and skill in writing does not develop as easily as skill in speaking. Vygotsky explains,

> Written speech is a separate linguistic function, differing from oral speech in both structure and mode of functioning. Even its minimal development requires a high level of abstraction. It is speech in thought and image only, lacking the musical, expressive, intonational qualities of oral speech. In learning to write, the child must disengage himself from the sensory aspect of speech and replace words by images of words. Speech that is merely imagined and that requires symbolization of the sound image in written signs (i.e., a second degree of symbolization) naturally must be as much harder than oral speech for the child as algebra is harder than arithmetic. (1962, pp. 98, 99)

Writing, getting ideas put down on paper, involves more than developing automatic encoding responses. Content must be thoughtfully dealt with; ideas and information must be clearly conveyed and logically organized. Even most adult writers find writing hard work. Professional writers have described the intense thought and decision-making they must go through in writing something for publication. Often page after page goes into the wastebasket as they struggle to blend their ideas into a "right" and satisfying composition.

Writing is a complex process. It involves generating and developing ideas, analyzing meanings, and making many decisions about content, form, organization, and style. Although the process may vary somewhat from one writer to another, it typically includes the following stages: prewriting, writing, and rewriting.

Prewriting

Before writers can write something down they must have something they want to say. The prewriting stage involves latching onto an idea or topic and getting ready to write about it. Henry James talks about the "germ" of a story and the importance of having "a good eye for a subject." Referring to his own writing, he says, "most of the stories straining to shape under my hand have sprung from a single small seed, a seed as minute and windblown as that casual hint . . . dropped unwittingly by my neighbor, a mere floating particle in the stream of talk" (1952, p. 147).

Once writers have an idea, they usually need an incubation period in which to mull it over in preparation for writing. Young children often draw pictures as a way of clarifying ideas. More experienced writers may simply think about the framework of their story: the characters, setting, and plot. Talking about their ideas is often important at this stage. Groups of children might share and discuss ideas and topics they are interested in, setting boundaries, establishing sequences, and finding expressive vocabulary and form. Discussion serves as a rehearsal, a time for clarifying, expanding, and refining thoughts and for trying out language.

Writing a report or essay, even when a topic has been assigned, involves a somewhat similar process. Once identified, the topic must still be brought into focus. During the prewriting time, writers may need to observe, read, listen, and reflect in order to set parameters and organize information to be presented.

Writing

In time, writers begin to feel ready to write. How long it takes one to move to this point depends on the individual and the nature of the writing project. Readiness to begin writing does not always mean that the composition is completely shaped, either in the writer's head or on notepaper. It means that the writer feels an urge to start getting something down. Dorothy Canfield describes her writing:

> Now the materials were ready, the characters fully alive in my mind and entirely visualized. . . . The story was now ready to write. I drew a long breath of mingled anticipation and apprehension, somewhat as you do when you stand, breathing quickly, balanced on your skis, at the top of a long white slope you are not sure you are clever enough to manage. (1952, p. 173)

Once sentences begin to come, it is important to get them down on paper. Form and spelling are secondary at this point; they can be dealt with later. Now the flow of words must take precedence. Because writing a composition involves deep concentration, children should have as few interruptions as possible. Translating their thoughts and feelings into words for an imagined audience involves children in a sort of mental role-playing. If they are disturbed at an intense moment they may never be able to recapture it in quite the same way again.

Rewriting

When the first draft is completed, writers tend to feel relief, but they may not feel satisfaction. Their thoughts have been given voice, but it may not be a particularly effective voice. *If the written composition is to be shared*, it will require some additional work to get it into "public" form. Each sentence needs to be read and reread with a listening ear and revised as necessary to make it clear and "right." Writing workshops involving a small group of peers can be very helpful at this stage. Children read their compositions aloud to the group, and peers offer feedback and suggestions. Members of the group may point out particularly well chosen words or effective sections. Or, they may question the logic of something or point out a part that doesn't "sound right." Together they try to solve the problem, offering suggestions and trying out optional approaches.

A sense of the need to rewrite develops as children become more aware of effective writing. Remember that the mere act of writing is difficult for young children; they tend to feel satisfaction from the fact that they have written *something*. Corrections and changes for them are minimal, perhaps a respelling here and a capital letter there. For older children, a need to say what they intended to say develops. They become aware that changes in wording and reorganization are sometimes necessary if their written product is to communicate their meanings and intentions.

Revision is a necessary aspect of good writing, and children may need to revise and rewrite their compositions more than once. Good writers usually do. However, it is important that revision be an outgrowth of children's own insights and critical reflection. Feedback from peers and teachers, extensive exposure to good literature, and discussions that cause children to think and evaluate are essential to developing a heightened awareness of effective writing, and hence, the need to revise. (It should be understood that the process described here refers to writing in which a *product* is the goal. Children write for many different reasons and they should not be expected to work all of their writing up to this final form.)

The Writing Environment

The classroom environment can be a powerful force in helping children develop writing competence. An ideal environment stimulates a flow of language and subtly shapes positive attitudes toward writing. It not only motivates children to write but provides a support system that makes satisfying experiences possible. Some important characteristics of this kind of environment are discussed here.

A good writing environment allows children to develop at their own pace. Teachers need to observe children very carefully and become aware of each child's developmental time line. They collect data by observing children at writing tasks, noting their queries and comments, and analyzing samples of their writing. With this knowledge teachers modify their expectations and responses, keeping in time with the child's internal clock. They should note which children need more prewriting discussion or prompts to generate ideas, which children need more input and encouragement during the writing stage, and which children are ready to thoughtfully analyze their work and rewrite. It is essential that children not be given too much instruction too early, but that they be guided through meaningful experiences that allow them to learn and grow as much as they are able.

A good writing environment provides intellectual stimulation. Interesting objects, books, pictures, and other resources that invite exploration and study ought to be in evidence in the classroom. For example, a special bulletin board might feature pictures and articles from the daily newspaper or from recent periodicals. There might be displays from the natural sciences (e.g., various kinds of rocks, geodes, seashells, molds, fungi, cones, leaves, grasses, insects). Posters, pamphlets, photographs, charts, and graphs offer other possibilities. Keeping these displays fresh is important. Items need to be changed or added frequently to keep interest high.

Interesting items in the room generate thought and spontaneous discussions quite naturally. Ideas and interaction may be further encouraged by labeling things (parts of a butterfly, a bicycle, diving equipment); adding captions ("This crater was formed by a meteor." "The Astrodome can hold 50,000 people."); and posing questions ("How are these leaves different?" "Which of these animals have backbones?").

A good writing environment is arranged spatially to facilitate several kinds of activities. Arranging the room to permit talk zones and quiet zones encourages ongoing verbal interaction. Materials and displays that are planned to stimulate talk should be placed in a part of the room where discussion will not interfere with other activities. Adequate space for children to group around displays is also important. Young children, especially, need to interact physically with objects. For example, feeling a texture is an integral part of "seeing" it.

Quiet zones are important; they allow children to get away from the mainstream of class activities to think and compose. Even visual barriers may be beneficial to some students; facing another child or sitting with a view of the playground can be distracting. Large packing crates may be used as writing carrels or small trifold cardboard screens may be set up on children's desks or tables to define their private work areas.

A good writing environment provides writing resources. Having writing supplies and reference materials readily available can be motivational as well as functional. These materials might include different sizes, shapes, and colors of paper and a variety of writing tools — pens, pencils, and typewriters. Adding-machine tape and colored ink sticks, for example, make comic strip story-writing a special delight. Reference materials such as a dictionary, a thesaurus, special word lists, punctuation and capitalization charts, and a proofreading checklist facilitate careful work and are valuable writing aids.

A good writing environment is noncritical and emotionally safe. A classroom atmosphere that is positive, objective, and expectant invites children to try out ideas and to experiment with language. Sharing an observation or a composition always involves risk. Unless children feel accepted and secure they will not be willing to risk expressing their personal knowledge and thoughts or revealing their level of writing competence. A supportive atmosphere is created by a teacher who accepts children's efforts, is sensitive to their needs, and encourages children to be considerate and accepting of one another. Such an atmosphere encourages them to try without fear of criticism or humiliation.

A good writing environment gives evidence that writing is valued. Displays of children's work and the sharing of apt phrases and well-written selections plus attention to helping children improve their skills all suggest that writing is a worthy activity. Children's efforts may be positively reinforced in many ways besides marks on their papers. Attentive listening as a child struggles to express an idea, a spontaneous chuckle in response to humorous writing; or a twinkle in the teacher's eye as a paper is read can all show a child that his or her work is valued.

Writing for Different Purposes

One of the problems in education has been that so much of what is done in school is related only vaguely, if at all, to real life. All too often children are asked to perform tasks that have little meaning or relevance for them personally. Under such circumstances learning tends to be mechanical, to consist merely of acquiring responses to given stimuli.

Writing is shaped (as speaking is) by purpose and intent. If children perceive the primary purpose of writing to be simply getting a job done, they are not likely to develop real language power. Perfunctory writing to fulfill an assignment encourages leaden and lifeless writing.

Competent writers are flexible and can write for different purposes and a variety of audiences. They know how one task varies from another and what forms and conventions pertain to each task. If we are to develop truly competent writers, we must include a range of purposeful, real-life writing activities in the language arts program. Here are some purposes for writing and some suggested writing activities:

Writing to describe or explain

the scene of an important event (busy intersection, sport contest)

a controversial or important personality (visitor, TV personality)

directions to a location (park, museum)

directions for playing a game (Go Fish, Monopoly)

directions for making or doing something (baking bread, building a bird house)

how something works (bicycle, paperclip)

opinion (letters to the editor, fan club letters)

requests or inquiry (letters of complaint, inquiry, application)

Writing to record

labels

lists

diaries

journals

biographies of famous people

autobiographies

surveys (opinion, use, differences)

interviews and conversations

news stories

minutes of a meeting

subject area reports (social studies, science)

book reports

Writing to convince

want ads

requests

campaign literature (for environmental concerns, for playground equipment)

editorials

commercials

Writing as a social courtesy

friendly letters (pen pals, relatives)

invitations

thank-you notes

congratulatory notes (for good sportsmanship, music ability)

letters of condolence (loss of a pet, contest)

Writing to entertain

stories

plays

skits

jokes

riddles

tongue twisters

The writing of very young children reflects their sense of purpose in writing, and teachers should strive to maintain and cultivate this attitude as children grow older. Young children should be encouraged to try to write on their own, and purposeful, child-initiated writing should be fostered throughout the grades. In addition to individual writing, group projects in which the teacher serves as the recorder provide important writing models. A first-grade class, for example, might cooperatively keep a record of the weather, invite another class to see a special exhibit, write news stories, or write a letter of appreciation to the school cook for a favorite dessert. Early group-writing activities can evolve naturally from discussions and can nudge children into thinking about the purpose and structure of writing tasks. Care must be taken, however, to give children enough time for personal writing. Engaging in writing of their own choosing provides important nourishment for children's unique development. Little by little the children will internalize the writing system and improve their written communication skills.

Teaching Expository Writing

Opportunities to describe, explain, propose, and report occur throughout the day, both in and out of school. Children may need to compose the daily news entry for the year-long file, write a note to a classmate to remind her of a committee meeting, or write a letter to the principal describing class plans and requesting permission for a school garden.

Teaching any form of writing begins by helping children conceptualize the nature of the writing task. Children need to understand both the purpose of writing and the subject they are to write about. An assigned topic (or even a self-selected one) is often vague at first. It has already been pointed out that oral language is an important prerequisite to writing; discussions are particularly important at this point. They allow children to share and explore what they know, and at the same time bring the writing task into focus.

Awareness of audience is also important. Visualizing their readers helps children direct what they write just as they direct their speech. Considerations such as the intended reader's age, interests, and knowledge make a difference in the amount and level of information needed and set the tone of the writing. Young children tend to write for a global (nonspecific) audience. Egocentric as they are, they are wrapped up in the doer rather than the receiver. Gradually, however, children come to realize that they are writing to tell someone something, and they consciously or unconsciously structure their compositions to that audience.

The actual development of a writing lesson varies with the task. If children are recording observations or writing invitations, for example, they have only to plan what they will write and begin writing. Reports, however, may require additional steps to collect, classify, and summarize information. Before children are ready to write they may need help in focusing on and defining the topic or idea they are going to write about. Writing down what they know, posing questions to be addressed, and making a list of words and phrases associated with the subject are possible approaches. Children may also need help in locating information, taking notes, and organizing content.

Locational skills help one to use an encyclopedia, an index, a library card file, and other reference materials such as almanacs and yearbooks. To help children learn to use references, you may need to do a mental walk-through of the way adults go about finding information. Then you can plan experiences to help children develop the same reference skills. Mastery of alphabetical order is especially useful because nearly all reference work involves alphabetical order in some way. Children also need to be able to recognize the way different references are organized (e.g., by alphabetical order, by subject) and to identify and use key words. If, for example, they are looking up information about raising cattle in Argentina they may need to look up *cattle, industries,* or *Argentina.* If an index covers several countries, children may find the information they are looking for listed as a subtopic under *Argentina.* If the entire reference is about Argentina, information about cattle-raising may be found as a subtopic of *industries.* Similar decisions need to be made in using the subject heading in a library card file.

The ability to take good notes is also important in functional writing. Note-taking requires considerable skill and practice and is something that must be learned. Children should soon realize the inefficiency of trying to copy information down word by word. Then, by summarizing paragraphs orally they can practice picking out main ideas. The number of words in a summary may be further reduced if children treat the paragraph as a news story and try to write a headline for it. They can also analyze which words in a sentence actually carry the meaning of the sentence and practice writing just those words (for example, in *The crew explored all along the coast looking for a safe harbor,* the key words are *Crew explored coast for safe harbor*). If children write notes on cards or small slips of paper it will be easier to organize the notes later on. They should also get in the habit of jotting down the source for notes. This will save time if they need to go back to find further information and will lead naturally to compiling a bibliography on their topic.

As soon as children have acquired adequate information they are ready to organize it and begin writing. When the topic is rather limited they may have little difficulty finding a logical organizational system. More involved topics, however, require children to categorize information according to a conscious pattern or scheme. In doing this they are creating a simple outline. At first children may list only the kinds of information they have found. For example, a plan for a report on snakes might look like this:

Report on Snakes

1. Kinds of snakes
2. Where snakes live
3. What snakes eat
4. How snakes help and harm

A more advanced outline for a report might look like this:

Sources of Pollution

I. Factories
   A. Energy smoke and fumes
   B. Disposal of waste products
   C. Noise pollution

II. Homes
   A. Disposal of packaging
   B. Food wastes
   C. Fuel burning exhaust and smoke
   D. Sewage

etc.

The second outline lists subtopics under major topic headings. This method of outlining helps children write more coherent and integrated paragraphs as they deal with more complex problems. The better their organization before writing, the less they will need to revise and rewrite later.

While writing a report, children may run into snags and need additional guidance. Rather than *tell* children what to do, it is better to *help* them think it through and get themselves going again. Questions may be used to direct children's thinking along productive channels ("What do you know about _____?" "How is _____different from _____?" "Why might _____be a problem?" "Is _____a result of _____?"). Using a problem-solving approach, children make their own decisions and not only feel greater satisfaction but also learn more about the processes involved in writing.

Once the report is written, it is best to let it lie for a day or two before getting back to it. It is very difficult to be objective about freshly created material, because much that went unsaid is still in the writer's head and closely associated with the written composition. Proofreading for content and the clarity of sentence structure is particularly important in writing reports. Reading aloud or discussing the paper with peers is often helpful in discovering areas that need more attention. Then, additional readings are necessary to discover conventional writing errors in preparation for making the final copy. (See the proofreading section later in this chapter.)

Once children have been guided through the process of writing a report, they may summarize the steps they followed in a chart. Doing so helps them become more aware of the process and also provides a guide for further work. One sixth-grade class, for example, developed the following chart:

Writing a Report

Step 1: Choose a topic and set the purpose.

Step 2: Think about the topic and what you might tell.

Step 3: Define the topic and subtopics.

Step 4: Find information and take notes.

Step 5: Organize the information.

Step 6: Write a draft of the report.

Step 7: Proofread and recopy the report in ink.

Teaching Narrative Writing

Telling stories is a uniquely personal and creative act. The content for a story may stem from a writer's experience or it may be born in his or her imagination. Once an idea is generated, the writer must then shape the plot, selecting elements of the story and deliberately arranging them according to some organizational scheme.

Children ought to have as much freedom as possible in selecting their own content for writing, yet on occasion a common stimulus may be desirable. Sharing a writing experience can help develop an appreciation for individual ways of thinking and structuring ideas. It can also give teachers an opportunity to work with small groups of children who need additional stimulation or help in planning a writing strategy. In addition, group writing experiences can provide encouragement and cross-fertilization of ideas among peers and aid in creative and logical thinking. On the other hand, too frequent structuring of writing experiences imposes constraints on children that can seriously impede their progress in recognizing story potential in the situations and problems they encounter in everyday activities. To become independent writers children must learn to look for ideas on their own.

Motivation and ideas for writing may come from many sources. Working with disadvantaged children in creativity workshops, Torrance (1970) found puppets and imaginative stories to be successful devices. Others have reported outstanding writing experiences arising from drama and sensory awareness exercises. By asking probing questions you can help children discover that they have something to say. For example, on first sight an old bicycle tire may do little to stimulate the imagination. Yet in responding to questions about it, children will perceive a plot for a story. (Look closely at this old bicycle tire. Is there any evidence to suggest where it has traveled? Who might have ridden the bike? Where do you suppose he or she might have gone? Do you think _____ would have gone there alone? What problems might they have had? How might they solve the problem?)

The following list contains ways to stimulate ideas and motivate children to write. These stimuli may be used to encourage a flow of oral language and mental associations. These may in turn lead to ideas for writing stories.

Sensory awareness

Single-sensory stimuli. Concentrated experiences in tasting, touching, hearing, smelling, and seeing; children discuss the sensation (e.g., touched with a feather) describing it ("It tickled." "It was soft."), comparing it ("It was like a soft blanket." "It wasn't rough like a stick."), and telling their response to it ("I wanted it some more." "It made me think of a cat or a pillow.").

Variation: A sequence of stimuli (e.g., a series of taste sensations — dill pickle, apple, bread, candy); or varying duration or intensity of a stimulus (e.g., sound: long–short, loud–soft; or fragrant flowers: close–far away, one–whole bouquet)

Multiple single-sensory stimuli. Concentration on input involving a variety of simultaneous single-sense stimuli (e.g., smell: perfume, onions, spices, wet feathers, oranges); children try to identify and describe each smell.

Multisensory stimuli. Observing through all the senses at once. Children may take up stations within the room (pet or locker area) or about the school (office, hallway, lunchroom, gym, etc.) and describe what they feel, hear, smell, and see (and taste, if appropriate).

Drama

Word associations. Recalling or imagining experiences associated with words: fear, funny, Grandmother, Saturday.

"Before" happenings. What happened before the accident, the party, the trip, etc.

Situations. Lost on a busy street, alone in a dark stairway, walking in a park, confronted about a broken window, etc.

"After" happenings. What happened after the end of a story, a movie, a picture, a comic strip, etc.

Ideas. How to make gum, how to make a burglar alarm, how to find lost treasure, how to teach a dog tricks, etc.

Objects

antiques (footwarmer, button hook, decorative comb, watch fob
    and chain, toy, etc.)
a worn shoe
an old tire
a hand-crafted item
an unusual art object
collection or hobby items
things from another country

Films

"Attic of the Wind" — Weston Woods
"Be Curious" — Encyclopaedia Britannica
"Let's Make Up a Story" — Coronet
"The Red Balloon" — Brandon Films
"Toes Tell" — Encyclopaedia Britannica
"A Time for Rain" — Encyclopaedia Britannica
"Tell Me About It: What Makes a Friend So Special?" — ACI
    Productions
"And Then What Happened?" — ACI Productions

Pictures

characters
animals
scenes
accidents
events
abstract art
enlarged segments of photographs

Beginning paragraphs

The day started out just like any other day. Peter helped his father do the chores and then he brought in enough wood to fill the big woodbox behind the stove. Then the family gathered around the long wooden table in the kitchen to eat their oatmeal and hot baking powder biscuits. He was almost finished eating before he remembered. How could he have forgotten?

Reg sounded a low, hesitant growl deep down in his throat. The sound trailed off, but the dog remained alert and watchful. We stopped walking and listened. Everything was quiet except for a car somewhere in the distance. A slight breeze ruffled the leaves. Reg's body grew more tense. Then he suddenly bounced to the end of the leash with a menacing sound, half-growl, half-bark. Someone or something was out there in the darkness, and Reg wanted to go after it.

"What if" situations

What might you do if you were invisible?
What might happen if all our television programs came from Mars?
What might happen if your favorite wish came true?
What might happen if all the fish and other seafood in the fish market came to life and could talk human language?
What would it be like if we didn't have telephones?
What might happen if you forgot your name?

Beginning sentences

Christie saw a little purse under the tree.
George burst through the door with exciting news.
A sign on the clubhouse read *On Vacation*.

The principal rubbed her eyes and took another look at the elephant standing by the tether ball.

Recordings

Peer Gynt Suite — Grieg
Pictures at an Exhibition — Musorgski
La Mer — Debussy
Firebird Suite — Stravinsky
The Sorcerer's Apprentice — Dukas

Poems

"Fog" — Carl Sandburg
"The Umbrella Brigade" — Laura Richards
"The Duel" — Eugene Field
"Doorbells" — Rachel Field
"The Moon's the North Wind's Cooky" — Vachel Lindsay
"Swift Things Are Beautiful" — Elizabeth Coatsworth

Titles

"My Funniest Experience"
"A Dream That Came True"
"Bugs Aren't My Favorite Creatures"
"Stalking a Bandzandritch"
"Why Crabs Walk Sideways"

"What is" questions

What is love? (or happiness, fear, loneliness, etc.)
What is a mother? (or father, sister, grandfather, etc.)
What is a friend?
What is morning?
What is rain? (or snow, wind, etc.)
What is school?

An awareness of other literary forms may be developed through similar activities. Working cooperatively with the children, you should help them first to become familiar with a number of stories structured around a particular pattern (e.g., fairy tales, nursery rhymes, tall tales, myths), then analyze the pattern or "formula" and prepare guidelines for writing such a story.

Writing Poetry

Poetry is somewhat difficult to define. It is more a feeling than a form. It is not written just to be read; it is written to be experienced. A poem reflects a poet's personal way of looking at something. It is his or her *response to something* rather than *a report of something*. Poetry gives the reader an intimate glimpse of a poet's inner feeling and reaction.

Poetry writing is a natural form of expression. It is found both in the sincere expressions of primitive societies and in the spontaneous utterances of children. Writing poetry involves capturing words as they surge from deep feelings and emotions. Notice, for instance, the strength and beauty of these lines elicited by the color red:

> Red is blood.
> Red is your heart.
> Red is love
> And red is your cheeks
>   after you have run through the wind.
> I love red.
>
> —Terri (nine years old)

The following poems resulted from a class gardening project in which one child's plant failed to grow. Notice the feeling in these second-graders' natural and unedited expressions.

Marygolds	*Marigolds*
I can see no Leafs	Why did you grow Pretty
just wet mudy Ground	Why did your Friend
just mud	die so soon.
there will not be leafs	Are you sorry plants?

When we help children write poetry we help them give voice to their feelings and emotions; we help them discover the songs in their minds. There is no simple formula; a feeling for poetry must grow from emotionally satisfying experiences. When children have little value for poetry we must move cautiously, sharing our enjoyment of it and encouraging them to hear and enjoy the voices of poets.

Poetry reading is important to poetry writing. Hearing a wide variety of poems helps children develop an appreciation of poetry. Because of the range of content and style to be found in poetry, all children ought to be able to find some poems that they genuinely like

FIGURE 7-1
One-Word Graphics.

and that especially speak to them. Just reading poetry may be enough to ignite a creative spark in some children and start them writing poetry. For many other children, however, writing poetry does not come so easily. It develops and flourishes only under the skillful encouragement and understanding of an empathetic teacher.

Encouragement to write poetry may take the form of readiness activities. Playing around with words tends to interest children in expressive language and to set the stage for creative endeavors. Children may, for example, explore the ten most beautiful words in the English language, the ten meanest words, the ten loudest words, or the ten softest words. They may search for particularly picturesque phrases to describe something or experiment with alliteration.

To develop an awareness of form in poetry children may try expressing ideas in one-word graphics as in Figure 7-1. Or, they may experiment with simple-shape poems (Figure 7-2).

Writing a group poem involves children in writing poetry in a highly supportive situation. One way to develop a group poem is for the teacher to act as the recorder, writing the lines dictated by various members of the group. For example, on a foggy day children might first talk about what it was like coming to school through the fog. In the guided discussion they could describe how the fog felt, how things looked, and the feelings and thoughts they had as they walked or rode along. Then the teacher could suggest that their experiences would make a good poem and ask volunteers to suggest phrases or sentences to write on the board.

Next, the teacher would record the children's words, free form, as the children say them. He or she may elicit certain kinds of responses to shape the poem if that seems necessary. Usually, however, children's natural responses to a moving experience produce a free flow of rhythmic and expressive language that needs little tampering. When enough lines have been recorded, the group reads the poem

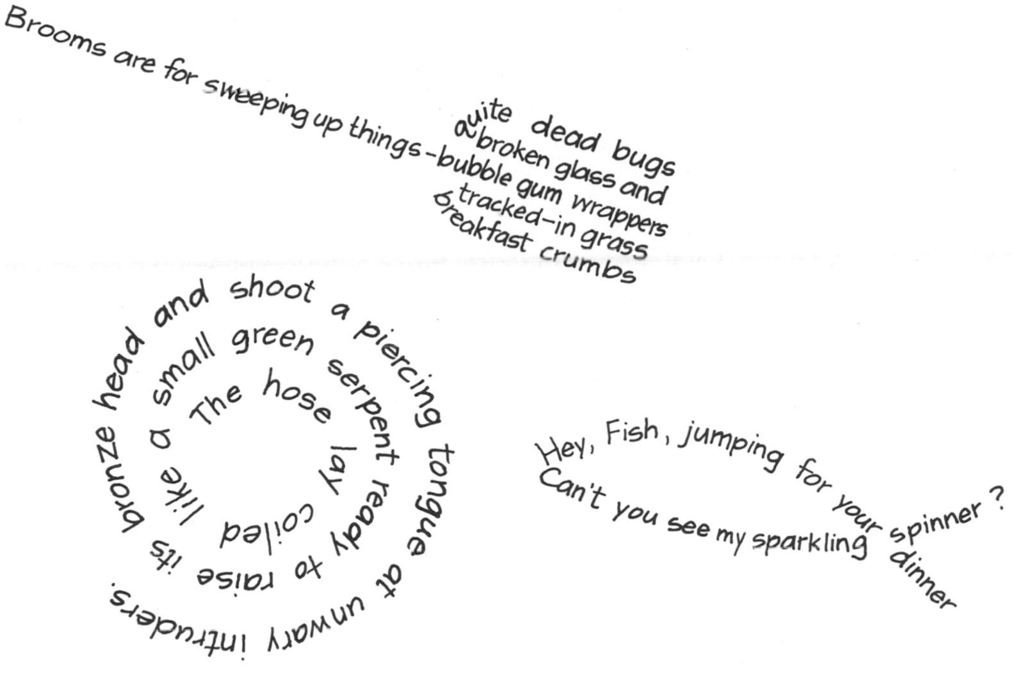

Brooms are for sweeping up things – bubble gum wrappers quite dead bugs broken glass and tracked-in grass breakfast crumbs

The hose lay coiled like a small green serpent ready to raise its bronze head and shoot a piercing tongue at unwary intruders.

Hey, Fish, jumping for your spinner? Can't you see my sparkling dinner

FIGURE 7-2
Simple-Shape Poems.

together and then suggests additions, deletions, or other changes
that might make it sound more like a poem. Any changes, of course,
should be acceptable to the original author of a phrase; they should
not change the intended meaning of the offering.

Another type of group poem involves short, individually written
responses combined into one poem. This sort of poem can be deliberately planned and developed from various media sources, discussions, or current topics of interest. Or, it too can be developed rather
spontaneously as a natural response to an emotional experience.
Children who have been studying slavery, for example, may be
guided quite naturally to express their feelings about it in a group
poem. Each child should write one or two lines (they may be rhyming
couplets) to describe slavery as he or she perceives it. The individual
contributions are then arranged into a group poem by the class or by
a small committee. Again, any editing to improve rhythm or to combine similar ideas should be cleared with the original writers.

Writing poetry that follows a pattern appeals to many children.
Young children especially enjoy writing rhyming couplets, and lim-

ericks and ballads tend to be favorites with middle-grade children. Cinquain and haiku are also popular. Even children in the lower grades can use these patterns successfully if they don't have to follow the syllable count exactly.

Although the set structure of certain kinds of poems may provide security for students who are hesitant to write poetry, too much attention to structure may lead to sterile, even inane, verse for the sake of meter and rhyme. In teaching poetry the teacher's primary focus should be on guiding children to find expression for their ideas; form should be a secondary consideration. Form poetry can, however, provide a most effective way to express ideas, and children generally enjoy such activities. There are several forms suitable for elementary children, some encouraging greater thought and expression of feeling than others.

Couplet The couplet is the easiest of verse forms. It consists of two lines with an end rhyme.

> Great grandfather sits in his old rocking chair;
> He rocks and he rocks all day there.

Tercet Tercets consist of three lines, rhymed or unrhymed. The most artistic form uses an *a a a* rhyme scheme. All the lines should have the same rhythm and length.

> The trapeze lady mounts the high wire,
> Graceful and dazzling in shiny attire,
> A sure-footed artist climbing higher and higher.

Quatrain The quatrain is a four-line verse pattern with many variations. Although all the lines may rhyme, it is difficult to find that many rhyming words. The pattern more often follows one of these rhyme schemes: *a b a b, a a b b, a b b a,* or *a b c b.*

> When Puppy jumps up on my bed,
> I know I'll not sleep one wink more.
> He nips at the pillow beneath my head,
> Playfully begging for a tug of war.

Ballad A ballad tells a story, simply and without emotion. Ballads were originally sung, and many of them have a refrain repeated after each verse. (Note: Writing parodies to familiar ballad tunes is one way to approach ballad-writing.)

> Jack came home one evening,
> Set his lunch bucket down by the sink.

He glanced at the breakfast dishes,
Saw blood that had dried black as ink.

Limerick A limerick is a humorous five-line poem with a strong rhythm and an interesting *a a b b a* rhyme scheme. It is catchy, and middle-grade children seem to have little difficulty picking up the pattern.

A mouse who was eating some cheese,
Paused a moment to sneeze a big sneeze.
Then he said with a wink,
"I really don't think
Yellow cheese quite becomes my gray knees."

Cinquain A cinquain is a poem in five lines that may be written with either a syllable count or a word formula. To use syllables, follow a 2-4-6-8-2 pattern. An easier, and probably more popular, version of cinquain uses whole words as follows:

Line 1: one word, the title
Line 2: two words, describing the title
Line 3: three words, expressing an action
Line 4: four words, expressing a feeling
Line 5: one word, a synonym for the title

Deer
Sleek, graceful
Running, leaping, prancing,
Happy to be free
Buck.

Haiku Haiku is a Japanese poetry form consisting of a total of seventeen syllables written in three unrhymed lines. It has five syllables in the first line, seven in the second, and five in the third. It gives but a brief glimpse, an insight into nature, and is rich in imagery.

One pink flower
among twisted vines and faded leaves,
A thing of beauty.

Tanka Another Japanese verse form is the tanka. It is like haiku, but it has two additional lines of seven syllables each to make a 5-7-5-7-7 pattern.

Snow falls soft and white
Covering rooftops and cars;

Angel wing feathers
That lazily, playfully
Drift in a silent ballet.

Diamante A diamante poem takes the shape of a diamond. It is more difficult than some of the other poems described here, but older children often find it fascinating. The poem is written in seven lines, beginning with a one-word line and ending with another one-word line that is the opposite of the first. For best results, begin by selecting two opposite ideas (nouns) and writing them in place at the beginning and at the end of a diamond shape. Develop the poem from the top through the fourth line, the transition, and then work toward the opposite idea word. Follow this pattern:

1 word: a noun, the subject
2 words: adjectives
3 words: participles
4 words: nouns related to the subject
3 words: participles
2 words: adjectives
1 word: a noun, opposite of the subject

Night
Dark, shadowy
Resting, tossing, waiting
Milkmen, farmers, animals, ants
Waking, stretching, moving
Sunny, warm
Day

Koch (1970) tells of his use of rules or direct form suggestions in teaching children to write poetry. He describes a class collaboration:

There were rules: every line had to begin with "I wish" and had to include a color, a comic-strip character, and a city or country. Many other good combinations are possible: any elements that will excite a child's imagination and test his ingenuity: animals, months, makes of automobile, planets, things to drink, birds, states. The children are likely to have good suggestions. After the lines were passed in, I read them aloud as a poem. It was a good first assignment; it made the children excited about writing poetry. (p. 64)

In another writing project on wishes, Koch's approach was somewhat different: "To help them with form I suggested that they begin every line with 'I wish,' and to make them feel free about what they said I suggested that they make their wishes as wild and crazy as they liked" (p. 86).

A more detailed account of a writing lesson about dreams is provided in this account of Gensler's (1975) teaching experience. Gensler writes from the point of view of a poet participating in a program in which poets go into public school classrooms.

> What I hope for today is an atmosphere of magic so authentic, so total, that you forget me and this classroom and the playground out there and your growling morning stomachs. Here and now, in the broad daylight of this fourth-grade classroom, in the fifty minutes between arithmetic and lunch, I have the colossal nerve to expect twenty-five children to write poems about falling asleep and dreaming. Somehow or other, I've got to transport them back to their beds; somehow I've got to recreate the landscape in which dreams occur.
>
> I unpack my props: three posters and a "model" poem. The posters are Magritte's *The Return*, Chagall's *Les Plumes en Fleurs* and Rousseau's *The Sleeping Gypsy*. The classroom teacher tacks up the posters on the chalkboard while I begin talking.
>
> I say: There's a part of everyone's life as real as seeing or hearing or touching, but it's stranger and more mysterious. I ask: What time do you go to bed? When do you get up? How many hours of sleep is that? How many hours are there in the day? So how much of the day do you spend sleeping? (Arithmetic in a poetry class?) The responses are quick and noisy: disagreement, fascination with other people's bedtime curfews, consensus. The teacher is particularly intrigued.
>
> More questions: Who sleeps on their stomach? Back? Side? Curled up? Who sleeps with a pillow? Who doesn't? Anyone take animals to bed with them? Real or stuffed? Anyone sleep in a bunk bed? Two to a bed? On the floor? Did you ever fall out of bed in the middle of the night? Sleepwalk? Does anyone yell in their sleep? (The teacher raises his hand; I raise my hand, too.) What's it like, falling asleep?
>
> The conversation is extraordinarily animated — even the shy ones get into the act. I continue the bombardment: What happens during all those hours while you're sleeping? Dreams, what are they like? ("Weird," "scary," "beautiful," "all of a sudden.") Who dreams in color? Hears sounds? Anybody have conversations in their dreams? See squiggles? What happens when a dream is full of monsters? We talk about the relief of waking up and going to the bathroom. We talk about night-lights and mothers.
>
> At last we look at the posters on the chalkboard. I discuss the paintings briefly — how I don't really know what they're about, but how they all share a dreamlike quality. How an artist sometimes paints his dreams. The children start to point out details in the painting. I interrupt them: Okay, you can write your poem in one of three ways:
>
> (1) Just hold your nose and jump into your dream with both feet.
> (2) Write about falling asleep, what it's like.

(3) Write about the paintings on the chalkboard.

Finally, before they begin writing (some have actually begun, others have gone up to the board to examine the paintings), I read them the model poem I brought with me. It could be a dream poem; this one happens to have been written by a fourth-grader in a nearby community:

The Bad Children Dream

The children that were never good
saw in a dream grass blowing
and lives flying away.

—Paul A.

The classroom is unnaturally quiet. Something is blowing through the room, the air of another place and time. I notice the classroom teacher — a long, lanky man — curled up at a standard fourth-grade desk, writing furiously. One by one the children hand me their poems and crowd around their teacher, trying to catch a glimpse of what he's writing. He shoos them away. As the bell rings, he hands me his opus and says, yes, I can duplicate it along with the children's poems. (pp. 1–3)

Evaluating Children's Writing

Past practices in evaluating children's writing have ranged from red-marking children's papers in judicious editing to resisting any direct form of evaluation on the grounds that it discourages children's effort and inhibits their creativity. In the midst of this confusion the question frequently asked by teachers today is "What shall I evaluate?" Perhaps a better starting point for a discussion of evaluation might be "*Why* should I evaluate?" To come to rational grips with the subject of evaluation and to put it into proper perspective, we first need to determine its purpose.

Generally speaking, evaluation of children's writing is done either at the program level or on the instruction level. At the program level children's growth is assessed over a period of time. The scores of each grade or school are then compared to its earlier scores, to determine overall growth in achievement. When different approaches are being used, achievement can be compared across programs. Program evaluation provides a profile of a school's or district's writing program and identifies effective instructional practices and areas of weakness.

Evaluation at the instructional level is concerned with diagnosing children's specific strengths and weaknesses for planning appropriate instructional activities. This kind of evaluation is immediate and is aimed at improving children's writing. The purpose may be lost, however, if teachers are unaware of the importance of assessing children's *strengths* as well as their *weaknesses.* Learning to write is a developmental process and instruction must complement each child's developmental level. Teachers need to know what children can do and then guide them in expanding that knowledge to new and related learning.

Evaluation aimed at improving the quality of children's writing ought to include both teachers and children. Teacher evaluation, of course, is necessary for some purposes. But when teachers take the responsibility for marking children's errors and then hand the paper back to be recopied without explanation, they are depriving children of meaningful learning opportunities. Such a procedure suggests that the purpose of rewriting is to please the teacher. Furthermore, when children mechanically copy what has already been edited for them, they need not understand the reasons for the changes. Evaluation of skills substantially beyond children's levels of awareness and understanding is meaningless and discouraging. Until children grasp the significance of a skill, practice on it is a mechanical response to teacher direction, and transfer of learning is therefore limited.

Evaluation to improve instruction ought to be viewed as an ongoing process, as a natural and integral part of the writing experience. In addition to day-by-day evaluation, examples of children's writing should be systematically collected and evaluated. By sitting down with an individual or a small group of children, a teacher can guide their discoveries and help them become more aware of effective writing techniques. Through such informal evaluation sessions teachers are able to develop skills inductively and also to plan additional strategies. The discoveries children make about effective writing help them develop better criteria for evaluating their own and others' writing.

Evaluation ought to emphasize effective writing. Capable writers capture the reader's interest and hold it not only through well-structured and mechanically correct paragraphs and sentences, but through fluency, variety, and originality. Such abilities should also be evaluated in children's writing. What is evaluated on their papers, of course, depends on their individual levels of ability and the purpose of the evaluation. At every level, however, evaluation should focus on more than just mechanical correctness, important as that element may be.

The list that follows is not intended to be used as a checklist. Rather, it is intended to suggest some elements of effective writing to consider in planning an individualized evaluation program.

relevancy of information

adequacy of coverage

quantity of data or ideas

validity and supporting evidence

logic and coherence of organization

unity

clarity

sincerity

rhythm and flow of language

novelty of approach, originality

sentence structure and variety

usage and grammatical relationships

spelling

capitalization and punctuation

appropriateness of style

appeal to reader

imagery

neatness

legibility

adherence to standard forms

Several approaches and scales for more formal evaluations of writing are to be found in published materials. Notable among them are Botel's (1972) syntactic complexity formula and Hunt's (1965) T-units to assess sentence maturity. Sager (1973) developed a rating scale for children's compositions — based on (1) vocabulary, (2) elaboration, (3) organization, and (4) structure — which children as well as teachers can use in evaluating compositions. Carlson (1973) adapted the Palo Alto Writing Analysis Guide. The revised scale includes categories for fluency, humor, reality, feeling, originality, and word usage. Carlson (1973) also developed a scale for measuring the originality of children's stories. These methods are useful for research or for objective evaluation of a school or class writing program.

Holistic scoring offers a quite different approach to evaluation. In holistic scoring raters read papers to gain an overall or "whole" impression. Papers are then rated on a numerical scale, commonly a range of one to four. Before the actual rating begins, experienced raters read a sampling of papers and identify "range finders," papers representative of each rating level. Once agreed on, these representative papers are used to train other raters in preparation for rating sets of papers. All papers are read by at least two trained raters and the ratings averaged to determine the final rating. (See Spandel and Stiggins, 1980, or Meyers, 1980, for more detailed information on holistic scoring.)

Developing Writing Skills

Children's writing skills develop through experiences with both the spoken and the written word. Using language orally provides opportunity to think and to verbalize ideas. An oral flow of language is important readiness for written expression. In addition, children must learn to put their ideas down in an appropriate written form. Learning to write effectively involves competence in using writing conventions and organizational structures. Children not only must have something to say; they must have the tools to say it. The discussion that follows addresses some important tools to be developed. They are not presented in a teaching sequence. Rather, they should be incorporated into the ongoing instructional program across the curriculum as appropriate to children's developmental levels.

Using Capitalization and Punctuation

Spoken language has an overlay of meaning made possible by the way in which something is said and by the facial expressions and body gestures that accompany the utterance. In writing, however, the rhythm and melody of the language are conveyed primarily through the use of punctuation marks, with some aid from capital letters at the beginning of sentences. Someone aptly summed it up metaphorically by saying, "Punctuation marks are a reader's hearing aid."

Learning to use capital letters at the beginnings of sentences and internal and terminal punctuation is largely a matter of hearing language in the mind and encoding its intonation patterns along with the words. To learn to capitalize and punctuate correctly, children need to develop an ear for the sound of language and to learn to translate the sounds into written symbols. Although the English language does not have a complete written system to signal intonation, effective use of capitalization and punctuation can greatly facilitate a reader's translation of printed material into meaningful communication.

It is important for children to recognize sentences as units of speech or writing if they are to learn to capitalize and punctuate sentences correctly. Reading and writing experiences provide important opportunities for children to make discoveries about relationships and to become aware of writing conventions. When teachers are taking dictation from young children, they may call attention to the capital letters and punctuation marks as they write them. Some teachers find it helpful to use traffic-light-colored chalk or ink as they write to signal the beginnings and ends of sentences. They write the beginning capital letters in green (for *go*) and the end punctuation in red (for *stop*). Later, when commas are introduced, they are written in yellow. Such experiences point up the purpose and use of capital letters and punctuation marks in sentences and help children learn to use them in writing their own stories.

Once children begin to notice and use capitals and punctuation at the beginnings and ends of sentences, they will likely notice additional uses of them in reading materials. Making a chart of their discoveries can be an open-ended activity leading to the development of a set of common capitalization and punctuation rules. If the rules are displayed in the room children can refer to them as they write or proofread.

Informal teaching of capitalization and punctuation is not likely to be adequate for all children; some will need specific help for mastery. Cooperative proofreading and correction of writing in pairs or small groups provide a meaningful laboratory learning experience. Then specific problems can be identified and taught; plans can be made for additional followup practice. One such exercise might be made from classroom materials by copying a selection with punctuation or capitalization deleted. Children correct the altered copy as a proofreading simulation. When they have finished the exercise, they check their work with the original. A supply of these kinds of exercises can be prepared in advance and placed in the writing center for independent work.

Children ought to master the more common uses of capitalization and punctuation first and then move on to more difficult skills as they are ready. In the following lists, the first gives skills that ought to receive primary emphasis in the early stages of writing, and the second gives skills for children to develop as they progress through the grades. Some children may develop proficiency in using certain skills in the second list before they have mastered all of those in the first, but, generally speaking, the more common skills should receive primary emphasis until they are mastered.

Beginning Skills	**More Advanced Skills**

Capitalize

the first word of a sentence.

proper names:
  people
  places
  holidays
  days of the week
  months of the year
  countries

the pronoun *I*.

titles:[1]
  stories
  books
  poems
  songs

Use a period

at the end of a sentence that tells something.

after initials.

after abbreviations.

Use a comma

between the city and state.

between the day and year in dates.

to separate items in a series.

Use a question mark

at the end of a request for information.

Use quotation marks

to enclose a direct quotation.

Use an exclamation point

to give unusual emphasis (to

Capitalize

the first word of a direct quotation.

names of special groups and organizations (*Methodist, Republican*).

titles and abbreviations used with proper names (*Dr. Jones, Captain Hook*).

important events and documents (*World War II, Bill of Rights*).

words referring to deity (*God, Christ*).

titles and words used as a name (*the President of the United States, a picture of Mother*).

words that came from proper names (*French cooking, English language*).

Use a comma

to set off *yes, no,* and *oh* in direct address.

to set off an adverbial clause at the beginning of a sentence.

to set off nonessential explanatory phrases and clauses.

to set off direct quotations.

before coordinating connectives (*and, but, for,* etc.).

Use quotation marks

to set off titles of stories and poems.

---

[1] the first and all important words

Beginning Skills

show fear, surprise, excitement, insistence).

More Advanced Skills

Use parentheses

to enclose information mentioned in passing.

Use a semicolon

to replace a period between closely related sentences.

Use a colon

after the greeting of a business letter.

to introduce a listing.

Writing Sentences

Constructing good sentences is often difficult for children in elementary school. Many young children do not recognize the difference between phrases and sentences. The complete sentences they do write are often short and choppy and contain few modifiers. Their writing lacks the melody and flow of their spoken language. For example, a seven-year-old wrote: "The bird has a big beak. The bird lived long ago. His name is Pete." Gradually, as children mature, they normally write longer sentences and incorporate more ideas in a single sentence. Given the same information, an older child might have written "Pete is a bird that lived long ago and he has a big beak," or "Pete, the bird with the big beak, lived long ago."

The ability to write more mature sentences does not necessarily develop automatically as children advance through the grades. Many, perhaps most, of children's attempts to write longer sentences show a lack of control over the organization and structure of sentences. A longer sentence may not be a better-constructed sentence. Quite typically children write longer sentences by merely adding coordinating conjunctions between kernel sentences. For example, one child wrote, "I go fishing in the summertime and I go swimming in the summertime too and when I try to swim backward I go under the water." This sentence is indeed long, but it is not well constructed.

To write well-formed sentences, children must develop a sentence sense. Attention to sentence structure ought to begin in the first grade and continue on through the grades, dealing with successively more complex constructions. Children develop an ear for sentences by listening to the sound and structure of sentences. Immerse them in quality language. Read to them, talk to them, and compose stories and reports together as a group. Through many such experiences children learn that a sentence tells something and they sense the closure or completeness of well-written sentences.

There are many helpful sentence activities. Children may analyze the basic components of a sentence, pick out the part that tells who or what — the subject or noun phrase — and the part that tells something about the subject — the predicate or verb phrase. Talking through a form story with children may also help them develop a concept of sentences. The teacher reads or tells the framework of a story, pausing to let children complete sentences. Here is an example:

> Juan and Juanita were on their way home from _____. Suddenly, a voice behind them said, "Give me your _____." Juan was very _____. He _____. Then he _____.
> Juanita felt _____. She _____. Together the children _____, and then they _____.

Another activity is to give one group of children strips of paper with sentence subjects written on them and a second group strips of paper with sentence predicates. Then children from the two groups try to match their sentence parts to make sentences that tell something. A set might look like this:

A boy	swam across the pool.
The little yellow duck	called to a friend.
Four of the men	got away.
The baby girl	woke up early.

Worksheets may also be made in which children draw lines to match up parts that form meaningful sentences.

Substituting words in sentence patterns provides oral practice to help children tune their ears to the sound of complete sentences. For example, children may suggest substitutions for elements in familiar sentences:

Humpty Dumpty sat on a *wall.*

Humpty Dumpty sat on a frog.

Humpty Dumpty sat on a chair.

etc.

or

Is the *pudding done?*

Is the turkey roasted?

Is the table set?

etc.

More complex sentence structure may be lifted from reading material for older children. These sentences from *Curious George Gets a Medal* by Rey,[2] for example, provide interesting sentence structures for children to analyze and imitate.

He lived with his friend, *the man with the yellow hat.* (p. 3)

He lived with his friend, the man with the black moustache.

He lived with his friend, the lady with the pink purse.

He lived with his friend, the teacher with the new car.

etc.

Then he *pulled the garden hose through the window, opened the tap,* and *sprayed water on the powder.* (pp. 8–9)

Then he lifted up the latch, opened the gate, and set the pigs free.

Then he jumped into the truck, hid himself, and rode to the museum.

etc.

While the guard was busy reading his paper, George *slipped inside.* (p. 30)

When the truck came down the road, George jumped aboard.

When the family looked at the dinosaur, George stood still.

etc.

Practice in sentence combining has been shown to improve the syntactical structure of children's writing significantly. Miller and Ney (1968), for example, conducted an experiment with fourth-graders, in which the children were given oral practice in combining sentences. The children gained practice in structuring sentences according to transformation rules, but grammatical terminology was not used in explaining or discussing the sentences. Samples of the children's writing were collected at the beginning and at the end of the experiment. The study showed that the children who had been

[2] Rey, H. A. *Curious George Gets a Medal.* Boston: Houghton Mifflin, 1957.

given practice in using the transformations wrote significantly more complex sentence structures than the children who had not received the practice. Similar results have been found by Mellon (1969) and O'Hare (1973).[3]

The following are some activities that might be used to help children develop more mature sentence structures:

Embedding kernel sentences

The birds looked strange.
The birds looked awkward.
The birds were wet.
The birds were newly hatched.

(The wet, newly hatched birds looked strange and awkward.)

Adding manner, time, and place adverbials

They walked.
They walked slowly.
They walked slowly through the woods.
They walked slowly through the woods in the early morning.

Reordering parts of sentences

They walked slowly through the woods early in the morning.
(Early in the morning they walked slowly through the woods.)

Through the woods they walked slowly in the early morning.
(Early in the morning they walked slowly through the woods.)

Coordinating sentences

The sun was up.
The woods were cool.

(The sun was up, but the woods were cool.)

Subordinating sentences

They came to a fork in the trail.
They weren't sure which path to take.

(When they came to a fork in the trail, they weren't sure which path to take.)

Adding explanatory phrases

Miss Jones took me to the concert.
Miss Jones is my former piano teacher.

(Miss Jones, my former piano teacher, took me to the concert.)

[3] In Mellon's study, students were given some instruction in transformational grammar.

Writing Paragraphs

Paragraphing is essentially a thinking process. To design and write paragraphs children must classify information and organize parts into wholes. Learning to use paragraphs is a complex skill and one that must be developed gradually. Merely telling children that "a paragraph is about one thing" is ineffective until they are able to make associations and form cognitive structures for understanding the use of paragraphs.

Children's first concepts of paragraphs are *visual*. They become acquainted with the appearance (the shape) of paragraphs in both reading and writing. In reading they learn that an indented line signals the beginning of a new paragraph. They must know this in order to respond when the teachers says "read the first paragraph" or "find out what happens in the second paragraph." Writing reinforces the visual concept of paragraphs. Many first-grade teachers have their children begin their writing a finger's width from the edge of their papers. Then, when the children advance beyond writing one-line stories, the teachers have them measure in the width of two fingers to begin the first word of the paragraph. (Children are invariably fascinated to know that *indent* comes from the same root as *dentist* and that the word is related to *tooth*. Having children think of indented paragraphs as tooth marks or notches down the side of a page helps them remember that an indented paragraph signals a new idea or another aspect of a topic.) As their experiences with paragraphs continue, children discover that a paragraph tells about one thing or idea.

Children usually need many experiences with paragraphs before they can conceptualize the *organizational structure*. By calling attention to the nature and content of paragraphs in written material you will help develop understanding and readiness for writing paragraphs. You might ask children to read a paragraph and then tell what the paragraph is about in their own words. Or, you might ask them to find the sentence that best summarizes the main idea in a paragraph (the topic sentence). They could then analyze how the rest of the paragraph relates to that sentence. Through such exercises children discover that most paragraphs move either from the topic sentence to supporting details or examples (deductively) or from specifics to a generalization (inductively).

Before planning a teaching strategy it is important to be aware that not all written material comes neatly organized around main points and topic sentences. The structure of paragraphs in fiction, for instance, may differ considerably from that in most expository writing. Paragraphing in fiction may occur more as waves of thought, to signal a change in speaker, or even to break up long passages for greater eye appeal. Some materials written for the content areas also follow a story form, and the paragraphs may not be developed around topic sentences. Because of these variations, paragraphs that are to be used as examples of structure need to be carefully selected. In time, children develop a paragraphing sense, and they learn to paragraph less tightly structured kinds of writing. Initially, however, instruction in paragraphing ought to include only the models that follow a pattern consistent with lesson objectives.

Initial teaching of paragraphs is probably most effective when children classify information and identify main ideas or topics in paragraphs. Structured lessons generally follow one of two designs. In the first, children work from specific to general. Given a quantity of information, they arrange it by categories and then summarize each category to arrive at main ideas. In the second design, children first identify main ideas and then flesh them out with supporting details. Using either design, children are ultimately guided to the understanding that a paragraph is about one thing and that the main idea is usually stated in a topic sentence at the beginning or end of the paragraph.

The following lesson shows how children's experiences with pet rabbits in the classroom were used to teach paragraphing. The objective of the lesson was to summarize children's observations of the rabbits by writing a class composition.

Step 1. The children discussed what they had observed. As they talked, the teacher made a list of their observations on the board.

Step 2. The entire list of observations was read aloud, and then the children were asked how they might group the information, which of their observations seemed to be related in some way. The children offered several suggestions, explaining their rationale for each grouping. At first some of the classifications were quite narrow and specific whereas others were more broad and general. The teacher encouraged the children toward the broader classifications to eliminate the need for too many different paragraphs. After considerable discussion, the class settled on three categories: descriptive information about the rabbits' appearance, information about the care and feeding of the rabbits, and information about the rabbits' habits and behavior.

Step 3. The children assigned each piece of observed information to one of the three categories.

Step 4. The children wrote a topic sentence for each category, expressing the main idea. Then they wrote supporting sentences using the observations in their list. As each paragraph was completed, it was carefully read and checked for clarity and unity. When the children had finished the entire composition they checked it for its overall effect and selected a title.

A teacher who had been using the second approach might have begun the lesson by asking children what kinds of things they had learned about the rabbits, in an effort to identify major concepts. If children responded with specific information, the teacher could then probe for a generalization, or could acknowledge the child's contribution by stating a category for that kind of information. For example, if a child said, "They eat green plants," the teacher might have asked "What *kind* of information would we call that?" or he might simply comment, "Yes, we have learned about their *eating habits*." Once the major concepts were identified and written on the board as topic sentences, children could then structure supporting sentences based on their observations to flesh out each main idea.

There are, of course, other organizational patterns for paragraphs. For example, a paragraph may be arranged sequentially to give procedural steps or stages in order. Or, a paragraph may be structured to show cause and effect or a comparison. The reasons behind the paragraphing in narrative material are often more difficult to define. In general, a new paragraph is begun to reflect a new speaker, a new idea, or a different aspect of an episode. Sometimes the paragraphs are merely for eye appeal, to break up large blocks of print. Writers simply have to develop a feeling for narrative paragraphs, to sense the ebb and flow of the story as it proceeds from paragraph to paragraph. Extensive reading of narrative material provides an excellent background of experience, especially if children read stories aloud and observe where the author chose to begin new paragraphs. Reading their own stories aloud with the teacher or a partner may also help them feel the slight pause or shift in the flow of language where a new paragraph would be appropriate.

Finding the Right Word

Good writing is clear and precise. The writer builds images and ideas through meaningful, well-chosen words. To do so he or she must have a large stock of words to choose from. Children encounter many words in their daily activities that they understand only vaguely or not at all. These words are most often ignored. A rich vocabulary begins with an awareness of words and an interest in them. Children need to be encouraged to tune in to words and to learn to use them appropriately.

A teacher's interest in words has a very positive effect on children's

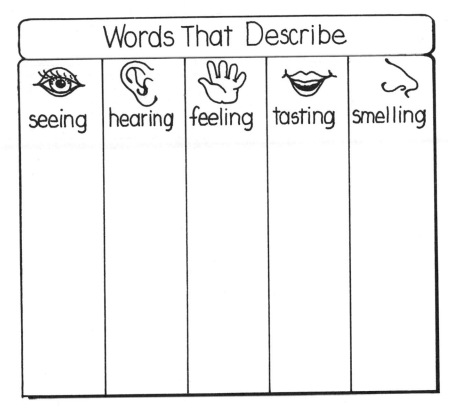

FIGURE 7-3

attitudes. Pausing to comment about a fascinating word or a word that is particularly well chosen suggests the importance of words and develops an appreciation of words as a writer's tool.

Vocabulary development should accompany and keep pace with experience. Children need labels for things and feelings; they need verbal symbols to express their perceptions of experience. Particular attention should be given to words for sensory input, because much of what is learned in the early years comes through the senses. Ability to write vivid description comes from observing and verbalizing appropriate sensory input: How does it look? How does it smell? How does it move? Frazier (1970) suggests a project for developing a vocabulary to describe sensory experiences. Children make a listing of sensory words and classify them in various ways. Using a similar idea, one intermediate-grade teacher constructed a large chart and asked the children to record all the words they could to describe different sensory experiences. (See Figure 7-3.) As the

FIGURE 7-4

length of each list on the chart grew, so did interest in using descriptive words.

Some primary-grade teachers make shape books, cutting large sheets of drawing paper in the shape of a sense organ, such as an ear. Children draw pictures of things that make sounds they like to hear on the shape sheets and write captions for their pictures using descriptive words or phrases: I like to hear _____ sounds. All the children's sheets are fastened together to make a class book and are titled *Sounds We Like to Hear*.

Teachers can encourage children to be word collectors in various ways. A "word of the day" or a "word of the week" is a good way to spark interest in words and add new words to children's vocabularies. Either reserve a spot on the chalkboard for the special word or use a small chart with a slot in which the word card may be placed (Figure 7-4). When a new word is presented it is defined and discussed and then the teacher and children try to use it as frequently as possible. An ongoing list of words that have been learned may be kept in a chart or diary form. These words can be worked into activities and games, or into challenge-word lists for good spellers, or they can merely be examined from time to time, savored, and enjoyed.

Young children enjoy making word banks of their new words. One idea is to make a word book in the shape of a piggy bank where children can collect and keep their new words (Figure 7-5).

Children also like to collect lists of words related to a topic or area of interest. First-graders might make an illustrated dictionary of farm words such as *pasture, barn, barnyard, hay, straw, stall, manger,* and *manure.* Older children might make a collection of space words — such as *rocket, retrorocket, launch, launch pad, trajectory, orbit, apogee, perigee* — and design a mobile to display them.

The English language has a rich vocabulary. It includes synonyms

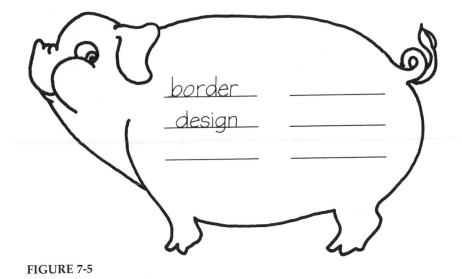

border
design

FIGURE 7-5

that children ought to learn to use to give their writing both variety and precision. Synonyms provide word options. A simple thesaurus is helpful in discovering these options (e.g., Schiller and Jenkins, 1982) and ought to be available to all middle- and upper-grade children. Most synonyms have similar but slightly different meanings. Children should be led to understand the different shades of meaning and the connotations of words. For example, if you regularly eat too much would you rather have someone describe you as *fat, heavy, round, plump, obese,* or *corpulent?* On the other hand, if food doesn't do much for you, would you prefer being called *skinny, lean, slim, slender, scrawny, emaciated, spare, lanky,* or *gaunt?*

Help your children develop a vocabulary of useful synonyms. Watch for synonyms in written materials and determine differences in meaning. Make a habit of looking up words in a thesaurus with children to discover what options are available. Encourage the children to make lists of synonyms for common or overused words. One such activity might be a "Synonym Search." Make worksheets for the children with key words written in each section. (See Figure 7-6.) The children carry the papers around throughout the day and record all the synonyms for each key word that they can find. If they want to, they could continue the activity over a period of time with many different words and then fasten the sheets together to make a thesaurus of their own.

Clear writing differentiates between general and specific words. To create clear images and concepts a writer must select words that convey specific meanings. Saying that a man ran into a building creates a vague image, but saying that a policeman ran into a church brings the image of the man and the building into sharper focus.

Give your children exercises to develop an awareness of general and specific words. For example, you might say a word and have the children describe the mental image that that word creates. As they compare images they discover that a word such as *piano* is more specific than *instrument* or that *screwdriver* is more specific than *tool*. A worksheet to develop awareness of general and specific words might also be used. Design the paper with sets of two columns as shown in Figure 7–7 and let the children fill in appropriate words.

Adding details brings images into sharper focus and fills in the gaps between ideas. Good writers remember that readers cannot look into their minds and see the images there. A writer's task is to create in the reader's mind the same image he or she has in mind, using the medium of words. Vividness results from well-chosen sensory words, words that stimulate the recall of sensory impressions. *A rainy day, the cool forest, a wrinkled coat, spring flowers,* or *a bloody knife* trigger associations built up from past experiences, causing the reader to create mental pictures and remember sensations. Children need to work on this skill to use it effectively, not with adjectives and adverbs heaped up until they spill over in redundancy and tedium, but with deftness and expertise.

Practice in writing descriptive details should begin with simple, concrete objects. For example, tell the children to look around the room or outside the window and select a single thing to describe, such as a tree. Discuss the general appearance of the tree and how it is different from others. Then have the children, working together, write a description of that tree, describing both its general and its unique appearance. They should include something about the setting to help a reader mentally locate the tree in space. Later, for followup practice, have each child select something and describe it in detail. For example, you might have a supply of twigs (or other small objects); each child would select one and write a description of it. Then all the papers would be shuffled and shared, and children would try to identify the twig described in the paper they read. Gradually children can learn to write more complex descriptions involving larger scenes, people, operations, and feelings.

Encourage children to use figures of speech; it not only makes their

FIGURE 7-6 *(facing page)*

walked

large

looked

said

Name _____
Date _____

GENERAL	SPECIFIC	GENERAL	SPECIFIC
building	*garage*	furniture	
car			rose
	Winnie the Pooh	school	
street			Easter
	Monopoly	fish	

FIGURE 7-7

writing more descriptive, but it speaks of originality. Children tend to use figures of speech quite naturally as they describe things. They particularly enjoy creating interesting comparisons: *sharp as broken glass, as hard as my fist,* or *as big as a skyscraper;* and sound words: *zrunk, skrink-skronk,* or *crickum, crickum.* Let them experiment freely, and provide many opportunities for them to give and get feedback among their peers. Teaching children the technical names for various figures of speech is not important, although children often enjoy being able to glibly identify a phrase by name. Stress freshness in figures of speech. Once readers become familiar with an expression, it loses its effectiveness and eventually becomes a cliché.

Similes are fun to write and probably suffer the most from overuse. Give the children a list of starter words and let them try to think of interesting comparisons.

as cold as _____

as soft as _____

as tired as _____

as excited as _____

as rough as _____

as dirty as _____

as juicy as _____

as sneaky as _____

as scary as _____

Work on the first comparison together: "What is the coldest thing you know? [List responses on the board.] Which of these things best describes cold? Have you ever heard that comparison before? Is it fresh and interesting?" Encourage the children to select something novel. Working on other similes in small groups may stimulate ideas, or children may prefer to work alone. In either case, the teacher should provide time to share and enjoy the similes.

Other common figures of speech that children may watch for or attempt to write include:

metaphor (an implied comparison, stated without using *as* or *like*)
He is a monkey.

personification (giving human characteristics to an inanimate thing)
friendly flowers

hyperbole (exaggeration for emphasis)
a million times

onomatopoeia (words that imitate sounds)
swish — bang

Using Conventional Forms

The conventions of writing include certain forms for the arrangement of words on a page. Although elementary schoolchildren are not likely to be engaged in sophisticated research papers or other advanced compositions, they should become aware of appropriate practices for their level of work and should establish correct habits.

Composition form Children should be expected to meet certain standards of writing from their earliest school experiences. By allowing them to hand in messy, rumpled papers you merely contribute to habits that will need to be corrected in later years. Standards for their papers ought to be kept simple and appropriate to their current needs, yet basic to future needs. In the elementary school years these standards might reasonably include:

leaving a margin on all sides of the paper

keeping straight side margins

writing the title in the middle of the first line

leaving a space between the title and the first paragraph

indenting the first word in each paragraph.

Letter forms   Children in the early grades write letters in a simple note form. In the first grade they usually use just the greeting, body, and signature. Later in the year, or in the second grade, they progress to adding the date and a closing before their signature. In the middle grades children use a complete heading with a full return address. Business letters are usually introduced in the fourth or fifth grade.

One way to teach the form of business letters is to show copies of letters on the overhead projector (or pass around several similar letters) and let children analyze the form used. A letter chart similar to the model in Figure 7-8 may then be developed and posted in the room for children to refer to as they write letters. Prelined paper consistent with the model developed (e.g., Figure 7-9) is often helpful for children to use while they are mastering the form.

Children also need to be taught how to address envelopes. The size limitations for writing the names and addresses can be a problem for them, particularly if they tend to write large. Talking about the size of an envelope and planning about how much area the address should cover and where to begin writing is often helpful. Children may need to practice on a piece of paper the same size as a regular envelope before they actually address a letter for mailing.

Children ought to understand why letters and envelopes are written in a particular way and why this is so important. They need to understand that being able to read a letter from a friend with ease adds to its enjoyment, and that legibility and conciseness in business letters is extremely important to busy office workers. Older children should realize that people often make judgments about the writer on the basis of their letter and these judgments may influence response. Furthermore, efficient mail service depends on standard form and legible writing.

Information about such things as undelivered mail, automation in the post office, and lost mail may be used to stimulate interest in their writing. A field trip to the post office or to a large office is also

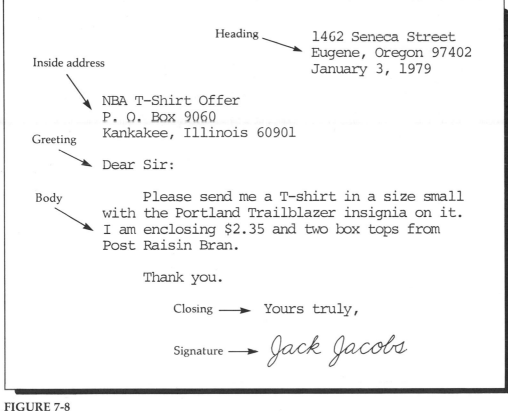

FIGURE 7-8
Letter Chart.

likely to help children develop new insights and recognize the importance of good letter writing.

It is important too that children have an immediate purpose for learning to write acceptable letters. They might carry on a correspondence with a pen pal or write a letter to the local newspaper editor, to a cereal company, or to a favorite author or television personality. The act of mailing a letter helps make the effort of learning to write worthwhile.

Bibliography form In writing reports, children seldom draw from more than a few resources. However, whenever they use an article or a book as resource material, they should list it at the end of the report in a bibliography. The entries should be arranged in alphabetical order by the author's last name. A simplified entry giving only the author and the title is usually adequate. Older children may

include the date of publication (it may be significant if current information is important) and the publisher.

Footnotes are seldom used in elementary school, but whenever children copy directly from a source, the source should be noted. Reference to footnotes may be indicated in the text of the report and the citation written at the bottom of the same page or at the end. The form is the same as for a bibliography entry, except that the page number of the quote is also given.

Proofreading

Proofreading is a complex skill. It requires highly critical reading with attention to detail. Both content and form must be thoughtfully scrutinized. When children proofread they need to read through their compositions several times, reading each time for a different purpose. They might read it

the first time to evaluate the total content of the composition (whether the topic is adequately covered and logically organized)

the second time to evaluate sentence and paragraph structures (whether each paragraph focuses on a main idea and sentences are complete)

the third time to evaluate the effectiveness of word choice (whether the words used create vivid images and convey appropriate shades of meaning)

the fourth time to check for correct spelling of words

the fifth time to check for correct uses of capitalization and punctuation

Although younger children cannot be expected to work on all these proofreading skills, they should establish proofreading habits at an early age. A reasonable task for first-graders might be to proofread for capitals at the beginning of each sentence and for end punctuation. Then, as their writing skills increase, they can gradually watch for more kinds of errors in proofreading their writing.

Reading aloud often increases children's accuracy in proofreading. Hearing what they have written makes errors more noticeable and

FIGURE 7-9 *(facing page)*
Prelined Letter Paper.

enables children to detect incomplete or poorly structured sentences. Hearing as well as seeing lets children listen for meaning and for the rhythm and flow of their compositions. Reading to a partner may be even more helpful. Having an audience tends to sharpen children's awareness of how their compositions sound and also provides valuable feedback from an outside source.

Children may use a simplified set of proofreading symbols in editing their compositions. Knowing that this is the way professional writers and editors work lends importance to the proofreading task and provides consistency in children's markings. A full set of proofreader's marks is included in many dictionaries and style manuals. Children might find it interesting to go through such a set and pick out the symbols they find most useful, or a set such as the one that follows may be presented for their use. Additional symbols may be added as needs arise.

℔	delete, take out
∧	insert
]	write farther to the right (to line up margins or to indent)
[	write farther to the left (to line up margins)
¶	begin a new paragraph
/	don't capitalize
≡	capitalize
◯ or ___	check spelling

Helping Reluctant Writers

A vital, purposeful writing program tends to get children involved cognitively and affectively. However, nearly every classroom has one or more children who write only with reluctance. For one reason or another these children find no satisfaction in writing. Perhaps the necessary stimulation to fill them with thoughts they want to express is missing. Perhaps they feel that their skills or ideas are inadequate, or negative feedback has convinced them that learning to write is an insurmountable task. Whatever the reasons behind their reluctance, they are not apt to be enthusiastic writers until they meet with success. Dealing with their negative attitudes requires patience, understanding, and positive persistence. Some suggestions to guide a course of action follow.

Set aside a definite time for writing. Some children never get around to doing things, even when they want to. Writing requires concentration and time to think and generate ideas. Having a set time to write, with other activities put aside, is often all that children need to get going. Some teachers have reported good results from a ten-minute writing period the first thing every morning. Children use this time for writing in their journals. Those who have nothing to say may copy poems or prose as long as they spend time writing. Before long they will be writing down their own ideas.

Expect all children to write. A positive attitude and an air of expectancy is infectious.

Spend more time in prewriting discussions to develop ideas for writing. Some children need more help than others to generate ideas. Pose thought-provoking questions that require critical and divergent thinking. Help children feel the excitement of ideas; build a flow of thought and language in preparation for writing.

Provide adequate structure to give children a feeling of security. Specific guidelines or models for children to pattern their work after make a writing task more concrete and less awesome.

Stress the importance of ideas. Lack of skills is a frequent deterrent to interest or effort in writing. Emphasis on content brings children's attention away from their lack of skills and leads to a better attitude toward writing. Skill development falls into proper perspective when children recognize the need for certain skills to express ideas.

Be accepting of children. Realize that children have different levels of ability and accept them where they are. Establish a skill baseline at that point and guide them upward from one successful step to the next. Let them know that you value their honest effort.

Stress the positive and build on success. Praise your children for whatever they do well, be it effort, ideas, or straight margins. Remember, however, that for praise to be effective it must be sincere. Children know very well when they deserve praise.

Plan appropriate amounts of writing. Children report not liking to write because they have so much of it to do. Check the amount of writing children are expected to do and find other activities if it is an inordinate amount. Children who tire easily or who are turned off to writing may become interested again if they can use a typewriter or a tape recorder. Dictating stories to the teacher or an aide is another possibility. Sometimes writing down just the first few lines is enough to get children writing on their own.

Write group compositions. Engage a group of children in a stimulating discussion and help them organize their ideas into a composition.

Write what they dictate neatly on the board, serving as the "secretary." Later, children may copy their story or it may be copied on a ditto. Watching as the teacher models writing can be a valuable learning experience.

Involve children in cooperative writing projects. Cooperative writing can have many positive effects. One idea stimulates others, and group work usually results in more interesting and better compositions. Children learn skills from each other and share in the laborious tasks of organizing and writing. The group shares responsibility for the composition, thus reducing the risk of criticism for an individual.

Approach writing through other art forms. Ideas may be expressed in various ways; writing is only one of them. Art, music, drama, and dance offer different possibilities for structuring and presenting ideas. They can lead quite naturally to related writing activities ranging from simple captions and labels to larger scripts, scores, program notes, or explanations.

Do not force children to share their written work with others. Recognize the risk involved in sharing individual work. Provide opportunities for children to share voluntarily what they have written in informal and natural situations; encourage but don't insist. When children discover how much fun it is to share, and how much attention is gained, they will begin to take their turns.

Planning and Individualizing Instruction

The goal of the writing program is to develop independent writers. To achieve this goal, children must experience purposeful writing. They must feel that what they write about is important and that it is directed to a real and particular audience. Purposeful writing puts children in the driver's seat and gives them a sense of control. It gives them a reason for prewriting, writing, and rewriting. Content and skills mesh into one comprehensive task.

The ability to write effectively develops over many years, and optimum progress during any period of time requires both guidance and practice. Although some linguistically gifted children may seem intuitively to use language well, they too need opportunities to expand and refine their writing ability. In defining and planning a writing program you will need to consider such things as the following.

Children have different interests and attitudes. Children need both a variety of approaches and frequent freedom of choice in selecting topics to write about. Their special interests can often be used to motivate writing experiences and foster positive attitudes. At the same time, children who do not enjoy writing may initially require greater guidance and structure in order to discover their natural tendencies and to achieve some satisfaction in writing.

Children ought to have a variety of writing experiences. A well-rounded program should go beyond children's immediate functional needs to acquaint them with other useful and enjoyable opportunities to write. Their use of writing should not be limited because of lack of experience.

Children's ability to write varies considerably at any given age level. All the children in a class should not be expected to write at the same level of proficiency. Although age may determine which motivational materials and planning activities are used, planning instruction requires the teacher also to assess individual skills to plan suitable experiences. However, individual learning can take place in a group situation. Therefore, an individualized program does not eliminate the grouping of children for appropriate learning activities.

Children's experiences should include both structured and unstructured writing times. A structured writing lesson permits the teacher to develop awareness of certain skills or techniques for developing a composition. A structured lesson need not preclude creativity. On the contrary, it may lead to greater creativity as a result of the teacher's skilled guidance and the quantity of ideas generated. In addition to teacher-directed activities, though, children should have many opportunities to select writing topics and develop ideas on their own.

Children can develop awareness of good writing by analyzing what other people have written. A wide acquaintance with literature provides a frame of reference for teaching writing skills and techniques. Literature provides examples of how recognized authors have achieved particular effects. And familiarity with different types of writing enables children to identify significant elements and to develop models to use in writing their own stories.

Learning to write inductively is usually more effective than memorizing rules. Discovery makes learning to write a higher-level thinking process and gives meaning to practice. Seeing writing as challenging and interesting work leads to positive attitudes and facilitates growth.

A writing center encourages growth. Writing centers are places for children to concentrate on and practice writing. A writing center calls attention to writing and lends importance to it. The center might contain: reference materials, writing assignments with accompanying stimulus questions and suggestions for developing a composition, skill cards or worksheets for practicing specific skills, stimulating multimedia resources, examples of effective writing, storage areas for children's writing folders, and a supply of materials for writing and illustrating original work. Such a writing center may be used as a scheduled part of the composition program or it may be used voluntarily during free time.

Writing workshops encourage children to learn from each other. A writing workshop draws a group of children together to read and discuss partial and whole compositions. Children who have run into a problem may bring their work to the group for evaluation and suggestions. In addition, the workshop may serve as a place to share finished compositions and to give and get feedback. In an informal but organized situation children have an opportunity to hear each other's work and react to it. The immediate and honest feedback from the group helps writers gain insights about which techniques are effective and which are not.

Rewriting is a part of writing. Good writing requires hard work. Professional writers often rewrite many times before offering a story or book for publication. Children need to become aware of an author's responsibility to his or her readers and of their own obligation to edit and polish compositions before offering them to their public.

Work that is to be shared should first be proofread thoughtfully and reworked as necessary. Then children should rewrite it neatly and in good form so that it represents their best effort. Some compositions, of course, do not reach this final stage. Writers need to do some playing around with ideas, and not all the papers children write will be written for others to read. It is important, however, that children meet reasonable standards in preparing compositions to be made public.

A writing file maintains a record of children's work. Whenever children write something it should be dated and placed in their files along with conference notes and records of skill practice. When children keep all their papers together they have a running record of their work and a reference of what they have learned; and as the volume of the file grows, they will develop a greater sense of the importance of writing. A file also allows them to go back through their papers and select ideas to put into finished form or to incorporate into other stories they are working on.

Teaching writing is a continual process. Teaching children to write is not limited to correcting their papers. Some of the most important teaching occurs before children write. Analyzing written materials, building an awareness of words and how they are used, helping children develop an ear for the sound of language, and providing instruction in specific writing skills all contribute to successful composition experiences. These helps, plus carefully structured prewriting lessons, enable children to use language effectively in writing their compositions and eliminate the need to deal with many errors after they have been committed.

Followup conferences help children recognize what makes their compositions interesting and effective, and they also provide opportunities to identify and record appropriate goals and skill needs. From this assessment the teacher and children can cooperatively plan, and perhaps contract, appropriate skill work and composition lessons in the writing center. The conference is the time for defining a child's individual program and what he or she is expected to do.

In Summary

Learning to write is a complex process that develops over a period of time. It is closely tied to the development of oral language and thought, and it also involves knowledge of an abstract set of symbols to express ideas. The classroom environment influences children's learning to write. The best classroom atmospheres stimulate children to think (so they will have something to write about) and encourage them to try.

All writing activities are not the same. Some are more functional, focusing on communication to record information, to convince someone of something, or to use language for social purposes. Creative writing, however, focuses on imaginative and artistic uses of language. Children need to have a variety of writing experiences so that they can meet their functional needs and derive pleasure from artistic expression.

Evaluation and the teaching of writing skills help in developing children's writing abilities and attitudes toward writing. Structured writing lessons are necessary to guide children through writing experiences and to help them grow in their ability to use written language. Learning the conventions and forms of writing and exploring expressive language provide tools and techniques that are important to good writing. Knowing how to write allows children freedom of expression to say the things they want to say in other unstructured writing situations.

Learning Objectives

COGNITIVE OBJECTIVES

Primary Grades

Children will

increase the quantity of their ideas.

be able to describe sensory experiences.

be able to relate events in sequence.

be able to express ideas in complete sentences.

be able to recognize relevant and irrelevant information.

be able to use beginning capitalization and end punctuation for all sentences.

be able to expand kernel sentences by adding descriptive words.

Intermediate Grades

Children will

maintain and improve their ability in all primary-grade objectives.

be able to use sentences with more complex structures.

be able to vary sentence structure.

be able to group pieces of information according to a logical plan.

be able to construct well-formed paragraphs.

be able to write clearly and convincingly.

be able to use words precisely to convey information and feelings.

be able to discuss and demonstrate various purposes for writing.

be able to use common capitalization and punctuation conventions.

know acceptable written forms and be able to use them.

be able to write imaginatively.

be able to develop an effective plot.

be able to communicate ideas and feelings through poetry.

be able to proofread compositions for mechanical errors, adequacy of content, organization, and style of writing.

AFFECTIVE OBJECTIVES

Children will

demonstrate a willingness to write.

take pride in the appearance and content of their written work.

gain confidence in their ability to write.

enjoy sharing what they have written.

appreciate the work of other children.

be supportive of the other children and be willing to give them appropriate help.

appreciate the value of writing both as a communication tool and as a means of deriving satisfying emotional experiences.

Suggested Learning Activities

Transplanted Characters. The children select a character from a story and transplant that character into another setting and time. Then they write an interesting story involving that person.

Personal Adventure. The children pick a favorite fictional character or famous person and write a story about something they do together.

Dream House. Have the children think about ways to improve their homes (new inventions, room size or arrangement, elevation, etc.). Then the children write a description of their dream house.

Modern Legends. Have the children select an unusual event that has recently taken place (something newly accomplished in space

travel, new athletic records, heavy snow or rain, etc.) and write it up as a legend that people a hundred or so years from now might tell.

Animal Why Stories. Have the children think of unusual characteristics of animals and make up stories about how they came to be. For example: "Why the Kangaroo Has a Pouch," "Why a Dachshund Looks Like a Hot Dog," or "Why the Skunk Has a White Stripe Down Its Back." The stories may be fastened together to make a book.

A Look at the Future. Nearly all children have ideas about what they want to be and do when they are grown. Talk about their plans and what it will be like to be grown-up. Have them pretend that they are grown and have them tell about their life.

Work Song. Do this as a group activity. First, select some work or a sport that has a definite rhythm or pattern, such as peddling a bicycle, scraping dishes, or raking the lawn. Develop a work chant to accompany the activity, using sounds or short words. Using the same rhythm, make up a poem. Some of the children may chant the rhythm while others say the poem. Variations of this idea: use the sounds made by machines (truck, cement drill, typewriter) or found in nature (wind, ocean, rain).

Pretending. Have the children pretend they are marbles, skateboards, pennies, or other objects and tell about something that happens to them.

Thoughts and Moods. Play a few measures of mood music or sound effects to set the scene and then let the children talk about their fears (or feelings, things they wonder about, etc.). Encourage them not only to tell what frightens them but to describe the feeling. (Here is a good opportunity to use comparisons.) Talk about how a poet might express fear, and record their suggestions. Most likely they will have created a poem. If not, they will still have had a worthwhile writing experience.

Genie in a Bottle. Make a collection of small and interesting bottles. Tell the children (or let them read) the story of Aladdin and his magic lamp. Pass out a bottle to each child and have him or her think about what it would be like to have a genie come out of the bottle — what the genie would look like, what the genie might do, an adventure they might have together, etc. When ideas are flowing let the children write a story about their special magic bottle and the genie that lives in it.

Obituary of a Flea (or other suitable creature). Watch for some rather interesting obituaries in the newspaper. Select obituaries that tell where the person was born and lived and some incidents in his or her life. Have these ready for reference if the children need them. Tell the children that you have a very special assignment for them: they are to imagine they are newspaper reporters with the unusual task of writing an obituary for a dead flea. Talk about the kinds of things usually included in an obituary and the kinds of things a flea might have done during his lifetime. Explain that the purpose of the writing assignment is really to entertain, that they will write in mock seriousness.

TV Summaries. Select an appropriate television program for all the children to watch and summarize. Let them read each other's summaries and critique them. By discussing different things that children included and the overall structure of the summaries, the children will gain insights and experiences in writing summaries.

Pick-a-Stick. Get a supply of popsicle sticks or tongue depressors. Make three groups of sticks by dipping the ends of some sticks in red, some in blue, and some in green (or whatever colors you have). Write a character on the plain end of the red sticks, give a setting on the blue, and tell what the character wants to do (his or her objective) on the green. Stand the sticks up in a can or other container, written ends down. Let each child draw a stick of each color and structure story to include all three things.

A Lemon to Remember. Pass a lemon to each child and ask the children to look at the lemons carefully, noticing everything they can about it. After a few minutes gather up all the lemons and then dump them out in a pile on a table. Have each child pick out his or her lemon. If a child thinks someone has his or her lemon they must explain why and try to convince the other person to give the lemon back.

Lemon Campaign. The idea of this creative writing assignment is to make people more aware of lemons and cause more people to buy them. Children are to make up songs, jingles, vignettes, or testimonials to advertise lemons and create a greater market for them.

Magic Mirror. If possible, procure enough small mirrors so that there is one for each child. If not, move around the group holding a large mirror so every child has a chance to see himself or herself for this lesson. Tell the children that this is a magic mirror. When someone looks into it it not only shows them how they look on the outside but has magical power to look inside them and see why they are special. Have each child look into the mirror and discover the nice things the mirror knows about him or her. Give the children time to think about it and then have them write down why they are special.

Note: Sharing this kind of writing may be threatening to children. Allow them their privacy if they wish. Also, some children may not be able to think of anything nice about themselves. Be ready with a few suggestions that the mirror might be saying.

Popcorn Antics. Bring a popcorn popper to class; put a few kernels of popcorn in it and let them pop *with the lid off.* Discuss how the popcorn looked as it popped. Think of vivid words and figures of speech to describe it. Compare the popcorn to Mexican jumping beans (if the children aren't familiar with them, explain). Then ask the children to imagine that the popcorn has something alive in it so that it keeps bouncing just as it did when it first popped. Talk about what might happen. Let them write a story about the popcorn that wouldn't stop popping.

Vivid Reporting. Select a news story and have the children rewrite it using vivid imagery. Have them imagine that they are there and ask them to think what they see, hear, and feel (and smell and taste if appropriate) and how they could describe the experience.

Ad Venture. Clip a variety of ads from the classified section — pets, job opportunities, cars, vacation homes, etc. Put the ads in a container and let each child draw one out. The children are to imagine they answer the ad and

purchase the item or get the job. They should then write a story of what happens as a result.

ZAP Books. Cut pieces of paper in half lengthwise to make strips about 4¼ × 11 inches. Have children fold the paper in thirds so that the two ends overlap completely, as shown in Figure 7-10. Then open the paper out and follow these directions:

Page 1: Children describe themselves, what they look like, like to eat and do, etc.

Page 2: Children write ZAP in bold lettering.

Page 3: Children describe what they have turned in to, how they look now and what they like to do, etc.

Tales from Heads. Cut out appropriate news stories and clip off the headlines. Pass out the headlines and let the children write the stories that could follow. Just for fun, let them read the original stories when they have completed their imaginary ones.

Historic News Story. Tie this activity into social studies. When the children are studying a historical event (e.g., the Boston Tea Party, the Battle at Bunker Hill, the invention of the sewing machine), have them write it up as a news story written at that time.

Hink-Pink. Ask the children to make up definitions for pairs of rhyming one-syllable words. For example, a carpet beetle would be a *rug bug,* a barren mountain top would be a *bleak peak,* a lady's wig would be *spare hair,* and a rodent cage would be a *mouse house.* To vary the exercise try two-syllable Hinky-Pinky (solid

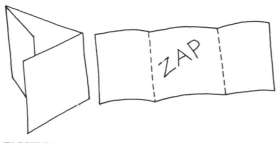

FIGURE 7-10

eating space: *stable table*, pair of tweezers: *sticker picker*, great spy: *sooper snooper*, etc.) or three syllable Hinkity-Pinkity (stubborn cactus: *truculent succulent*, astounding detail: *terrific specific*, etc.).

Geographic Riddles. Let the children look at a map of their state and then write a riddle to describe a town or a geographic feature (waterfall, mountain, lake, etc.). Have them exchange riddles and try to identify the place.

Euphuistic Proverbs. Ask the children to rewrite common proverbs in high-sounding phrases. For example, "The feathered vertebrate who arrives before the appointed time ensnares the annelid," for "The early bird catches the worm."

Green Hair. Imagine a child whose hair turns green whenever he or she says something that isn't true. Talk about what it would be like. Do people ever say something that isn't true without knowing it? Is there ever a time when a person might not tell the truth to keep from hurting someone? Write a story about something that could happen to the child whose hair turned green.

Pioneer Letters. Have children pretend they are pioneer children on the Oregon Trail and have them write a letter to grandmother back home.

Post Office. Make a classroom post office. Let the children send notes back and forth to each other and provide for "Out of Town" deliveries to permit them to send letters to the principal, cooks, and others in school. Special assignments or announcements may also be sent to children through the mail.

Weather Diary. Have the children keep a daily record of the weather in diary form.

Cartoon Conversations. Cut the conversation balloons from cartoons, leaving just the shapes of the balloons. Paste the comic strip on pieces of white paper to form blank balloon spaces. Have the children study the strips and write in the conversation they think the characters might be having.

Diary of the Month. Make a calendar on the bulletin board large enough so that each day's square is the size of a piece of writing paper. Have the children write about each day's activities, and then pin all the papers up together in that day's square. (This activity is especially interesting to parents at an open house.)

Colorful Expressions. Every family uses certain expressions that may or may not be common to other families in the area (such as *for pity's sake, crooked as a dog's hind leg, ready for bear,* or *fit as a fiddle*). Have the children listen to the language around them and bring interesting expressions to class. They can write the expressions on strips of colored paper and arrange them around the caption "Colorful Expressions" on the bulletin board.

Paragraph Match. Find a selection with well-written, fairly short paragraphs (at least as many sentences as there are children in your class). Type each sentence separately on a slip of paper. Pass the slips out to the children and let them find the children whose sentences go with theirs to make a paragraph. (Some children may be given two slips to make the paragraphs come out right.)

Suggestions for Further Reading

Carlson, Ruth Kearney. *Sparkling Words: Two Hundred and Twenty-Five Practical and Creative Writing Ideas.* Geneva, Ill.: Paladin House, 1973.

Cooper, Charles, and Lee Odell. *Research on Composition.* Urbana, Ill.: National Council of Teachers of English, 1978.

Haley-James, Shirley, Ed. *Perspectives on Writing in Grades 1-8.* Urbana, Ill.: National Council of Teachers of English, 1981.

Lickteig, M.J. "Research-based Recommendations for Teachers of Writing," *Language Arts* 58 (January 1981): 44–50.

Smith, Frank. *Writing and the Writer.* New York: Holt, Rinehart and Winston, 1982.

8
Spelling

Few people go through life without the need to spell some words quickly and accurately. . . . Writers with limited spelling skills frequently choose easily spelled, less precise, and less effective words to express their ideas because they are unable or unwilling to consult spelling resources. Incorrect spelling *marks an individual as careless, inaccurate, and perhaps illiterate, and often as one who lacks pride in his written communication.*

Boyd and Talbert (1971, p. 2)

CHAPTER PREVIEW

If yoo kan rede this, yoo mite bee abul too rede and rite ae foenetik speling sistum. But duzn't it look funee? Perhaps you have lamented the seeming inconsistencies of our orthographic system and have wondered why we spell as we do. If so, this chapter is especially for you. It will also bring you up to date on what is known about the teaching of spelling and will help you plan a spelling program.

QUESTIONS TO THINK ABOUT AS YOU READ

Why is American English spelled the way it is?

Does knowledge of phonics help children spell words correctly?

Which words are most important for children to learn to spell?

What should be the goals of a spelling program?

Which other language arts are related to spelling?

How do children learn to spell?

What kinds of errors do they make?

How can I individualize spelling instruction in my class?

The teaching of spelling is often a difficult and controversial aspect of language instruction. Seeming inconsistencies in the way words are spelled challenge systematic and meaningful mastery. Yet ability to spell continues to be important both in and out of school. In his introduction, Allred states, "Accurate spelling is important at all levels of written composition. A writer's creativity and effectiveness are influenced greatly by spelling ability. Good spellers are able to express their thoughts on paper freely while poor spellers are hampered in their ability to communicate in writing" (1977, p. 7).

In a very practical sense, the ability to spell often influences judgments about a person's educational level and general ability. Spelling errors stand out in writing. They are more obvious, for instance, than a poorly organized paragraph or an illogical statement. Frequent misspellings connote carelessness and create a negative attitude toward work that is otherwise good. This, in addition to the difficulty a poor speller has in communicating ideas, can limit opportunities.

Helping children learn to spell can be a difficult task. It is important for teachers to gain as much insight into the spelling system of our language as possible and to become knowledgeable about the spelling process. Effective instructional strategies require an understanding of what to teach and the ways children learn.

A Look at Spelling History

The spelling of American English is a record of the history of the language as it emerged and grew through hundreds of years of change. A study of spelling reveals change from one period of time to another and variation among writers during each period. Furthermore, an individual writer's spelling often varied from one manuscript to the next. Knowing this, it is perhaps little wonder that a cursory assessment of the way words are spelled today suggests a confusing system with little "rhyme or reason." Beneath the seeming inconsistencies of the language, however, lies a rich heritage and many colorful stories of the past.

Skeat explains,

> We find that the reason for the actual spelling of every word can almost always be discovered. . . . If I know . . . both the form and the sound of [a word] at its first introduction into the language, and next the various ways in which both the form and the sound gradually changed, through all the centuries, down to the present day, I am *then* in a position to understand the modern spelling of the word. (1924, pp. 30–31)

A few of the highlights of spelling history are given here as examples of the reasons behind our spelling system. This limited overview should shed some light on why our words are spelled as they are. It may also show not only that our spelling system is a medium through which our heritage has been recorded, but that it exemplifies that heritage.

The spelling of Old English generally followed a close phoneme-grapheme correspondence. Through the years, as pronunciations changed, there was not always a corresponding change in spelling. This fact accounts for many of the silent letters in our language today. For example, both the *k* in *knee* and *knife* and the *l* in *walk* and *half* were once pronounced. Some spellings, of course, did change as sounds were dropped. Old English included words beginning with *hl*, *hn*, and *hr* in which the *h*, no longer pronounced, has been dropped (*hlædel*–ladle, *hnutu*–nut, and *hring*–ring). A similar sound spelling pattern, *hw*, was retained but respelled as *wh* (*hwæt*–*what*).

With the coming of the Normans to England as we saw in Chapter 2, Norman French became the official language. Many changes in both the French and English languages resulted. The Anglo-Saxons refused to give up their language during the period of Norman rule, and the Norman rulers found it necessary to learn some English if they were to communicate with the common people. Toward the end of the fourteenth century, when the English again gained control of the country and restored English as the official language, the language had changed not only in vocabulary but in spelling. Some of the changes made by the French were:

ou replaced *ū* (*hūs*–*house, lūs*–*louse*)

qu replace *cw* (*cwēn*–*queen, cwic*–*quick*)

th replaced *ð* and *þ*(*ðis* or *þis*–*this*)

c at the beginning of words (which had always had the sound of /k/ in Old English) was often replaced by *k* (*cyn*–*kin*)

/s/ was spelled *c* before *e* and *i*

u and *y* were often used as consonants

the elongated *i* (*j*) was added to the language to spell a new sound, /j/ as in *joy*

new diphthongs were added: *ai, ay, ei, ey, ew, oi*

new consonant digraphs were added: *ch, th,* and *sh*

gu was never followed by a vowel in Old English, but the Norman scribes added new words such as *guard* and *guise,* and changed the spelling of Old English words *gæst* to *guest* and *gild* to *guild*

Spelling elements that date back to the Middle English period include the silent *gh* and the *ee* and *oo* spellings. In Old English, *night* was spelled *niht,* the *h* representing a sound not found today. The spelling of the sound was later changed to *gh.* Although the sound gradually died out, the spelling remained. Furthermore, as similar-sounding words were added to the language (e.g., *tight, delight*), they were spelled to correspond to the Old English words *night* and *light.* The *double e* and *double o* spellings were used to indicate long vowel sound. However, *a, i,* and *u* were not doubled.

The spelling of such words as *love, some,* and *son* also date back to Middle English. The vowel sound had been spelled *ū* in Old English, but during the Middle English period the angular style of writing made the *u* difficult to read before certain letters. Hence the *u* was changed to *o* to reduce the ambiguity.

The advent of the printing press in the fifteenth century had a considerable influence on spelling. As more written materials became available, the printers themselves usually set the patterns of spelling. The way they spelled was not always consistent or logical. In setting type by hand they frequently altered the spelling of a word merely to fit the space available. The letter *e,* for example, was sometimes added to the end of a word to fill space and justify the right-hand margin. Skeat describes the influence of printing: "The invention of printing began to petrify the forms of words, and retard useful change. The use of an idle final *e* in the wrong place, as in *ranne* for Middle English *ran* became extremely common; and the use of *y* for *i* was carried to ridiculous excess" (1924, p. 39).

The Renaissance brought about the respelling of many words to give them a Latin look. Some letters were inserted, though never pronounced, to correspond to similar Latin words. Examples of such spelling changes include *de[b]t, dou[b]t, indi[c]t, su[b]tle, recei[p]t,* and *vi[c]tual.* Quoting again from the candid Skeat: "French words were often ignorantly and pedantically altered, in order to render their Latin origin more obvious *to the eye.*" (1924, p. 39)

During the Renaissance another change in spelling occurred that eventually led to a change in pronunciation as well: the insertion of *h* after *t* in a number of words. Words such as *throne, theater, anthem,* and *apothecary* were originally spelled with only *t.* (Although the spelling of such names as *Catherine* and *Anthony* followed the change, the nicknames retained the old spelling and pronunciation: *Kate, Tony.*)

In America the English language was enlarged by words from other languages; in most cases the colonists borrowed the spelling as well as the pronunciation. Because the native Indians had no alphabet, the words they gave us came to be spelled according to the language of the white men who first borrowed the Indian words. Thus we have words of Indian origin with French, Spanish, and English spellings.

Spelling Reform

Various spelling reforms have been proposed to simplify the spelling system. Essentially, these would establish a consistent phoneme-grapheme correspondence so that each sound would always be spelled the same way. There are many problems with any such plan, however. One major concern has to do with the quantity of materials already written. A change to another orthographic system would make materials in traditional orthography inaccessible to most readers. If they were to be read, either the materials would have to be rewritten in the new orthography or readers would need to have special training in reading the outdated code.

Dialect is another concern. Imagine the spelling confusion if every writer encoded his or her personal speech sounds precisely. Papers written by a person in one section of the country might require laborious reading by readers outside that dialect area. On the other hand, if words were spelled according to one "standard" dialect, there still would not be a perfect one-to-one phoneme-grapheme correspondence for speakers of variant dialects.

High-Frequency Word Lists

Several research projects have been undertaken to determine which words in our language are used most frequently. One of the earlier and better-known word counts was that done by Horn (1926). Horn's project analyzed 5 million running (consecutive) words written by adults and found a total of 36,000 different words. The study showed that of this number, 4,000 to 5,000 constituted a common core of frequently used words.

Other studies, such as those by Rinsland (1945) and Fitzgerald (1951a), sought to identify the words most frequently used by children. These studies, based on similar large samples of running words, also found a core of high-frequency words. Such studies have been very helpful in selecting words to teach in the elementary school.

In view of the knowledge explosion that we are continuing to experience, the validity of these word lists for today's children might be questioned. It might seem, for instance, that today's writer would need different words from those used by writers in the 1920s, 1940s, or 1950s. To test this theory, Hollingsworth (1965) replicated Horn's study. His study was done on a smaller scale but used the same criteria and the same source of words as the Horn study. Hollingsworth found only sixteen words that were not on Horn's list in some form. Furthermore, Hanna and Hanna (1959) suggest that the words on Horn's list have most likely been high-frequency words for some time in American English. They report, "Of 100,000 running words occurring in the letters of Benjamin Franklin, 97 percent of those he used 10 or more times are found in Horn's basic writing vocabulary." (p. 10)

TABLE 8-1. THE 100 WORDS MOST FREQUENTLY USED IN THE WRITTEN WORK OF CHILDREN IN THE UNITED STATES

1. the	26. school	51. would	76. now
2. I	27. me	52. our	77. has
3. and	28. with	53. were	78. down
4. to	29. am	54. little	79. if
5. a	30. all	55. how	80. write
6. you	31. one	56. he	81. after
7. we	32. so	57. do	82. play
8. in	33. your	58. about	83. came
9. it	34. got	59. from	84. put
10. of	35. there	60. her	85. two
11. is	36. went	61. them	86. house
12. was	37. not	62. as	87. us
13. have	38. at	63. his	88. because
14. my	39. like	64. mother	89. over
15. are	40. out	65. see	90. saw
16. he	41. go	66. friend	91. their
17. for	42. but	67. come	92. well
18. on	43. this	68. can	93. here
19. they	44. dear	69. day	94. by
20. that	45. some	70. good	95. just
21. had	46. then	71. what	96. make
22. she	47. going	72. said	97. back
23. very	48. up	73. him	98. an
24. will	49. time	74. home	99. could
25. when	50. get	75. did	100. or

From Folger, Sigmund, "The Case for a Basic Written Vocabulary," *The Elementary School Journal* 47,1 (1946). Copyright © 1946 by The University of Chicago. All rights reserved. Reprinted by permission of The University of Chicago Press.

One useful piece of information from word list research is that a few words are used over and over again in writing and that these account for a high percentage of a writer's total running words. In analyzing Rinsland's word list, Folger states,

> The first 10 words comprise almost 25 per cent of all the words reported by Rinsland; the first 25 words, more than 36 per cent of all the words; the first 50 words, almost 47 per cent of all the words; and the 100 words comprise over 52 per cent of all the words reported. (1946, p. 47)

The words he has identified as having highest frequency are given in Table 8-1.

Allred (1977) also points out the high utility of a comparatively small number of words in Rinsland's list. He states,

1,000 words account for 89 percent of all words that children use in their writing (89 percent usage for 1,000 words), 2,000 words account for 95 percent (a 6 percent usage gain for the second 1,000 words), and 3,000 words account for 97 percent (only a 2 percent gain for the third 1,000 words. (p. 16)

In addition to determining the words children most frequently use, Fitzgerald (1951a) also identified the 100 words most frequently misspelled at each grade level. These lists were then combined into one master list of 222 Spelling Demons (Table 8-2). He explains that the words in the list are not the most difficult words children write, but because they combine difficulty and frequency of use they account for a majority of children's spelling errors.

The Spelling Regularity of English Words

When we consider the diverse origins of American English words and the influences that have contributed to the development of the language, we may logically assume that such a language would lack consistency in spelling. This point of view has indeed been commonly held and is reflected in programs that teach spelling on a word-by-word basis. At the same time, however, many teachers have held to the belief that a knowledge of phonics helps children spell. They have urged children to "sound out the word and spell it like it sounds," and have rigorously drilled them on spelling rules. An objective analysis of many of those spelling rules riddles them with exceptions and raises serious doubt about their value.

The spelling of American English is based on an *alphabetic system.* That is, sounds of the language are represented in writing by letters of the alphabet. If there were a perfect one-to-one match between sounds and letters, the task of learning to encode the language in correct spelling would seem to be reasonably simple. But the sounds of language may be represented by one or more written symbols. To spell correctly, the writer often has to select the one acceptable form from among several options.

Studies to identify phoneme-grapheme correspondences in traditional orthography (Horn, 1957, Soffietti, 1955) indicate many ways to spell certain sounds. Using a corpus of 10,000 words, Horn (1957) tabulated how the sounds in the words were spelled and the percentage of occurrences for each spelling. Slightly abridged data from that study are shown in Table 8-3. Such evidence seems to cast doubt on the theory of phoneme-grapheme regularity that some writers have advocated.

Other researchers have carried the study of phoneme-grapheme

TABLE 8-2. 222 SPELLING DEMONS FOR SECOND, THIRD, FOURTH, FIFTH, AND SIXTH GRADES

about	come	has	Mar.	said	think
address	coming	have	maybe	Santa Claus	thought
afternoon	couldn't	haven't	me	Saturday	through
again	cousin	having	Miss	saw	time
all right	daddy	he	morning	school	to
along	day	hear	mother	schoolhouse	today
already	Dec.	hello	Mr.	send	together
always	didn't	her	Mrs.	sent	tomorrow
am	dog	here	much	sincerely	tonight
an	don't	him	my	snow	too
and	down	his	name	snowman	toys
answer	Easter	home	nice	some	train
anything	every	hope	Nov.	something	truly
anyway	everybody	hospital	now	sometime	two
April	father	house	nowadays	sometimes	until
are	Feb.	how	o'clock	soon	vacation
arithmetic	fine	how's	Oct.	stationery	very
aunt	first	I	off	store	want
awhile	football	I'll	on	studying	was
baby	for	I'm	once	summer	we
balloon	fourth	in	one	Sunday	weather
basketball	Friday	isn't	our	suppose	well
because	friend	it	out	sure	went
been	friends	it's	outside	surely	were
before	from	I've	party	swimming	we're
birthday	fun	Jan.	people	teacher	when
bought	getting	just	play	teacher's	white
boy	goes	know	played	Thanksgiving	will
boys	going	lessons	plays	that's	with
brother	good	letter	please	the	won't
brought	good-by	like	pretty	their	would
can	got	likes	quit	them	write
cannot	grade	little	quite	then	writing
can't	guess	lots	receive	there	you
children	had	loving	received	there's	your
Christmas	Halloween	made	remember	they	you're
close	handkerchiefs	make	right	they're	yours

From Fitzgerald, James A. *A Basic Life Spelling Vocabulary* (Milwaukee: The Bruce Publishing Company, 1951), pp. 144–50. Reprinted by permission of the Glencoe Press.

correspondence still further. They have sought to discover how predictable the spelling of a word is when other variables are taken into consideration (e.g., whether the syllable ends in a vowel or a consonant). Studies of this nature indicate that the phoneme-grapheme relationships in our language are more consistent than previously

TABLE 8-3. COMMON SPELLINGS IN 10,000 WORDS

SOUND	NUMBER OF OCCURRENCES OF THE SOUND	NUMBER OF DIFFERENT SPELLINGS	MOST COMMON SPELLINGS	EXAMPLES	NUMBER OF OCCURRENCES	PERCENT OF OCCURRENCES
ā	1237	14	a-e	date	636	51.40
			a	angel	249	20.13
			ai	aid	192	15.52
			ay	day	89	7.19
ē	859	14	ea	each	263	30.62
			ee	feel	221	25.72
			e	evil	176	20.49
			e-e	these	56	6.52
			ea-e	breathe	34	3.96
ĕ	1917	7	e	end	1763	91.97
			ea	head	86	4.49
ō	691	15	o	go	333	48.19
			o-e	note	179	25.90
			ow	own	95	13.75
			oa	load	54	7.81
ô	497	11	o	office	281	56.54
			a	all	83	16.70
			au	author	60	12.07
			aw	saw	30	6.04
o͝o	108	4	oo	book	61	56.48
			u	put	36	33.33
			ou	could	7	6.48
			o	woman	4	3.70
o͞o	371	16	u	cruel	93	25.07
			oo	noon	87	23.45
			u-e	rule	61	16.44
			o-e	lose	30	8.09
			ue	blue	27	7.28
			o	to	19	5.12
			ou	group	15	4.04
ŭ	721	6	u	ugly	548	76.01
			o	company	126	17.48
			ou	country	30	4.16
stressed syllabic r	430	12	er	her	160	37.21
			ur	church	93	21.63
			ir	first	63	14.65
			or	world	34	7.91
			ear	heard	26	6.05
			our	courage	24	5.58
unstressed syllabic r	1044	11	er	better	720	68.97
			or	favor	165	15.80

TABLE 8-3. COMMON SPELLINGS IN 10,000 WORDS (*continued*)

SOUND	NUMBER OF OCCURRENCES OF THE SOUND	NUMBER OF DIFFERENT SPELLINGS	MOST COMMON SPELLINGS	EXAMPLES	NUMBER OF OCCURRENCES	PERCENT OF OCCURRENCES
			ure	picture	72	6.90
			ar	dollar	62	5.94
oi	107	2	oi	oil	63	58.88
			oy	boy	44	41.12
ou	225	2	ou	out	165	73.33
			ow	cow	60	26.67
u	376	11	u	union	167	44.41
			u-e	use	130	34.57
			ue	value	29	7.71
			ew	few	17	4.52
syllabic l	478	10	le	able	247	51.67
			al	animal	163	34.10
			el	cancel	34	7.11
			il	civil	16	3.35
syllabic n	171	8	en	written	79	46.20
			on	lesson	33	19.30
			an	important	18	10.53
			in	cousin	17	9.94
			contractions	didn't	12	7.02
			ain	certain	10	5.85
ch	357	5	ch	church	212	59.38
			t(u)	picture	91	25.49
			tch	watch	42	11.76
			ti	question	11	3.08
f	1117	7	f	feel	936	83.80
			ff	sheriff	91	8.15
			ph	photograph	57	5.10
j	484	10	ge	strange	161	33.26
			g	general	138	28.51
			j	job	118	24.38
			dge	bridge	26	5.37
k	2613	11	c	call	1681	64.33
			k	keep	290	11.10
			x	expect, luxury	164	6.28
			ck	black	159	6.08
			qu	quite, bouquet	113	4.33
l	2590	5	l	last	2205	85.14
			ll	allow	294	11.35
			le	automobile	84	3.24
m	1712	7	m	man	1500	87.62

TABLE 8-3. COMMON SPELLINGS IN 10,000 WORDS (*continued*)

SOUND	NUMBER OF OCCURRENCES OF THE SOUND	NUMBER OF DIFFERENT SPELLINGS	MOST COMMON SPELLINGS	EXAMPLES	NUMBER OF OCCURRENCES	PERCENT OF OCCURRENCES
			me	come	112	6.54
			mm	comment	66	3.86
n	4007	8	n	no	3724	92.94
			ne	done	170	4.24
ng	998	3	ng	thing	880	88.18
			n	bank, anger	116	11.62
s	3846	9	s	sick	2568	66.77
			ce	office	323	8.40
			c	city	315	8.19
			ss	class	299	7.77
			se	else	149	3.87
			x(ks)	box	140	3.64
sh	829	17	ti	attention	423	51.03
			sh	she	242	29.19
			ci	ancient	47	5.67
			ssi	admission	36	4.34
t	4277	6	t	teacher	3522	82.35
			te	definite	424	9.91
			ed	furnished	179	4.19
			tt	attend	145	3.39
y[a]	530	13	u	union	190	35.85
			u-e	use	155	29.25
			y	yes	55	10.38
			i	onion	44	8.30
			ue	value	42	7.92
			ew	few	17	3.21
z	1792	8	s	present	1473	82.20
			se	applause	183	10.21
			ze	gauze	64	3.57

[a] The *y* sound is the first element in the diphthongal sound long *u*. In many words where the long *u* sound follows a consonant — for example, d(duty) and t(tune) — the sound of *y* occurs in only one of two or more pronunciations.

thought, and that it is possible to learn to spell words correctly most of the time by learning to use certain linguistic cues. Those cues may be primarily associated with specific phoneme-grapheme correspondences or they may involve larger linguistic structures.

A major spelling research project was conducted at Stanford University under the direction of Paul R. Hanna (1966). In the first phase of the project, the researchers examined the consistency of phoneme-grapheme relationships in 17,000 words, and analyzed the various structures of American English orthography. In the second phase they programmed a computer to spell the 17,000 words according to the information gained from the first phase.

The results of Hanna's study proved to be most interesting. By considering (1) phonological factors (position, stress, and surrounding environment of letters); (2) morphological factors (compounding, affixation, and word families); and (3) syntax (the way words are arranged in sentences), the researchers were able to devise an *algorithm* (a set of rules) that resulted in very accurate spelling. Summarizing the study, Hodges and Rudorf (1965) report, "Individual phoneme-grapheme relationships, *though not in terms of whole* <u>*words*</u>, can be predicted with an accuracy of 89.6 percent by use of the phonological cues contained in the algorithm" (1965, p. 532; italics added for emphasis).

Carol Chomsky (1970) believes that the orthographic system of American English is quite optimal and that it is more regular than commonly thought. The way words are spelled reflects relationships beneath the surface level of phoneme-grapheme correspondence. She states, "The conventional spelling of words corresponds more closely to an underlying abstract level of representation within the sound system of the language, than it does to the surface phonetic form that the words assume in the spoken language" (p. 288).

For example, Chomsky points out that when suffixes are added to words, the vowel sound in the stem often undergoes a pronunciation shift (*sane–sanity, extreme–extremity, wide–width, compose–composite*). Chomsky explains, "This type of vowel alternation is . . . in fact an integral feature of the phonological system of the language which speakers of English have internalized and which they use automatically in producing and understanding utterances" (p. 289). In our current spelling system, the relationships of pairs of words, such as those just cited, are retained even though the pronunciation changes. This is a significant and desirable feature. It allows speakers and writers to recognize variant forms of the same word.

Chomsky further notes that this consistency in the form of words, regardless of pronunciation, allows writers to deduce the spelling of one word by generalizing on the basis of their knowledge of the spelling of related words. This is particularly helpful in the spelling of unaccented syllables in which a pronunciation shift results in a schwa-sounded vowel (*illustrate–illustrative*), in words with silent letters (*muscle–muscular*), and in other words that change pronunciation when affixes are added (*right–righteous*).

Spelling and Other Language Abilities

There is an underlying and recurrent theme running through spelling research *and* the experiences of classroom practitioners: spelling ability is related to children's overall language ability. The way children make correct spelling choices appears to be tied to their intuitive knowledge of certain key features of language and their ability to respond to significant language cues. Whether children learn to apply a spelling rule consciously or unconsciously to the surface structure of words or whether they intuitively search beneath the pronunciation of a word for abstract phonological and lexical relationships, their success in spelling, as in other language arts, will be influenced by their overall language competency.

Correlation studies consistently indicate the interrelationship of spelling ability and the other language arts. These studies suggest the need to teach spelling in the context of a strong language arts program. Children who are good readers tend to be good spellers. A good reader may occasionally be a poor speller, but a poor reader is rarely a good speller. Writing on the psychological bases of spelling, Hodges asserts,

> Because there is ample linguistic evidence to support the position that oral language is primal to written language and that the written code is in large part a reflection of the oral code, it becomes clear that aural-oral abilities have the highest priority in the spelling process. The development of these abilities suggest that initial spelling instruction might emphasize children's analysis of the written code in relation to the previously established phonemic habits. (1965, pp. 6–31)

Spelling and reading, though different in some respects, are mutually supportive from the earliest stages.

Correlations between speech and spelling ability are significant. Incorrect pronunciation or careless articulation reduces the number of oral cues children have to aid them in translating spoken language into written symbols. The child who says "runnin" or "gonna" has fewer regularized phoneme-grapheme correspondences to use in spelling the word. Whenever oral cues to phoneme-grapheme correspondence are reduced, children must put greater reliance on the recall of visual forms.

Visual memory contributes significantly to good spelling. Although some words can be spelled by listening to the sequence of sounds and applying phonic generalizations, it is not always possible to spell correctly on that basis alone. As seen in the Horn study cited earlier, some sounds have several common spellings plus others that are less common. When children encounter irregularly spelled words, they must rely on their visual memory.

Correlations are also found between handwriting and spelling. Letters that are illegibly formed cannot be considered to be spelled correctly. In addition, slow and laborious writing may detract from concentration on the spelling of a word before a child has finished writing it. Poorly formed words make visual imagery less exact, reducing this channel for learning.

Other correlates of spelling ability include both intelligence and motivation. The conceptualization and utilization of a spelling system requires abstract thinking. In deciding how to spell words children must generalize about available cues and relate them to previous language experiences. Less able children find these tasks more difficult and tend to rely on other, less efficient ways to spell words (e.g., rote memorization). Motivation, however, is a powerful force, and some able children who are indifferent to the need for correct spelling may do poorly. On the other hand, children of average or below-average ability may be so highly motivated that they achieve surprisingly well.

Spelling as a Developmental Process

Recent studies indicate that in learning to spell children go through a developmental process quite similar to the process for learning oral language (Beers and Beers, 1981; Beers and Henderson, 1977; Clay, 1975; Gentry, 1981). Their progress typically proceeds through predictable stages indicative of their cognitive strategies and linguistic awareness.

In summarizing research studies Beers and Beers (1981) identified four stages of development common to children from grades one to ten. (See Table 8-4.) The *prereading stage* consists of two steps. In the first step children group letters incidentally; in the second they begin to represent consonant sounds correctly. Between the first and third grade, approximately, children pass through the *phonetic stage.* This stage is characterized by the use of letter names for sounds[1] and the omission of preconsonant nasals (*cids/kinds; jupt/jumped*).

The *orthographic stage* commonly occurs between second and fourth grade. During this stage children demonstrate an awareness of word features and spelling generalizations but may not be able to apply

---

[1] Gentry (1981) supplies this favorite example: *ade lafwts kramd ntu a lavatr* for *Eighty elephants crammed into a[n] elevator.*

TABLE 8-4. DEVELOPMENTAL SPELLING STAGES

1. Prereading Stage
   a. Prephonetic level
      ABDG — *Wally*   11 + OZ — *cat*
   b. Phonetic level
      WTBO — *wally*   HM — *home*
      KT   — *cat*   GT — *get*

2. Phonetic Stage
   GAT   — *get*   FRMR — *farmer*   SCARD — *scared*
   TREP   — *trip* CIDS — *kinds*   JUPT   — *jumped*

3. Orthographic Stage
   GAETT — *gate* SPATER — *spatter*   SITTING — *sitting*
   MAIK   — *make* RIDDER — *rider*   CANT   — *can't*

4. Morphemic and Syntactic Stage
   a. Control on doubling consonants
      HAPPY   SMATTERING
   b. Awareness of alternative forms
      MANAGERIAL *manage*
      REPETITION   *repeat*
   c. Awareness of syntactic control on key elements in words
      SLOW*LY*   FAST*ER*   REST*ED*
      PASS*ED*   SAV*ED*   SLEEP*ING*

From Beers, Carol Strickland, and James Wheelock Beers. "Three Assumptions about Learning to Spell," *Language Arts* 58 (May 1981):573–80. Reprinted by permission.

them accurately. For example, their spelling may show an awareness of silent letters related to pronunciation, but the silent letters may be written in the wrong place in the word (*gaett/gate*). Children may also have difficulty knowing when to double a consonant (*spater/spatter*). They do, however, spell short vowels correctly with greater frequency.

The *morphemic and syntactic stage* occurs from approximately fifth grade on. By this time children are more aware of the regular and consistent features of English orthography. They generally know when to double consonants (*smattering*), and are more cognizant of alternate forms of the same word (*judge–judgment*), and associate the spelling of a word with other words having similar meaning (*photographic, photography*) instead of being solely dependent on pronunciation. They also gain control of morphological endings of words such as *-er*, *-ly*, and *-ed*. Beers and Beers say, "When older students have gained an understanding that English spelling is controlled by meaning and grammatical structure in addition to phonology they have mastered the 'real' spelling rules for written English" (1981, p. 577).

Planning the Spelling Program

Goals of the Spelling Program

The major goal of the spelling program is to develop able and independent spellers. The goal is not an end in itself, but it is part of the schools' goal of developing able and independent writers. More specific long-range goals for the spelling program include

1. Children will learn to spell most frequently used words.
2. Children will develop and use an effective method for learning to spell new words.
3. Children will recognize misspelled words.
4. Children will use the dictionary to determine the correct spelling of words.
5. Children will value correct spelling and will strive to improve their own spelling ability.

Important Considerations for Teaching Spelling

Several research studies on the teaching of spelling have been reported in educational publications. From them we have gathered the following generalizations about good spelling programs.

Extensive reading and writing experiences help children become good spellers. As children read they come in contact with words, words they will sometime want to write. Through reading children gain a basic understanding of the written code of language. Writing is also an essential and complementary activity. Just as reading creates the need to think about how words and letters are pronounced, writing creates the need to think about how words and sounds are spelled. Writing requires children to formulate hypotheses about spelling; reading supplies the data either to support their hypotheses or to suggest modifications.

The purpose of spelling instruction is to help children spell words accurately in actual writing situations. Attention to spelling should not be limited to specific periods of the day. Children need help in processing information relative to spelling throughout the day and they need to apply their knowledge of spelling to written work outside of spelling class. Although teachers should not place undue stress on spelling, they should realize that learning to spell a word in isolation has little value unless it is related to meaningful writing experiences.

Understanding the meaning of words is important. The words children learn to spell should be words they already know orally. Unless children know the meaning of a word they will have no use for it in writing; hence, they will see no reason for learning it. Homonyms illustrate the need for meaning. Rote memorization of *pair, pear,* and *pare* will be of little value unless children associate meaning with each word.

Children vary in aptitude for spelling. Some children seem to be "natural born spellers." They have apparently developed a cognitive structure that allows them to assimilate the spelling of words very easily. At the other end of the spectrum are those children who must work hard to learn to spell words and who have difficulty remembering from one day to the next how a word is spelled.

Children vary in the way they learn. Some children find one learning modality more efficient, whereas other children learn best in another way. Spelling is commonly thought of as an auditory-visual learning process, but it should not be limited to those channels. Some children learn best through kinesthetic channels.

The spelling program should provide for individual differences in children. Both the content of the spelling program (*what* children learn) and the scope of the program (*how much* children learn) should be flexible. The program should be planned to provide a variety of approaches at different levels of difficulty, so that all children can experience satisfaction and success.

Studying lists of words has been found to be an efficient way to learn to spell words. Learning to spell a difficult word requires concentration. Studying a few troublesome words at a time allows children to focus their complete attention on each word, thus facilitating mastery. Once learned, however, words should be used in context to ensure assimilation and integration of skills.

The test-study approach is generally more efficient than a study-test approach. By giving a pretest on a list of words, the teacher identifies the words the children do not know. Then the study of those words becomes purposeful. Studying words one already knows how to spell is a waste of time.

Children need to acquire a system for learning to spell words. It is virtually impossible to know which words children will need in a lifetime. It is therefore important to teach them a way to learn words on their own so that they can systematically learn to spell whatever words they need.

Requiring children to write each word ten times is an inefficient way to study words. It is possible to copy words with little or no cognitive involvement. Given a word such as *little* to write, children have been known to make a column of *l*'s, then a column of *i*'s beside the *l*'s and so on. They fulfill the writing requirement without learning.

Calling children's attention to hard spots in words should be avoided. Teachers should not assume that children will have trouble spelling a particular word. What is difficult for one child may not be difficult for another. By pointing out a potential difficulty you may actually cause children to become confused about something that might have been no problem.

Instruction and practice should focus on helping children write *words.* Practice that emphasizes spelling words orally is of questionable value. The real test of competency is the ability to *write* words correctly in context.

Spelling skills need to be reinforced. Knowledge of words and generalizations is maintained and strengthened through frequent use. A good spelling program provides review cycles of learned words and provides opportunities for children to use their full range of spelling knowledge in a variety of writing situations.

Not more than seventy-five minutes per week should be used for spelling instruction. Research has shown that children gain little when spelling instruction exceeds seventy-five minutes. Learning to spell requires concentration; a short period of directed attention yields the best results.

Ability to proofread accurately is an important spelling skill. Even good spellers occasionally make a careless spelling error. However, good spellers catch those errors by carefully proofreading what they have written. Instruction in spelling ought to include attention to proofreading and should help children develop "a good eye" for errors.

Skills Important to Learning to Spell

Formal spelling lessons are usually not begun until the end of first grade or the beginning of second grade. Before children are ready to *study* spelling, they must accumulate experiences with language. Through many informal experiences hearing, speaking, reading, and writing words they begin to develop basic concepts about print and become interested in knowing more about it. Important signs of readiness include:

1. Ability to enunciate words clearly.

2. Ability to name and write the letters of the alphabet.

3. Ability to identify letters correctly in a word in sequence.

4. Ability to copy words accurately.

5. Ability to read simple stories.

6. Desire to write words and stories independently.

The following skills may to some extent be prerequisites for learning to spell and to some extent concomitant learnings or results of learning to spell. In any case, teachers should be aware of their importance and attend to the acquisition of these skills by individual children.

Visual discrimination Children must learn to look closely at words and to notice the letters and the sequence of letters in words. To develop this skill, they might be given exercises in which they find words that are the same or different. A domino game with words instead of dots may be used for matching words that are the same. Worksheets may also be made with key words for children to find among a list of other words.

come	home	come	came	calm
said	sail	soil	same	said

Visual memory Children need to form a visual image of words and be able to remember how a word looks. One exercise for developing this skill is to hold up a word on a flash card and have the children concentrate on it for a few seconds. Then remove the flash card and ask the children either to write the word or to find it in a list or in a story.

Auditory discrimination If children are to use phonic cues to help them spell words, they must be able to distinguish both the individual sounds in words and the correct sequence of the sounds. Children need many exercises in identifying words that are alike or different, that rhyme, that begin the same, or that end with the same letter. Saying words slowly helps children hear that words are made up of separate sounds and provides readiness for phonics. It also helps older children hear the sequence of sounds in words and use their phonic knowledge in spelling words.

Using phonic generalizations A basic knowledge of phoneme-grapheme correspondences is an important aid to good spelling. Activities such as cutting out pictures of things that begin alike, writing word lists, and making alphabet books help develop letter-sound associations. It may also be helpful for children to form a key association or referent for each letter sound through stories or activities. For example, children might model a snake out of clay in the shape of an *s* or they might be given an olive and note that it has the shape and sound of *o*.

Using structural and morphemic analysis Learning to recognize and spell parts of words helps children deal with longer words. By saying words in syllables and writing each syllable as they pronounce it children learn to listen more closely and accurately. Recognizing familiar roots or affixes in words that they already know how to spell also helps children spell successfully and builds spelling confidence.

Teaching Generalizations

There is little question that a general knowledge of phonics is helpful in spelling. Many of the phonic generalizations or "rules" traditionally taught in relation to reading, however, are based on *decoding* rather than *encoding* and offer little direct help for generating the spelling of words. For example, if children have discovered the generalization that when the vowel combination *oa* appears in a word, the first vowel is usually long and the second is silent, they can apply the generalization and decode the word *boat* correctly even if they have never seen it before (if, of course, they also can decode the *b* and *t*).

Generalizing about the spelling of the same sound is a different matter. Imagine, for example, that a child does not know how to spell a similar word with a long vowel in medial position, /r/ /ō/ /d/. The first and final sounds would most likely pose no problem, but the vowel sound in the middle would not be so easy. There is no generalization that reliably indicates the correct spelling of /ō/ in medial position; there are only options. The child might, for example, generalize the spelling of the sound from the *o* in *go,* the *oa* in *boat,* the *o—e* pattern in *note,* the *ow* in *own,* the *ew* in *sew,* or even the *eau* in *beau.* If the children were not familiar with the less common spellings or knew that the *o* spelling usually occurs only in the final position of a syllable, they would eliminate some of the options. A child who had a background of reading experiences and a good visual memory might be able to narrow the spelling options to *road* and *rode.* Then, choosing between the two spellings would require semantic knowledge that would, in turn, depend on the context in which the word was used: syntactic cues. Thus we see that a generalization about the pronunciation of *oa* offered little help in *generating the spelling* of a word containing the /ō/ sound.

The question of which spelling generalizations to teach has stimulated a great deal of discussion. Although the Stanford research project shed considerable light on the consistency of American English orthography, the extensive set of spelling rules (the algorithm) that was programmed into the computer does not provide a succinct set of generalizations to be taught in the elementary school. Rather, in suggesting a program based on that research, Hanna, Hanna, Hodges, and Rudorf advocate a spelling program that encompasses a broad language study approach in which children "develop a cognitive map of the powerful patterns and principles (phonological, morphological and contextual) by which we encode language" (1966, p. 115).

Most of us recall memorizing a great many spelling "rules" in elementary school. But if we can still remember those rules, we are also aware of numerous exceptions to them. There seems to be little justification for teaching a spelling rule, or generalization, unless it applies to many words and has few exceptions. Few generalizations meet those criteria. Those generally considered to be worth teaching include:

1. One-syllable words or longer words accented on the last syllable that end with a single consonant preceded by a single vowel, usually double the final consonant before adding a suffix beginning with a vowel (*run–runner, sit–sitting, hop–hopping*).

2. Words ending in silent *e* usually drop the *e* before adding a suffix beginning with a vowel, but keep the final *e* if the suffix begins with a consonant (*bake–baking, hope–hoping; sincere–sincerely, hope–hopeless*).

3. Words ending in *y* preceded by a consonant usually change the *y* to *i* before adding suffixes that begin with a vowel unless the suffix begins with *i* (*deny–denial, envy–envious; fry–fried–frying, empty–emptied–emptying*).

4. Words ending in *y* preceded by a vowel are not changed when a suffix is added (*monkey–monkeys, delay–delays, play–played*).

5. *Q* is always followed by *u* in English words (*quiet, quick, quilt*).

6. Plurals of nouns are formed by adding *s* with two exceptions: words ending in *s, z, x, sh,* or *ch* add *es;* and words ending in *y* preceded by a consonant usually change the *y* to *i* and add *es* (*boy–boys, pencil–pencils;* but *fox–foxes, bush–bushes; sky–skies, army–armies*).[2]

Children begin to generalize about the spelling of words as soon as they start writing on their own. Allowing them to try to spell words encourages them to develop an attitude of inquiry and to be alert to orthographic features that may provide significant spelling help. Thinking about similarities and forming tentative generalizations, whether it results in the formulation of a concise grapheme-phoneme generalization or not, is an aid to good spelling. It is

---

[2] Notice the difficulty in trying to pronounce words ending in *s, z, x, sh,* and *ch* without adding *es* to make another syllable.

important, too, to remember that any generalization must be considered tentative until adequate data have been collected either to substantiate or to invalidate it.

Activities based on word patterns or "families" can provide opportunities for children to generalize from the spelling of one word to others. Through awareness of groups of words that end with the same sound, they can use one spelling pattern to spell a number of words (e.g., *day: way, say, play, may, tray,* etc.) Exercises in hearing and writing rhyming words give children practice in auditory discrimination and develop the concept that spelling is encoding language sounds. There are many word endings that may serve as patterns for such exercises. Some of the more common ones include:

at	ed	id	ot
ail	et	ing	ong
ate	eat	ine	ort
ain	it	ick	ow
an	in	ite	ug
ang	ip	ice	up

Many of the spelling generalizations children discover do have several exceptions and require extensive modification (or elimination) on the basis of additional data. However, the discoveries they make in the process of formulating generalizations are of greater value than the net total of reliable generalizations. One value that must not be overlooked is the discovery of spelling options. Identifying variant spellings can lead to a deeper understanding of linguistic influences that control which grapheme is appropriate under which circumstances (e.g., the *gh* spelling of /f/ appears only at the end of certain words). In this way children discover that spelling options, too, are often predictable and that they depend on linguistic cues derived from the total language system.

Young children as well as older ones are capable of seeing certain consistent patterns and relationships. Children of any age, however, are apt to miss learning opportunities unless they have guidance in developing a system for analyzing data. A procedure for developing a generalization might follow these steps:

1. The teacher identifies a generalization to teach.

2. A list of known words that exemplify the generalization are presented to the children and pronounced orally.

3. The teacher asks "What do you notice about all these words?" or "How are all these words alike?"

4. The children are guided in stating the generalization.

5. The children are given an opportunity to test the generalization on additional words.

One teacher, for example, noticed that several children asked for words beginning with /sh/ while they were writing stories. When the children had finished their stories, the teacher wrote the words they had asked her to spell for them on the board: *show, ship, shell, shook.* The children said each word as the teacher wrote it. Then the entire list was read again, and the teacher told them to listen carefully as they pronounced each word. The teacher asked what sound they heard in all the words, then what letters spelled that sound. A child was selected to go to the board and underline the letters that spelled the /sh/ sound while the class once again read through the list. The children suggested other words they knew that began with the same sound, and the teacher wrote them on the board. Finally, the words that had been requested during the story-writing were added to their weekly spelling list. Those words were selected from the total list of /sh/ words because they were the words the children actually used.

Once children have formulated a generalization they should have periodic opportunities to practice and reinforce what they have learned. Games offer one way to provide this practice. Another way is to write the generalization on the board or on chart paper and ask the children to list examples of words or to add pictures that illustrate the generalization.

The Dictionary and Spelling

A dictionary can be a valuable spelling resource. For someone with a basic knowledge of sound spelling options, the dictionary provides a way to find an unknown spelling or to check the accuracy of an uncertain spelling. The habit of looking words up in a dictionary is a good one to establish early and reinforce throughout the school experience. There are suitable dictionaries for every age — dictionaries for young children, beginning dictionaries, junior and intermediate dictionaries, and others on through collegiate editions.

In addition to commercial dictionaries, children, particularly young children, ought to have their own alphabetized word lists. Their personal lists contain words they need to write most frequently. One useful resource is a personal word box with words arranged in alphabetical order. A word box can be made for each child from a small box (two-pound cheese boxes work well). Cut slips of paper slightly smaller than the box and make alphabetical dividers from heavy

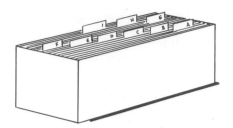

FIGURE 8-1

paper or cardboard. After you attach lettered tabs the box is ready to use (Figure 8-1).

A child who doesn't know how to spell a word should first check the word box to see if it is there. If not, the teacher or an aide writes the word neatly on one of the slips of paper while the child watches. Then the child copies the word onto his or her paper and files the slip behind the appropriate divider in the word box. Soon children's files contain most of the words they use regularly. As they repeatedly use these words, they learn how to spell them and no longer need to look them up and copy them.

A similar word source can be made by stapling paper together to make individual word books. The procedure is similar to that for the word box, except that the words children request are written in their word books on the appropriate page. Older children may prefer to keep word lists in their notebook. They may compile these lists themselves or they may use published word lists available in many school-supply sections of stores. The latter come already punched and ready for insertion in notebooks. Small paperback word books such as those designed for secretarial use are also favorites.

Word boxes and word books teach alphabetizing as well as spelling. Younger children file their words by the first letter only; older children gradually learn to alphabetize to the third letter of words or even to a letter further in.

Learning alphabetical order is an essential skill for using a dictionary. An alphabet displayed conspicuously in the classroom provides children with a ready reference. As soon as children have learned to recognize all the letters, they can play alphabet games, sing alphabet songs, and participate in activities that require the use of alphabetical order. A teacher might have them line up in alphabetical order or take turns doing something in alphabetical order. Or, children may help alphabetize such things as groups of papers, lunch tickets, or new library books. Another way to help young children develop a

TABLE 8-5. SOUND SPELLINGS

SOUND	KEY WORD	POSSIBLE SPELLING
/sh/	ship	sh (bush), s (sugar), ch (machine), ss (fissure), sch (schwa), ce (ocean), ci (ancient)
/ā/	ate	a (able), ai (maid), ay (day), ea (break), au (gauge), ei (veil), ey (hey), uet (bouquet), et (buffet)

sense of the alphabet is to say a letter and have the children chant the alphabet up to that letter, taking one jump forward as each letter is said. This activity is particularly good to help children conceptualize the position of letters in the alphabet. When they must jump many times before they come to a letter they know that it is near the end of the alphabet and that words beginning with that letter will be found toward the back of the dictionary.

Being able to use a dictionary to find the spelling of a word is not always a simple matter of knowing alphabetical order, however. To use a dictionary, children must have some knowledge of the way a word is spelled. They must be familiar with spelling options and proceed to look up each possible spelling until they find the word. It is often useful to have a ready reference of possible sound spellings. As a class activity the children might develop a list of both common and uncommon spellings of sounds in chart form. They could continue to add to the chart as they discover other spellings for sounds. Such a chart might look like Table 8-5.

Textbooks and the Instructional Program

Earlier in this chapter we have seen that learning to spell is directly related to children's awareness and utilization of phonic, morphological, and syntactic cues. Because of this, a spelling program must be broadly based. It must include attention to the characteristics of written language and assist children in formulating generalizations they can apply in writing words. In addition, decisions must be made about the specific content of spelling instruction and how it should be taught.

In many school districts the adopted spelling textbooks become the spelling program. As with any such materials, the teacher must analyze the philosophy and content of the books and determine their usefulness for his or her spelling program. Some current textbooks, for example, emphasize knowledge of phonic and structural patterns of spelling. The weekly lists of words and exercises are selected to illustrate specific spelling patterns. In this approach one assumes that once children know the common patterns in the spelling system, they will be able to spell an infinite number of words.

A good spelling program ought to include attention both to the immediate writing needs of children and to long-range spelling goals. It should not be limited to the rote memorization of a prepackaged weekly list of words or to chance discovery of phoneme-grapheme relationships through writing. Hanna, Hodges, and Hanna suggest, "An effective spelling program should be based on a carefully laid out *scope and sequence chart* showing how the most important phoneme-grapheme correspondences, word-building generalizations, and contextual cues can be introduced and then repeated at higher levels with words that have more complex spelling patterns" (1971, p. 11). They further suggest that a spelling program should include experiences under these seven spelling related categories: sound-to-letter correspondences, word-building, meaning, the history of words, the study of language, dictionary usage, and writing conventions (p. 119).

Published spelling programs offer a sequential approach to teaching spelling skills and usually include words selected on the basis of use and utility. They are organized around a weekly lesson plan and provide all necessary materials. Therefore they can save the teacher a great deal of time. An example of a weekly lesson plan is given in Figure 8-2. This plan follows a study-test approach but it could easily be modified to a test-study-test plan by testing children on the words before they are introduced. According to the printed plan in this spelling series, the list of words is introduced on the first day (part *A*) and followed up with additional exercises for each of the other days of the week (parts *B*, *C*, and *D*). A mastery test is given on the fifth day.

A teacher-designed spelling program might follow a similar plan, or it might be organized as follows:

Day 1. Test children on the list of words for the week. Let them check their tests and prepare a personal list of words they need to study.

Day 2. Independent or small-group study with teacher-directed instruction. Children work on developing visual imagery of

FIGURE 8-2 (*pages 287–290*)

From *Spelling: Words and Skills*, Book 5 by Ronald L. Cramer, et al. Copyright © 1978 by Scott, Foresman and Company. Reprinted by permission.

1. _____
2. _____
3. _____
4. _____
5. _____
6. _____
7. _____
8. _____
9. _____
10. _____
11. _____
12. _____
13. _____
14. _____
15. _____
16. _____
17. _____
18. _____
19. _____
20. _____

LESSON 29

The Consonant Sounds
/kw/, /ks/, and /f/

Part A

Say the words in the list below. Write the words.

1. quit
2. quite
3. quiet
4. square
5. question
6. aquarium
7. fox
8. sixth
9. axle
10. excited
11. exercise
12. galaxy
13. physical
14. pheasant
15. photograph
16. elephant
17. telephone
18. trophy
19. coordination *
20. extinct *

● Write the first two words in which /kw/ is spelled **qu**.

_____   _____

● Write the first two words in which /ks/ is spelled **x**.

_____   _____

● Write the first two words in which /f/ is spelled **ph**.

_____   _____

✻Wild Words   Be careful not to run the first two syllables of *coordination* together when you say it: pronouncing it with /kw/ leads to spelling errors. The first **o** stands for /ō/, and the second **o** stands for /ô/. Learn the word parts: *co or di na tion*.

The sound /ks/ in *extinct* is spelled **x**. Use the study steps to learn the word.

Test Score:_____ —20   **116**   Part A Score:_____ —6

Part B

1. Write the list words with the spelling patterns shown.
   a. /ks/ spelled **x**   b. /kw/ spelled **qu**   c. /f/ spelled **ph**

   _____   _____   _____
   _____   _____   _____
   _____   _____   _____
   _____   _____   _____
   _____   _____   _____
   _____   _____

2. Write a list word that goes with each meaning.
   a. working together   b. no longer existing   c. thrilled

   _____   _____   _____

   d. a group of stars   e. bar on which wheels   f. of the body
                             turn

   _____   _____   _____

3. Write the words that name the pictures on this page.

   a   b   c

   d   e   f

   a. _____
   b. _____
   c. _____
   d. _____
   e. _____
   f. _____

What's the Big Idea?

Some consonant sounds have unusual spellings: /ks/ may
be spelled **x**; /kw/ may be spelled **qu**; /f/ may be spelled **ph**.

pre sent (pri zent′ *for
1*; prez′nt *for 2*).
1 give: *They presented
flowers to their teacher.*
2 thing given; gift: *a
birthday present.* 1 *v.,* 2
n.

re cord (ri kôrd′ *for 1*;
rek′ərd *for 2*), **1** set
down in writing so as
to keep for future use:
*Record what the
speaker says.* **2** a thin,
flat disk, usually of
vinyl or other plastic,
with narrow grooves on
its surface, used on a
phonograph. 1 *v.,* 2 *n.*

square (skwer *or*
skwar), **1** a plane figure
with four equal sides
and four right angles
(□). **2** having this
shape: *a square box.* 1
n., 2 *adj.*

Part C
Dictionary

If a word may be pronounced in more than one way, more
than one pronunciation is shown in a dictionary entry. Say
the two pronunciations for *square.* Both are correct.

Sometimes the pronunciation of a word depends upon its
meaning. Notice that the first pronunciation for *present* is
used with meaning 1 and the second pronunciation is used
for meaning 2. *I'll (pri zent′) a (prez′ nt) to Dad.*

Read each sentence. Then write *1* or *2* to show which
pronunciation and meaning is correct for the underlined
word.

_____ 1. Mom gave me a nice birthday <u>present</u>.

_____ 2. The mayor will <u>present</u> a trophy to our team.

_____ 3. Pamela put a <u>record</u> on the phonograph.

_____ 4. Mr. Garcia will <u>record</u> the minutes of the meeting.

Handwriting

_____ *N*   *X* _____

The letters **v** and **x** begin with overhill strokes. Be sure to
cross the **x** with a straight line stroke. Write *exercise* and
vetoes.

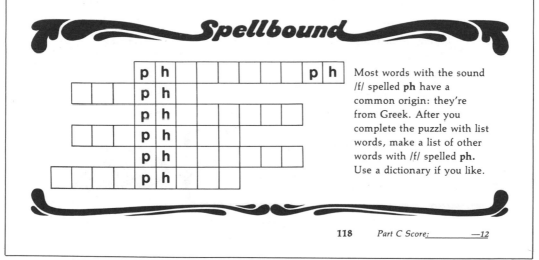

Most words with the sound
/f/ spelled **ph** have a
common origin: they're
from Greek. After you
complete the puzzle with list
words, make a list of other
words with /f/ spelled **ph.**
Use a dictionary if you like.

118   *Part C Score:_____ —12*

Part D

Choose the list or lists of words you want to learn. Then complete the activities next to each list you choose.

---

1. Make a phrase by writing each word below with a review word that rhymes with it. Example: *rough enough*

a. double   b. warning   c. tough   d. steak

a. _____

b. _____

c. _____

d. _____

2. Make a crossword puzzle with the review words.

Review Words

enough
trouble
break
morning

---

1. Use the glossary to choose the word that goes with each meaning.

a. to make aware or inform _____

b. a group of words _____

c. to be better than _____

d. to tell the meaning of _____

2. Write a short paragraph. Use each word in it.

Big Idea Words

acquaint
excel
explain
phrase

---

1. Which two words name something worn on the head?

_____   _____

2. Which words name types of material used for clothing?

_____   _____

3. Write *suede* and circle the letter that spells /w/.
4. Write *beret* and circle the letters that spell /ā/.

Challenge Words

suede
turban
corduroy
beret

Study Hint!

Say each word that is difficult for you and look carefully at the letters that spell the sounds. Write the word without looking at it. Check the spelling.

119

words and auditory and visual discrimination, and on analyzing phonic and structural spelling cues in their personal word lists.

Day 3. Trial test on the entire list of words to check progress and determine mastery. Children again correct their tests and prepare a personal list of words for further study.

Day 4. Concentrated independent or peer tutor study for children who have not mastered all spelling words. Children who have attained mastery level on the trial test may engage in enrichment exercises (study of etymology, word puzzles, morphology, proofreading, dictionary work, etc.)

Day 5. Final test.

Teaching and Learning Strategies

Research tends to favor a test-study-test approach in which children are tested on a list of words before studying them. That test is followed by time to study the words they miss, and then the children are retested on the entire list. This plan seems most efficient because it allows children to spend their study time working on words they don't know. Study then becomes more purposeful. The plan also permits greater individualization of spelling, freeing more able spellers to engage in more challenging activities.

For accurate assessment of known words the test should be given without children looking over the words to refresh their memories. The test should be conducted informally, yet in a businesslike and predictable manner. Children should not comment on or discuss words during a test. Not only does this detract from concentration but it tends to make the test unnecessarily tedious. A three-step procedure provides pronunciation and meaning cues for children and simulates an actual writing experience.

1. Pronounce the word distinctly but without unnatural emphasis.

2. Use the word in a meaningful sentence.

3. Pronounce the word again.

The pace of a spelling test is important. It should allow a reasonable time for children to write a word yet maintain a brisk enough pace to encourage attention to the task. When children know how to spell a word they are able to write it quickly. Using a word in a sentence indicates its meaning and thus alleviates need for further clarification.

To maximize the learning experience, children ought to check their own papers. They may do so as the teacher spells each word slowly aloud or as they compare their papers against a printed list. Identifying the words they have misspelled gives children immediate feedback and promotes learning. Horn states, "When corrected by the pupils and the results are properly utilized, the test is the most fruitful single learning activity (per unit of time) that has yet been devised" (1967, pp. 17–18).

Teaching children to spell involves helping them to associate printed symbols with words. To do this they need to develop a way of studying words. For example, they may use

Visual memory: looking at the whole word and trying to form a visual image of it.

Structural analysis: listening to and analyzing the parts of a word, its syllables, roots, and affixes.

Phonic analysis: listening to the sounds in the words and associating letters with sounds.

Rote memory: remembering the sequence and clustering of letters in words.

Kinesthetic response: physically responding to a word by writing it.

The following study plan combines all these approaches and provides a comprehensive method for learning to spell a word.

Step 1. Look at the word and pronounce it slowly, listening to the natural grouping of sounds into syllables as you pronounce it.

Step 2. Find the root word(s). Do you know any other words with the same root? If so, what are they? Are there any prefixes or suffixes? If so, what are they? Is the root changed when suffixes are added? If so, how? Spell each part.

Step 3. Close your eyes and try to see how the word looks. If you can't remember all of it, take another look. Then close your eyes and try again.

Step 4. Now write the word without looking at it in the book. Check each letter to see if you wrote the word correctly. If not, go back to the first step again.

Step 5. Cover up the word and write it again, saying the sounds slowly to yourself as you write. Check for correct spelling. If you wrote it correctly, write the word two more times without looking.

The final test over the week's spelling list indicates children's mastery after study. If you are concerned about the children's ability to correct their tests accurately, you may spot-check their work, you may check them yourself, or you may let the children check their work in pairs. Although this test is called *final,* you should not infer that incorrectly spelled words are ignored at this point. Words that are misspelled should be added to the list for study during the following weeks until they are mastered. Periodic review tests, usually at six-week intervals, should also be given to reinforce the learning of words. And, to reiterate a previous point, children must be given ample opportunity to use spelling in purposeful writing activities. The time set aside for specific instruction will not achieve its intended goal unless children relate what they are doing to actual language use.

Developing a Spelling Conscience

A spelling conscience has to do with children's personal concern for correct spelling. It evolves from their ability to distinguish between correct and incorrect word forms and from their desire to spell correctly. A spelling conscience in children is directly related to the pride they take in their work. When they value correct spelling they are more apt to respond positively to learning opportunities and to apply what they learn to their writing.

Establishing pride in correct spelling is not always easy. Children need to realize that spelling is an essential part of our communication code and that failure to spell correctly hampers communication. Even though poorly written material can sometimes be decoded, misspellings detract from the message. Children need to realize, too, that when words are misspelled readers tend to make negative assumptions about the writer. From a practical standpoint, poor spelling may limit opportunities both in and out of school. One large firm, for example, reportedly screened applicants for janitorial positions partially on their spelling ability. Whenever a task requires writing, spelling becomes an important prerequisite for success and poor spellers are quickly eliminated. Although some people doubtlessly find spelling easier than others, poor spellers can improve if they are willing to work at it.

If children are to value correct spelling and to want to spell correctly, they need to experience the intrinsic rewards of doing quality work. Initially teachers may have to set high standards for children and insist that they meet them. Teachers must also help children find ways to achieve success. For example, one technique that has been effective involves a system for indicating possible spelling errors while children are writing. Whenever they are not certain of the spelling of a word, they write it as nearly correctly as they can, draw a line under it, and go on. When they are finished writing and have their ideas down on paper, they go back over their paper and look up the correct spellings of all the underlined words. Such procedures help children become aware of correct spelling without burdening them with corrections while they are concentrating on a flow of thought. At the same time, they shift the responsibility for correct spelling from the teacher to the learner. Accepting responsibility is an important step for children in developing a spelling conscience.

Individualizing Instruction

A spelling program may be modified in several ways to accommodate students' individual needs and abilities. The guiding principle for an individualized program is to tune in to children and find out where they are and how they learn. Observing, discussing, and sampling are important ways to assess their skills and understandings. When you have this knowledge you can plan instruction. The following aspects of a spelling program can be adapted for individual differences.

Selection of Words

If a commercial spelling program is used, examine the list carefully to determine whether the words are those which your children most need to spell now. To give the children spelling confidence and to motivate them to want to learn, you should choose words with high personal utility now and in the foreseeable future. The level of difficulty of the words is also important. Modify the list (or create a new one) by substituting more or less difficult words appropriate to individual children. A spelling list should offer a comfortable but not impossible challenge.

Number of Words

An individualized list of words ought to represent a reasonable goal. In other words, the number of words children are expected to master in a given period of time should be governed by their individual learning capacities. The net gain for poor spellers is apt to be greater when they concentrate on fewer words at a time. If they try to learn too many words at once, their efforts may be spread so thin that they are unable to master any (or master only a few) of them.

Study Procedures

Suggested learning procedures may be modified for individual children. The child with a high spelling aptitude will most likely master words without going through all the suggested study steps. However, repeated practice on a particular step may prove particularly beneficial for other children. Some children, for example, learn to spell words best through the physical activity of writing words. Thoughtful writing practice brings together sounds and letters through children's eyes, ears, and muscles. Writing a word over and over while attending to its sounds and letters trains the arm and fingers to respond to certain words by producing a correct sequence of letters.

A tape recorder is a useful tool for modifying instructional procedures. Prerecorded direct instruction may be used by children who require help in developing efficient study habits. Tests may also be recorded so that children can use them as a study technique. Or, a tape recorder may be used with more able children to test them on individualized lists of words, to provide dictation practice, or to present enrichment activities.

Spelling Games

Hodges (1981) states, "The value of word games in the teaching of spelling lies not only in the enjoyment they offer young children but in their potential to promote inquiry and experimentation. In addition they provide opportunities for students to practice word formation in settings that are challenging and exciting rather than rigid and monotonous. . . . In sum, word games encourage the formulation of generalizations about the written code and the classification of information within those concepts" (p. 15).

For games to be effective instructional aids, they must fit the learner's abilities and needs. Games should never be used indiscriminately; the teacher should be sure that they will give the kind and amount of practice needed by specific children. In choosing games keep the following criteria in mind:

1. Games should supply as much practice to as many participants as possible. Games where one child performs while others wait a turn supply limited practice.

2. Games stressing oral spelling should be used only rarely. Spelling is primarily a writing skill.

3. Avoid games that place poor spellers in embarrassing or high-risk situations.

4. Avoid games that give the child who already knows how to spell the most practice and the greatest incentives.

Mnemonic Aids

Mnemonic aids are memory crutches; they require children to remember a particular association that, in turn, serves as a clue to the spelling of a word. For example, to spell *principal* correctly, children may remember the saying, "The princi*pal* is a *pal*"; to remember not to put a *t* in *bachelor*, they may remember, "A bachelor doesn't like tea"; or the spelling of *abundance* may be aided by forming a mental image of a bun dancing.

Although mnemonic aids may help some children remember a particularly troublesome part of a word, they can be a nuisance for other children and may even cause unnecessary confusion. An association that works for one person may not for another. Sometimes children remember an association but can't remember what it is supposed to help them remember. The best memory crutches are those which children discover for themselves, those which have personal meaning.

Evaluation of Spelling

Sources for Evaluation

Standardized tests Standardized tests are routinely given in many schools, and they offer one means of evaluating children's spelling ability. They have limited value, however, for spelling assessment, and should not be relied on too heavily. The nature of the spelling task makes it difficult to design an objective test that can be machine scored and still adequately measure spelling ability. On most standardized tests the spelling section asks children to pick out the correct spelling of a word from among several choices. This tests their ability to identify correctly spelled words rather than testing their ability to generate correct spellings as they must do in normal writing activities. Children may be able to pick out an incorrectly written word even though they are unable to write the word correctly.

Word list tests The most common testing situation is the weekly spelling test. In this type of test children are required to write words from a list they have studied in advance. Some children memorize the list so completely that they are able to write the whole list from memory without anyone having to pronounce the words for them. Getting the words correct on a weekly spelling test does not guarantee that children will be able to write the words correctly in actual use. When they have crammed for a test, they may hold the words in short-term memory for a limited period of time. They will need additional practice and use to ensure mastery of the words.

Written work The way children spell in their everyday written work provides valuable data for assessing children's spelling strategies and evaluating their spelling skills. How well children spell in practical situations is a good indication of how well they have internalized the spelling of specific words and the spelling system in general. Practical application of spelling is the real test of children's spelling ability. This does not mean, however, that evaluation of the spelling in children's writing should be allowed to negatively influence what children write. Pressure to conform to inappropriate standards may cause them to lose their freedom of expression and result in an unnaturally simplistic language that they feel is safe.

Purposes of Evaluation

Evaluation of spelling serves two purposes. It measures progress and it provides a means for improving spelling ability. Evaluation not only identifies where children are on a continuum of learning, but it also indicates the kinds of problems that account for their placement. A spelling test or other evaluation should not be seen as an end in itself. Rather, it is a diagnostic tool and a progress report.

Analysis of Errors

Evaluating children's spelling ought to be more than merely counting the number of words correct. To be genuinely helpful, evaluation needs to get at the kinds of errors children make. Quite often children get most of a word right; it is only one small part that they need to improve. Knowing the type of error they have made allows them to concentrate on eliminating that problem. Some of the more common types of errors and suggestions for remediating them are listed in Table 8-6.

Record-Keeping

A record of children's progress is essential in planning appropriate instruction. It should indicate not only how well children do on the weekly spelling list but the kinds of errors children make in their tests and in their daily lessons. For the sake of teacher time and efficiency, records must be kept simple. Running notes may be kept on a 5 × 8 card for each child, or checklists of common errors (see Table 8-6) may be used for the class.

Children should also be encouraged to keep a list of the words they misspell on their tests and in daily writing. Then, as they master the spelling of those words, they can draw a single line through them. This list makes an interesting record of their progress and of the words that they have learned and that need to be reinforced from time to time.

Many teachers record children's weekly test scores on special charts displayed in the room. These charts range from rockets shooting to the moon to the traditional one with gold stars. Charts provide a form of extrinsic reward and are intended to motivate children to improve their spelling scores. Sometimes, however, they have the opposite effect and actually discourage poor spellers. Children may find little incentive even to try to propel their rocket into space when they are convinced that they will never get the necessary score. Whenever extrinsic rewards are used they must be based on realistic and attainable goals. A goal of seven words correct may be a challenge for the poor speller. Achieving that goal is as worthy of praise as a score of twenty by a student who already knew most of the words before the lesson began.

In Summary

American English orthography reflects the history of the language from very earliest times. It is a record of the influences and political powers that have gradually shaped the language into its present form. Although the orthographic system does not have a perfect one-to-one phoneme-grapheme correspondence, some linguists believe that the spelling of English is a nearly optimum system. To spell all

TABLE 8-6. COMMON SPELLING ERRORS

TYPE OF ERROR	EXAMPLE	REMEDIATION
inaccuracy in regular phoneme-grapheme correspondence	*teta* for *baby*	auditory-visual training of basic phonic elements; interrelation of reading and spelling instruction
wrong choice of spelling option	*wead* for *weed*	teaching of most common spellings of sounds; stress on visualization of words
omission of a pronounced letter	*pay* for *play*	checking for correct pronunciation of word; auditory training in listening for sounds; practice in writing other words containing omitted sound
omission of silent letter	*ofen* for *often*	visual imagery training; kinesthetic practice; breaking longer words into syllables with common patterns involving silent letters identified (e.g., *-ble*); study of word history; possible mnemonic aids
insertion of a letter	*molst* for *most*	auditory and visual training; careful enunciation of individual sounds; matching up phonemes and graphemes in word
reversal of letters	*form* for *from*	auditory and visual training; serial memory work; kinesthetic practice
use of wrong vowel in unaccented syllable	*inturesting* for *interesting*	breaking word into syllables; pronouncing and analyzing parts separately; visual memory; listing other forms of the word
confusion in using homonyms	*ware* for *wear*	writing pairs of words; defining; using in sentences; visual memory training; possible mnemonic aids
confusion between words with similar pronunciation	*except* for *accept*	clarifying pronunciation; noticing differences in pronunciation and meaning; oral and written practice in using words in sentences
suffixes added to roots	*surly* for *surely*	generalizations; collecting examples of correctly spelled words using structural element
double consonants	*baloon* for *balloon*	analysis of pronunciation of double consonants (usually only the first is sounded); breaking words into syllables; sharpening visual imagery of word; possible mnemonic aids (e.g., "a *ball*oon is like a *ball*")

TABLE 8-6. COMMON SPELLING ERRORS (*continued*)

TYPE OF ERROR	EXAMPLE	REMEDIATION
plural forms involving *es*	*brushs* for *brushes*	auditory-visual training; pronouncing singular and plural forms; counting syllables; identifying last syllable of plural form
irregularly formed plurals	*mouses* for *mice*	list of irregular plural forms; chant lists; making up riddles, poems, and songs
poor handwriting	*cloor* for *door*	analyzing the formation of letters; checking writing against a model; practice on poorly formed letters; personal checklist for proofreading

words phonetically would destroy the visual cues that indicate variant forms of base words. For example, the common base of *relate* and *relative* would no longer be evident if each word were spelled exactly as it sounds.

Spelling ability has a high correlation with other language abilities. Children who read well are most often good spellers also. This fact is not surprising, because common language skills are involved: visual and auditory perception, visual memory, and phonemic and morphemic knowledge and application. Aural and oral uses of language, wide reading, writing, and an understanding of the sound and structure of English words provide an important background for spelling.

The spelling program in the elementary school ought to focus on lists of words selected on the basis of frequency of use and level of difficulty. Words with common linguistic features are frequently grouped and taught in units. The teaching of generalizations is limited to those which are consistent and apply to a large number of words. Learning has been found to be more efficient when words are studied in lists. It is important, however, that children have opportunity to use the words in meaningful writing situations.

Because children cannot learn all the words they will ever need to use, they need to develop a system for learning new words on their own. A typical learning strategy includes visual, auditory, and kinesthetic learning modes. Developing a spelling conscience is a major goal of spelling programs. Children's attitude toward spelling is of utmost importance. To be good spellers they not only must develop skills, but they must value the ability to spell and assume a sense of pride and responsibility for their work.

Learning Objectives

COGNITIVE OBJECTIVES

Primary Grades

Children will

develop skill in analyzing the spelling of words.

be able to recognize patterns of words.

be able to generalize about spelling on the basis of common patterns.

develop visual and auditory memory of words.

be able to write the most common spelling of American English language sounds.

be able to use alphabetical order to locate words in simple dictionaries.

become aware of how they learn to spell new words.

Intermediate Grades

Children will

meet all primary-grade objectives.

be able to recognize misspelled words.

be aware of a range of spelling options that can assist them in locating words in the dictionary.

be able to use a dictionary to check correct spelling of words.

be able to make tentative spelling generalizations, search out additional data, and modify the generalizations appropriately.

be able to recognize and encode common morphemes whether in stressed or unstressed syllables.

develop a personalized and effective method for learning to spell.

be able to spell whatever words are needed to express ideas and information.

develop a sense of the factors that influence the spelling of words.

AFFECTIVE OBJECTIVES

Children will

want to spell correctly.

seek to improve their spelling through study and practice.

apply spelling competency to all written work.

demonstrate a willingness to assist other children in learning to spell words correctly.

choose to use the dictionary to check unknown or doubtful spellings.

recognize the importance of legible handwriting in correct spelling.

Suggested Learning Activities

See It; Spell it. To practice visual imagery of words with young children have them take a good look at a word and then try to "see" it written in unusual places.

Teacher: Can you see the word *may* on the ceiling?
Child: Yes.
Teacher: How is it spelled?
Child: M-a-y.
Teacher: Good. Can you see the word *under* on your shoe?
etc.

Flannelboard Spelling. Have a supply of letters and let the children "write" their words on the flannelboard.

Lost Letters. To help the children focus attention on the spelling of words give them a prepared list of spelling words with missing letters (e.g., com__, fo__r, etc.). The children should refer to their spelling list, fill in the missing letter and then write the whole word.

Camera. The children should shut their eyes while the teacher writes a word on the board.

When they open their eyes they are to take a picture of the word before the teacher erases it. Then they develop their film and tell how the word was spelled.

Alphabet Soup Spelling. The children should arrange letters from dry alphabet soup mix to spell their list of words. Words may either be lined up on the children's desks and then later returned to the container, or they may be glued to a paper or cardboard for future reference. Smooth rocks may also be used as a base. These make interesting paperweights.

Riddle Me a Word. The teacher or leader describes a spelling word. A child who guesses the word goes to the board and writes it correctly.

Ghost Hunt. Ghost letters are described as the silent letters in words that appear but make no sound. Give the children lists of words containing silent letters and let them draw a ghost shape around the silent letters in the words.

k n o w   o f t e n

Put It Back. This activity begins with spelling words randomly written on the board. The children put their heads down while the teacher erases one word. Then they try to recall the erased word and how to spell it. They then try to replace the missing word by writing it correctly. When they are successful, the activity continues with other words.

Spelling Detective. Give the children a short story in which some words are misspelled. They are to find the misspelled words, circle them, and write them correctly.

Hangman. The leader draws a hangman's noose on the board and a dash for each letter of the word he has chosen from the spelling list, as in Figure 8-3. In turn, children call out letters with which to spell the word. If their letter is a part of the word, the leader writes it in the appropriate blank. If not, the head is drawn. The game continues until the word is spelled or the body — head, trunk, legs, arms, hands, and feet — is completed.

Pair Tree. Make a bare tree trunk and limbs. Ask the children to find pairs of homonyms, write them on pear-shaped pieces of colored paper, and fasten them to the tree. Vary the activity for other pairs (antonyms, synonyms, etc.).

Crossing the Creek. Draw a simple creek scene with stepping stones going across it. Write words from the spelling list on each stepping stone. To get across the river, a child stands with his back to the board and spells each word as it is pronounced. This game may also be played with partners or in small groups with children taking turns crossing the creek and pronouncing words.

Post Office. Before this game is played, have a number of jokes cut from old children's magazines and pasted on sheets of paper, one per sheet, and fold the sheets like a letter. Then write spelling words on other pieces of paper.

One child is chosen to be the postmaster. One by one the children go to the postmaster and ask, "Have you any mail for me?" The postmaster replies, "What is your name?" The child then gives a word from the spelling list, and the postmaster finds it on one of his cards. The postmaster asks, "How do you spell it?" and the child must spell the word correctly. If the child is right he or she gets a "letter" with a joke in it. If not, the child gets the card with the word written on it to study some more.

Target Spelling. Selected words (from weekly list or challenge list) are written on a target; harder words are closer to the bull's-eye. The children toss an art gum eraser at the target and must spell the word they hit. Words may be assigned scores, and individuals count up their total points in a game.

Spelling Search. Make a word search game of current spelling words. Write the words vertically, horizontally, or diagonally on squared paper, one letter per square. A letter may be part of more than one word. Then fill in the leftover blank squares with random letters. Have the children circle whole words and then write them on the bottom of the sheet. Figure 8-4 shows an example.

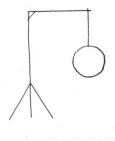

FIGURE 8-3
Hangman.

w	n			c	o	m	e
b	o	o	k		e		
		r			n		
			d	o	o	r	t
		a					
	y			r	a	t	e

FIGURE 8-4
Spelling Search.

Spotted Bugs. To practice word patterns or families, select a pattern and have the children think of words whose spelling follows the pattern (e.g., *-in; pin, win, tin,* etc). Draw a large ladybug on the board. As children think of a pattern word draw a spot on the ladybug and write the word in the spot. The children try to see how many spots they can give the ladybug.

Double Consonants. Declare a "Double Consonant Week." The children collect words that are spelled with double consonants and display them on the bulletin board.

Alphabet Shuffle. Prepare two complete sets of alphabet cards, writing one letter on each card. Put all the A–M cards in one deck and the N–Z cards in another deck. The children will play with only one deck at a time (but the deck has two cards of each letter).

Shuffle one deck of cards and deal five to each player. The rest of the deck is stacked upside down in a stockpile. The object of the game is to make "books" of cards by getting any three cards in sequential alphabetical order. To start play, the child to the left of the dealer names a letter and asks another player to give it to him. If the child has it, he or she must give it up. If not, the caller draws a card from the stockpile and play goes to the next player. If, however, the child gets the card that was asked for, he may call for another until he misses. When no more sequences are possible the children count their "books," and the child with the most is the winner.

Animal Alphabet. Give the children pictures of animals and have them arrange the pictures in alphabetical order according to the name of the animal. (Check inexpensive books in vari-ety stores for pictures, if you don't draw well.) Variation: Use only pictures of animals that make well-known sounds. Have the children arrange the picture alphabetically according to the *sound* each animal makes (cow–"moo"; sheep–"baa"; etc.).

Suggestions for Further Reading

Allred, Ruel A. *Spelling: The Application of Research Findings.* Washington, D.C.: National Education Association, 1977.

Boyd, Gertrude A., and E. Gene Talbert. *Spelling in the Elementary School.* Columbus, Ohio: Charles E. Merrill, 1971.

Forester, Anne D. "Learning to Spell by Spelling," *Theory Into Practice* 19 (Summer 1980): 186–93.

Frith, Uta, ed. *Cognitive Processes in Spelling.* London: Academic Press, 1980.

Gentry, J. Richard. "Learning to Spell Developmentally," *Reading Teacher* 34 (January 1981): 378–81.

Hanna, Paul R., Richard Hodges, and Jean S. Hanna. *Spelling: Structure and Strategies.* Boston: Houghton Mifflin, 1971.

Hodges, Richard E. *Learning to Spell.* Urbana, Ill.: Clearinghouse on Reading and Communication Skills and National Council of Teachers of English, 1981.

Zutell, Jerry. "Some Psycholinguistic Perspectives on Children's Spelling," *Language Arts* 55 (October 1978): 844–50.

9
Handwriting

"The moving finger writes and having writ moves on" — *and on, and on. The history of handwriting is as old as the history of man, i.e., the recorded history of man. Though alphabets have undergone great changes down through the ages and though a variety of alphabets have caused great differences in the way we put our letters together, the fact remains handwriting is, and always has been, a major preoccupation of civilized man.*

Andersen (1965)

CHAPTER PREVIEW

Imagine trying to write a term paper in pictures. Could you? Our use of writing is so automatic that we seldom stop to think about the convenience of being able to write. The "invention" of writing was surely one of man's great achievements. This chapter is about our writing system and handwriting instruction. It begins with a brief history of writing and then gets into specifics for helping today's children learn to use writing effectively as a communication tool.

QUESTIONS TO THINK ABOUT AS YOU READ

How did our writing system develop?

What ought to be the emphasis of handwriting instruction?

What does learning to write involve?

What form of writing is taught in the primary grades?

How is manuscript taught?

How is cursive writing taught?

How does the writing of left-handed children differ from that of right-handed children?

Should writing speed be stressed in the elementary school?

What are the characteristics of good writing?

What are some common writing problems?

How can I help children improve their writing?

A Look at the History of Writing

Writing grew out of drawing and progressed through various stages of development to the present alphabetic system. The story of writing most likely begins very early, somewhere in prehistory, when people

307

began drawing or carving on the walls of caves and on rocks. The paintings in the Altimira Caves in Spain are some of the most famous examples of this ancient era. It is not known why such early pictures were drawn or what they represented, but it is hypothesized that they were some kind of record or that they served some magical purpose.

People on down through the ages continued to draw pictures much as we might record an event through photography. Sometimes an artist-scribe drew a series of pictures to show a sequence of actions or events. Gradually such drawings were simplified, becoming more stylized or conventional. In time, many of the picture symbols bore little resemblance to the original object.

The early picture writing was limited for communication, because it could only deal with concrete things. Eventually a system of combining picture symbols to represent abstract ideas was developed. In this system drawings of a foot and a mountain might be used to convey the idea of a journey across a mountain or drawings of an eye and rain (for falling tears) might mean sorrow. This kind of writing is called an *ideogram.*

Although the development of ideograms to represent abstract ideas was an important step in written communication, the system often resulted in ambiguity. Reading an ideogram required interpretation of the symbols, and not everyone interpreted a message in the same way. Just imagine, for example, trying to "read" a message from this interesting ideogram found in New Mexico: A rock drawing near a steep mountain trail showed a mountain goat standing in an upright position and beside it was a horse and rider upside down. The intended message was that the trail was so steep it could only be traveled by a mountain goat. A man on a horse would not be able to travel it.

The next important stage in the development of writing was a system of picture symbols to represent the sounds of words rather than their meanings. This system resulted in a *sound syllabary,* or *rebus writing.* For example, if we were using this writing system to write American English, we could use the picture symbol for pin (e.g., ⟋) not only to write the word *pin* but to write the sound of /p/ /i/ /n/ whenever it occurred as a syllable in another word such as pinto (⟋ỏ⟋), pinfeather (⟋🖋), or pinwheel (⟋⊗). Although a syllabic writing system required fewer symbols than the earlier picture writing, it still required many symbols and was far more cumbersome than our present alphabetic system.

Syllabic systems have been used in writing several languages. Children find the story of Sequoya and his "talking leaves" particularly fascinating. Briefly, a Cherokee Indian named Sequoya invented a writing system for his people that required only eighty-five symbols. Using the materials at hand, he wrote the syllables on leaves and taught the Cherokees how to read and write. With Sequoya's writing system they were able to publish newspapers and books in their own language.

The development of writing up to the present time involved one more significant step: the development of an alphabet. For this we are indebted to the Phoenicians, a Semitic group of people who lived along the eastern coast of the Mediterranean Sea. Instead of using picture symbols to represent whole words or syllables, the Phoenicians developed a system in which a symbol represented only the first sound of a word. For example, their word for head was *resh* and the written symbol for it was $\triangleleft$. In the Phoenician alphabet, then, $\triangleleft$ stood for only the r sound at the beginning of the word. Thus whole words could be written as a series of symbols for the separate sounds.

The Phoenician alphabet consisted of twenty-two sound symbols depicting common objects such as a camel, a house, a tooth, a monkey, and a fish. The symbols were extremely simplified pictures, and many of them required a good imagination to see any relationship to the original thing. Their word *nun*, for example, meant "fish," and the written symbol for the word is thought to suggest an open mouth of a fish: γ. *Aleph*, an approximation of their word for "ox," pictured the head of an ox: $\forall$; *beth*, meaning "house," was represented by a symbol suggesting a rounded roof: $\ni$; and *daleth*, meaning "door," was represented by $\triangle$.

The Greeks adopted the writing system from the Phoenicians including the symbol names, which were meaningless in the Greek language. They altered many of the symbols and changed the letter names to conform to Greek phonic patterns. Thus *nun* became *nu*, *aleph* became *alpha*, *beth* became *beta*, and *daleth* became *delta*.

Vowel symbols were an innovation of the Greeks. The Phoenician alphabet had more than enough symbols for the Greek consonant sounds, but it didn't have any symbols for their vowels. Hence, the Greeks simply used the extra Phoenician consonant symbols.

The Greek alphabet was adopted by the Romans by way of the Etruscans. The Romans modified the alphabet to fit their language and rounded the shapes of many of the letters (e.g., delta: D and gamma: G). The Roman alphabet consisted of only capital letters for hundreds of years. Gradually, lowercase letters were developed from the capital letters. These letters made the copy work of manuscripts easier and permitted scribes to write more words in less space.

The Roman alphabet was widely disseminated throughout the

Western world and became the basis for most of the Western languages in use today. The writing used in Old English manuscripts was based on an Irish modification of the Roman alphabet and included a few symbols from the runic alphabet. Changes in the English writing system that were brought about through the Norman invasion and the various Renaissance influences were less drastic, because the languages involved were also based on the Roman alphabet. Thus the alphabet we use today is still known as the Roman (or Greek-Roman) alphabet.

Developing a Philosophy for Teaching Handwriting

Handwriting is an important skill in our modern world. In spite of the widespread use of typewriters, word processors, and other mechanical writing devices, there are times when virtually everyone needs to be able to write. Most schoolchildren are totally dependent on handwriting.

The major purpose of handwriting is communication. Clearly, if it is to serve this function, what is written must be legible. It is not enough merely to encode a message; the message must also be readable. We have only to look at the problems created by poor handwriting to recognize the importance of legibility. For example, consider the inconvenience and other negative consequences of illegibly addressed mail, illegible requests for goods or services, illegible assignments, or illegible job applications.

Young children living in a print environment show a natural curiosity about writing and proceed predictably through developmental stages of acquiring the writing system to which they are exposed (Clay, 1975; DeFord, 1980). Similar patterns of development have been found in various countries of the world. Scribbling gives way to letterlike shapes and finally to formations approximating those used in the native language.

In working with young children teachers should see their role as facilitators of the developmental process. Left to their own resources, young children may develop awkward, inefficient movements and poor formations that later require remediation. Instruction throughout the grades should help children refine and maintain their handwriting skills. Without continued instruction, their writing often becomes tedious, if not impossible, to read.

Instruction in specific handwriting skills, though essential for most children, must be kept in perspective. If children are to understand the communicative purpose of writing, instruction and practice must be related to something that is meaningful to them. For example, once young children have mastered the basic formation of letters, they find writing the word *me* more interesting practice than simply writing disconnected *m*'s and *e*'s. Writing practice for older children might include copying a favorite poem or joke. When remediation of a specific letter formation is needed, concentration on the problem element should always be followed by practice in using the correct formation in a purposeful context.

Handwriting in the Total Curriculum

A good handwriting program teaches skills and reinforces them through meaningful practice. Learning to write is much like learning other skills and requires the same initial attention to important specifics. It is similar in many ways, for example, to learning to drive a car. You must first learn how to drive, and then you must practice driving until turning the steering wheel or putting your foot on the brake becomes an unconscious act. It is only when you have mastered the skills of driving that you are free from operational pressures and concerns and can use a car as a functional and satisfying mode of travel.

Handwriting requires more attention in the primary grades than in the middle grades. It is recommended that primary children have approximately ninety minutes of instruction per week and that the time be decreased in the middle grades to no more than sixty minutes. How much time is spent depends on the needs of the children at that point in their development. Children who are just learning to write will obviously need more instruction than children who have mastered the basic skills and need only a maintenance program.

Handwriting instruction ought not to be seen only in terms of a specific time period, however. Attention to quality and efficiency in handwriting should be maintained throughout the entire school day. To become proficient and to value good writing, children need to practice their writing skills in many practical and pleasurable ways. Maintaining consistent standards for writing throughout the day helps children to develop an awareness of good writing and to realize intrinsic rewards for quality work.

Characteristics of Good Writing

Several factors contribute to legibility and general ease in reading handwritten material, whether manuscript or cursive. They include:

1. *Formation of letters.* Although there is considerable variation in the way letters are made, good writing adheres closely enough

to conventional forms to make recognition easy. Children should not adopt personal styles of writing that distort standard forms of letters and create reading difficulty. Older children also need to understand that unconventional joinings of cursive letters can cause illegibility.

2. *Spacing*. Studies show that the spacing between, above, and below letters greatly influences legibility. Good writers do not run letters together or stretch them out unnecessarily. They also leave space between lines. All spacing should be even and should consistently signal which letters are grouped together into words.

3. *Size*. As a general rule, larger writing is more distinct and easier to read. In writing on prelined paper, however, a writer must coordinate size with space available. Lines of too large writing run together; in very small writing, details become obscure. Either extreme makes reading difficult. Beginning manuscript paper is ruled to guide the size of letters and provide extra space between lines. In addition, young children are usually taught to leave the width of a finger between words. More mature writers use regular lined paper and use one-third to one-half space for the base of letters with stems and tails extended above or below.

4. *Alignment*. Words "sit on the line." All letters stop at the baseline with the exception of tail letters, which extend below the line.

5. *Slant*. The degree of slant may vary from one individual to another. However, a good writer consistently slants all down strokes to form parallel lines.

6. *Line quality*. Good writers control the amount of pressure applied to the writing instrument and maintain evenness in writing. The quality of their writing is neither exceptionally light nor very dark.

Teaching Handwriting

Developing Writing Readiness

Recent research (Kirk, 1980) indicates that learning to write involves cognitive development as well as motor skills. The seemingly simple task of copying a letter requires more than control of movement. It is essentially a cognitive task governed by rules. Kirk reports, "Copying is a complex task that requires visual analysis of component parts, recognition of the relationship between parts and the whole, and a plan of action. To copy, a child must know where to start, in what direction to move, where to stop and change directions" (p. 30).

Children need many experiences with written language in preparation for writing. Through these experiences they become aware of significant features of letters (shapes, orientation, relation to line, starting point, and progression of formations), of words (the progression from left to right, the clustering or joining of letters, and the recombinations of letters to form new words), and of sentences (word order, continuous lines of print, and punctuation). Activities such as reading to children or recording stories they tell and then reading the stories back to them help to establish a conceptual link between writing and speech. Such experiences stimulate children's interest in learning to write and motivate them to acquire the skills that will make written communication possible.

Perceptual competency Writing requires close observation of the shape and formation of letters. It also requires that children be able to distinguish significant features of letters and to perceive differences and similarities both in the shape of letters and in the sequence of movements used in forming letters. Children must also perceive the importance of spacing between letters and words, and the upright positioning of letters along a line.

Children need many opportunities to develop and practice visual discrimination. Verbalization of differences and similarities enhances learning and provides information about children's perceptions. For example, given a set of shapes or letters in which one is different from the others, children might be asked to pick out the one that is different and to explain how it is different. Or, they might watch the teacher write two letters (e.g., *b* and *p*) and explain the differences in writing them. If children have difficulty, the teacher should help them discover the significant differences and provide additional practice in a similar situation.

Visual and kinesthetic memory Writing requires children to remember how letters look, to hold an image in mind while the fingers and hands reproduce the mental image on paper. Holding a shape in memory, the brain sends messages to the finger and hand muscles to move in a certain way. At first, writing is a slow, deliberate act. Gradually the visual and kinesthetic memory channels become so well developed that writing becomes an automatic response. Activities in which children identify shapes or make simple drawings from memory may be useful prewriting activities. A variety of activities might evolve from looking around the room for round objects or curved or straight surfaces. Other ideas include showing children a round cookie or a domino (with a low number of dots) and having them draw the object from memory.

Eye-hand coordination Getting the hand to cooperate in producing a visual image can be difficult for young children. A child must exercise and train small muscles for writing just as an adult must develop muscle strength and control to serve a tennis ball with precision. Once children have a clear image of the letter they want to write, their eyes and hands need to work in close harmony to produce that image. To create a match between the visual model and what is actually written, the brain must respond to the image relayed through the eye and must set the appropriate muscles into action. Cutting, pasting, modeling, and painting activities provide practice in eye-hand coordination in preparation for specific writing tasks.

The basic shapes and strokes of manuscript writing can be developed in various prewriting activities. Through simple games of "writing play" children can practice using an instrument and making the shapes they will later use in actual manuscript writing. For example they might make the following:

balls	○	ladders	
donuts	◉	beds	
apples		fences	
grapes		houses	⌂
lollipops		canes	
flowers		monkeys' tails	
moons	○	trees	△
boxes	▢	wigwams	△
telephone poles	†	wagons	
chairs	⊢	table settings	

Any of these prewriting activities should emphasize the place to begin circles and lines and the direction of movements, as in Figure 9-1.

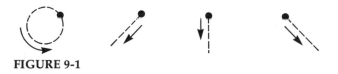

FIGURE 9-1

Handwriting elements may also be practiced by illustrating little stories with simple line drawings. For example, as the teacher tells the following story and makes the drawings on the board, the children draw the lines and shapes on their papers to make a picture story.

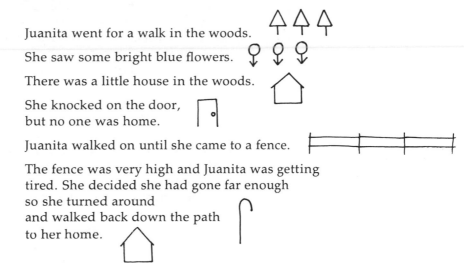

Juanita went for a walk in the woods.

She saw some bright blue flowers.

There was a little house in the woods.

She knocked on the door,
but no one was home.

Juanita walked on until she came to a fence.

The fence was very high and Juanita was getting tired. She decided she had gone far enough
so she turned around
and walked back down the path
to her home.

Teaching Manuscript Writing

Manuscript, or *print-script* as it is sometimes called, was developed in England and was first introduced in this country in 1922. Prior to that time, beginning writers learned to write in the same style that adults use. Since that time, manuscript has gained wide acceptance and has been taught in most schools as the first writing system that children learn. Reasons for its popularity include the following:

1. Manuscript is easy to write. Because it is based on short lines and circles, many teachers feel that even children with poor coordination can write it successfully.

2. Manuscript is similar to the print that children encounter in books. There is no need to learn two separate alphabets, one for writing and one for reading.

3. The form of each letter is distinct and separate, making manuscript easy to read and errors in the formation of letters easy to detect.

Although manuscript alphabet charts are prominently displayed in virtually all primary classrooms, it is inevitably the teacher who serves as the most significant writing model. Teachers model handwriting informally throughout the day. For example, whenever they help children write a caption for a picture they have made or encode their oral stories for them, teachers demonstrate the art of writing. In addition, the formal writing lesson requires the teacher to demonstrate letter formation for children to observe and practice. Thus it is important that teachers become thoroughly familiar with the manuscript form adopted in the district so they can provide a consistent model for children. A common manuscript alphabet is shown in Figure 9-2.

When teachers model manuscript for children, they need to be careful to begin each letter at the proper starting point and write the parts of the letters in correct sequence. Teachers need to be aware that when children are initially learning to write they are apt to misinterpret a slight deviation or idiosyncratic stroke as a significant feature of a letter. Seeing letters formed in a consistent and specific way helps children develop sharp mental images and lessens the possibility of ambiguities.

Materials for Manuscript Writing Most paper designed for beginning manuscript has wide lines and an additional light or dotted line to indicate the correct height of letters. (See Figure 9-2.) The paper is placed on the desk or table in front of the child so that the bottom edge of the paper is parallel to the edge of the desk. Placement is the same whether the child is right- or left-handed.

Young children frequently use a primary pencil for beginning writing. Because it has a larger diameter than a standard pencil, some teachers believe it is easier for young children to grasp and use. Research, however, does not lend support to this theory (Cole, 1980). Children past the beginning stage of writing often consider primary pencils "babyish," and prefer using a regular-sized pencil.

The way children hold their writing instrument is important to control and ease of writing. One effective way is to place their index finger on the top of the pencil, put their thumb on the side, and curve their other fingers underneath to give a firm support area. The eraser end of the pencil points over the shoulder, the right shoulder for right-handed children and the left for left-handed children. (See Figure 9-3.) This position facilitates muscle action to pull on downward strokes and to push up or out in other strokes. Some children have a tendency to grasp the pencil near the lead, creating a tense grip and tiny writing. It may be helpful to wrap a rubber band just

FIGURE 9-2 *(facing page)*

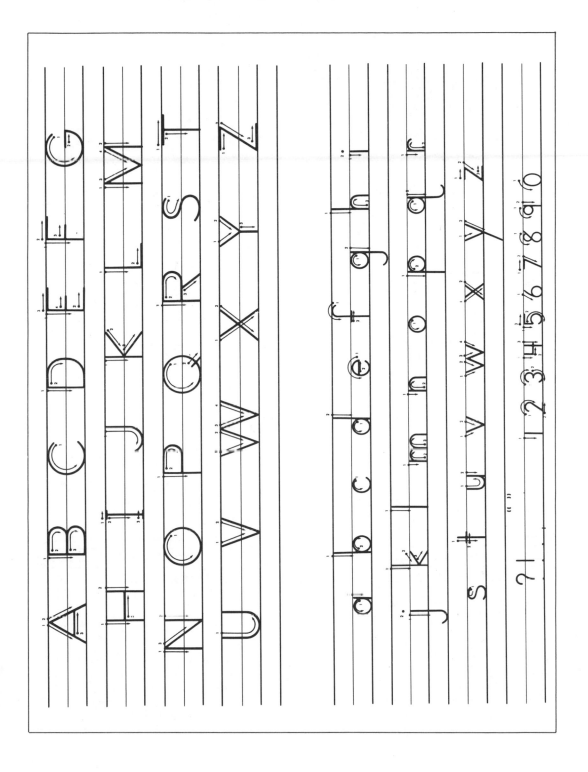

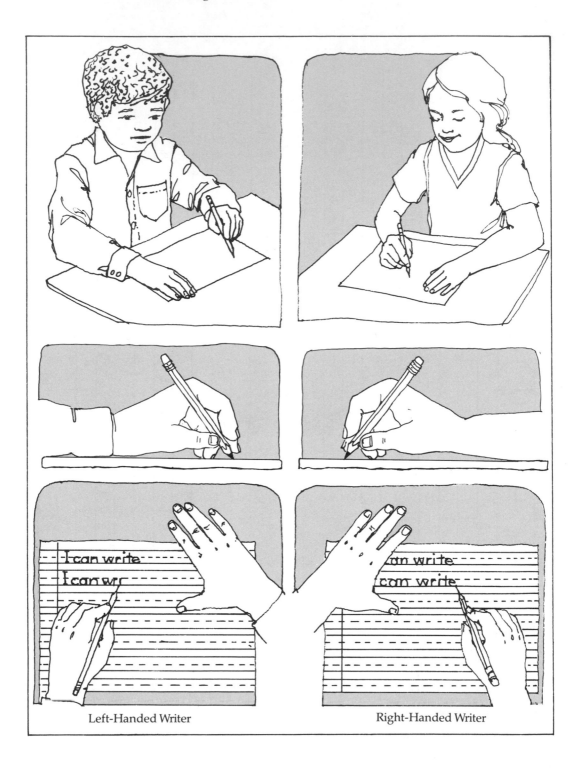

Left-Handed Writer   Right-Handed Writer

above the sharpened surface of their pencil as a guide to where they should hold it.

As mentioned earlier, most classrooms are equipped with an alphabet chart. It is also helpful for young children to have their own alphabet displayed across the top of their desk for ready reference. The letters can be duplicated on heavy paper and taped above the writing area.

Teaching Techniques

If children have not learned to write their names before they come to school, that is the first thing they ought to learn to write. It will give them great satisfaction and will relieve the teacher of having to write their names on paintings and other papers.

It is a good idea to introduce any new writing skill to children at the chalkboard. The teacher can then observe children's letter formations and correct any errors immediately. Writing at the board also allows children freedom of movement while they are learning. In teaching children to write their names, the teacher should work with each child individually, writing his or her name at eye level on the board and talking about how each letter is made. Marking the beginning of each letter with a dot helps children remember where to start the letters; they can continue to practice from the model while the teacher gets other children started.

Lines permanently drawn on the chalkboard provide a helpful guide for children's writing. Initially, however, children are concentrating on the formation of letters, and the size of their letters will probably vary considerably. In subsequent lessons the teacher will need to help them refine their name-writing skills and practice writing their names at their seats. A card with the child's name on it should be prepared in advance so that a child can refer to it until he or she can write the name without help.

Writing on regular manuscript paper helps children control the size and alignment of their letters. The middle line provides a boundary within which to write. Establishing a label for each line permits discussion of how high letters should be and where the tails should be drawn. Some teachers refer to the lines as the *baseline*, the *midline*, and the *topline*. Others compare the lines to parts of the children's bodies: *toeline*, *waistline*, and *headline*. Verbalizing the starting point, the direction of movement, and the shape of letters as they are made

FIGURE 9-3 (*facing page*)

helps children form concepts and gain control of writing movements. ("The letter *o* begins at one o'clock . . . curves back up to the beltline . . . now it's rounded down to the toeline . . . and a nice round curve up to the starting point.")

There is no set order in which letters ought to be taught. The lowercase letters are often taught first so that children can begin writing words as soon as possible. Only one or two letters that follow a similar pattern should be taught at one time. If children have not previously learned to read the letters of the alphabet or if writing is difficult for them, their pace will be slower to ensure mastery of each lesson. The following is one possible sequence of instruction.

1. The basic forms used in manuscript:

2. Letters made with straight lines:

3. Letters made with circles or parts of circles:

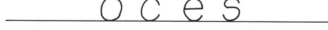

4. Letters made with similar circle and line movements:

5. Letters made with clockwise circle and line movements:

6. Letters with straight and slant lines:

Any of the letters with low utility, such as *q*, may be left until the last to teach.

A similar grouping of capital letters is also possible.

1. Letters made with circles and parts of circle:

2. Letters made with lines and clockwise circle movements:

3. Letters made with lines:

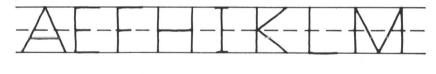

Reversal problems are fairly common in the early grades. Lowercase *b* and *d* are particularly apt to cause trouble. To avoid reversal problems, similar letters should be taught with a lapse of time between them. For example, the *d* could be taught first and thoroughly mastered. Then, after an interval of a week or so, the *b* could be taught. If children still have difficulty with these two letters it may be helpful to teach the capital *B* and show them that the lowercase *b* is like the capital letter with the top circle removed. Another common problem involves letters with tails that extend below the baseline or above the midline. These letters are frequently more difficult for children to write than others. Talking children through the formation of a difficult letter as they are learning to make it is often helpful.

Learning to write well takes practice; a time should be set aside each day for *teacher-directed instruction and practice*. Children must not be left "to figure out how to make letters" on their own. When all the letters have been introduced and children are able to write words and sentences, they still need help in evaluating their writing and in correcting faulty practices before habits are firmly established. Specific evaluation will be discussed later in this chapter.

Cursive Writing

The word *cursive* means "running." Hence, cursive writing is a curved and flowing style. It is different from manuscript in that the letters slant forward and are joined together in flowing strokes. The transition time from manuscript to cursive varies, but most schools begin teaching children cursive writing in the latter part of second grade or in the first part of third grade. This practice stems from the belief that manuscript is easier for children to write and to read. By second or third grade their eye-hand coordination and reading ability allow them to read and write a different style of writing easily.

There appears to be no valid educational reason for transferring children from manuscript to cursive. Manuscript is a legible and efficient way of writing. Research indicates that when children continue to use manuscript, they develop unique styles of writing and are able to write as quickly in manuscript as in cursive. Occasional review of manuscript writing and continued use of it will be helpful to upper-grade children. They will find it useful in many contexts. A number of students in the late elementary and secondary school years (particularly boys) adopt a type of print-script writing style on their own. Cursive writing, however, continues to be the traditional form, and both parents and children seem to think of cursive writing as "real writing."

Children indicate their readiness for using cursive by their general educational and physical development and by their attitude toward writing. Good coordination and ability to read are important signs. This is borne out in research indicating that children who read and write manuscript well have little difficulty with cursive. A tendency to slant manuscript and an interest in trying to write in cursive on their own are other indications of children's readiness.

Teaching Cursive Writing The transfer to cursive writing requires children to learn alternate letter formations and joining strokes. (See Figure 9-4.) In addition, they learn to position their papers at an angle to their bodies for cursive writing. Right-handed children place their paper so the lower left-hand corner points toward their body; left-handed children place it so the lower right-hand corner points toward them. The opposite hand rests on the top of the paper to hold it in place. (See Figure 9-5.)

One way a teacher might introduce cursive is to write a word in manuscript on the chalkboard and then draw in the connecting lines between letters.

Tracing over the whole word again without lifting the pencil from the board helps children conceptualize the cursive writing process.

Instruction usually begins with individual letters. Groups of letters that begin or end with the same motion may be taught together, a few letters at a time. Children first observe closely while the teacher demonstrates how to write a letter and then describes it. Verbalizing the process provides a check of the accuracy of their observation and also enhances their learning.

Lowercase letters are usually taught first because they have the greatest utility for children's daily writing needs. One possible sequence is given here.

1. Downcurve letters that rest on the baseline:

2. Downcurve letters that extend below the baseline:

FIGURE 9-4 *(page 324)*

FIGURE 9-5 *(page 325)*

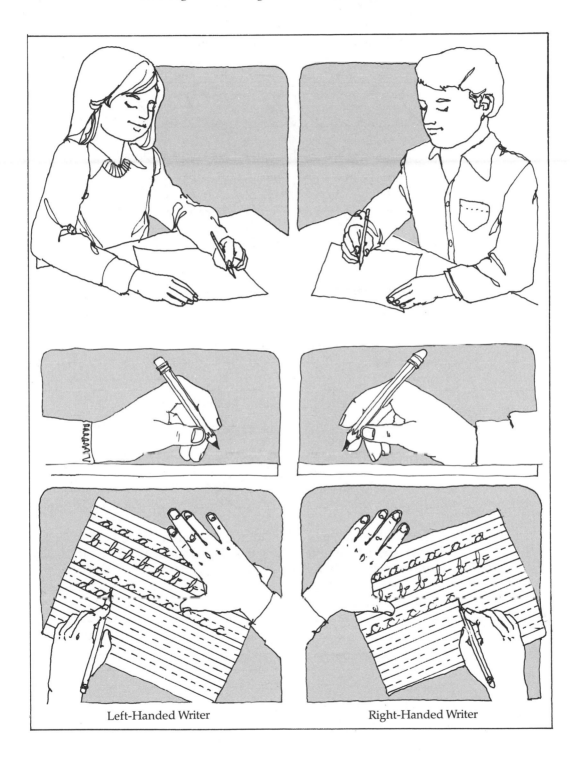

Left-Handed Writer   Right-Handed Writer

3. Undercurve letters that extend to the midline:

4. Undercurve letters that extend above the midline:

t l b f h j k

5. Overcurve letters that extend to the midline:

m m v x

6. Overcurve letters that extend below the baseline:

y z

   Some letters are more difficult to join than others and will need to receive special attention. The letters *b, v, w,* and *o* end up off the line and will most likely require extra practice.

FIGURE 9-6

In analyzing the formation of these letters children should realize that the end stroke is a significant part of their form. Careful attention to this detail will help eliminate legibility problems later.

Capital letters may also be grouped according to similarity of formation for teaching. One possible sequence would be to teach the capital letters that begin with a "cane" and then proceed to other groups as shown in Figure 9-6.

Alternate Writing Systems

Teachers have frequently voiced concern about teaching children one writing system (manuscript) and then requiring them to learn a quite different system (cursive) as they progress through the grades. In response to these concerns, several new programs have been developed and placed on the market in recent years. Two of the programs are briefly summarized here.

D'Nealian Handwriting

The beginning D'Nealian alphabet differs rather significantly from conventional manuscript alphabets, but the cursive forms retain the general appearance of current writing systems. Letters in the manuscript alphabet are more oval than round, and they are slanted rather than vertical. Most lowercase letters are written with one continuous stroke, retracing lines as in cursive writing. This simplifies the transition to cursive considerably because children do not have to learn significantly altered forms of letters. In most cases they merely add joining strokes. A D'Nealian alphabet is reproduced in Figure 9-7.

Italic Handwriting

Italic handwriting is described by Dubay and Getty (1980) as "an old approach to handwriting that has been revitalized. It is based on 16th century letterforms that first developed in Italy and were also used in England and Europe." They explain that "the contemporary italic handwriting system presents one simple lowercase alphabet that is cursive in nature to begin with — the letters are based on the elliptical shape. Italic letterforms have a slight slope and require few lifts of the writing tool. These assist the natural, rhythmic movements of the hand in the act of writing, and fulfill the requirements for both legibility and speed." (p. 1) Figure 9-8 shows the basic and cursive italic alphabet, and includes directions for making and joining each letter.

FIGURE 9-7 *(facing page)*

From *D'Nealian™ Handwriting* by Donald N. Thurber. Copyright © 1978 by Scott, Foresman and Company. Reprinted by permission.

FIGURE 9-8 *(page 330)*

From Instructional Manual, *Italic Handwriting Series* by Inga Dubay and Barbara Getty. Portland State University, Portland, Oregon, 1980. © 1980 by Barbara M. Getty and Inga S. Dubay.

D'Nealian™ Manuscript Alphabet

a b c d e f g h i
j k l m n o p q r
s t u v w x y z

A B C D E F G H I
J K L M N O P Q R
S T U V W X Y Z

D'Nealian™ Cursive Alphabet

a b c d e f g h i
j k l m n o p q r
s t u v w x y z

A B C D E F G H I
J K L M N O P Q R
S T U V W X Y Z

D'Nealian™ Numbers

0 1 2 3 4 5 6 7 8 9

D'Nealian Handwriting, Book 2. ©Scott, Foresman and Company.

BASIC/CURSIVE ITALIC
lowercase and capitals · stroke sequence of each letter, and joins

BASIC ITALIC LOWERCASE

a a b b c c d d e e e *be sure to overlap 3 over stroke 1* f f g g

2 strokes

All letters are 1 stroke except: e, f, i, j, k, t & x

h h i i j j k k l l m m n n o o p p q q

r r s s t t u u v v w w x x y y z z .

a) b h m n p r

a) Downstroke goes to base line, then retraces up to the branching line – a point half way between base line and waist line – then branches up to the right.

b) The upstroke branches into the stem which is then retraced on the downstroke. (see arrow)

b) a d g q u y

"e" closes on branching line e

BASIC ITALIC CAPITALS

A A B B C C D D E E F F

G G H H I I J J K K L L M M

N N O O P P Q Q R R S S T T *or*

U U V V W W X X Y Y Z Z .

CURSIVE ITALIC LOWERCASE

na nb nc nd ne nf ng nh ni n

"n" chain showing all joins

nj nk nl nm nn no np nq nr ns nt n

nu nv nw nx ny nz or nx nz . *no join into f or from g, j, q · y*

CURSIVE ITALIC CAPITALS

A B C D E F G H I or I J or J

K L M N O P Q R R S T U

V W X Y Z .

5mm

The Left-Handed Writer

Enstrom (1962) reports that approximately 11 percent of elementary schoolchildren prefer to write with the left hand. The number might be higher if all children were allowed to use whichever hand they preferred. For the most part, these children learn to work and play in a right-handed world and do so with a minimum of difficulty. No significant difference has been found in the quality of writing produced by left-handed writers as long as they have been properly instructed. They also write as easily and quickly as right-handed writers.

In working with left-handed children it is well to keep in mind that it is the brain which determines the hand they use and that handedness is not simply a habit they have acquired. Neural messages for movements on the right side of the body are processed in the left hemisphere of the brain; movements of the left side of the body, in the right hemisphere. Therefore, it is not wise to try to change the handedness of children. To do so may lead to psychomotor confusion and learning difficulties. However, children who do not demonstrate a definite preference for either hand may be encouraged to use the right.

Determination of handedness may be made by observing which hand a child consistently uses in nonwriting situations. For example, the teacher might observe which hand a child uses

to hold a spoon or fork in eating

to throw a ball

to bounce a ball in place

to string beads

to hammer or saw

to reach for something

to cut something with scissors

Left-handed writers use the same letter formations and sequence of movements when they write, but their physical orientation to the task is different. In writing from left to right, right-handed writers move *away from* the center of the body; left-handed writers write *toward* the center of the body. Not only does this mean that right- and left-handed individuals utilize a different movement in relation to their body, but right-handed children leave a trail of writing in the open space behind their instrument. Unless left-handed children learn to position their paper and hold their instrument properly they have difficulty seeing what they have written. Many left-handed writers develop the habit of hooking their wrist to bring their hand above the line of writing. Such a position is not only awkward but it necessitates rubbing the hand across the writing. The positions described in an earlier section of this chapter should be carefully monitored while children are forming their writing habits, for once formed, these habits are very difficult to break. Any tendency to curve the hand or wrist should be corrected before the pattern becomes set.

Speed in Writing

Speed in writing should receive little stress in the elementary school, particularly in the primary grades while children are just learning to write. Learning the skill of writing requires children to pay attention to detail and to give conscious effort to producing correctly formed letters. Emphasis on speed at this point creates pressure and tension, which can be detrimental to learning.

In the middle grades, when children are able to form letters with ease, some attention may be given to improving the rate of production. The volume of writing increases as children get older, and thus the ability to write faster is an advantage. However, studies show that when speed is unduly increased, legibility decreases. If speed of writing is taught, it should not be emphasized to the point of affecting quality. Noble and Noble provide the following chart as a guide to the approximate speed to expect of children (1971, book 2, p. T8).

GRADE	LETTERS PER MINUTE
1	5–20
2	15–25
3	25–35
4	35–55
5	64
6	71
7	76
8	79

These norms may be helpful in determining whether a child has an inordinate amount of difficulty with the motor aspect of writing. Accommodations in the amount of copy work for such children are strongly recommended.

There is some controversy about the use of rhythmic devices (music, counting, etc.) to increase speed. Analysis of time and type of movement in producing different parts of letters shows considerable variation. Attempting to fit these movements to a steady rhythm is therefore difficult and often sets an artificial objective. Because writing is such an individual process, using rhythm patterns as a teaching technique is a questionable practice.

Evaluating and Individualizing Instruction

Manuscript

In considering the individualization of instruction in manuscript writing, thorough initial teaching of letter forms cannot be overstressed. Presenting too much too fast results in poor conceptualization of letter formation and inadequate training in eye-hand coordination. The variation in the amount of time and practice children need to learn a given writing task is a related factor. Letter forms also present varying degrees of difficulty. For example, a study by Lewis and Lewis (1964) found that children consistently find some letters more difficult than others. They list the following ranking of letter difficulty, from most to least difficult (p. 858):

q	u	K	F
g	M	W	P
p	S	A	F
y	b	N	X
j	e	C	I
m	r	f	v
k	Z	J	i
U	n	w	D
a	s	h	H
G	Q	T	O
R	B	x	L
d	t	c	o
Y	z	V	l

Helping children overcome problems is a matter of helping them replace incorrect habits with correct ones. Remediation begins with an analysis of their writing in terms of some standard or model. A checklist based on an analysis of the writing process may be used as a guide for identifying children's manuscript difficulties. The following list is an example.

A Checklist for Manuscript

		Yes	No
1.	Is the bottom of the paper parallel to the edge of the desk?	___	___
2.	Is the left hand (right hand for left-handed children) placed at the top of the page to hold it in place?	___	___
3.	Is the pencil held approximately one inch back from the tip with the index finger on top and the thumb on the side?	___	___
4.	Do the arm and hand rest on the desk?	___	___
5.	Are curved letters appropriately round?	___	___
6.	Are all round parts of letters closed?	___	___
7.	Is a clockwise motion used to form the circle part of the letters *b* and *p?*	___	___
8.	Is a counter-clockwise motion used to form the circle part of *a, c, d, e, g, o,* and *q?*	___	___
9.	Are all straight lines straight?	___	___
10.	Do pointed letters come together in sharp points?	___	___
11.	Do separate strokes and parts of letters connect?	___	___
12.	Are letters properly oriented in terms of position and line?	___	___
13.	Do all lowercase letters touch the waistline and toeline with stem letters properly extended above or below?	___	___
14.	Are words written with even spacing between the letters?	___	___
15.	Is the amount of space between words adequate to show word units without spreading the writing out unnecessarily?	___	___

Once problems have been identified, the next step is to plan appropriate teaching strategies. Some problems, such as those having to do with placing the paper or holding the writing instrument, may not require specific lessons. Being alert to such problems and making certain that children use the proper position is likely to be all that is necessary to form good habits. Problems such as those related to letter formation, however, require planned reteaching strategies.

Children with the same problems may be grouped together for direct instruction, or the teacher may work with children individually. Most letter-formation problems stem from poor visualization or poor memory of letter forms. Observing, verbalizing, and writing letter forms help children improve mental images of letters and develop correct writing habits. A teacher-directed lesson to improve children's visualization and production of a letter should include the following steps:

1. The teacher demonstrates letter formation for the children.

2. The children analyze and describe how the letter is made.

3. The children copy the letter.

4. The children compare what they have written with the teacher's model.

5. The children practice writing the letter several times.

6. The letter is written in the context of one or more known words.

Some children benefit from tracing a letter model that is grooved, raised, or texturized (made from sandpaper, velvet, etc.). Another kinesthetic and tactile suggestion is to write letters in cornmeal or sand boxes. Close supervision of children's practice is essential so that errors may be called to their attention and correct formation practiced.

Reversals and positioning problems are also apt to be a matter of poor visualization or visual memory or both. Having children describe the way letters look and the way they are made helps fix letter images in their minds. Children should observe the way letters face and should notice any features that extend below the line of writing. Again, verbal analysis should be followed up with writing practice plus additional kinesthetic practice as necessary. Teachers should not be unduly alarmed by reversals at this stage. Consistent spatial orientation is a new concept for most children. Prior to learning to write they have largely to ignored orientation differences in their perception of objects.

A study by Zaslow (1966) found it helpful for children who have reversal problems to write with their paper placed on the side of the body opposite the normal position. This position causes children to cross the midline of their body as they write. The study also suggested that starting letters from the bottom rather than from the top may help remediate more serious reversal problems.

Cursive

A few kinds of errors have been found to account for most illegibilities:

1. Failing to close letters (e.g., d made like cl , k made like h , g made like y).

2. Closing top loops (e.g., l made like t , e like i).

3. Making unnecessary loops (e.g., t made like l , i like e).

4. Failing to use round strokes appropriately (e.g., h made like li , c like i , n like u).

5. Failing to complete end strokes properly (e.g., o made like a , v like u).

6. Crossing the *t* carelessly (e.g., t , $\mathcal{T}$).

Just four letters — *a, e, r,* and *t* — account for almost 50 percent of all illegibilities. The letter *r* creates the greatest problem among lowercase letters, and the letter *I* among capital letters (Myers, 1963). In addition, letters that are joined above the baseline — *b, o, v,* and *w* — also present particular writing difficulties (e.g., br , ou , ve).

By the middle grades most children have mastered the basic forms of writing and have established firm writing habits. Attempting to change those habits is usually futile unless children have a strong motivation to do so. Pride in workmanship ought to be encouraged in all possible ways. Writing letters, preparing material for display, and recording information for others to read give meaning to quality writing and an incentive to improve written communication skills. Without constant attention to and reinforcement of good writing, the quality is almost certain to break down with the increased volume of writing children are expected to do as they move through the grades.

Writing is a highly personal skill, but children need to be aware of the significance of their writing habits and style. According to graphologists (persons who study handwriting), handwriting reveals a great deal about a person and it is possible to analyze the characteristics of individuals from handwriting samples. It is not necessary, however, to be skilled in graphology to generalize about a person's handwriting. Good writing indicates that a writer understands the purpose of writing and is trying to facilitate reading. Poor writing indicates a conscious or unconscious lack of concern for the reader and a faulty conceptualization of writing as communication.

A program to improve children's writing begins with their awareness of need. Awareness develops when children are able to recognize qualities in their own writing that detract from legibility and when they have a desire to improve. Diagnosis of errors is essential to progress, and it is most effective when children are directly involved in the process. One technique is to guide children in analyzing anonymous specimens of good and poor handwriting to determine the qualities that constitute good writing. Examples of this technique may be found in some commercial writing programs. One provides a description of qualities found in good handwriting (Figure 9-9) followed by examples of handwriting (Figure 9-10) for children to evaluate and discuss (Figure 9-11).

Samples of children's writing, both from specific writing lessons and from other classwork, should also be evaluated. Children may cooperatively develop their own checklist or use one from commercial materials. An example of a checklist developed by children follows.

A Self-Evaluation of Handwriting

1. Are my letters correctly formed?

2. Do I close my letters?

3. Do I leave loops open?

4. Do I cross my *t*'s and dot my *i*'s and *j*'s?

5. Are my letters properly joined?

6. Do all my letters rest on the baseline?

7. Are all my short letters the same height?

8. Are all my tall letters above the midline?

9. Are all the tails of letters below the baseline?

10. Do I space letters evenly?

11. Do I leave just enough space between words?

12. Are all my downstrokes parallel?

FIGURE 9-9   (*page 338*)

From *Writing Our Language*, Book 5 by Marion Monroe. Copyright © 1973 by Scott, Foresman and Company. Reprinted by permission.

FIGURE 9-10   (*page 339*)

From *Writing Our Language*, Book 5 by Marion Monroe. Copyright © 1973 by Scott, Foresman and Company. Reprinted by permission.

FIGURE 9-11   (*page 340*)

From *Writing Our Language*, Book 5 by Marion Monroe. Copyright © 1973 by Scott, Foresman and Company. Reprinted by permission.

The Six S's of Superior Handwriting

Stroke, size, slant, space, shape, and style are the *Six S's of Superior Handwriting*. When you check handwriting samples, you must think of each of the *Six S's*.

STROKE: Beginning and ending strokes should be made correctly. Letters should be joined carefully.

SIZE: The letters should be uniform in size. The writing should not be too large or too small for the paper. The **d, t,** and **p** should be taller than the small letters (**a, c, e,** etc.), but smaller than the tall letters (**b, f, h,** etc.). The tall letters should not quite touch the line above.

SLANT: Letters should slant slightly to the right. The slant should not be extreme. Keep all the letters slanting the same amount.

SPACE: Joining strokes should leave enough room between each letter so the letters are legible. A slightly larger space should be left between words and sentences.

SHAPE: Letters should be made in the correct shape. They should not be too tall and thin, or too short and wide. Each letter should be clear and legible.

STYLE: Words and sentences should be written neatly with correct capitalization and punctuation. Margins should be kept even. Paragraphs should be indented. Erasures should be clean and complete. The writer's handwriting should be easy for others to read.

Read the story written below. Then use the
check list of the *Six S*'s on the opposite page to
rate the handwriting in the story. Which letters
and words need improvement in each of the
Six S's?

The electric brain in
my bedroom had just
finished my homework when
my Mother called me. She
was getting supper ready
and needed some fresh dates and asked
me to get in our rocket
which was parked on the
roof and pick up some
in Sun Valley, California
and on the way back, she
wanted me to stop in Racine,
Wisconsin for some cheese.
    I got started   all right
but I forgot the rocket was
headed East and landed in Switzerland,
instead of California. So I
bought Swiss cheese, stopped in
Spain for the   dates and got
back in time for supper.

Check List

The Six S's of Superior Handwriting

Date ——————————— Rated by ———————————————

Use the list below to decide how the sample writing on page 10 could be improved. After you have rated the sample, copy the story on a separate piece of paper. Then make a list of the *Six S*'s you need to improve in your own handwriting.   Answers will vary.

1. **Stroke**
   - [ ] beginning strokes
   - [ ] ending strokes
   - [ ] joining strokes
   - [ ] alignment

2. **Size**
   - [ ] too large
   - [ ] too small
   - [ ] not uniform

3. **Slant**
   - [ ] too far toward right
   - [ ] too far toward left
   - [ ] not uniform

4. **Shape**
   - [ ] letters too tall and thin
   - [ ] letters too low and wide
   - [ ] letters illegible
   - [ ] **a** and **o** too much alike
   - [ ] **cl** and **d** too much alike
   - [ ] **n, r,** and **v** too much alike
   - [ ] others too much alike

5. **Space**
   - [ ] letters too far apart
   - [ ] letters too crowded together
   - [ ] words too far apart
   - [ ] words too crowded together
   - [ ] lack of uniformity
   - [ ] ascenders touching descenders from above

6. **Style**
   - [ ] too many erasures
   - [ ] margins too wide
   - [ ] margins too narrow
   - [ ] margins not uniform
   - [ ] paragraphs not indented
   - [ ] errors in punctuation
   - [ ] errors in capitalization

General Comments

What is your general impression of this sample of handwriting?   Is it poor, average, good, or superior?

The next step is for children to list their deficiencies and plan how they will try to improve their writing. They may, for example, enter into a contract that specifically states what they will do. (See Figure 9-12.) A contract places the responsibility for improvement on children and provides motivation for specific practice.

Handwriting Contract

I, _____ , need to improve
(*Name of student*)

_____ .

For the next _____
                    (*Number of days or weeks*)

I will _____

_____

to help me become a better writer.

Signature: _____

Date: _____

FIGURE 9-12

Using Handwriting Scales

Handwriting scales are useful tools for modeling and evaluating children's handwriting. These scales give examples of handwriting that demonstrate graded levels of performance. Children's writing is compared to the examples and scored according to comparable overall quality. Such a scale may be found in the Zaner-Bloser (1975) handwriting materials. There are scales for both manuscript and cursive writing. A range of five levels of writing specimens is given for each grade level.

A Handwriting File

A handwriting file provides a record of children's writing progress. It should include randomly selected samples of both daily work and "best" writing papers. If children evaluate each sample against a scale or checklist before it is filed, they will be able to see their progress over a period of time. This in itself can be an incentive for improving their writing.

Guidelines for a Handwriting Program

As we suggested throughout this chapter, an effective handwriting program entails more than initial instruction in manuscript and cursive letter formation, important as that may be. The program should also reflect an understanding of program goals, children's needs, and learning theory. Some key points are listed here.

1. One style of writing should be used consistently with children who are just learning to write. It is a good idea to send a copy of the alphabet, showing the formation of letters, home to parents of primary-age children.

2. A handwriting program should provide specific instruction in the techniques of letter formations and joinings, followed by appropriate practice.

3. Whenever possible, children should be allowed to copy material of high interest to them during handwriting practice.

4. Excess amounts of copy work should not be required at any age.

5. Handwriting skills should be reinforced throughout the school day.

6. Individual difference and special needs of children require that instruction and expectations be modified appropriately.

7. Handwriting instruction in the middle grades should follow a diagnostic approach.

8. Handwriting exercises should never be used as punishment.

9. Children's writing should be displayed prominently about the classroom.

10. Legibility should be the primary concern of any handwriting program.

In Summary

The first form of written communication consisted of simple drawings such as those found in early caves and on rocks. Later, pictures were drawn to represent ideas as well as things. In the next stage of writing development, picture symbols were used to stand for syllables. Eventually a picture symbol came to stand for a single language sound. These symbols were the beginning of the alphabetic system of writing. Our alphabet is thought to have its origin in the Phoenician alphabet, coming to us through the Greeks, the Etruscans, the Romans, and then the English.

Handwriting is a basic communication skill. Proficiency in writing requires specific teaching and a great deal of practice. Usually, young children first learn to read and write manuscript. Toward the end of the primary grades, children are introduced to cursive writing. Instruction throughout the rest of the elementary school years generally focuses on helping children improve their skill in cursive writing. Because the primary purpose of writing is communication, the emphasis in handwriting instruction is on legibility. Ease and efficiency in forming and joining letters are also important.

Developing good handwriting involves helping children to recognize the differences among letters and the factors that significantly influence legibility, to discover and practice efficient ways to write and join letters, and to want to write well. Thorough initial instruction provides a necessary foundation for success. Improvement and maintenance of skills depends on purposeful practice and continual evaluation. Consistent standards throughout the total curriculum help children become aware of the importance of good writing and foster positive attitudes toward writing.

Learning Objectives

COGNITIVE OBJECTIVES

Primary Grades

By the end of grade 2 children will

know how to hold a writing instrument.

know the appropriate position for their writing paper.

be able to follow specific writing directions.

be able to identify correctly all capital and lowercase manuscript letters and describe the process for making them.

be able to recall and demonstrate the correct formation of all capital and lowercase manuscript letters.

be able to visualize and execute appropriate spacing between written letters and words.

demonstrate an understanding of writing as communication.

be able to use manuscript to record short stories and communications.

By the end of grade 3 children will

be able to demonstrate all grade 1 and 2 objectives

be able to identify all capital and lowercase cursive letters.

be able to recall and demonstrate the correct formation of all capital and lowercase cursive letters.

use correct strokes to join letters.

be able to use cursive writing in practical and creative writing situations.

Middle Grades

Children will

demonstrate all grade objectives.

know and be able to explain criteria for good writing.

be able to identify variations in spacing, size, alignment, and slant of writing.

be able to evaluate their own writing through the use of handwriting models and scales.

be able to identify needed improvement in their writing and to suggest appropriate remediation techniques.

AFFECTIVE OBJECTIVES

Children will

recognize the importance of legible writing.

willingly follow instructions for placing their paper and holding their writing instrument.

try to form and join letters correctly.

recognize the importance of consistent spacing, letter size, alignment, and slant in writing.

demonstrate a desire to improve their writing.

show pride in neat, legible writing.

appreciate the efforts of other children who are trying to improve their writing.

Suggested Learning Activities

Name Designs. Cut butcher paper or other smooth finished paper into approximately 9″ × 15″ sheets. Pass a sheet to each child and have children fold the paper the long way. Then using the fold as the writing line, have the children write their names with paint and immediately fold the paper and press. The paint rubs off on the opposite side, and the mirrored name creates an interesting design.

Clay Tablets. Have each child grease a shallow box with petroleum jelly and mold soft clay or wax into it to form a "tablet." When the tablet has hardened, let the children incise a message into it.

Reports. Have children look up information about a writing-related subject and report what they find to the class. Ideas include:

the Braille writing system

cuneiform

the alphabet

runic writing

the Rosetta Stone

Sequoya

early counting and record-keeping systems, e.g., notches on a stick, pebbles, knots (quipus), etc.

Rebus Writing. Let the children try writing their own and others' names using a rebus system. For example, they might make a picture of a tom-cat and someone fishing for the name Tom Fisher.

Picture Writing. If there is someone in your community who writes Chinese invite him or her to demonstrate and explain the system.

Silent Roll Call. Have young children practice writing their names by "signing in" in the morning. Place a paper on a desk by the door or on a designated spot on the bulletin board. Keep the sign-in sheets for a record of daily attendance.

Cheer Cards. Whenever someone is ill, have the children design a cheer card for them and carefully write a message inside. Cheer cards may also be made for residents of local nursing homes or hospitals.

Recipe Book. Have each child bring a favorite recipe to school. Have the children copy each recipe carefully to make recipe books.

Poetry File or Book. Make a file or book of the children's favorite poems. After several poems have been read in class, ask each child to select the one he or she likes best. Then have the children copy their favorite poems giving credit to the poet but indicating that it is the favorite poem of _____. Assemble all the poems to make a class file or book of favorite poems.

Polka-dots. To give young children practice in making the circle part of manuscript letters, give them a large, simple outline drawing of Daddy's tie, Mother's scarf, a clown suit, etc. and let them decorate it with polka-dots.

Circle Animals. Have children draw animals using only circles. They may use different sized circles for different parts of the body and may use half-circles for feet, hands, etc.

Alphabet Border. Let children experiment with various kinds of letters and marks to make border designs.

Address Book. Have each child write his or her name and address neatly on the board. Then have the children copy them, arrange them in alphabetical order, and fasten them together to make a class address book.

Early American Sampler. Give the children squared paper (¼") and have them plan and make an alphabet sampler. The letters of the alphabet should be neatly written in the center of the paper and a cross-stitch design made as a border.

Posters. Have the children select a favorite saying, motto, or short verse and neatly write it as a poster.

Master Sentence. The sentence "A quick brown fox jumps over the lazy dog," contains all the letters of the alphabet. Have the children practice writing the sentence.

Variation: Have the children try to construct an original sentence that contains all the letters of the alphabet.

Note: "Write On! Creative Handwriting in the Classroom" in *Language Arts* 54 (March 1977: 294–96) is an excellent source of interesting and creative handwriting activities.

Suggestions for Further Reading

Andersen, Dan W. *What Research Says to the Teacher: Teaching Handwriting.* Washington, D.C.: National Education Association, 1968.

De Ford, Diane E. "Young Children and Their Writing," *Theory into Practice* 19 (Summer 1980): 157–62.

Enstrom, E.A. "The Left-handed Child," *Today's Education* 58 (April 1969).

Enstrom, E. A., and Doris C. Enstrom. "In Print Handwriting: Preventing and Solving Reversal Problems," *Elementary English* 46 (October 1969).

*Irwin, Keith Gordon. *The Romance of Writing from Egyptian Hieroglyphics to Modern Letters, Numbers and Signs.* New York: The Viking Press, 1956.

*Ogg, Oscar. *The 26 Letters.* New York: Crowell, 1948.

Petty, Walter T. "Handwriting and Spelling: Their Current Status in the Language Arts Curriculum," in *Research on Handwriting and Spelling,* ed. Thomas D. Horn. Urbana, Ill.: National Council of Teachers of English, 1966.

* Easy books.

10
Reading

Fundamental to a clear understanding of the process of teaching reading is an awareness on the part of the teacher of the close relationship among all four facets of the language arts — listening, speaking, reading, writing. A reading program that ignores the fact that reading is inextricably interwoven with the other language arts not only defeats, in part, its own purpose but also seriously jeopardizes the success of the programs in oral communication and in writing.

Dallmann (1974)

CHAPTER PREVIEW

If you ask preschool children why they want to go to school, their answer is apt to be "To learn to read." Learning to read, like growing up, holds a sense of magic and importance. To know the secret for finding stories among the pages of a book is indeed a wondrous thing. Mastery over print is a developmental process. In this chapter we will deal with that process and the factors involved. We will discuss significant reading skills and describe how those skills may be developed in various reading programs.

QUESTIONS TO THINK ABOUT AS YOU READ

How is reading related to the other language arts?

What factors influence children's ability to read?

How may reading readiness be developed?

What skills help children recognize words?

What is involved in comprehension?

How is reading in the content areas different from narrative reading?

What are some approaches to teaching reading? How do they differ?

What is meant by readability? How is it determined?

What are some ways to assess children's reading ability?

How might I organize my reading program?

When Napoleon's men discovered the Rosetta Stone in 1799, the officer in charge surmised that the inscription on the stone must bear some message, but he was unable to read any part of it. Hampered by a lack of knowledge of the languages involved (there were three) and the language symbols used to encode the languages, he was unable to read a single word. In time a scholar was found who could read the portion inscribed in Greek. Then, little by little, after painstaking years of work, the inscriptions in Demotic and Ancient Egyptian hieroglyphics were decoded and translated.

Reading involves a process of deriving meaning from symbols. Today's printed page holds no more inherent meaning than the ancient writing on the Rosetta Stone. There is no meaning in print itself; printed symbols merely represent the sounds of language. To derive meaning from print, a reader must translate the written symbols into the sound symbols of language and utilize his or her knowledge of language to reconstruct the writer's message.

Reading As a Language Art

We read language. At first this statement seems too obvious to be worthy of mention. However, as we begin to understand the nature of the reading task and the factors that influence success, we will begin to realize the profundity of the statement and what it implies for the teaching of reading.

Children bring all of their language experiences to the reading task. Unless those experiences provide an adequate language background for the material children are expected to decode and understand, progress in reading will be slow. What children gain from the reading encounter is directly related to the language competency they already possess. Reporting on a thirteen-year study of children's language development, Loban says, "It is of special note that those superior in oral language in kindergarten and grade one *before they learned to read and write* are the very ones who excel in reading and writing by the time they are in grade six. Our data show a positive relationship of success among the language arts" (1976, p. 71).

Reading is a communication process. It requires readers to reconstruct encoded messages, to "hear" in their minds what the writer says. All that is involved in reading is not completely understood, however. Britton comments, "The process of learning to read is one that has appeared to grow longer and longer as we have come to understand more fully what is involved in reading itself" (1970, pp. 159–60).

Schema Theory

Recent advances in understanding the nature of comprehension have resulted in what is called *schema theory*. Very briefly, this theory "seeks to explain how new information acquired while reading is meshed with old information already in our head" (Strange, 1980, p. 393). Durkin (1981) also describes it as being concerned with how knowledge is stored in the brain. She states, "[The] basic assumption is that what is experienced (learned) is organized and stored in the brain not in a static, unchanging form but in a way that permits modification through further development. Development occurs, the theorists say, when what is known (about an object, an event, a role, a process, or whatever) interacts with what is new but related" (p. 25).

A schema is something like a concept, but it involves much more. And, just as concepts are interrelated, schemata (the plural form) apparently form a hierarchically arranged network of concepts. Hacker (1980) offers the following example for *going swimming:*

> The top level representation of a schema for "going swimming" would include the general description of swimming as a sport involving immersion of the body in some form of water. This top-level schema will specify the interrelationships between its underlying components (sub-schemata). Schemata at a lower level of the "going swimming" hierarchy would include more specifics such as going swimming in a pond or going swimming in the country club pool. At the bottom-most level, the schemata apply to unique perceptual events. (p. 867)

The implications of schema theory for reading instruction are significant. Schema theory suggests that reading is an interactive process, that what readers already know influences their ability to get meaning from print. Each schema is incomplete and can be added to or modified as the result of new information. For example, if we are reading about the desert, the printed word *desert* triggers the recall of information about conditions in the desert that we have previously stored up as a schema. Let's assume that our existing schema includes such attributes as hot, sandy, dry, and barren. As we read, new information about severe wind storms in the desert can be understood and incorporated into our existing schema. It should also be noted that stored *mis*information may be recognized and corrected when the newly gained information is incompatible with existing schema.

Schema theory lends new support to arguments for a meaning-based reading program. Most young children have well-established schemata that they use in processing oral language. A meaning-based emphasis in reading instruction builds on existing structures. Schema theory, however, does not appear to exclude the teaching of specific skills. Skills, *when taught in meaningful contexts*, provide important new information that children can use to expand and refine their existing schemata.

Factors That Influence Reading

How well children are able to read depends on several factors. These may be categorized according to whether they relate to the reading material, the reader, or the teaching strategies. Through an understanding of the relationships among these factors we gain valuable insights about how to set optimal conditions for teaching children to read.

Factors Related to Reading Material

Vocabulary Words are said to be the building blocks of language. They stand for objects and ideas; they form a link between print and concept. For children to learn to read they must be able to associate visual symbols (printed words) with the things themselves (the referents). Unless the words children read have meaning for them they lack a basis for forming associations, and comprehension is impaired. Successful reading is possible only when most of the vocabulary in a reading selection is familiar.

Sentence structure The sentences children are asked to read should be structured similarly to those they use or comprehend orally. Materials for beginning readers are usually written in short sentences and are composed primarily of nouns and verbs. Materials for readers at successively higher levels contain noticeably longer sentences. This practice reflects an awareness of children's language development and is an attempt to match the language level of reading materials with that of children's oral language. For example, a sentence such as "So while the children swam and played and splashed water at each other, Wilbur amused himself in the mud along the edge of the brook, where it was warm and moist and delightfully sticky and oozy"[1] obviously requires greater linguistic competence than a sentence such as "They climbed the fence." By adding descriptive words and phrases to kernel sentences, compounding subjects and predicates, and coordinating and subordinating ideas, one creates longer and more complex sentences and increases the reader's processing load.

Content of material It is easiest for children to read material on a subject they know a great deal about. If, for example, they have watched a car being assembled in a factory, they will already have a frame of reference to which they can relate the information in an article about assembly-line procedures in a Detroit factory. The type of material also affects reading difficulty. Informational reading usu-

---

[1] White, E. B. *Charlotte's Web.* New York: Harper & Row, 1952.

ally requires greater concentration and cognitive processing than fiction. One must remember, organize, and relate concepts in order to grasp what the writer has said. In fiction the story line moves the reader along at an easier conceptual pace with less need to identify and relate specific details consciously.

The appearance of print The format of a story or article influences ease in reading. Spacing, print, and the number of words per page are important. Such factors as the style and size of print, the length of lines and the amount of empty space or number of illustrations influence how well a reader moves through a page. Small print and a high density of words tend to discourage less capable readers. On the other hand, print that older children associate with primers is offensive to them, and although it may be clear and legible, they may reject it.

Factors Related to the Reader

Experiential background Children collect information about the world through experience. As they have more and more experiences, they not only gain more bits of knowledge, but they begin to see how the bits relate to each other. They develop a cognitive framework, or schema, to organize information. Their ability to read, to make sense out of print, is directly related to the match between the reading material and their experiential background. If, for example, children are told to read a story about the beach and they have never been to a beach, they are not likely to have developed a schema adequate for understanding the story.

Language background Children's language background is a significant factor in their ability to decode and comprehend writing. The more children bring to the reading act, the more they will derive from it. Children with mature speech patterns and large vocabularies are well on the way to successful reading experiences. When a child's personal stock of words and language patterns differs from that of printed materials, comprehension is more difficult. The black child, for instance, who says, "It don't be all her fault," or the Spanish child who says, "Maria no is here," is unable to make a one-to-one match between the language of speech and the language of print. For reading to be a meaningful experience these children have to translate the words they read into their own linguistic framework.

Physical and emotional well-being of children The human organism is an integrated being. Hence, the condition and functioning of one part directly affects the other parts. Empty stomachs, itching heads, cold bodies, and hurting psyches command attention that may crowd out intellectual pursuits. To function well in the classroom children need to feel physically well and emotionally secure. Unless their basic needs are met it is very difficult for them to become mentally involved in reading.

Auditory and visual perception Language is made up of a system of sounds that, when combined in certain sequences, represent objects and ideas. In order to read, children must be able to hear significant differences in the sounds of language and to see significant differences in the shapes of letters. These things are difficult for some children, particularly those whose personal language differs from that in common use or those who have not developed a sensitivity to aural and visual differences in language. For example, children may not hear a difference between *pin* and *pen* or between *pad* and *pat* if they are not accustomed to distinguishing the words in pronunciation. Others may have difficulty seeing the significant difference between words such as *these* and *there*, *came* and *cane*, or *saw* and *was*. When children read for meaning, however, they bring all their linguistic knowledge to bear on the reading task, and precise pronunciation of print becomes less important. Noting contextual as well as phonic clues reduces errors in reading.

Intellectual development Reading is an intellectual process. It requires the reader to interact with print. In order to decode and derive meaning from print, readers are continually involved in such mental activities as recalling and associating; translating and interpreting; analyzing, synthesizing, and generalizing; and evaluating. Reading is an active mental process in which readers must think ahead and think back in the quest for meaning.

Ability to attend to a reading task is necessary for reading success. Concentration allows readers to recognize more meaning clues and to use a range of reading and thinking skills selectively. Inattentive children face the task of reconstructing meaning from print with a haphazard disarray of clues caught in passing.

Interest and attitude Purpose and enjoyment in reading provide a favorable mind set for reading. When children read because they want to, they bring to the printed page expectancies that facilitate the reading process. Interest in reading creates an alert mental attitude. This attitude in turn leads to a higher level of interaction with what is read; the result is that children are more aware of and receptive to significant content.

Factors Related to Teaching Strategies

Setting purposes for reading Learning is maximized when children are aware of an activity's purpose. To know whether they are working to acquire a particular decoding skill or reading to solve a problem, to identify a propaganda technique, or simply to find out what happens next in a story is important. Purposeful effort sharpens children's mental processes and helps them channel their efforts in a productive direction.

Skill development Mastery of reading skills and abilities is essential to good reading. Although some children seem to learn to read on their own, their reading ability is increased through appropriate instruction to develop systematic strategies for dealing with new material. Teaching strategies ought to be based on a good understanding of the skills children need to acquire. Adequate instruction ensures development of those skills.

Developing Reading Skills

Reading Readiness

The term *reading readiness* is most often applied to the period of instruction preceding the formal teaching of reading. It can also be used to describe the development of prerequisite skills for successively more complex learning in a developmental reading program. For our purposes here, however, reading readiness will be limited to preparation for initial reading instruction and we will turn to a task analysis to explore aspects of readiness that directly affect children's success in reading.

Language development Because children read language, the ability to use language receptively and expressively is an important background skill for reading. Language readiness activities include listening to stories and poems, verbalizing about field trips and other activities, conversing informally with attention to both talking and listening, dictating stories to the teacher, and observing through all the senses. Such activities give children opportunities to hear and use language in formal and informal contexts, to expand their vocabulary, and to develop competence in using the language system.

Auditory discrimination In preparation for phonics, children must learn to listen to the sounds of language and be able to identify similarities and differences. Discrimination activities include repeating words accurately, listening to a sequence of words to find one that is pronounced twice, hearing or suggesting words that begin with the same sound, picking out rhyming words, and listening for specific words in a story (e.g., "Raise your hand every time you hear the word *puppy*."). Even children who speak a variant dialect may be able to discriminate sounds and words, although they may not differentiate them in their own speech.

Visual discrimination Before children can learn to read words, they must be able to distinguish differences in the features of letters and in whole words. Exercises such as the following may be used for discrimination practice.

Finding and circling letters that are the same:	m	m	o	w	m	g
	p	l	p	y	g	p

Finding and circling words that are the same:	cat	day	cat	lamp
	boy	box	bag	boy

Finding and circling letters that are different:	r	r	t	r	r	r
	a	a	a	s	a	a

Finding and circling words that are different:	top	toy	top	top
	was	was	saw	was

Intellectual development Learning to think about language and learning to use language to verbalize thinking are important dimensions of reading readiness. Planning, organizing, classifying, and predicting offer many opportunities to develop intellectual abilities. For example, children might classify pictures of objects, placing all the toys in one group, all the tools in another, and so on. They might arrange a series of pictures in a story sequence, predict what will happen next in the story, or experience and describe cause and effect relationships ("The plant didn't get enough water so it died.") Or, they might identify things that are a particular color ("How many red things can you see?"), things that are a particular shape ("What is round?"), or quiet things and noisy things.

Concepts of print Children must develop certain concepts about print before they can read. For example, they need to understand that the print and not the pictures on a page tell the story, that reading follows a left-to-right and top-to-bottom progression, and that space between groups of letters indicates word boundaries. The *Sand Test*, devised by Clay (1975) provides a good assessment of these and other concepts children have about print.

Reading readiness tests are available as predictive measures of children's readiness to read. These tests usually measure such aspects of readiness as visual and auditory discrimination, ability to follow directions, knowledge of letter names, vocabulary, and auditory blending. *Gates-McGinitie Reading Tests: Readiness Skills* (Teachers College Press, Columbia University), *The Metropolitan Readiness Tests* and *The Murphy-Durrell Reading Readiness Analysis* (Harcourt Brace Jovanovich) are examples of these tests.

Teachers' observations also provide information about children's readiness to read. An informal reading-readiness checklist such as the one devised by Rouch may be helpful for this purpose (Dallmann, 1978).

	Satisfactory	Unsatisfactory

Interest in Reading
1. Listens attentively to stories read
2. Is interested in picture books
3. Is curious about symbols and letters
4. Seeks out books to take home

Oral Language
1. Has command of a large number of words
2. Can communicate effectively
3. Speaks distinctly

Auditory Discrimination
1. Distinguishes between sounds heard
2. Can hear rhyming words
3. Distinguishes differences in sounds represented by letters

Visual Discrimination
1. Recognizes colors
2. Can see differences in unlike geometric shapes
3. Can see differences in unlike letters

Listening
1. Recalls stories heard
2. Can follow simple directions
3. Can recall a sequence of events

Left-to-Right Orientation
1. Identifies left from right hand
2. Scans a series of pictures from left to right
3. Recognizes the left-to-right sequence of letters within words

Social and Emotional Factors
1. Shares with others
2. Can work in groups
3. Displays self-control
4. Works independently
5. Attends to task

Word Recognition Skills

Sight recall As adult readers, we instantly recognize most of the words we encounter. We do not have to stop to figure out words, because we already know them. Many children have begun to acquire such a sight vocabulary even before they come to school. Repeated experiences in associating words on packages, labels, and books with the objects they represent develop the ability to identify certain words.

Despite the volume of research on word recognition processes, we still do not clearly understand how words are learned and recognized in rapid processing. We do know that longer words are often easier for children to learn than shorter ones. They may have little difficulty recognizing words such as *elephant* or *Halloween*, yet be unable to remember *was* or *more*.

Children remember words better when they associate an experience or referent with them. Words that stimulate intense mental or emotional responses seem considerably easier to remember. Sylvia Ashton-Warner (1963), for example, found that Maori children were most successful in learning key words that elicited strong feeling, such as *love, ghost,* and *kiss.* Function words such as *the, this, that,* and *there* lack specific meaning and are more difficult for children to remember. Children often have difficulty reading function words in isolation, yet they are able to pronounce them in context. When children read for meaning, insignificant words take on the same role that they do in oral language, and children usually pronounce them correctly because the words "belong there."

Building a store of words recognized at sight is an integral component of learning to read. Words that children encounter again and again ought to be known as *sight words.* Although high-frequency words tend to be learned quite readily, it may sometimes be desirable to give special attention to helping children acquire a basic sight vocabulary. A list such as the Kucera-Francis word list in Table 10-1 provides a useful source of high-frequency words children will encounter. It is usually best to provide concentrated practice on these particular words when children experience difficulty with them, rather than to drill children on isolated words in lists. Once a word has been taught, word games, puzzles, and various activities may be used for additional practice and mastery.

Phonic analysis The word *phonics* comes from the Greek *phone* meaning "sound." In the context of reading it refers to letter-sound associations. To teach phonics is to teach children to associate sounds of language with letters. The purpose of phonics instruction is to help children develop the ability to figure out the pronunciation of printed words that they don't already know as sight words.

TABLE 10-1. THE 220 MOST FREQUENT WORDS IN THE KUCERA-FRANCIS CORPUS

1. the	45. when	89. many	133. know	177. don't
2. of	46. who	90. before	134. while	178. does
3. and	47. will	91. must	135. last	179. got
4. to	48. more	92. through	136. might	180. united
5. a	49. no	93. back	137. us	181. left
6. in	50. if	94. years	138. great	182. number
7. that	51. out	95. where	139. old	183. course
8. is	52. so	96. much	140. year	184. war
9. was	53. said	97. your	141. off	185. until
10. he	54. what	98. may	142. come	186. always
11. for	55. up	99. well	143. since	187. away
12. it	56. its	100. down	144. against	188. something
13. with	57. about	101. should	145. go	189. fact
14. as	58. into	102. because	146. came	190. though
15. his	59. than	103. each	147. right	191. water
16. on	60. them	104. just	148. used	192. less
17. be	61. can	105. those	149. take	193. public
18. at	62. only	106. people	150. three	194. put
19. by	63. other	107. Mr.	151. states	195. thing
20. I	64. new	108. how	152. himself	196. almost
21. this	65. some	109. too	153. few	197. hand
22. had	66. could	110. little	154. house	198. enough
23. not	67. time	111. state	155. use	199. far
24. are	68. these	112. good	156. during	200. took
25. but	69. two	113. very	157. without	201. head
26. from	70. may	114. make	158. again	202. yet
27. or	71. then	115. would	159. place	203. government
28. have	72. do	116. still	160. American	204. system
29. an	73. first	117. own	161. around	205. better
30. they	74. any	118. see	162. however	206. set
31. which	75. my	119. men	163. home	207. told
32. one	76. now	120. work	164. small	208. nothing
33. you	77. such	121. long	165. found	209. night
34. were	78. like	122. get	166. Mrs.	210. end
35. her	79. our	123. here	167. thought	211. why
36. all	80. over	124. between	168. went	212. called
37. she	81. man	125. both	169. say	213. didn't
38. there	82. me	126. life	170. part	214. eyes
39. would	83. even	127. being	171. once	215. find
40. their	84. most	128. under	172. general	216. going
41. we	85. made	129. never	173. high	217. look
42. him	86. after	130. day	174. upon	218. asked
43. been	87. also	131. same	175. school	219. later
44. has	88. did	132. another	176. every	220. knew

Source: Johnson, Dale D., "The Dolch List Reexamined" in *Reading Teacher* 24 (1971): 455-456. Reprinted with permission of Dale D. Johnson and the International Reading Association.

Burmeister lists twelve categories of phonics to be taught in the reading program (1975, p. 5):

1. **Consonants**
   a. single consonants (*b, c, d, f,* etc.)
   b. consonant blends (*bl, cl, dr, sm, spl,* etc.)
   c. consonant diagraphs (*ph, sh, ch, th, ng*)
   d. silent consonants (*-mb, -lm; wr-, kn-,* etc., and one of two consecutive like consonants, e.g., *balloon, rabbit*)

2. **Vowels**
   a. single vowels (*a, e, i, o, u, y*)
   b. final single vowel-consonant-*e* (*-ape, ice,* etc.)
   c. vowel clusters (*ai, oa, oi, ou, ei,* etc.)
   d. the *r* control (*car, her, hear, care,* etc.)
   e. "consonantizing" of *i* in the following situations: *-tio, -tia, -cio, -cia, -sio* (*mansion, action, vision, fusion, caution,* etc.)

3. **Phonic syllabication in the following patterns:**
   a. vowel-consonant-consonant-vowel (*aster, silver*)
   b. vowel-consonant-vowel (*razor, lemon*)
   c. final consonant-*l-e* (*maple, cable*)

Many children pick up a knowledge of phonics with little effort. Some children seem to develop a sense of letter-sound relationships almost intuitively in much the same way that they learn to string words together to form sentences. Other children need repeated practice to make phonics a useful reading tool. Wide experiences with letter-sound correspondences, both in reading and in writing, help children formulate generalizations they can apply to unknown words. Activities such as listing words that begin alike, comparing the spelling of rhyming words, and analyzing the sounds that single consonants, blends, digraphs, and diphthongs signal when found in different environments, strengthen children's phonics knowledge in meaningful ways.

Morphemic analysis It is possible to predict the pronunciation and meaning of many unfamiliar words from known parts. Longer words often contain a familiar base word, but it may be masked by its combination with other morphemes. Activities need to be planned to help children increase their awareness of the more common base words, affixes, and inflections and how they can be combined to form new words. Experiences should include work within each of the following categories from primary grades on. A sampling of possible activities is included for each category.

Compound words
Match up sets of base words to form compound words (*play/ground, tree/top, day/time*).
Build as many compound words as possible from a given base word (<u>out</u>: *outside, outdoors, outdo, outwit, outstanding;* <u>over</u>: *overcome, overflow, overlook, overpower, overseas*).

Plural forms
Categorize words by plural formation (words ending with -<u>s</u>, words ending with -<u>es</u>, and <u>irregularly formed</u> plurals such as <u>mice</u> and <u>women</u>).
Complete cloze sentences that require the selection of appropriate plural forms (*Mary ate two dish_ of ice cream.*).

Contractions
Match up sets of word phrases and their contracted forms (*cannot/can't, do not/don't*).
Rewrite sentences using contractions when appropriate (He <u>does</u> <u>not</u> like fish/He *doesn't* like fish.).

Prefixes and suffixes
Watch for examples of prefixes and suffixes in reading materials (basals, magazines, or newspapers) and tally the number of times each is used.
Write sets of words using a particular prefix, suffix, or base word (<u>re</u>turn, <u>re</u>do, <u>re</u>cycle; <u>un</u>known, <u>un</u>kind, <u>un</u>friendly).

Possessives
Match corresponding illustrations with the correct possessive form in sentences (The dog<u>s'</u>/dog<u>'s</u> chain was caught.)
Collect sentences containing possessive forms and list the possessives under <u>singular</u> or <u>plural</u> headings (*mother's, Mark's, flower's, girls', children's, teachers'*), then justify placement.

Contextual analysis When children come to a word they do not know, contextual clues can help them narrow down the number of possible words. Children may not be able to explain why a word seems right in a given sentence, but when they are meaningfully engaged in reading, their intuitive knowledge of language facilitates their use of contextual clues to identify unknown words. Suppose, for example, that Mary is reading along and comes to an unknown word in the following sentence:

Brian stopped to look at the posters of the Pink Panther outside the _____.

Try to imagine the thoughts (most likely unconscious ones) that flit through her mind as she mentally searches through her storehouse of knowledge to solve the linguistic puzzle. It might go something like this: "*The* is a determiner used before nouns so the word must be a noun. . . . The Pink Panther is a character in movies so Brian must be looking at movie posters. . . . The posters are outside something, probably a building. . . . Movie posters are displayed outside theaters. . . . The word I don't know must be *theater*." In the brief span of a moment Mary's semantic background and intuitive knowledge of language have produced enough clues to enable her to derive meaning from print without the aid of other word attack skills.

The use of contextual clues potentially involves the full range of a reader's knowledge of language. It encompasses knowledge of the meaning of words, word order, grammatical structures, and intonation. The better grasp children have of language, the better they are able to determine unknown words through contextual clues.

Using the dictionary The dictionary offers yet another way to determine the pronunciation of a word. Familiar words can usually be recognized by applying one or more of the other word-recognition skills, but when a word is not in the reader's listening or speaking vocabulary, looking it up in the dictionary becomes necessary. Thus the ability to use a dictionary is also important for word recognition. To be able to look up words and arrive at the correct pronunciation quickly requires a thorough knowledge of alphabetical order, phonetic respellings, and stress indicators. Because phonetic symbols and systems for indicating stress vary from one dictionary to another, children need to learn how to use the pronunciation key and explanations in the dictionary available to them.

Learning to use the dictionary to decode unknown words must include attention to the structure and meaning of a word as well as to its pronunciation. Children may note morphemic parts (*rowdiness: rowdy + ness*) and related forms of the word (*rowdy, rowdily, rowdyish, rowdyism*). They also need to read the definition carefully and apply that definition to the reading context.

When several definitions are given for a word, children must analyze the context carefully to determine which definition applies. Sometimes, too, the same spelling of a word may be pronounced in more than one way (*con'tent, con · tent'*) and children must be aware of the meaning of the word in order to select the correct pronunciation in the given sentence.

Developing Comprehension

Reading is much more than decoding printed symbols. The symbols of reading provide a way to get the author's message. They are not the message. It is indeed a grave mistake to place so much emphasis on decoding skills that children see the end product of reading as being a puzzle instead of a message.

Comprehension of a reading selection requires an understanding of the meaning of words. However, words often have many dimensions of meaning, and to really know a word one must be exposed to that word many times in different contexts. Knowing a "dictionary definition" is only the beginning. Developing a broader understanding of a word may be facilitated by exploring different facets of its meaning. For example, some of the following activities might be used where appropriate:

> identifying and discussing morphemes in the word (*chalk + board*)
>
> relating words with similar meaning (*tiny/minute*)
>
> contrasting words of opposite meaning (*loose/tight*)
>
> describing physical properties (size, color, texture, shape)
>
> explaining how something is different from something that is similar (*turkey/chicken*)
>
> identifying attributes or characteristics (*candy: sweet; miser: stingy*)
>
> relating whole and parts (*foot: toe*)
>
> relating one part to another (*wheel: tire*)
>
> identifying use or function (*shovel: dig with it*)
>
> identifying the user (*cleaver: butcher*)
>
> classifying (*sparrow: bird*)
>
> associating mood (*Halloween: goblins and witches*)
>
> noting other forms of the word (*knit, knitted, knitting*, etc.)
>
> recognizing several meanings of the word (*run: a kind of movement, to compete, to come unknit, to spread over an area*, etc.)

In addition to an understanding of the meaning of individual words, comprehension requires an understanding of larger units. Readers must be able to integrate the meanings of all the words in a sentence — to understand the function of each word and how the words are interrelated. They also need to understand the organizational structure of a paragraph. They must be able to relate the parts — the sentences — to the larger unit. Furthermore, each paragraph is but a subunit of the whole story, and readers must be able to analyze and synthesize a story as a total work. To do so they must consider the sequence of events, the influence of one event on another, the relationships between characters, setting as it affects plot development, etc. Thus, comprehension involves an expanding store of specific knowledge and a webbing of interrelationships within the whole.

The purpose for reading influences what and how children read. Comprehension is facilitated when readers have a clear understanding of the purpose of reading and genuinely want to achieve that purpose. Purpose causes readers to anticipate, to set their minds toward accomplishing a particular goal. They will then filter the intake of ideas and information, to screen out whatever is irrelevant to the purpose. At the same time, they will have a greater receptivity for processing whatever is compatible with their purpose.

The skills of comprehension are defined in various ways. Some textbooks offer long lists of very specific skills; others consider comprehension in more general terms.

Smith and Johnson have identified ten comprehension skills that they believe should be taught in the elementary school (1976, pp. 176–77):

1. To read sentences with the appropriate intonation patterns.

2. To form mental pictures of situations or conditions that are described in a sentence or a longer passage.

3. To answer questions about the facts or details presented in a sentence or longer passage.

4. To recall, with a minimum of prompting, the facts or details in a sentence or longer passage.

5. To paraphrase the central thought or main ideas in a passage.

6. To identify cause-effect, comparison-contrast, sequential happenings, and other relationships between and among ideas.

7. To summarize the content of a passage.

8. To test the information or assertions given by an author against personal observations, logic, or the information and assertions given by other authors.

9. To use a literary character, a description, or an opinion as a point of departure for creative thinking that goes beyond the presentation of an author (e.g., the creation of lines of dialog between two characters, an extension of a story, a diary entry of a historical figure).

10. To identify specific characteristics of an author's craft (e.g., exaggeration, use of figurative language, deductive or inductive reasoning, detailed descriptions, vivid characterization, emotional appeals).

Barrett has developed a taxonomy of reading comprehension. It includes the following levels (Smith and Barrett, 1979, pp. 63–66):

1.0 Literal recognition or recall
    1.1 Recognition or recall of details.
    1.2 Recognition or recall of main ideas.
    1.3 Recognition or recall of sequence.
    1.4 Recognition or recall of comparisons.
    1.5 Recognition or recall of cause and effect relationships.
    1.6 Recognition or recall of character traits.

2.0 Inference
    2.1 Inferring supporting details.
    2.2 Inferring the main idea.
    2.3 Inferring sequence.
    2.4 Inferring comparisons.
    2.5 Inferring cause and effect relationships.
    2.6 Inferring character traits.
    2.7 Predicting outcomes.
    2.8 Inferring about figurative language.

3.0 Evaluation
    3.1 Judgments of reality or fantasy.
    3.2 Judgments of fact or opinion.
    3.3 Judgments of adequacy or validity.
    3.4 Judgments of appropriateness.
    3.5 Judgments of worth, desirability, or acceptability.

4.0 Appreciation
    4.1 Emotional response to plot or theme.
    4.2 Identification with characters and incidents.
    4.3 Reactions to the author's use of language.
    4.4 Imagery.

Barrett points out that "the tasks listed within each category should not be thought of as discriminate comprehension subabilities to be specifically developed; rather, they should be viewed as examples of tasks that will contribute to the development of the general ability designated by the category" (p. 58).

Teacher guidance is essential in developing comprehension skill.

The kind of instruction children receive channels their thinking and orients them to the reading task. Thus it can either cause them to refine and expand their thinking and comprehension or it can limit their progress. The kinds of questions teachers ask are particularly important in focusing and directing comprehension. Children must have a base of knowledge before they can compare or evaluate that knowledge. They must, for example, know what an author has said before they can identify his or her purpose, point of view, or biases.

Spache and Spache have developed a questioning strategy model to assist teachers in constructing reading comprehension questions at different levels. The model provides a set of versatile question patterns that capture the essence of Sanders's (1966) hierarchical categories (Spache and Spache, 1977, pp. 455–57).

Questioning Strategies for Comprehension

1. *Memory* — recognizing or recalling information as given in the passage. Sanders distinguishes four kinds of ideas on the memory level of thinking:

   a. facts —
      Who did ___?
      When did ___?
      How many ___?
      What are ___?

   b. definitions of terms used, and perhaps explained, in the text —
      What is meant by ___?
      What does ___ mean?
      What meaning did you understand for ___?
      Define ___.
      Explain what we mean by ___.

   c. generalizations — recognizing a common characteristic of a group of ideas or things
      What events led to ___?
      In what three ways do ___ resemble ___?
      How did ___ and ___ effect (cause) ___?

   d. values — a judgment of quality
      What is said about ___?
      Do you agree?
      What kind of a boy was ___?
      What did ___ do that you wouldn't?

2. *Translations* — expressing ideas in different form or language
      Tell me in your own words how ___.
      What kind of a drawing could you make to illustrate ___?

How could we restate ___?
Could we make up a play to tell this story?
How?
What does the writer mean by the phrase ___?
Write a story pretending you are ___.

3. *Interpretation* — trying to see relationships among facts, general-izations, values, etc. Sanders recognizes several types of inter-pretation:

   a. Comparative — are ideas the same, different, related, or op-posed
      How is ___ like ___?
      Is ___ the same as ___?
      Why not?
      Which three ___ are most alike in ___?
      Compare ___ with ___ in ___.
      How does ___ today resemble ___ in ___?

   b. Implications — arriving at an idea that depends on evidence in the reading passage
      What will ___ and ___ lead to?
      What justification for ___ does the author give?
      If ___ continues to ___, what is likely to happen?
      What would happen if ___?

   c. Inductive thinking — applying a generalization to a group of observed facts
      What facts in the story tend to support the idea that ___?
      What is the author trying to tell you by ___?
      What does the behavior of ___ tell you about him?
      What events led to ___?
      Why?

   d. Quantitative — using a number of facts to reach a conclusion
      How much has ___ increased?
      What conclusions can you draw from the table (graph) on page ___?
      How many times did ___ do ___? Then what happened?
      How many causes of ___ can you list?

   e. Cause and effect — recognizing the events leading to a hap-pening
      Why did the boy ___?
      How did the boy make ___ happen?
      What two things led up to ___?
      When the girl ___, what had to happen?
      Why did ___ happen?

4. *Application* — solving a problem that requires the use of generalization, facts, values, and other appropriate types of thinking

How can we show that we need a traffic policeman at the crossing at the south end of our school?

If we want to raise hamsters in our classroom, what sort of plans will we have to make?

John has been ill for several days. What could we do to help him during his illness? To show him we think of him?

5. *Analysis* — recognizing and applying rules of logic to solution of a problem; analyzing an example of reasoning

Discuss the statement, "All teachers are kind and friendly."

Some people think that boys can run faster than girls. What do you think?

John was once bitten by a dog. Now John dislikes all dogs. Is he right or wrong in his feelings? Why?

6. *Synthesis* — using original, creative thinking to solve a problem

What other titles could you think of for this story?

What other ending can you think of for this story?

If John had not ___, what might have happened?

Pretend you are a manufacturer of pencils who wishes to produce a much better pencil. Tell what you might do.

7. *Evaluation* — making judgments based on clearly defined standards

Did you enjoy the story of ___? For what reasons?

What do you think of ___ in this story? Do you approve of his actions?

In the textbook, the author tells us that ___ felt ___. Is this a fact or the author's opinion? How do you know?

This story has a very happy ending. Should all stories end happily? Why not?

The author of our textbook apparently believes that the American colonists were right in their actions. Do you agree? What do you suppose the British said about the colonists?

Write a short story about your favorite person in history. Tell why this person is your favorite.

Reading in the Content Areas

Reading in the content areas (e.g., math, science, and social studies) differs significantly from reading stories. First of all, content area materials contain a greater density of concepts, and a thorough understanding of each important concept is essential to an understanding of the whole. The information in paragraphs must be processed and organized according to some hierarchy or system as it is read. Thus, concepts must not only be understood but remembered and related to other concepts. For example, to understand a paragraph, children need to recognize the main idea and relate details to the larger concept.

The vocabulary used in content area materials also differs from that in stories. Whereas a story may have a core of common vocabulary words, each subject area has a specialized vocabulary peculiar to it. Sometimes familiar words also have specific meanings for a particular subject area. Words such as *axis, gravity, rotation, apogee, planet, satellite,* and *umbra* are easily recognized as belonging to science. In addition, words such as *attract, force, influence, system, position, crust,* and *body* have both common and science-specific meanings. To comprehend materials in a content area, children must have a thorough understanding of word meanings and processes related to that area. This understanding must be developed through demonstrations, illustrations, and discussions.

To be successful in reading in the content areas, children need to develop a systematic approach for previewing, reading, and summarizing. Previewing is important to gain an overview of materials and establish a conceptual framework for associating and processing information. It involves becoming familiar with typographic signals of size and type of print. Reflecting about and summarizing what they have read helps children relate and organize information. Robinson's (1962) SQ3R formula has been widely used as a systematic approach to effective study reading. It consists of five steps as follows:

1. *Survey.* Children glance through the entire selection to get a general impression of what it is about, noting headings and other print cues and illustrations.

2. *Question.* Children formulate questions they think might be answered in the selection.

3. *Read.* Children read carefully and purposefully to answer the questions.

4. *Recite.* Children recite from memory what they learned, either to themselves or to someone else.

5. *Review.* Children review the selection to clarify any concepts not understood or to fix ideas and details in mind.

Flexibility in rate is also important in study reading. Some materials need to be read much more slowly than normal if children are to understand them. For other reading tasks, skimming or scanning are most appropriate. To get the gist of something, children need to be able to skim material quickly. *Skimming* is fast reading in which children read headings and topic sentences and spot-read parts of paragraphs. *Scanning* is glancing through a page to locate a particular kind of information. For example, children might scan through names in a telephone directory to locate a friend's name, or they might scan a paragraph to find where an event took place. Scanning requires the reader first to identify key words or phrases related to the information sought and then to focus on just those words as he or she glances over a page. Moving a finger ahead of the eyes in a straight downward motion helps to pace scanning and assists in a methodical coverage of print. Children need considerable guidance in adjusting their reading rate to their purposes in reading and to the nature of the material.

Information is often given in the form of maps, graphs, charts, or diagrams in content materials. Children need to know how to read and interpret them. They should be able to use keys to translate symbols and to understand significant features of various kinds of visuals. For example, in reading maps children need to understand differences in color coding, size of print, scale, direction, and other special features peculiar to maps. In reading line graphs children need to be able to identify and combine the various kinds of information provided such as year and country, or group and dollars, or vehicle and gallons, and to understand the comparison of the two components and thus the meaning of the graph.

Locational skills are another important aspect of study reading. Whether children are looking up information in a single text or have access to an entire library, they need to know where and how to look for information. For example, they need to know that a book's table of contents can tell them how that book is organized and the kinds of information they will find in it. They also need to know the differences between a table of contents and an index. The ability to locate information includes several skills: picking out key words, recognizing classifications of information, using cross-references, and being aware that information may be listed by subject, author, and title. Locational skills are best developed through meaningful projects that require children to become familiar with the various parts of a book and to use a variety of reference sources such as encyclopedias, almanacs, different types of guides to periodicals, and the card catalog found in most libraries.

Some Approaches to Reading Instruction

Given what we know about reading, it seems perfectly clear that a viable reading program must be language based. Reading is a *language* art, and the language children already possess provides the natural and logical foundation for an effective reading program to be developed in the classroom.

Some educators have postulated that teaching children to read is a two-step process: teaching them to decode and teaching them to comprehend. This is an oversimplification. Reading does not involve two distinct sets of behaviors, but a continual interplay of factors in both categories. The skills of reading evolve from the language system itself, and like those for speaking, involve a network of interdependent skills. Developing a specific competency is facilitated by the possession of other related knowledge and abilities. For example, having a personal set of meanings for a word affects the ease with which children remember that word. When children "know" a word — that is, when the word elicits vivid memories or feelings — learning to recognize it is easier.

A good reading program provides both cognitive and affective learning based on children's practical and aesthetic needs. Succinctly stated, the ultimate goal of a reading program is to help children become readers. This means not only that children will be *able* to read but that they will *want* to read. To accomplish such a goal, a reading program must (1) provide continuous growth in the skills of reading, (2) provide opportunity for children to use their reading skills in both functional and pleasurable situations, and (3) foster positive attitudes toward reading.

The three aspects of a reading program are important and interrelated. Without adequate training in skills, children will be unable to read for information and enjoyment. On the other hand, unless children see the utility of the skills they are taught, they will have little interest in acquiring or using them.

The teaching of reading may be approached in several ways. Some of the more common ways are discussed in the pages that follow. The approaches represent different points of view, different materials, and different structures. They are all potentially effective methods: children have been taught to read in these types of programs. As you consider each approach, try to see how the reading skills and abilities presented earlier in this chapter might be developed. Consider also how well the approach fits reading into the framework of a *language* art.

A Language Arts Approach

A language arts approach, sometimes called *language experience,* uses an integrative model to teach reading in the context of the other language arts. Children's experiences provide the content for listening, speaking, writing, and reading activities. Children discuss, write, and read. In group situations the teacher serves as the scribe, modeling writing and calling attention to features of language and print as she writes. At other times, children record experiences, first in pictures and later in writing. Material thus produced is "read" with the teacher's assistance. Little by little children make connections between print and oral language and begin to recognize words by sight both in the material they have written and in other print sources.

Schemata necessary for processing and understanding class-produced writing are well established during the discussion and writing stages of the activity. Hence, children can attend to the content of the message and the coding aspect of written language as they read.

Clay points out another important plus for integrating writing with reading. She states,

> In writing, the child must construct his own words, letter by letter. The attention of eye and brain is directed to the elements of letters, to letter sequences and to spatial concepts. The child who writes a simple story is caught up in a process of synthesizing words and sentences. This building-up process is an excellent complement to the visual analysis of text in his reading book, which is a breaking-down process. By these two processes the child comes to understand the hierarchical relationships of letters, words and utterances. He also confirms that a left-to-right constraint is applied to lines of print, to words within lines, and to letters within words. (1979, p. 124)

The language arts approach to reading has sometimes been criticized for the very fact that it utilizes children's language. Its critics contend that it limits vocabulary and skill development. This need not be the case. Meaningful language is always related to experiences, real or vicarious. Because experience is the source of language, language development is limited only by a lack of resourcefulness in the teacher. It is the teacher's task to guide children into new experiences and to help them discover appropriate matches between words and experiences. A language arts approach does not limit children to reading what they have written. Rather, it accepts their language as the regulator for decoding and comprehending the world of print. A language arts approach uses children's language as the base from which reading and reading-related experiences grow and develop.

A language arts approach builds on a solid foundation of concepts and attitudes about reading. These are developed through such pre-reading activities as

listening to stories and poems

listening to find words that begin alike

listening or looking for words that begin with the same letter as a child's name

thinking of words that rhyme

listening to "read along" recordings of stories and following along in the book

looking at books

acting out experiences or stories

telling about or explaining something

discussing ideas

making plans

discussing the meanings of interesting words

telling stories

drawing pictures or shaping models to tell about something

writing and reading children's names

making charts of classroom helpers

labeling objects in the room and in children's pictures

dictating captions for artwork

making lists of things to do, then reading and checking off the things as they are done

composing and writing group stories

dictating and copying individual stories

One of children's first writing and reading experiences usually comes about through art. Given a paintbrush and easel, children seldom have difficulty thinking of something to make. Drawing is a natural expression and precedes writing as a graphic form of communication. Even though the product may appear meaningless to the untrained eye of an adult, children's artwork is an expression of their feelings and thoughts, uniquely encoded in color and line.

The transition from drawing to writing as the major form of written communication requires careful guidance. The child who has worked diligently at the easel may become discouraged if the teacher asks "What is it?" The teacher who asks children to tell about their pictures, instead, elicits a verbalization of their ideas without suggesting adult interpretations or standards. When children have told about their pictures the teacher can increase the importance of what they have created and lead into a reading experience by saying something such as, "That is interesting. Let's write that down so others can read what you said." Then, as the child dictates, the teacher writes a sentence or two on the bottom of the picture or on a separate piece of paper. To extend this into a reading situation, a strategy such as the following might be used.

> The teacher and child "read" the story together and then the child is helped to focus in on a key word.
>
> *Teacher:* The word says *tent.* You slept in a *tent.* Look closely at the word. What letter do you see at the beginning and at the end of the word?
>
> *Child:* T.
>
> *Teacher:* That's right. Listen to the sound *t* spells as I say the word. *Tent.* Now you say it and listen to the *t* at the beginning and ending of the word.
>
> *Child:* Tent.
>
> *Teacher:* Can you think of some words that rhyme with *tent?* [Writes the word on the board.]
>
> *Child:* *Went.* [Teacher writes *went* under *tent.*] *Tell.*
>
> *Teacher:* Does *tell* rhyme with *tent* and *went?* Does it end the same?
>
> *Child:* No.
>
> *Teacher:* Can you think of another word that rhymes with *tent?*
>
> *Child:* *Bent.* [Teacher gives approving nod and writes *bent.*] *Tent, went, bent, . . . cent!* A penny.
>
> *Teacher:* [Writes *cent.*] Good. You thought of three words that rhyme with *tent.* Notice that they are spelled alike except for the first letter. [Underlines *ent* in each word as she pronounces them.] Show me the word *tent* in your story. [Child points.] That's right. Now let's read your story again. [They "read" and when they come to the word *tent,* the teacher lets the child read the word alone.]

The picture and story are then displayed on the bulletin board or put into a book along with pictures and stories by other children. Reading for meaning develops from many such group and individual experiences incorporated into activities throughout the day.

Reading experiences may be generated from various class activities. Going on a field trip, for example, requires thorough planning and lends itself to writing and reading summaries, lists, journal entries, letters, and books. These materials may be read and reread in the course of the activity or in related followup activities. Some activities might involve the whole class working cooperatively on a group composition, whereas others might have children working independently.

The following example illustrates a writing and reading activity that developed from a visit to a dairy. After the visit, the class decided to make some butter. They discussed how butter was made and planned what they would do. The teacher wrote the directions on the board as the children dictated. When the directions were complete, each child made a personal copy of them to read and use in making butter (Figure 10-1).

A language arts approach is theoretically sound. It assumes little or no prior knowledge; it provides experiences, develops language necessary to communicate about experience, and uses the child's own language for reading and writing. Because of this it may be used effectively with all types of children. Children for whom English is a second language, children from limited experiential and language backgrounds, speakers of divergent dialects, and children with advanced language skills can all be accommodated. Furthermore, as Hall points out,

> Although this approach has its greatest application in the prereading and beginning reading stages of instruction, it can be applied selectively for students needing corrective or remedial help, and can be used with other methods as well as being used in conjunction with language programs to further creativity and fluency in written expression. (1978, p. 89)

Although a language arts approach seems to offer a near optimal approach, it is not without possible pitfalls. First of all, because it is unstructured in terms of a set scope and sequence of instruction — the teacher has enormous responsibility for monitoring the development of children and making certain each child engages in activities that will lead to maximum growth. This means that teachers must have a thorough understanding of the skills of reading, know when and how to teach them in the context of various activities, and have an extensive knowledge of library books and other materials to supplement and extend the materials created by children. They must be skilled in developing children's ability to think. They must be able to guide children to probe, analyze, and organize experiences and to communicate their ideas. In addition, they must be especially percep-

Let's Make Butter

1. Wash the churn.
2. Pour cream in the Churn. 3. Work the dasher. 4. See the butter Come.! 5. Pour off the buttermilk. 6. Put the butter in a a bowl.
7. Work and wash the
8. butter. add Salt. ?
9. Shage butter inot a cube.

tive of children's interests and have a good memory of what children have done both experientially and academically.

Another related pitfall of a language arts approach lies in the amount of systematic instruction and practice children receive. Some children seem to learn best in a less global and more structured approach. These children need explicit instruction that is limited to one or a few skills at a time and is followed up with carefully monitored practice. For some children the instructional sequence may need to be repeated a number of times and be followed by a set reinforcement schedule. Although it is possible to meet their needs with language arts approach, time constraints and the demands on the teacher may make it difficult to give children the necessary time.

A Basal Reader Approach

A basal reader approach utilizes a set of reading books and supplementary materials designed to teach children all the important skills of reading. It is an attempt to provide a complete reading program. The materials are organized by levels from readiness through either sixth or eighth grade. They usually include a readiness workbook, several preprimers, a primer, and one or more readers for each level. Each level of pupils' material is accompanied by a comprehensive teacher's manual with specific helps for teaching, organizing, and evaluating the reading program. There are also workbooks for each level and other optional teaching materials such as filmstrips, charts or reader boards, supplementary readers, and ditto master skill sheets.

Basal programs generally provide a developmental sequence of skills and have a controlled vocabulary so that reading is learned in small steps. They typically offer a readiness program to develop children's skills in auditory and visual discrimination, knowledge of letter names, and ability to follow directions, to sequence events, to use left-to-right progression, and to understand concepts such as *over*, *under*, *in*, *around*, and *between*. Some basal programs differ in initial teaching procedures, particularly those for developing sound-symbol relationships. In what is commonly called a *meaning-based* basal, children begin by reading simple stories and learn a core vocabulary of sight words through contextual reading activities. Once they have conceptualized the process of reading and can read a few words, the words they know are used as the base for teaching phonics induc-

FIGURE 10-1 (*facing page*)

tively. For example, words such as *boy, ball,* and *baby* may be used to teach the spelling of the /b/ sound. Children pronounce the words, listen to the beginning sound, and identify the spelling of the sound. Then they think of other words that begin with /b/ and add those to the list. Or, they might listen as the teacher pronounces a word and decide whether or not the word begins with *b* (e.g., <u>b</u>attle, <u>b</u>unch, <u>h</u>andle). The oral part of the lesson would then be followed up with an exercise in the workbook or a ditto sheet to provide individual practice. Later lessons would teach other phonic elements in a similar way. This approach is called an *analytic approach* because sound-symbol correspondences are taught by analyzing sounds in the context of whole words.

Some approaches to beginning reading place greater emphasis on teaching letter-sound relationships from the very first. These are referred to as *code-based* basals. One such approach teaches the common sounds of high-frequency letters in isolation and then teaches children to combine sounds into words. For example, in learning /m/ children might listen to a story associating the letter and the sound (something that tastes good makes a character in the story go "M-m-m-mm") followed by drill:

[The teacher writes *m* on the board.] This letter spells /m/.

Say it. [Response]

Look at it carefully. Now watch as I write it.

[Writes the letter] Now you write it. [Response]

What letter did you write? [Response]

What sound does the letter *m* spell? [Response]

When children have learned several letter-sound correspondences they are given flash card drills on the letters for further practice and taught to blend the sounds:

[The teacher writes the word *mat.*] Look at this word.

[Pointing to *m*] What is this letter? [Response]

What sound does *m* spell? [Response]

[Pointing to *a*] What is this letter? [Response]

What sound does *a* spell? [Response]

[Pointing to *t*] What is this letter? [Response]

What sound does *t* spell? [Response]

Now let's put all these sounds together to make a word. Say each sound as I point to it. Ready . . . [Points to each letter and children respond]

Again, and this time we'll say the sounds faster. Ready . . . [Points quickly from letter to letter and children respond.] Now read the whole word. . . . [Moves hand under the word in a continuous motion as children read]

Teaching children individual phoneme-grapheme correspondences and then combining sounds into whole-word reading is called a *synthetic approach* to teaching phonics.

The synthetic approach has been criticized on several counts. First, it places heavy emphasis on the mechanical process of sounding out words. Second, when sounds are learned separately children do not have the benefit of contextual cues to help them make sound associations. Perhaps an even more important consideration lies in the difficulty of uttering individual speech sounds without distortion. Sounds such as /b/, /d/, /g/, and /t/ are particularly difficult and may lead to gross difficulty in trying to apply knowledge of phonics to the pronunciation of words (e.g., *bit* as *buh-i-tuh* or *tree* as *tuh-r-ee*).

Another code-based approach is referred to as the *linguistic approach*. This approach to beginning reading teaches sound-symbol relationships through consistent word patterns. Words are grouped according to phoneme-grapheme correspondence patterns and taught in a hierarchical order of difficulty. For example, children's first reading experiences focus on a consonant-vowel-consonant pattern and they learn words such as *man, ran, pan, fan, tan.* In this way they learn letter-sound associations but always in the environment of naturally occurring language patterns. Sentence practice is included in this approach by combining known words and a few structure words such as *the, in,* and *a* to form simple sentences. Some advocates of the linguistic approach believe pictures in children's reading books hamper mastery of letter-sound relationships because children tend to tell the story from the pictures. For this reason some linguistic materials have only colorful decorations on the pages and no pictures.

By the middle grades, basal reading programs introduce children to many kinds of reading. Newer books contain a range of subject area selections as well as stories, biographies, and other literary materials. Special attention is given to developing oral and silent reading, reading rates, comprehension, critical reading, and study skills.

In short, these materials are designed to teach children the necessary reading skills and habits for effective adult reading. They should also acquaint children with good literature and develop positive attitudes toward reading.

The teacher's manual that accompanies basal materials provides detailed instructional plans. These plans include step-by-step procedures for teaching each lesson either to small groups of children or to a whole class; usually there are also suggestions for ways to adapt lessons to the needs of slower and faster learners. A typical basal reading lesson contains the following elements:

1. *Preparation for reading.* Introducing a story and setting the scene for a successful reading experience is especially important when a story requires understanding of something outside the children's background of experiences. In this step the teacher guides children's discussion about pictures in the story, what they already know, and what they think the selection will be about. New words are introduced and the meanings established.

2. *Guided reading.* Under the guidance of the teacher, children read parts of the selection to verify their predictions and to find specific information (e.g., what a character does, what happened next).

3. *Silent reading.* Children read the story through without interruption for continuity.

4. *Skill practice.* Specific skill-building exercises provide practice to reinforce skills as needed or to teach new ones.

5. *Enrichment activities.* Suggestions are given for children to use information or skills in other situations (e.g., in supplementary books, workbooks, games) or to engage in reading-related activities (e.g., creative writing, puppets, murals).

A basal reading program can be a great help to the busy teacher, but one must recognize that it is neither a cure-all nor a complete program. To use the program wisely you will need to observe the following cautions:

1. Basal readers are aimed at a broad range of audiences, and certain stories and activities may not be appropriate for a particular group of children. Be selective, particularly in the use of workbooks; don't feel you have to use everything.

2. Basal readers are primarily designed to be used during the scheduled reading class period. However, content area reading

occurs at various times of the school day. Do teach skills whenever they are needed and in meaningful contexts. Don't be a slave to the program outlined in the basal.

3. Children vary widely in their ability to read. Sole dependence on material at one grade level will at best be appropriate only for the average readers. Do substitute or at the very least supplement the basal with material at levels appropriate for more advanced and less able readers.

4. The content of basal readers includes but a sampling of the world of books and other reading materials. Don't confine children to one book; help them broaden their reading interests through a wide range of reading materials.

5. Using a similar teaching format for each lesson can become tiresome. Set objectives appropriate to your group of children and then devise other alternate teaching strategies to achieve your objectives.

6. Since most basal series are designed as *reading* textbooks, they may do little if anything to integrate the language arts. Let the teaching of reading spill out into other subject areas. In particular, make certain the skills taught in listening and spelling complement those taught in reading.

7. Using a basal program can give teachers a false sense of having "covered all the bases" in reading. Know the skills children need and then assess their strengths and weaknesses, keep a record of their progress, and individualize instruction as indicated.

A Personalized Approach

A personalized reading program emphasizes self-directed and purposeful reading experiences. It is not prestructured, but is planned for and with children on the basis of individual interests and needs. It also stresses general language development as a prerequisite for successful reading experiences and develops readers through natural, purposeful activities. To develop and manage a personalized reading program, teachers must know all the skills of reading and be prepared to diagnose and teach them as needed. A personalized reading program places a large responsibility on the teacher for the content and structure of the program, but it also requires children to share responsibility for their own progress.

Because a personalized reading program develops around studies in other areas of the curriculum and around children's interests, it utilizes a variety of reading materials at several levels of difficulty. To get such a program started, teachers need to assemble a sizable classroom library, including books on topics being studied, as well as children's magazines, reference materials, and any other pertinent resource materials. The classroom library forms the core of the reading program, so it should contain something every child can read and will want to read. Once they have gathered materials, teachers need to become thoroughly familiar with them. Discussion questions may be prepared for specific materials, or reading may be guided through more general questions determined at the time of the conference ("How did a colonial home differ from yours today?" "What is the floor of the ocean like?") Prepared discussion questions and language activities may be kept in a handy reference file with easy access to children.

Word recognition and comprehension skills are usually taught in small groups. Job cards provide additional practice. Exercises and activities covering all the skills should be designed and placed in a file so that children who need practice on specific skills can work on them independently or with a peer tutor. (See Figure 10-2.) Planning for the use of these exercises is done with children during the individual conference. It is important to have enough job cards available when children need them; the file will no doubt need to be added to periodically to ensure fresh and appropriate skill lessons. To save preparation time and materials, the cards may be covered with clear plastic so that answers can be wiped off and the cards reused.

Plans for the reading period are made with the whole class and during individual conferences. Although much of the reading period is taken up in reading self-selected materials, children also participate in other reading-related activities: reading aloud, holding conferences, discussing, writing, making, planning, and sharing. Organization is a key element in a smoothly running program. Any activity that involves more than one person must be scheduled in advance so as not to interfere with the work of others. Children must also learn to plan how they will spend a block of time and must be held responsible for their activities. The teacher should maintain a schedule of conferences with individuals and groups, but leave some time available for direct instruction and incidental help. Small groups with similar interests or needs may be formed so that the teacher can work with several children at once.

The teacher-student conference is the main thrust of instruction,

FIGURE 10-2 (*facing page*)
Job Cards.

Job Card # _____

Find 5 words that begin with each of these consonant clusters.

bl   pl   sl   cl

___ ___ ___ ___

___ ___ ___ ___

___ ___ ___ ___

___ ___ ___ ___

___ ___ ___ ___

Job Card # _____

Find 10 words that were used to describe a character.

_____

_____

_____

_____

_____

_____

_____

_____

_____

_____

Job Card # _____

Compound words are made by combining shorter words. Someone, <u>playground</u>, and <u>sometimes</u> are compound words.[*] Make compound words from the words below. Write them on the lines.

out   *hook*

time   *line*

fish   *table*

*The word <u>breakfast</u> was made by combining two words. Can you explain what it means?

Job Card # _____

Write a synonym for each word below. A dictionary or a thesaurus will help you.

pleasant   _____

famished   _____

simple   _____

enormous   _____

beautiful _____

```
┌─────────────────────────────────────────────────────────┐
│                          Name _____   │
│                          Date _____   │
│   Personal Reading Plan                                   │
│   For the next __ days I will read _____  │
│   _____ │
│   I will also improve _____  │
│   by _____  │
│                        (Signed) _____   │
└─────────────────────────────────────────────────────────┘
```

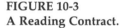

FIGURE 10-3
A Reading Contract.

and conferences should be scheduled frequently with each child. During the conference the teacher may pose questions to help children explore ideas and interpretations, listen to them read a passage orally, check their vocabulary and comprehension, probe their thinking to clarify concepts and facilitate new insights, assess their progress and needs, motivate, plan learning experiences, or check their reading journals. The conference should not be longer than five to ten minutes. Before it is concluded, however, the teacher and child should have laid out plans for future work. When the child is found to need special help or skill work, specific plans should be made for special instruction. This will usually entail working with a group of children having similar needs and following up the instruction with additional independent work through job cards or skill worksheets. Plans for the next block of time may be made in the form of a contract as in Figure 10-3.

Record-keeping is an important part of a personalized reading program. Children may keep daily records or journals of their work. They should include the title of the reading material, pages read, troublesome words, learning activities, and types of sharing experiences. Their record-keeping should not be allowed to become cumbersome, however, or it will detract from the reading program. A sample journal that requires only a few minutes each day to complete is shown in Figure 10-4. Children can also keep track of troublesome

FIGURE 10-4 *(facing page)*

READING JOURNAL   Name _____

Date	Title	Pages Read	New Words	Activities	Comments

words as they read along by writing them on an oversized bookmark that they keep in their book. Such a list provides a simple inventory of children's word-recognition skills and suggests needed skill instruction. Meanings of the words on the list may also be identified and used in activities that help children conceptualize the word and incorporate it into their vocabulary (e.g., acting out, constructing sentences, finding synonyms and antonyms).

Teachers also need to keep records of children's progress. This is best done during the individual conference. As children read aloud the teacher can note word-identification errors. Through discussions and other reading activities teachers can note comprehension problems or readiness for more advanced work. Some teachers prefer to keep an anecdotal record, whereas others prefer a checklist such as the one in Figure 10-5. Although it would not be possible to assess everything on the checklist at each conference, the list does remind the teacher of the range of reading skills that must be attended to, and it provides a comprehensive record-keeping system. Having such a record is important for guiding children's selections of reading materials and activities and for planning appropriate group and individual learning experiences.

Language activities are an integral part of a personalized approach to reading instruction. Children need to have many opportunities to react to and interpret what they read. Engaging in a discussion or an activity related to what they have read motivates children's reading and brings the printed page to life. When children elect to read a whole book, as they often do, it is a good idea to plan activities for sharing and interacting with other children or with the teacher at intervals throughout the reading of the book. Becoming mentally involved in reading tends to stimulate a desire for oral or active response. Children might draw, discuss, debate, construct, act out, write poetry or songs, read aloud, or respond in any other way that seems appropriate. Children who are caught up in a story and encouraged to read creatively seem to have little difficulty thinking of interesting ways to share what they read.

An effective personalized reading approach places heavy demands on the instructional and management skills of the teacher. It also requires quantities of materials, and children who take a greater share of the responsibility for their own learning. Clearly, this approach is not suitable for all teachers; as with the language arts ap-

FIGURE 10-5 (*facing page*)
A Reading Skill Checklist.

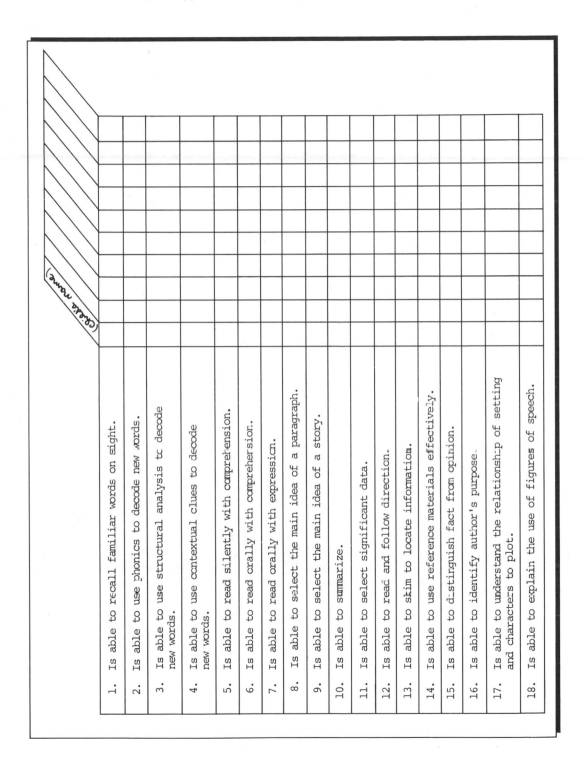

(Child's name)

1. Is able to recall familiar words on sight.

2. Is able to use phonics to decode new words.

3. Is able to use structural analysis to decode new words.

4. Is able to use contextual clues to decode new words.

5. Is able to read silently with comprehension.

6. Is able to read orally with comprehension.

7. Is able to read orally with expression.

8. Is able to select the main idea of a paragraph.

9. Is able to select the main idea of a story.

10. Is able to summarize.

11. Is able to select significant data.

12. Is able to read and follow direction.

13. Is able to skim to locate information.

14. Is able to use reference materials effectively.

15. Is able to distinguish fact from opinion.

16. Is able to identify author's purpose.

17. Is able to understand the relationship of setting and characters to plot.

18. Is able to explain the use of figures of speech.

proach, some children may not make as much progress as they would in a developmental program emphasizing a tightly structured sequence of skills and more teacher-directed instruction.

Determining Readability

It is important that children be given reading materials at an appropriate level of difficulty for all their developmental, functional, and recreational reading. To do so requires a knowledge of the level of difficulty for given materials. This may be determined by using a readability formula. The Estimate of Readability by Fry in Figure 10-6 is comparatively easy to use and is suitable for reading materials at all levels.

Assessing Pupils' Progress

There are many widely different reading tests on the market; they are designed to provide information ranging from children's recognition of individual letter sounds to general ability in comprehension. Most schools have an established testing program that is administered through the school district office at specific intervals. Such testing programs usually utilize a standardized survey test, such as the *Gates-McGinitie Reading Test* (Teacher's College Press), *Metropolitan Achievement Tests: Reading* (Harcourt Brace Jovanovich), or the *Stanford Achievement Test: Reading* (Harcourt Brace Jovanovich). These tests yield an average or general reading ability score and permit comparisons between classes or schools. Although they may be helpful in indicating children's overall competency or the success of a particular reading program, most tests of this type offer little help for planning specific instruction. Diagnostic tests such as the *Doren Diagnostic Reading Tests of Word Recognition Skills* (American Guidance Service) or the *Stanford Diagnostic Reading Test* (Harcourt Brace Jovanovich) may also be part of a district's program. This type of test gives more specific information about children's skills and abilities. However, because of the nature of the tests and the fact that they are administered infrequently (often only once during the school year),

FIGURE 10-6 (*facing page*)
Graph for Estimating Readability.
From Edward Fry, *Elementary Reading Instruction* 1977. Copyright © McGraw-Hill, p. 217. Reprinted by permission of McGraw-Hill Book Company.

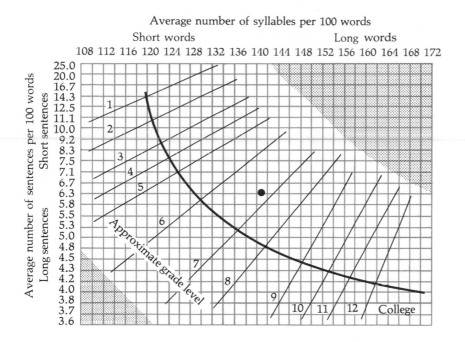

Average number of syllables per 100 words

Directions

Randomly select three 100-word passages from a book or an article. Plot average number of syllables and average number of sentences per 100 words on graph to determine the grade level of the material. Choose more passages per book if great variability is observed and conclude that the book has uneven readability. Few books will fall into the gray area, but when they do grade level scores are invalid.

Example

	Syllables	Sentences
First hundred words	124	6.6
Second hundred words	141	5.5
Third hundred words	158	6.8
Average	141	6.3

Readability 7th grade (see dot plotted on graph)

Additional Directions for Working Readability Graph

1. Randomly select three sample passages and count exactly 100 words beginning with a beginning of a sentence. Don't count numbers. Do count proper nouns.
2. Count the number of sentences in the hundred words, estimating length of the fraction of the last sentence to the nearest 1/10th.
3. Count the total number of syllables in the 100-word passage. If you don't have a hand counter available, an easy way is to simply put a mark above every syllable over one in each word, then, when you get to the end of the passage, count the number of marks and add 100.
4. Enter graph with average sentence length and number of syllables; plot dot where the two lines intersect. Area where dot is plotted will give you the approximate grade level.
5. If a great deal of variability is found, putting more sample counts into the average is desirable.

they provide limited information for instruction. Because children's reading skills are continually changing, evaluation needs to be an integral and ongoing part of the reading program. The most effective instruction is based on children's current and individual needs.

The Informal Reading Inventory

An Informal Reading Inventory (IRI) is a series of short passages taken from books or materials at successively more difficult levels. Children read the selections and then answer questions about what they have read. The teacher records vocabulary and composition errors and converts the children's scores into percentages. This information provides data on the kinds of errors children make and indicates the levels at which they can read for different purposes. An IRI is, as the name suggests, an informal assessment, and the results are subject to teacher interpretation. Although it is not a standardized test, it is a handy assessment tool. Many basal reading series include an IRI for placement in the program. When one is not available the teacher can easily prepare one.

Preparing the inventory To prepare an IRI you will need a series of graded books with a range of difficulty from at least two levels below to two levels above a child's estimated reading level. Word lists from the series may be used to determine the child's approximate level. Select a sample of 100 to 150 words near the middle of the book for each level. The number of words may be less for easier material; 50 to 75 words should be adequate at early primary levels. Be careful to select a part of the book that makes sense in isolation and to extend the passage through a sentence or paragraph where a natural break occurs. Count the number of words in each selection.

Prepare eight to ten comprehension questions for each passage, possibly less for easy selections. Include a variety of questions to check different kinds of comprehension: vocabulary, factual, inferential, and evaluative. Make a copy of the selections and the questions so that you can write on them. Children may either read directly from the book or from a copy that does not include questions.

Administering the inventory Before administering the IRI to a child, the teacher needs to memorize a simple marking code for errors as follows:

Omissions. Circle the word omitted.

He saw (some) lions.

Additions. Insert a caret and write the word.

big
Jack ate a ˄ red apple.

Substitutions. Cross out the word and write the word pronounced.

The door ~~was~~ open. *(went)*

Unknown words. Write *P* above words pronounced by the teacher.

Into the woods ran the gnome. *(P)*

Repetitions. Underline a repeated word or phrase.

I want some of that <u>big</u> cheese.

The IRI should be administered in a normal reading situation without interruption. Help the children feel at ease by explaining what is expected and telling them that some of the material will be fairly difficult but that you want them to read it as well as possible. Very briefly establish the background and purpose for reading each excerpt ["This is a story about . . . " "Let's see what happens to the . . . (or when the . . .)"]. Then, as the children read, mark your copy using the marking code. Errors involving proper nouns and variant pronunciations typical of a child's dialect are not counted. Do not hurry the children or help them decode words. When they come to a word they don't know, pause a few seconds and then simply tell them the word so they can go on. After they have finished reading, ask the questions and write down their answers. Writing down the answers instead of merely marking questions right or wrong is often useful to reveal patterns of children's thinking. Watch for signs of tension as the children read (frowning, squinting, wiggling, hesitant speech, etc.).

Start children reading at a level about two grades below the level you think they are able to read. Have them proceed through successive levels until they experience obvious difficulty. Reading at a more difficult level yields data on their word-recognition skills. Children may be asked to read both an oral and a silent selection at each level. You can then compare oral and silent comprehension, and this comparison may be desirable for some children. However, using only an oral selection is usually adequate and saves time.

Computing reading levels and analyzing results To compute the results of the word-recognition part of the IRI, subtract the number of errors from the total number of words in the selection. The answer is the number of words correctly pronounced. Divide the number of correct words by the total number of words in the selection to find the percentage correct. Next, find the percentage of comprehension by dividing the number of correct responses by the number of questions. (If both an oral and a silent selection are given, find the average of the two.) The two percentage figures are interpreted according to the following range for each type of reading:

> *Independent reading level*
> 98% or above on vocabulary
> 90% or above on comprehension

> *Instructional reading level*
> 90% to 97% on vocabulary
> 75% to 90% on comprehension

> *Frustration reading level*
> below 90% on vocabulary
> below 50% on comprehension

Various factors influence how a child reads at any given time, and you will need to take any unusual circumstances into consideration in deciding children's placement. Signs of tension or poor phrasing, for example, would suggest an easier level. A completed IRI selection is shown in Figure 10-7.

Analyzing miscues The errors or *miscues* on an IRI provide important information about children's reading. Some miscues are more significant that others. Of primary concern is the degree to which a particular miscue results in loss of meaning. The child who reads *Sam had a big ugly scarecrow in front of his house* as *Sam had an ugly big scarecrow in front of his house* has not read the sentence correctly, yet the miscues have not caused a loss of meaning. On the other hand, a child who reads "Sam had a big guy carcow in from his house" has not derived the intended meaning from print.

Further analysis of miscues involves looking at children's ability to use three kinds of cueing systems: phonic, semantic, and syntactic. Begin by making a list of the words that a child mispronounced. Then write the child's pronunciation beside each word. Compare the two lists to determine the child's use of word-recognition skills: Can any of the mispronunciations be accounted for by dialect differences? Were consonants pronounced correctly? Were there vowel errors? Did the child pronounce common morphemes correctly? Then check the errors to see if they make sense semantically: Does the mispronounced word sound similar to the word? Does it have a similar meaning? (Remember that if children think a word makes sense in context they seldom stop to apply other word-recognition strategies.) Finally, check each error to see if it is related to children's syntactic awareness, their sentence sense: Does the mispronounced word fit the grammatical structure of the sentence? Was the mispronounced word

Doug stripped off his sweat shirt and began to put on his diving gear. "I sure hope I can find some lobsters today," he said. "Not many around, though, I guess. The fish markets in Seaview are really paying a good price for lobsters. And I can use a little money. I've got a chance to get a paper route. But I've got to have a bike to do it. Bikes cost money."

Stan didn't mention how badly he, too, needed spending money. School was about to start again. What clothes he hadn't ~~outworn~~ *worn out* during the summer, he had outgrown. At the age of thirteen he seemed to be growing faster than Iowa corn in July.

Questions:

1. What were the boys getting ready to do? *go diving*
2. What is a lobster? *like a big crawdad*
3. What does diving gear look like? *fins, mask, oxygen tank*
4. Where do you think the boys lived? *Seaview*
5. Why did Doug want to catch lobsters? *to get a bike*
6. What did Stan plan to spend his money on? *school*
7. Why did Stan want new clothes? *he'd outgrown his old ones*
8. What does the phrase "growing faster than Iowa corn in July" mean? *that's when corn grows fast*

Vocabulary: Number of words correct _____ ÷ 116 = *98* %

Comprehension: Number of questions correct *7½* ÷ 8 = *94* %

Reading level of selection: 4th Grade

Level of difficulty: *Independent*

Comments: *good expression*

Reading selection from *Excursions* by Ira E. Aaron et al. Copyright © 1976 by Scott, Foresman and Company. Reprinted by permission.

FIGURE 10-7
Sample IRI Worksheet.

the same part of speech? The results of these kinds of analyses indicate what kind of help children need, which skills they need to be taught or to have reinforced.

The Cloze Procedure

The cloze procedure is another informal means of matching material and reader. It utilizes the principle of *closure* to measure comprehension on a particular passage. In this procedure every *n*th word of a passage is deleted and readers must supply the missing words.

Bormuth (1975) recommends using a selection of about 250 words with every fifth word deleted. The material should be something children have not read before.

To prepare a cloze test, select an adequate passage and type the material on a sheet of paper, leaving a blank space in place of every fifth word. Any one of the first five words that is not essential to meaning may be deleted. Then count every fifth word and type a blank line. Make all the blanks equal in length.

Children read through the selection, writing whatever word they think fits in the blank. To check their answers, Bormuth recommends that only the exact word be counted correct. The score is computed by dividing the number of correct responses by the number of blanks. A score of 44–57 percent is comparable to the instructional level on an IRI; above 57 percent to the independent level.

You will notice that to supply the missing words one relies heavily on contextual clues. Therefore the cloze procedure has also been used to develop an awareness of meaningful comprehension clues. Analysis of children's responses on the cloze procedure provides information about their sense of semantic and syntactic appropriateness. Compare their choices for each blank with the correct words to see if they have given synonyms or other meaningful responses and whether they have used words that are the same part of speech.

The following passage from North, "Little Rascal," is a brief example of a cloze exercise.

> Then, with a picnic _____ filled with sandwiches and _____ few bottles of cold _____ beer and pop, my _____ and Rascal and I _____ clamber happily into the _____ seat of the big _____ passenger Oldsmobile, with the _____ back and the windshield _____.
>
> All three of us _____ goggles — Rascal's being natural, _____ course. He liked to _____ between us on the _____ of the seat, gazing _____ ahead as my father _____ from low into second _____ from second into high, _____ up the river road _____ Lake Koshkonong.

Grouping for Reading Instruction

Children with similar abilities may be grouped together for instruction. In a basal reading program children are usually placed in high-, average-, and low-ability groups. These groups are determined on the basis of children's average reading ability. This plan permits the teacher to work with each group each day for a period of direct instruction. While the teacher is working with one group, the other children are reading and working independently on skill sheets, in workbooks, at a learning center (see Chapter 13), or in a creative or enrichment activity. A basic daily schedule might look like this:

Group A	Teacher-directed instruction	Independent skill or enrichment activities	Silent reading
Group B	Silent reading	Teacher-directed instruction	Independent skill or enrichment activities
Group C	Independent skill or enrichment activities	Silent reading	Teacher-directed instruction

Such a schedule may be varied one or more days a week to allow for large-group activities such as going to the school library or sharing projects, or for special language-related experiences.

A language arts or personalized reading approach lends itself to a variety of grouping procedures. For example, small groups of children may work cooperatively on a writing or reading activity, interest groups may meet to share information or read aloud together, or needs groups may be formed to work on particular skills. In addition, children may group informally with the teacher at various times during the day to plan or work together.

It is important to remember that children's reading ability varies in many ways. Hence having three reading groups or any other fixed grouping is inadequate to serve their needs completely. At the same time, managing a great number of reading groups is difficult; having too many groups may well decrease the overall efficiency of the reading program. One way to accommodate individual differences while maintaining a three-group structure is through the use of individually prescribed skill work. Packets of worksheets, selected workbook pages, or multimedia materials may be planned for individuals to work on during the independent work period.

Regardless of the major approach used to teach reading, grouping procedures must be flexible so that children can move from one group to another as necessary to find a "best fit." Achievement grouping is at best only an approximation. One child may be capable in one aspect of reading and less able in another; another may demonstrate the reverse skills. Still, their test scores can average out at the same level. Maximum growth requires continual assessment and planning on an individual basis.

In Summary

Children's success in reading is closely related to their other language competencies. Their oral language provides the foundation for developing skill in reading. Their knowledge of vocabulary and grammar allows them to derive meaning from print. Their ability to listen to language and to discriminate among sounds facilitates their acquisition of word-recognition skills. Writing and reading are closely related in that they are reciprocal language skills and abilities.

The reading process involves the use of a complex set of interrelated skills and abilities. These include the ability to identify words by sight, by phonic analysis, by structural and morphemic analysis, by contextual analysis, or by looking them up in the dictionary. It also involves organizing and assimilating what is read. These activities require a complex of thinking skills. Materials may be understood at various levels of comprehension depending on the kind of thinking skills the reader employs. One comprehension taxonomy identifies four levels: literal, inferential, evaluative, and appreciative. Reading in the content areas requires special attention inasmuch as expository material differs from narrative in significant ways.

Many factors help to determine children's readiness for reading instruction. Because they bring all of their experiences to the reading task, all their social, emotional, physical, and intellectual experiences directly or indirectly affect their degree of readiness. However, factors such as language development, auditory discrimination, visual discrimination, and general intellectual development are particularly important.

Some of the more common ways to teach reading include a basal reader approach, a language arts approach, and a personalized approach. A basal series provides a structured reading program and is the most widely used throughout the country. A language arts approach integrates listening, speaking, reading, and writing. Children first learn to read what they themselves have written. In a personalized reading program children select their own reading material, and instruction is based on individual needs. Both the language arts and personalized approaches place responsibility for organization and skill development on the teacher.

Tests and other evaluation instruments provide information about children's reading ability. Commonly used instruments are either survey or diagnostic tests. Survey tests indicate children's general reading ability and provide a means of determining reading gain for an individual or for comparing individuals or groups. Diagnostic tests usually identify children's abilities more specifically. Informal Reading Inventories may be used to assess children's instructional level. A cloze procedure measures comprehension and suggests appropriate levels of reading material.

Learning Objectives

COGNITIVE OBJECTIVES

Primary Grades

Children will

enlarge their sight word vocabulary.

expand their understanding of specific words.

conceptualize reading as a communicative act.

be able auditorily and visually to perceive significant aspects of language.

be able to use word-recognition skills to identify unknown words.

be able to integrate the meanings of words in phrases and sentences.

be able to summarize the content of stories.

be able to tell the sequence of events in stories.

be able to make inferences from information given.

be able to associate personal experiences with what is read.

be able to distinguish fact from fantasy.

be able to explain cause and effect.

be able to read with expression.

be able to react creatively to what is read.

Middle Grades

Children will

expand primary-level objectives.

be able to summarize the main idea of a paragraph.

be able to organize details and factual information around main ideas.

be able to read for different purposes.

be able to distinguish fact from opinion.

be able to make comparisons of the characters, settings, and plots of stories.

be able to relate what is read to personal problems.

be able to recognize mood and explain its contributing influence in stories.

be able to evaluate the author's purpose.

be able to recognize and explain figures of speech.

AFFECTIVE OBJECTIVES

Children will

listen to stories with interest.

seek out information in printed materials.

find pleasure in reading.

appreciate characterizations in stories.

share reading experiences spontaneously.

develop goals for reading that include both skill improvement and personal gain.

read widely.

Suggested Learning Activities

Sound Bingo. Make Bingo cards with small pictures of things that begin with common consonant sounds. Print consonants on small cards. To play the game, hold up a consonant card and have the children look for a picture of something on their card that begins with that sound. The children then place a marker on the picture. The first one to form a row of markers wins the game.

Trip Phonics. Make simulated suitcases out of heavy tagboard, and write a common consonant sound on each. (You will probably want to use the most troublesome ones.) Begin the game by saying, "I am going on a trip. This is my [J] suitcase and I'm going to pack it with things that begin with [J]. I will take [jacks] in my [J] suitcase." The suitcase is passed around the group, and each child in turn says, "I will take _____ in my _____ suitcase."

Change. Make up phonic puzzles in which children change one letter at a time to make a new word.

HIKE		**Key:**
_ _ _ _	enjoy something	like
_ _ _ _	body of water	lake
_ _ _ _	put together or construct	make
_ _ _ _	cook in an oven	bake
_ _ _ _	the bottom of something	base
_ _ _ _	enjoy the sun	bask
_ _ _ _	opposite of front	back
_ _ _ _	put lunch in	sack

(Children can make these up for each other.)

Cereal Box Readers. Have the children bring the boxes from their favorite cereals to school (empty). Let them get together in groups or with partners to read their boxes. The children should make a list of all the words they don't know and then employ all their word attack skills (phonics, structural analysis, contextual clues) to arrive at their best "guesstimate" of the correct pronunciation. Children in other groups will most likely have the same words on their lists and they can compare pronunciations and explain why they thought their pronunciation was a good "guesstimate."

Dictionary Code. Pass out slips of papers with interesting or funny sentences written on them (or let children make up their own). The children should look up each word in the dictionary and copy the phonetic pronunciation down on another piece of paper. Then they exchange papers and read what is written. For example, "A rolling stone gathers no moss," might look like this:

ə rōl´ing stōn găth´ərz nō môs.

Synonym Concentration. Prepare a deck of cards that consists of pairs of synonyms. To play the game, the cards are placed singly, face down, on the desk. The children take turns picking up a card and then trying to find its mate. Each child is allowed to pick up two cards. If the cards make a synonym pair, the child gets another turn. If not, both cards are laid back down and the next child takes a turn. The child with the most pairs wins.

Scavenger Hunt. Prepare lists of questions that the children can find in classroom reference materials (e.g., Who wrote *Brighty of the Grand Canyon*? How many people live in England? Who discovered penicillin?). Children work in small groups to complete all the information on their sheet.

Storytime. "Buddies" select a story they like and practice reading it aloud until they can read it with fitting expression. When they are well prepared let them hold a "storytime" for peers or younger children. It is usually effective to alternate the reading of paragraphs between the children but they may wish to break up the reading in some other way.

Chalk Talk. Have the children draw pictures to illustrate stories as they are telling them. For example, if Susi goes skipping down a country path, the picture of Susi in the country is drawn as the scene is described. When she comes upon a magic coin in the path, the coin is drawn in, etc.

Lost Character. The children pretend that a character from a story is lost. They write a newspaper ad describing the character for a Lost and Found column.

Peep Show. Use a shoe box or other box about that size. Cut a hole in the top to let light in and a small hole in front to "peep" through. Make a scene in the box with cutouts to illustrate a story. The outside of the box may be covered or painted and the name of the story neatly lettered across the front.

Two-Word Summaries. When children have finished a story, have them describe the story in just two words.

Act It Out. When you are reading to the children, stop reading and let them get into small groups to discuss what they think will happen next. Then let them plan and act it out.

Newspaper Scramble. Clip interesting articles from the newspaper. Cut off the headlines and mix up articles and headlines. Have the children read and try to match them up.

Fact and Opinion. Bring editorials or letters to the editor to class. Have the children underline facts in red and opinions in blue.

Alliteration. Guide the children to discover the use of alliteration in stories and poems. To strengthen the concept, have them write sentences using the same letter to begin every word or nearly every word.

Examples: Naughty Norris knows now not to be naughty any more.
Tongue twisters twist tongues terribly tight.

Treasure Hunt. Prepare slips of paper with clues to the "treasure." Hide them about the room or school grounds and let the children read and search.

Musical Background. When the children have finished reading a story with a pronounced mood, let them select or create mood music to illustrate it. If a piano is available, they can make up a variety of simple music even though they are unable to read music. Just one note played at a time offers infinite variation.

Comic Strip Sequence. Glue comic strips to heavy paper. Then cut them apart into separate frames and mix them up. The children must then figure out the sequence of the story and arrange the frames in correct order.

Homographs. Give the children a list of homographs and let them write a single sentence to illustrate the different meanings (e.g., The author was content with the content of the article. The manager will object to this object being in his office.). Suggested words: *wind, conduct, lead, perfect, live, rebel, read, subject, produce, convict,* and *content*.

Sports Page Compounds. Have the children look through the sports page of the newspaper and list all the compound words they find (e.g., *fisherman, football, basketball,* etc.).

Password. Children play this game in pairs. Provide each child with a copy of current vocabulary words, but a different list for each of the pair. Using one word at a time from his or her list, a player gives one-word clues and the other player tries to guess the word. Alternate turns between players.

Ballads. Have the children write a story summary in ballad form. They may or may not sing it to music. If they choose to sing it, however, "On Top of Old Smokey," "My Bonnie Lies Over the Ocean," or "Yankee Doodle" are possible tunes to use.

Pick-a-Pair. Bring a bare branch to school and anchor it in a pot. Cut out shapes of pears and fasten a string through them so they will hang on the branch. Write pairs of words that sound alike but are spelled differently (homonyms) on each branch. Children pick a pear and then use each word in a sentence to illustrate its meaning. If they can do so correctly, they keep the pear. If not, they must put the pear back on the tree. Each child gets one pear per turn. The game ends when all the pears have been picked.

Story Map.   Have the children draw a map to illustrate where a story took place. First, study various maps to become familiar with symbols. Then decide how to make the map so it will show all the physical features of the story.

Suggestions for Further Reading

Clay, Marie M. *Reading: The Patterning of Complex Behavior.* Exeter, N.H.: Heinemann Educational Books, 1979.

Durkin, Dolores. *Strategies for Identifying Words.* Boston: Allyn and Bacon, 1980.

Goodman, Kenneth S., and Olive S. Niles. *Reading: Process and Program.* Urbana, Ill.: National Council of Teachers of English, 1970.

Hall, Mary Ann, and Christopher J. Ramig. *Linguistic Foundations for Reading.* Columbus, Ohio: Charles E. Merrill, 1978.

Smith, Frank. *Understanding Reading,* 3rd ed. New York: Holt, Rinehart and Winston, 1982.

Stauffer, Russell G. *Directing the Reading-Thinking Process.* New York: Harper and Row, 1975.

Weaver, Phyllis. *Research Within Reach.* Washington, D.C.: National Institute of Education; U.S. Department of Health, Education, and Welfare, 1978.

11
Children's Literature

All that people have ever thought, done, or dreamed lies waiting to be discovered in a book. Literature begins with Mother Goose. It includes Sendak as well as Shakespeare, Milne as much as Milton, and Carroll before Camus. For children's literature is a part of the mainstream of all literature, whose source is life itself.

Huck (1976, p. 3)

CHAPTER PREVIEW

Can you remember your favorite story when you were a child? Was it one you read yourself, or did someone read it to you? Either way, reading or listening, good stories often afford such realistic adventures that they are not easily forgotten. Children's literature is an immense universe with something for everyone. Within the pages of a book children may delve into the past, explore the present, peek into the future, or step into the realm of maybe. Virtually nothing is out of reach. This chapter is designed to acquaint you with the delightful world of children's literature, for surely no language arts program can be complete without it. In this chapter we offer help in selecting stories and poems for use with children and suggest ways to enhance their literary experience.

QUESTIONS TO THINK ABOUT AS YOU READ

How has the field of children's literature developed?

Why is children's literature important in the language arts curriculum?

What types of literature are available for children?

How can I recognize good literature?

How can I stimulate children's interest in reading and help them understand what they read?

Why are enrichment activities important?

What must I do to learn to tell stories to children?

How can I enhance children's enjoyment of poetry?

How might I evaluate my literature program?

School libraries and the children's sections of public libraries are filled with books to delight the eye and stimulate the mind of every child.

401

In addition, various other media such as records, films, and television offer countless opportunities for encounters with children's literature. A broad range of print and nonprint material beckons children to vicarious experiences in faraway places or in the house next door, or to transcend time and peer into the past or the future, or to envision the fantastic or come to a rational understanding of common experiences. Children's literature can satisfy every interest and whet the appetite for countless new intellectual pursuits.

Modern communication systems hold the potential for providing children with a wealth of literary experiences. This great potential, however, cannot be realized through quantity alone. Now more than ever children need to develop tastes for good literature so that they can judiciously select from among the wide array of offerings and spend their reading, listening, and viewing time to good advantage. This is not a small order, to say the least, but it is a most gratifying one. By introducing children to the range of literary forms and helping them to understand and appreciate quality literature, teachers can help them build a foundation for life-long enjoyment of good literature.

A Look at the History of Children's Literature

Literature for children has been around as long as children themselves. Children were told tales by adults, mostly about their heritage or everyday experiences, at least as long as history has been recorded. Centuries ago monks who taught boys in England's monastery schools, wrote stories and printed little books by hand long before printing presses were ever invented. Writing for children is thought to have begun as far back as A.D. 600. However, very few books were written for children before the nineteenth century. The few that were intended for children did not entertain them, but rather taught them how to behave or what to believe, or simply taught them subjects such as reading, penmanship, or history. Then in the 1800s people became interested in children's reading and began to create children's books. These books were intended to entertain children, both through the way language was used and by the inclusion of illustrations. As children demonstrated a desire for books, the number of publications steadily grew.

The 1800s were an important period in the history of children's literature. Many books were written during that period, and some of the great children's classics came into being. Illustrators appeared for the first time, and many of them are still considered among the greatest. Writers soon recognized children's short interest span and thus wrote collections of short stories or tales to appeal to children.

The Grimm brothers, Jakob and Wilhelm, for example, compiled the first collection in which "Hansel and Gretel" appeared. Peter Asbjornsen collected Norwegian tales. One of them was "The Three Billy Goats Gruff." Simultaneously, Joseph Jacobs's English tales, including "Jack and the Beanstalk" and "The Story of the Three Little Pigs," appeared. There were many others that are familiar to young and old alike today.

Some of the greatest masterpieces of longer fiction also appeared. Not all of them were originally intended for children, but because of the fantasy elements they contained, they appealed to young readers and have become associated with children's literature. Some of the well-known books written during the 1800s include *Hans Brinker of the Silver Skates* by Mary Mapes Dodge (1865), Lewis Carroll's *Alice's Adventures in Wonderland* (1871), and Johanna Spyri's *Heidi* (1884). Few of today's children or adults have not read or at least heard of *Black Beauty*, by the English author Anna Sewell (1862), a sad story of the cruel treatment a beautiful horse receives from his masters. Other perennial favorites are *Little Women* by Louisa May Alcott (1869), a novel about a New England family with four daughters; and Mark Twain's *The Adventures of Tom Sawyer* (1876) and *The Adventures of Huckleberry Finn* (1884). *Treasure Island* (1883) and *Kidnapped* (1886), both by Robert Louis Stevenson, were popular adventure stories as was Jules Verne's *20,000 Leagues Under the Sea* (1864). All of them are still enjoyed as books and in television shows. They are called *classics* because of their lasting popularity.

A wide variety of poetry was also written for children during the 1800s. Some of children's enduring favorites include Jan Taylor's "Twinkle Twinkle Little Star" (1804), Clement Moore's "A Visit from St. Nicholas" (1822), and Eugene Field's "The Duel" (1896). Volumes of poetry also appeared by favorite writers Edward Lear (1846), Christina Rossetti (1872), Robert Louis Stevenson (1885), and James Whitcomb Riley (1891).

Illustrations of this period were limited by the available media and printing processes. Yet some of the great early illustrators produced admirable art despite those limitations. For example, works by Randolph Caldecott, Kate Greenaway, Walter Crane, and Beatrix Potter are still highly regarded. For the most part these illustrations appeared in delicate colors and portrayed happy, peaceful scenes and children.

As might be expected, more children's books have been published since 1900 than in all the previous years combined. Increased interest is not the only reason. Development of educational theories, constantly improved printing and art techniques, emphasis on the importance of reading, persistent and varied methods of advertising and merchandising have all contributed to the increased interest in and market for children's books. Quantity is no guarantee of quality, however, and there has been an unfortunate increase in the number of poorly written books on the market. Although this is a very real concern, it should also be noted that there are still a great many excellent books being written for children. Examples of newer books that have already proved their worth include Katherine Milhous's *The Egg Tree* (1950), Beverly Cleary's *Henry Huggins* (1950), E. B. White's *Charlotte's Web* (1952), Laura Ingalls Wilder's *Little House on the Prairie* (1953), Scott O'Dell's *Island of the Blue Dolphins* (1960), Madeleine L'Engle's *A Wrinkle in Time* (1962), and Robert O'Brien's *Mrs. Frisby and the Rats of NIMH* (1971).

The past quarter-century has also seen some significant new entries into the field of children's literature. Among them are the wordless picture books. These books are designed to promote interpretive and creative thinking. They are used to stimulate both children's oral language and creative writing. Another newer concept in children's books is the easy-to-read book for beginners or less able readers. Most of these little books fall somewhere between picture books and reading textbooks, yet they are neither. They are meant not to be read to children but for children to read themselves. The easiest books contain a very limited vocabulary and much repetition. The books progress in difficulty for older readers but maintain a proportionate high interest–low vocabulary reading level.

Children's magazines, although introduced two centuries ago, belong almost entirely to the current period. *St. Nicholas* was published from approximately 1870 to 1940, and a few others, such as the official Girl Scout and Boy Scout magazines *American Girl* and *Boy's Life,* appeared in the early part of the twentieth century. Subsequently, a greater variety of children's periodicals began to emerge. Now the choices range from *Children's Playmate Magazine* to *American Junior Red Cross.* Included in the list are periodicals on diverse subjects such as animals (*Zoonooz*), current events (*Geographic World*), science (*Popular Science*), automobiles (*Hot Rod*), history (*Cobblestone*), and many others. On the whole, the general literary quality of children's magazines is excellent. Some, such as *Cricket, Humpty Dumpty's Magazine,* and *Jack and Jill,* are even classified as literary magazines. One magazine, *Kids,* is written for children by children. Magazines are an important source of children's literature in that they provide a current, periodic publication with short articles, poems, and items of interest for the young, and they motivate many who ordinarily are not avid readers to pick up a magazine and read for a short period of time. A personal magazine subscription is a relatively inexpensive gift that can be enjoyed throughout the year.

Several recent trends may be noted in the content of children's books and materials. Among these are the increase in books about minorities, a reflection of greater social awareness and a search for identity. Women play a greater role in books and stories as a result of the feminist movement. An increasing number of books may be found that deal with various physical and mental handicaps. Death, divorce, sex, and parental rejection are no longer ignored. Informational books continue to be produced at a fast pace. These range from books on outer space to pollution and conservation, from life among the Ibus to how to repair a bicycle. Poetry books are also experiencing a rise in popularity.

Children's Literature in the Classroom

Literature is used almost constantly in the classroom as a teaching tool. Textbooks, supplementary materials, reference books, and other reading materials provide information on arts, sciences, social sciences, historical data, and many other areas of study. Although some of these materials may differ considerably from the exciting adventures of fictional heroes and imaginative accounts of good fairies and evil witches, they too are literature. Reading materials that are used as teaching aids are selected primarily for their value in helping children discover information in a given subject area. Yet they are generally attractive and well written. Twenty or so years ago there was little concern for the attractiveness, style, illustrations, action, or other interest-catching features in informational books. During the past few years, however, textbooks and other classroom reading materials have acquired new dimensions in child appeal. At the same time, the emphasis in schools on self-directed learning, inquiry, and independent study has given new purpose and prestige to reading.

There are many reasons for children's increased use of literature. Among them are:

1. The expanded use of various kinds of instructional materials. Textbooks alone are inadequate to meet today's educational needs. Hence the trend is to supplement textbooks with materials from the wider offerings of trade books.

2. The availability and use of other forms of media in school programs. Filmstrips, tapes, kits, records, and television are used along with more traditional materials.

3. The inclusion of supplementary books in basal reading programs. They are usually in the form of reading labs or sets of individual storybooks grouped by reading level.

4. The increased number and variety of books available. Because of improved mass-production techniques, more books are being printed and sold.

5. A greater availability of children's books. For example, they are now found in many grocery and drug stores.

6. The expansion of motivational reading materials. These materials include word cards, games, and manipulative devices.

Today's children enjoy greater opportunity and freedom of choice than ever before. This often extends into the classroom and their use of learning materials. Inherent in this situation, however, is the problem of making selections from an almost overwhelming quantity of print and nonprint materials. Thus it is more important than ever that children have the opportunity to learn about good children's literature and how to distinguish the good from the poor, the noteworthy from the mediocre. They also need help in exploring other media such as tapes, television, films, and filmstrips and deciding which to use to gain whatever information they need.

Types of Children's Literature

Children's literature can be divided into five main categories:

1. Fiction

2. Information books

3. Folklore

4. Biography

5. Poetry

Fiction

Many of the categories of literature overlap or interrelate. Fiction is mainly for recreational reading and includes a wide range of materials. Fantasies such as *The New Wizard of Oz* by L. Frank Baum (1955) recounts the exciting adventures of a girl who is carried from her home in Kansas to a land of magic in a dream. This story comes under the heading of fiction. So do adventure stories such as Jean L. Latham's *Carry On, Mr. Bowditch* (1955). Animal stories are another type of fiction that is guaranteed to attract children. One well-known animal story is *The Incredible Journey* by Sheila Burnford (1961). This story tells of the adventures of two dogs and a cat who travel a great distance and suffer many hardships to find the human friends they love. Historical fiction also comes under this category. Alice Dalgliesh wrote several novels for young readers about life in colonial times. *The Courage of Sarah Noble* (1954) is one. Also popular and in constant demand are mystery and detective stories. In *The House of Dies Drear* by Virginia Hamilton (1968) a thirteen-year-old black boy finds buried treasure in a mysterious old house. Science fiction is a fairly recent addition to the fiction category. One of the first science fiction books to be written especially for children was *The Space Ship Under the Apple Tree* by Louis Slobodkin (1967). The book is about a boy named Eddie who is vacationing on his grandmother's farm and is visited by Marty, a little man from Martinea. More recently, social issues and personal problems of children have been dealt with realistically in fiction. For example, Marie Hall Ets's *Bad Boy, Good Boy* (1967) is about the problems of a Mexican child; Natalie Carlson presents insights about integration in *The Empty Schoolhouse* (1965); Beth Goff's book *Where Is Daddy?* (1969) is about divorce; and Patricia Hermes's *What If They Knew?* (1980) describes how a girl coped with epilepsy.

Information Books

Information books are typically nonfiction works that, if well written, are read with enjoyment. Information books open the door to the whole world of learning. Nearly every subject appearing in adult literature is also found in materials for children at a manageable reading level. There are books about how our government is run, the wonders of prehistoric animals, the science of our discovery of outer space, the fascination of learning about and seeing close-up photography of insects, and even simple recipe books for cooking delicious meals. All of these and more can enthrall children, satisfy their natural curiosity, and at the same time expand their horizons.

Available information books also include material on contemporary social problems and they are generally accurate and responsibly written. *What You Should Know About Drugs* (1970) by Charles Gorodetzky is one such book written for young people. It describes types of drugs and tells how each can be abused. *Tear Down the Walls!* (1968) by Dorothy Sterling describes the history of the black civil rights movement in America.

Folklore

Sutherland and Arbuthnot describe folklore as "accumulated wisdom and art. . . . In the broadest sense of the word, folklore includes superstitions, medicinal practices, games, songs, festivals, dance rituals, old tales, verses, fables, myths, legends, and epics. Folklore is sometimes called the 'mirror of a people' " (1977, p. 142). Dorson points out that " 'folklore' usually suggests the oral traditions channeled across the centuries through human mouths. . . . The scientific folklorist seeks out, observes, collects, and describes the inherited traditions of the community" (1959, p. 2). True folklore, then, is not consciously invented by a writer; it is *collected and recorded*. Folklore embraces a wide range of literature. Some of the common classifications of stories are discussed here.

Folktales Nearly every major culture has a heritage of one or more collections of folktales that are still widely read. For example, the ever-popular *Arabian Nights*, published by several publishing houses on many different dates is a collection of ancient folktales from parts of Asia and North Africa. The collection includes such famous tales as "Aladdin and the Wonderful Lamp" and "The Seven Voyages of Sinbad the Sailor." Andrew Lang, a Scottish poet and anthropologist, is well known for his studies of folklore. He espoused the theory that folktales originated in many different and widespread places and were not disseminated from one common source as was previously thought. Lang rewrote many collections of traditional English and Scottish stories for children based on folktales in that part of Europe. *The Blue Fairy Book* (1889) is one of those.

American folktales are also numerous, and many of them have been gathered and written down by various authors. Some folktales are heard only in a given area of this country. Others have been widely disseminated and are generally familiar, although perhaps with slight variations. American folktales often recount unusual circumstances and events including witchcraft, apparitions, and instances of superhuman strength, or they deal with customs and traditions of groups of people at all levels of society.

Joel Chandler Harris ranks as one of the best known of American students of folk literature. While he was living on a southern plantation, he listened to many folktales told by black people. He used these stories in his *Uncle Remus* short-story collections. These collections were written in the latter part of the nineteenth century in Negro dialect. In the early part of this decade, publishers were beseiged with demands to cease printing Harris's works because of the way blacks were portrayed.

It is interesting to note the threads of similarity in plot that weave through all folktales: the conquest of evil by good, humor through exaggeration, and emphasis on a moral involving human behavior.

Myths It is difficult to classify the types of folklore precisely, and this is particularly true of myths. Simply stated, myths deal with the supernatural. They often tell a story based on man's search for explanations of his own behavior or on imaginative conjectures about his ultimate destination. Myths usually lean toward religion or toward beings with godlike attributes. In the far distant past, before scientific studies provided explanations for such inquiries as what causes rain or snow, how earthquakes occur, and why eclipses take place, stories were developed attributing these and other phenomena to gods and other beings. These myths were intended to answer questions about unexplainable natural phenomena and events.

One well-known Greek myth tells how Persephone, the daughter of the goddess Demeter, was abducted by Pluto and taken away to his underground kingdom. Blaming the earth for the loss of her daughter, Demeter cursed the earth with drought and famine. Finally, the gods on Olympus helped locate the forlorn and unhappy Persephone in the underworld. The Fates would not allow her to return to the earth permanently, though, because she had eaten some pomegranate seeds while there. Instead, they decreed that Persephone must spend a part of every year with Pluto in his underground kingdom. However, she might spend the rest of the year with her mother on the earth. Each year her return to the earth brought warmth and new stirrings of life. The grass turned green, flowers came into bloom, and the bleakness of winter disappeared. Then at the end of the period, when she returned to the underworld, things on the earth again stopped growing and winter appeared. Hence, Persephone's coming and going between the earth and the underworld explained the seasonal changes.

Other myths portrayed the folly of arrogant and selfish ways. There was Phaeton who drove his golden chariot too close to the sun; Arachne who challenged Athena at weaving and was turned into a spider; Narcissus who was so engrossed in love of self that it ultimately destroyed him; King Midas who turned all that he touched into gold, including his daughter, Marygold; and the talkative Echo who always had to have the last word and who was meted out the punishment of saying *only* last words.

The godlike qualities of characters are found in myths of various cultures. Once children have been introduced to almost any of these myths, they usually become intensely interested in this category of literature. Older children are particularly fascinated by the similarities among myths from different cultures. Also, older children usually enjoy *epics*, a type of literature closely related to myths. Sutherland and Arbuthnot describe epics as "tales of human heroes buffeted violently by gods and humanity but daring greatly, suffering uncomplainingly, and enduring staunchly to the end. Such tales, having a human hero as the focus of the action and embodying the ideals of a culture, are called epics" (1977, p. 191).

The best-known epics are the *Iliad* and the *Odyssey*, apparently written by an ancient Greek poet named Homer. The *Iliad* recounts the final period of the Trojan War between Greece and Troy, which centered around Helen of Troy, supposedly the most beautiful woman in the world. The *Odyssey* tells of the travels and wandering of King Odysseus during his return home from the war. *King Arthur and His Knights of the Round Table,* describing the adventures of Sir Galahad, Sir Lancelot, and the magician Merlin, deal with British lore and customs. Many epics were written in verse form as ballads, and these are particularly enjoyable when read aloud. *Robin Hood* is a special favorite. Children also enjoy the modern prose version, *The Merry Adventures of Robin Hood,* by Howard Pyle, an American author and illustrator.

Fairy tales A fairy tale is an imaginative story with a touch of magic or a dreamlike quality. Some of the characters are usually fairies, gnomes, trolls, elves, or other fanciful beings with special powers. In the end good usually prevails over evil or gentleness over wickedness. The witch casts a spell over the good princess, but a handsome prince breaks the spell, freeing the princess and punishing the witch.

It must be remembered that no authors are identified for the traditional fairy tale such as "Sleeping Beauty" and "Snow White." Many compilers of fairy tales rewrote the information they had gathered, but the plots and characters had been used by generations of storytellers. The popularity of the old fairy tale gave rise to the modern fairy tale, which bears the same characteristics except that the creators of the stories are known. Hans Christian Andersen, author of "The Ugly Duckling," "The Emperor's New Clothes," and a host of other widely known stories is credited with introducing children to the modern fairy tale. Andersen's stories do contain supernatural beings, but they aren't always apparent. Like Shakespeare, Andersen wrote his fairy tales with deeper hidden meanings relating to the hypocrisy and strange standards of society. It was a little child who pointed out honestly and without pretense that the Emperor was not wearing new clothes at all; he was wearing no clothes. "The Nightingale" portrayed the contempt Andersen felt for those who prefer the mechanical and the gaudy to the real and beautiful. Andersen's fairy tales are sad and somewhat introspective. He wrote of tragedy and death, but with beauty and simplicity that children easily relate to and enjoy. Andersen's tales have been illustrated by many different artists. Adrienne Adams, for example, used bright and sparkling watercolors to portray "Thumbelina" in her tiny world. The artist visited Denmark, Andersen's native land, to capture the Danish traditions and put them into her art.

Another modern fairy tale writer who retained the "Once upon a time" opening line of the old fairy tale is Phyllis McGinley. In her "Plain Princess" she transforms a plain princess into a beautiful one, and the story ends happily as most fairy tales do. The illustrations in a fairy tale have a tremendous effect on the reader's enjoyment, as in Fiona French's *The Blue Bird*. An evil enchantress puts a spell on all birds including a young girl's blue bird friend who used to sing to her. A young student discovered the reason for the spell and destroyed it, setting the blue bird and all other birds free to sing once again. The oriental setting is reflected in the blue porcelain illustrations.

Fables *Aesop's Fables* are probably the best known of all fables. A fable is a very short story with a moral, and it often uses animals as characters. Somewhat like a parody, it contains a message and gives that message briefly but poignantly. In "The Fox and the Grapes," one of Aesop's fables, the fox made many attempts to reach the grapes. When he was convinced that it was impossible, his retort was that he didn't really want them anyhow. Although fables were originally intended for adults, children enjoy them too, and readily grasp the moral whether it is stated or implied. This is doubtlessly due to the animal characters, the simple plot, which usually contains only one incident or event, and the clear examples of right and wrong. Many of our proverbs, such as "Please everyone, please no one," and "Don't count your chickens before they are hatched," originated in fables.

Legends Historical events have frequently been recounted as legends. As a matter of fact, a legend that has been heard time and again may be difficult to separate from historical truth. John Chapman (1774–1845), commonly referred to as Johnny Appleseed, was a real person but quite different from the character portrayed in legend. Some of the stories written about Johnny Appleseed were based on fact — he did plant apple trees — whereas others are pure fantasy. This combination is a natural outgrowth of repeating interesting historical facts.

Another historical character who easily became the subject of legendary lore was Davy Crockett (1786–1836). He was a good-natured frontiersman, hunter, politician, congressman, and soldier. Stories of his brave and rugged adventures, climaxed by his heroic death at the Alamo, gave voice to the spirit of the western frontier and set his name in the folklore of his country. Other legendary characters such as Paul Bunyan, Pecos Bill, Old Stormalong, Joe Magerac, and Febold Feboldsen never existed and are based on little or no oral tradition. According to Dorson "These heroes originated in the brains of journalists and authors. . . . The nation demanded demigods, to reflect its massive triumphs in subduing the continent and conquering its foes, and professional writers furnished them ready made" (1959, p. 215). Although the tales are not true folklore, they have found their way into many folklore collections, and are the favorites of many children.

Biography

In all types of literature for children, biographies hold a particular place of importance. They introduce children to noteworthy living men and women or to those who have lived in the past. There are biographies about many different kinds of people from a variety of settings and experiences. Biographies teach children about such famous individuals as explorers, scientists, religious leaders, athletes, government officials, writers, and entertainers. Although some of these people have a greater attraction for the very young than others, there are certain to be "real heroes" of interest to every child of any age.

James Daugherty is an American author who has written and illustrated many favorite biographies. *Abraham Lincoln, Daniel Boone,* and *Henry Thoreau* are a few of his biographies that usually appeal to children. A skillful biographer can take the life story of a notable individual in nearly any field and turn it into exciting and lively reading. A well-written biography can read like a fiction book, and yet bring to life the story of "people who really lived." The introduction of biography into children's reading experiences is essential for several reasons. Besides the fact that it offers a departure from fiction and thereby an introduction to nonfiction, biography serves as a source of identification for children. Reading of the accomplishments of others is a means of finding satisfaction and encouragement. Through suggestion, children can dream of possible careers, contributions they might make to society, or new endeavors they could pursue.

Careful selection of biographies for children is important. They must be fast-moving, fictional in style, and exciting. The facts should be there, but they should appear casually and coincidently with the flow of the story. Biography may be fictionalized, in which case the facts are authentic but the episodes are dramatized and embellished. Biographical fiction is a reconstruction or imaginative narrative based on the life of a noted person. For example, Robert Lawson's hilarious *Ben and Me* is told in the words of a mouse named Amos who lived in Benjamin Franklin's old hat. This rollicking example of biographical fiction will hold the attention of any group or class of children if used by the teacher in reading sessions.

Poetry

Children's tastes in poetry may be quite different from those of adults. Although they like poems of quiet moments of thought, they are generally unimpressed with the sentimental or moralistic poem. Fortunately, there are poems about every subject imaginable, and therefore something that will appeal to every child. Poems range in subject matter from simple and honest statements about every-day things to creative or profound wonderings about science and nature.

Poetry sets words to music in the minds and hearts of children. Their liking for poetry is often unconscious. They only know that poems, like Myra Cohn Livingston's *Whispers,* "tickle in the ears." Poems appeal to children for many reasons. Poems that tell a story are particular favorites. Simple story rhymes such as "Simple Simon," "Little Bo Peep," and "The Three Little Kittens" are well known and loved by most young children. As children get a little older they enjoy the gingham dog and the calico cat in Eugene Field's "The Duel." Longfellow's tale of "Paul Revere's Ride," Robert Browning's account of "The Pied Piper of Hamlin," and James Weldon Johnson's "The Creation" become other favorites.

The rhythm and melody of poems give them a singing quality that children enjoy. Although these elements are found in virtually all poetry, some poems have an especially appealing sound. Eve Merriam's "Mean Song" fairly speaks to children to chant along. E. R. Young's "Railroad Reverie" and David McCord's "The Pickety Fence" recall vivid experiences through reconstructed sound images. Henry Wadsworth Longfellow's "Hiawatha's Childhood" has an infectious quality that invites children to "sing along."

Poems containing vivid sensory images cause children to recall experiences and relive them with the poet. "Snow" by Dorothy Aldis, "Fog" by Carl Sandburg, and "Butterfly" by William Jay Smith capture moments of intense feeling and wonder. In "A Modern Dragon," Rowena Bastin Bennet uses metaphor to describe a train passing by. The robust poem stimulates vivid visual and auditory response and associated memories. In the same way, Edward Lueders recreates a scene in "Rodeo" that will bring back vivid memories to anyone who has sat in the stands on a hot, dusty day and watched cowboys in action.

Humor also appeals to children, and it abounds in poetry. Kaye Starbird's "Eat-it-all Elaine" tells an amusing camp story about a girl who literally ate everything including a bug. Her "Don't Ever Cross a Crocodile" is another favorite. Laura Richards's "Eletelephony" continues to delight new generations, and young and old alike get a good chuckle out of Arthur Guiterman's irreverent "Ancient History."

Animals and pets are particularly popular with children. Old favorites include Marchette Chute's "My Dog," Eleanor Farjeon's "A Kitten" and "Mrs. Peck-Pigeon," Rose Fyleman's "Mice," and Vachel Lindsay's "The Little Turtle." Older children enjoy Theodore Roethke's "The Bat," Rosalie Moore's "Catalogue," and Robert Frost's "The Runaway."

People, things in nature, sports, and ideas generated by modern technology are subjects that children can relate to and enjoy. Dorothy Aldis's "Little" has strong appeal to children who have new babies at home. Aspects of nature such as the sea, wind, rain, and snow are things that children know about. John Updike's "Sonic Boom," Marcie Hans's "Fueled," and May Swenson's "Southbound on the Freeway" are poems of today that speak to children about their world. There are poems for quiet moments, mad moods, and seasons of laughter. As Arbuthnot, Broderick, Roote, Taylor, and Wenzel state, "The range of poetry is so vast, its forms so diverse, and its pleasures so gratifying that no child should grow up without being given an opportunity to appreciate it" (1976, p. 2).

Identifying Good Literature

In order to identify good literature you must read, browse through, handle, thumb through, scan, and read snatches of books and become generally acquainted with authors and illustrators. It is important to notice the style of the writing and to look for evidence that the writer understands children — their hopes, dreams, fantasies, imagination, excitement, wonder, delight, and curiosity. The vocabulary and sentence structure and the author's choice of words must also be appropriate to the level of the intended reader. The message ought to be clear and appealing; the title and the first few words should capture the reader's interest and create a desire to read further. The following are some important points.

Criteria for Identifying Good Literature

1. *Quality of literary values*
   a. Are the characters realistically portrayed? Do you discover what becomes of them as the story unfolds?
   b. Are slang and poor grammar used only where warranted, not as general practice?

    c. Is the plot construction and development proportionate with the reading level?

    d. Do works of fantasy have as much clarity as other types of fiction?

    e. If the book is nonfiction, does it also possess literary qualities?

    f. Is the style lively and interesting?

2. *Quality of content*

    a. Does it contribute to the child's well-being?

    b. Are the facts or concepts accurate and dependable?

    c. Is the presentation clear and geared to the child's stage of development?

    d. Is the vocabulary consistent in difficulty?

3. *Quality of format*

    a. Has the size of type and the layout been selected for its appeal to a specific age group?

    b. Do the illustrations go with the text, and provide the child with a variety of art forms?

4. *Level of maturity*

    a. Does the reading level go with the subject interest?

    b. Does it contain those elements which help children grow in understanding themselves as individuals and as members of society?

5. *Other qualities*

    a. Does it have appeal for children?

    b Does it stimulate the child to seek other books on the same subject?

    c. Does it evoke questions like, Are there any other books by this author?

To relate the general criteria to the specific two types of literature, fiction and fact, teachers need to examine the types of material for certain characteristics. Fictional materials should be judged on the basis of children's interests, liveliness of plot, excellence of characterization, and literary quality, as described earlier. Books in subject areas should be judged for timeliness, accuracy, organization and effectiveness, and clarity of presentation. Books on several levels of reading difficulty should be made available on a given subject to allow for individual differences in reading skill. Books that discuss sensitive subjects should present facts objectively and encourage open-mindedness. The same quality in a book that would attract an adult might not appeal to a child. This accounts for the fact that awards are sometimes given for children's books that do not appeal to children at all. The reason is that adults often judge children's books on the merits of adult criteria.

Awards for Noteworthy Children's Books

A considerable number of awards or prizes or honors have been established over the years for outstanding children's books. Illustrators as well as authors have received recognition in this area. Some of the more notable awards are mentioned here. (See also Appendix A.)

Caldecott Medal

The Randolph J. Caldecott Medal has been awarded annually since 1938 to the illustrator of the most distinguished picture book for children published in the United States during the preceding year. The award is made under the supervision of the American Library Association Children's Services Division. Announcement of the winner is made in January along with one or more runners-up. Winners must be citizens of the United States.

Newbery Medal

The Newbery Medal is an award to the author whose work is judged the most distinguished contribution to children's literature. The award has been given annually since 1922 in honor of John Newbery (1713–67), the first English publisher of children's books. The winner and runners-up are also selected by a committee of the Children's Services Division of the American Library Association and announced in January for the preceding year.

Hans Christian Andersen Award

This award has been given biennially since 1956 to one author and one illustrator in recognition of all his or her endeavors in the field. Unlike the Caldecott and Newbery Awards, which go to United States citizens only, this award goes to people in other countries as well. For example, in 1956 the award went to Eleanor Farjeon of

Great Britain, and in 1964 it went to Rene Guillot of France. The award is sponsored by the International Board on Books for Young People.

Child Study Association Children's Book Award

This award is given annually in March for the best book of the previous year. The subject must deal realistically with some problem in the child's contemporary world. One such award went to Margaret and H. A. Rey for their story *Curious George Goes to the Hospital* (1972).

Other Book Awards

Outstanding authors of children's books appear frequently as winners or runners-up for many different awards. These people obviously are highly skilled in their ability to appeal to children, and their books are worthy of note. For further information on honors bestowed on authors and illustrators, the Children's Book Council (175 Fifth Ave., New York, NY 10010) publishes a pamphlet entitled *Children's Books, Awards, and Prizes.*

Children and Books

It is important for teachers to understand the nature of literary experience. Children's literature should not be thought of in terms of the materials alone. Literature is actually two-dimensional. It consists not only of the printed word and the accompanying illustrations, but of the experiences of individuals as they interact with the words or pictures and interpret them in highly personal and unique ways. Literature recalls and simulates experience. Therefore children think about and interpret what they read in terms of their own limited experiences, and these are different for each child.

Literature, both written and illustrated, has a profound influence on readers, especially on children. Their limited experiences cause them to be impressionable and less capable of discrimination and evaluation in their reading choices. Because children relate literature to their own reality, dreams, feelings, and curiosities, it can be used effectively with children who have special problems. A child whose parent has died, for example, may find comfort in a book character who has had a similar experience. Bibliotherapy is often used effectively in counseling. Sutherland and Arbuthnot note that

> Books are no substitute for living, but they can add immeasurably to its richness. When life is absorbing, books can enhance our sense of its

significance. When life is difficult, they can give a momentary relief
from trouble, afford a new insight into our problems or those of others,
or provide the rest and refreshment we need. (1977, p. 4)

Illustrations play an important role in children's literary experience. Pictures are much more important in books written for children
than in those for adults. The pictures in children's books often contribute as much to the enjoyment of the book and even to the comprehension of the content as the written text. Children enjoy
illustrations in any of the many possible media. Some of the more
common include watercolors, silkscreen, woodcuts, pen and ink
sketches, charcoal, oils, lithography, collage, and photography. Children undoubtedly prefer color to black and white, yet some of the
most popular picture books have black and white pictures. Robert
McCloskey's *Make Way for Ducklings*, Lynd Ward's *The Biggest Bear*,
and the hilarious illustrations found in *The Story of Ferdinand* by
Munro Leaf could hardly be improved on by color. Using color is no
guarantee that the book will be a success. However, neither Gerald
McDermott nor Nonny Hogrogian would have received Caldecott
Awards for *Arrow to the Sun* and *One Fine Day*, respectively, without
the brilliant use of color in their illustrations. Pictures in children's
books not only afford enjoyment but expose children to a wide variety of art forms and styles. Because appreciation of art as well as
literature is learned and experiential, beautifully illustrated books can
serve many purposes simultaneously.

The appropriateness of style (arrangement of mass or line and
color) for the age of the intended readers of a book is also important.
For example, illustrations should reflect an awareness of the fact that
children's eyes gradually mature until around the age of eight or
nine. Detail is important, but a distracting background may be confusing to young children and discourage them from reading further
in an otherwise good book. Incomplete pictures (a hand missing
because it is at the edge of the page and not seen) or perspective (a
person at a distance who looks out of proportion) is also distracting.

Guiding Children's Selection of Books

Helping children discover literature that appeals to them requires a
thorough knowledge of both children and books. Teachers need to
know children's interests, fears, and dreams. They need to know
how well children can read and the kind of format they find attractive
in books. Listening to children in class discussions and in informal
conversations, noting their involvement in various topics and stud-

ies, and observing which kinds of books they reach for first when several choices are available all offer insights into their reading background and preference. By listening to children read orally and analyzing their comprehension in reading assignments a teacher can learn what level of material they can read successfully.

The best way to get to know books is to examine them personally. With the number of volumes available, however, this is more idealistic than realistic. Over a period of time teachers can read and become acquainted with many books. Reading the blurbs on book jackets and noting what children say about the books they have read are possibilities. Two kinds of published aids are also available: periodicals, which review current publications; and selected bibliographies, which generally include materials that have been on the market for some time and have been reviewed by groups of experienced professionals.

Following are some periodicals that review children's books and offer articles on the subject of children's literature.

> *Calendar.* Children's Book Council, 67 Irving Place, New York, NY 10003 (quarterly). This is especially useful for teachers. In addition to reviews, it gives such information as titles of award-winning books and lists of recent material concerning children's literature.
>
> *Childhood Education.* Association for Childhood Education International, 3615 Wisconsin Avenue, NW, Washington, DC 20016 (monthly).
>
> *The Horn Book Magazine.* Horn Book, Inc., Park Square Building, 31 St. James Avenue, Boston, MA 02116 (bimonthly).
>
> *Instructor.* The Instructor Publications, Inc., 7 Bank Street, Danville, NY 14437 (monthly).
>
> *Language Arts.* National Council of Teachers of English, 1111 Kenyon Road, Urbana, IL 61801 (monthly).
>
> *The New York Times Book Review.* Contains a section of reviews devoted to children's books (weekly).

Here are some general and special subject lists that are invaluable in guiding children toward good literature.

> *Adventuring with Books* (1981). National Council of Teachers of English, 1111 Kenyon Road, Urbana, IL 61801. This list is periodically revised. Gives information about the story, age, level, publisher, and awards.

Best Books for Children: Pre-School through Middle Grades (1978). Titles are annotated and arranged by age levels.

The Best in Children's Books: The University of Chicago Guide to Children's Literature, 1966–72 (1973). Zena Sutherland, ed. University of Chicago Press, Chicago, IL 60637. Selected reviews from the *Bulletin of the Center for Children's Books.* Indexed by title, developmental values, curricular use, reading level, subject matter, and type of literature.

The Best in Children's Books: The University of Chicago Guide to Children's Literature, 1973–78 (1980). Zena Sutherland, ed. University of Chicago Press, Chicago, IL 60637.

Children's Books Too Good to Miss, 7th ed. (1979). May Hill Arbuthnot et al. Case Western Reserve University Press, 2029 Adelbut Road, Cleveland, OH 44106. This is a highly selective list of classics and recent publications with annotations. Books are classified by age group and type of book.

Children's Catalog (1976). Barbara Dill, ed. The H. W. Wilson Co., 950 University Avenue, Bronx, NY 10452.

Choosing Books for Children: A Commonsense Guide (1981). Betty Hearne. Delacorte Press. 1 Dag Hammarskjold Plaza, 245 E. 47th St., New York, NY 10017.

Good Reading for Poor Readers (1974). George D. Spache. Garrard Publishing Company, 1607 N. Market Street, Champaign, IL 61820. Annotated bibliography giving both reading level and interest of each book.

Reading Ladders for Human Relations, 6th ed. (1981). Eileen Tway, ed. National Council of Teachers of English, 1111 Kenyon Road, Urbana, IL 61801. Extensive annotated bibliography with titles arranged by maturity level.

Other lists may be found in *Aids to Media Selection for Students and Teachers* (1979), compiled by Beatrice T. Simmons and Yvonne B. Carter. (U.S. Department of Health, Education, and Welfare, Washington, D.C.)

Matching children and books, that is, deciding whether a particular book seems "right" for a particular child, involves decisions with a particular child in mind. The following questions may be used as guidelines.

1. Is the story or the subject matter appropriate for the reader? In other words, does it fall within the realm of the reader's experience? A book, even simply written, on philosophy or statistics

would have little meaning or interest for a child in the primary grades. Yet a profusely illustrated book with simple vocabulary on space travel, animals that are an endangered species, or children in China would probably hold considerable fascination for that child in spite of limited firsthand experience. Television viewing, conversations at home, stories, and various other factors provide many vicarious experiences for children and whet their curiosity.

2. Is the story interesting and understandable? Will it elicit vivid imagery and hold attention?

3. If the material is factual, is the text accurate and up-to-date?

4. If the material is imaginative or fanciful, does it encourage appreciation of good literature and positive attitudes?

5. Is the style of writing appropriate for the reader? Sometimes a noteworthy picture book is published, obviously designed for the primary student, but with language and vocabulary on an intermediate or even secondary level. It may use simple vocabulary generally, but difficult words and complex sentence structures from time to time. The difficult passages interfere with comprehension and discourage younger readers.

6. Will it develop qualities such as appreciation of art, music, science, or those characteristics of people, animals, and plants which are part of our world?

7. Will it contribute to the development of positive attitudes toward self and recognition of personal abilities, interests, and problems?

8. Will it develop an understanding of others?

9. Will it encourage creative reading and generate additional story-related activities?

Stimulating Interest and Understanding

Setting the Scene

Space and attractive surroundings are the first requisites for a desirable reading atmosphere. Displays of attractively illustrated, colorful books grouped together with an artifact, a bowl of fresh flowers or a plant or an object may call attention to books nearby on that subject. For example, there might be a pair of spurs, a rope, and a pair of cowboy boots arranged on a saddle blanket together with several horse stories and books on the settling of the West. Colorful props can attract children who may be aimlessly seeking a book to read.

A portion of a classroom can be set aside as a reading nook or browsing areas. A small rug, one or two chairs or floor pillows, and a table or bookshelf with some attractive reading materials can provide the opportunity for individual exploration. A quantity of books should be kept in the classroom, and books either from the room or the central school media center should be available for borrowing to take home. These collections of books must not become stagnant; they need to be changed frequently to whet the students' curiosity for new reading adventures.

Bulletin board displays attract many otherwise disinterested students. These may be created with book jackets, catch captions, posters, and original art work. One teacher made an eye-catching bulletin board with "These Books Are Tops" as a caption. The bulletin board displayed toy tops cut out of colored paper spinning in and out among colorful book jackets with interesting titles. Children also enjoy creating and arranging bulletin boards on their own to feature their favorite books.

Reading and Thinking

One of the best ways to stimulate interest in reading is simply to provide time for children to read. Setting a time for reading when no other activity is permitted gives children an opportunity to read enough to become involved with a book. If the book is a really good one children will have difficulty putting it down at the end of the period and will be motivated to pick it up again later. In many classrooms a time is set aside each day in which everyone, including the teacher, reads. Such programs are often referred to by initials: USR (*Uninterrupted Silent Reading*), SSR (*Sustained Silent Reading*), or DEAR (*Drop Everything And Read*).

Children should also be read to. Hearing a story aloud in a group is different from reading a story silently to oneself. Some teachers like to read to children right after lunch or a play period. Others set aside the last fifteen to twenty minutes of the day for reading. A book that holds children's interest may be read completely through by the teacher. Or, one may read only the first part of a book and then the book is put in the reading corner for children to finish on their own. Children may also suggest books they think the class would enjoy having the teacher read. It is also a good idea for children to read aloud to each other in pairs or in small groups. However, throughout the grades the teacher should read to the class on a regular basis.

Talking about books stimulates interest and understanding. With young children, a discussion might be structured along a story line, giving the sequence of events in the story. Children might also describe the characters and talk about what they were like, whether they were funny, sly, frightening, lazy, etc. Young children tend to take a story quite literally, but they can also see relationships ("Why did . . . ?") and speculate ("What if . . . ?") and interpret the mood of the story ("How did it make you feel?"). Discussing, interpreting, and enjoying the illustrations also add interest and understanding to the story.

In discussions older children might further analyze the story using a model such as this:

1. *Identify the setting*

   Where did the story happen?

   What do you know about [the place]?

   What time of day/year was it? How do you know this?

2. *Identify the main character(s)*

   Who is the story about?

   What do you know about him/her?

3. *Identify the problem*

   What did [the character] want to do?

   Why couldn't he/she?

   What did he/she try to do to solve the problem?

4. *Diagram the plot*

   Now we have the main elements of the story. Let's make a diagram of the plot.

   (Draw ascending and descending lines of plot diagram.)

   How did the story begin? What did the main character want to do?

   (Write response at base of ascending line.)

   What was the climax of the story? What was the most exciting moment?

   (Write response at apex of figure.)

   What events led up to the climax? What problems or events occurred to make the story interesting?

   (Write responses in sequential order on ascending line.)

   How did the story end?

   (Write response at bottom of descending line.)

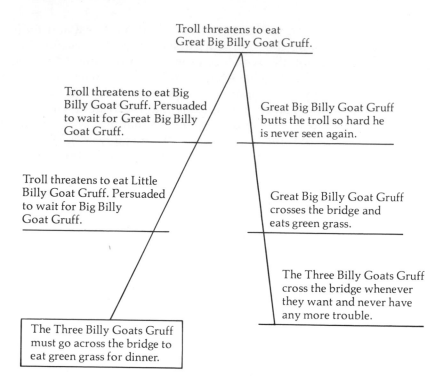

FIGURE 11-1

What happened to make the story end this way? How was the problem solved?

(Write responses in sequential order on descending line.)

A plot diagram for "The Three Billy Goats Gruff" is shown in Figure 11-1.

Additional discussion might be elicited with such questions as these:

How important was the setting in this story? Could it have happened anywhere else? Why?

When did you begin to think you knew what was going to happen? What made you think of this?

Now that you know how the story ended, can you look back and see that the author gave you hints about how it would end?

What kind of a person was [a character]? How did this affect the story?

How did you feel about [a character or an event or issue]?

How did the story make you feel?

Who seemed to be telling the story? Why do you think this?

Enriching Literature Experiences

Activities related to books and stories enhance the reading experience in two ways: using or applying information or ideas gained from the story helps children clarify their understanding of the story, and sharing a personal response to a story heightens children's enjoyment of it. In addition, enthusiasm is contagious, and reluctant readers often become infected with a desire to read when they see their peers having a good time with books. Perhaps more important is the fact that such activities provide a natural vehicle for purposeful practice of oral and written language skills and abilities. Several types of enrichment activities are suggested in the paragraphs that follow. More detailed information about many of them may be found in earlier chapters of this book.

Art Art activities are a natural way for children to express their interpretation of literature. Colored paper, chalk, crayons, paint, and various scrap materials such as bits of wood, plastic, cloth, yarn, buttons, and spools can stimulate creative art ideas for a particular story. Children's work can then be displayed along with the book in an appropriate niche in the classroom or in the school media center.

Murals provide an opportunity for a small group of children to work together on an art project. A chapter or an entire story can be illustrated on a large sheet of paper by identifying the parts of the story to include in the mural and then marking the paper off, with a section for each part. Flannel or magnet boards offer other possibilities. Children can draw characters and scenery and then "build" the scene as they tell the story. They can make the story elements out of ordinary heavy paper and then glue strips of flannel or little magnets on the backs of them. To share a story, small children will need to work in pairs with one telling the story and the other putting up the story parts; it is difficult for them to concentrate on both at once.

Drama Dramatic activities are among the most popular with children of all ages. Storybook charades, pantomimes of characters or events, or a dramatization of an interesting part of a story are all possibilities. A range of puppets may also be used effectively to tell stories. (See Chapter 6 for more suggestions.)

Simplified Readers' Theater Dramatic reading of selected parts of a story provides excellent practice of oral reading skills, and arouses listener interest. The analysis necessary to prepare such renditions also heightens and extends comprehension. In readers' theater two or more voices read alternating parts of the selection, using voice and facial gesture to suggest action. A narrator may be used to read descriptive or explanatory sections.

Music Incorporating music into literature can be an enriching experience. The children may listen to music or actually learn and sing some songs related to what they are reading. Occasionally, songs may be found about a particular character. For example, songs have been written about some legendary figures such as Daniel Boone and Johnny Appleseed. There is a whole songbook to accompany Winnie the Pooh stories. Often, a song may be found from a particular historical period or geographic area to complement a story. Ballads are meant to be sung and are best studied that way. Both folk and contemporary ballads are readily available in music form, and although they may not be the same ballads children are currently reading, a musical experience with one can stimulate interest in another.

Oral language As mentioned earlier in this chapter, children like to talk about the stories they are reading. Round-table discussions on a common book, quiz shows about famous authors or characters, and book talks are some of the activities that might be used.

Creative writing After reading a book, children may be motivated to write a letter to the author, the illustrator, or the publisher to comment on it. Or, they may write a different ending to the story, write a sequel, or make the story into a play.

Records, tapes, and films Audio-visual materials are excellent for bringing a good story to life, particularly for less able readers. Hearing a recording of a story, listening to a taped story while reading along in the book, or viewing a film of or about a story can be richly rewarding. *Pagoo* by H. C. Holling is an excellent example of a film made by an author while writing a book. In the film, Holling tells of his research and shows the tasks he had to perform in order to write his book on ocean life. Dr. Seuss stories have been televised and have become popular on the screen as well as in print. (See the resources in Appendix B.)

Sharing Stories with Children

Storytelling

Skill in telling stories can be attained by anyone. Somehow the thought of "telling" a story seems to make many people feel uneasy. Perhaps it might help to realize that storytelling is a natural activity in everyday life. A child walking to school with a friend and recounting what she did the evening before is actually "telling a story." When teachers describe something they did on a trip, they too are telling a story.

Storytelling permits a face-to-face experience with the audience. Teachers can maintain continual eye contact with children and pace or modify the story appropriately for specific groups of children. Unfamiliar concepts may be explained or developed more thoroughly than in the original story. Many good stories lend themselves to being told, but others are really better read aloud. Because stories are *told*, not *memorized*, those which have particularly rich and vivid language may lose important qualities in telling. Also, if the book is extensively illustrated, it may be better to read the story to permit stopping to enjoy and discuss the pictures.

Skill in oral storytelling is an art teachers should strive to develop, not only to entertain children and introduce them to literature, but also to encourage children to try this activity themselves. Storytelling has tremendous potential for developing oral language skills.

In storytelling, the first step is to select the story. It should be lively with a well-defined story line and short enough for the age of the audience. Kindergarten listeners can tolerate little more than a five-minute story. When a story is too long, of course, the storyteller can usually condense it satisfactorily. To prepare the story, read it through silently and comprehensively twice. Then "tell" yourself the story aloud before a mirror. Read the story once more silently and then tell it once more to your image in the mirror. When telling the story to the class, it is usually best to avoid using notes or referring to the book unless there is a particular illustration you wish to show the children for special effect or emphasis.

The place where the story is told should be quiet and have few visual distractions. Children enjoy sitting on the floor as much as they do sitting in chairs. A soft rug makes an excellent informal gathering spot. The storyteller can stand, lean against a table, or sit on a small chair if the children are seated on the floor. Developing skill in storytelling takes practice, and with practice comes self-confidence. It's a good idea to develop a repertoire of stories so that if you are begged to "tell us another story" you have an encore handy.

The following factors should be considered in developing skill in storytelling:

1. Voice is important. The tone should be conversational, but loud enough to reach all listeners. Care should be taken to vary the intonation and thereby avoid a monotonous drone. If adventurous or exciting incidents are part of the story, the voice should take on a quick note of excitement. When a character whispers,

the storyteller should use a "stage whisper," perhaps holding up a forefinger.

2. Facial expression and gestures should be natural. If a good choice is made in selecting a story to tell, facial expressions and natural motion will hold the group's attention as the story unfolds. Too much "acting" or forced grimacing detracts from the interest in the story and should be avoided.

3. Maintain contact with the children. The storyteller should try to look at each child individually as the story progresses. At a crucial point in the story, children may be drawn into the story with questions. For example, if the listeners are primary children, the storyteller might ask, "And what do *you* think the owl said?" and give several children a chance to reply. Another way is to use the name of a child who has momentarily let his thoughts (or his hands) wander: "And Billy, you can imagine how good that fish tasted. . . ."

4. A good way to introduce a story is with a catch phrase from the story itself. For example, if you were telling Lynd Ward's *The Biggest Bear*, you might say, "It's better to find a bear in the orchard than an Orchard in the bear." (The hero's name in the story is Johnny Orchard.)

5. Once the climax is reached, wind up the story quickly.

Reading a Story

Teachers ought to have read a story before they read it to children. Being thoroughly familiar with a story allows you to anticipate what is coming next and to use good expression. Some books lend themselves to being read a part or chapter at a time. When books are read on a continuing basis, it is important to stop during an exciting episode. Then the audience will look forward to the next reading period with anticipation.

Children ought to hear much good literature. It not only helps them develop many concepts and background knowledge, but it provides a model of reading for them to emulate. They understand the purpose for developing good reading skills and acquire positive attitudes toward reading. Educators recognize the importance of reading to children at an early age, even before the child is one year old. Although infants' comprehension is limited, reading to them gives them an educational advantage. Looking at pictures, associating words with books, and watching the lines of print all help children develop cognitively and affectively.

Teaching Poetry

Poetry is a natural expression of children. From their earliest listening experiences they delight in the rhythmic flow of "Bye, baby bunting," "Three blind mice," "Ride a cockhorse to Banbury Cross," and countless other favorites. They enjoy the sound of poetry long before the words have meaning. When children learn to speak, chants and catchy phrases readily become a part of their linguistic experience. Taunts, jump rope rhythms, and tongue-twisters fascinate them.

Somewhere along the way, many children get turned off to poetry. It gradually loses the charm that made it a part of early childhood. Something happens to disrobe poetry of its vitality and appeal. This is sad, for to miss out on poetry is to miss out on language in its most appealing and expressive form. Poetry captures the essence of life's special moments, couching them in words that prose cannot match.

To make poetry experiences enjoyable teachers need to consider the following points.

1. *Read poetry aloud to children.* Because the rhythm and sound of poetry is important, children ought to have many experiences in hearing poems. When they become more competent readers and are able to "hear" poetry in their minds, they may derive pleasure from reading it silently.

2. *Present poetry in small "doses."* Slip in a special poem now and then rather than "doing a poetry unit." Tantalize children with interesting poems too great to miss. Never read so many poems at one time or discuss one poem so long that children become weary. By stopping while interest is still high you will help children anticipate the next poetry experience with pleasure.

3. *Select poems carefully.* Find poems that relate to children's interests. Action poems generally appeal to children, and there are many good ones on sports and other activities. If in doubt, test a poem out on a small group before presenting it to the class. You might even form a poetry selection committee to help you decide which poems to read.

4. *Avoid poems that are sentimental or abstract.* They mean little to most children.

5. *Don't hurry through the reading of poems or rush into discussing them.* Give children time to form images and let the poem settle in their minds before you talk about it. Sometimes they may want to hear the poem again before they even comment on it.

6. *Don't overanalyze a poem.* Enhance it; don't kill it.

7. *Be cautious about requiring children to memorize poetry.* They may enjoy committing a favorite to memory but *having to* can reduce the task to drudgery.

8. *When the situation is appropriate, share choice phrases from poetry that you remember* (e.g., Ogden Nash's "In spite of her sniffle,/Isabel's chiffle." Rosalie Moore's "Cats sleep fat and walk thin." Carl Sandburg's "Arithmetic is where numbers fly like pigeons in and out of your head").

9. *Don't expect every child to like every poem.* Remember that poetry is very personal, and respect children's right to their own opinion. Be objective.

10. *Provide a warm and rich environment that encourages children to read and write poetry.* Have many colorful and interesting poetry books available in the classroom library. On occasion, use a poem or a poetry theme in a bulletin board display. Develop an appreciation of language by developing sensory awareness — see, hear, feel, smell, and taste — and searching out precise, image-eliciting words to describe experiences. Help children savor the excitement of apt expressions.

11. *Encourage the children to move out beyond themselves.* Help them get inside someone or something else and see and feel from that vantage point. Or, help them stretch their imaginations, to soar beyond reality and peer into other worlds of thought.

Teaching poetry is at once a challenging and a richly satisfying experience. Children *do* like poetry, but some of them don't know that they like it. It is up to the teacher to reacquaint those children with the delights of poetic expression.

Studying poetry isn't really "studying" at all, it is "experiencing." Poetry paints pictures and opens the floodgate of memory. Poetry *suggests* rather than *tells*. The language of the poet has the power to evoke, in a few well-chosen words, countless images and associations that go beyond the actual words spoken. Thus the enjoyment and interpretation of poetry is a very private affair. It is never quite the same for any two people. And therein lies much of its charm. To probe too deeply into that private experience may destroy it. *Let* children enjoy poetry — in their own way.

Teaching poetry involves a delicate balance between leaving children to their own interpretations of poems and guiding them toward knowledge that enhances their poetry experiences. Poems are meant to be enjoyed. Nothing done in the name of teaching should be allowed to destroy that.

There are many ways to look at a poem to enhance children's understanding and enjoyment of it. The list that follows suggests possible conversations with children about poems. The ideas should, of course, be used selectively. The poem you choose, the children you have, and the situation all determine which, if any, of the techniques are appropriate. Teaching a poem should be simply helping children think about a poem.

1. *The content of the poem*

   What is the poem about?

   What did the poet want to tell you?

   What did you find out about [the character(s)] in the poem?

2. *The situation in the poem*

   Where did the poem take place?

   What time of year (day) was it?

   What was happening?

   What was [the situation] like? Can you describe the setting?

3. *The mood and feeling expressed in the poem*

   How does the poem make you feel?

   What mood is expressed in the poem?

   Do you think the poet wanted you to feel happy? sad?

   If you were making this poem into a movie, what kind of background music would you use?

4. *The speaker in the poem* (The narrator, or reporter, who tells the poem is not necessarily the same person as the poet.)

   Who seems to be telling the poem?

   Is [the speaker] talking out loud or just thinking to himself?

   What do you know about [the speaker]? How old do you think [she] is? What does [she] like (or like to do)?

   Does [the speaker] know much about [snow]? Do you think [he] has ever [really felt snow on his face]?

   How does [the speaker] feel about [the snow]?

   Whom do you think [the speaker] is talking to?

5. *The words of the poem* (Word choice and metaphor)

   What word (or group of words) makes a picture in your mind?

   Why is [meandering] a particularly good word?

When you hear [pines], what does it make you think of?

Why do you think the poet used the word(s) [stately pines] instead of [tall pines]?

What other "just right" words did the poet use?

What does [gold] mean? What else can it mean? What is associated with [gold]?

What does the poet say [the sky] is like?

What does the poet compare [the snow] to?

Is [snow] really [a blanket]?

Is [a tree] really [as tall as the sky]?

What comparison helps you [see, feel, hear] something better?

How does the poet help you know [how cold it is]?

Find two or more words right together that begin with the same sound.

6. *Rhythm of the poem*

   How should this poem be read, fast or slow?

   Should any part of it go faster or slower?

   What words (or syllables) in [line 1] are stressed?

   How many stressed syllables are there in that line?

   Do all the lines have the same number?

7. *Rhyming words in the poem*

   Which words rhyme?

   Can you find a pattern to the words that rhyme?

   Do you think the rhythm is more important in this poem than what [the speaker] is saying?

   Would you like the poem better if it did (or didn't) rhyme?

8. *Personal response to the poem*

   Do you like the poem?

   What part of the poem do you like best?

   Does this poem remind you of an experience you have had? someone you know?

   How do you think the poet might have described [a local setting, object, or character]?

   Who do you think might enjoy this poem?

Posing questions causes children to think. Encourage them to talk about their ideas and to share their feelings about the poem.

Choral Reading

Choral reading can be a delightful way to help children interpret and share prose and poetry. It has many values. When children plan and read a selection expressively together, they must think about its meaning and how they can use their voice as an artist's tool. They must think about the rhythm and sound of each line or sentence, intuiting the grammatical structures and noting which words they need to stress and where pauses most naturally fall. Choral reading helps children learn to enunciate clearly and to vary the volume, tempo, and quality of their voices for special effects.

Choral reading is rewarding to children in many ways. Not only is it a creative and enjoyable activity, but it helps them learn to plan and work together. Shy children tend to lose their shyness and speak out in the safety of a group. All children learn the importance of cooperation as they take turns or blend their voices in group response. Choral reading also gives poorer readers opportunity to practice sight vocabulary in the reading and rereading of selections. Types of choral reading are described here.

Refrain This type involves a narrator reading the storyline of the selection with the group joining in on the refrain. Poems such as the well-known "Poor Old Woman," Laura Richards's "The Umbrella Brigade," or Beatrice Brown's "Jonathan Bing" lend themselves to this type of choral reading.

Line-a-child Individuals or groups are assigned to read lines or sentences. Eve Merriam's "Hurry," Coleridge's "The Months," or Whitman's "I Hear America Singing" are appropriate poems.

Antiphonal Children are divided into two groups and take turns reading parts. Traditionally, this type of choral reading was used with two groups of voices, one heavy and one light. Various groupings are possible, however. The class might be divided into boys and girls or into geographic sections in the room. Rossetti's "Who Has Seen the Wind?" might be used in this way. Patricia Hubbell's "When Dinosaurs Ruled the Earth" is also effective in two parts, with the heavier voices chanting each introductory chorus and the lighter voices reading the story verses.

Unison Unison is actually the most difficult type of choral reading, because it requires children to stay together for longer periods. However, nearly any selection lends itself to unison reading, and the opportunities for interpretation are many. Story poems such as Kaye Starbird's "Eat-it-all Elaine," Eugene Field's "The Duel," or Karla Kuskin's "I Woke Up This Morning" are interesting to try.

A combination of types More than one type of choral reading may be used in the same selection for interesting and dramatic interpretations. For example, "Three Little Kittens" might utilize the whole class on the narrative part with one child reading the mother cat's part and three children reading the kittens' speeches. In John Godfrey Saxe's "The Blind Men and the Elephant" the narration might be read by the whole class with each of six children reading a solo part and a small group of light voices reading the moral at the end. Vocal interpretations of selections may also be accompanied by sound effects for additional accent or atmosphere.

Select a poem that you think will appeal to children and that has a good rhythm to follow. Give each child a copy of the selection or show it on the overhead projector. (I prefer the overhead projector. Children can see where you are pointing and seem to keep together better.) Read the selection to the children, using good expression, and then discuss difficult vocabulary and clarify the meaning of the selection as necessary.

If the selection is easy or there is a chorus, you may simply indicate the parts for children to join in on and proceed to reread the selection. If the selection is fairly difficult you will probably want to make rather careful plans for children's participation before rereading the selection, noting the rhythm and the words to stress. Children may, if they wish, reread the selection several times, each time discussing and evaluating the interpretation and making further plans for changing, adding to, or otherwise improving their reading of it. Children need not perfect each selection, and it is well to stop the activity before they tire of it. They often get caught up in the interpretive process, however, and want to read a selection again and again so they can try out different effects. Some poems, of course, are available already marked for choral reading; these may be good to use in the beginning if you are unfamiliar with this form of expression.

Evaluating the Literature Program

Literature is usually seen as an ongoing and developmental activity. All too often, however, it is given only peripheral attention in the busy language arts curriculum. Traditionally, literature programs, if evaluated at all, have been measured solely on the basis of the number of books children read. Although number of books may indicate their interest in reading, it is by no means an adequate or reliable evaluation tool by itself. In evaluating a literature program one also ought to look closely at children's reading behavior. One should consider what children read, how well they understand what they read, what their attitude is toward literature, and how they respond creatively and applicatively to literature.

Periodically, classroom teachers need to stand back and take an objective look at what is happening in literature in their classrooms. The following questions may be helpful in taking this look.

1. Are the children reading materials in addition to assignments in textbooks?

2. Is oral reading of carefully selected selections included in the daily lesson plans?

3. Are the children being introduced to a wide variety of literature and to many authors and illustrators?

4. Are the children being encouraged to read widely and to vary the types of literature they read?

5. Are the children cognizant of the different types of literature and able to discuss them?

6. Do the children read willingly on their own?

7. Are the children enthusiastic about what they read, and do they want to share it with others?

8. Do the children recognize possible connections between what they read on their own and in the content of other subject areas?

9. Does the children's reading motivate creative responses? Do they interpret what they read artistically through drama, art, and music?

10. Does the children's reading help them better understand themselves, others, and the world in which they live?

In Summary

Children's literature began long ago as oral stories told to children by their elders. The first *written* stories for children are placed at about A.D. 600. However, there were very few books written for children before the nineteenth century. The few that were written were not intended to be entertaining, attractive, or interesting by modern standards. The contribution of nineteenth-century authors resulted in some of the greatest masterpieces of children's literature ever written. They included fairy tales, full-length novels, and poetry. This period was also marked by outstanding illustrators of children's books. During the twentieth century the number of books written for children continued to increase steadily; many fine books were written and illustrated.

Children's literature may be classified into five main categories: fiction, information books, folklore, biography, and poetry. These classifications overlap. For example, either biography or historical fiction may contribute a considerable amount of information about a person, subject, or event. It is important that children become acquainted with books in each category and develop an understanding of the characteristics and contributions of each.

Literature ought to be a vital part of every child's school experience. Teachers need to become acquainted with a wide range of quality children's literature at various levels of difficulty so they can guide children toward appropriate selections. A stimulating classroom environment, time to read, discussions, supplementary audiovisual materials, and enrichment activities all help to create children's interest in literature and enhance their literary experiences. Teacher-guided discussions help children develop important concepts about literature. Enrichment activities develop understanding and facilitate children's enjoyment. Storytelling and oral reading of stories are especially important classroom activities and ought to be included in each school day.

Learning Objectives

COGNITIVE OBJECTIVES

Primary Grades

Children will

become familiar with many good books and stories.

be able to retell stories.

develop concepts of people, places, and things outside their environment.

be able to compare stories.

expand and refine their vocabulary.

be able to respond creatively to stories through art, music, drama, writing, and dance.

become familiar with different kinds of stories (e.g., fairy tales, fables, myths, etc.).

Middle Grades

Children will

continue to develop all primary-grade objectives.

be able to describe the plots of books and stories.

be able to explain the interrelationships of characters and events in books and stories.

be able to relate books and stories to their own problems.

be able to compare stories within the same category.

be able to identify and discuss various types of literature (biography, myths, legends, etc.).

recognize literature as a mirror of a culture.

be able to evaluate and discuss the literary merits of particular books and stories.

AFFECTIVE OBJECTIVES

Children will

enjoy reading and listening to literature.

engage in informal discussions of literature.

develop an appreciation of other people through literature.

elect to read books and stories on their own.

seek out and observe enacted forms of good literature (e.g., plays, films).

Suggested Learning Activities

Book Tree. "Plant" a bare branch or bring in a small artificial Christmas tree. Cut tagboard circles for ornaments and string colorful yarn through them. When a child has read a book, he or she writes the title, author, and the reader's name on one side of an ornament. On the other side the child draws a picture of a scene from the book. Then the child hangs the ornament on the tree.

Book Mobile. Ask the children to write the title of a book on a long strip of cardboard and then write single words that describe the book on smaller strips of cardboard. String the strips together to make a mobile.

Clothesline Book Review. When the children have completed their books they should find and cut words from headlines in the newspaper to describe the books. They should paste their words on a piece of paper and then pin the papers to a clothesline strung across the room.

Book Report Collage. Have the children cut pictures from magazines to illustrate the mood of the book they have read. They should paste the pictures on a large piece of paper to form a collage, then cut out letters to make the title of the book and paste it boldly across the collage.

Book Auction. Hold a book auction for children to auction off good books they have read. The children take turns being the auctioneer and try to stimulate interest so that someone in the class will "buy" their book. Play money may be allotted to each child to make the bidding more realistic.

Interview the Author. Pair up children who have read books by the same author. Let them research the author and then plan and produce an interview in which one of them is the interviewer and the other the author.

Time Line. Ask the children to draw a line across a piece of paper to represent the span of time covered in a book. Then they should divide the line into segments of time, with the dates written below the line and an illustration of what happened on that date above the line.

Book Jackets. Have the children design book jackets for their favorite books. A brief summary of the story is written on the front inside flap and a short sketch of the author on the back inside flap.

Stage Set. Have the children construct a miniature stage set to go with a story. They may make furniture and other props from cardboard or balsawood from the hobby store.

Dramatic Book Report. Let the children select small groups to work with them in dramatizing an interesting part of a book.

Letters to the Author. Have the children write letters to the authors of their favorite books. They might tell why they liked the books, the best parts, etc. Letters sent to an author in care of the publishers will be forwarded.

Cartoons. Help the children identify the conflict in a book they have read. Then let them make a cartoon to illustrate the conflict.

Library Orders. Have the children plan a speech to the librarian in which they try to convince him or her to buy additional copies of a particularly good book.

Book Boxes. Have the children make book boxes to exchange with each other. To make a book box they select a subject or a theme and find several books about it. These are placed in a box and the box decorated in keeping with the theme. They also think of activities appropriate to the books and put those in the box. Additional items might include bookmarks, games, or puzzles that go along with the theme. Boxes may be made in various shapes to add interest.

Reading Wheel. To encourage children to read from several kinds of literature, make charts such as the one in Figure 11-2 for each child. As they read a book from a particular category, they color in that section of the wheel.

Character's Log. The children pretend they are a character in the story and write a log describing the events in the story.

Good Writer's Awards. The children select a paragraph that they feel illustrates excellent writing and nominate the author to the Writers'

Hall of Fame. Each child in turn reads the selected paragraph and explains why he or she thinks it is well written.

Caldecott Winners. Older children can enjoy the winning books by sharing them with younger children. Let the children read the books and plan a presentation for (or simply read them to) younger children.

Poetry Pockets. Make pockets out of scraps of cloth or old jeans, one for each child. Fasten the pockets to the bulletin board and when a child finds a poem he or she particularly likes, have the child copy the poem on a card and put it in the pocket.

Suggestions for Further Reading

Arbuthnot, May Hill, Dorothy M. Broderick, Shelton L. Roote, Jr., Mark Taylor, and Evelyn L. Wenzel. *The Arbuthnot Anthology of Children's Literature,* Rev. by Zena Sutherland. Glenview, Ill.: Scott, Foresman and Co., 1976.

Bauer, Caroline Feller. *Handbook for Storytellers.* Chicago: American Library Association, 1976.

Huck, Charlotte S. *Children's Literature in the Elementary School,* 3rd ed. New York: Holt, Rinehart and Winston, 1976.

Lamme, Linda Leonard, ed. *Learning to Love Literature: Preschool through Grade 3.* Urbana, Ill.: National Council of Teachers of English, 1981.

Sebesta, Sam Leaton, and William J. Iverson. *Literature for Thursday's Child.* Chicago: Science Research Associates, 1975.

Smith, James A., and Dorothy M. Park. *Word Music & Word Magic: Children's Literature Methods.* Boston: Allyn and Bacon, 1977.

Sutherland, Zena, and May Hill Arbuthnot. *Children and Books,* 5th ed. Glenview, Ill.: Scott, Foresman, 1977.

FIGURE 11-2 *(facing page)*

Name _____

Reading Wheel

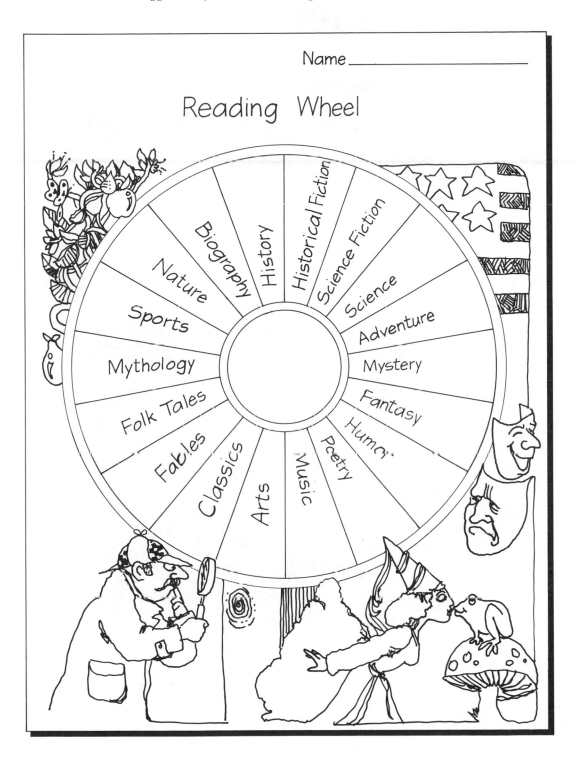

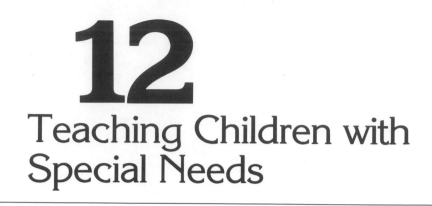

12
Teaching Children with Special Needs

Regardless of the causes, there are differences in the ways in which children approach learning, and teachers need to know the general characteristics of these variations on a theme. All children learn by doing (theme), but the learning pace, sequence, and actual doing will not always be the same (variations).

(Hansen-Krening, 1979, p. 206)

CHAPTER PREVIEW

Try to remember what it was like to be a child. Were there some things you didn't have that you wanted? Were there some things you wanted to do but never got to do? This chapter is about the special children in school, those children who would like to run and play, or get a perfect paper, or just be able to talk to the child in the next chair. Classrooms are filled with all kinds of children. This chapter is about the special ones.

QUESTIONS TO THINK ABOUT AS YOU READ

What are some instructional implications of PL 94-142?

What kinds of children might I find in a *mainstreamed* classroom?

What are the special needs of special children?

What is an IEP?

What are gifted and talented children like?

How might a language arts program be modified for gifted and talented children?

In 1975, Public Law 94-142 was passed mandating that all children be provided free public education in an appropriate and "least restrictive environment." This meant that many handicapped children who had previously attended special schools were "mainstreamed" into regular classrooms. Prior to this, provisions for the handicapped varied from one state to another, and the "mainstreaming law," as it is now commonly called, was a major step in equalizing opportunity.

The last decade has also witnessed another trend with considerable influence on our schools. Large numbers of people from non–English speaking countries, particularly from Asian and Latin countries, have emigrated to the United States. Many of these people have settled in smaller towns and rural areas where multicultural populations were formerly less common. Economic conditions and personal preferences have also resulted in the migration and relocation of many people from one part of the United States to another. The effect of these changes has been to create a school population with great diversity, and hence, the need for programs responsible to the needs of a wide range of children.

Some of the children in our schools differ from the majority in certain important ways. Among this group are children who are mentally or physically handicapped, those who have had limited learning experiences, those who come from culturally different groups or homes in which standard English is not spoken as the primary language, and those who possess abilities beyond their peers'. Providing effective instruction for these children in a regular classroom is obviously a big challenge for today's teachers.

Looking at the Needs of Special Children

The many common characteristics of children everywhere make any attempt to classify them into "special" groups artificial at best. Lines of difference are not clear-cut; there are only degrees of difference. Furthermore, we must be very careful about labeling children. Labels can become self-fulfilling prophecies or they may contribute to a child's further sense of being different. The discussion that follows, then, should be considered as a discussion of types of differences and needs among children, rather than as classifications or labels for groups of learners.

The Physically Handicapped

Children with physical handicaps are usually intellectually able students, and they should be encouraged to participate in activities as fully as possible. Teaching them in a regular classroom involves adjusting the learning situation to allow alternatives within their capabilities. When regular classroom activities present difficulties beyond the physical limits of children, they may be able to perform different but related and important tasks. For example, children who are unable to move about without aid may be unable to participate in the dance part of a literary dramatization. Instead they might be able to create a new character with a less strenuous role or assume a production task such as that of director. Multimedia activities also offer many possibilities for less mobile children.

The Hearing Impaired

Children who are hearing impaired may not be as far advanced in language development as other children their age. The ability to hear language affects the ability to speak unless children have been given special training from a very early age. Assess children's language learning carefully to provide appropriate help. If in doubt, check with the specialist for your district.

Some children suffer from partial impairment. For example, they may have a high-frequency loss, or only a percentage of normal hearing. Detection of such problems is difficult and will require special consultation. Such losses can have a serious effect on the development of language and literacy.

Many hearing-impaired children, even those fitted with a hearing aid, are adept at lip reading. Make sure they are seated where they can see your lip movements clearly. Don't continue talking when you turn your back to write on the board. If possible, use an overhead projector so you can face the children while you write and speak. Because hearing impaired children must attend more closely, they often tire more readily than other children. Provide alternate sources of information and individual activities that they can do on their own.

The Visually Impaired

Many visually impaired children are fitted with glasses that enable them to function normally in the classroom. Others may need special materials such as large-print books and a typewriter, or perhaps, Braille materials. Although it is important for these children to learn to read and write independently, assignments may need to be modified so that they do more of their work orally. They will also need to sit where they can see the board and to be within the necessary visual range for presentations. Once other children understand the problems faced by those who are unable to see well, they will think of numerous ways to help.

The Mentally Handicapped

Children less academically able learn at a slower pace and show limited ability to deal with abstract concepts. Therefore, they need to begin their learning at lower levels than their age mates, and they need to have learning tasks broken down into very small steps and carefully sequenced to build a gradual continuum of learning. Instruction in speaking and listening should be associated with concrete learning experiences: doing, seeing, handling, and using things and materials. Multisensory learning experiences are important. Children need to verbalize their activities and to have many opportunities to practice and reinforce skills.

Mentally handicapped children often need encouragement to participate in group and individual learning activities. Left to themselves, they tend to lack focus and purpose in assigned tasks. Short, rewarding experiences are best. Because their attention span is short, they require more supervision or peer support to remain at task. These children tend to forget easily; what is learned today may not be remembered tomorrow. Progress is slow; they take many steps backward in the course of going forward.

The Learning Disabled

Learning disabled children possess normal intelligence, yet perform below their expected level for reasons that are not clearly understood. Their learning problems do not stem from the previously mentioned handicapping conditions, but rather from a malfunction of one or more basic learning processes (Woolfolk and Nicolich, 1980).

Woolfolk and Nicolich explain, .

> Children must receive, make sense of, and express the events in their world. . . . Learning is complex. Sometimes we must take information in visually but express it vocally or we must take information in through hearing but express it in writing. Some students have great difficulty converting from one modality to another.
>
> In between the reception and expression of information is the processing. People must integrate, analyze, synthesize, store, and retrieve information. We must make sense of our world. A child who has difficulty with perception, integration, storage, retrieval, or expression of information will have problems with learning, especially in school. Students with learning disabilities may experience difficulties in one or several of these areas. (1980, p 573)

The Emotionally Handicapped

Emotionally handicapped children may manifest some behaviors similar to those of mentally handicapped children. Their attention spans are generally short, and they have difficulty concentrating on the task at hand. Emotional problems take precedence over attending to their schoolwork. Some emotionally handicapped children may also have difficulty controlling themselves, and they may create a disturbance for other children. Some, on the other hand, are overly quiet and withdrawn. The very fact that they are among so large a group of children can often overwhelm them and produce tension.

Emotionally handicapped children need a very consistent and secure environment with many opportunities to succeed and to feel good about themselves. Because it is difficult for them to concentrate on a task for very long, they need to be able to move frequently from one task to another, yet they should be encouraged to remain at a task for progressively longer periods of time. Highly motivational activities and those that involve movement of larger muscles or gross body movements are apt to be more successful. Experiences in separate learning activities must be planned so that they are cumulative and organized to contribute to larger language learning objectives.

The Economically Limited

Davis (1972) discusses the large numbers of poor people living in the United States. He states,

> The disadvantaged poor are very unevenly distributed geographically and ethnically. They include the chronically unemployed coal miners in such pockets of poverty as the southern mountains, sharecroppers, migrant farm workers, and the ever-increasing masses of urban poor. Ethnically they are Negro; Puerto Rican; Spanish-speaking Mexican-American and wetbacks; American Indians; they are immigrants and old American stock. (p. 42)

Fundamental differences in values underlie many of the problems associated with education in poverty areas. Although some children from impoverished homes have good intellectual stimulation from their families and environment, the values of a large number of poor tend to differ in significant ways from those of middle-class oriented schools. Concern for basic economic needs has necessarily taken precedence over less urgent matters. Children of poor parents often express a hopeless attitude toward their future and show little interest in learning anything that they do not see as utilitarian. Thus they may appear apathetic toward academically oriented learning activities. Poor parents may value ultimate educational achievement for their children but be naive about how to help them realize these ideals. Teaching these children initially involves igniting their spirits and helping them discover both practical and enjoyable reasons for learning to use language. Motivating them to learn often rests on helping them understand and value the acquisition of additional language skills. They need to experience language as a means of opening up opportunities for them and transcending the barriers and gloom of poverty.

School can be a bewildering and discouraging encounter for children reared in poverty. Because they have limited experiences on which to draw, the places and things they find pictured and written about in many of their school books are simply beyond their frame of reference. Their language, though perfectly adequate for communication within their homes, often proves inadequate for the receptive and expressive communication required of them at school. Economically limited children who have not had the advantage of books and stimulating adult language need many opportunities to develop awareness and competency in using oral language. Speaking and listening activities are a prerequisite for success in written language experiences. These children need to experience adult language through conversations and through listening to stories and books. They also need opportunities to verbalize meaningful, concrete experiences of their own. They need to build and expand their vocabularies and to develop more complex and interesting sentence structures. Stimulation of creative thought is essential throughout activities. Encouraging children to be curious and to creatively solve problems challenges them to go beyond the known to reach new levels of understanding and self-fulfillment.

The Ethnically Different

Children who come from different ethnic groups bring a variety of backgrounds to the classroom. The problems of some of these children are roughly equivalent to those of children in an economically depressed area. These are the children of ethnic minorities who live in poverty and who have little opportunity or incentive to extend their learning beyond that demanded by their immediate environment. Some minority children, however, may have other problems. Those from newly integrated cultural groups within the United States or those who are recent emigrants from foreign countries must often cope with a range of problems. Their language, experiential background, family expectations, attitudes toward their teachers and their peers, or the kind and amount of responses they have been trained to give may be quite different from those of the other children.

Language is often the most obvious problem of ethnically different children. Some of them speak standard English only as a second language, if at all, and are seriously limited in both their receptive and expressive communication ability. Ching points out that:

> The bilingual child's vocabulary may be inadequate because concepts which he has developed may have labels or names which are unique

within his own culture. For example, when the Black child asks, "Will you *carry* me to school?" he means "Will you *take* me to school?" . . . The child may have no names or labels at all for certain concepts since he has not had opportunities to communicate about them with anyone. For example, when the child enters kindergarten he may not know the names of the various parts of his body because he has not talked about them with anyone at home. In homes where both English and another language are spoken, the child may have learned the Chinese or Spanish word for a concept rather than the English word and thus be handicapped when he is confronted with unfamiliar words in the English language. (1976, p. 5)

In considering the teaching of special children, it is important to remember that children are more alike than different. They all share a common need for physical comfort — for adequate food, clothing, and shelter — and for love and acceptance by their social group. Furthermore, it is important to realize that any differences among children stem from psychological, physical, or environmental variables over which the children themselves have no control.

A positive self-concept is important for everyone, child or adult. All children need to experience a warm and friendly classroom environment, but it is particularly important for those who, for various reasons, feel different from other children. A sense of security is essential for them to adjust to differences and to feel good about themselves. Helping these children fit into the group and experience success can also be a rewarding learning experience for other children, broadening and enriching their lives and their sense of humanity. A teacher who accepts and respects all children sets the tone for the classroom and paves the way for learning.

Children gain a sense of well-being when they know they are contributing to their society. By observing children closely you can discover their strengths and help them excel in those areas. One newly mainstreamed child with muscular dystrophy was found to have a nice voice. He was invited to join the school choir and beamed with pride each time the group sang for a special program.

Teaching Special Children

The Learning Environment

Nowhere is the need for experience-based language learning more important than in working with special children, particularly those children with limited experiential background and those with limited use of English. Regardless of the age of the children with whom you work, you will need to continually assess their understanding and ability to use English. Some children may need to make very basic connections between "words" and "things" and to learn the rhythm and melody of language.

Working with diverse students in a regular classroom may at first seem an overwhelming responsibility. Although these children do indeed present some interesting challenges, it is important to remember that the reason they are there is to give them the opportunity to experience regular classroom activities. The experiences they have in the classroom should not be totally different from those of other children. Rather, special children should participate in the ongoing classroom program to the extent that they are able, with activities modified as necessary to accommodate their special needs.

Individualizing Instruction

It is especially important to be aware of the unique learning patterns and abilities of individual special children. Even children with a similar handicapping condition tend to vary in a number of ways, and no one method of instruction is best for all of them. Still, data from many sources make some generalizations possible.

For example, learning disabled children, and others who for one reason or another find learning difficult, seem to learn concepts and skills more easily in a structured, teacher-directed situation. Lowenbraun and Afflect explain, "In learning a new skill or concept, a child progresses through three stages, *initial acquisition, proficiency*, and *maintenance*" (1976, p. 48). To maximize learning during the acquisition phase of instruction, they suggest the following.

> The first component of direct-teacher instruction is the providing of instructional input on how to perform the desired skill or the components of a new concept. Instructional input is usually provided in the regular classroom through verbal instruction. The usefulness of verbal instruction can be maximized if you:
> 1. insure that the children are attending to the instruction
> 2. use a balance of teacher presentation and child activity during the instructional period
> 3. provide visual stimuli in addition to verbal instruction
> 4. use consistent, simple vocabulary
> 5. present information in an organized, logical fashion
> 6. demonstrate the desired behavior (p. 53)

Additional practice is needed to develop proficiency and to maintain skills. By selecting appropriate materials and establishing procedures, you can help children to learn to practice independently. This also frees you to work with other children. Lowenbraun and Affect suggest these additional guidelines for independent-child activities:

1. Focus on skills at the level of proficiency or maintenance.
2. Provide equivalent or analogous exercises for a specific objective.
3. Insure independence of task completion.
   a. Use simple directions.
   b. Use one task per page or assignment.
   c. Use standard formats that the child can recognize.
   d. Insure that the child knows the exact demands of the task and when she has completed the task.
   e. Use responses that can later be corrected by the teacher.
4. Insure success on the child-directed tasks.
   a. Use visual prompts.
   b. Use verbal prompts.
5. Provide feedback on responses made. (p. 63)

In some ways physically handicapped or severely visually impaired children seem easier to teach than other special children simply because their handicaps are obvious. We are more readily aware of their limitations. Conversely, children who sit quietly and look attentive are more easily neglected. That may be particularly true for hearing impaired children. In severe cases of hearing loss children have no idea what they are missing, so they have no way of knowing how to respond or question.

Teachers must assess and remember each child's physical and educational capabilities and make certain that every child engages in appropriate learning activities. Both children's learning aptitude and the type and degree of their handicapping condition are significant for determining the program modifications that will be necessary. One possible approach is to think in terms of *input to children* and *output from children*. Conditions for input: How can the child receive information and instruction? What conditions will help them learn? Conditions for output: How can the child respond? What aids, if any, are necessary or advantageous? Given adequate input, hearing impaired children may be able to respond in the same manner as their peers most of the time. Severely visually handicapped children may respond orally, in typewriting, or, when available and appropriate, with manipulative materials (blocks, letters, three-dimensional models, etc.).

Understanding Culturally Different Children

In considering one group of special children, the ethnically different, a word of caution may be in order: minority children are not necessarily handicapped. Actually, the opposite may be true. In some instances these children might well be considered advantaged in that they are familiar and at ease in, not one, but two cultures and are able to communicate effectively in more than one dialect or language. The special children we are concerned with in the context of this chapter are those ethnically different children who are handicapped in terms of school achievement because of cultural or language differences that impede their progress in learning within the classroom. These children need experiences in which they can develop concepts for English words and become thoroughly familiar with syntactic patterns of English. They need many opportunities to hear and use language in nonthreatening situations such as listening to stories, memorizing finger plays and poems, singing, and participating in choral speech.

Cultural differences that are less obvious than those of language may also contribute to children's attitudes and learning behaviors in the classroom. For example, Jones points out other cultural characteristics that affect Indian children's learning. Among these are the following (1976, p. 140):

> anxieties, taboos, mores, aspirations, religion and behavior patterns of their culture
>
> concept of time
>
> social withdrawal when unfamiliar with acceptable social behavior
>
> observation or visual means of learning rather than verbal
>
> listening to older tribal members
>
> preference for private recognition rather than public announcement
>
> low self-image

Children's cultural expectations often differ sharply from those of the school. This difference can create a serious conflict for children caught between the two worlds. Sometimes, acceptance of new ways and new ideas results in criticism or even alienation from the child's family or larger cultural group. To work successfully with ethnically different children, the teacher needs to become knowledgeable about other cultures and aware of differences in values and attitudes that may affect children's participation and response in learning activities.

Cheyney states that "Teachers and children have cultural walls separating them. The burden for tearing down the walls lies with the teacher'' (1976, p. 35). He suggests the following guidelines as a first step in coping with problems (Dawson, 1974).

Do's and Don'ts for Teachers in Multicultural Settings

DOs

1. Do use the same scientific approach to gain background information on the culture of multiethnic groups as you would to tackle a complicated course in science, mathematics, or any subject area in which you might be deficient.

2. Do engage in systematic study of the disciplines that provide insight into the cultural heritage, political struggle, contributions, and present-day problems of minority groups.

3. Do try to develop sincere personal relationships with minorities. *You can't teach strangers!* Don't give up because *one* black or other minority person rejects your efforts. All groups have sincere individuals who welcome honest, warm relationships with members of another race. Seek out those who will accept or tolerate you. This coping skill is one that minorities have always used.

4. Do recognize that there are often more differences within a group than between two groups. If we recognize diversity among races, we must also recognize diversity within groups.

5. Do remember that there are many ways to gain insight into a group. Visit their churches, homes, communities; read widely and listen to various segments of the group.

6. Do remember that no one approach and no one answer will assist you in meeting the educational needs of all children in a multicultural society.

7. Do select instructional materials that are accurate and free of stereotypes.

8. Do remember that there is a positive relationship between teacher expectation and academic progress.

9. Do provide an opportunity for minority group boys and girls and children from the mainstream to interact in a positive intellectual setting on a continuous basis.

10. Do use a variety of materials and especially those that utilize positive, true-to-life experiences.

11. Do provide some structure and direction to children who have unstructured lives, primarily children of the poor.

12. Do expose all children to a wide variety of literature as a part of your cultural sensitivity program.

*13. "Do remember that in spite of the fact that ethnic groups often share many common problems their specific needs are diverse."

*14. "Do utilize the rich resources within your own classroom among various cultural groups."

15. Do remember that human understanding is a lifetime endeavor. You must continue to study and provide meaningful experiences for your pupils.

*16. "Do remember to be honest with yourself. If you can't adjust to children from multicultural homes get out of the classroom."

DON'Ts

1. Don't rely on elementary school textbooks, teachers' guides, and brief essays to become informed on minorities. Research and resources will be needed.

2. Don't use ignorance as an excuse for not having any insight into the problems and culture of Blacks, Chicanos, Native Americans, Puerto Ricans, Asian Americans, and other minorities.

3. Don't rely on the "expert" judgment of *one minority person* for the answer to all the complicated racial and social problems of his/her people. For example, Blacks, Mexicans, Indians, and Puerto Ricans hold various political views on all issues.

4. Don't be fooled by popular slogans and propaganda intended to raise the national consciousness of an oppressed people.

5. Don't get carried away with the "save the world concept." Most minorities have their own savior.

6. Don't be afraid to learn from those who are more familiar with the mores and cultures than you.

7. Don't assume that you have all the answers for solving the other man's problems. It is almost impossible for an outsider to be an expert on the culture of another group.

8. Don't assume that all minority group children are culturally deprived.

* Helpful suggestions of "DOs and DON'Ts" were made by Delores Fitzgerald and Robin Kovats of St. Paul the Apostle School and Raven Oas of St. Columba School, both in New York City.

9. Don't develop a fatalistic attitude about the progress of minority group pupils.

10. Don't resegregate pupils through tracking and ability grouping gimmicks.

11. Don't give up when minority group pupils seem to hate school.

12. Don't assume that minorities are the only pupils who should have multicultural instructional materials. Children in the mainstream can be culturally deprived in terms of their knowledge and understanding of other people and their own heritage.

13. Don't go around asking parents and children personal questions in the name of research. Why must they divulge their suffering? It is obvious.

14. Don't get hung up on grade designation when sharing literature that provides insight into the cultural heritage of a people.

*15. "Don't try to be cool by using the vernacular of a particular racial group."

16. Don't make minority children feel ashamed of their language, dress, or traditions.

Materials for and About Special Children

A number of materials have been written for and about children with various handicapping conditions. Books, stories, and newspaper and magazine articles that show the problems children and adults face and how they learn to accept and deal with them can be of great value. Reading about problems associated with someone outside the classroom is one way to introduce what may be a sensitive topic and objectify discussion. The understandings children gain will help them openly discuss and deal with problems experienced by people they know.

By reading about the accomplishments of other people with handicapping conditions or special needs, children can gain a sense of worth and encouragement. Literary sources available to children should include people from different ethnic and ability groups who have made significant contributions, whether or not you have children with similar talents or backgrounds in your classroom. Reading about cultures in other countries further expands children's awareness of differences and provides yet another way to develop understanding and respect for humankind. (See Chapter 11 for references.)

IEPs — Individualized Education Programs

To implement PL 94-142, schools are required to plan an Individualized Education Program (IEP) for each handicapped child. Based on a thorough, objective evaluation of the child's needs and abilities, the plan establishes the child's placement in a mainstreamed classroom or a special resource room. It delineates a plan of instruction for a given period of time and the school personnel responsible for teaching the child and monitoring the program.

When children have been mainstreamed into a regular classroom, it is highly desirable for the classroom teacher to take an active part in planning the IEP. The classroom teacher in this case is the person working most closely with the child, and he or she is most likely to be knowledgeable about the child's patterns of daily work.

Teaching the Gifted and Talented

A gifted and talented child is defined as "any child whose performance in a worthwhile type of human endeavor is consistently or repeatedly remarkable" (Witty, 1971). This definition suggests that children with special talents have a wide range of abilities and that they should not be thought of as a homogeneous group. Children demonstrate their talents in various ways. However, they consistently show conceptual abilities beyond their age group and tend to be linguistically advanced. Their speech and writing characteristically demonstrates larger vocabularies, longer sentences, and generally more advanced thinking strategies.

Instruction for gifted and talented children ought to be directed both to the ways in which children are like their peers and to the ways in which they are different. Although they may be academically advanced and able to deal with more abstract concepts than other children their age, they are still children and should not be expected to behave as miniature adults. Although they need stimulation in order to grow and develop at a rate commensurate with their ability, they also need to maintain their identity with their normal social group and to learn to live and work with different kinds of people.

The program for gifted and talented children ought to be highly individualized. These children need to be encouraged to pursue their special abilities beyond usual grade- or age-level expectations. Because they learn quickly and tend to be advanced in general language skills, grade-level activities may not be purposeful for them. They need the additional challenge of enrichment activities and advanced work. Classtime should not be spent doing "more of the same"; it should be structured to stimulate their special talents and to broaden their knowledge. Wide reading, speaking, and writing offer many opportunities for gifted and talented children to encounter ideas and develop their thinking skills.

As with any child, instructional planning for gifted and talented children begins with an assessment of their strengths and weaknesses. Teachers too often assume that these children possess skills and understanding which they do not in fact have. Thus their program should include attention to basic skills as well as to advanced work. Experiences that equip them to learn and progress independently are particularly important. These include skills related to procuring, selecting, interpreting, organizing, and presenting a broad range of information. All areas of the language arts — listening, speaking, reading, and writing — need to be advanced. For example, some children may need to learn how to ask questions, how to phrase a question to get the information they seek. Or, they may take too narrow a focus and ignore significant information when they listen or read.

A background rich in the knowledge of one's literary heritage is a distinct asset and advanced units of study are excellent fare for gifted and talented children. Literary analysis develops critical thinking skills and a greater understanding of other people. Tracing their own or their country's historical roots also offers children many possibilities for learning basic skills and gaining new insights. Because writing is such an important mode of expression, it is important that these children who are capable of making significant contributions to society be especially well trained in that art.

Programs for gifted and talented children need to be flexible enough to allow them a wide range of exploration. At the same time, children need to learn the importance of commitment to a specific task and to develop the necessary skills for pursuing a study in depth.

In Summary

The passage of Public Law 94-142 was responsible for allowing many handicapped children to attend regular public schools for the first time. These children come with a variety of physical, mental, and emotional handicaps. At the same time, similarities with other children in the classroom are marked. Most handicapped children can profit from public school attendance if modifications are made in the program to accommodate them.

Minority children are also found in public school classrooms. Any problems they might have are apt to be related to cultural and language differences. Patterns of behavior are quite different for children in some cultures, and it is important for teachers to become aware of cultural expectations.

Gifted and talented children excel beyond their peers, yet they too are growing and developing and require instruction. However, they learn at a fast pace and should not be discouraged with work that is too easy.

Suggestions for Further Reading

Cheyney, Arnold B. *Teaching Children of Different Cultures in the Classroom, A Language Approach*, 2nd ed. Columbus, Ohio: Charles E. Merrill, 1976.

Hansen-Krening, Nancy. *Competency and Creativity in Language Arts: A Multiethnic Focus*. Reading, Mass.: Addison-Wesley, 1979.

Knight, Lester N. *Language Arts for the Exceptional: The Gifted and Linguistically Different*. Itasca, Ill.: F. E. Peacock, 1974.

Lowenbraun, Sheila, and James Q. Affleck. *Teaching Mildly Handicapped Children in Regular Classes*. Columbus, Ohio: Charles E. Merrill, 1976.

Renzulli, Joseph S. *The Enrichment Triad Model: A Guide for Developing Programs for the Gifted and Talented*. Mansfield Center, Conn.: Creative Learning Press, 1977.

Renzulli, Joseph S., and Linda H. Smith. *A Guidebook for Developing Individualized Educational Programs for Gifted and Talented Students*. Mansfield Center, Conn.: Creative Learning Press, 1979.

Urzua, Carole. "A Language-Learning Environment for All Children," *Language Arts* 57 (January 1980): 38–44.

13

The Language Arts Program

The idea that "English" includes whatever one does with language (maybe even: whatever one does with symbols) has broadened the activities of the English classroom beyond what most of us would have envisaged ten years ago. "Dramatic" activities, such as improvisation and the enactment of literary texts, are now encouraged; oral language is for many teachers as much of a concern as written language, and for some teachers even more of a concern. . . . At the same time, many teachers are asserting that one goal of English must be to teach students the basic skills of listening, speaking, reading, and writing, and are voicing concern over test scores which imply that these skills are not achieved.

(Statement of the Preparation of Teachers of English and the Language Arts, NCTE, 1976, pp. 1–2.)

CHAPTER PREVIEW

Imagine trying to devise a formula for a language arts program. "Take 28 parts children and one part teacher. Place ingredients in one crowded classroom and add . . ." But that is really too simplistic; the processes of teaching and learning are not easily expressed in this manner. An effective language arts program is flexible. It is designed to meet the diverse needs and abilities of children and to further their cognitive and affective growth. In this chapter you will find a discussion of different kinds of planning and the variables that influence language arts programs. The chapter also includes resources you might utilize and suggestions for grouping, organizing, and evaluating instruction.

QUESTIONS TO THINK ABOUT AS YOU READ

What kinds of planning are necessary for an effective language arts program?

What principles of learning ought to be reflected in a language arts program?

What is meant by the *teaching cycle?*

How may children be grouped for instruction?

What are some pointers for effective classroom management?

What kinds of materials are available for teaching language arts?

How can I know which materials to use?

What is the role of electronic technology in the classroom?

How might learning centers be set up and used?

How is children's progress evaluated?

This is an age of new linguistic and technological awareness, fraught with implications for elementary language arts programs. A greater consciousness of our linguistic heritage, the structure of English, the development of language in children, the nature of receptive and expressive language processes, the range of language diversities, and the importance of language to society are reflected in contemporary language arts programs. A cursory examination of recently published program guides and learning materials reveals the broad scope of content in today's language arts programs and the influence of current research on teaching and learning.

Teaching the language arts is a process that involves helping children develop their knowledge, appreciation, and skillful use of language. Teaching thus requires a master plan to stimulate language awareness and provide opportunities for children to use language purposefully. Language learning is an active process, one that depends on cognitive responses to stimuli. What and how much children learn is directly related to their opportunities to learn. Guiding and encouraging children's language growth means involving them in activities with people, things, and ideas that generate language and facilitate growth in using it effectively.

An analysis of activities in a typical elementary school day makes the importance of the language arts in the total elementary school curriculum quite clear. Virtually all that children do involves receptive or expressive language in some way. Therefore, elementary classrooms are a potential laboratory for developing a range of language knowledge and skills. It is not enough, however, to assume that because children are using language they are developing the understandings and competencies they need now and later on. If we are to maximize learning, we need to realize that although children's natural encounters with language may form the core of the language arts program, their language experiences ought to be carefully inventoried and thoughtfully structured to ensure a sound developmental program.

Planning for Instruction

Planning for instruction should be both long-range and specific. In *long-range planning* one considers desirable outcomes over a period of time — what children ought to know about language, what they ought to be able to do with language, and how they ought to feel about the skillful use of language. However, adequate planning also involves formulating explicit plans for immediate instruction. *Specific planning* focuses on concrete learning objectives from which lesson plans may be developed. In actual practice, of course, the two kinds of planning are interrelated and interdependent. A statement of long-range goals provides the framework for developing more specific plans. At the same time, it is through planning for sequential, day-by-day language experiences that long-range goals are attained.

Long-Range Planning

Most school districts are required (or at least expected) to develop a set of written goals for each curriculum area. A statement of goals for the language arts addresses each of the major strands to be developed — listening, speaking, reading, and writing — and includes both cognitive and affective outcomes. Goals are broad statements of learning to be accomplished over a period of time. The following are examples of goals:

> The student will acquire, interpret, and evaluate information through purposeful and critical observation and listening.

> The student will interpret literature and the humanities as a reflection of the life, values, and ideas of this and other cultures.

In formulating goals one takes into account the abilities and understandings that children need both now and in the future. If school is preparation for life, then what children learn in school ought to help them feel confident in using language correctly in common life situations and to set the stage for continued positive, creative uses of language.

Goals for children's language development are cultural. First, they are based on the unique features of the language and the competencies children have and need in order to effectively use a particular language in a particular society. Second, goals reflect the values of a group of people and the aspirations they hold for their children. Every community has expectations of schools that reflect the dominant thinking of that group. These expectations constitute an unwritten set of guidelines on which the community's acceptance and support of a school's program depend. All these factors must be considered in formulating a set of language arts goals.

In planning long-range language arts goals, it is important to determine what children need to achieve if they are to meet the community's expectations and aspirations for them. Input from school patrons and students as well as professionals is both necessary and desirable. At the same time, goals should not be stated so narrowly as to restrict children to a particular language community. Care must be taken to ensure that children acquire a range of competencies adequate to meet their functional needs in broader social settings and to facilitate their use of language in personally satisfying and pleasurable ways.

Specific Planning

When general program guidelines have been established through long-range planning, the next step is to analyze what is involved in reaching those goals and to identify specific learning objectives. Suppose, for example, one goal is "to acquire knowledge through listening." In order to attain this goal, children need to acquire competencies such as the following:

a general knowledge of language (e.g., vocabulary, syntax, intonation)

ability to pick out main ideas and supporting details

ability to recognize fact, inference, and opinion

ability to compare and contrast

ability to recognize relationships

ability to generalize

Each of these competencies in turn suggests a more finite learning continuum. Few children, if any, are able to learn "to pick out main ideas and supporting details" in one lesson. Rather, such an ability is developed through a series of learning experiences that gradually build competency in the larger learning objective. Possible learning activities include listening: to find out who or what a story is about, to find the main events in a story, to suggest headlines for a newsstory, to complete a list of relevant details, to match supporting details with previously stated main ideas, or to make a simple outline of a speech.

It is also important in planning specific instruction to notice where objectives in one area overlap those in another and to use that overlap to interrelate the language arts. For instance, listening for main ideas and supporting details parallels a similar skill in reading comprehension. Hence the concept may be advantageously developed and practiced in more than one context.

Stating objectives in behavioral terms provides greater specificity and clarifies the criteria for determining when children have achieved a satisfactory level of competency. A *behavioral objective* is a concise statement of what the learner will be able to do in a given situation under particular conditions (e.g., "After listening to a one- to two-minute speech that is organized around three main ideas, the learner will be able to state the three ideas expressed in the speech").

Planning based on specific learning outcomes is frequently associated with the specific skill areas of the curriculum. However, since learning objectives are, in effect, statements of the purpose or intent of a learning activity, they can be used with expressive and creative activities as well. For example, in oral language an objective might simply be that a nonparticipant make a contribution to a class discussion. In creative drama an objective might be that children demonstrate their ability to concentrate by moving their bodies to simulate real-life experience. Or, in writing, an objective might be that children will be aware of alternate ways to begin a story and will make a conscious decision about which one to use. If the objective is exploratory, a right or wrong answer is not appropriate. Also, learning objectives are not necessarily achieved in one lesson. A period of experimentation and practice is often a requirement for development.

Learning objectives provide an organized way of directing children's acquisition of language skills, abilities, and attitudes. Clearly stating what children are expected to learn provides direction and purpose for specific lesson-planning. Once the teacher has identified an objective, his or her next task is to find an efficient and interesting way for children to develop the skill and demonstrate mastery. Teachers may use a lesson in a language arts textbook or in a language learning center activity, a teacher-directed lesson, or an independent study sheet.

Planning with Children

Children, too, should be involved in planning. Under the guidance of the teacher, they can begin to share the responsibility for their educational experiences at an early age. Such activities as planning for wise use of free time, choosing learning centers or other appropriate activities for work periods, checking work independently, completing and analyzing attitude surveys, stating learning objectives, making contracts for independent study projects, and planning creative ways to share activities offer a number of opportunities to involve children of various ages in planning their language experiences.

When children help to shape their experiences, learning takes on new meaning. Children usually become more conscious of the purpose of assignments rather than merely trying to get the assignments done. Furthermore, while assessing their personal needs and in planning appropriate activities, they exercise their cognitive skills to solve meaningful problems and thus develop their ability to think logically and creatively.

Teaching and Learning

Helping children to learn is a complex task. How well and how fast they learn depends on more than the quantity of their experience. What they gain from a learning activity is directly related to the quality of the experience and their responses to it. Superficial experiences result in limited learning. Maximum learning occurs when children acquire an understanding of the concept or skill that is taught and incorporate that knowledge into their previously formed cognitive structures.

Principles of Learning

Analysis of children's learning reveals several factors that enhance the teaching-learning process. Teachers need to be aware of them as they plan instruction and develop teaching strategies. Some of the more significant principles follow.

Learning patterns are highly individualistic Psychologists have identified children's stages of development, yet within each stage there is a considerable variation among individuals. Just as children differ physically in size and body build, they also differ psychologically in aptitude and mode of learning. This is true even of children reared in the same family: they also develop individual interests, attitudes, and ways of doing things.

Each child in a classroom represents a unique bundle of native endowment plus an array of perceptions gleaned from his or her background of social, emotional, and educational experiences. All these factors, combined and interrelated in complex ways, influence how children respond to learning situations. Every new experience is filtered through a child's individual experiential screen. Therefore, children who participate in a common learning experience will probably not all develop the same concepts or degree of skill.

Learning is developmental Learning is a building process. It develops gradually as new concepts are added to what is already known — to the schemata previously established. However, the extent to which children are able to perceive and process significant information at any time is apparently governed by their cognitive ability. Piaget and others have described the stages children pass through and the marked qualitative differences in their thinking at each stage (see Chapter 4).

The rate at which children grow is usually influenced by the sequence and structure of their experiences. Most learning is incremental; each additional knowledge or ability adds to and expands previously acquired knowledge and abilities. Thus it is possible to structure learning sequences from easy to complex and to guide children along a continuum at their own individual pace. In this way, each level of achievement provides the necessary readiness for successful achievement at the succeeding level of difficulty.

Learning is more efficient when it has meaning The human mind seeks closure; it strives to associate and organize information into meaningful wholes. Information that can be assimilated into an existing schema is learned more easily and retained longer. Associational thinking allows children to see relationships between old and new information, making this process work better. Skills learned in isolation require minimal cognitive activity, and thus the amount and practicality of learning is limited. By relating specific information or skills to broader contexts one begins to see a reason for learning and to develop associations that facilitate learning and retention.

Motivation affects learning Everything a person does consciously is done for some reason. The reasons may range from "because I have to stay after school if I don't" to "because I want to." Today's children present special challenges for motivation in schools. They have grown up with the glamor and passivity of television, and some may never have experienced the satisfaction of setting and achieving personal learning goals. The task of guiding children through rewarding learning experiences and helping them develop positive attitudes is at once a challenge and a necessity.

Creative teaching offers many possibilities for catching children's interest and helping them discover the utility and intrinsic value of learning. Exposure to children's literature, for example, may help children discover reading as a worthwhile use of time. Learning to listen to others and to express their own thoughts clearly may pave the way for exploring interests with others. To become motivated from within, children need to feel that what they are doing is important and to derive satisfaction from their accomplishments.

Learning requires reinforcement Knowledge or skills that are learned but not used move quickly out of the conscious mind. Once children have learned a concept or skill, they need many additional opportunities to use it in meaningful situations to make the skill fully theirs. Until a skill becomes automatic, ways must be found to keep it at the conscious level, continually and positively reinforcing its use.

It is important that children receive frequent feedback on their work. Positive feedback is encouraging and emphasizes correctness. At the same time, identification of errors allows children to correct them before they have been reinforced through practice. When children do something well they ought to be sincerely praised. Not all feedback needs to come from the teacher, however. Peer tutors, self-correcting games and exercises, self-assessment checklists, and cooperative work projects permit informal input from a number of sources.

The Role of the Teacher

The language arts program in any classroom is ultimately the teacher's responsibility. Even when schools have an adopted course of study, it is up to individual teachers to translate that content into actual lessons. How they do so will naturally vary from one teacher to another as a result of varying backgrounds of knowledge, philosophy, and teaching styles. It is important, however, that good instructional practices be incorporated into whatever individual approaches teachers develop. Specific tasks of the teaching-learning situation follow.

Providing good language models Children do not acquire language skills they have never met. Frequent exposure to good models is therefore essential if children are to become familiar with a wider range of language and personally adopt more complex forms of communication. Children need to hear and read a variety of good prose and poetry. In addition, because the teacher is apt to provide the most dominant example of language usage, it is important that every teacher inventory his or her personal habits and strive for language performance worthy of emulation.

Providing language stimulation Language develops through interaction with environmental stimuli. To expand and refine their language, children need many experiences that elicit and encourage language use. A wide range of realia and multimedia materials are available and may be used to stimulate ideas and to establish a laboratory situation for developing language.

Encouraging development of appropriate personal language Through extended language experiences children may be guided to recognize other uses of language and to set personal goals for increasing their individual communication potential. Children's goals will vary in accordance with their background and exposure to language. However, if children are to communicate effectively in the mainstream of society they must become adept in using common forms and conventions of language. For this reason they should be encouraged to acquire a broad language competence.

Planning and providing instruction Effective instruction maximizes language development and causes children to learn. To think of instruction in this way suggests an organized plan for guiding children's learning. At the same time it leaves the door open for using any instructional approach that effects learning.

Providing maximum opportunity for children to use language

Language develops through use. The broader that use, the greater the opportunity for development and expansion. Children need to listen, talk, read, and write language in a variety of contexts. Listening to and talking with adults as well as peers, reading widely, and sharing and discussing what they have written point up to the functional and aesthetic uses of language and develop children's oral and written fluency.

Creating a need for additional language skills With skillful teaching, the classroom can provide opportunities and experiences that require new skills or new levels of performance. Real-life situations provide meaningful learning experiences and motivation for learning new skills.

Recognizing the global nature of language Building language expertise ought to be viewed as an integral part of the total educational process. Opportunities to expand and refine language are by no means limited to activities in which a language competency is specifically stated as the primary objective. Language learning is ongoing. Teaching language in the context of science or mathematics is merely recognizing and utilizing a language situation that already exists.

The Teaching Cycle

Instruction begins with diagnostic assessment of children's abilities. Once the desired objectives have been identified, teachers need to know just where children are in relation to achieving those objectives in order to begin instruction at an appropriate point. There are several informal ways to determine children's strengths and weaknesses. Teachers often make important discoveries about children's abilities through casual day-by-day observations of their work and their attitudes toward what they do. In addition, more precise information may be gained by checking for specific skills in daily oral and written work, by giving informal tests, or by having children assess their own skills and abilities.

Assessment records are essential to the instructional cycle. It is virtually impossible to remember all that pertains to children's progress without writing it down. Anecdotal records, checklists, and class charts are some of the ways in which teachers keep track of children's progress. Some teachers, for example, maintain a file folder for each child. They carry a small pad with them and quickly jot down the child's name, the date, and pertinent information about the child's learning behaviors. These observations are filed, along with information from informal teacher-made tests. Such a file not only provides a record of children's progress over a period of time, but it often reveals patterns in the individual's unique learning process.

A lesson typically consists of three parts: *presentation*, *application* or study, and *summation*. In the first step the teacher sets the stage for learning and develops the concept. Frequently it involves separating a concept from its larger context for special attention (e.g., ''Yesterday we read a story in which the characters did a lot of talking. How did the writer show us the exact words the character said?''). In other instances the teacher may present a concept as an enabling activity (e.g., ''If you're going to write your mother a letter for Mother's Day, you'll have to know how to write a letter.''). Or in the case of literature the teacher might establish the background and vocabulary for a given story as a means of building interest in reading the story and facilitating the reading process.

The second part of a lesson involves helping children practice or use the concepts developed in the first part. Continuing the examples cited, children might write sentences in which they use direct quotations, write a letter in acceptable form, or read a story. It is a work time for children, with the teacher providing guidance or clarification as necessary and reteaching concepts to those children who need additional help.

The final step gives closure to the lesson and assesses learning. Summation may include an informal discussion of the questions raised during the introductory or work period or a carefully structured sequence of questions aimed at assessing children's understanding and comprehension. This step provides important direction for further instruction. If responses indicate that the children have accomplished the lesson objective(s), the teacher may feel that they are ready to go on to other concepts. If not, additional instructional activities may be planned for the next day. Sometimes an expansion of the activity, such as dramatizing, drawing, reading, or writing creatively may be deemed an appropriate followup activity.

Response and interaction are important elements of instruction. Throughout the teaching cycle teachers seek to involve children and promote interaction with concepts and ideas. They pose problems, elicit ideas, create a need to summarize and organize, and challenge children to evaluate. For example: ''How might an author reveal what a character is like without really telling?'' ''What else might the little boy have done?'' ''How many different scenes were there in the story? What were they?'' ''Are all the words spelled correctly in this paper?''

Grouping for Instruction: Within the School

Children may be grouped for instruction in several different ways. Which grouping to use is usually determined by considering the needs of children, the facilities — both space and materials available — and teachers' competencies and preferences. The organizational structure may provide for children to be grouped either homogeneously or heterogeneously and to be with one or more teachers during the day. Some possible grouping plans follow. They may be used alone or in combination with other plans.

Self-contained classroom The self-contained classroom is an organizational plan whereby one teacher and a group of children are together for the entire day. Teachers are responsible for the children's total learning experience and teach all areas of the curriculum. Children may be assigned to self-contained classrooms on the basis of age or ability.

The self-contained classroom allows maximum flexibility for comprehensive planning based on children's special abilities and needs. It enables teachers to get to know children well and to individualize instruction throughout the school day. Subjects may be integrated into larger units of study. Because of the breadth of school programs, however, such an approach requires teachers to have a wide range of expertise.

Ungraded classroom An ungraded classroom is much like a self-contained classroom with the exception that there is a planned range of ages among students. Six-, seven-, and eight-year-olds may all be assigned to one teacher for a year or more. One such plan places incoming first-graders with a teacher and an approximately even number of both second- and third-graders. At the end of the year the third-graders move on to an intermediate classroom, creating room for a new group of first-graders in the fall. Children remain with the same teacher for three (possibly even four) years. Part of the reasoning behind this plan is that it allows children to learn from each other and that it leads to greater individualization of instruction.

Joplin plan In the Joplin plan, children are regrouped for specific instruction on the basis of ability. For example, a school may assign children in the fifth and sixth grades to language arts classes according to their achievement test scores and teacher judgment. Thus, children of different ages and grade levels might be in the same class for the reading period.

This approach is intended to reduce the range of differences among children in a given class. However, children vary in many ways and hence will still need individualized help. Because the teachers work with each group of children for only one period of the day, it is difficult to integrate subject matter or to extend skill learning to other times of the day.

Departmentalization Teachers in the middle grades sometimes prefer to teach in a particular area of specialization. For example, one teacher might teach science classes to several groups of children, another might teach social studies, and another language arts. In this arrangement children move from teacher to teacher for each class just as they do in junior or senior high schools.

The advantage of this plan is in utilizing teachers' particular strengths and interests. Theoretically, children should receive better instruction when teachers teach in their area of expertise. Disadvantages include the possibility of lack of coordination of subject matter and developmental skill work throughout the day, and tendencies for departmental teachers to stress subject matter at the expense of accommodation to individual learning needs.

Team teaching Team teaching maintains the usual ratio of teachers to children, but it differs in that two or more teachers are assigned to one larger group of children. This approach permits flexibility in regrouping and working with children within a classroom. One teacher may supervise a large number of children during a recreational reading time while another works with a small group of children on a particular skill. For team teaching to be effective the teachers involved must get to know a large number of children and must work together closely to coordinate their teaching efforts.

Grouping for Instruction: Within the Classroom

Once class groups have been determined, children are usually grouped within the classroom for instructional purposes. Efficient use of a teacher's time suggests that children who share learning objectives be taught as a group rather than individually. The teacher thus avoids repeating the same instruction for each child. In addition, children are stimulated by interactions with their peers and learn from each other. Some common types of groups are defined in the following paragraphs. Several of these groups may be found in a classroom at the same time. For example, some children from an achievement group may be placed in a needs group to work on a particular skill, yet remain members of the larger group.

Whole class Many learning activities lend themselves to total class participation. Storytelling or reading stories aloud, drama, creative writing, film viewing, and choral speaking are examples. For such activities, larger groups are a distinct asset. They enhance enjoyment by creating a corporate air of anticipation and offering a wider range of interpretation. At the same time, large groups are inappropriate in activities requiring a great deal of individual help at different levels of ability.

Achievement groups Children at similar levels of achievement may be grouped for certain activities. For example, three or more spelling groups may be organized to facilitate the use of appropriate teaching strategies and materials. Children who are already good spellers then work with more challenging lists of words and engage in advanced enrichment activities. Poorer spellers can be given fewer words and have many experiences in using words in context to promote transfer of learning.

Needs groups Children with similar needs may be grouped together for concentrated instruction and practice. Needs groups may help children learn to write letters, to capitalize, to find words in a dictionary, or to use the telephone. As soon as children have reached the target set for the group they leave it, and ultimately the group disbands.

Interest groups Children who share interests may form a group to study and discuss information and work together on activities. For example, a number of children may collect poems about sports and periodically get together to read and discuss the poems they each enjoy. A group of children may form a book club in which each child reads the same book and then participates in a round-table discussion. Or, some children may decide to work together to make a roller movie of a story that the teacher has read to the class. An interest group may be formed for a specified period of time or it may continue to meet until its objective is realized.

Group or individual projects Sometimes one child or a small group of children have goals or interests that are not shared by other members of the class. When this situation occurs, provision may be made for those children to pursue a study or project independently. Independent study entails careful planning to delineate the scope and sequence of the project and requires frequent checkpoints to assess progress. An example of this type of activity might be recording daily observations of a classroom pet or engaging in a research project about famous women.

Classroom Management

A well-organized classroom gives children a secure base of operation. They know what is expected and can get on with the task of learning. However, organization need not imply a rigid schedule and a quiet classroom. Rather, it suggests the need to plan adequately for activities. Space, time, and materials must be considered as well as the skills and concepts children are to be taught. Areas of the room may be designated for different kinds of activities. One corner may be used for exhibits and displays that are likely to generate conversation and discussion, another area may be used for silent reading, and another for art or other work activities. Such planning of space allows children to carry on a range of appropriate activities without disturbing others or being disturbed themselves.

Planning how time is to be spent helps children develop expectancies and learn to use their time productively. When they know they have a certain amount of time to complete a task they work with a purpose and become more efficient in using their time. Careful planning is necessary to ensure that all the components of the language arts are included in the program. Thus, timing must be flexible to accommodate different kinds of activities without eliminating others. When a large block of time is needed for preparing and sharing stories, for example, other skill activities must be shortened. Then, when the sharing activities are completed, the skills are given greater time and emphasis. How the teacher's time is to be spent must also be considered so that all children have their share of direct instruction and teacher interaction.

Thorough planning includes having materials ready when they are needed. Books, papers, films, and projectors ought to be secured well in advance of a lesson to ensure that they will be available at the appropriate time. The management of materials is also important. It includes planning an efficient way to distribute and collect materials (e.g., assignments) and finding ways to minimize ineffective uses of materials (e.g., overuse of worksheets).

In planning the teacher should seek a balance between receptive activities (reading, listening, viewing) and expressive activities (talking, writing, dramatizing, painting, etc.). He or she should also consider children's need for alternating amounts of physical activity. Periods of sustained quiet activities such as reading or writing need to be interspersed with physical movement to provide a change of pace and mental relaxation. Creative dramatics, music, art, and physical education provide breaks in paper-oriented activities. It is a good idea to have some action songs, finger plays, choral verse, riddles, or mental puzzles ready when children need a brief moment of diversion or when there are a few minutes between scheduled activities. Thorough yet flexible planning contributes to a functional and satisfying learning experience and results in a minimum of discipline problems.

Teaching Resources

Materials

A wide variety of materials is available in the language arts area. Some are designed for direct teacher instruction and others are intended to be used independently by children. The possible use and value of any of these materials depends on the objectives of a given lesson and the level and background of the learner. Whether materials for independent learning or direct instruction are "best" depends on the classroom organization and the learning styles and needs of the children involved.

To use materials effectively, teachers need to become thoroughly familiar with them. They need to know the scope and the level of the materials and how the materials were designed to be used. With this background, teachers will often be able to adapt materials effectively for children's specific learning needs. Let us look at some common types of materials.

Textbooks Sets of language arts textbooks and workbooks are available in most classrooms. These books are sequentially developed by levels to provide what is considered to be a basic program in the language arts. Language arts textbooks generally reflect the cooperative efforts of a team of competent teachers and writers. The lessons offer a sequence of structured learning activities intended to develop a range of language arts competencies and appreciations. Often the lessons have been developed and field-tested with elementary schoolchildren in a variety of settings.

By their very nature, textbooks place more emphasis on specific skills and on language conventions to be learned than on expressive activities. The teacher must be ready to plan dramatics, writing, discussions, and other expressive activities in addition to textbook lessons.

In selecting and using a textbook, teachers need to keep in mind that no one book, not even a good one, will fill the needs of all children. A textbook should not be allowed to become the language arts program but should be regarded as a teaching tool. Selection and use of a textbook requires careful examination to determine whether the scope and sequence of the skills and concepts presented complements the needs of children and the established program goals and objectives of the school. With careful selection, a "best fit" may be found and then supplemented with additional materials as necessary.

Supplementary books and other print materials Library books, workbooks, skill books, and activity books of all kinds are available to supplement materials found in adopted textbooks. Various other separate booklets are available for developing specific skills (e.g., those designed to be used in creative writing and those for teaching study skills).

Library books offer many possibilities for expanding vocabulary and other skills and appreciations. These are books for all interests and all levels of ability. Wide reading improves children's thinking and conceptualization and helps them develop a general awareness of the relationship and structure of ideas. Quality books acquaint children with good expository and creative writing and help them develop a cognitive framework for self-expression.

Newspapers and magazines also offer possibilities for teaching the language arts. With the exception of a few such materials designed specifically for children's use in schools, the use of most of these materials depends on the creativity and resourcefulness of the classroom teacher. For example: Paragraphs from articles may be cut up into separate sentences for children to organize and arrange into paragraphs again. Children may look for words in headlines or titles that describe sounds, objects, people, places, or feelings. They may look for words containing certain roots or having certain inflected endings. They may look for words that follow a particular spelling pattern or that begin with a particular letter. They may listen while the teacher reads, to discover specific uses of words or for certain kinds of information. A supply of newspapers and magazines in the classroom stimulates reading and oral discussion. They present an open invitation to children to explore many current topics. They also encourage children to be curious and thoughtful learners.

Multimedia materials A wide range of multimedia resources is available commercially to supplement print materials in the classroom. Television programs, slides, films, recordings, the overhead projector, and various kinds of games offer many possibilities for varying instruction and developing meaningful concepts. Many of these materials include an instructional plan specifically designed for use by teachers. Before using one of these materials, however, teachers need to judge its value for a particular learning situation. By carefully selecting materials that are appropriate to the teacher's learning objectives and the level of the learners involved, teachers may effectively utilize the materials to motivate children and to enrich their learning experience.

Teacher-made materials Creative teachers devise many clever learning aids to use in their classrooms. Such aids range from specific skill worksheets to innovative games and teaching devices. Old socks become hand puppets, the carton from a new mattress becomes a game board that first-graders can actually sit or walk on, plastic egg cartons hold letters for spelling games, and the attics of friends yield interesting old clothes to turn a child into a wicked witch or into a rugged pioneer. Teacher-made materials are limited only by the imagination and time of the teacher. A few moments to ponder the learning needs of children or a concept that is to be developed is often all it takes to generate creative approaches to learning.

Evaluation of Materials

All learning materials need to be carefully evaluated in terms of the objectives of language arts program. Before textbooks or other materials are purchased, they should be carefully scrutinized to determine the appropriateness of their use in a particular school setting. One should consider, for example, the philosophy, content, readability, organization, and physical attributes of the material, and the teaching aids and suggestions. The sample evaluation form in Table 13-1 suggests possible points to consider in selecting or using textbooks and other materials.

TABLE 13-1 EVALUATION OF LANGUAGE ARTS MATERIALS

Philosophy

The material	Excellent	Poor
is compatible with knowledge of children's language development.		
can be adapted to individual interests, needs, and abilities of children.		
provides for continuous and well-rounded growth in using and enjoying language.		

Content

The material

	Excellent	Poor
is appropriate in range and level of concepts.		
has well-defined learning objectives.		
uses a developmental approach.		
is intellectually stimulating.		
utilizes subject matter of interest to children.		
offers supplementary and enrichment activities.		
provides variety in the types of learning activities.		
is free from bias.		

Readability

The material

	Excellent	Poor
uses appropriate vocabulary and syntax.		
uses an interesting and appropriate writing style.		
is printed in type that is clear and easy to read.		

TABLE 13-1 EVALUATION OF LANGUAGE ARTS MATERIALS (*continued*)

Organization

The material

is systematically organized.   _____

has an adequate index and table of contents.   _____

contains effective visual organization cues (boldface
type, symbols, etc.).   _____

Physical Attributes

The material

is durable.   _____

is generally attractive.   _____

has a variety of appealing illustrations.   _____

uses an appropriate size and style of print.   _____

Teaching Aids and Suggestions

The material

includes adequate explanation of the format and
philosophy.   _____

includes appropriate background information.   _____

includes suggestions for adapting materials to
children's individual needs.   _____

includes suggestions for integrating concepts into
other areas of the curriculum.   _____

includes helpful references and resource materials.   _____

includes evaluation procedures.   _____

Auxiliary Personnel

Specialists, teacher aides, and volunteers are important personnel
resources for teachers. Wherever language arts specialists or other
trained personnel are a part of the school staff, they may be called in
for consultation and help in developing programs or in working with
individual children. In some schools teacher aides are employed to
help with some of the "behind-the-scenes" work of teaching. Sometimes, too, parents or other adults in the community are willing to
donate their time to help at school. These volunteers are often talented and highly capable individuals who simply enjoy spending a
few hours regularly in the school. Examples of the kinds of tasks they

may volunteer to do include playing the piano, typing, making games and other instructional aids, preparing bulletin boards, helping individuals or small groups, talking and listening to children, and sharing interesting experiences.

Before volunteers and other untrained people are ready to perform tasks in the school, they need to know exactly what they are to do and they need to be trained in the proper procedures and techniques. Adequate preparation is important if children are to benefit from the efforts of volunteers and the volunteers themselves are to feel good about their contribution.

Electronic Technology in the Classroom

Shane (1982) identifies four distinct revolutions in the history of human communication. The first was the development of complex human speech; the second, the development of writing; the third, the invention of the printing press; and the last, what he refers to as the *silicon chip revolution.* He explains, "Although the telegraph, telephone, and radio play an important role, not until the last decade has our globe begun to become a 'wired planet' — an information society created by the microchip" (p. 303).

The technological advances to which Shane refers, though still in their infancy, seem to offer limitless possibilities for information gathering, processing, storing, and use. It is staggering to realize that things not even imagined as recently as ten years ago are today a reality. Furthermore, if this trend continues, what is new today is likely to be outdated tomorrow. Nevertheless, the effect of electronic technology has clearly begun to be felt in our public school classrooms and it is almost certain to play an increasing role in instruction.

In order to keep up with the changing influence of technology on the classroom, teachers can contact an educational software company or subscribe to a computer periodical geared toward the teacher.

Educational Software Companies

Educational Software, P.O. Box 746, McMinnville, OR 97128.

Microdynamics Educational Systems, Inc., 2360 S.W. 170th Ave., Beaverton, OR 97005.

MicroMedia, Inc., P.O. Box 17, Valley Cottage, NY 10989.

Milliken Publishing Co., 1100 Research Blvd., St. Louis, MO 63132.

Opportunities for Learning, Inc., 8950 Lurline Ave., Dept. 26C, Chatsworth, CA 91311.

Computer Periodicals for Teachers

Calculators and Computers Magazine. Published by Dymas, P.O. Box 310, Menlo Park, CA 94025.

The Computing Teacher. Published by The Department of Computer and Information Science, University of Oregon, Eugene, OR 97403.

Electronic Learning. Published by Scholastic Inc., 50 West 44th St., New York, NY 10036. Communications relating to subscriptions to: Electronic Learning, 902 Sylvan Ave., Englewood Cliffs, NJ 07632.

Instructional Innovator. Published by The Association for Educational Communications and Technology, 1126 Sixteenth St., NW, Washington, DC 20036.

Popular Computing. Published by BYTE Publications, Inc., 70 Main St., Peterborough, NH 03458. Communications relating to subscriptions to: Popular Computing, P.O. Box 307, Martinsville, NJ 08836.

Microcomputers

Microcomputers are currently making their way into classrooms at a rapid rate. A number of language arts programs are available, and more are being developed. Software, the term for computer programs, generally come in one of three instructional forms: drill and practice, tutorial, or simulations. Drill and practice programs provide specific practice in basic skills. Their primary use is to diagnose children's errors and provide needed practice. Tutorials teach concepts. Through carefully sequenced steps, children respond and receive feedback. In addition to telling them whether or not their response was correct, the computer may also include an explanation of why the response was right or wrong. Children are then directed to the next activity. If their response was incorrect they will be given additional activities at the same level until they demonstrate mastery of that step. If their response was correct they will be told to proceed to the next step in the learning sequence. The graphic capability of computer programs permits instruction to include drawings and other illustrations as well as words on the screen. Simulations allow children to solve problems and manipulate variables that are not ordinarily available to them in the classroom. Although many simulation programs focus on social science or science content, the functional and creative uses of language are an integral part of the simulations and may be explored to advantage.

Programs may be put directly into a computer by typing the information on the special keyboard. This approach does, however, assume knowledge of both programming procedures and computer language. Also, since storage capacity is limited, only a certain number of programs can be kept for future use (depending on the length of the program and the particular computer). Other input systems include the cassette tape recorder and the disk drive. Programs may be stored on a casette tape, and then by typing a few simple commands, the program is sent from the tape to the computer for processing. The disk drive functions in a similar way. The device plays a floppy disk somewhat similar to the way in which a record player plays a record. Programs are stored on the disk and then sent into the computer. Commercially developed language arts programs are available in both forms.

Microcomputer programs are relatively easy to use and are highly motivational for children. As they work through a program, children tend to respond to the computer as to another person. They often talk back to it in a conversational mode. Some programs are designed to include children's names in accepting and responding to their input. For example, the computer may print, "That's right, Mary." or "That was hard, wasn't it Mark!" But whether or not children respond to the computer overtly, it elicits a flow of internal speech

Software for classroom use must be carefully selected to serve educational purposes. Many available computer programs were not designed for schools and have little if any educational value. Even programs specifically designed for school use may be seriously flawed. *Electronic Learning* (vol. 1, 1981) lists the following criteria for quality software.

Software should
1. Be free of technical or pedagogical errors.
2. Take advantage of the machine's unique capabilities without substituting flash for substance.
3. Provide positive reinforcement, and, at the same time, help students to understand wrong answers.
4. Include some diagnostic and branching features.
5. Be creative, stimulating creativity among users.
6. Allow for easy teacher modification.
7. Provide clearly written support materials and activities. (p. 34)

Word Processors

The word processor offers one of the most interesting innovations in today's world of technology. It allows the writer to delete or add words, sentences, or paragraphs; rearrange the order of sentences or paragraphs; or correct typographical and spelling errors through the use of simple "commands" to the computer. Other possible changes include making margins wider or smaller, changing the spacing between lines, and adding or deleting headings. When the copy that appears on the screen satisfies the writer, the text can be printed on paper.

A word-processing computer makes it easy to correct mistakes, and the professional-looking print seems to add to children's interest in writing. They not only write longer compositions, but they revise more. Research indicates that "writers tend to do more experimenting and rewriting. While young children generally focus on insert and delete options, older students appreciate the capacity for moving sentences and sections of text around" (Daiute, 1982, p. 30).

The possibilities for using computers in the classroom are mind-stretching. What is only thought about today may be commonplace tomorrow. Daiute suggests that "writing on the computer may actually change the nature of writing, as voice typewriters are introduced. The writer will talk into the computer and then receive a hard copy (a print out) instantly. It remains to be seen, though, whether writers prefer producing written words from a silent voice or a spoken one" (1980, p. 31). Only through continued use can we gain insights about the computer's long-range value. Questions to be answered include whether currently reported results are primarily attributable to the novelty of computers, whether the use of computers requires a modification of the writing process, and whether skills developed at the computer are transferable to writing on paper.

Videodiscs

Videodiscs have been hailed as the most important teaching tool since the book. Wallman (1981) describes it well: "The disc player itself is a table-top device that, when attached to a TV set, plays video programs that are stored on record-like 12-inch discs, capable of reproducing both picture and sound. Each disc can hold 54,000 picture frames of information (about 900 slide carousels' worth), making the disc the densest form of information storage available" (p. 39).

Videodiscs are available in two formats, and a third is expected to be available soon. The capacitance electronic disc (CED) system uses a stylus to pick up audio and visual information stored in the grooves of the disc. The optical system stores information on a flat, grooveless metal disc, which is then read by a laser beam. A video high density system is scheduled in the near future.

A videodisc offers highly individualized learning. It may be either slowed down or "frozen" on a particular picture for careful study. When hooked up to a microcomputer, the system becomes an interactive learning center. Wallman explains, "The computer-controlled videodisc has the 'intelligence' to move ahead with new material if a student answers a question correctly or automatically go to a point on the disc which gives remedial instruction when the response is wrong" (p. 40). Assuming that appropriate programs are available for a given child, the immediate feedback and error remediation of this system seem to make it a highly desirable way to augment the limited instructional time presently possible in most classrooms.

Television

Although the effect of commercial television on children remains unclear, the fact that children spend large amounts of time viewing television has been well established. Singer, Singer, and Zuckerman report, "The average number of hours spent viewing television varies from about 3 hours a day for preschoolers to 5 hours a day for elementary school-aged children. We also know that poor and black children spend even more time — approximately 5½ to 6 hours per day — before the television set" (1981*b*, p. 19).

Many concerns are voiced about the time children sit in front of a television set. Of primary concern is the realization that televiewing is a spectator sport; it requires only passive listening to programs that are aimed at an impersonal "anyone" audience. Little if any cognitive demands are placed on the viewer. Whatever is learned is by absorption rather than through interaction. What children do learn from television is often clouded by misconceptions and stereotypic thinking. To combat the adverse effects of television and to make viewing time a more positive learning experience, teachers need to teach *about* television and challenge children to become interactive viewers.

Teaching television literacy involves developing consumer awareness. One of the problems children have is in separating reality and fantasy in programs. Things that could never happen are presented realistically on the screen. Time is also distorted. One group of sixth-graders who spent a half-day in an actual courtroom were amazed at what really happened in a trial and were bored by the slow pace of the proceedings. Their frame of reference came solely from experiences with television in which complete trials were cleverly presented and neatly wrapped up in an hour's time. Children need to understand both the constraints on television programming (e.g., the need to give audiences the kind of entertainment they want, fitting programs into allocated time slots, and telecasting to a nonresponsive audience) and the illusory potential of television (e.g., using unusual camera angles, fading images in and out, and zooming in on a small part of an image). A trip to a television studio to watch an actual filming is excellent. If that is not possible, you might discuss how much of what the children have seen could really have happened and hypothesize how technicians were able to create the illusions.

Learning about commercials is another important aspect of television literacy. As in other forms of propaganda, commercials employ a range of persuasive techniques to sell products. Among these are testimonials by well-known people or "just plain folks" (like you and me), card-stacking (half-truths and omissions), and bandwagon psychology (everyone else uses this). Touting the superiority of one product over another, particularly the nutritional value of food, is a favorite scheme.

McGarvey (1980) suggests a simple TV Advertising Test to help children become aware of the techniques advertisers use. Once children begin to notice the subtleties of advertising (*virtually* spotless, *see* how luxurious hair *feels*), they collect and analyze other commercials to become more aware of advertising fallacies. Singer, Singer, and Zuckerman (1981*b*) also point out the effect of the context in which products are presented (e.g., happy people make the product seem like fun) as well as the use of catchy advertising jingles that cause people to remember products.

On the more positive side, television exposes children to language not used in their community. Thus it contributes to the development of larger vocabularies and expanded sentence patterns. In addition it can be used as a motivational force and as a source of information. Winkeljohann reports that "librarians all over the country were swamped with children the next day after Fonzie got a library card in an episode of Happy Days" (1981, p. 100). Programs such as the "Little House on the Prairie" series have been a common motivator. Many teachers have used the Little House series as a springboard to further reading of Laura Ingalls Wilder's books or to a study of pioneer life. Special programs about the universe, outer space, or the human body have prompted extensive discussion, reading, and writing.

Television stories can be used in many ways. For example, they can be used to develop an understanding of literary genre. Children can analyze the design and key elements of stories they watch on television and then categorize the stories by types. Comparisons are then made with types of stories children have read, such as fables, myths, fairy tales, and science fiction. Once defined, the story form can be used as the model for writing an original story. Another activity is to write a sequel or another episode for a current television story.

Learning Centers

Learning centers are just what the name implies, centers or designated areas where children go to learn. Kaplan, Kaplan, Madsen, and Taylor define a learning center as "an area in the classroom which contains a collection of activities and materials to teach, reinforce, and/or enrich a skill or concept" (1973, p. 21). Physically, the learning center may be a table pushed against a wall, a large carton cut to create a folding screen with pockets glued to it, a big box on the floor, or a lovely corner fixed up as a miniroom with a rug and comfortable tables and chairs. It is possible to improvise learning centers in nearly any spare space with little more than scrounged materials and a creative teacher. If possible, there should be enough space for children to actually work in the center. When that isn't possible, an alternate plan is for children to make their selections from the center and then take the materials back to their desks.

Learning centers focus on a particular skill or concept. They contain several activities (five is considered a bare minimum) such as worksheets, puzzles, activity cards, audio-visual aids, posters, and charts to help children attain certain objectives. Some learning centers, particularly those which focus on specific skills, require a sequence of activities so that the child can work through the sequence in a developmental manner. Other types of centers offer a variety of ungraded activities from which children may make personal choices. Whenever possible, activities should either be self-correcting (e.g., color-coded, numbered, etc.) or have keys available so that children can correct their own work. Some teachers have one child designated to check all the work and record the activities completed by each child on a master chart.

A step-by-step procedure for preparing a learning center follows.

1. Identify the concept(s) or skill(s) to be developed in the center.

2. Select a title or label for the center (a catchy one if you can think of one).

3. Collect and make a variety of activities for the center, including answer keys whenever possible.

4. If sequence is important, label the activities in the order in which they are to be completed.

5. Determine how many children may work in the center at one time and decide how groups will be determined (a sign-up sheet or appointment).

6. Devise a record-keeping system for keeping track of each child's activities.

7. Prepare a chart or card giving specific directions for using the center.

8. Arrange the materials center attractively: title, activities and answer keys, supplies, directions for use, and record chart.

9. Introduce the center to the children by explaining how, when, and by whom it is to be used.

It is best to begin with only one or two learning centers at first and then gradually develop additional ones. If a particular center (e.g., a listening center) is to be used continually, activities must be added or changed from time to time to keep it fresh and interesting. Many centers serve their purpose in a few weeks and need to be completely replaced with another center.

Integrating the Language Arts

Language is a part of all that we think or do. It is learned during various activities and is not limited to instruction parceled out on a given schedule. Learning to listen, talk, read, and write always involves *something* — some content to listen, talk, read, or write about. A course labeled art or science, then, is an ideal setting in which to learn to use language more effectively.

An integrated approach capitalizes on the centrality of language. Skills are developed in a natural way, as part of an ongoing project. Suppose, for example, a class (of any age) is studying career awareness in social studies. To gather information, they will read (or have read to them) books and other materials; they will interview parents, friends, and business and professional people; and they will view films and television. As a final project they will contribute short reports to a "Careers" book and collaborate in making a roller movie to be presented to other classes. Each day spent on the unit would involve purposeful, integrated uses of language such as *listening* for information, to compare, evaluate, and plan; *talking* with peers and adults, explaining, and reporting; *writing* lists, notes, letters, outlines, summaries, reports, and scripts; and *reading* signs, brochures, newspapers, magazines, and books. Skill would be taught throughout the unit whenever needed.

This approach does not preclude the formal teaching of a particular skill to a group or to the whole class. If, for example, children have had little or no experience in interviewing, a carefully sequenced lesson designed to meet specific objectives would certainly be appropriate for the entire class. On the other hand, if only a few children were unfamiliar with using the telephone, small-group instruction for those children would be indicated.

An integrated instructional model for the language arts requires careful planning and implementation. The teaching of skills cannot be left to chance. Skills to be taught must be clearly defined and consciously included in setting-up activities. Because learning follows a less formal structure, teachers must be diligent in assessing what children are able to do well and what they need to ensure maximum growth.

Evaluation of Children's Progress

Evaluation is an essential component of the instructional program. Through evaluation teachers become aware of children's strengths and weaknesses so that they can plan appropriate learning experiences for them. Evaluation also provides a measurement of children's progress. It can take different forms to serve different purposes. Teachers may be evaluating when they observe children at work, casually listen to children's comments, ask informal questions, check written work, administer a teacher-made or published test, or engage children in self-evaluation assessment. Evaluation in some form should be continual.

Evaluation falls loosely into one of two categories: formal and informal. In a formal evaluation program one uses scientifically constructed tests, usually developed commercially, which are administered regularly according to a particular schedule or plan. Informal evaluation, on the other hand, includes the use of a range of less sophisticated tests and other assessment techniques from day to day as a part of the instructional cycle.

The Formal Testing Program

In many schools the formal testing program consists of administering batteries of commercially published tests. Sometimes it may also include tests that have been developed locally. The tests used depend on the purpose for testing. Some tests are designed to measure children's general level of achievement, whereas others are diagnostic and yield more specific information.

Achievement tests Achievement tests are standardized tests designed to assess children's general achievement in specified areas (e.g., reading, language arts, mathematics). Before achievement tests are published they are carefully standardized to ensure validity and reliability. National norms are also established for translating children's raw scores into age or grade levels. This translation is done by administering the test to large numbers of children in various parts of the United States. Data from all the test scores are then treated statistically to establish *norms,* or normal distribution patterns of children's scores. These norms provide a yardstick for measuring the achievement level of subsequent children who take the test. The term *norm-referenced* refers to the practice of comparing children's scores to the norms established for the test.

The primary purpose for administering norm-referenced achievement tests is to quantify progress levels of groups of children. More specific information can, of course, be determined by delving into children's responses to individual items. Test information is most frequently used, however, for such things as assessing individual growth over a period of time, comparing a child's achievement level with that of others in the class, comparing one class with another, or determining school or district levels of achievement by age or grade group. The administration of standardized achievement tests permits a school to describe individual and group achievement in terms of the norming population for the test.

Diagnostic tests Diagnostic tests are designed to assess children's strengths and reveal their weaknesses. The primary purpose of a diagnostic test is to identify the skills children have and have not acquired. Although some diagnostic tests may be norm-referenced, such information is apt to be of secondary importance. Generally, a diagnostic test is administered to measure children's skill level as an aid to instruction. The results are usually stated in terms of certain standards or criteria.

Criterion-referenced tests Criterion-referenced tests compare a child's performance to a standard of performance, rather than to the performance of other children. They grew out of the nationwide attention to competency-based education. The concept of *competency-based education* requires children to demonstrate mastery of certain knowledge, skills, and abilities deemed important to their educational experience. It emphasizes children's individual mastery of each competency in terms of specifically stated criteria. Thus criterion-based tests indicate whether children meet the competencies at a uniform level.

Informal Tests

Informal testing includes a variety of nonstandardized measures. These measures range from a weekly list of spelling words to a teacher-made test of punctuation skills. Most informal tests are directly related to specific instruction, and as such are important components of an ongoing language arts program. Some tests are designed to be used before instruction is begun to determine children's placement and need. Others are given at the end of a unit of work to assess children's learning.

Teacher-made tests can serve several functions. They provide a measure of children's knowledge or skills. They suggest concepts and skills that need to be taught or retaught. They also provide feedback to teachers regarding the effectiveness of instructional materials and techniques. Ideally all test errors would be analyzed with an eye to determining why children made particular errors. This would provide important information for planning further instruction and remediation.

The Value of Tests

Although language arts tests yield important information about children's progress, testing is not without its problems and concerns. In selecting or using test instruments to assess children's abilities in the language arts, it is important to understand what is measured by the tests and to be aware of the problems inherent in formal assessment. Typical achievements test items in the language arts include word-recognition skills, vocabulary, and comprehension in reading; capitalization; punctuation; spelling; usage; parts of speech; sentence structure; and reference skills. Unfortunately, many aspects of language, particularly those pertaining to oral language skills and those attitudes and values classified in the affective domain, are not measurable through ordinary testing procedures. They are important, however, and ought to be a part of a language arts program. When they are not part of the assessment program they often lose instructional emphasis. Some of these abilities and attitudes must develop over a period of time. Others simply do not lend themselves to paper-and-pencil tests. Loban states his concern,

> Emphasis on oral language development is essential to any reformed curriculum. An important reason for its present neglect is the complete absence of oral language in all language testing whether it be college

entrance examinations or elementary school testing. Yet, oral language, by its very nature, cannot be reduced to paper and pencil tests, nor do we know of any variables, amenable to paper and pencil testing, which correlate with oral language power. (1976, p. 46)

The content of achievement tests for the language arts — *what* is measured — raises serious questions about the validity of using the scores as the measure of children's language proficiency. For example, children who are unfamiliar with test-taking procedures are at a distinct disadvantage. Test items may also be culturally biased. What is measured in a standardized test — the range of assessment — tends to be restrictive in comparison to children's actual use of language in functional settings. There is obviously much more to language development than these tests are able to measure. However, it is recognized that assessing and quantifying certain aspects of skills, abilities, and attitudes pose a genuine problem. Because of the difficulties, it is essential to recognize the limitations of language arts tests and to interpret scores appropriately.

Evaluation of the Language Arts Program

Evaluation of the total language arts program is essential to effective teaching and learning. By stepping back and looking at the whole program objectively you can identify a program's strengths and weaknesses, which otherwise might be overlooked. Program evaluation goes beyond the assessment of children's specific skills and abilities. It does, of course, include those findings, but only in the perspective of the whole program.

Deciding *what* to assess is the first step in program evaluation. The stated goals and objectives that underlie the program provide a good starting point. They delineate the program and provide a framework for ongoing evaluation. They inherently contain the philosophy of the program and identify what it is that children are expected to learn. Further evaluation ought to focus on *how* learning is accomplished. It would include assessment of teaching procedures, facilities, and resources (both of material and personnel). Ultimately, evaluation ought to attend to any facet of the teaching and learning situation that might in some way influence the program's effectiveness.

Specific evaluation criteria will, of course, vary with the program and setting. The following list of questions suggests possible criteria.

1. Does the program guide children to a concept of language as being alive, interesting, and functional?

2. Does the program recognize the importance of oral language development as the basis for other language competencies?

3. Is the program developed from an experiential (concrete) base?

4. Are children working toward stated goals and objectives?

5. Does the program provide a continuum of learning so that children can progress at their own rates?

6. Does the program provide opportunities for developing competency in both receptive and expressive language skills?

7. Are children's strengths and weaknesses being continually evaluated?

8. Does the program provide for instruction in specific language skills?

9. Are adequate and up-to-date records of children's progress maintained?

10. Are there many opportunities to practice skillful use of language in practical situations?

11. Does the program stimulate children's thinking and foster creative uses of language?

12. Does the program foster enjoyment and appreciation of language?

13. Are the quantity and quality of material resources adequate to meet the needs of children at various levels of development?

14. Are resources, both of material and personnel, used creatively and effectively?

15. Are parents aware of the program's goals and objectives, and are they kept informed about their children's progress?

16. Is the program flexible and subject to change whenever change is indicated to better meet the needs of children?

Once the pertinent aspects of a language arts program have been defined for evaluation, the next step is to seek out evidence to determine how well the program meets the criteria. In informal and ongoing evaluation, teachers continually watch for children's reactions to various learning materials and situations. They note any inconsistencies or problems and keep track of them. They analyze available resources and materials to determine their adequacy and most appropriate use. As they consider their observations as a whole, they see strengths and weaknesses of the program. As soon as a weakness becomes evident, teachers take steps to remediate the problem as expediently as possible. When time is required to effect change (e.g., for budget items or outside resources), existing conditions are adjusted as much as possible to maximize learning.

Evaluation should not focus on weaknesses to the exclusion of a program's strengths, however. Successful program components are perhaps even more important, because they indicate what works well and thus they may serve as models for other effective practices. *Exceptional programs* develop and grow by expanding and adding to *good programs*.

In Summary

A well-planned language arts program gives direction to teaching and learning. Such a statement suggests the need for long-range planning to identify goals that children should be expected to achieve over a period of time. In addition, it involves identifying the component skills, abilities, and attitudes that make achievement of the goals possible. Once this framework has been established, teachers have a clearer view of what children need to learn and can set about planning developmental learning activities. How well children learn is governed by natural laws or principles of learning. Among these are: (1) children learn in different ways and at different rates; (2) learning is developmental; (3) learning is more efficient when it is meaningful; (4) motivation affects how well children learn; and (5) to be retained, learning must be reinforced.

Children may be grouped for instruction in different ways. Frequently they are assigned to self-contained classrooms in which the same teacher remains with a group of children for all subjects. Children may be assigned to a self-contained classroom on the basis of either age or ability. An ungraded classroom is similar but has a wider range of ages and abilities. Ungraded classrooms usually include children from two to three grade or age levels. In the Joplin plan, children are regrouped by ability level for specific subjects or blocks of time. Other grouping possibilities include departmentalizing for instruction and team teaching. Once children have been assigned a classroom for all or part of the day, they may then be taught as a whole group, or regrouped according to achievement, need or interest, or for a special project.

Instructional resources include textbooks, supplementary workbooks, library books, newspapers, magazines, slides, films, recordings, and learning games. Often, community volunteers or teacher aides are available to gather or make materials and assist children in using them. The newest teaching materials are associated with electronic technology. Though this field is still in its infancy, many classrooms now have access to microcomputers and other electronic learning aids. Learning centers may be set up for individualizing instruction. Organization of time and resources is essential for a smoothly running classroom. Children need to have clearly established objectives for each activity and to know how to use learning resources effectively.

The language arts teacher ought to be sensitive to children with special needs and individualize activities as necessary to facilitate children's learning. The teacher would consider the needs of children who are physically handicapped, mentally handicapped, emotionally handicapped, economically limited, and ethnically different. Children who are gifted and creative also need an individualized program that is purposeful and challenging for them.

Evaluation of the language program is essential. Such assessment depends on clearly identified criteria. Aspects of the program that ought to be considered include the achievement of major goals and objectives; teaching effectiveness; and the adequacy and use of resources, both material and human. Ultimately, evaluation of an existing program identifies the strong features of the program, which may in turn be used as the base for further program planning and development.

Suggestions for Further Reading

Forte, Imogene, and Mary Anne Pangle. *More Center Stuff*. Nashville, Tenn.: Incentive Publications, 1976.

Denham, Carolyn, and Ann Lieberman, *Time to Learn*. Washington, D.C.: The National Institute of Education, 1980.

Larson, Carl, Phil Backlund, Mark Redmond, and Alton Barbour. *Assessing Functional Communication*. Urbana, Ill.: Clearinghouse on Reading and Communication Skills, 1978.

Mager, Robert F. *Preparing Instructional Objectives*. Palo Alto, Calif.: Fearon, 1962.

Mandel, Barrett J., ed. *Three Language-Arts Curriculum Models: Pre-Kindergarten through College*. Urbana, Ill.: National Council of Teachers of English, 1980.

Sleisenger, Lenore, and Joyce Lancaster. *Guidebook for the Volunteer Reading Teacher*. Thorofare, N.J.: Charles B. Slack, 1979.

Appendix A
Selected Multimedia Resources

The following is a partial listing of multimedia materials that may be used in teaching and learning the language arts. The code given in parentheses after each item indicates its possible use.

Code:

CW — creative writing
DR — creative drama
LN — study of language
LS — listening
LT — children's literature
OL — oral language development
PO — poetry
PP — puppets
SS — specific skills
ST — storytelling
RD — reading
WR — writing

FILMS

American Tall Tale Heroes. Coronet. 15 minutes, color, grades 3–8. (LT, ST, CR, D)
 Features adventures of Stormalong, Paul Bunyan, John Henry, and Pecos Bill.

Arrow to the Sun. Texture Films. 12 minutes, color, grades 3–7. (LT, DR, ST)
 Based on the book by the same title. Acoma Pueblo Indian tale about a boy's search for his father, the Lord of the Sun, and his return to earth to spread the Sun's warmth.

The Baggs. Film Fair Communications. 12 minutes, color, grades 1–6. (OL, CW)
 A nonnarrative fantasy about two sacks of junk that come alive and escape from their collector.

Buttercup. Churchill Films. 11 minutes, color, all ages. (CR, OL, DR, ST)
 A buttercup starts out in a clear stream and floats downstream into a polluted industrial area.

Communications: A First Film. Bailey Films. 9 minutes, color, grades 1–3. (LN)
 Discusses the importance of communication and the mass media. Shows how communication involves the use of symbols — music, designs, numbers, colors, written and spoken words.

Creative Writing, A Series. Churchill Films. 4 films of 16 minutes each, color, grades 3–6. (CW)
 Involves audience in creative thinking and writing along with demonstration class on the films.

The Deer and the Forest: A Story Without Words. Encyclopaedia Britannica. 16 minutes, color, grades 4–adult. (OL, CW, ST, DR)
 Uses music and photography of natural phenomena to dramatize the many moods evoked by deer in the forest. A film essay from Hungary.

Dictionary for Beginners. Coronet. 11 minutes, color, grades 1–3. (SS)

Shows young children choosing words, alphabetizing them, writing definitions, finding or drawing pictures, and using guide words as they make a dictionary.

Discovering Language Series. Coronet. Color. (LN)
> *How English Borrowed Words.* 11 minutes, grades 4–8.
> *How English Changed in America.* 11 minutes, grades 4–8.
> *How Words Are Made.* 14 minutes, grades 4–9.
> *How Words Get Their Meanings.* 11 minutes, grades 4–8.
> *The Alphabet Story.* 14 minutes, grades 4–9.

Dream of the Wild Horses. McGraw-Hill. 9 minutes, color, grades 4–adult. (OL, CW, PO)
> Cinematic poem using slow motion and soft focus camera to evoke the wild horses of the Camarque district of France, showing them as they roam on the beach.

Fun with Words Series. Coronet. 11 minutes each, color, grades 1–3. (LN, SS)
> *From Words to Sentences*
> *Word Twins*
> *Words That Add Meaning*

Hailstones and Halibut Bones, Part I. Sterling. 5 minutes, color, grades K–6. (PO)
> Original impressionistic drawings illustrate poems from Mary O'Neil's book. Poems define color in terms of imaginary sounds, feelings, and moods.

Hailstones and Halibut Bones, Part II. Sterling. 8 minutes, color, grades 3–6. (PO)
> Presents five poems from Mary O'Neil's book to show how a writer uses colors to convey feeling and emotion.

The Haunted House. Encyclopaedia Britannica. 14 minutes, color, grades K–3. (DR, OL, ST, CW)
> Story with three different endings.

Leaf. Pyramid. 7 minutes, color, grades K–12. (OL, CW)
> Follows the path of an autumn leaf as it soars on the wind in a Yosemite canyon and floats down a stream. No narration.

The Learning to Look Series. McGraw-Hill. Color, primary grades. (OL, CW, LS)
> *All Kinds of Buildings.* 8 minutes.
> *Just Like in School.* 8 minutes.
> *Learning to Look at Hands.* 8 minutes.
> *Let's Find Some Faces.* 9 minutes.
> *On Your Way to School.* 8 minutes.
> *What Is a Family?* 7 minutes.

Let's Make up a Story. Coronet. 11 minutes, color, grades 2–5. (CW, SS)
> How to make up a story with individual characters and settings.

Let's Try Choral Reading. McGraw-Hill. 12 minutes, color, grades 2–6. (OL, PO)
> Experiences in choral reading.

Let's Write a Story. Churchill. 11 minutes, color, grades K–6. (OL, CW)
> A boy and his dog have series of adventures, each of which is designed to motivate and facilitate oral and written language experiences.

Listening. Churchill. 14 minutes, color, grades 3–6. (LS, SS)
> Designed to develop auditory awareness.

Magic Moments, A Visual Language Experiences Series. Encyclopaedia Britannica. Primary grades. (OL, DR, ST, CW)
> A series of 20 short films developed in collaboration with Roach Van Allen.
> *Bang!* 3 minutes.
> *Choosing Up.* 7 minutes.
> *Clap!* 5 minutes.
> *Fantasy of Feet.* 8 minutes.
> *Follow Me.* 6 minutes.
> *Getting Along.* 3 minutes.
> *Getting Even.* 4 minutes.
> *Guessing Game.* 7 minutes.
> *Hands Grow Up.* 7 minutes.
> *Holding On.* 5 minutes.
> *Join Hands — Let Go!* 9 minutes.
> *Lopsideland.* 5 minutes.
> *Magic Hands.* 7 minutes.
> *Magic Sneakers.* 9 minutes.
> *Matching Up.* 5 minutes.
> *Me, Too?* 4 minutes.
> *Toes Tell.* 7 minutes.
> *What If?* 4 minutes.
> *What's Happening?* 5 minutes.
> *Whose Shoes?* 4 minutes.

Making Haiku. Encyclopaedia Britannica. 8 minutes, color, grades 2–6. (PO, CW)
> Explains haiku form and encourages students to compose their own.

Orange and Blue. McGraw-Hill. 15 minutes, color, grades K–6. (OL, DR, CW)
> Two bouncing balls, one orange and one blue, representing the essence of childhood,

explore and play in a junk surplus yard. A nonverbal film.

People Soup. Learning Corporation of America. 14 minutes, color, grades 2–adult. (OL, ST, CW)

A fantasy in which two brothers, using household ingredients, mix a magic potion that turns one into a sheepdog and the other into a chicken.

The Practical Princess. Sterling. 20 minutes, color, grades 1–6. (RD, OL, CW, SS)

Designed to stimulate reading and classroom discussion of plot, character development, emotions, and other elements of writing by telling a story about a practical princess who evades a wicked suitor and marries a handsome prince.

Puppets You Can Make. Coronet. 16 minutes, color, grades 4–9. (PP)

Demonstrates how to make workable hand puppets using assorted odds and ends and shows how to work with puppets.

The Red Balloon. Brandon Films. 34 minutes, color, K–adult. (OL, ST, DR)

Fantasy about a boy who makes friends with a balloon, playing with it in the streets of Montmartre, Paris, and trying unsuccessfully to elude a gang of urchins trying to destroy it.

Soopergoop. Churchill Films. 13 minutes, color, K–adult. (OL, DR, ST, CW)

Animated story in which two characters concoct a TV commercial for a cereal.

Speak Up. McGraw-Hill. 13 minutes, color, grades 2–5. (OL)

Explores the importance, pleasures, and varieties of oral expression. Shows how speech can be used to exchange information, express feelings, convey ideas, and interact with others.

Watch. Encyclopaedia Britannica. 12 minutes, color, grades 4–6.

A boy, home alone, lets a friend in. The friend breaks a gold pocket watch. As the boy holds the watch, his mother returns. What happens next?

Wizard of Words Series. McGraw-Hill. Color, grades 4–6. (LN, SS)

The Wizard, an invisible but always present grammar guide, and Harvey, a silent partner in the style of Buster Keaton, are the catalysts in these stimulating grammar lesson films.
NOUNS AND ADJECTIVES. 9 minutes.
PREPOSITIONS. 10 minutes.
VERBS AND ADVERBS. 9 minutes.

Wordwise: Suffixes. Bailey Film Associates. 12 minutes, color, grades 3–6. (LN, RD, SS)

Presents 13 suffixes and shows the basic rules for affixing suffixes to words. Uses a mystery story set in the Hawaiian Islands to carry the story line.

Write On. McGraw-Hill. 14 minutes, color, grades 3–6. (WR)

Children are exposed to a full range of purposes for writing.

Writing Different Kinds of Letters. Coronet. 11 minutes, color, grades 4–6. (WR)

Uses four common situations to show how to write different types of letters, including the personal letter, the business letter, the letter of invitation, and the thank you letter.

Your Communication Skills Series. Coronet. 11 minutes each, color, grades 4–9. (OL, LS, RD, WR)
Exchange of Ideas
Listening
Reading
Writing

FILMSTRIPS

Award Libraries. Weston Woods. All levels. (LS, LT, DR, CW)

Sound filmstrips of selected Caldecott and Kate Greenaway award winning books.

Basic Study Skills I, II, and III. Miller-Brody. Intermediate. (SS)

Three sets of four filmstrips with two cassettes each. Teaches outlining, taking notes, using reference books, etc.

Children's Literature Filmstrips. Random House. (LS, LT)

Extensive listing of filmstrips and accompanying records or cassettes.

Classic Fairy Tales. Encyclopaedia Britannica. Grades K–6. (LT, ST, DR, CW)

Ten filmstrips and audiodiscs.
Story of Aladdin
Story of Cinderella
Story of King Midas
Story of Little Red Riding Hood

Story of Little Thumb
Story of Puss in Boots
Story of Sinbad the Sailor
Story of Snow White
Story of the Little Mermaid
Story of the Pied Piper

Discovering Spelling Patterns. McGraw-Hill.
Intermediate. (SS, LN)
  Thirty-six filmstrips.

Episodes from Famous Stories. Encyclopaedia
Britannica. Intermediate. (LT, OL, ST, DR)
  Series of six filmstrips. Highlights from
  stories such as *Robinson Crusoe* and *Treasure
  Island.*

Folktales from Many Lands. McGraw-Hill.
Grades K-6. (LT, ST)
  Filmstrip series.

How A Picture Book is Made. Weston Woods.
(CW, LT, OL)
  Author-illustrator Steve Kellogg describes
  the steps involved in creating *The Island Of
  The Skog,* a picture book relating the
  adventures of a group of mice on a faraway
  island.

How to Use the Card Catalog. Society for Visual
Education. Intermediate. (SS)
  Sound filmstrip to teach use of the card
  catalog.

How to Use the Encyclopedia. Society for Visual
Education. Intermediate. (SS)
  Sound filmstrip to teach use of an
  encyclopedia.

Listen: There Are Sounds Around You. Guidance
Associates. Grades K–3. (LS, SS)
  Sound filmstrip program to increase
  auditory awareness and improve auditory
  discrimination.

Meet the Newbery Author Series. Random
House. (LT, LS)
  Filmstrips with record or tape provide
  portraits of authors chosen for Newbery
  recognition.

Monster Filmstrips. Bowmar, Beginning
readers. (RD, OL, ST, CW)
  Three sets of filmstrips to accompany
  Monster Books.
  Set 1: *Monster Comes to the City*
          Monster Looks for a House
          Monster Cleans His House
          Monster Looks for a Friend

Set 2: *Monster Meets Lady Monster*
        Monster and the Magic Umbrella
        Monster Goes to the Museum
        Monster on the Bus
Set 3: *Monster Goes to School*
        Monster at School
        Monster Has a Party
        Monster Goes to the Zoo

Nonverbal Filmstrips. Weston Woods. Primary.
(OL, DR, CW, ST)
  A Flying Saucer Full of Spaghetti
  Bubble Bubble
  The Silver Pony
  The Bear and the Fly

Primary Language Arts Kit. Encyclopaedia
Britannica. Primary. (OL)
  Eight filmstrips and four records to
  stimulate use of language.

Improve Your Handwriting. Young America
Films/McGraw-Hill. Intermediate. (SS)
  A color filmstrip designed to improve
  writing.

Using Colorful Language. Learning Corporation
of America. Intermediate. (OL, WR, SS)
  A color filmstrip and record designed to
  help children use language more effectively.

RECORDS AND TAPES

Adventures of Robin Hood. Caedmon.
Intermediate. (LT, LS)

African Village Folktales, Volumes I, II, and III.
Caedmon. Intermediate. (LT, LS, ST)

American Indian Tales for Children. Miller-Brody.
Grades 2–6. (LT, LS, ST)

Americans Speaking. National Council of
Teachers of English. Intermediate to adult.
(LN, LS)
  A dialect recording of English as it is spoken
  in different parts of the United States.

The Best in Children's Literature. Bowmar. K–6.
(LT, PO, OL, DR, ST)
  The four series include 374 selections. They
  introduce children to some best-known
  stories and poems. (14 records or cassettes)

The Best in Children's Literature Series. Troll
Associates. Primary. (LT, OL, DR, ST)
  Recorded on cassettes for young listeners.

Caddie Woodlawn. Miller-Brody. Intermediate.
(LT)

Carl Sandburg's Poems for Children. Caedmon. Grades 2–6. (PO)

Carry on, Mr. Bowditch. Miller-Brody. Intermediate. (LT)

The Changing English Language. Folkway Records. Intermediate. (LS, LN)
Readings in Old, Middle, and Modern English to illustrate changes.

Countdown for Listening. Educational Activities. Grades 3–5. (LS, OL, DR)
Audio presentation of 24 lessons on speech improvement and dramatization. Includes six cassettes with four lessons each.

Door in the Wall. Miller-Brody. (LT)

Extending Comprehension Through Listening. Miller-Brody. Grades 4–6. (LS, SS)
Includes four records with teacher's manuals.

Listening Time. Bowmar. Primary. (LS, OL)
Three recordings and a picture book.

Picture Book Parade. Weston Woods. Primary. (LT, LS)
Recordings of selected picture books. Available in cassette or LP record.

Poems for the Very Young. Bowmar. Primary. (LS, PO)
Interpretive readings of poems with related music.

Scholastic Record and Book Companion Series. Scholastic Records. Grades K–3. (LT, LS, ST)
Each set includes a Scholastic paperback and a seven-inch record.

Soundways to Reading. Listening Library, Inc. Grades 3–6. (RD, LS)
Cassettes with book. Reader narrates the story up to interesting part. Children finish on their own.

Switched on Bach. Columbia Records. Grades 4–9. (LT, DR, CW)
Walter Carlos performing on the Moog synthesizer provides music for creative interpretation.

Talkstarters. Scott, Foresman. Primary. (OL, CW)
Books and records to stimulate language.

You Read to Me, I'll Read to You. Miller-Brody. Primary. (PO, LS)
John Ciardi reads his poems for children.

NOTE: *For more complete lists of records, films, and filmstrips of children's literature consult publishers' catalogs. The following companies offer extensive selections:*
Bowmar Records
Caedmon Records
Capitol Records
Columbia Records
Coronet Instructional Films
Disneyland Records
Miller-Brody Productions
Weston Woods Studios

KITS AND OTHER MATERIALS

ABC Serendipity. Bowmar. Grades 2–6. (OL, DR, CW, RD)
A reading, writing, talking, acting, doing series for language study. Contains 6 books and 66 activity cards.

The Art of Learning Through Movement. Bowmar. Grades K–6. (DR)
Book and record set includes games, fantasy, and dramatic play ideas.

Breakthrough to Literacy. Bowmar. Primary. (OL, LN, RD, WR)
Materials for beginning reading and writing. Includes children's books, word and sentence makers, story figures, and teachers' resource book.

A Child-Centered Language Arts Program. Curriculum Associates. Grades 3–8. (OL, LS, RD, WR)
Includes activity cards for individual, small-group, larger-group, and whole-class self-directing activities.

Continuous Progress in Spelling. The Economy Company. All levels. (SS)
Kit includes all materials for an individualized spelling program.

Developing Listening Skills. Leswing Press. Grades K–6. (LS, SS)
Contains puppets, student activity sheets, and lesson plans to improve listening skills.

Elaborative Thinking Sets. Curriculum Associates. Sets for both primary and intermediate. (OL, CW)
Includes activity cards, spirit masters, introductory cards, and teacher's guide.

Information Fast. Lakeshore Curriculum

Materials. Intermediate. (SS)
Contains 125 information-gathering activities for gifted children.

Interaction. Houghton Mifflin. Level 1 for K–3 and Level 2 for 4–6. (OL, DR, CW, LS, RD, SS)
James Moffett's student-centered language arts and reading program. Includes activity cards and games at both levels.

Language Arts Box. Lakeshore Curriculum Materials. Intermediate. (OL, WR)
Contains 150 ideas for language arts.

Language Stimulus Program. Bowmar. Levels 3–8 (Grades 3–8). (OL, PO, DR, RD, WR, PP)
Kit contains highly visual materials, including books, activity cards, personal language checkbooks, and teacher's guidebook.

Letter Sounds All Around. Bowmar. Primary. (OL, RD, SS)
A multimedia program that explores the alphabet and the sounds that each letter represents.

Listen and Think Program. Educational Development Laboratories. Levels 1–9 (Grades K–9). (LS, SS)
Developmental sequence of 15 listening comprehension and thinking skill lessons at each level. Kit includes tapes or cassettes, individual lesson books, and teacher's guide.

Listening to the World. American Guidance Service. Primary. (LS)
Program includes audio-cassettes, gameboards, posters and sound book. Teaches auditory and memory skills.

On Stage: Wally, Bertha, and You. Encyclopaedia Britannica. Grades K–3. (OL, LS, DR)
Kit contains puppets, activity cards, and teacher's handbook.

Oral Language Skills Series. Leswing Press. Grades K–6. (OL, PP)
Contains book, stick puppets or felt cutouts, and lesson plans.

The Outlining Kit. Curriculum Associates. Intermediate. (WR, SS)
Instructs students to organize good outlines for clear writing. Includes activity cards, spirit masters, teacher's guide, and classroom box.

Peabody Language Development Kits. American Guidance Service. Primary. (OL, LS, PP)
Includes posters, puppets, stimulus cards, recordings, etc. Three kits cover a mental age range of 4½ to 9½. Each kit includes 180 daily lessons.

Phonics and Word Development: Basic Elementary Spelling Skills. Miller-Brody. Grades 2–6. (SS)
Five records or cassettes, self-checking exercises, and teacher notes.

Rainbow Activities: Multicultural Experiences. Lakeshore Curriculum Materials. (OL, LS)
Games, puzzles, songs and art activities allow children to explore cultural pluralism, self-image, feelings and values.

Reading Incentive Program. Bowmar. Grades 3–12. (OL, RD, SS)
A multimedia reading program with high interest content and easy-to-read vocabulary. Includes books, sound filmstrips, spirit master skill development sheets, and teacher's guide.

Right Is Write. Curriculum Associates. Elementary to high school. (WR, SS)
A simulation game that develops writing skills. Mechanical writing skills are practiced as students simulate roles of writers, agents, editors, and publishers.

Sound, Order, Sense. Follett. Primary. (LS)
Developmental auditory perception program. Kit.

SRA Listening Skills Program. Science Research Associates. Various levels. (LS)
Kit includes a set of 36 LPs and teaching materials.

SRA Reading Laboratories. Science Research Associates. Various levels. (RD, SS)
Each kit contains comprehension exercises, rate builders, pupil booklets, and teacher's guide.

SRA Writing Skills Laboratory. Science Research Associates. 2 levels. Series II for Grades 5 and 6. Series III for Grades 7 and 8. (WR, SS)
Includes exercises in writing narration, description, and exposition.

Terry the Terrible Troll Series. Media Materials. Primary. (SS)
Set of ten learning packages helps children learn basic study skills. Includes cassette, student booklets, teacher's guide, posttest, and set of library reference cards.

The Writing Bug. Random House.
Intermediate. (CW, WR)
  Kit includes filmstrips, cassettes, charts, and teacher's guide.

ADDRESSES OF MULTIMEDIA PUBLISHERS AND DISTRIBUTORS LISTED

American Guidance Service, Inc., Publishers' Building, Circle Pines, MN 55014

Bailey Fill Associates, 11559 Santa Monica Blvd., West Los Angeles, CA 90025

Bowmar Publishing Corporation, 622 Rodier Dr., Glendale, CA 91201

Bowmar Records, 12 Cleveland St., Valhalla, NY 10595

Brandon Films, Inc., 211 West 57th St., New York, NY 10019

Caedmon Records, 505 Eighth Ave., New York, NY 10018

Churchill Films, 662 North Robertson Blvd., Los Angeles, CA 90069

Columbia Records, 799 Seventh Ave., New York, NY 10019

Coronet Instructional Media, 65 East South Water St., Chicago, IL 60601

Curriculum Associates, Inc., 5 Esquire Road, North Billerica, MA 01862

Disneyland Records, Walt Disney Educational Materials, 800 Sonora Ave., Glendale, CA 91201

The Economy Company, P.O. Box 25308, 1901 North Walnut, Oklahoma City, OK 73125

Educational Activities, Inc., Freeport, NY 11520

Educational Development Laboratories, 284 Pulaski Road, Huntington, NY 11744

Encyclopaedia Britannica Educational Corporation, 425 North Michigan Ave., Chicago, IL 60611

Film Fair Communications, 10820 Ventura Blvd., Studio City, CA 91604

Folkway Records, Record, Book and Film Sales, 121 W. 47th St., New York, NY 10036

Follett Publishing Co., 1010 West Washington Blvd., Chicago, IL 60607

Lakeshore Curriculum Materials Co., 2695 E. Dominguez St., P.O. Box 6261, Carson, CA 90749

Learning Corporation of America, 711 Fifth Ave., New York, NY 10022

Leswing Press, 750 Adrian Way, San Rafael, CA 94903

Listening Library, Inc., 1 Park Avenue, Old Greenwich, CT 06870

McGraw-Hill Films, 1221 Avenue of the Americas, New York, NY 10020

Media Materials, Inc., 2936 Remington Ave., Dept. K8, Baltimore, MD 21211

Miller-Brody Productions, 711 Fifth Ave., New York, NY 10022

National Council of Teachers of English, 1111 Kenyon Rd., Urbana, IL 61801

Pyramid Films Corporation, P.O. Box 1048, Santa Monica, CA 90406

Random House Educational Media, 400 Hahn Rd., Westminster, MD 21157

Scholastic Records, Scholastic Magazines, AV Department, 50 West 44th St., New York, NY 10036

Science Research Associates, 259 East Erie St., Chicago, IL 60611

Scott, Foresman and Co., 1900 E. Lake Ave., Glenview, IL 60025

Society for Visual Education, 1345 Diversey Parkway, Chicago, IL 60614

Texture Films, 419 Park Avenue South, New York, NY 10016

Troll Associates, 320 Route 17, Mahwah, NJ 07430

Weston Woods, Weston, CT 06880

Young America Films, McGraw-Hill Co., 330 West 42nd St., New York, NY 10036

Appendix B
Award-Winning Books for Children

THE NEWBERY MEDAL

1922 *The Story of Mankind* by Hendrik Willem van Loon (Liveright)
HONOR BOOKS:
The Great Quest by Charles Hawes (Little, Brown)
Cedric the Forester by Bernard Marshall (Appleton-Century-Crofts)
The Old Tobacco Shop by William Bowen (Macmillan)
The Golden Fleece and the Heroes Who Lived Before Achilles by Padraic Colum (Macmillan)
Windy Hill by Cornelia Meigs (Macmillan)

1923 *The Voyages of Doctor Dolittle* by Hugh Lofting (Lippincott)
HONOR BOOKS: No record

1924 *The Dark Frigate* by Charles Hawes (Atlantic/Little, Brown)
HONOR BOOKS: No record

1925 *Tales from Silver Lands* by Charles Finger (Doubleday)
HONOR BOOKS:
Nicholas by Anne Carroll Moore (Putnam)
Dream Coach by Anne Parrish (Macmillan)

1926 *Shen of the Sea* by Arthur Bowie Chrisman (Dutton)
HONOR BOOK:
Voyagers by Padraic Colum (Macmillan)

1927 *Smoky, the Cowhorse* by Will James (Scribner)
HONOR BOOKS: No record

1928 *Gayneck, The Story of a Pigeon* by Dhan Gopal Mukerji (Dutton)
HONOR BOOKS:
The Wonder Smith and His Son by Ella Young (Longmans)
Downright Dencey by Caroline Snedeker (Doubleday)

1929 *The Trumpeter of Krakow* by Eric P. Kelly (Macmillan)
HONOR BOOKS:
Pigtail of Ah Lee Ben Loo by John Bennett (Longmans)
Millions of Cats by Wanda Gäg (Coward, McCann & Geoghegan)
The Boy Who Was by Grace Hallock (Dutton)
Clearing Weather by Cornelia Meigs (Little, Brown)
Runaway Papoose by Grace Moon (Doubleday)
Tod of the Fens by Elinor Whitney (Macmillan)

1930 *Hitty, Her First Hundred Years* by Rachel Field (Macmillan)
HONOR BOOKS:
Daughter of the Seine by Jeanette Eaton (Harper and Row)
Pran of Albania by Elizabeth Miller (Doubleday)

Jumping-Off Place by Marian Hurd
McNeely (Longmans)
Tangle-Coated Horse and Other Tales by Ella
Young (Longmans)
Vaino by Julia Davis Adams (Dutton)
Little Blacknose by Hildegarde Swift
(Harcourt Brace Jovanovich)

1931 *The Cat Who Went to Heaven* by Elizabeth
Coatsworth (Macmillan)
HONOR BOOKS:
Floating Island by Anne Parrish (Harper
and Row)
The Dark Star of Itza by Ralph Hubbard
(Doubleday)
Mountains Are Free by Julia Davis Adams
(Dutton)
Spice and the Devil's Cave by Agnew
Hewes (Knopf)
Meggy Macintosh by Elizabeth Janet Gray
(Doubleday)
Ood-Le-Uk the Wanderer by Alice Lide and
Margaret Johansen (Little, Brown)

1932 *Waterless Mountain* by Laura Adams
Armer (Longmans)
HONOR BOOKS:
The Fairy Circus by Dorothy P. Lathrop
(Macmillan)
Calico Bush by Rachel Field (Macmillan)
Boy of the South Seas by Eunice Tietjens
(Coward, McCann & Geoghegan)
Out of the Flame by Eloise Lownsbery
(Longmans)
Jane's Island by Marjorie Allee (Houghton
Mifflin)
*Truce of the Wolf and Other Tales of Old
Italy* by Mary Gould Davis (Harcourt
Brace Jovanovich)

1933 *Young Fu of the Upper Yangtze* by
Elizabeth Foreman Lewis (Holt,
Rinehart and Winston)
HONOR BOOKS:
Swift Rivers by Cornelia Meigs (Little,
Brown)
The Railroad to Freedom by Hildegarde
Swift (Harcourt Brace Jovanovich)
Children of the Soil by Nora Burglon
(Doubleday)

1934 *Invincible Louisa* by Cornelia Meigs (Little,
Brown)
HONOR BOOKS:
The Forgotten Daughter by Caroline
Snedeker (Doubleday)

Swords of Steel by Elsie Singmaster
(Houghton Mifflin)
ABC Bunny by Wanda Gág (Coward,
McCann & Geoghegan)
Winged Girl of Knossos by Erik Berry
(Appleton-Century-Crofts)
New Land by Sarah Schmidt (McBride)
Big Tree of Bunlahy by Padraic Colum
(Macmillan)
Glory of the Seas by Agnes Hawes (Knopf)
Apprentice of Florence by Anne Kyle
(Houghton Mifflin)

1935 *Dobry* by Monica Shannon (Viking)
HONOR BOOKS:
Pageant of Chinese History by Elizabeth
Seeger (Longmans)
Davy Crockett by Constance Rourke
(Harcourt Brace Jovanovich)
Day on Skates by Hilda Van Stockum
(Harper and Row)

1936 *Caddie Woodlawn* by Carol Brink
(Macmillan)
HONOR BOOKS:
Honk, the Moose by Phil Stong (Dodd)
The Good Master by Kate Seredy (Viking)
Young Walter Scott by Elizabeth Janet
Gray (Viking)
All Sail Set by Armstrong Sperry (Holt,
Rinehart and Winston)

1937 *Roller Skates* by Ruth Sawyer (Viking)
HONOR BOOKS:
Phebe Fairchild: Her Book by Lois Lenski
(Stokes)
Whistler's Van by Idwal Jones (Viking)
Golden Basket by Ludwig Bemelmans
(Viking)
Winterbound by Margery Bianco (Viking)
Audubon by Constance Rourke (Harcourt
Brace Jovanovich)
The Codfish Musket by Agnes Hewes
(Doubleday)

1938 *The White Stag* by Kate Seredy (Viking)
HONOR BOOKS:
Pecos Bill by James Cloyd Bowman
(Little, Brown)
Bright Island by Mabel Robinson
(Random House)
On the Banks of Plum Creek by Laura
Ingalls Wilder (Harper and Row)

1939 *Thimble Summer* by Elizabeth Enright
(Holt, Rinehart and Winston)

HONOR BOOKS:
Nino by Valenti Angelo (Viking)
Mr. Popper's Penguins by Richard and
Florence Atwater (Little, Brown)
"Hello the Boat!" by Phyllis Crawford
(Holt, Rinehart and Winston)
*Leader by Destiny: George Washington, Man
and Patriot* by Jeanette Eaton (Harcourt
Brace Jovanovich)
Penn by Elizabeth Janet Gray (Viking)

1940 *Daniel Boone* by James Daugherty
(Viking)
HONOR BOOKS:
The Singing Tree by Kate Seredy (Viking)
Runner of the Mountain Tops by Mabel
Robinson (Random House)
By the Shores of Silver Lake by Laura
Ingalls Wilder (Harper and Row)
Boy with a Pack by Stephen W. Meader
(Harcourt Brace Jovanovich)

1941 *Call It Courage* by Armstrong Sperry
(Macmillan)
HONOR BOOKS:
Blue Willow by Doris Gates (Viking)
Young Mac of Fort Vancouver by Mary
Jane Carr (Crowell)
The Long Winter by Laura Ingalls Wilder
(Harper and Row)
Nansen by Anna Gertrude Hall (Viking)

1942 *The Matchlock Gun* by Walter D. Edmonds
(Dodd, Mead)
HONOR BOOKS:
Little Town on the Prairie by Laura Ingalls
Wilder (Harper and Row)
George Washington's World by Genevieve
Foster (Scribner)
Indian Captive: The Story of Mary Jemison
by Lois Lenski (Lippincott)
Down Ryton Water by Eva Roe Gaggin
(Viking)

1943 *Adam of the Road* by Elizabeth Janet Gray
(Viking)
HONOR BOOKS:
The Middle Moffat by Eleanor Estes
(Harcourt Brace Jovanovich)
Have You Seen Tom Thumb? by Mabel
Leigh Hunt (Lippincott)

1944 *Johnny Tremain* by Esther Forbes
(Houghton Mifflin)

HONOR BOOKS:
These Happy Golden Years by Laura Ingalls
Wilder (Harper and Row)
Fog Magic by Julia Sauer (Viking)
Rufus M. by Eleanor Estes (Harcourt
Brace Jovanovich)
Mountain Born by Elizabeth Yates
(Coward, McCann & Geoghegan)

1945 *Rabbit Hill* by Robert Lawson (Viking)
HONOR BOOKS:
The Hundred Dresses by Eleanor Estes
(Harcourt Brace Jovanovich)
The Silver Pencil by Alice Dalgliesh
(Scribner)
Abraham Lincoln's World by Genevieve
Foster (Scribner)
Lone Journey: The Life of Roger Williams by
Jeanette Eaton (Harcourt Brace
Jovanovich)

1946 *Strawberry Girl* by Lois Lenski
(Lippincott)
HONOR BOOKS:
Justin Morgan Had a Horse by Marguerite
Henry (Rand McNally)
The Moved-Outers by Florence Crannell
Means (Houghton Mifflin)
Bhimsa, the Dancing Bear by Christine
Weston (Scribner)
New Found World by Katherine Shippen
(Viking)

1947 *Miss Hickory* by Carolyn Sherwin Bailey
(Viking)
HONOR BOOKS:
Wonderful Year by Nancy Barnes (Julian
Messner)
Big Tree by Mary and Conrad Buff
(Viking)
The Heavenly Tenants by William Maxwell
(Harper and Row)
The Avion My Uncle Flew by Cyrus Fisher
(Appleton-Century-Crofts)
The Hidden Treasure of Glaston by Eleanore
Jewett (Viking)

1948 *The Twenty-one Balloons* by William Pène
du Bois (Viking)
HONOR BOOKS:
Pancakes-Paris by Claire Huchet Bishop
(Viking)
Li Lun, Lad of Courage by Carolyn
Treffinger (Abingdon)

*The Quaint and Curious Quest of Johnny
     Longfoot* by Catherine Besterman
     (Bobbs-Merrill)
*The Cow-Tail Switch, and Other West
     African Stories* by Harold Courlander
     (Holt, Rinehart and Winston)
Misty of Chincoteague by Marguerite
     Henry (Rand McNally)

1949 *Kind of the Wind* by Marguerite Henry
     (Rand McNally)
     HONOR BOOKS:
     Seabird by Holling C. Holling (Houghton
         Mifflin)
     Daughter of the Mountains by Louis
         Rankin (Viking)
     My Father's Dragon by Ruth S. Gannett
         (Random House)
     Story of the Negro by Arna Bontemps
         (Knopf)

1950 *The Door in the Wall* by Marguerite de
     Angeli (Doubleday)
     HONOR BOOKS:
     Tree of Freedom by Rebecca Caudill
         (Viking)
     The Blue Cat of Castle Town by Catherine
         Coblentz (Longmans)
     Kildee House by Rutherford Montgomery
         (Doubleday)
     George Washington by Genevieve Foster
         (Scribner)
     Song of the Pines by Walter and Marion
         Havighurst (Holt, Rinehart and
         Winston)

1951 *Amos Fortune, Free Man* by Elizabeth
     Yates (Aladdin)
     HONOR BOOKS:
     Better Known as Johnny Appleseed by
         Mabel Leigh Hunt (Lippincott)
     Gandhi, Fighter Without a Sword by
         Jeanette Eaton (Morrow)
     Abraham Lincoln, Friend of the People by
         Clara Ingram Judson (Follett)
     The Story of Appleby Capple by Anne
         Parrish (Harper and Row)

1952 *Ginger Pye* by Eleanor Estes (Harcourt
     Brace Jovanovich)
     HONOR BOOKS:
     Americans Before Columbus by Elizabeth
         Baity (Viking)
     Minn of the Mississippi by Holling C.
         Holling (Houghton Mifflin)

The Defender by Nicholas Kalashnikoff
     (Scribner)
The Light at Tern Rock by Julia Sauer
     (Viking)
The Apple and the Arrow by Mary and
     Conrad Buff (Houghton Mifflin)

1953 *Secret of the Andes* by Ann Nolan Clark
     (Viking)
     HONOR BOOKS:
     Charlotte's Web by E. B. White (Harper
         and Row)
     Moccasin Trail by Elois McGraw (Coward,
         McCann & Geoghegan)
     Red Sails to Capri by Ann Weil (Viking)
     The Bears on Hemlock Mountain by Alice
         Dalgliesh (Scribner)
     Birthdays of Freedom, Vol. 1 by Genevieve
         Foster (Scribner)

1954 *. . . and now Miguel* by Joseph Krumgold
     (Crowell)
     HONOR BOOKS:
     All Alone by Claire Huchet Bishop
         (Viking)
     Shadrach by Meindert DeJong (Harper
         and Row)
     Hurry Home Candy by Meindert DeJong
         (Harper and Row)
     Theodore Roosevelt, Fighting Patriot by
         Clara Ingram Judson (Follett)
     Magic Maize by Mary and Conrad Buff
         (Houghton Mifflin)

1955 *The Wheel on the School* by Meindert
     DeJong (Harper and Row)
     HONOR BOOKS:
     The Courage of Sarah Noble by Alice
         Dalgliesh (Scribner)
     Banner in the Sky by James Ullman
         (Lippincott)

1956 *Carry on, Mr. Bowditch* by Jean Lee
     Latham (Houghton Mifflin)
     HONOR BOOKS:
     The Secret River by Marjorie Kinnan
         Rawlings (Scribner)
     The Golden Name Day by Jennie Lindquist
         (Harper and Row)
     Men, Microscopes, and Living Things by
         Katherine Sheppen (Viking)

1957 *Miracles on Maple Hill* by Virginia
     Sorensen (Harcourt Brace Jovanovich)

HONOR BOOKS:
Old Yeller by Fred Gipson (Harper and Row)
The House of Sixty Fathers by Meindert DeJong (Harper and Row)
Mr. Justice Holmes by Clara Ingram Judson (Follett)
The Corn Grows Ripe by Dorothy Rhoads (Viking)
Black Fox of Lorne by Marguerite de Angeli (Doubleday)

1958 *Rifles for Watie* by Harold Keith (Crowell)
HONOR BOOKS:
The Horsecatcher by Mari Sandoz (Westminster)
Gone-Away Lake by Elizabeth Enright (Harcourt Brace Jovanovich)
The Great Wheel by Robert Lawson (Viking)
Tom Paine, Freedom's Apostle by Leo Gurko (Crowell)

1959 *The Witch of Blackbird Pond* by Elizabeth George Speare (Houghton Mifflin)
HONOR BOOKS:
The Family Under the Bridge by Natalie S. Carlson (Harper and Row)
Along Came a Dog by Meindert DeJong (Harper and Row)
Chicaro: Wild Pony of the Pampa by Francis Kalnay (Harcourt Brace Jovanovich)
The Perilous Road by William O. Steele (Harcourt Brace Jovanovich)

1960 *Onion John* by Joseph Krumgold (Crowell)
HONOR BOOKS:
My Side of the Mountain by Jean George (Dutton)
America is Born by Gerald W. Johnson (Morrow)
The Gammage Cup by Carol Kendall (Harcourt Brace Jovanovich)

1961 *Island of the Blue Dolphins* by Scott O'Dell (Houghton Mifflin)
HONOR BOOKS:
America Moves Forward by Gerald W. Johnson (Morrow)
Old Ramon by Jack Schaefer (Houghton Mifflin)
The Cricket in Times Square by George Selden (Farrar, Straus & Giroux)

1962 *The Bronze Bow* by Elizabeth George Speare (Houghton Mifflin)
HONOR BOOKS:
Frontier Living by Edwin Tunis (World)
The Golden Goblet by Eloise McGraw (Coward, McCann & Geoghegan)
Belling the Tiger by Mary Stolz (Harper and Row)

1963 *A Wrinkle in Time* by Madeleine L'Engle (Farrar, Straus & Giroux)
HONOR BOOKS:
Thistle and Thyme by Sorche Nic Leodhas (Holt, Rinehart and Winston)
Men of Athens by Olivia Coolidge (Houghton Mifflin)

1964 *It's Like This, Cat* by Emily Cheney Neville (Harper and Row)
HONOR BOOKS:
Rascal by Sterling North (Dutton)
The Loner by Ester Wier (McKay)

1965 *Shadow of a Bull* by Maia Wojciechowska (Atheneum)
HONOR BOOK:
Across Five Aprils by Irene Hunt (Follett)

1966 *I, Juan de Pareja* by Elizabeth Borten de Trevino (Farrar, Straus & Giroux)
HONOR BOOKS:
The Black Cauldron by Lloyd Alexander (Holt, Rinehart and Winston)
The Animal Family by Randall Jarrell (Pantheon)
The Noonday Friends by Mary Stolz (Harper and Row)

1967 *Up a Road Slowly* by Irene Hunt (Follett
HONOR BOOKS:
The King's Fifth by Scott O'Dell (Houghton Mifflin)
Zlateh the Goat and Other Stories by Isaac Bashevis Singer (Harper and Row)
The Jazz Man by Mary H. Weik (Atheneum)

1968 *From the Mixed-Up Files of Mrs. Basil E. Frankweiler* by E. L. Konigsburg (Atheneum)
HONOR BOOKS:
Jennifer, Hecate, Macbeth, William McKinley, and Me, Elizabeth by E. L. Konigsburg (Atheneum)
The Black Pearl by Scott O'Dell (Houghton Mifflin)

The Fearsome Inn by Isaac Bashevis Singer (Scribner)

The Egypt Game by Zilpha Keatley Snyder (Atheneum)

1969 *The High King* by Lloyd Alexander (Holt, Rinehart and Winston)
HONOR BOOKS:
To Be a Slave by Julius Lester (Dial)
When Shlemiel Went to Warsaw and Other Stories by Isaac Bashevis Singer (Farrar, Straus & Giroux)

1970 *Sounder* by William H. Armstrong (Harper and Row)
HONOR BOOKS:
Our Eddie by Sulamith Ish-Kishor (Pantheon)
The Many Ways of Seeing: An Introduction to the Pleasures of Art by Janet Gaylord Moore (World)
Journey Outside by Mary Q. Steele (Viking)

1971 *Summer of the Swans* by Betsy Byars (Viking)
HONOR BOOKS:
Kneeknock Rise by Natatlie Babbitt (Farrar, Straus & Giroux)
Enchantress from the Stars by Sylvia Louise Engdahl (Atheneum)
Sing Down the Moon by Scott O'Dell (Houghton Mifflin)

1972 *Mrs. Frisby and the Rats of NIMH* by Robert C. O'Brien (Atheneum)
HONOR BOOKS:
Incident at Hawk's Hill by Allan W. Eckert (Little, Brown)
The Planet of Junior Brown by Virginia Hamilton (Macmillan)
The Tombs of Atuan by Ursula K. Le Guin (Atheneum)
Annie and the Old One by Miska Miles (Atlantic/Little, Brown)
The Headless Cupid by Zilpha Keatley Snyder (Atheneum)

1973 *Julie of the Wolves* by Jean George (Harper and Row)
HONOR BOOKS:
Frog and Toad Together by Arnold Lobel (Harper and Row)
The Upstairs Room by Johanna Reiss (Crowell)

The Witches of Worm by Zilpha Keatley Snyder (Atheneum)

1974 *The Slave Dancer* by Paula Fox (Bradbury)
HONOR BOOK:
The Dark is Rising by Susan Cooper (Atheneum/Margaret K. McElderry)

1975 *M. C. Higgins, the Great* by Virginia Hamilton (Macmillan)
HONOR BOOKS:
Figgs & Phantoms by Ellen Raskin (Dutton)
My Brother Sam is Dead by James Lincoln Collier and Christopher Collier (Four Winds)
The Perilous Gard by Elizabeth Marie Pope (Houghton Mifflin)
Philip Hall Likes Me, I Reckon Maybe by Bette Greene (Dial)

1977 *Roll of Thunder, Hear My Cry* by Mildred D. Taylor (Dial)
HONOR BOOKS:
Abel's Island by William Steig (Farrar, Straus & Giroux)
A String in the Harp by Nancy Bond (Atheneum/A Margaret K. McElderry Book)

1978 *Bridge to Terabithea* by Katherine Pattison (Crowell)
HONOR BOOKS:
Ramona and her Father by Beverly Cleary (Morrow)
Anpao: An American Indian Odyssey by Jamake Highwater (Lippincott)

1979 *The Westing Game* by Ellen Raskin (Dutton)
HONOR BOOK:
The Great Gilly Hopkins by Katherine Paterson (Crowell)

1980 *The Gathering of Days* by Joan W. Blos (Scribner)
HONOR BOOK:
The Road from Home: The Story of an Armenian Girl by David Kherdian (Greenwillow)

1981 *Jacob Have I Loved* by Katherine Paterson (Crowell)
HONOR BOOKS:
The Fledgling by Jane Langton (Harper)

A Ring of Endless Light by Madeleine
L'Engle (Farrar)

1982 *A Visit to William Blake's Inn: Poems for
Innocent and Experienced Travelers* by
Nancy Willard, illus. by Alice and
Martin Provensen (Harcourt)
HONOR BOOKS:
Ramona Quimby, Age 8 by Beverly Cleary,
illus. by Alan Tiegreen (Morrow)
*Upon the Head of the Goat, A Childhood in
Hungary, 1939–1944* by Aranka Siegal
(Farrar)

THE CALDECOTT MEDAL

1938 *Animals of the Bible* by Helen Dean Fish,
illus. by Dorothy P. Lathrop
(Lippincott)
HONOR BOOKS:
Seven Simeons by Boris Artzybasheff
(Viking)
Four and Twenty Blackbirds by Helen Dean
Fish, illus. by Robert Lawson (Stokes)

1939 *Mei Li* by Thomas Handforth
(Doubleday)
HONOR BOOKS:
The Forest Pool by Laura Adams Armer
(Longmans)
Wee Gillis by Munro Leaf, illus. by
Robert Lawson (Viking)
Snow White and the Seven Dwarfs by
Wanda Gág (Coward, McCann and
Geoghegan)
Barkis by Clare Newberry (Harper and
Row)
Andy and the Lion by James Daugherty
(Viking)

1940 *Abraham Lincoln* by Ingri and Edgar Parin
d'Aulaire (Doubleday)
HONOR BOOKS:
Cock-A-Doodle Doo . . . by Berta and
Elmer Hader (Macmillan)
Madeline by Ludwig Bemelmans (Viking)
The Ageless Story by Lauren Ford (Dodd,
Mead)

1941 *They Were Strong and Good* by Robert
Lawson (Viking)
HONOR BOOK:
April's Kittens by Clare Turlay Newberry
(Harper and Row)

1942 *Make Way for Ducklings* by Robert
McCloskey (Viking)
HONOR BOOKS:
An American ABC by Maud and Miska
Petersham (Macmillan)
In My Mother's House by Ann Nolan
Clark, illus. by Velino Herrera (Viking)
Paddle-to-the-Sea by Holling C. Holling
(Houghton Mifflin)
Nothing at All by Wanda Gág (Coward,
McCann & Geoghegan)

1943 *The Little House* by Virginia Lee Burton
(Houghton Mifflin)
HONOR BOOKS:
Dash and Dart by Mary and Conrad Buff
(Viking)
Marshmallow by Clare Turlay Newberry
(Harper and Row)

1944 *Many Moons* by James Thurber, illus. by
Louis Slobodkin (Harcourt Brace
Jovanovich)
HONOR BOOKS:
Small Rain: Verses from the Bible selected
by Jessie Orton Jones, illus. by
Elizabeth Orton Jones (Viking)
Pierre Pigeon by Lee Kingman, illus. by
Arnold E. Bare (Houghton Mifflin)
The Mighty Hunter by Berta and Elmer
Hader (Macmillan)
A Child's Good Night Book by Margaret
Wise Brown, illus. by Jean Charlot
(W. R. Scott)
Good Luck Horse by Chih-Yi Chan, illus.
by Plao Chan (Whittlesey)

1945 *Prayer for a Child* by Rachel Field, illus. by
Elizabeth Orton Jones (Macmillan)
HONOR BOOKS:
Mother Goose, illus. by Tasha Tudor
(Walck)
In the Forest by Marie Hall Ets (Viking)
Yonie Wondernose by Marguerite de
Angeli (Doubleday)
The Christmas Anna Angel by Ruth
Sawyer, illus. by Kate Seredy (Viking)

1946 *The Rooster Crows . . .* (traditional Mother
Goose) illus. by Maud and Miska
Petersham (Macmillan)
HONOR BOOKS:
Little Lost Lamb by Golden MacDonald,
illus. by Leonard Weisgard
(Doubleday)

Sing Mother Goose by Opal Wheeler, illus.
by Marjorie Torrey (Dutton)
My Mother is the Most Beautiful Woman in the World by Becky Reyher, illus. by
Ruth Gannett (Lathrop)
You Can Write Chinese by Kurt Wiese
(Viking)

1947 *The Little Island* by Golden MacDonald,
illus. by Leonard Weisgard
(Doubleday)
HONOR BOOKS:
Rain Drop Splash by Alvin Tresselt, illus.
by Leonard Weisgard (Lathrop)
Boats on the River by Marjorie Flack, illus.
by Jay Hyde Barnum (Viking)
Timothy Turtle by Al Graham, illus. by
Tony Palazzo (Viking)
Pedro, the Angel of Olvera Street by Leo
Politi (Scribner)
*Sing in Praise: A Collection of the Best Loved
Hymns* by Opal Wheeler, illus. by
Marjorie Torrey (Dutton)

1948 *White Snow, Bright Snow* by Alvin
Tresselt, illus. by Roger Duvoisin
(Lathrop)
HONOR BOOKS:
Stone Soup by Marcia Brown (Scribner)
McEligot's Pool by Dr. Seuss (Random
House)
Bambino the Clown by George Schreiber
(Viking)
Roger and the Fox by Lavinia Davis, illus.
by Hildegard Woodward (Doubleday)
Song of Robin Hood ed. by Anne
Malcolmson, illus. by Virginia Lee
Burton (Houghton Mifflin)

1949 *The Big Snow* by Berta and Elmer Hader
(Macmillan)
HONOR BOOKS:
Blueberries for Sal by Robert McCloskey
(Viking)
All Around the Town by Phyllis McGinley,
illus. by Helen Stone (Lippincott)
Juanita by Leo Politi (Scribner)
Fish in the Air by Kurt Wiese (Viking)

1950 *Song of the Swallows* by Leo Politi
(Scribner)
HONOR BOOKS:
America's Ethan Allen by Stewart
Holbrook, illus. by Lynd Ward
(Houghton Mifflin)

The Wild Birthday Cake by Lavinia Davis,
illus. by Hildegard Woodward
(Doubleday)
The Happy Day by Ruth Krauss, illus. by
Marc Simont (Harper and Row)
Bartholomew and the Oobleck by Dr. Seuss
(Random House)
Henry Fisherman by Marcia Brown
(Scribner)

1951 *The Egg Tree* by Katherine Milhous
(Scribner)
HONOR BOOKS:
Dick Whittington and His Cat by Marcia
Brown (Scribner)
The Two Reds by Will, illus. by Nicolas
(Harcourt Brace Jovanovich)
If I Ran the Zoo by Dr. Seuss (Random
House)
The Most Wonderful Doll in the World by
Phyllis McGinley, illus. by Helen
Stone (Lippincott)
T-Bone, the Baby Sitter by Clare Turlay
Newberry (Harper and Row)

1952 *Finders Keepers* by Will, illus. by Nicolas
(Harcourt Brace Jovanovich)
HONOR BOOKS:
Mr. T. W. Anthony Woo by Marie Hall Ets
(Viking)
Skipper John's Cook by Marcia Brown
(Scribner)
All Falling Down by Gene Zion, illus. by
Margaret Bloy Graham (Harper and
Row)
Bear Party by William Pène du Bois
(Viking)
Feather Mountain by Elizabeth Olds
(Houghton Mifflin)

1953 *The Biggest Bear* by Lynd Ward
(Houghton Mifflin)
HONOR BOOKS:
Puss in Boots by Charles Perrault, illus.
and tr. by Marcia Brown (Scribner)
One Morning in Maine by Robert
McCloskey (Viking)
Ape in a Cape by Fritz Eichenberg
(Harcourt Brace Jovanovich)
The Storm Book by Charlotte Zolotow,
illus. by Margaret Bloy Graham
(Harper and Row)
Five Little Monkeys by Juliet Kepes
(Houghton Mifflin)

1954 *Madeline's Rescue* by Ludwig Bemelmans
(Viking)
HONOR BOOKS:
Journey Cake, Ho! by Ruth Sawyer, illus.
by Robert McCloskey (Viking)
When Will The World Be Mine? by Miriam
Schlein, illus. by Jean Charlot
(W. R. Scott)
The Steadfast Tin Soldier by Hans
Christian Andersen, illus. by Marcia
Brown (Scribner)
A Very Special House by Ruth Krauss,
illus. by Maurice Sendak (Harper and
Row)
Green Eyes by A. Birnbaum (Capitol)

1955 *Cinderella, or the Little Glass Slipper* by
Charles Perrault, tr. and illus. by
Marcia Brown (Scribner)
HONOR BOOKS:
Book of Nursery and Mother Goose Rhymes,
illus. by Marguerite de Angeli
(Doubleday)
Wheel on the Chimney by Margaret Wise
Brown, illus. by Tibor Gergely
(Lippincott)
The Thanksgiving Story by Alice Dalgliesh,
illus. by Helen Sewell (Scribner)

1956 *Frog Went A-Courtin'* ed. by John
Langstaff, illus. by Feodor
Rojankovsky (Harcourt Brace
Jovanovich)
HONOR BOOKS:
Play With Me by Marie Hall Ets (Viking)
Crow Boy by Taro Yashima (Viking)

1957 *A Tree is Nice* by Janice May Udry, illus.
by Marc Simont (Harper and Row)
HONOR BOOKS:
Mr. Penny's Race Horse by Marie Hall Ets
(Viking)
1 is One by Tasha Tudor (Walck)
Anatole by Eve Titus, illus. by Paul
Galdone (McGraw-Hill)
Gillespie and the Guards by Benjamin
Elkin, illus. by James Daugherty
(Viking)
Lion by William Pène du Bois (Viking)

1958 *Time of Wonder* by Robert McCloskey
(Viking)
HONOR BOOKS:
Fly High, Fly Low by Don Freeman
(Viking)

Anatole and the Cat by Eve Titus, illus. by
Paul Galdone (McGraw-Hill)

1959 *Chanticleer and the Fox* adapted from
Chaucer and illus. by Barbara Cooney
(Crowell)
HONOR BOOKS:
The House that Jack Built by Antonio
Frasconi (Harcourt Brace Jovanovich)
What Do You Say, Dear? by Sesyle Joslin,
illus. by Maurice Sendak (W. R. Scott)
Umbrella by Taro Yashima (Viking)

1960 *Nine Days to Christmas* by Marie Hall Ets
and Aurora Labastida, illus. by Marie
Hall Ets (Viking)
HONOR BOOKS:
Houses from the Sea by Alice E. Goudey,
illus. by Adrienne Adams (Scribner)
The Moon Jumpers by Janice May Udry,
illus. by Maurice Sendak (Harper and
Row)

1961 *Baboushka and the Three Kings* by Ruth
Robbins, illus. by Nicolas Sidjakov
(Parnassus)
HONOR BOOK:
Inch by Inch by Leo Lionni (Obolensky)

1962 *Once a Mouse . . .* by Marcia Brown
(Scribner)
HONOR BOOKS:
The Fox Went Out on a Chilly Night by
Peter Spier (Doubleday)
Little Bear's Visit by Else Holmelund
Minarik, illus. by Maurice Sendak
(Harper and Row)
The Day We Saw the Sun Come Up by Alice
E. Goudey, illus. by Adrienne Adams
(Scribner)

1963 *The Snowy Day* by Ezra Jack Keats
(Viking)
HONOR BOOKS:
The Sun is a Golden Earring by Natalia M.
Belting, illus. by Bernarda Bryson
(Holt, Rinehart and Winston)
Mr. Rabbit and the Lovely Present by
Charlotte Zolotow, illus. by Maurice
Sendak (Harper and Row)

1964 *Where the Wild Things Are* by Maurice
Sendak (Harper and Row)
HONOR BOOKS:
Swimmy by Leo Lionni (Pantheon)
All in the Morning Early by Sorche Nic

Leodhas, illus. by Evaline Ness (Holt, Rinehart and Winston)

Mother Goose and Nursery Rhymes, illus. by Philip Reed (Atheneum)

1965 *May I Bring a Friend?* by Beatrice Schenk de Regniers, illus. by Beni Montresor (Atheneum)
HONOR BOOKS:
Rain Makes Applesauce by Julian Scheer, illus. by Marvin Bileck (Holiday House)
The Wave by Margaret Hodges, illus. by Blair Lent (Houghton Mifflin)
A Pocketful of Cricket by Rebecca Caudill, illus. by Evaline Ness (Holt, Rinehart and Winston)

1966 *Always Room for One More* by Sorche Nic Leodhas, illus. by Nonny Hogrogian (Holt, Rinehart and Winston)
HONOR BOOKS:
Hide and Seek Fog by Alvin Tresselt, illus. by Roger Duvoisin (Lathrop)
Just Me by Marie Hall Ets (Viking)
Tom Tit Tot, ed. by Joseph Jacobs, illus. by Evaline Ness (Scribner)

1967 *Sam, Bangs & Moonshine* by Evaline Ness (Holt, Rinehart and Winston)
HONOR BOOK:
One Wide River to Cross by Barbara Emberley, illus. by Ed Emberley (Prentice-Hall)

1968 *Drummer Hoff* by Barbara Emberley, illus. by Ed Emberley (Prentice-Hall)
HONOR BOOKS:
Frederick by Leon Lionni (Pantheon)
Seashore Story by Taro Yashima (Viking)
The Emperor and the Kite by Jane Yolen, illus. by Ed Young (World)

1969 *The Fool of the World and the Flying Ship* by Arthur Ransome, illus. by Uri Shulevitz (Farrar, Straus & Giroux)
HONOR BOOK:
Why the Sun and the Moon Live in the Sky by Elphinstone Dayrell, illus. by Blair Lent (Houghton Mifflin)

1970 *Sylvester and the Magic Pebble* by William Steig (Windmill)
HONOR BOOKS:
Goggles! by Ezra Jack Keats (Macmillan)

Alexander and the Wind-Up Mouse by Leo Lionni (Pantheon)
Pop Corn & Ma Goodness by Edna Mitchell Preston, illus. by Robert Andrew Parker (Viking)
Thy Friend, Obadiah by Brinton Turkle (Viking)
The Judge by Harve Zemach, illus. by Margot Zemach (Farrar, Straus & Giroux)

1971 *A Story — A Story* by Gail E. Haley (Atheneum)
HONOR BOOKS:
The Angry Moon by William Sleator, illus. by Blair Lent (Atlantic/Little, Brown)
Frog and Toad Are Friends by Arnold Lobel (Harper and Row)
In the Night Kitchen by Maurice Sendak (Harper and Row)

1972 *One Fine Day* by Nonny Hogrogian (Macmillan)
HONOR BOOKS:
If All the Seas Were One Sea, by Janina Domanska (Macmillan)
Moja Means One: Swahili Counting Book by Muriel Feelings, illus. by Tom Feelings (Dial)
Hildilid's Night by Cheli Duran Ryan, illus. by Arnold Lobel (Macmillan)

1973 *The Funny Little Woman* retold by Arlene Mosel, illus. by Blair Lent (Dutton)
HONOR BOOKS:
Anansi the Spider adapted and illus. by Gerald McDermott (Holt, Rinehart and Winston)
Hosie's Alphabet by Hosea, Tobias and Lisa Baskin, illus. by Leonard Baskin (Viking)
Snow-White and the Seven Dwarfs translated by Randall Jarrell, illus. by Nancy Ekholm Burkert (Farrar, Straus & Giroux)
When Clay Sings by Byrd Baylor, illus. by Tom Bahti (Scribner)

1974 *Duffy and the Devil* by Harve Zemach, illus. by Margot Zemach (Farrar, Straus & Giroux)
HONOR BOOKS:
Three Jovial Huntsmen by Susan Jeffers (Bradbury)

Cathedral: The Story of Its Construction by David Macaulay (Houghton Mifflin)

1975 *Arrow to the Sun* adapted and illus. by Gerald McDermott (Viking)
HONOR BOOK:
Jambo Means Hello by Murial Feelings, illus. by Tom Feelings (Dial)

1976 *Why Mosquitoes Buzz in People's Ears* retold by Verna Aardema, illus. by Leo and Diane Dillon (Dial)
HONOR BOOKS:
The Desert Is Theirs by Byrd Baylor, illus. by Peter Parnall (Scribner)
Strega Nona retold and illus. by Tomie de Paola (Prentice-Hall)

1977 *Ashanti to Zulu: African Traditions* by Margaret Musgrove, illus. by Leo and Diane Dillon (Dial)
HONOR BOOKS:
The Amazing Bone written and illus. by William Steig (Farrar, Straus & Giroux)
The Contest retold and illus. by Nonny Hogrogian (Greenwillow)
Fish for Supper written and illus. by M. B. Goffstein (Dial)
The Golem written and illus. by Beverly Brodsky McDermott (Lippincott)
Hawk, I'm Your Brother by Byrd Baylor, illus. by Peter Parnall (Scribner)

1978 *Noah's Ark* by Peter Spier (Doubleday)
HONOR BOOKS:
Castle by David Macaulay (Houghton Mifflin)
It Could Always Be Worse by Margot Zemach (Farrar, Straus & Giroux)

1979 *The Girl Who Loved Wild Horses*, by Paul Goble (Bradbury)

HONOR BOOKS:
Freight Train by Donald Crews (Greenwillow)
The Way to Start a Day by Byrd Baylor, illus. by Peter Parnall (Scribner)

1980 *Ox-Cart Man* by Donald Hall, illus. by Barbara Cooney (Viking)
HONOR BOOKS:
Ben's Trumpet by Rachel Isadora (Greenwillow)
The Garden of Abdul Gasazi by Chris Van Allusburg (Houghton)
The Treasure by Uri Shulevitz (Farrar)

1981 *Fables* by Arnold Lobel (Harper)
HONOR BOOKS:
The Bremen-town Musicians retold and illus. by Ilse Plume (Doubleday)
The Grey Lady and the Strawberry Snatcher by Molly Bang (Four Winds)
Mice Twice by Joseph Low (McElderry/Atheneum)
Truck by Donald Crews (Greenwillow)

1982 *On Market Street* by Arnold Lobel, illus. by Anita Lobel (Greenwillow)
HONOR BOOKS:
Outside Over There by Maurice Sendak (Harper)
A Visit to William Blake's Inn: Poems for Innocent and Experienced Travelers by Nancy Willard, illus. by Alice and Martin Provensen (Harcourt)
Where the Buffaloes Begin by Olaf Baker, illus. by Stephen Gammell (Warne)

NOTE: *In entries where an illustrator is not specifically named, the book was written and illustrated by the same person.*

Selected References

CHAPTER 1: The Nature of Language and Language Teaching

Altmann, S. A., ed. *Social Communication Among Primates.* Chicago: University of Chicago Press, 1967.

*Amon, Aline. *Reading, Writing, Chattering Chimps.* New York: Atheneum Publishers, 1975.

Bloom, Benjamin, et al., eds. *Taxonomy of Educational Objectives: Cognitive Domain.* New York: David McKay, 1956.

Boyd, Gertrude. *Linguistics in the Elementary School.* Itasca, Ill.: F. E. Peacock, 1976.

Burns, Paul C. "Linguistics: A Brief Guide for Principals," in *Linguistics for Teachers, Selected Readings.* Chicago: Science Research Associates, 1973.

*Castle, Sue. *Face Talk, Hand Talk, Body Talk.* Garden City, N.Y.: Doubleday, 1977.

*Chase, Stuart. *Danger — Men Talking! A Background Book on Semantics and Communication.* New York: Parents' Magazine Press, 1969.

*Cohen, Daniel. *Talking with the Animals.* New York: Dodd, Mead, 1971.

Denham, Carolyn and Ann Lieberman, eds. *Time to Learn.* Washington, D.C.: National Institute of Education, 1980.

DeStefano, Johanna S. *Language, the Learner and the School.* New York: John Wiley and Sons. 1978.

———. "Research Update: Demonstrations, Engagements and Sensitivity: A Revised Approach to Language Learning — Frank Smith" *Language Arts* 58 (January 1981): 103–112.

*Children's books

*Epstein, Sam, and Beryl Epstein. *The First Book of Codes and Ciphers.* New York: Frank Watt, 1956.

Fries, Charles Carpenter. "Language Meaning and Language Signals," Chapter 3 in *Linguistics and Reading.* New York: Holt, Rinehart and Winston, 1963.

Frings, H., and M. Frings. *Animal Communication.* New York: Blaisdell, 1964.

*Gallant, Roy A. *Man Must Speak: The Story of Language and How We Use It.* New York: Random House, 1969.

*Gans, Roma. *Bird Talk.* New York: Crowell, 1971 (Easy)

*Gilbert, Bill. *How Animals Communicate.* New York: Pantheon Books, 1966.

Goyer, Robert S. "Communication, Communicative Process, Meaning: Toward a Unified Theory," *Journal of Communication* 20 (March 1970): 4–16.

*Gross, Ruth Belov. *What Is That Alligator Saying?* New York: Hastings House, 1972 (Easy).

Halliday, M. A. K. *Learning How to Mean — Explorations in the Development of Language.* London: Edward Arnold, 1975.

Hockett, C. F. "The Origin of Speech," *Scientific American* 203 (September 1960): 89–96.

*Hofsinde, Robert. *Indian Sign Language.* New York: Morrow, 1956.

Jacobs, Francine. *The Secret Language of Animals.* New York: William Morrow, 1976.

Krathwohl, D. R., B. S. Bloom, and B. B. Masia. *Taxonomy of Educational Objectives Handbook II: Affective Domain.* New York: David McKay, 1968.

Lefevre, Carl A. "Communication, Language, American English," Chapter 2 in *Linguistics, English, and the Language Arts.* Boston: Allyn and Bacon, 1970.

Lindauer, Martin. *Communication Among Social Bees.* Cambridge, Mass.: Harvard University Press, 1961.

Mager, Robert F. *Preparing Instructional Objectives.* Palo Alto, Calif.: Fearon Publishers, 1962.

Monod, Jacques. *Chance and Necessity.* New York: Alfred A. Knopf, 1971.

*Patent, Dorothy Hinshaw. *How Insects Communicate.* New York: Holiday House, 1975.

*Pei, Mario. *All About Language.* Philadelphia: J. B. Lippincott, 1954.

Premack, D. "The Education of Sarah: A Chimp Learns the Language," *Psychology Today* 4(September 1970):54–58.

Sebeok, Thomas A. *Perspectives in Zoosemiotics.* The Hague, Netherlands: Mouton, 1972.

*Selsam, Millicent E. *The Language of Animals.* New York: Morrow, 1962.

Strehlo, Kevin. "Talk to the Animals," *Popular Computing* vol. 1, no. 8 (June 1982):102–108.

von Frisch, Karl. *The Dancing Bees.* London: Methuen, 1954.

CHAPTER 2: Our English Language

*Alexander, Arthur. *The Magic of Words.* Englewood Cliffs, N.J.: Prentice-Hall, 1962.

Alexander, Henry. *The Story of Our Language.* Garden City, N.Y.: Doubleday, 1969.

*Asimov, Isaac. *Words from the Myths.* Boston: Houghton Mifflin, 1961.

*———. *Words on the Map.* Boston: Houghton Mifflin, 1962.

Baugh, Albert C. *A History of the English Language,* 2nd ed. New York: Appleton-Century-Crofts, 1957.

*Benagh, Christine L. *100 Keys: Names Across the Land.* Nashville: Abingdon Press, 1973.

Boyd, Gertrude. *Linguistics in the Elementary School.* Itasca, Ill.: F. E. Peacock, 1976.

Bryant, Margaret M. *Modern English and Its Heritage,* 2nd ed. New York: Macmillan, 1962.

*Epstein, Sam, and Beryl Epstein. *The First Book of Words.* New York: Franklin Watts, 1954 (Easy).

*Funk, Charles Earl, and Charles Earl Funk, Jr. *Horsefeathers and Other Curious Words.* New York: Harper and Brothers, 1958.

Gleason, H. A. *Linguistics and English Grammar.* New York: Holt, Rinehart and Winston, 1965.

Jespersen, Otto. *Growth and Structure of the English Language,* 9th ed. Garden City, N.Y.: Doubleday, 1955.

*Laird, Helene, and Charlton Laird. *The Tree of Language.* Cleveland: World Publishing Company, 1957.

*Lambert, Eloise, and Mario Pei. *Our Names, Where They Came From and What They Mean.* Lothrop, Lee and Shepard, 1960.

Loughead, Flora Haines. *Dictionary of Given Names.* Glendale, Ill.: Arthur H. Clark, 1974.

Malmstrom, Jean. *Understanding Language, A Primer for the Language Arts Teacher.* New York: St. Martin's Press, 1977.

*Mathews, Mitford M. *American Words.* New York: World Publishing Company, 1959.

Mencken, H. L. *The American Language.* New York: Alfred A. Knopf, 1960.

Morris, W., and M. Morris. *Dictionary of Word & Phrase Origins.* New York: Harper and Row, 1967.

*Pizer, Vernon. *Ink, Ark, and All That: How American Places Got Their Names.* New York: G. P. Putnam's Sons, 1976.

Pyles, Thomas. *The English Language: A Brief History.* New York: Holt, Rinehart and Winston, 1968.

———. *The Origins and Development of the English Language.* New York: Harcourt Brace Jovanovich, 1964.

Smith, Elsdon C. *The Story of Our Names.* New York: Harper and Row, 1950.

———. *American Surnames.* Radnor, Pa.: Chilton Book Company, 1969.

———. *New Dictonary of American Family Names.* New York: Harper and Row, 1973.

*Sparke, William. *Story of the English Language.* New York: Abelard Schuman, 1965.

*Stewart, George R. *Names On the Land.* Boston: Houghton Mifflin, 1958.

*Waller, Leslie. *Our American Language.* New York: Holt, Rinehart and Winston, 1960 (Easy).

CHAPTER 3: Grammar, Usage, and Dialects

Bailey, Richard W., and Jay L. Robinson, eds. *Varieties of Present Day English.* New York: Macmillan, 1973.

Boyd, Gertrude. *Linguistics in the Elementary School.* Itasca, Ill.: F. E. Peacock, 1976.

Chomsky, Carol. *The Acquisition of Syntax in Children 5 to 10.* Cambridge, Mass.: M.I.T. Press, 1969.

Chomsky, Noam. *Syntactic Structures.* The Hague: Mouton, 1957.

————. *Reflections on Language.* New York: Pantheon Books, 1975.

Davis, A. L., ed. *Culture, Class, and Language Variety.* Urbana, Ill.: National Council of Teachers of English, 1972.

DeStefano, Johanna S. *Language, the Learner and the School.* New York: John Wiley and Sons, 1978.

————. "Research Update: Linguistic Consciousness Raising in Children — Carol Chomsky," *Language Arts* 58(May 1981):607–612.

Elgin, Suzette Haden. *A Primer of Transformational Grammar for Rank Beginners.* Urbana, Ill.: National Council of Teachers of English, 1975.

Frazier, Alexander, ed. *New Directions in Elementary English.* Urbana, Ill.: National Council of Teachers of English, 1967.

Fromkin, Victoria, and Robert Rodman. *An Introduction to Language*, 2nd ed. New York: Holt, Rinehart and Winston, 1978.

Gleason, H. A., Jr. *Linguistics and English Grammar.* New York: Holt, Rinehart and Winston, 1965.

Guth, Hans P. *English for a New Generation.* New York: McGraw-Hill, 1973.

Hook, J. N., and Michael G. Crowell. *Modern English Grammar for Teachers.* New York: Ronald Press, 1970.

Jespersen, Otto. *Growth and Structure of the English Language*, 9th ed. Garden City, N.Y.: Doubleday, 1955.

Joyce, William W., and James A. Banks. *Teaching the Language Arts to Culturally Different Children.* Reading, Mass.: Addison-Wesley, 1971.

Labov, William. "The Logic of Nonstandard English," in *Language and the Language Arts.* Johanna S. DeStefano and Sharon E. Fox, eds. Boston: Little, Brown, 1974.

Lefevre, Carl A. *Linguistics and the Teaching of Reading.* New York: McGraw-Hill, 1964.

————. *Linguistics, English, and the Language Arts.* Boston: Allyn and Bacon, 1970.

Liles, Bruce L. *An Introductory Transformational Grammar.* Englewood Cliffs, N.J.: Prentice-Hall, 1971.

Malmstrom, Jean. *Understanding Language, A Primer for the Language Arts Teacher.* New York: St. Martin's Press, 1977.

Malmstrom, Jean, and Annabel Ashley. *Dialects — U.S.A.* Urbana, Ill.: National Council of Teachers of English, 1963.

Pooley, Robert C. "Teaching Usage Today and Tomorrow," in *Language Arts Concepts for Elementary School Teachers.* Paul C. Burns, J. Estill Alexander, and Arnold R. Davis, eds. Itasca, Ill.: F. E. Peacock, 1972.

Reed, Carroll E. *Dialects of American English*, rev. ed. Amherst, Mass.: University of Massachusetts Press, 1977.

Roberts, Paul. *English Syntax.* New York: Harcourt Brace Jovanovich, 1964.

Ross, Charles S., and Mary M. Ross. "Linguistics in the Elementary School," in *Language Arts Concepts for Elementary School Teachers.* Paul C. Burns, J. Estill Alexander, and Arnold R. Davis, eds. Itasca, Ill.: F. E. Peacock, 1972.

Savage, John F. *Linguistics for Teachers, Selected Readings.* Chicago: Science Research Associates, 1973.

Shuy, Roger W. *Discovering American Dialects.* Urbana, Ill.: National Council of Teachers of English, 1967.

Sledd, James. "Doublespeak: Dialectology in the Service of Big Brother," in *Varieties of Present Day English.* Richard W. Bailey and Jay L. Robinson, eds. New York: Macmillan, 1973.

Smith, Frank. *Psycholinguistics and Reading.* New York: Holt, Rinehart and Winston, 1973.

Smitherman, Geneva. *Talkin and Testifyin.* Boston: Houghton Mifflin, 1977.

Tiedt, Sidney W., and Iris M. Tiedt. *Language Arts Activities for the Classroom.* Boston: Allyn and Bacon, 1978.

Weaver, Constance. *Grammar for Teachers, Perspectives and Definitions.* Urbana, Ill.: National Council of Teachers of English, 1979.

CHAPTER 4: Oral Language

Bellugi, Ursula, and Roger Brown. *The Acquisition of Language.* Chicago: University of Chicago Press, 1964.

Black, Janet K. "Those 'Mistakes' Tell Us a Lot," *Language Arts* 57(May 1980):508–513.

Bloom, Benjamin S. *Taxonomy of Educational Objectives.* New York: David McKay, 1956.

Bloom, Lois. *One Word at a Time.* The Hague: Mouton, 1973.

Book, Cassandra, and Kathleen Galvin. *Instruction In and About Small Group Discussion.* Urbana, Ill.: ERIC Clearinghouse on Reading and Communication Skills, 1975.

Braine, M.D. "The Acquisition of Language in Infant and Child," in *The Learning of Language.* Caroll E. Reed, ed. New York: Appleton-Century-Croft, 1971.

Broman, Betty L. "Too Much Shushing — Let Children Talk," *Childhood Education* 46(December 1969):132–34.

Brown, Roger. *A First Language*. Cambridge, Mass.: Harvard University Press, 1973.

Buckley, Marilyn Hanf. "A Guide for Developing an Oral Language Curriculum," *Language Arts* 53(September 1976):621–27.

Cazden, Courtney. *Child Language and Education*. New York: Holt, Rinehart and Winston, 1972.

———. ed. *Language in Early Childhood Education*. Washington, D.C.: National Association for the Education of Young Children, 1972.

Chomsky, Carol. *The Acquisition of Syntax in Children from 5 to 10*. Cambridge, Mass.: M.I.T. Press, 1969.

———. "Language Development After Age Six," in *Language and the Language Arts*. Johanna S. DeStefano and Sharon E. Fox, eds. Boston: Little, Brown, 1974.

Clark, Eve. "What's In a Word? On the Child's Acquisition of Semantics in His First Language," in *Cognitive Development and the Acquisition of Language*. Timothy E. Moore, ed. New York: Academic Press, 1973.

Dale, Philip S. *Language Development*, 2nd ed. New York: Holt, Rinehart and Winston, 1976.

Denes, Peter B., and Elliot N. Pinson. *The Speech Chain*. Garden City, N.Y.: Anchor Books, 1973.

DeStefano, Johanna. *Language, the Learner and the School*. New York: John Wiley and Sons, 1978.

Elgin, Suzette Haden. *What Is Linguistics?* Englewood Cliffs, N.J.: Prentice-Hall, 1973.

Florio, Susan and Jeffery Shultz. "Competence at Home and at School," *Theory into Practice* 18(October 1979):234–239.

Genishi, Celia. "Language Across the Contexts of Early Childhood," *Theory into Practice* 20(Spring 1981):109–115.

———. "Young Children Communicating in the Classroom: Selected Research," *Theory into Practice* 18(October 1979):244–250.

Ginsburg, Herbert, and Sylvia Opper. *Piaget's Theory of Intellectual Development*. Englewood Cliffs, N.J.: Prentice-Hall, 1969.

Grayson, Marion F. *Let's Do Fingerplays*. Washington, D.C.: R. B. Luce, 1962.

Henry, Mabel Wright, ed. *Creative Experiences in Oral Language*. Urbana, Ill.: National Council of Teachers of English, 1967.

Hunkins, Francis P. *Questioning Strategies and Techniques*. Boston: Allyn and Bacon, 1972.

Klein, Marvin L. "Designing a Talk Environment" *Language Arts* 56(September 1979):647–656.

———. *Talk in the Language Arts Classroom*. Urbana, Ill.: ERIC Clearinghouse on Reading and

Communication Skills and National Council of Teachers of English, 1977.

Lenneberg, Eric H. "The Biological Foundations of Language," in *Language Arts Concepts for Elementary School Teachers*. Paul C. Burns, J. Estill Alexander, and Arnold R. Davis, eds. Itasca, Ill.: F. E. Peacock, 1972.

Lindfors, Judith. *Children's Language and Learning*. Englewood Cliffs, N.J.: Prentice-Hall, 1980.

Loban, Walter. *Problems in Oral English*. Urbana, Ill.: National Council of Teachers of English, 1966.

———. *Language Development: Kindergarten through Grade Twelve*. Urbana, Ill.: National Council of Teachers of English, 1976.

McNeill, David. *The Acquisition of Language: The Study of Developmental Psycholinguistics*. New York: Harper and Row, 1970.

Malmstrom, Jean. *Understanding Language, A Primer for the Language Arts Teacher*. New York: St. Martin's Press, 1977.

Menyuk, Paula. *The Acquisition and Development of Language*. Englewood Cliffs, N.J.: Prentice-Hall, 1971.

———. *Language and Maturation*. Cambridge, Mass.: M.I.T. Press, 1977.

Naylor, Rex V. "Helping the Stutterer," in *Readings in the Language Arts*, 2nd ed. Verna Dieckman Anderson, Paul S. Anderson, Francis Ballentine, and Virgil M. Horves, eds. New York: Macmillan, 1968.

Petty, Walter T., ed. *Research in Oral Language*. Urbana, Ill.: National Council of Teachers of English, 1967.

Phillips, John L., Jr. *The Origins of Intellect: Piaget's Theory*. San Francisco: W. H. Freeman, 1969.

Piaget, Jean. *The Language and Thought of the Child*. Trans. M. Gabian. London: Routledge & Kegan Paul, 1926.

Pinnell, Gay Su, ed. *Discovering Language with Children*. Urbana, Ill.: National Council of Teachers of English, 1980.

Platt, Nancy G. "Social Context: An Essential for Learning" *Language Arts* 56(September 1979):620–627.

Possien, Wilma M. *They All Need to Talk*. New York: Appleton-Century-Crofts, 1969.

Reed, C. E. *The Learning of Language*. Urbana, Ill.: National Council of Teachers of English, 1971.

Richmond, P. G. *An Introduction to Piaget*. New York: Basic Books, 1970.

Russell, David H. *Children's Thinking*. Lexington, Mass.: Ginn, 1956.

Sanders, Norris M. *Classroom Questions: What Kinds?* New York: Harper and Row, 1966.

Scott, Louise Binder. *Rhymes for Fingers and Flannelboards.* St. Louis: Webster Publishing Co., 1960.

Smith, Frank. "The Language Arts and the Learner's Mind" *Language Arts* 56(February 1979):118–125 ff.

Taba, Hilda. "The Teaching of Thinking," *Elementary English* 42(May 1965):534–42.

Templin, Mildred C. *Certain Language Skills in Children: Their Development and Interrelationship.* Minneapolis: University of Minnesota Press, 1957.

Tiedt, Sidney, and Iris M. Tiedt. *Language Arts Activities for the Classroom.* Boston: Allyn and Bacon, 1978.

Tough, Joan. *The Development of Meaning: A Study of Children's Use of Language.* New York: Wiley, 1977.

Vygotsky, Lev Semenovich. *Thought and Language.* Trans. Eugenia Hanfmann and Gertrude Vakar. Cambridge, Mass.: M.I.T. Press, 1962.

CHAPTER 5: Listening

Canfield, Robert. "How Useful Are Lessons for Listening?" *The Elementary School Journal* 62(December 1961):147–51.

Denby, Robert. "Report on Research in Listening and Listening Skills," *Elementary English* 46(April 1969):511–17.

Duker, Sam. *Listening Bibliography.* New York: Scarecrow Press, 1964.

———. *Listening: Readings.* Metuchen, N.J.: Scarecrow Press, 1966.

———. *Listening: Readings,* Vol. 2. Metuchen, N.J.: Scarecrow Press, 1971.

Fawcett, Annabel E. "Training in Listening," *Elementary English* 43(May 1966):473–76.

Frazier, Alexander. "The Teaching of Listening: A Memo to Teachers," *Elementary English* 35(February 1958):111–12.

Hall, Edward T. "Listening Behavior: Some Cultural Differences," *Phi Delta Kappan* 50(March 1969):379–80.

Harris, Mary Imogene. *A Handbook of Speaking and Listening Activities for Elementary School.* Minneapolis: T. S. Denison, 1971.

Horrworth, Gloria L. "Listening: A Facet of Oral Language," *Elementary English* 43(December 1966):856.

Keller, Paul W. "Major Findings in Listening in the Past Ten Years," *Journal of Communication* 10(March 1960):29–38.

Kopp, O. W. "The Evaluation of Oral Language Activities," *Elementary English* 44(February 1967):114–23.

Landry, Donald. "The Neglect of Listening," *Elementary English* 46(May 1969):599–605.

Lundsteen, Sara W. "Critical Listening: An Experiment," *Elementary School Journal* 66(March 1966):311–15.

———. *Listening: Its Impact on Reading and the Other Language Arts,* rev. ed. Urbana, Ill.: National Council of Teachers of English, 1979.

Nichols, Ralph G. "What Can Be Done About Listening," *The Supervisor's Notebook* 22, No. 1. Glenview, Ill.: Scott, Foresman (undated).

———. *Are You Listening?* New York: McGraw-Hill, 1967.

Pratt, E. "Experimental Evaluation of a Program for the Improvement of Listening," *The Elementary School Journal* 56(March 1956):314–20.

Russell, David H., and Elizabeth F. Russell. *Listening Aids Through the Grades,* 2nd ed. New York: Teachers College Press, Columbia University, 1979.

Smith, Robert W. L. *American Language Today, Purple Sand.* New York: Webster/McGraw-Hill, 1974.

Taylor, Stanford. *Listening: What Research Says to the Teacher.* Washington, D.C.: National Education Association, 1973.

Tiedt, Sidney W., and Iris M. Tiedt. *The Elementary Teacher's Complete Ideas Handbook.* Englewood Cliffs, N.J.: Prentice-Hall, 1965.

———. *Language Arts Activities for the Classroom.* Boston: Allyn and Bacon, 1978.

Wagner, Guy. *Listening Games.* Darien, Conn.: Teachers Publishing Corporation, 1962.

Wilt, Miriam. "Study of Teacher Awareness of Listening as a Factor in Elementary Education," *Journal of Educational Research* 43(April 1950):626–36.

Wolvin, Andrew D. and Carolyn Gwynn Coakley. *Listening Instruction, Theory and Research into Practice.* Urbana, Ill.: ERIC Clearinghouse on Reading and Communication Skills, 1979.

CHAPTER 6: Creative Drama

Blackie, Pamela, Bess Bullough, and Doris Nash. *Drama.* New York: Citation Press, 1972.

Blank, William Earl. "The Effectiveness of Creative Dramatics in Developing Voice, Vocabulary, and Personality," *Speech Monographs* 21(August 1954):190.

Busching, Beverly A. "Readers Theatre: An Education for Language and Life," *Language Arts* 58(March 1981):330–338.

Carleton, Lessie, and Robert H. Moore. *Reading, Self-Directive Dramatization and Self-Concept.* Columbus, Ohio: Charles E. Merrill, 1968.

Chambers, Dewey W. *The Oral Tradition — Storytelling and Creative Drama,* 2nd ed. Dubuque, Iowa: William C. Brown, 1977.

Complo, Sister Jannita Marie. *Dramkinetics in the Classroom.* Boston: Plays, Inc., 1974.

Courtney, Richard. *Play, Drama and Thought: The Intellectual Background to Dramatic Education.* London: Cassell and Company, 1968.

Dillon, David A., "Perspectives: Drama As a Sense of Wonder—Brian Way," *Language Arts* 58(March 1981):356–362.

Ehrlich, Harriett, ed. *Creative Dramatics Handbook,* 2nd rev. ed. Philadelphia: School District of Philadelphia, 1974.

Gillies, Emily P. *Creative Dramatics for All Children.* Washington, D.C.: Association for Childhood Education International, 1973.

Heathcote, Dorothy. "How Does Drama Serve Thinking, Talking, and Writing?" *Elementary English* 47(December 1970):1077–81.

Heinig, Ruth Beall, and Lyda Stillwell. *Creative Dramatics for the Classroom Teacher,* 2nd ed. Englewood Cliffs, N.J.: Prentice-Hall, 1981.

Hoetker, James. *Dramatics and the Teaching of Literature.* Urbana, Ill.: National Council of Teachers of English/ERIC, 1969.

Lightwood, Donald. *Creative Drama for Primary Schools, A Handbook of Activities.* London: Blackie and Son, 1970.

McCaslin, Nellie. *Creative Dramatics in the Classroom,* 2nd ed. New York: David McKay, 1974.

McIntyre, Barbara. *Creative Drama in the Elementary School.* Itasca, Ill.: F. E. Peacock, 1974.

Mandelbaum, Jean. "Creative Dramatics in Early Childhood," *Young Children* 30(January 1975):84–92.

Moffett, James. *A Student-Centered Language Arts Curriculum, Grades K–13: A Handbook for Teachers.* Boston: Houghton Mifflin, 1973.

Osten, Gwen. "Structure in Creativity," *Elementary English* 46(April 1969):438–43.

Ross, Elinor P., and Betty D. Roe. "Creative Drama Builds Proficiency in Reading," *The Reading Teacher* 30(January 1977):383–87.

Schwartz, Dorothy Thames, and Dorothy Aldrich, eds. *Give Them Roots and Wings: A Guide to Drama in the Elementary School.* Washington, D.C.: American Theater Association, 1972.

Schwartz, Sheila. "Involving Students in the Drama Process, K–12," *English Journal* 64(May 1975):32–38.

Siks, Geraldine Brain. *Children's Literature for Dramatization.* New York: Harper and Row, 1964.

———. *Drama with Children.* New York: Harper and Row, 1977.

Slade, Peter. *Child Drama.* New York: Philosophical Library, 1955.

Stewig, John W. "Creative Drama and Language Growth," *Elementary School Journal* 72(January 1972):176–88.

———. *Informal Drama in the Elementary Arts Program.* New York: Teacher's College Press, 1983.

———. "Drama: Integral Part of the Language Arts," *Elementary English* 51(January 1974):66–71.

Wagner, Betty Jane. *Dorothy Heathcote: Drama as a Learning Medium.* Washington, D.C.: National Education Association, 1976.

Ward, Winnifred. *Playmaking with Children from Kindergarten through Junior High School,* 2nd ed. New York: Appleton-Century-Crofts, 1957.

Way, Brian. *Development through Drama.* London: Longman, 1967.

Woolf, Gerald, and Mary Jane Myers. "The Effect of Two Ear Training Procedures on the Improvement of Auditory Discrimination and Articulation," *Exceptional Children* 34(May 1968):659–65.

Puppets

Alkema, Chester Jay. *Puppet Making.* New York: Sterling, 1971.

Gardner, Richard. *101 Hand Puppets.* New York: David McKay, 1962.

Paludan, Lis. *Playing with Puppets.* Boston: Plays, Inc., 1975.

Pels, Gertrude Jaeckel. *Easy Puppets.* New York: Crowell, 1951.

Ross, Laura and Frank Ross, Jr. *Finger Puppets: Easy to Make, Fun to Use.* New York: Lothrop, Lee and Shepard, 1971.

Weiger, Myra. "Puppetry," *Elementary English* 51(January 1974):55–65.

CHAPTER 7: Written Composition

Applebee, Arthur N. "Children's Narratives: New Directions," *Reading Teacher* 34(November 1980):137–142.

———. *The Child's Concept of Story: Ages 2–17.* Chicago: University of Chicago Press, 1978.

Applegate, Mauree. *Freeing Children to Write.* New York: Harper and Row, 1963.

Botel, Morton. "A Formula for Measuring Syntactic Complexity," *Elementary English* 49(April 1972): 513–16.

Burrows, Alvina Treut, Doris C. Jackson, and Dorothy O. Saunders. *They All Want to Write*, 3rd ed. New York: Holt, Rinehart and Winston, 1964.

Canfield, Dorothy. "How Flint and Fire Started and Grew" in *The Creative Process* by Brewster Ghiselin. New York: Mentor Books, 1952.

Carlson, Ruth Kearney. *Language Sparklers*. Berkeley, Calif.: Wagner, 1972.

———. *Sparkling Words: Two Hundred and Twenty-Five Practical and Creative Writing Ideas*. Geneva, Ill.: Paladin House, 1973.

Clay, Marie M. "Learning and Teaching Writing: A Developmental Perspective," *Language Arts* 59(January 1982):65–70.

Cooper, Charles and Lee Odell. *Research on Composing*. Urbana, Ill.: National Council of Teachers of English, 1978.

Cramer, Ronald. *Children's Writing and Language Growth*. Columbus, Ohio: Charles Merrill, 1978.

Crowhurst, Marion. "The Writing Workshop: An Experiment in Peer Response to Writing," *Language Arts* 56(October 1979):757–762.

DeHaven, Edna P. "A Questioning Strategy Model for Creative Writing," *Elementary English* 50(September 1973):959–61, 987.

Evertts, Eldona, ed. *Explorations in Children's Writing*. Urbana, Ill.: National Council of Teachers of English, 1970.

Frazier, Alexander. "A Vocabulary of the Senses," *Elementary English* 47(February 1970):176–84.

Furner, Beatrice. "Creative Writing Through Creative Dramatics," *Elementary English* 50(March 1973):405–08.

Gensler, Kinereth. "Dreams Poems in Broad Daylight," *Poemmaking: Poets in Classrooms*. Ruth Whitman and Harriet Feinberg, eds. Lawrence, Mass.: Massachusetts Council of Teachers of English, 1975.

Glaus, Marlene. *From Thoughts to Words*. Urbana, Ill.: National Council of Teachers of English, 1965.

Graves, Donald. "An Examination of the Writing Processes of Seven-Year-Old Children," *Research in the Teaching of English* 9(1975):227–241.

———. "Let Children Show Us How to Write," *Visible Language* vol. 13, no. 1:16–28.

Haley-James, Shirley, ed. *Perspective on Writing in Grades 1–8*. Urbana, Ill.: National Council of Teachers of English, 1981.

———. "Revising Writing in the Upper Grades," *Language Arts* 58(March 1981):562–566.

Hennings, Dorothy Grant, and Barbara M. Grant. *Written Expression in the Language Arts*, 2nd ed. New York: Teacher's College Press, 1981.

Hunt, Kellogg. *Differences in Grammatical Structures Written at Three Grade Levels*, NCTE Research Report No. 3. Urbana, Ill.: National Council of Teachers of English, 1965.

———. "Teaching Syntactic Maturity," in *Language and the Language Arts*. Johanna S. DeStefano and Sharon E. Fox, eds. Boston: Little, Brown, 1974.

James, Henry. "Preface to the Spoils of Poynton," in *The Creative Process* by Brewster Ghiselin. New York: Mentor Books, 1952.

Jett-Simpson, Mary. "Writing Stories Using Model Structures: The Circle Story, *Language Arts* 58(March 1981):293–299.

King, Martha L. "Learning How to Mean in Written Language," *Theory into Practice* 19(Summer 1980):163–169.

Koch, Kenneth. "Syllogisms and Superstitions: The Current State of Responding to Writing," *Language Arts* 59(May 1982):464–471.

———. *Wishes, Lies, and Dreams*. New York: Vintage Books, 1970.

Larson, Rich L. *Children and Writing in the Elementary School*. New York: Oxford University Press, 1975.

Lickteig, M. J. "Research-based Recommendations for Teachers of Writing," *Language Arts* 58(January 1981):44–50.

Livingston, Myra C. *When You Are Alone/It Keeps You Capone: An Approach to Creative Writing with Children*. New York: Atheneum, 1973.

Lundsteen, Sara W., ed. *Help for the Teacher of Written Composition (K–9)*. Urbana, Ill.: National Council of Teachers of English, 1976.

Mearns, Hughes. *Creative Power: The Education of Youth in the Creative Arts*. New York: Dover Publications, 1958.

Mellon, John C. *Transformational Sentence-Combining: A Method for Enhancing the Development of Syntactic Fluency in English Composition*. Urbana, Ill.: NCTE Research Report No. 10. 1969.

Meyers, Miles. *A Procedure for Writing Assessment and Holistic Scoring*. Urbana, Ill.: ERIC Clearinghouse on Reading and Communication Skills and the National Council of Teachers of English, 1980.

Miller, Barbara, and James Ney. "The Effect of Systematic Oral Exercises on the Writing of Fourth-grade Students," *Research in the Teaching of English* 2(Spring 1968):44–66.

O'Donnell, Roy C., William J. Griffin, and Raymond C. Norris. *The Syntax of Kindergarten and Elementary*

School Children: A Transformational Analysis, NCTE Research Report No. 8. Urbana, Ill.: National Council of Teachers of English, 1967.

O'Hare, Frank. *Sentence-Combining: Improving Student Writing without Formal Grammar Instruction.* Urbana, Ill.: National Council of Teachers of English, 1973.

Pease, Don. *Creative Writing in the Elementary School.* New York: Exposition Press, 1964.

Perron, Jack. "Beginning Writing: It's All in the Mind," *Language Arts* 53(September 1976):652–57.

Petty, Walter T., and Mary E. Bowen. *Slithery Snakes and Other Aids to Children's Writing.* New York: Appleton-Century-Crofts, 1967.

Pratt-Butler, Grade K. *Let Them Write Creatively.* Columbus, Ohio: Charles E. Merrill, 1973.

Sager, Carol. *Improving the Quality of Written Composition through Pupil Use of a Rating Scale.* Doctoral dissertation, Boston University School of Education, 1973.

Schaefer, Charles E. *Developing Creativity in Children.* Buffalo, N.Y.: D.O.K. Publishers, 1973.

Schiller, Andrew and William A. Jenkins. *In Other Words: A Beginning Thesaurus.* Glenview, Ill.: Scott, Foresman and Company, 1982.

———. *In Other Words: A Junior Thesaurus.* Glenview, Ill.: Scott, Foresman and Company, 1982.

Smith, Frank. *Writing and the Writer.* New York: Holt, Rinehart and Winston, 1982.

Spandel, Vicki and Richard Stiggins. *Direct Measures of Writing Skill: Issues and Applications.* Portland, Or.: Northwest Regional Educational Laboratory, 1980.

Torrance, E. Paul. *Encouraging Creativity in the Classroom.* Dubuque, Iowa: William C. Brown, 1970.

Tway, Eileen. "Teacher Responses to Children's Writing," *Language Arts* 57:(October 1980):763–772.

Whitman, Ruth, and Harriet Feinberg, eds. *Poemmaking: Poets in Classrooms.* Lawrence, Mass.: Massachusetts Council of Teachers of English, 1975.

Wilde, Jack and Thomas Newkirk. "Writing Detective Stories," *Language Arts* 58(March 1981):286–292.

Vygotsky, Lev Semenovich. *Thought and Language.* Cambridge, Mass.: M.I.T. Press, 1962.

CHAPTER 8: Spelling

Allred, Ruel A. *Spelling: The Application of Research Findings.* Washington, D.C.: National Education Association, 1977.

Baugh, Albert C. *A History of the English Language,* 2nd ed. New York: Appleton-Century-Crofts, 1957.

Beers, Carol Strickland and James Wheelock Beers. "Three Assumptions about Learning to Spell," *Language Arts* 58(May 1981):573–580.

Beers, James Wheelock and E. H. Henderson. "A Study of Developing Orthographic Concepts among First Grade Children," *Research in the Teaching of English* 11(Fall 1977):133–148.

Boyd, Gertrude A., and E. Gene Talbert. *Spelling in the Elementary School.* Columbus, Ohio: Charles E. Merrill, 1971.

Chomsky, Carol. "Reading, Writing, and Phonology," *Harvard Educational Review* 40(May 1970):287–309.

Chomsky, Noam, and M. Halle. *The Sound Patterns of English.* New York: Harper and Row, 1968.

Clay, Marie. *What Did I Write?* Exeter, N.H.: Heinemann Educational Books, 1975.

Fitzgerald, James A. *A Basic Life Spelling Vocabulary.* Milwaukee, Wis.: Bruce Publishing Co., 1951a.

———. *The Teaching of Spelling.* Milwaukee, Wis.: Bruce Publishing Co., 1951b.

Folger, Sigmund. "The Case for a Basic Written Vocabulary," *Elementary School Journal* 47(September 1946):43–47.

Forester, A. D. "Learning to Spell by Spelling," *Theory Into Practice* 19(Summer 1980):186–193.

Frith, Uta, ed. *Cognitive Processes in Spelling.* London: Academic Press, 1980.

Ganschow, Leonore. "Discovering Children's Learning Strategies for Spelling through Error Pattern Analysis," *Reading Teacher* 34(March 1981):676–680.

Gentry, J. R. "Learning to Spell Developmentally," *Reading Teacher* 34(January 1981):378–381.

Graves, Donald H. "Research Update: Spelling Tests and Structural Analysis Methods," *Language Arts* 54(January 1977):86–90.

Greene, Harry A. *The New Iowa Spelling Scale.* Iowa City, Iowa: University of Iowa, 1955.

Hanna, Jean, and Paul R. Hanna. "Spelling as a School Subject: A Brief History," *The National Elementary Principal* 38(May 1959):8–23.

Hanna, Paul R., and Jean S. Hanna, "The Teaching of Spelling," *The National Elementary Principal* 45(November 1965):19–28.

Hanna, Paul R., Jean Hanna, Richard E. Hodges, and Edwin H. Rudorf, Jr. *Phoneme-Grapheme Relationships Basic to Cues for Improvement of Spelling.* USOE Cooperative Research Project No. 1991. Washington, D.C.: Government Printing Office, 1966.

Hanna, Paul R., Richard Hodges, and Jean S. Hanna. *Spelling: Structure and Strategies*. Boston: Houghton Mifflin, 1971.

Hillerich, Robert L. *Spelling: An Element in Written Expression*. Columbus, Ohio: Charles E. Merrill, 1976.

Hodges, Richard E. *Learning To Spell*. Urbana, Ill.: Clearinghouse on Reading and Communication Skills and National Council of Teachers of English, 1981.

————. "The Psychological Bases of Spelling," *Elementary English* 42(October 1965):629–35.

Hodges, Richard E., and E. Hugh Rudorf. "Searching Linguistic Cues for the Teaching of Spelling," *Elementary English* 42(1965):527–33.

Hollingsworth, Paul M. "Spelling Lists — Outdated?" *Elementary English* 42(1965):151.

Horn, Ernest. *A Basic Writing Vocabulary*. University of Iowa Monographs in Education No. 41. Iowa City: University of Iowa Press, 1926.

————. "Phonetics and Spelling," *Elementary School Journal* 57(May 1957):424–32.

————. *What Research Says to the Teacher: Teaching Spelling*. Washington, D.C.: National Education Association, 1967.

Horn, Thomas D., ed. *Research on Handwriting and Spelling*. Urbana, Ill.: National Council of Teachers of English, 1966.

Lamb, Pose. "Linguistics and the Teaching of Spelling," Chapter 2 in *Linguistics in Proper Perspective*, 2nd ed. Columbus, Ohio: Charles E. Merrill, 1977.

Marino, Jacqueline L. "Spelling Errors: From Analysis to Instruction," *Language Arts* 58(May 1981):567–572.

Pyles, Thomas. *The Origins and Development of the English Language*. New York: Harcourt Brace Jovanovich, 1964.

Reed, Charles. *Children's Categorization of Speech Sounds in English*. Urbana, Ill.: National Council of Teachers of English, 1975.

Keith, Herbert, et al. "Influence of Distributed Practice and Daily Testing on Weekly Spelling Tests," *The Journal of Educational Research* 68(October 1974):73–77.

Rinsland, Henry A. *A Basic Vocabulary of Elementary School Children*. New York: Macmillan, 1945.

Skeat, Walter W. *A Primer of English Etymology*. Oxford: The Clarendon Press, 1924.

Soffietti, James P. "Why Children Fail to Read: A Linguistic Analysis," *Harvard Educational Review* 25(Spring 1955):73–84.

Sorenson, Marilou R. and Kristen Jeffers Kerstetter. "Phonetic Spelling: A Case Study," *Language Arts* 56(October 1979):798–803.

Venezky, Richard L. *The Structure of English Orthography*. The Hague, Netherlands: Mouton, 1970.

Zutell, Jerry. "Some Psycholinguistic Perspectives on Children's Spelling," *Language Arts* 55(October 1978):844–851.

————. "Spelling Strategies of Primary School Children and Their Relationship to Piaget's Concept of Decentration," *Research in the Teaching of English* 13(February 1979):69–80.

CHAPTER 9: Handwriting

Andersen, Dan W. "Handwriting Research: Movement and Quality," *Elementary English* 42(January 1965):45–53.

————. *What Research Says to the Teacher: Teaching Handwriting*. Washington, D.C.: National Education Association, 1968.

————. "What Makes Writing Legible," *Elementary School Journal* 69(April 1969):364–69.

Burns, Paul C. *Improving Handwriting Instruction in Elementary Schools*, rev. ed. Minneapolis, Minn.: Burgess Publishing Company, 1968.

Cahn, William, and Rhoda Cahn. *The Story of Writing*. Irvington-on-Hudson, N.Y.: Harvey House, 1963 (Easy).

Clay, Marie. *What Did I Write?* Exeter, N.H.: Heinemann Educational Books, 1975.

————. "Research Update: Learning and Teaching Writing: A Developmental Perspective," *Language Arts* 59(January 1982):65–70.

DeFord, Diane E. "Young Children and Their Writing," *Theory into Practice* 19(Summer 1980):157–162.

Dubay, Inga and Barbara Getty. *Italic Handwriting Series: Instructional Manual*. Portland, Or.: Portland State University/Division of Continuing Education, 1980.

Enstrom, E. A. "The Relative Efficiency of the Various Approaches to Writing with the Left Hand," *Journal of Educational Research* 55(August 1962):573–77.

————. "The Left-handed Child," *Today's Education* 58(April 1969):43–44.

Enstrom, E. A., and Doris C. Enstrom. "In Print Handwriting: Preventing and Solving Reversal Problems," *Elementary English* 46(October 1969):759–64.

————. "Signs of Readiness," *Elementary English* 48(February 1971):215–20.

Fairbank, Alfred. *The Story of Handwriting: Origins and Developments.* New York: Watson-Guptill Publications, 1970.

Freeman, Frank N. *Guiding Growth in Handwriting.* Columbus, Ohio: Zaner-Bloser, 1964.

———. "A New Handwriting Scale," *Elementary School Journal* 59(January 1959):218–21.

Furner, Beatrice Ann. "The Development of a Program of Instruction for Beginning Handwriting Emphasizing Verbalization of Procedures to Increase Perception and an Analysis of the Effectiveness of this Program with a Commercial Method." Doctoral dissertation, University of Iowa, 1967.

Graham, Steve and Lamoine Miller. "Handwriting Research and Practice: A Unified Approach," *Focus on Exceptional Children* 13(October 1980):1–16.

Hanson, Irene W. "Teaching Remedial Handwriting," *Language Arts* 53(April 1976):428–31, 469.

Hofsinde, Robert. *Indian Picture Writing.* New York: William Morrow, 1959 (Very easy).

Irwin, Keith Gordon. *The Romance of Writing from Egyptian Hieroglyphics to Modern Letters, Numbers and Signs.* New York: The Viking Press, 1956 (Easy).

Kirk, Ursula. "Learning to Copy Letters: A Cognitive Rule-Governed Task," *The Elementary School Journal* 81(September 1980):28–33.

Lehman, Charles. "Teaching and Learning the Craft of Handwriting," *The Education Digest* 45(May 1980):50–52.

Lewis, Edward R. and Hilda P. Lewis. "Which Manuscript Letters Are Hard for First Graders?" *Elementary English* 41(December 1964):855–58.

Monroe, Marion. *Writing Our Language.* Glenview, Ill.: Scott, Foresman, 1973.

Myers, Emma Harrison. *The Whys and Hows of Teaching Handwriting.* Columbus, Ohio: Zaner-Bloser, 1963.

Noble and Noble. *Better Handwriting for You.* New York: Noble and Noble, 1971.

O'Donnell, Peg and Karen F. Duncan. "I Won't Write — But I'll Do Calligraphy," *The Pointer* 24(Spring 1980):4–11.

Ogg, Oscar. *The 26 Letters.* New York: Crowell, 1948 (Easy).

Petty, Walter T. "Handwriting and Spelling: Their Current Status in the Language Arts Curriculum," in *Research on Handwriting and Spelling.* Thomas D. Horn, ed. Urbana, Ill.: National Council of Teachers of English, 1966.

Pyles, Thomas. *The Origins and Development of the English Language.* New York: Harcourt Brace Jovanovich, 1964.

Rodgers, Frances. *Painted Rock to Printed Page.* Philadelphia: J. B. Lippincott, 1960 (Easy).

Russell, Solveig Paulson. *A is for Apply and Why.* New York: Abingdon Press, 1959 (Very easy).

Tawney, Shirley. "An Analysis of the Ball Point Pen Versus the Pencil as a Beginning Handwriting Instrument," *Elementary English* 44(January 1967): 59–61.

Thurber, Donald N. *D'Nealian Handwriting.* Glenview, Ill.: Scott, Foresman, 1978.

UNESCO (United Nations Educational, Scientific, and Cultural Organization), *The Art of Writing,* 1965.

Yee, Albert H., and Personke, Carl. "Teaching Handwriting: Why and How:" *Instructor* 77(November 1967):126–27.

Zaner-Bloser. *Creative Growth with Handwriting.* Columbus, Ohio: Zaner-Bloser, 1975.

Zaslow, Robert. "Reversals in Children as a Function of Midline Body Orientation," *Journal of Educational Psychology* 57(June 1966):133–39.

CHAPTER 10: Reading

Allen, P. David, and Dorothy J. Watson, eds. *Findings of Research in Miscue Analysis: Classroom Implications.* Urbana, Ill.: ERIC/National Council of Teachers of English, 1976.

Ashton-Warner, Sylvia. *Teacher.* New York: Simon and Schuster, 1963.

Bormuth, John R. "The Cloze Readability Procedure," *Elementary English* 45(April 1968): 429–36.

———. "The Cloze Procedure," *Help for the Reading Teacher.* William D. Page, ed. Urbana, Ill.: National Conference on Research in English, 1975.

Britton, James. *Language and Learning.* Baltimore, Md.: Penguin Books, 1970.

Burmeister, Lou. *Words — From Print to Meaning.* Reading, Mass.: Addison-Wesley, 1975.

Burns, Paul C. and Betty D. Roe. *Informal Reading Assessment.* Chicago: Rand McNally, 1980.

Ching, Doris C. *Reading and the Bilingual Child.* Newark, Del.: International Reading Association, 1976.

Clay, Marie. *Concepts about Print Test: Sand.* Exeter, N.H.: Heinemann Educational Books, 1972.

———. *Reading: The Patterning of Complex Behavior.* Exeter, N.H.: Heinemann Educational Books, 1979.

Cullinan, Bernice E., ed. *Black Dialects & Reading.* Urbana, Ill.: ERIC/National Council of Teachers of English, 1974.

Dallmann, Martha, Roger L. Rouch, Lynette Y. C. Char, and John DeBoer. *The Teaching of Reading,* 5th ed. New York: Holt, Rinehart and Winston, 1974.

Dean, Loraine. "Increase Vocabulary with the Word Elements, Mono Through Deca," *Elementary English* 47(January 1970):49–55.

Durkin, Dolores. "Phonics: Instruction That Needs to Be Improved," *The Reading Teacher* 28(November 1974):152–56.

————. *Strategies for Identifying Words*. Boston: Allyn and Bacon, 1976.

————. "What Is the Value of the New Interest in Reading Comprehension?" *Language Arts* 58(January 1981):23–43.

Freedman, Glenn and Elizabeth G. Reynolds. "Enriching Basal Reader Lessons with Semantic Webbing," *Reading Teacher* 33(March 1980):677–684.

Frith, Uta and Juliet M. Vogel. *Some Perceptual Prerequisites for Reading*. Newark, Delaware: International Reading Association, 1980.

Fry, Edward. *Elementary Reading Instruction*. New York: McGraw-Hill, 1977.

Goodman, Kenneth S. "Effective Teachers of Reading Know Language and Children," *Elementary English* 51(September 1974):823–28.

————. "Reading: A Psycholinguistic Guessing Game," *The Journal of the Reading Specialist* 4(May 1967):123–135.

Goodman, Kenneth S., ed. *Miscue Analysis*. Urbana, Ill.: ERIC/RCS/National Council of Teachers of English, 1973.

Goodman, Kenneth S., and Olive S. Niles. *Reading: Process and Program*. Urbana, Ill.: National Council of Teachers of English, 1970.

Hacker, Charles J. "From Schema Theory to Classroom Practice," *Language Arts* 57(November/December 1980):866–871.

Hafner, Lawrence E. *Patterns of Teaching Reading in the Elementary School*. New York: Macmillan, 1972.

Hall, Mary Ann. *Teaching Reading As a Language Experience*. Columbus, Ohio: Charles E. Merrill, 1976.

Hall, Mary Ann, and Christopher J. Ramig. *Linguistic Foundations for Reading*. Columbus, Ohio: Charles E. Merrill, 1978.

Heilman, Arthur W. *Phonics in Proper Perspective*. 4th ed. Columbus, Ohio: Charles E. Merrill, 1981.

————. *Principles and Practices of Teaching Reading*, 5th ed. Columbus, Ohio: Charles E. Merrill, 1981.

Heilman, Arthur W., and Elizabeth Ann Holmes. *Smuggling Language Into the Teaching of Reading*. Columbus, Ohio: Charles E. Merrill, 1972.

Johnson, Dale D. "The Dolch List Reexamined," *Reading Teacher* 24(February 1971):449–57.

Judd, Dorothy H. "Avoid Readability Formula Drudgery: Use Your School's Microcomputer," *Reading Teacher* 35(October 1981):7,8.

Laffey, James L., and Roger Shuy, eds. *Language Differences: Do They Interfere?* Newark, Del.: International Reading Association, 1973.

Lamb, Pose, and Richard Arnold, eds. *Reading: Foundations and Instructional Strategies*. Belmont, Calif.: Wadsworth, 1976.

Loban, Walter. *Language Development: Kindergarten through Grade Twelve*. Urbana, Ill.: National Council of Teachers of English, 1976.

McCracken, Robert A., and Marlene J. McCracken. *Reading Is Only the Tiger's Tail*. San Rafael, Calif.: Leswing Press, 1972.

Otto, Wayne, and R. Chester. "Sight Words for Beginning Readers," *Journal of Educational Research* 65(1972):425–43.

Page, William D., ed. *Help for the Reading Teacher*. Urbana, Ill.: ERIC/RCS/National Council of Teachers of English, 1975.

Pearson, P. David. "A Psycholinguistic Model of Reading," *Language Arts* 53(March 1976):309–314.

Ransom, Grayce A. *Preparing to Teach Reading*. Boston: Little, Brown, 1978.

Robinson, Francis P. *Effective Reading*. New York: Harper and Row, 1962.

Roeder, Harold H., and Nancy Lee. "Twenty-five Teacher-tested Ways to Encourage Voluntary Reading," *The Reading Teacher* 27(October 1973): 48–50.

Rosso, B. R. and Robert Emans. "Children's Use of Phonic Generalizations," *Reading Teacher* 34(April 1981):756–761.

Sanders, Norris M. *Classroom Questions, What Kind?* New York: Harper and Row, 1966.

Silvaroli, Nicholas J. *Classroom Reading Inventory*, 4th ed. Dubuque, Iowa: William C. Brown, 1982.

Smith, Frank. *Understanding Reading*, 3rd ed. New York: Holt, Rinehart and Winston, 1982.

Smith, Richard J., and Thomas C. Barrett. *Teaching Reading in the Middle Grades*. Reading, Mass.: Addison-Wesley, 1979.

Smith, Richard J., and Dale D. Johnson. *Teaching Children to Read*. Reading, Mass.: Addison-Wesley, 1976.

Spache, Evelyn B. *Reading Activities for Child Involvement*. Boston: Allyn and Bacon, 1976.

Spache, George D., and Evelyn B. Spache. *Reading in the Elementary School*, 4th ed. Boston: Allyn and Bacon, 1977.

Stauffer, Russell G. *The Language Experience Approach to the Teaching of Reading.* New York: Harper and Row, 1970.

———. *Directing the Reading-Thinking Process.* New York: Harper and Row, 1975.

Strange, Michael. "Instructional Implications of a Conceptual Theory of Reading Comprehension," *Reading Teacher* 34(January 1980):390–397.

Van Allen, Roach. *Language Experiences in Communication.* Boston: Houghton Mifflin, 1976.

Veatch, Jeannette, Florence Sawicki, Geralding Elliott, Eleanor Barnette, and Janis Blakey. *Key Words to Reading.* Columbus, Ohio: Charles E. Merrill, 1973.

Weaver, Constance. *Psycholinguistics and Reading: From Process to Practice.* Cambridge, Ma.: Winthrop, 1980.

Weaver, Phyllis. *Research Within Reach.* Washington, D.C.: National Institute of Education, 1979.

Zintz, Miles V. *The Reading Process,* 3rd ed. Dubuque, Iowa: William C. Brown, 1980.

CHAPTER 11: Children's Literature

Applebee, Arthur. "Children and Stories: Learning the Rules of the Game," *Language Arts* 56(September 1979):641–646.

Arbuthnot, May Hill, and Shelton L. Roote, Jr. *Time for Poetry.* Glenview, Ill.: Scott, Foresman, 1968.

Arbuthnot, May Hill, Dorothy M. Broderick, Shelton L. Roote, Jr., Mark Taylor, and Evelyn L. Wenzel. *The Arbuthnot Anthology of Children's Literature.* Rev. by Zena Sutherland. Glenview, Ill.: Scott, Foresman, 1976.

Arnstein, Flora. *Adventure into Poetry.* Palo Alto, Calif.: Stanford University Press, 1951.

———. *Poetry in the Elementary Classroom.* New York: Appleton-Century-Crofts, 1962.

Bamman, Henry A., Mildred A. Dawson, and Robert J. Whitehead. *Oral Interpretation of Children's Literature,* 2nd ed. Dubuque, Iowa: William C. Brown, 1971.

Bauer, Caroline Feller. *Handbook for Storytellers.* Chicago: American Library Association, 1976.

Bettelheim, Bruno. *The Uses of Enchantment.* New York: Alfred A. Knopf, 1976.

Blackburn, Thomas, ed. *Handbook for English Teachers: Presenting Poetry.* London: Methuen Educational, 1971.

Catterson, Jane H., ed. *Children and Literature.* Newark, Del.: International Reading Association, 1970.

Chambers, Dewey W. *Children's Literature in the Curriculum.* New York: Rand McNally, 1971.

Cleland, Craig J. "Highlighting Issues in Children's Literature through Semantic Webbing," *Reading Teacher* 34(March 1981):642–646,

Coody, Betty. *Using Literature with Young Children.* Dubuque, Iowa: William C. Brown, 1973.

Cook, Elizabeth. *The Ordinary and the Fabulous: An Introduction to Myths, Legends and Fairy Tales for Teachers and Storytellers.* London: Cambridge University Press, 1969.

Dorson, Richard M. *American Folklore.* Chicago: University of Chicago Press, 1959.

Egoff, Sheila, G. T. Stubbs, and L. F. Ashley, eds. *Only Connect: Readings on Children's Literature.* New York: Oxford University Press, 1969.

Favat, F. Andre. *Child and Tale: The Origins of Interest.* Urbana, Ill.: National Council of Teachers of English, 1977.

Hoffman, Miriam, and Eva Samuels. *Authors and Illustrators of Children's Books: Writings on Their Lives and Works.* New York: R. R. Bowker, 1972.

Hopkins, Lee Bennett. *Pass the Poetry, Please!* New York: Citation Press, 1972.

Huck, Charlotte S. *Children's Literature in the Elementary School,* 3rd ed. New York: Holt, Rinehart and Winston, 1976.

Karlin, Robert. *Teaching Elementary Reading,* 2nd ed. New York: Harcourt Brace Jovanovich, 1975.

Lamme, Linda Leonard, ed. *Learning to Love Literature: Preschool through Grade 3.* Urbana, Ill.: National Council of Teachers of English, 1981.

Larrick, Nancy. *A Parent's Guide to Children's Reading,* 4th ed. New York: Doubleday, 1975.

Lonsdale, Bernard J., and Helen K. Mackintosh. *Children Experience Literature.* New York: Random House, 1973.

Odland, Norine. *Teaching Literature in the Elementary School.* Urbana, Ill.: National Council of Teachers of English, 1969.

Paulette, Nancy. *E Is for Everybody: A Manual for Bringing Fine Picture Books into the Hands & Hearts of Children.* Metuchen, N.J.: Scarecrow Press, 1976a.

———. *Reading Guidance in a Media Age.* Metuchen, N.J.: Scarecrow Press, 1976b.

Ross, Elinor. "Comparison of Folk Tale Variants," *Language Arts* 56(April 1979):422–426.

Sawyer, Ruth. *The Way of the Storyteller.* New York: The Viking Press, 1962.

Sebesta, Sam Leaton, and William J. Iverson. *Literature for Thursday's Child.* Chicago: Science Research Associates. 1975.

Smith, James A., and Dorothy M. Park. *Word Music & Word Magic: Children's Literature Methods.* Boston: Allyn and Bacon, 1977.

Sutherland, Zena, and May Hill Arbuthnot. *Children and Books,* 5th ed. Glenview, Ill.: Scott, Foresman, 1977.

Tanyzer, Harold, and Jean Karl, eds. *Reading, Children's Books and Our Pluralistic Society.* Newark, Del.: International Reading Association, 1972.

Vandergrift, Kay E. *Child and Story: The Literacy Connection.* New York: Neal-Schuman Publishers, 1981.

Ziskim, Sylvia. *Telling Stories to Children.* New York: H. W. Wilson, 1976.

CHAPTER 12: Teaching Children with Special Needs

Abrahams, Roger D., and Rudolph C. Troike, eds. *Language and Cultural Diversity in American Education.* Englewood Cliffs, N.J.: Prentice-Hall, 1972.

Allen, Harold B., ed. *Teaching English As a Second Language.* New York: McGraw-Hill, 1965.

Cassidy, Jack. "Inquiry Reading for the Gifted," *Reading Teacher* 35(October 1981):17–21.

Cheyney, Arnold B. *Teaching Children of Different Cultures in the Classroom, A Language Approach,* 2nd ed. Columbus, Ohio: Charles E. Merrill, 1976.

Ching, Doris C. *Reading and the Bilingual Child.* Newark, Del.: International Reading Association, 1976.

Davis, A. L., ed. *Culture, Class, and Language Variety,* Urbana, Ill.: National Council of Teachers of English, 1972.

Dawson, Martha E., ed. *Are There Unwelcome Guests in Your Classroom?* Washington, D.C.: Association for Childhood Education International, 1974.

Edelsky, Carole and T. J. Rosegrant. "Language Development for Mainstreamed Severely Handicapped Non-Verbal Children," *Language Arts* 58(January):68–76.

Foerster, Leona M. and Dale Little Soldier. "Classroom Communication and the Indian Child," *Language Arts* 57(January 1980):45–49.

Gillies, Emily. *Creative Dramatics for All Children.* Washington, D.C.: Association for Childhood Education International, 1973.

Gonzales, Phillip C. "Beginning English Reading for ESL Students," *Reading Teacher* 35(November 1981):154–162.

Hammill, D. D., and N. R. Bartel. *Teaching Children with Learning and Behavior Problems.* Boston: Allyn and Bacon, 1975.

Hansen-Krening, Nancy. *Competency and Creativity in Language Arts: A Multiethnic Focus.* Reading, Mass.: Addison-Wesley, 1979.

Johnson, Kenneth R. *Teaching the Culturally Disadvantaged: A Rational Approach.* Palo Alto, Calif.: Science Research Associates, 1970.

Jones, Reginald L., ed. *Mainstreaming and the Minority Child.* Minneapolis, Minn.: Leadership Training Institute/Special Education, University of Minnesota, 1976.

Joyce, William W., and James A. Banks. *Teaching the Language Arts to Culturally Different Children.* Reading, Mass.: Addison-Wesley, 1971.

Knight, Lester N. *Language Arts for the Exceptional: The Gifted and Linguistically Different.* Itasca, Ill.: F. E. Peacock, 1974.

Kohl, Herbert. *36 Children.* New York: Signet Books, 1967.

Labuda, Michael, ed. *Creative Reading for Gifted Learners: A Design for Excellence.* Newark, Del.: International Reading Association, 1974.

Lowenbraun, Sheila, and James Q. Affleck, eds. *Teaching Mildly Handicapped Children in Regular Classes.* Columbus, Ohio: Charles E. Merrill, 1976.

McGee, Lea M. and Gail E. Tompkins. "Concepts About Print for the Young Blind Child," *Language Arts* 59(January 1982):40–45.

Mangold, S. S. "Tactile Perception and Braille Letter Recognition: Effects of Developmental Teaching," *Journal of Visual Impairment and Blindness* 72(1978):259–266.

Manson, Martha. "Explorations in Language Arts for Preschoolers (Who Happen to be Deaf)," *Language Arts* 59(January 1982):33–39 +.

Materials on Creative Arts (Arts, Crafts, Dance, Drama, Music, Bibliotherapy) for Persons with Handicapping Conditions, rev. ed. Washington, D.C.: American Alliance for Health, Physical Education, and Recreation, 1977.

Miller, Robert. "The Mexican Approach to Developing Bilingual Materials and Teaching Literacy to Bilingual Students," *Reading Teacher* 35(April 1982):800–804.

Monson, Dianne and Cynthia Shurtleff. "Altering Attitudes Toward the Physically Handicapped Through Print and Non-Print Media," *Language Arts* 56(February 1979):163–170.

Renzulli, Joseph S. *The Enrichment Triad Model: A Guide for Developing Programs for the Gifted and Talented.* Mansfield Center, Conn.: Creative Learning Press, 1977.

Renzulli, Joseph S. and Linda H. Smith. *A Guidebook for Developing Individualized Educational Programs for*

Gifted and Talented Students. Mansfield Center, Conn.: Creative Learning Press, 1979.

Stanford, Gene (chair) and the NCTE Committee on Classroom Practices. *Classroom Practices 1980–1981: Dealing with Differences*. Urbana, Ill.: National Council of Teachers of English, 1980.

Sutherlin, S., ed. *The Most Enabling Environment: Education Is for All Children*. Washington, D.C.: Association for Childhood Education International, 1979.

Taylor, Gail Cohen. "ERIC/RCS REPORT: Creative Dramatics for Handicapped Children," *Language Arts* 57(January 1980):92–97 + .

Urzua, Carole. "A Language-Learning Environment for All Children," *Language Arts* 57(January 1980): 38–44.

Wagener, Elain H. "Language Arts for the Visually Impaired Child," *Language Arts* 53(April 1976):432–434.

Witty, Paul A. "Education of the Gifted and the Creative in the U.S.A.," *The Gifted Child Quarterly* 15(Summer 1971):109–16.

———, ed. *Reading for the Gifted and Creative Student*. Newark, Del.: International Reading Association, 1971.

Woolfolk, Anita E. and Lorraine McCune Nicolich. *Educational Psychology for Teachers*. Englewood Cliffs, N.J.: Prentice-Hall, 1980.

CHAPTER 13: The Language Arts Program

Bruner, Jerome S. *The Process of Education*. New York: Vintage Books, 1960.

Burns, Paul C. *Diagnostic Teaching of the Language Arts*. Itasca, Ill.: F. E. Peacock, 1974.

Day, Barbara. *Open Learning in Early Childhood*. New York: Macmillan, 1975.

Daiute, Colette. "Word Processing: Can It Make Even Good Writers Better?" *Electronic Learning* 1(March/April 1982):29–31.

Denham, Carolyn and Ann Lieberman, eds. *Time to Learn*. Washington, D.C.: The National Institute of Education, 1980.

DeStephano, Johanna S. "Research Update: Demonstrations, Engagement and Sensitivity: A Revised Approach to Language Learning — Frank Smith," *Language Arts* 58(January 1981):103–112.

Evertts, Eldonna. "Minimal Professional Reference Library on the Language Arts for Elementary School Teachers," *Language Arts* 58(February 1981):225–248.

Forte, Imogene, and Mary Anne Pangle. *More Center Stuff*. Nashville, Tenn.: Incentive Publications, 1976.

Forte, Imogene, Mary Ann Pangle, and Robbie Tupa. *Center Stuff for Nooks, Crannies, and Corners*. Nashville, Tenn.: Incentive Publications, 1973.

Goodman, Yetta and Kenneth Goodman. "Twenty Questions about Teaching Language," Educational Leadership 48(March 1981):437–442.

Greff, Kasper N., and Eunice N. Askov. *Learning Centers, An Ideabook for Reading and Language Arts*. Dubuque, Iowa: Kendall/Hunt, 1974.

Grommon, Alfred H., ed. *Reviews of Selected Published Tests in English*. Urbana, Ill.: National Council of Teachers of English, 1976.

Hennings, D. G. "Input: Enter the Word-Processing Computer," *Language Arts* 58(January 1981):18–22.

Kaplan, Sandra Nina, Jo Ann Butom Kaplan, Sheila Kunishima Madsen, and Bette K. Taylor. *Change for Children: Ideas and Activities for Individualizing Learning*. Pacific Palisades, Calif.: Goodyear, 1973.

Lange, Bob. "Television's Role in Education: Is There an Artful Balance?" *Language Arts* 58(January 1981):93–99.

Larson, Carl, Phil Backlund, Mark Redmond, and Alton Barbour. *Assessing Functional Communication*. Urbana, Ill.: Clearinghouse on Reading and Communication Skills, 1978.

Loban, Walter. "Language Development and Its Evaluation," in *Reviews of Selected Published Tests in English*. Alfred H. Grommon, ed. Urbana, Ill.: National Council of Teachers of English, 1976.

McGarvey, Jack. "Cross-Examining the Commercials," *Media and Methods* 16(January 1980):47–49.

McNeil, John D. *Designing Curriculum: Self-Instruction Modules*. Boston: Little, Brown, 1976.

Mager, Robert F. *Preparing Instructional Objectives*. Palo Alto, Calif.: Fearon Publishers, 1962.

Mandel, Barrett J., ed. *Three Language-Arts Curriculum Models: Pre-Kindergarten through College*. Urbana, Ill.: National Council of Teachers of English, 1980.

May, Jill P. *Films and Filmstrips for Language Arts: An Annotated Bibliography*. Urbana, Ill.: National Council of Teachers of English, 1981.

Musgrave, G. R. *Individualized Instruction: Teaching Strategies Focusing on the Learner*. Boston: Allyn and Bacon, 1975.

Petreshene, Susan S., *The Complete Guide to Learning Centers*. Palo Alto, Calif.: Pendragon House, 1978.

Platt, Nancy. "Social Context: An Essential for Learning," *Language Arts* 56(September 1979):620–627.

"Quality Software: How to Know When You've Found It," *Electronic Learning* 1(November/December 1981):33–36.

Rankin, Pauline and Charlie W. Roberts. "Television and Teaching," *Reading Teacher* 35(October 1981):30–32.

Shane, Harold G. "The Silicon Age and Education," *Phi Delta Kappan* 63(January 1982):303–308.

Singer, Dorothy G., Jerome L. Singer and Diana M. Zuckerman. *Getting the Most Out of TV*. Santa Monica, Ca.: Goodyear Publishing Company, 1981a.

Sleisenger, Lenore and Joyce Lancaster. *Guidebook for the Volunteer Reading Teacher*. Thorofare, N.J.: Charles B. Slack, Inc., 1979.

Smith, Frank. "The Language Arts and the Learner's Mind," *Language Arts* 56(February 1979):118–125.

Stibbs, Andrew. *Assessing Children's Language — Guidelines for Teachers*. London: Ward Lock Educational Limited, 1979. (Available from National Council of Teachers of English.)

Torrance, E. Paul, and R. E. Myers. *Creative Learning and Teaching*. New York: Dodd, Mead, 1970.

Winkeljohann, Sister Rosemary. "What Is the Role of Television in the Language Arts Program?" *Language Arts* 58(January 1981):100–102.

Wollman, Jane. "The Videodisc: A New Educational Technology Takes Off," *Electronic Learning* 1(November/December 1981) 39,40.

528

Index